Myself When I Am Real

Myself

OXFORD
UNIVERSITY PRESS

When I Am Real

The Life and Music of
Charles Mingus

Gene Santoro

OXFORD
UNIVERSITY PRESS

Oxford   New York
Athens   Auckland   Bangkok   Bogotá   Buenos Aires
Cape Town   Chennai   Dar es Salaam   Delhi   Florence   Hong Kong   Istanbul
Karachi   Kolkata   Kuala Lumpur   Madrid   Melbourne   Mexico City   Mumbai
Nairobi   Paris   São Paulo   Shanghai   Singapore   Taipei   Tokyo   Toronto   Warsaw

and associated companies in
Berlin   Ibadan

Copyright © 2000 by Gene Santoro

First published by Oxford University Press, Inc., 2000
198 Madison Avenue, New York, New York 10016

First issued as an Oxford University Press paperback, 2001

Oxford is a registered trademark of Oxford University Press

Library of Congress Cataloging-in-Publication Data
Santoro, Gene.
Myself when I am real : the life and music of Charles Mingus / Gene Santoro.
p. cm.
Includes bibliographical references and index.
ISBN 0-19-509733-5 (Cloth); ISBN 0-19-514711-1 (Pbk.)
1. Mingus, Charles, 1922–79. Jazz musicians—United States—Biography. I. Title.
ML418.M45 S26 200
781.65'092—dc21
[B]   99-046734

Book design & composition by Mark McGarry
Set in the Scala family of types

10 9 8 7 6 5 4 3 2 1

Printed in the United States of America
on acid-free paper

Contents

Preface

CHARLES MINGUS, jazz's legendary Angry Man, lured me into writing this book, relentlessly, seductively, finally, just as he'd gotten what he needed from so many others while he was still alive.

I was a fan of his music; that was why I wanted to do the book at all. I admit I didn't realize right away how lucky or right I was to choose Mingus as my biographical subject. The famed, even notorious composer-musician turned out to be more fascinating and complicated than I'd guessed or hoped. His messy, sprawling life, his endless quests, his acute self-awareness and persistent involvement in so many facets of his time gave me a huge and ambitious canvas to work on—the best of my life, as I soon began to find out.

The music drew me in, but the people and places hooked me. Once I was into the couple of hundred interviews that help buttress this book, talking with Mingus's families and friends and peers and colleagues and sidemen and behind-the-scenes and in-the-know types, poking around the Mingus Archives at the Library of Congress and the Institute for Jazz Studies at Rutgers University, digging up background material on this and that, it hit me like a sap swung by a Raymond Chandler cop. The stories I knew, the tales widely retold around the jazz world about this Gargantuan character were often myths. Sometimes they distorted facts; sometimes they were just made up. Even the true tales, I saw, offered only glimpses of the man's apparently hydra-headed personality. And there were, I was finding, a lot of other tales not in the dossier.

Here's Charles Mingus, standard-issue thumbnail sketch. A fat, bristling, light-skinned black guy who busted people on the bandstand, who stopped his shows midstream if a cash register rang or a fan or musician said or did something that set him off. If he was set off enough, he yelled at or lectured or swung on or pulled a blade on the offender like he was the 240-pound wrath of Zeus. Sometimes he connected. Sometimes he got backed down by somebody with a gun or a knife. In a rage, he once tossed a $2,200 bass, one of his prized instruments, onto a nightclub floor to shatter at a groupie's feet. In a similar rage, he once yanked the tight-wound, wire-sharp strings out of a club piano with his bare hands, and then shoved the piano down the stairs. He made a movie of himself being thrown out of his downtown loft and carted off by the New York Police Department. His mouth was always running off about racism, about some kind of mistreatment or misunderstanding or persecution or lack of recognition. He had a lot of fans who dug his shows. Important and influential critics and record company heads dug his music. He was rich. He died broke. He'd erupt in volcanic passions for dim (if any) reasons. Erratic. Unpredictable. Mood swings. Evil. His ego was a blimp, like the rest of him. He ate like a pig. He loved fine wines and aged steaks and exotic cuisines. He chased women constantly. Women, especially white women, adored him. He acted like a pimp. He brooded. He didn't hang out. He talked nonstop. Everyone was scared of him. He hated white guys. He was mean and hard and cheated people and put his name on music he had others write. He was an endless self-promoter. He always bragged he was one of jazz's greatest composers, the successor to Duke Ellington. He wrote some amazing stuff, he couldn't write a standard pop tune, he couldn't read music or keep time, he was a bass virtuoso but he was lazy. He always had an edge to him. He said a lot of things that needed saying when nobody else was saying them. Maybe he was a genius and maybe he wasn't. Nobody could play his music right. He made a big impact. People liked him or hated him, avoided him or played with him. Sometimes— a lot of times—they hated him *and* played with him. He was Jazz's Angry Man.

But, a lot of the people who actually knew him were saying, what about *Mingus?* What about his devastating grin, his crackling electricity, the voice that leaped yelping intervals, the charm, intelligence, humor, vulnerability, verbal dexterity, flashes of insight, volatility, childishness, and sheer charismatic pull we all felt and saw and loved in the complicated Mingus *we* knew? And the stories would follow.

Meanwhile, I'd gone back to listen to Mingus music. I let its panoramic sweep wash over me instead of going for my favorite fishing holes. And in the process a nagging problem that wouldn't go away became the wellspring for this book.

Here's the problem. Mingus music is overwhelming in its torrent of musical styles and psychological switchbacks and emotional punch, its tumble of raucous gospel swing, luminous melodies, European classical threads, bebop tributes, Mexican and Colombian and Indian music and sounds from anywhere and everywhere. He had incredibly sharp and open-minded ears, for a violent, self-obsessed asshole who may have been a genius.

Genius. How else to explain all this huge sonic crazy quilt that is Charles Mingus's art, and why it could, and still does, touch a lot of listeners?

So then, if all this stuff—these ridiculously diverse sounds full of majesty and humor, buoyant joie de vivre and tidal waves of pain, lyrical yearning and satiric edge all powered by a scary willingness to tackle any emotion head-on— if all this *stuff* didn't come out of Charles Mingus, standard issue, where did it come from?

As it turns out, for me that problem was irresistible. You're holding my solutions, what made me write this book this way.

An old saw says biography is detective work. Out of stacks of witness testimony and historical records and research, cross-referenced and cross-linked and I hope not too crossed up, a historical narrative started to cohere around this hero with more sides than a polyhedron. The plots and subplots of Charles Mingus's life's drama unfold from before his birth on April 22, 1922, till just after his death of Lou Gehrig's disease on January 5, 1979. Like him, like his 300-odd compositions and dozens of albums, they take in a lot of ground.

Creativity isn't necessarily straightforward in its dealings with the world. To put it another way, no one has ever convinced me that the geniuses who have the lasting human touch we call art are either monsters or role models, or even that they should be. Shamans don't have to be horrible or nice. They just have to work effectively in their surroundings, account for some of the planet's mysteries in ways the people they live among can understand.

What counts about artists is that they perceive reality differently. In any clinical sense, they're not schizophrenics (although historically some of them have been that too) because they produce something coherent in its own terms that is valued by their communities—their art, their strikingly individual contributions to human culture. Artists don't simply reflect their lives and times like mirrors, but if they're worth anything they light some way we haven't seen from quite that angle before. That takes a genius; otherwise everybody would be doing it.

Mingus's strange and wonderful gift let him take his all-too-human self, his tangle of desire and hope and need and strength, and translate it all into a special place that others, too, can enter, in the magical way of art, when they listen to his music. It's not a paradox to say that Mingus was most fully himself in his music. It was his lamp unto the world.

He saw himself as the Romantic larger-than-life hero of an always in-process living theater, and so his life and his art became deeply entwined. His lamp burns so intensely because, being Mingus, he never separated what he did and thought and said and wanted and needed—his life—from what he made—his art. He used everything he saw or heard, felt or even misunderstood as ingredients in a constant creative process. He transformed it all into something that moves people still, thanks to his uncanny gift of tongues in a language called music. This is the lasting human touch his art bequeathes. No matter if it comes out caress or belly laugh or fist in your face; that's part of how each piece of his music tells us, "Charles Mingus made me."

So this book is not a psychobiography. It couldn't and doesn't try to reduce Mingus's art to a reflection of his neuroses, psychoses, childhood beatings, or ferocious need for love and attention, although it portrays all those. It's just that everything about Mingus was too big to be shoehorned into that sort of sideshow.

But I have tried to let Mingus unfold as who he was, in his special moment in American history's flow. And I hope that captures how a fragile, fertile network of real people and places and a lifetime of encounters and events allowed Mingus to be Mingus—which is to say, one of the most important composers, pivotal artistic figures, and magnetic characters from the wild renaissance explosion of talented oddballs who rumbled across the arts in the post–World War II United States. In its own unique way, Charles Mingus's quest was as American as it gets.

I've tried to get a solid grip on all the fine details and big brushstrokes that make this book, but I'm sure I've been thrown to the mat sometimes during the match. I take full credit for any falls. But I also have to insist, hopefully politely, that this portrait of Charles Mingus lives up to its title—*his* title for one of his richest, most telling pieces of music.

Myself When I Am Real

Introduction

CELIA MINGUS ZAENTZ, *second wife*: From the time he picked up an instrument, he got into the band, and then the high school band, and then he went on the road. And that's how a real artist is: artists think by going on with their life and their work. They're driven. They couldn't imagine anything else.[1]

JUDY STARKEY MINGUS McGRATH, *third wife*: It was so important to him to have his music heard, to be taken seriously. And that piece "Half Mast Inhibition"—when you really listen to it and realize it was this young black kid in Watts hearing these things and composing this music, it has to blow you away.

SUSAN GRAHAM UNGARO MINGUS, *fourth wife*: He felt that he was a vessel for music that came from somewhere else. He always took credit for his bass playing and virtuosity, but he always said the melody comes from God. He said the music was waiting for him on the piano keys.

Charles Mingus Jr. struck everyone he met hard, whether it was for the first time or the thousandth. Insisting he was five-foot-ten, though he was at least an inch shorter, rolling back and forth between 180 and 250 pounds, and packing the coiled intensity of a rattler about to strike, Mingus projected even bigger. He engulfed people, things, conversations, ideas. People describe him like he was ready for a National Football League front line.

Driven, indeed. As a young man, he practiced his bass for hours a day to

3

master his chosen craft, taping his strongest fingers to force the weakest to get stronger, more agile, more useful. For the rest of his fifty-six years, he pounded the piano for hours a day, at home, in studios, other people's homes, hotels, wherever he happened to be, pouring out the music endlessly cycling inside his restless imagination, to release as many of the angels circling him and demons haunting him that day as he could.

Real and projected, Mingus's guiding spirits drove him to produce one of the most far-reaching bodies of music of the postwar era. In the course of his decades of creating and reworking it, its raw materials came from pop and blues and European, African, Indian, and Hispanic sounds. He fed it all through a jazz-shaped sensibility that put a premium on the hard-learned art of improvisation—the art of expressing yourself on the spur of the moment.

His ongoing conversation with the world around him—Mingus music—embraces a panorama of human feeling from yearning romanticism to bitter irony, all drawn from the never-extinguished interior dialog among Mingus's various selves. For Mingus his art was his life, translated, and his focus on it was possessed, Dionysiac, total. It shouldn't be a surprise that he then demanded extraordinary commitment to that art from its performers and audiences alike. Nor that he demanded drama, even if it was only melodrama, on a monumental scale in the world around him, to keep his attention, to keep him at the center of attention, to offer reassurance, to infuriate him—above all, to inspire him to transmute those raw materials into more of the timeless cultural dialog we call art.

For he saw his life—and his music reflected this—as a now-simmering, now-roiling drama of wildly mixed ingredients that only he could reconcile. And because his consuming curiosity about anything and everything guaranteed that his life was very much a part of his times, his music and his writings and his performances speak of how one gifted man saw America, the planet, the universe, and even the mind of God during his time here.

He was born in Nogales, Arizona, on April 22, 1922—a Taurus, determined and driven and sexual, whose birthdate was a numerologist's delight he enjoyed playing with for the rest of his days. But Charles Mingus Jr. grew up in Watts, outside Los Angeles, when it was still country and racially diverse. His half-white, half-black father, a former noncommissioned officer in the U.S. Army, was a bully with a bourgeois life. His half-black, half-Indian stepmother, a well-meaning but superstitious and easily dominated woman, tried ineffectually to protect the Mingus kids from the old man's iron hand. Until high school the boy grew up isolated, thanks to his family's convoluted racial politics, which often encapsulated the prejudices and confusions of America at large.

Young Charles started music early, but he had bad teachers who screwed him up. Inadvertently, though, they taught him to rely on his quick ears rather than music on paper. He found his instrument—the bass—and good teachers and colleagues near the end of high school. Some of his confusion was racially caused. He started by playing the cello and European classical music, which had a near-unbreakable color bar. So the sixteen-year-old switched to jazz, and the bass, because there black Americans had more freedom to create—and the chance to earn real money and recognition and fame. Being a musician meant cash and glamor and women, status plus a shot at playing out the sounds in your head.

In his teens and early twenties, Mingus wound his way through the convoluted Los Angeles scene in full swing on Watts' Central Avenue, then called "Brown Broadway." The great musicians of both the swing and postwar jazz eras all hung around and passed through, and he found them, unerringly, to learn what there was to learn. But he also met Hollywood stars and sound track composers, vaudeville strippers and comics, pimps and gangsters and white heiresses. He was seventeen when one of his first tours as a sideman brought him to San Francisco, where he walked into the prewar Bohemian scene that set the stage for the Beat Generation. Allen Ginsberg and Charles Mingus bumped into each other repeatedly over thirty years.

All his life, Mingus was expansive in his curiosity and insatiable in acting on it. That only accelerated after he moved to New York in 1951. He read nearly constantly into the 1960s—poetry, history, philosophy, psychology. He called painters and poets his friends, and spent a lot of time cruising galleries and readings and artist haunts. He recurrently worked in multimedia situations, hitching his music (or vice versa) to the spoken word, drama, film, TV.

In the mid-1950s, while still married to his first white wife, he began writing a book he called *Memoirs of a Half-Schitt-Colored Nigger*. It started as straight autobiography, full of satiric jabs and stream-of-consciousness and purple prose about love and mystical ruminations and scornful fusillades about the music industry. Gradually it swelled into thousands of pages and was drastically edited and reedited and written and rewritten as it traveled, at times in a suitcase, in search of a publisher for over a decade and a half.

Driven. Mingus had no use for people he thought were looking for handouts or free rides, but he knew firsthand how racism in America blunted the chances for a person classified as black. And so he spoke out, often screaming, on political and social points: racism, the Vietnam War, economic injustice, Nazis, whatever swam into his purview. His titles often reflect that: "Fables of Faubus," after the 1950s racist Arkansas governor who barred integrated schools, or "Remember Rockefeller at Attica," for the 1960s New York governor who ordered the National Guard to storm a prison gripped by a racially motivated riot.

Mingus was nagged by racial prejudice, constantly triggered by dull and grinding details—cabs that wouldn't stop for him, restaurant owners who wondered if he could cover the tab, the differential calculus of pay scale and recognition in force between black and white musicians. But he loved and married three white women and loved a few more and was most comfortable in interracial spheres like Greenwich Village. Some of his closest friends were white. His bands were usually integrated. And they were usually full of younger musicians he could train to play his demanding, rewarding music. It was the School of Mingus.

He called his outfits Jazz Workshops, and he meant it in the same sense as drama workshops—a performance tryout in the moment, as actors say. Workshop shows were a process unfolding rather than a finished product unveiled. In that way, Mingus's conception was in tune with the postwar American Renaissance—Abstract Expressionism and Pop Art, rock and roll, confessional poetry, Beat literature, conceptual art, psychedelia, you name it. You could say Mingus reconceived jazz as performance art, so that the process at the music's heart—spontaneous composition, as he called it—was dramatized. At a Workshop set, anything could happen onstage. He might slap down a sideman, or flip into a diatribe, or rehearse a piece over and over, or storm off. One night, he sat and had dinner while he played records for the audience. But his fans expected weirdness. It was part of the show.

During the 1950s and 1960s, Charles Mingus produced some of his best-known and most popular music. Singles like the gospel-blues rocker "Better Get It in Your Soul," sold well and forged some new crossover ideas. Never content to pursue one path, Mingus always saw his music as multifaceted. So even as he delved into the "roots" music that powered his most popular cuts, he continued writing in almost every format possible, from classical to pop, and invented his own unclassifiable ideas as well. As his notoriety and popularity grew from the late 1950s, he insisted on pushing the envelope further. So at Town Hall in October 1962, he tried to record the process of an orchestra making a live record in front of an audience, which became a disaster on several levels, for several reasons. Just two years later, he was ushered into the jazz pantheon with a tumultuous triumphant performance at the landmark Monterey Jazz Festival. In his characteristic entrepreneurial fashion, he recorded the concert and then distributed the two-disc set, via mail-order, on his own Charles Mingus Enterprises label.

Mingus wrote reams of music. They've made him an immortal. So who was he? In his quest to become a legend, Mingus created his own myths. His autobiography, *Beneath the Underdog,* distorts, rearranges, and frames facts in service of different agendas. Some of his best writing and most salient points, especially about the music industry surrounding him, disappeared under the misguided eyes of a couple of dozen editors, pros and volunteers. And Mingus was continuously spinning yarns for lovers, his closest friends, in front of cameras or on tape or onstage.

His friends were black and white, and came from many separate spheres. He kept himself the only real link. That way, he composed his life as a work of art, just like he did his music, from a nourishing diversity of raw thematic materials. Nobody had to know all the threads that went into weaving his web. Cover the bones, he told one of his arrangers, and then he threw a lot of razzle-dazzle into a chart that he felt made all too clear some of the sources underlying that piece of Mingus music.

He had near-photographic absorption abilities, the persistent discipline of the dedicated craftsman, and the piercing insight and transmuting touch of genius. He was also mercurial, erratic, prone to violent blowups. He developed a dependency on benzedrine and a bagful of uppers and downers, and after one of his breakdowns spent an extended period on mellaril, a thorazine-type antipsychotic. Possible overdose side effects: lightheadedness, sedation, agitation, confusion, restlessness, disorientation, convulsions, fever, and coma. Among other risks: retinitis pigmentosa leading to blindness, and dangerously lowered blood pressure.

Mingus had big ideas and loved to think he could see behind the machinery of society, from corporate get-aheads to the Central Intelligence Agency (CIA) and the Federal Bureau of Investigation (FBI), that stage-managed life for most people. But the written and spoken record of his opinions, ideas, idées fixes, and free associations mixes daunting and telling insights about Big Issues like racism, war, and love with hare-brained schemes, paranoid fantasies, and a lurking, smoldering sense of being hurt, even abused.

Nobody, not even a genius, is 100 percent right.

Still, someone with Mingus's sense of history and perspective and insight had a lot to talk about about. Race in America, a subject brimming with a history of pain, was a big part of his tale, and his family's. The Mingus clan's story encapsulated this country's racial struggle—progress and setbacks, tragedies and triumphs. Multiracial by birth, black in America, Mingus fought for recognition and belittled racial copouts. But he also knew how to mau-mau the flak-catchers: he could inject race into any situation to try to fix it so he came out the aggrieved party. Everything in his life was an instant cosmic metaphor.

Paradoxically, maybe, that left him vulnerable. For all his noisy raunch and bluster, Charles Mingus was a real Romantic, a pudgy and avid talker who cast

victim. More than a few wags wondered how the famously volatile composer-bassist, widely known for his quick temper and fighting words and physical outbursts, dealt with the concept, central to Hinduism, of Ahinsa. Ahinsa means noninjury to living creatures, one taproot of Mohandas Gandhi's famed nonviolent resistance as a mode of social and political protest.

Sue Mingus, the musician's last wife and widow, accompanied his ashes on the journey from Mexico, where he died on January 5, 1979, back through New York, where he'd lived for most of his life, to the upper reaches of the Ganges River, east of Delhi, where he'd never been, except in his boundless imagination.

Atlantic Records, the last label Mingus had a contract with, paid for the sad pilgrimage. But when Jody DeVito, Sue's daughter-in-law and assistant, picked up the tickets from the label's New York offices, she found they were for coach. Sue, arriving in New York, went ballistic, insulted at the slight to her barely dead husband. "Charles," she sputtered through gritted teeth, "never flew coach." The tickets were quickly upgraded.

She let no one, not even customs, touch the beautiful antique silver box the size of a pet coffin. Lined in velvet, it held Mingus's ashes along with the chunks of bone and flesh that remained because of the low-temperature method of cremation traditionally practiced by Hindus.

Sue wrapped the box in the kind of Mexican blanket on display at every marketplace in turista Mexico, and put it on a small luggage wheelie. She flashed the death certificate and her temper, when anyone tried to tamper with her husband's remains.

When Roberto Ungaro, her son, and Jody met her at the International Arrivals terminal at Kennedy Airport in New York, they were stunned to see Mingus so reduced, riding on a collapsible pullcart. He really was dead after all.

From there, Jody joined Sue on the last, sad leg of the journey for India. Once they were there, the female duo decided that, much as he loved silver and velvet, the box just wasn't really Charles. So they got a handwoven basket, emptied the ashes into a piece of handmade Indian linen, taking care to get all of it, bones and everything. Nobody wanted Mingus to reincarnate without a right arm or an eye or something.

Then they tossed the precious antique box off a high bridge, and watched it flip and tumble through the long, seemingly eternal descent.

Sue and Jody found a hotel with a balcony in Delhi, India's capital, sited at the western end of the Ganges plain. The city was a maze of colorful bazaars and narrow winding roads and pressing hordes of people; it always seemed on the edge of chaos, but it was fascinating, distracting. With all its history, it doubled as northern India's modern travel hub, a tourist draw in itself that sits just up the road from tourist destinations like Agra's Taj Mahal and the ghats of Varanasi.

The Brahmins Jody had quizzed about proper procedure for a Hindu funeral warned her that the ashes could not be kept inside a structure; if they were, they would trap the spirit inside too. Hence the balcony.

Sue and Jody got a cart to take them and the basket to the ashram at Rishikesh, an ancient religious center on the Ganges near Haridwar and about 220 kilometers from Delhi. The small town's river banks are lined with ashrams and places of worship.

For three or four days Sue could not part with what was left of Mingus's once overwhelming physical presence. Finally, with no warning, she roused Jody and said, "Let's do it." They found a Brahmin, and Sue gave him $500— a fortune in that part of India—after some marketplace haggling.

Rishikesh had seen many Westerners trying to find their own paths through the ancient ways of the Orient's religious rites, the mystic pull that lured Western intellectuals and artists as believers or wannabes with increasing frequency from the 1920s through the 1960s. Tourist hotels dot its streets.

The women went to the marketplace to buy clothes—not saris, but dhotis, the loose white clothes of men, since white in Hindu symbolology is the color of death. They each wore a bindi, the dot of red or black powder Hindu women put on their foreheads as marks of beauty. Then they went out to a rock overlooking the Ganges, and Sue made a circle with the ashes, and threw them in.

With that, Charles Mingus Jr., one of the most revolutionary thinkers and foremost composers and performers in jazz during the explosive postwar American cultural Renaissance, became the stuff of legend.

1 *Growing Up Absurd*

THE BABY, barely three months old and pudgy but with bright eyes and an inquiring air, was the center of attention as he fussed on the hot train. He was riding with his parents and two older sisters as they traveled from Fort Huachuca, the dusty desert army post outside Nogales, a grubby, boiling speck on the Arizona-Mexico border.[1]

Nogales was where the baby, Charles Mingus Jr., had been born on April 22, 1922.

The Mingus family was heading to a larger dusty desert town—Los Angeles, California. For a decade, L.A. had rocketed through boomtown expansion fueled by a new industry called Hollywood. Like Nogales and the entire southwestern United States, it was part of the Spaniards' New World colonial legacy. Later, the baby would sometimes claim Mexican blood. Like many of his claims, he justified this one by his reading of his history and experience, even if it wasn't, strictly speaking, true.

ESTELLA WILLIAMS, *first cousin*: He had a guilt complex: he felt he had killed his mother. He said that to me many times, sitting in his car. It seemed to affect him greatly. Sometimes he was on the verge of tears. Aunt Mamie was the only mother he knew. He said his father was really nasty, too harsh. The color differences, these can be serious things. My mother was very light and married a dark man. So my brothers and I came out on the dark side. Now, the Minguses all have different shades of lightness. Vivian was the lightest. But to me Grace looks like a dark white woman.

The baby's mother, a light-skinned attractive black woman named Harriet Sophia Mingus, née Phillips, was almost forty. She got sick on the train and complained about her stomach and feeling generally poorly. Her spit-and-polish husband of five years, Staff Sergeant Charles Mingus of the U.S. Army Quartermasters Corps, didn't know that she was dying.

The couple met and married in Brackettville, Texas, on April 14, 1917. It was eight days after the United States entered World War I, and a blink after the career military man divorced his first wife, Mary Taylor. He'd married Taylor in Gallup, New Mexico, and shed her in Holbrook, Arizona, as he went from post to post. In between, she bore him two daughters, and she kept them when he left. All that remained of Sergeant Mingus's first family was a picture that later sat on his second family's mantel.

In his characteristic gruff, taciturn way, Mingus Sr. never explained the framed, faded photo. The people in it looked like white folks to his second set of kids as they grew up in Watts, outside Los Angeles. Only when they were nearly teens did the children discover the picture's cryptic historical significance, deciphered by their resentful and jealous stepmother.

The Mingus family was riding the train to join Harriet's family in Los Angeles. There they, like the thousands and thousands of others who would double the Los Angeles population in the 1920s, meant to settle. There the forty-five-year-old ex-army lifer would collect his pension, find another government job, and raise his second family. But on September 7, 1922, Harriet died of myocarditis, or heart inflammation—and the tentative new world of the Mingus family tilted.[2]

Around his family, Sergeant Charles Mingus Sr. was easily angered and often violent and closemouthed the rest of the time, except when he gave orders in a stentorian voice that carried the assumption of command. And he avoided telling his children much about his life. When he did, he altered and embroidered his stories.

Storytellers often see to the heart of the matter at hand. It's why books are still being written and read, tales still being told and heeded. As it happens, the tales of the Mingus dynasty encapsulate a lot of American history.

Springing from immigrant pioneers and slaves, the Mingus dynasty traced the twists and turns of American race relations firsthand. They mingled races and heritages in a literal rendition of the American melting pot. So as Charles

Mingus Jr. walked the racial and cultural borders of America, he had repeated chances to see and experience what W. E. B. Du Bois at the turn of the century famously called "double consciousness."[3]

For Du Bois, all Americans of color were fundamentally split psychologically; they saw themselves at least partly through the eyes of the dominant culture, which excluded them and disparaged or patronized their ways of life. Ironically, being marginalized meant they could see the foundations, self-deceptions, and limits of the larger society in ways its more privileged members rarely could.

With jazz as his main vehicle and his life as his inspiration, Charles Mingus Jr. would transform that double-edged gift into a lifetime's worth of adventures, and his own expansive, quintessentially American art.

Charles Mingus Sr. was born in Swain County, North Carolina, on February 4, 1877, the great-great-grandson of the family's founding patriarch, Jacob Mingus. Jacob and his wife Sarah were among the first whites to settle in North Carolina's Oconaluftee valley around 1790. By most accounts, Jacob was a German immigrant. But when the forty-year-old enlisted in the military in 1814, he declared he'd been born in Berks County, Pennsylvania. He could have migrated from there to Tennessee, then to the Blue Ridge of Carolina.[4]

Jacob and Sarah's youngest son, whom everybody called Doctor John, was, by his own accounts, born in either North Carolina or Tennessee on September 15, 1798. The only one of five siblings to remain on the family homestead, he became fairly wealthy. John expanded the Mingus Corn Mill (its slogan: Great Smokies, Great Pancakes), which still draws 1,000 visitors a day in Great Smoky Mountains National Park.

In the hilly country that the Mingus clan settled, slaves were few, far from the hundreds that worked the flatland cotton plantations. Bookkeeping was rigorous in cotton country; the highly developed economic and social bureaucracy of slavery demanded a precise accounting. In the Blue Ridge, things were more casual. And so slave records are fragmentary.

Besides, North Carolina wasn't pure pro-slave country. It had a history of internal divisions over slavery, and initially opposed southern secession in 1861. After the Civil War, it supported Radical Reconstruction. Many local leaders were businessmen rather than planters; they were less interested in slavery than protective tariffs and northern investment in railroads. But when the state constitution of 1868 established black suffrage, fierce Ku Klux Klan violence erupted. Within a few years, the state government was run by conservatives.

A man of Doctor John's standing experienced all this firsthand. According to the 1870 census, David Mingus, age thirty-five, black, was working on John's farm. The 1880 census lists Daniel Mingus, black and probably the same person as David, married to Sarah, white. Their children were listed as mulatto. Miscegenation, the Old South's not-so-secret fear, was close by John Mingus. And would get closer still.

John and Mary's granddaughter Clarinda lived in the big homestead with her grandparents. Like many southern white women, she had her own ideas about race. At nineteen, she conceived a child, possibly by Daniel. The baby had her fair skin and blue eyes, with barely a hint of his father's color or features. He was named Charles and was raised as a family member. The census of 1880, which lists him as John's grandson, does not mark him as mulatto or colored. It may have made a difference that Charles's great-uncle Abraham, unmarried and living with his parents at age fifty-three, was the local census enumerator.

Charles Mingus Sr. told his children almost none of this. But like his son, he regularly substituted psychological and emotional truth for accuracy.

GRACE MINGUS, *sister*: What he told us was, he was born on a plantation, and his father was an African, and he got one of the slaveowner's daughters pregnant. He said Mingus was an African name.

So after a while, he didn't like the situation up there at the plantation, so he put his age up and joined the service. Somebody sent word to him in the service, and he went back one time on leave, and they had a big celebration. But he was leery of staying there; he was afraid for his life, because of the racial thing. So he left and went back into the service. During that time, he said he didn't know if he'd wake up dead or what.

He looked like a white man. I have a picture of him and some of the buddies he was in the service with. I didn't know which was him because they were all so white.

VIVIAN MINGUS, *sister*: My dad said when he was small—this is translated from my stepmother, now—that he was treated so bad because he had black in him, that he ran away when he was about fourteen and joined the army. Then he went back and they treated him bad, and he swore that if he was going to go back he was going to kill them all. So he wrote them a letter and said he was coming back. He said when he got there they had a banquet table in one room with all kinds of food and stuff. He said they treated him so good, like a king coming home, he didn't have the nerve to even harm them.

Mingus Sr. enlisted in the army at Richmond, Virginia, on December 30, 1897; he was twenty. His mother had married when he was fourteen. Did he leave the family estate again because of his stepfather? Or was it because of the Ku Klux Klan's dominance? Whatever happened, his first three-year hitch probably included a stint in the Tenth Cavalry in the Philippines during the Spanish-American War. Then he was discharged from Fort Wright in Washington.

He was out of the service for eighteen months, long enough to head back to the Mingus family homestead to see where he fit, if at all. His stories make his ambivalence clear. What is known is that on June 12, 1902, he reenlisted, this time in the 24th Regiment of Infantry—a colored outfit, as it was called then. With it, he'd move from Montana to New York to the Southwest, until his twenty-year-plus time in was up and his second wife wanted to move to Los Angeles to be with her family.

Harriet Sophia Phillips Mingus was, like her husband, multiracial. Her father, John, was Chinese from Hong Kong and a British subject; her mother was black. Charles Jr. and his sisters would dimly remember her almond-shaped eyes, her yellow-toned skin, her gentle voice—and not much more. Physically they'd all resemble their father, who was five feet, eight-and-a-half inches tall and heavyset. But their skin had a hint of hers—light with a yellowish cast. Her famous son, who inherited his father's extremely bowed legs, would later use as a working title for his autobiography *Memoirs of a Half-Schitt-Colored Nigger*.

Grace, the oldest of the three children, sketchily remembers the trip to Los Angeles, to her grandmother's house at 1545 East 52nd Street. She recalls her mother complaining on the train ride, and says wistfully, "Her pictures show a beautiful woman."

Several weeks after Harriet's death, Staff Sergeant Charles Mingus Sr. retired from the army, after logging in twenty-seven years, eleven months, and twenty-one days—including his two years, one month, and twenty-seven days in the Philippines. (Foreign service counted for double time; Sergeant Mingus actually spent some twenty-three years on active duty.) So he was entitled to a full pension.

Two days after his son was born, he'd joined the Benevolent Proud Order of Elks. Once Harriet died, he showed up at the Los Angeles lodge, and also joined the Masonic Order, where he'd eventually rise to the twentieth degree. And he signed on at the post office right after his discharge.

These posts and his passion for bridge, a long-standing hobby from his army career, were the pillars of his daily life. Twenty years as a high-ranking NCO in the daily grind of the peacetime army quartermaster's corp left him with a clear sense of his right to command. Unbuffered by his children's mother, he usually ordered them around, and often bullied them.

Enter Mamie Newton Carson Mingus, his third and final wife. Born in South Carolina, half black and half American Indian, barely five feet tall, Mamie added another darker strain to the Mingus household's racial melange. Her arrival on the scene—along with her son Odell, a dozen or more years older than the Mingus kids and disliked by them and their father—rerouted the family's always fragile internal dynamics.

VIVIAN MINGUS: She told my daddy she'd had a dream. The Lord had told her she'd be the one to take care of his children; she'd dreamt she had Charles in her arms. And then she turned out to be a witch.

GRACE MINGUS: Mamie was crazy about my brother. She called him Baby. I thought Mama was a beautiful person to take a man's three children and raise them up, dedicate her life to that. She didn't go anywhere. Daddy, he'd go out and play bridge with his friends and Mama would stay with us. We were no kin to her. She was just good like that.

When the Reverend Holbrook married Mamie and Charles Mingus Sr. on July 1, 1923, they seemed like the odd couple. Mingus's bulk and carefully invulnerable air of frowning authority contrasted sharply with the tiny Mamie's passivity. The gulf in personality eventually helped undermine their marriage. It could sour even the good times with tensions and arguments and frustrations.

But they started off well-meaning enough. Mamie was plain and downhome, but she was willing to mother three kids who weren't hers in exchange for financial security. That Mingus Sr. could provide. He would rise to supervisor at the post office. His circle of old army buddies and his fraternal orders' memberships created a network of friends. Playing bridge with them would more and more keep him out of the new Mingus home.

Right after the wedding, the family moved into a bungalow at 1621 East 108th Street. It was large enough to fit them comfortably, even with Mamie's son Odell. In the early 1920s, Watts, like most of the region around Los Angeles, was still semirural. Its population was racially mixed—blacks, Mexicans, Japanese, whites. Most of them gardened on their land to supplement storebought groceries.

Thanks to Mamie, the Minguses had a bountiful truck farm. The arbor in the backyard doubled as a playhouse; beneath the hanging grapes, Vivian and Charles, thick as thieves, would play house or preacher, taking turns as the man of God. Near the garage stood the fig tree, then the pond, then the peach trees farther back. Chickens and turkeys and ducks shared the plot with the crops: corn, string beans, tomatoes, and the usual greens, including collard greens. Says Vivian, "White people would come by and ask for them, they'd be so tall, so high. Mama'd give them some."

Mamie seems to have done her best for the Mingus children, though she could sometimes be as gruff and dismissive in her peevish way as their father. But she'd also make them treats and tip them for doing errands or tasks for her. And she tried to shield them, usually ineffectually, from their father's furious temper. The confrontations could explode into beatings. Grace says her father hit her last when she was sixteen.

Charles Jr. grew up relatively coddled and indulged. He bore the brunt of his father's rage less than the girls. As the sole boy, Charles was the apple of his father's eye. Not for nothing was he called Baby by his family until he was in his early teens. "We were raised to stay kids, even when we got big," says Vivian. For Sergeant Mingus, it was another form of control.

Most of Baby's early adventures were trivial, typical exurban childhood escapades. He'd climb up onto the kitchen counter and eat the stuffing out of Mamie's delicious sweet potato pies, or catch a cat or a field mouse and toss it against the side of the house. He'd wet the bed, and his father's temper would flare, and he'd get a whipping. He'd disappoint his sister Vivian by telling her there was no Easter Bunny, despite their parents' elaborate charades. He'd go pony-riding at a neighbor's.

He was Baby, a pudgy, bowlegged child so much the center of attention that any threat to his well-being was seen as a catastrophe. If he got a stomachache or got clawed, it was his sisters' fault, and they'd get hit. "Girls were nothing," recalls Vivian. "He was the prize. He was carrying the Mingus name."

When Baby was three or four, the Mingus kids were playing tag inside the house. To escape his sisters, Baby lunged into the corner of a dresser, opening a small gash over his eye. With all the blood, the family thought he was dying. They raced him to the doctor, where he got a couple of stitches, leaving a small scar.

Only a couple of years later, Baby was at a Tom Thumb wedding, a widespread church event for kids, when he fell in love with Mary Ellen Kelly, daughter of a local cop. She was the first in a long, long series of females to fix Charles Mingus Jr.'s focus.[5]

One of the harshest punishments the boy got from his father was caused by girls. Around third grade, Baby started looking up girls' dresses in class, in the schoolyard, in the playground. Some girls told the teachers. Baby was sent home from school, and his father was called in to see the principal. Mingus Sr.

was incensed: his sense of morality ran deep and conservative, even if he didn't always apply it to himself. And so he came home from the principal's office and shaved his son's gentle curls to shame him.

"He sat in the back of church all embarrassed," remembers Vivian. For the congregation at the African Methodist Episcopal (AME) church around the corner from the Mingus house, shaving your head meant physically defiling your body, God's temple. It was a vivid sign of Baby's sinful ways, a scarlet A.

Every Sunday, the Mingus family went to the AME church. The music at the services went from the old hymnals to Baptist-style shouts, while the sermons touched the usual chords of hellfire and damnation.

For the Mingus children, the weekly churchgoing became an empty ritual of righteousness. For years, each Sunday morning before church, their house rocked with their parents' bitter arguing. Sometimes things got physical. Mamie started dressing more and more like a mammy, acting more and more down-home country, knowing it enraged and disgusted her husband. She took a fancy new dress he bought her and cut it up into underwear. She nagged him about being away so much, about running around. One Sunday, Sergeant Mingus hit her, and she ran around to show and tell all the neighbors.

She started going to other churches beside the AME, including the Baptist Church. She was superstitious. For her, evil was a vivid presence in the world.

When the kids were almost teenagers, the main source of argument between Mamie and Sergeant Mingus was one Miss Garrett, choir member at the AME church. By the time Baby was in high school, the goings-on between his father and Miss Garrett had long been an open secret.

Baby never stopped wanting female attention. Growing up with his mother dead, a doting if unpredictable stepmother, and two sisters made him aware early of the opposite sex. They protected him, cuddled him, solved his problems when they could. He didn't have to compete with them. They listened to him, hung on his bright sayings, cheered his triumphs, like his getting honorable mention in a Community Chest poster contest for coining the slogan, "Give and let live."[6] For the rest of his life, he'd trust women instinctively and generously, with little hesitation.

Males were a different matter. Lots of things provoked his father. But then the old man sometimes backed him to the hilt. The way he remembered it, his grade-school teachers thought "he was dumb. And he wasn't learning much. It was decided to send him to a dumb school, as he described it. Mingus's father, light-skinned and scornful of the intelligence of most whites, came to instruct the principal." When they checked the boy's IQ scores, his father told him, "Even by white man's standards, you're a genius."[7]

Then there were the boys at school, who called him names and left him out of recess games and stole his lunch almost every day. They inspired only dreams of revenge.

Life for the Mingus children was materially comfortable and relatively unde-manding. There were weekend outings to Lincoln Park and Santa Monica, where they'd picnic and their father would swim and terrorize them into try-ing. Neither Vivian nor Baby learned. But the boy loved to watch the shows on the Santa Monica pier.

Every year, the three children had to go to the Colosseum, where Los Ange-les veterans marched and caroused to honor themselves and their memories. "My daddy would put his uniform on, with all the stripes and ribbons," says Vi-vian. "He seemed to have a lot of friends." His old-boy network dictated the children's caroling rounds every Christmas. Every year on Christmas morning, he'd get up early and make egg nog, with the bottle of whiskey, not rum, he'd buy once a year just for that. He'd leave a little; spiked with sugar, it doubled as cold medicine year-round. Every year, after they drank the eggnog on Christ-mas morning, their father took them and a couple of friends to sing at veter-ans' homes.

Sergeant Mingus's world ran on rails, and on time.

VIVIAN MINGUS: He didn't like people disagreeing with him. Very stern. He just sorta delivered orders. Every day, he'd come home, and we'd open the gate, and he'd come in. He'd take his shoes off and put his house shoes on, every day. He'd take the newspaper and start reading, every day. There wasn't much communication. Me, I was the type of person who wanted to be affectionate. But when I'd sit on his lap, my stepmother would make me get off. She broke up the relationship between my father and me. She didn't like it. I thought it was kind of evil.

Baby's bicycle gave him enviable freedom; the girls, who weren't allowed to go out alone, got in trouble if they didn't stay together or wandered too far. Their father would send them to look for his son, calling "Baby" along the streets—though they never knew where they'd find him. He wandered all over the neighborhood, and sometimes made it clear into L.A.

He met some interesting characters. A local autodidact recited excerpts from the encyclopedia about far-flung topics like Julius Caesar and Buffalo Bill. Fascinated, Baby started reading the encyclopedia at home. He began going to the library.

Then there was Sabato, better known as Simon, Rodia, the builder of the

now-famed Watts Tower. The old Italian immigrant built a castlelike forti-
fication around his house, a maze of birdbaths and fountains and the like
topped by towers stretching skyward. He worked texture and color into the
mortar and cement with heterogeneous bits of found junk, from seashells and
stones to busted chunks of Phillips' Milk of Magnesia bottles. Slowly, over
thirty-three years, the towers arose as Rodia worked slowly, steadily, all by himself, all by hand. Now the Towers, with their sprawling rhythms and triumph
of romantic artistic vision over formalism, are a monument to so-called primitive art, a tourist stop that's an ironic Disneyland. Don DeLillo has aptly
dubbed it a "jazz cathedral."[8] In Depression-era Watts, though, Rodia was just
another local eccentric. Like other local kids, Baby earned pennies and nickels
for bringing him anything from soda bottles to bits of tile and glass or pebbles
for his ever-growing sculpture.

All the Mingus household studied music. In the 1920s, radio was still more
idea and hobby than business. As the children grew, it matured into mass
media. In any case, Sergeant Mingus was uninterested in it. But studying
music—European classical music—had status, bourgeois respectability. Besides, music lessons were easily available, thanks to cheap itinerant teachers,
who varied wildly in talent. And then there were the public schools, where
music lessons were free, as part of the curriculum with accredited activities
like orchestra.

GRACE MINGUS: My father's the one that started all of us on music. For him,
it was part of being an educated person. He didn't seem to care about music
himself. He never played an instrument. I never even heard him try to sing. But
you had to be doing something with music: Charles on the trombone and me
on the violin, my sister on the piano. I hated it.

Grace wanted to sing, but her father insisted on the violin. Vivian wanted to
paint and draw, but Mingus Sr. made her study piano. When he was eight or
so, Charles took up the trombone—his father got him one via the Sears-Roe-
buck catalogue—for a few weeks and dropped it, then picked up the cello. He
was surprisingly quick at it; he had natural talent, an ear. His first teacher was
a mediocre itinerant. But Vivian's teacher, an African woman named Miss
Loketi, was a disciplined pedagogue. Soon Baby too was studying with her.

He liked music—the rising and falling cadences at church, the crackly
broadcasts of big bands like Duke Ellington's. When he was twelve, he heard
Ellington over the radio and fell instantly in love with Duke's music. It was just
around then, when Charles Mingus Jr. hit junior high school, that he decided
he was black.

During Baby's childhood, the black population in Los Angeles nearly doubled. The largest influx of immigrants came, like Sergeant Mingus, from the Southwest, especially Texas, and brought the blues to Los Angeles as they looked for work. The railroads helped draw them. Blacks worked on the Santa Fe and Southern Pacific, which nineteenth-century Anglos had built with Irish, Chinese, and black labor to connect L.A. with the rest of the former Spanish New World.

Still, the City of Angels was pretty strictly segregated. There was zoning and restricted housing, housing covenants. It wasn't southern Jim Crow, where the streets had to be cleared at sundown. But the strong streak of nativism in the local white Anglo-Saxon Protestant (WASP) elites ensured that blacks and whites mixed freely only in out-of-the-way, limited sites.

As black immigrants poured into South Central Los Angeles, it changed from a racially mixed semirural exurb to a predominantly black, increasingly lower-class suburb. Where the Mingus family lived, in Watts, would change color and be absorbed as a result.

Mingus Sr. had it good: an enviable government job and an army pension. In Depression-era Watts, he was solidly bourgeois. To some kids, the Mingus kids were rich. They had milk every day.

Their father had ambitions for them, aspirations that suited his memories of childhood, his sense of entitlement and worth. Music was only part of them. Grace recalls, "When me and my sister were maybe twelve or thirteen, he would introduce us to different young men, from families that were upper-crust. 'Miz so-and-so's son is gonna be a doctor or lawyer.' He was ambitious for us."

W. E. B. Du Bois wrote, "The problem of the twentieth century is the problem of the color-line."[9] The Mingus family lived that problem.

VIVIAN MINGUS: Grace was the darkest. We always called her the blackest one in the family. Charles and I were always picking on her. My momma had to come in there and whip all three of us, break up the fight.

GRACE MINGUS: My sister was more or less Daddy's girl. I always thought my daddy didn't like me, because I was the darkest one. They used to kid me: blackest in the family. And I grew up and found out I wasn't black, and I used to cry like a baby.

Sergeant Mingus kept his two daughters close and carefully monitored their friends. "He didn't want us playing with certain kids," says Grace. "He'd say, 'I don't want you playing with those black niggers.'" Yet she also recalls how he fought to amalgamate the separate-but-equal unions at the post office, heavy since Reconstruction with black workers: "Daddy had friends who were dark-skinned and light-skinned. I could never understand that."

Vivian never reconciled her father's membership in the National Association for the Advancement of Colored People (NAACP) with his wanting his daughters to marry white men. When she brought home her first dark boyfriend, Sergeant Mingus blustered at her about having black children. When she met a few members of her extended family, she got more confused. Part of her mother's family came from New Mexico and spoke Spanish; her uncle looked white. Her New York cousins, Rudy and Estella Williams, were dark black.

And then there was Mamie. Vivian recalls, "It's sad. I remember how, just walking down the streets of Watts, Mama would say, 'Those two little black kids look like monkeys to me. And you belong to that race.' I felt real bad. It was because of my father's attitudes. He didn't like people disagreeing with him."

Nor did his son—particularly about race. For Charles Mingus Jr., the neurotic contradictions of American racism were personal—highly personal. Paradox was at the heart of his darkness. He talked about it endlessly, not always coherently, at times thoughtfully, often provocatively. Race was painfully complex for him, though that complexity came out at times as self-contradiction. It was a matter of fierce pride and bitter resentment because his appearance could be so racially ambiguous—because his skin was not black.

2 Black Like Me

BABY WORKED hard on the cello, despite teachers like the racist Italian Signor Lippi in junior high school, whom he would later mostly belittle. Music came easy to him, and he liked that. His father complained whenever he was around about the kids sawing away on the instruments he insisted they study. But Sergeant Mingus was proud that Charles was a prized member of the Los Angeles Junior Philharmonic, and he made sure to come to the performances. For Charles, anything that kept the feisty old man off his back and on his side was worth doing well.

During his last couple of years in grade school, though, when the boy was lugging his cello back and forth every day, he felt like a target. And in the complicated cultural geography and hierarchies that multiplied as Watts grew denser, he didn't fit neatly anywhere.

He'd discovered that the hard way: he'd become the butt of threats and beatings and name-calling and put-downs from most of Watts's ethnic groups. The bullies and gangs whose paths inevitably crossed his included Mexicans, whites, and blacks. He was called nigger for the first time by Mexicans, and wondered how he could be something his father hated so much. When white bullies chased him, they complained about miscegenation, although Baby and his paramour were nine years old. When blacks picked on him, the confrontations turned on his color and sissyhood.

He couldn't have been more of an outsider.

Two years later, Baby's world tilted. The Great Long Beach Earthquake of

1933 shook his grade school at 103rd Street and leveled the small shops, clustered around it, that served Watts. Structural damage at the school forced the pupils to transfer elsewhere. Like many, Baby ended up trudging with his cello three miles each day down the San Pedro tracks, to the 111th Street School. There the population was overwhelmingly black. It was a situation he'd never faced before.

He didn't start well. Not long after he arrived, he called David Bryant a black motherfucker. *Black* wasn't a cool term in the 1930s. Bryant, another sissy by reputation who played the violin, punched him in the stomach, and Baby went over like a punctured balloon.[1]

Cornered by gangs day after day, Charles made new friends—a Japanese family, the Okes. The gangs congregated in front of their store, and one of the Oke kids was among the few nonblacks at Charles's new school. The boys taught Charles about judo. It was enough to shock the gangs, who were used to his timidity. They also introduced him to Japanese food, his first culinary adventure. He basked in the glow of familial warmth missing in his own home. The contrast was stark. When Charles had asked Sergeant Mingus to teach him to fight, his father head-butted him across the room and announced, "That's your first lesson, son."[2]

Driving Charles to learn self-defense was a gang leader named Coustie.[3] A few years older, he was a classic bully, using his size and reputation to scare smaller kids. Charles was an easy target.

Coustie was a long nightmare, someone who knew the sissy grade-school Baby's reputation. He called Baby a "half-schitt colored nigger" and regularly threatened and teased him, sometimes slapped him around. And there he was, to greet Charles on his new school's opening day.

BUDDY COLLETTE, *musician and friend*: I'd heard about Mingus before I'd met him. We were going to Jordan High School, and he was actually walking on 96th and Compton after school one day. And he had a shoeshine box over his shoulder; he had a strap. It was a tall kind of box, three feet tall; it had legs on it rather than a flat bottom. It was different from all the others I'd seen—and I'd seen them all. A lot of us were shining shoes for extra money—for reeds, mouthpieces, you know. But his looked like a chicken coop, or something birds would fly into. But it still had the footrest on top.

So I said, "You got to be Mingus." And he said, "Yeah, well, how did you know?" This stuff he was doing, the way he looked—it was easy enough to pick him out. He was bowlegged. He was heavy. And he was definitely pigeon-toed. He was bigger and bowlegged and pigeon-toed and light-complexioned—a different look than most of the kids of the same size. His hair was kind of wavy, but it was more into a Latin look than black. So I told him, "Well, they said you'd be different, look different." He didn't know how to take that. He figured I was putting him on. So I kidded around with him a little bit. I said, "I don't know why you have this shine box so tall." He said, "The reason is that so people I shine shoes for can sit on the hood of the car. That way their feet reach." I thought, Boy, this guy is really something.

Nobody in the Jordan High School yard looked like him in 1936, but lots of the other kids noticed him. They couldn't miss him. He looked like an amalgam of leftover parts—the baby-fat body perched on bowlegs and pigeon-toes, the hot-combed-and-greased Spanish hair, the saffron-meets-taffy complexion. Then there was his weird, hard-to-take attitude. He was like a current crackling between poles of arrogant flamboyance and sissy crap. Charles Mingus Jr. was unique. He knew it. So did they.

To most teenagers, uniqueness sounds cool but doesn't feel cool. In the cruel calculus of teenhood, almost all feel they don't measure up to something. At thirteen, entering Jordan Junior/Senior High School, Charles Mingus Jr. had real reasons for feeling left out. He was a loner who had girlfriends. Males were baffling and potentially dangerous. The world he carried in his head was still inchoate, a whispered promise. But it was where he'd done most of his living. If that made everything that touched him seem bigger than life, it also made him uncertain, erratic, always ready to be hurt when he faced the outside world.

On opening day at Jordan, the older boys traditionally hazed new kids by stealing their pants and running them up the school flagpole. Charles had a bright idea born of fear: he flushed his underpants down the toilet, then ran to the principal's office to ask for protection for his cello. Instead, Principal Doherty good-naturedly handed him over the the mob led by Coustie.

For the first time, Charles took charge by wielding a clever idea with instinctive timing that played to a hostile audience. He dared the boys to pants him and leave him naked. That, they all knew, would bring the cops. When they hesitated, he yelled, "Go for the chicks, you dumb bastards." So they did. And then they waited for orders. He told them to take the girls' underpants.

He saw them in a new light.

CHARLES MINGUS: A mob is a large cowardly animal with several heads and each head has a large, loud mouth backed by strong lungs and a frightened, overworking heart.[4]

Up till then, he'd nearly always flunked the tribal schoolyard rituals boys work on each other to establish pecking orders and relationships. He was lousy at sports and didn't like doing things he couldn't pick up quickly. After years of being chosen out of schoolyard games or becoming their butt, he wasn't interested. Besides, he didn't like competing when it wasn't something that mattered to him.

He did like to talk and show off, once he got started, which was usually around the girls. But even then he came off as a sissy and superior—lethal around the boys. He watched small knots of them slouching in corners or milling around the schoolyard or the park, and he didn't feel any way to connect. He didn't understand them. He couldn't see what there was to compete with them about.

That first day in the Jordan High schoolyard taught him the first of a lifetime's lessons in leadership, but it took him another couple of years to get over what one of his first real pals calls "his complexes."

BRITT WOODMAN, *musician and friend*: The kids in grade school used to take his lunch. He was very timid then. And very bowlegged. So they made fun of him. And he played cello. I was in the senior orchestra. And when he found that out, I think in his second semester, he signed up to play in the junior orchestra. This is in high school. They said he played well enough that the next semester they transferred him to senior orchestra, which is where I met him and we became friends.

Two years older than Charles, sixteen-year-old Britt Woodman already played trombone. It was the first instrument the younger boy tried, and he'd always loved the sound. Good-natured and mischievous, Britt felt sorry for the strange but strangely interesting new kid. So he invited Charles back to the Woodman gas station to shoot some hoops and hang out after school. Few people visited the standoffish Mingus home, but the boy seized any chance to see how others lived. And so, through the Woodmans, he entered the world of Watts, with its dirt streets that rain still turned to mud, the Largo and Yeager theaters that on Saturdays drew local kids with cowboy pictures and cartoon shorts, and the 22nd Street gang called the Tarzans, who had regular run-ins with white and Mexican gangs from Los Angeles trying to take some of their turf.

William Woodman, father of the Woodman brood, had played with Duke Ellington. In that pre-TV era, he saw music as a family activity that doubled as entertainment, but he also knew it was a door to a better world. In the 1920s and 1930s, jazz attracted the college-educated black elite. It opened a way into the lucrative entertainment industry. So Woodman trained his kids and formed the Woodman Brothers Orchestra, billed as "The Biggest Little Band in the World." All his kids played more than one instrument; Britt learned clarinet and tenor sax as well as trombone.

They played on weekends at weddings and dances. Charles came by and watched them rehearse. As he and Britt became close, the Woodmans worked on his poor music-reading skills. They helped train his sensitive ear to work with written music. But he'd never be able to read a score easily on first sight.

Britt tried to open other doors to teen social life.

BRITT WOODMAN: I was an expert on the rings, and gymnastics, at athletics— Ping-Pong, horseshoes, basketball. So I showed him all that. I liked to play him Ping-Pong with my left hand because he couldn't never really play. He used to get mad at me and say, "Play with your right hand." And I'd say, "You got to learn."

I always told him, "Charles, everything you do, the rings, basketball, horseshoes, there's an art to it." I never showed him what it was for arm-wrestling, so I could beat him twelve times with my right hand, and nine times with my left. I didn't weigh but 125, but I had lifted weights, and I was pretty strong. But it was an art. Like basketball—we'd play different fellas, pickup games, at 21, for a nickel. Mingus had this play where he'd run under the basket and throw the ball back out, and I'd shoot. He had that down. I had a shot with my left hand, and they'd think I was gonna shoot with my right. So we beat most of the fellas we played. So he got pretty good at basketball, but the other sports, he never really got.

Woodman's acceptance touched some chord in his young and moody friend. He joined the football team, started telling jokes with Britt in the schoolyard. Then Britt took Charlie, as the boy's new friends called him, to the Woodman family's Holiness church at 79th and Watts, where the music swelled and the congregation rocked. It unlocked another world he'd only glimpsed at his family's church. He absorbed it greedily.

The Woodman family, and soon the Collette family, became his safe havens, his alternatives to the Mingus family. And from then on, Britt Woodman and Buddy Collette were among the few people Charlie Mingus almost never took on in an explosive rage. When he needed their help in a jam, he usually pictured himself as the victim of racism.

Buddy Collette was eight months older than Charlie. Like Britt, he came from a supportive musical family, an open and loving environment leavened with his dad's playful sense of humor. Charlie was hit by the contrast with home.

BUDDY COLLETTE: His family wasn't the everyday kind. The mother was very quiet. She was very nice. She used to fix us lunch, stuff like that. The father was very stern. He didn't seem to have a lot of love for Mingus. He didn't show it. My dad was more talkative, funlike, telling stories and stuff—the way Mingus showed him in *Beneath the Underdog* [Mingus's autobiography].

I don't know the relationship between the mother and father. It was almost like they didn't talk very much. But the dad seemed to be taking care of business, going to work. But they wouldn't be like, "I'll miss you, honey." Not a warm kind of thing. Mingus chose music and they stayed out of his way. They wanted him to play, but it wasn't like they were sitting there saying, "Charles, you've got to practice."

It was Collette who suggested the pudgy yellow fourteen-year-old turn in his cello for a bass. The suggestion turned on race. Classical music, Collette underlined for him, was closed to nonwhites. Jazz, on the other hand, could take a talented black man to the top—or at least make him a living. "Learn to slap that bass," Collette told his friend, "and you'll always be able to get work."

Pushing him from the other side was the teacher who led the Jordan High School orchestra, Mr. Joseph Louis Lippi. The boy had jumped from junior to senior symphony, where the music was more demanding. Charlie's lack of training at reading scores made him stumble at the first rehearsal. Mr. Lippi announced loudly and condescendingly, "I've noticed that most Negroes can't read."

CHARLES MINGUS: Il Signore had a Florentine bias against any possible descendants of the great Hannibal of Carthage. . . . It is historical fact that the young white ladies and women looted and raped the black soldiers for their *hardwares*, which may account for certain very dark Italian offspring down to this very day.[5]

From then on, Mingus regularly translated his confrontations into racial conflicts. Since he was yellow, he had to be louder, harder, and angrier about being black.

BUDDY COLLETTE: The greatest thing about going to Jordan High was they had all the races there. You grew up without any prejudices. You almost had to. There's Chinese and Japanese and Mexican and white. We all had to go to the same school. And nobody was any better; you better not call any racial names.

And a lot of times he thought more was happening about that than there was; he'd concentrate on it all the time and make it stronger. The racial thing was there, and he was very light-skinned. So a lot of times people didn't know; they might have talked in racial terms. He'd say, "God, those guys look like they don't like me." And then part of the reason would be they might not know what he was. He's saying, "I'm black." They could have said, "You don't look it." That was happening a lot.

Buddy had his own reasons for suggesting that Charlie try the bass. His band had lost its tuba player, and he wanted to replace the old-fashioned oompah with a string bass. He didn't know anybody else who played the cello, and figured if you could play one, you could pick up the other. Besides, Charlie didn't seem that attached to the cello. He told his new pal he wasn't too impressed with the family string trio, that he was just doing it to please his parents. So when Buddy suggested that Sergeant Mingus trade the cello in for a bass so Charlie could could join his band, the pudgy boy's face opened and lit up. From then on, Buddy Collette could do virtually no wrong.

A band meant making money, anything from fifty cents to a couple of dollars. School lunch cost about a dime. A hot dog was a nickel. And playing music beat shining shoes. At first the youngsters played for neighborhood house parties thrown by their parents and parents' friends. This gave them a chance to meet girls outside of school hallways or between-class breaks. Musicians, they knew, attracted women. The power was the stuff of myth among them, up there with the legend of Peatie Wheatstraw letting the devil tune his guitar to make him a virtuoso.

But in 1930s Watts, there were limits to sexual exploring.

BUDDY COLLETTE: In his book, those parts where he was dating one girl and went and had sex with three or four and stuff like that, a lot of that he used to dream about. The stuff he said about us doing wild things—we didn't do them. If you were dating at fifteen or sixteen then, you didn't have much leeway to keep her out very late. Things were really strict. You could be in a shotgun marriage. Sure, there'd be kissing and touching. But you knew that if you made that girl pregnant, you were going to marry her. The fathers were very strict. We could sneak away a little bit, in the summer. But everybody was on a schedule. Some baloney and cheese and crackers, a couple of bottles of Coke—that was a party. But when he was writing the book, he blew these things up, and they were more exciting. Give it a little zip.

When Charlie told his parents he wanted a bass, Mamie told him they couldn't afford it. Britt, now a regular visitor, chimed in that Charlie's quick ear would make him a very good bassist. He had a real future in music. Sergeant Mingus listened, and acted.

A couple of weeks after Buddy's offer, Charlie called Britt, told him he'd gotten a bass, and asked him to help lug it to Jordan. Then he found Buddy during lunch. He was ready to start. "He just gripped that bass and got going, like with the rings and basketball," says Woodman. Most lunchtimes found Buddy and the Bledsoe brothers rehearsing, and he joined in, feeling his way through the simple chords of popular hits like "The Music Goes Round and Round" and "I'm an Old Cowhand." A week after he first sat in, the band did its first gig.

Until Woodman graduated, he and Buddy and Charlie were always hanging around together. They'd hop the trolley that plied Central Avenue between downtown L.A. and Watts, part of the light rail system that still crisscrossed America then. Buddy and Charlie would ride for hours and practice their instruments. They'd play their tunes and pick up spare change from riders, and swap daydreams of what they'd do beyond Watts. The trio made a solemn pact that they'd always pursue music.

The bass became the core of who Charles Mingus was.

BRITT WOODMAN: He got over being bowlegged once he got his bass. He came to school with a beige zoot suit. All of a sudden, he was growing out of all his complexes. He had a piano at home, and he had a record of Duke Ellington, and he played me the introduction on the piano. Brilliant.

He started fighting around then, and I think I'm the one who caused it. We got a big bag and stuffed it, and put it in our garage, and showed him how to box. I said, "Charles, these cats are picking on you every day, so we'll show you the one-two punch." And he started fighting with people, even my friends. He never had control over himself. No discipline over his emotions—it was one of his downfalls.

One of his first targets was Coustie.

His confidence was rapidly inflating. His sense of himself seemed to be coalescing. He was trusting his impulses, letting them go, becoming utterly spontaneous. Everything he did became a statement of self-expression and a demand for the spotlight. Toward the end of his time at Jordan High School he stripped and walked naked along the street, just to draw attention to himself.

3 Making the Scene

CHARLES MINGUS JR. slid listlessly through the academic side of Jordan High. His intellectual curiosity went into reading books he got from the library, the encyclopedia at home, odds and ends he picked up in his wanderings around Los Angeles. His heart went into learning to play the bass. He played along with songs on the radio and learned more tunes from the other boys. Like most beginners, he concentrated on flashy moves, playing fast.

It got him attention and approval, and girls. But he also was a perfectionist. He was driven to succeed. Right away, he wanted to be the best. And so Buddy Collette and Britt Woodman helped him study, to practice, deepen his technique and musical understanding.

After all, music was his way out—out of Watts and L.A., out of the post office future his father envisioned, maybe even out of the bars of race.

He could cross those barriers with the music within him. He'd spent years playing European concert music. He loved Richard Strauss's *Death and Transfiguration*, with its weighty themes and rich melodies. The bittersweet Romantic lyricism of the Impressionists drew him, especially the mournful cello works of Debussy and Ravel. The cello had also introduced him to Bach, the master performer who wrote down his improvisations, who outlined modern Western ideas of harmony as well as thematic development. And the knotty ensembles of Beethoven's string quartets spoke deeply to him.[1]

He saw how the notions of thematic development and improvisation were linked. He was discovering that beyond the swing-era hits he and his pals loved to play unfolded a dimly lit region where black composers from Scott Joplin to his hero Duke Ellington had mapped out extended musical works. He needed to know more about what they were doing, and how. He needed to know what to do about the music that was starting to fill his head, like a personal, ever-changing soundtrack.

He needed a teacher—a real teacher.

LaRue Brown Watson, *widow of trumpeter Clifford Brown*: In Los Angeles at that time, there were two teachers who were always referred to as Mister—Mr. Lloyd Reese and Mr. Samuel Browne. They taught absolutely everybody who would be anybody, including Mingus.

Across Depression-era America, urban public schools offered music programs. They were once as common as gym and shop, and they helped train an entire generation of young black American musicians who became jazz players.

Sam Browne taught at Jefferson High School. There were classes in theory and basic musicianship, and there were two bands. The school marching band played light classics; the swing band played stock charts of Count Basie and Benny Goodman hits. His students used to call him Count Browne, partly because he led so many bands, partly because he kept the wild young Watts dudes not only in line, but interested.

There were plenty of other teachers. Al Adams led a band that met weekly at the Ross Snyder playground in Watts, and played affairs at the Elks Hall on 40th and Central. Adams's band once held a battle of the bands with George Brown's there. It was the night a young alto saxist named Illinois Jacquet switched to tenor.

All this hustle and playing plus the kids' own bands, like the Woodman Brothers, gave them a taste of what it was like to be professional, even during high school.

Chico Hamilton, *musician and friend*: We got together when Buddy was playing with his band in Watts. And I wanted to play. So I asked Buddy to sit in, and he said okay. I was a sharp-looking little cat. They were playing swing, popular tunes. Buddy later joined the band we started in Jefferson High. Charlie was hanging around with Buddy.

We auditioned for a spot at the Million Dollar Theater, in downtown L.A. That and the Lincoln Theater on Central Avenue both had shows, like burlesque and vaudeville. When the bands came to L.A. they'd play one or the other or both. Every band had its own show—a line of girls, singers, dancers, comedians— that it brought in. So we got the gig, but to get it we combined Buddy's band

and mine. Illinois Jacquet was in that band. We were all fifteen or sixteen at the time. And we stayed together. The union came and made us a proposition 'cause we raised so much hell, so we joined the union—for seven dollars. What happened was, all the gigs in town, if a union band was playing, we'd play cheaper—a dollar, five dollars cheaper.

Buddy was the first of us to hit the big time in L.A. He got the job with the number one local band, playing at this big nightclub with a show. He had a car, a big Pontiac. He was the only guy who could control Mingus, cool him down.

Britt Woodman was the first to go professional. He spent his senior year at Jordan playing half-days at the Pollux Theater, where his father had played for years. He got $21 a week, plus house passes he lavished on his pals.

BRITT WOODMAN: One time the comedian on the bill, his name was Rooney. He was Mickey Rooney's dad. So Mickey Rooney came by the theater one day for a matinee, and that's when I met him. It's when he was doing the Andy Hardy series. I would tell Charles the jokes from the show during recess at school, and we'd have the kids gathered around us. Years later, when we'd do that, the musicians working for him were amazed. They never saw him like that before they saw him with me or Buddy.

Charlie talked about Buddy Collette nonstop to everybody he met. He was constantly comparing everybody to his best friend. Technique and discipline? Tone and articulation? Dedication and originality? Nobody touched Buddy. "Buddy Collette could do that," was his standard comeback in jam sessions and rehearsals. Collette met musicians who were sick of hearing his name before they'd met him.

Sergeant Mingus had always wanted his son to take the post office test. It was a steady job with good pay and a good pension, the best future for a boy with shaky grades and artistic ambitions. What else could a man shunted to the black side of the tracks in America hope to do? Working for the feds was a black tradition since Reconstruction days. It was security in an insecure world, where anything from race to the Depression crushed the less nimble. And it had been good enough for him.

So Charles was set in his senior year to take the test. At the last minute, he decided not to show up. When he finally admitted the truth to his father, he told the old man he wanted to be a musician. Sergeant Mingus didn't reach for his belt. He looked at his son and said, "All right. What do we need to make you a success?" His son didn't miss a beat: "A really good instrument and a good teacher." Sergeant Mingus nodded. His son got both.

Buddy told him he had to practice hard and regularly to become the world's greatest bassist, and so he started. For hours a day, he scoped his way around the bulky strings and recalcitrant fingerboard, developing tricks and techniques, learning unusual fingerings and positions, learning to use the big bass like a cello. He taped his index and middle fingers together to hobble them, forcing his ring finger to build strength and agility. Of all his musical playmates, only a kid named Eric Dolphy, who played the clarinet, matched or exceeded his intensity.

They met through their teacher, a dark-skinned, round-faced, serious-looking man, a chainsmoker with perfect pitch who reminded acquaintances of Count Basie. His name was Lloyd Reese.

BUDDY COLLETTE: Lloyd was more like a professor or doctor. He wanted to make sure you had the right sound, were tuned, make sure you knew the right chords. I don't think he was so much into saying what you should play. He was just trying to make you have the best knowledge and then allow you to have your own style. It was something you needed, because other than that, you take a few lessons with somebody and you're on your way. But he said, "Let's take 'Body and Soul' in this key." Then he taught you how to transpose with a Roman numeral. He showed us how to think and apply this stuff—intervals and scales and long tones. It's like the foundation for a house.

Lloyd Reese was black bourgeoisie. His father was an architect in New Orleans; Reese had graduated with a conservatory degree from the University of Southern California. He'd played with Red Nichols and worked at Warner Brothers in the studios—an exceptional achievement for a black musician. An urbane man, he crossed color lines in a day when the L.A. musicians' unions were segregated. He knew Los Angeles's expatriate artists, Nazi-fleeing luminaries like composer Arnold Schoenberg. With his sophisticated attitude toward race and life, he had the sort of polish and élan Ellington projected.

In his well-furnished home on Jefferson Avenue off Central Avenue, Reese held a kind of cross between a musical salon and a school. Star musicians like Ellington hornmen Rex Stewart and Ben Webster dropped by, sometimes to take some notes, sometimes to swap jazz gossip. The alcove outside the room where Reese taught great and small alike was stacked high with copies of *Down Beat* and other jazz magazines.

As a teacher, Reese emphasized the full range from basic musicianship and theory to arranging and composition. During his lessons, he'd refer to anything from the classics and jazz to film scores. Then to illustrate his point, he'd pull the records out of his big collection and let students take them home to study. Art Tatum was one of his favorites: he loved to assign challenging Tatum piano solos like "Elegie" that strode deep into the harmonic language of classical European styles. Besides jazz, Ravel and Debussy, Stravinsky and Schoenberg, Bach and Beethoven, and works such as "Contrasts," the trio piece Benny Goodman had commissioned from composer Béla Bartók and recorded with Bartók and famed violinist Joseph Szigeti, found a home on Reese's shelves.

Every Sunday, the maestro led a rehearsal band of his students at the black musicians' union hall on Central. Mingus and Collette and Dexter Gordon, a future star soloist who got constantly razzed about his poor reading skills, were in the cast. This was a proud and competitive group, eager to strut what they learned. They used musical arrangements—charts—that Reese had. These weren't stock stuff off the shelves, but challenging music, some from bands he had worked with.

For an ambitious and open-eared student musician, Lloyd Reese could open doors to a lot of different worlds.

Charlie Mingus needed a better musical foundation, and he knew it. But he only took casual lessons with Reese. Mostly he hung around, absorbed by the salon aspect of Reese's work. He loved to talk. He felt he'd found his element, swapping ideas and information and gossip about jazz stars and soloists. And he learned about what Hollywood musicians and film scorers did, and began mixing with them at Reese's.

He listened to Reese and thought about the dapper man's criticisms and praise for the pieces of music he brought in. But he was less interested in exercises than in being praised and finding a mentor, a model, an illustration of what he could become. He watched Reese closely.

The bass was a different story. There he knew he needed drill, and found himself a hands-on teacher. Red Callender was barely out of high school himself and only three years older than Mingus, but he was already established as a serious musician.

Mingus was mastering the bass fingerboard and working relentlessly on speeding up his fingers. Callender's focus on the unwieldy bass, used then almost entirely to keep time, was to make the instrument sing. For the ex-cellist, studying with Callender was a perfect match, and in several ways.

RED CALLENDER, *musician and friend*: One morning there's a knock on my door on 20th Street. It's Mingus, saying he wants to study with me. He was

seventeen, still in high school. I told him I was no teacher, that I was still studying myself, but he persisted. That was typical of him; Mingus would go through
walls to get what he wanted. . . . Mingus knew little about the bass, but even
then he knew what he aspired to be: the world's greatest bass player. He practiced seventeen hours a day.[2]

At the time I was playing melodies on the bass, which was very unusual in
those days. Mingus was fascinated. . . . The bass was almost new to him; the
cello was his ax. He was very fast by ear. Mingus would come for a lesson and
we'd sit around for a long time talking about racial injustice. 1940s L.A. was
hopeless for black people, especially [for] studio work.[3]

For young Charlie Mingus, race and the bass were entwined, and young
Red Callender would soon spearhead early attempts to desegregate the Los Angeles music scene. So his pupil's agitated questions—how does this black
man, this black man's music, fit into white America?—spoke to his heart. But
to polish Mingus's skills, Callender sent him to his own teacher.

Herman Rheinschagen, a white bassist, had performed with the New York
Philharmonic. David Bryant, who later studied with Rheinschagen, says Mingus argued with him during lessons. "You're supposed to do it this way." "Well,
man, you can do it this way too."[4]

Technique in music could be color-blind, even if the music business wasn't.
And already Charlie refused to accept the way things were. Instead, he was
finding options.

He was inventing a character, a multilayered collection of personalities, that
his music would reflect. And at the foundation of his character was an undeniable impulse: to improvise life as he did music, to compose his history.

BUDDY COLLETTE: He did a lot of crazy things. One day we were standing out
in Oakland. We were playing with Floyd Ray's band. We were just talking outside
the theater and he just took off, and started running, and went over the top of
the car, stepped up on the hood, stepped on the top, and then came back. And
when the owner of the car saw him, he said, "You bent my car." Mingus was very
heavy then. And he said, "I'm sorry. I didn't know what I was doing. I just felt
like doing it." That was Mingus. He did things in a spontaneous way.

Floyd Ray's outfit wasn't the big leagues, but that didn't matter to Collette
and Mingus and Chico Hamilton. They were on top of the world. They were
pros. They held down three key chairs while the fifteen-piece band toured theaters and clubs up and down the valley stretching between Los Angeles and

Oakland, the other great West Coast railroad terminus that drew black immigrants like a magnet. For the teenagers, it was a taste of life on the road, an inexpressible mix of cut-rate glamor and daily grind.

CHICO HAMILTON: We went on tour with a midget, Sugar Charles Robinson. He was eight years old, and he could play the boogie-woogie on piano—that was it. He was a sensation. So we toured up and down the coast, and he headlined. The opening act was a dance team named the Will Mastin trio, featuring Sammy Davis Jr.

Charlie grew a pencil mustache, and he had his first casual sexual experiences with the girls with names like Tempest Storm who worked the shows. He lived through the crowded, dusty car trips that hauled too many people too far for a day's time over the pre-interstate roads of California. He sat through the nights of abusive or responsive audiences. And he didn't go home every night. He had no one to watch out for him.

Except, of course, his close pal Buddy. Collette was the straight man to Charlie's wild man. He was more self-possessed. You had to know how to handle Charlie. One night, Mingus smart-assed Brother Woodman, one of Britt's siblings. Brother, who'd been boxing and wrestling with Charlie since Britt first brought him home, just picked the fat boy up and held him over his head until he calmed down.

Collette's bemused attitude often led Charlie to curb his more outrageous impulses. Buddy seemed unerringly able to tune into things that the young man himself felt most torn about, his mass of often contradictory impulses.

He talked all the time to Buddy about Mary Ellen Kelly. The Tom Thumb lovers had reunited at the end of high school, but her father broke up their budding relationship.

As excited as he was to be on the road with a band in Oakland, as erotic as the burlesque shows and his dreams about of them could be, he was shattered by the loss of his long-time dream girl.

He was a Romantic.

CHARLES MINGUS: I didn't think I dug life the way other people did. I didn't have any lust or love for life. I dug breathing and all that but I thought something must be wrong with life and there must be a better place to go.[5]

But as his life expanded beyond Watts, he stopped confiding everything in Buddy and Britt. He began keeping separate the different worlds he was entering. Friends from various sectors rarely met. He was their nexus point, the composer-arranger.

That way, he also protected himself.

And so he never told Buddy he'd seen a white man named Trent Frakes tip over a car in San Francisco—part of what inspired his outburst in Oakland. He certainly didn't mention that he met Trent at a big party thrown by a white artist across the Bay.

At seventeen, Charles Mingus Jr. stood at a crossroads in a changing world. A world war loomed in the shadows of the Great Depression. Almost as rebuttal, the twin World's Fairs in New York and San Francisco celebrated the accelerating triumph of technology. Among the displays was television, which would make radio's reach into American homes seem like a gentle knock.

San Francisco, the City by the Bay, stood for Culture in the minds of most Angelenos then. Sited on man-made Treasure Island, an exit off the just-finished Bay Bridge, San Francisco's 1939 Golden Gate International Exposition celebrated the completion of the Bay and Golden Gate bridges. Treasure Island was filled with modern marvels and hordes of tourists and other delights that seemed almost irresistible to young Charlie.

The main causeway, lavishly decorated with murals, greeted visitors. The food courts served up exotic cuisines from Java and the Netherlands East Indies and the Philippines. The Gayway Fun Zone bustled with burlesque strippers and vaudeville shows, headlined by the famed fan-dancer Sally Rand. There was Billy Rose's Aquacade, which showed off Hollywood stars like Johnny Weissmuller and Esther Williams. And the period's reigning big bands, like Benny Goodman and Duke Ellington and Count Basie, all played the Expo, then played the ballrooms and clubs of San Francisco and Oakland.

It was like the old Santa Monica pier gone humongous.

Charlie never described what happened next to Buddy Collette. Maybe he needed to keep his mentors separate, or he just might have guessed what Buddy's reactions would be. When he started to tell Britt Woodman, his church-going friend was horrified at the non-Christian blasphemous beliefs he had absorbed from his new mentor, painter Farwell Taylor.

SHELLEY TAYLOR, *friend*: Mingus was at my parents' apartment almost every weekend from before I was born, in 1942. I knew him all my life. In his twenties he was handsome, dapper, always dressed in a suit. Dashing, like Orson Welles. I saw him all the time. He was like another father to me.

Charlie and my dad were so much alike. Farwell was always getting away with things. Charlie had deep beliefs, but people didn't find out about them because he was so big, they didn't go beneath the surface. People think that jazz musicians are simple people, drug addicts, whatever, who just pick up their instruments and play. But they're complex, or at least the best of them are. They have a wide range of knowledge about a lot of things. Otherwise how could they play the way they do?

In her paintings, my mother could capture future things. Farwell had that ability too, and Mingus shared it.

Farwell Taylor was thirty-four, big and noisy and scruffy looking and widely read and given to expansive, dramatic gestures. He could dominate a room just by entering it. He was an artist with a reputation. He'd painted murals along the causeway for the World's Fair, and his North Beach studio was a hangout for jazzers and bohemians, even celebrities and politicians. His name was known all over the city. When Charlie Mingus first met him, he was creating the small but vital underground salon culture that, after the war, nurtured the Beat Generation. Taylor knew how to live in the slippery interstices between the marginal bohemians and their monied patrons and admirers.

Besides the artist's personal magnetism and social impact, the seventeen-year-old found his Vedanta Hindu beliefs and his part-American Indian background fascinating. Maybe they explained why Taylor was so tolerant and accepting of others, unprejudiced. "Everyone is a child of God," he said all the time. It was only one of a trunkload of his repeated and forceful opinions.

His new young admirer couldn't help noticing and absorbing all he did, and how, in his intuitive spongelike way.

CHARLES MINGUS: I liked his work immediately. It moved me. I couldn't say why I liked it—I didn't know terms like perspective—except to say that what he painted was living off the paper.[6]

That was what Charlie wanted for the snatches of sounds he was hearing more and more in his head. Could a black person become a respected musical artist? Being black, what kind of music should he write? Taylor was the first person outside music he talked to about his ambitions, his hopes and fears for his music.

Born in Oklahoma in 1905, Taylor was the oldest boy of eight brothers and sisters. The family moved to Truro, and he landed scholarships all through art school, though he was fond of bragging he hadn't finished third grade. He met Faye Morgan at the San Francisco School of Fine Arts, and they married in 1932. Five years younger, she came from a nouveau-riche shipbuilding family.

Her father adored her, but her mother nearly disowned her when Taylor married her rather than going to Rome on an art scholarship. There was always tension between Faye's mother and Farwell, even scenes at parties.

Charlie absorbed this tale as if it were mythic. He'd use it, like he used others, as a model for his own life. Sometimes he just acted like the stories were his.

Farwell and Faye settled into San Francisco, and Taylor drew cartoons for the *Chronicle* and *Examiner*. Like thousands of artists, he was part of the New Deal's arts programs, and he painted murals around the Bay area. His sister Anne, a gorgeous redhead, stayed close to him even after she moved to L.A., went into the movies, and met celebrities. Some made their way to Farwell's place, a magical doorway into a transcendent spot where art met money and drugs, where race and politics and religion were topics for boisterous debate, where the food was succulent and offbeat, where the music went on all night.

On the Nob Hill corner of Taylor and Washington loomed the Casbah, a luxury building of fifty or so apartments. It took up nearly the whole corner, and its brick stairs led into a sumptuous lobby. Farwell and Faye made their home in a dazzling penthouse, complete with marble fireplaces, high ceilings, and wraparound bay windows overlooking both the city and the water.

The place was free, because Farwell doubled as the building's superintendent. He fixed leaky faucets and stopped-up toilets, and Faye sewed curtains and draperies. They sold their paintings out of Farwell's North Beach studio, and that paid for everything else.

Both of them loved to cook, so they started organizing weekend parties stuffed with food. They set out huge buffets that included anything from cabbage juice and sesame seed buns to whole pigs and hash cookies. Their apartment quickly turned into a floating open house with jam sessions and high-powered conversation about politics and religion and the arts. People just kept coming back. Some of them were Eleanor Roosevelt, Billie Holiday, Kenneth Rexroth, and Ernest Hemingway.

SHELLEY TAYLOR: Charlie was a regular. I can remember, from the time I was three or four years old, musicians playing all night. Much of the time, I'd be in my crib, and every morning, my mother would find me and my crib clear across the room, from me rocking myself to sleep to the music. See, I always loved to dance. My mother taught me to dance when I was very young to Stravinsky's music: I'd be this little bud, and she'd dance around me and be the rain and the sun, and I would unfold, you know, and start dancing. So as far out as Charlie's music could get, it wasn't that far out to me. And I could always dance to it— and would.

The tie between Mingus and my parents was artistic and religious. He was struggling with where his place was as a black person, and Farwell would tell him we're all God's people, skin color doesn't make any difference. Charlie was asking questions like, "Am I different because I'm black?" Still, they'd argue sometimes. I don't think Farwell was prejudiced at all, but there were things that came out. People sometimes work like sandpaper against each other. I guess that's why they were such buddies, because they could argue about things and always come out okay, and understand each other.

He moved in with the Taylors briefly, slept in the North Beach studio, then kept coming back. He read Freud's *Interpretations of Dreams*, H. G. Wells's *Outline of History*, Dostoyevsky's *Crime and Punishment*. Thanks to Pocket Books and Penguin, founded in the 1930s, paperbacks of classic titles, even of poets from Homer to Rilke, were cheap. Taylor had tons of them, and Charlie began collecting them.

Farwell began his lifetime project of encouraging Mingus. "The greatest," he would say over and over, popping into a room and speaking to Charlie, "You're the greatest. Remember that." He recognized the Watts' boy's shrewd intuitive intelligence, his ability to drink in ideas. He saw him flip through book after book, read a few chapters, and talk as if he'd studied it cover to cover. It was a spark of genius, and Taylor fanned it. If Charlie thought he wanted to be a composer, then that's what he should be. Classical or jazz—what's the difference? Be who you are.

Taylor's tolerant openness was rooted in his beliefs in Vedanta, a form of Hinduism that first took root among American artists and intellectuals at the turn of the century.

In 1893, Swami Vivekananda arrived at the World Parliament of Religions in Chicago, held there in connection with that year's World's Fair. He wanted to bring India's spiritual outlook to America and to learn more about the West's science and technology. Though he was unknown in America, his speech to 7,000 intellectuals, philosophers, and theologians made him instantly famous and won him fans like William James.

Vivekananda's master, Sri Ramakrishna, preached that all religions embraced truth. Religion was simply the manifestation of the divine spark within man. Like all Hindus, Sri Ramakrishna believed that an eternal spirit without beginning or end permeated the entire universe and was its animating principle. Different deities just embodied manifestations of the one God. Truth, for the Vedanta adherent, is universal, and every faith offers valid ways for its followers to uncover it.

Vedanta tells its followers to suppress their lower natures and manifest their higher natures through unselfish work, worship, contemplation, and psychic control, or philosophy. In that way, they gain access to the underlying and unifying spirit of the universe.

They could feel the Zeitgeist.

Taylor's Vedanta beliefs echoed throughout Mingus's life. Even if he didn't practice it regularly, Vedanta fit his Romantic nature.

CHARLES MINGUS: I learned through meditation the will to control and actually feel calmness. I found a thing that made me think I could die if I wanted to. And I used to work at it. Not death and destruction but just to will yourself to death.[7]

For him, death was transcendent, not a threat. It brought peace from inner turmoil, the process of becoming himself in the world. At seventeen, Charlie Mingus was at the peak of adolescent self-dramatization. He wanted to walk to the edges of life. It was his prime form of self-expression. In many ways, it would always be.

When he went back to Watts after his eighteenth birthday, he brought with him unfinished compositions he called "Half-Mast Inhibition" and "Chill of Death." He'd given up sex for eight months while he studied with Taylor. He later said that when he'd finished "Inhibition," he lay down to die. "I had a funny little thing in there like 'jingle bells, jingle bells' . . . not funny style but because it represented Christ and Christmas."[8] This was the Christ honored by Vedantists as one of the great leaders who tried to bring humanity a universal message of love.

The boy became a mystic. He believed he was one of the special people who saw things—visions that revealed the future, insights into people and places he knew. When Taylor taught him yoga meditation, it let him feel those transcendent moments he'd glimpsed in music when it truly moved him.

For a moody and sensitive teen, self-obsession is inevitable. In isolation, it can deepen easily into depression. Back in Watts, Charlie Mingus had nobody he could share his new mystical understandings with. And he couldn't shake the feeling that death was waiting for him. That feeling would recur throughout his life.

CHARLES MINGUS: While I was lying there, I got to such a point that it scared me and I decided I wasn't ready. And ever since, actually, I've been running because I saw something I didn't want to see. I felt I was too young to reach this point. Then I found something else, a little girl named Jeanne who I fell in love with. I started to write again, and write out of that.[9]

With the same inspiration that filled the poet Dante when he first spied the mystical love of his life, Beatrice, Charlie suddenly acknowledged his craving for female love and attention. Women were his muses. They distracted him from the magnetic gaze of his own death. He pursued them with a passion all his life and named musical pieces after some of the central objects of his desire.

Charlie Mingus had begun his lifelong process of reinventing himself—of moving, as his hero Duke Ellington put it, "beyond category."

4 Life During Wartime

WHEN DUKE ELLINGTON'S band released "Jumpin' Punkins" in early 1941, the remarkably flexible, almost hornlike bass of a twenty-two-year-old named Jimmy Blanton rippled across Harlem and Watts and other jazz hot points like an electrical storm.

In Watts, Blanton's virtuosity, riveting from the time he'd joined Ellington a year earlier, sharpened Charles Mingus's aspirations. Years of playing the cello had taught him how expansive melodies could lie beneath his fingers even on an instrument that wasn't among the front-rank for soloists. "I played jazz cello long before Pettiford," he once said, referring to his friendly bass rival, Oscar Pettiford.[1]

But until Blanton, for Charlie the bulky bass had its limits. It was great for socializing and fun, but it couldn't sing the way his cello or even Britt's trombone could. So once he heard Blanton's agile expression, something in him pivoted and opened. He spent hours listening to such Blanton vehicles as "Jack the Bear" on the jukeboxes in late-night Watts hot spots like Central Avenue's 54th Street Drugstore at two or three in the morning. Blanton was barely his senior, but what he could do mesmerized Mingus.

Then, early in 1941, Ellington's band landed in Los Angeles and moved in and out for months as Duke worked on several L.A. projects. Blanton had lots of time to hang out, which meant he joined drummer Lee Young and others for jam sessions at the black union hall and the many after-hours clubs around Central Avenue in Watts. Somehow the clubs flourished despite the mayor's attempt in May 1940 to shut them down for selling alcohol after 2:00 A.M.[2]

Also in Los Angeles was Charlie Christian, the young guitarist Benny Goodman had recently hired, who had revolutionized the role of the electric guitar in jazz as Blanton had done for the bass. Blanton and Christian moved from session to session. They joined in a Labor Day jam session, part of the black musicians' union celebration that included a Central Avenue parade, with Nat King Cole and Illinois Jacquet.

Jazz was about to change, and some of the emerging young men with new ideas who would change it came through Charlie's hometown.

Charlie—some people, his family and female friends, called him Charles—always wanted lessons. His early disappointments with his teachers were more than overcome with Callender and Rheinschagen, who for months had him walking around the neighborhood flexing his hands with rubber balls. Britt Woodman and Buddy Collette and Lloyd Reese and Farwell Taylor instilled in him a sense of discipline and craft in service of a vision.

That, and the stream of music that would pour more steadily through him from now on, helped center him. With his volatile sensitivity, that was no easy task, even with music as his gyroscope.

His hyperbolic nature, mingling its prickly insecurities and massive self-assurance, could lapse into laziness. His quick intuitive intelligence and sharp ears allowed him to grasp ideas in a kind of flash; he got the overall picture and didn't feel he needed to dot all the I's and cross all the T's.

But he was always open and ready for the flow of inspiration. When he wasn't sharpening his bass chops, he spent hours at the piano, teaching himself to play so he could follow better the harmonic and melodic flow of hits and classics alike.

In jazz, if he wanted to be a composer, he also had to be a working musician. All the greatest, from Jelly Roll Morton to Duke Ellington, led their own bands, where they played their own music. It wasn't like the classical world. Composers made their own way, with no formal structures for financial support, no symphony orchestras and halls subsidized by wealthy patrons and tax dollars. And so he seized the bass as his vehicle with a passion born of his unyielding sense of his own future greatness.

KATE MULHOLLAND, *friend*: I met Mingus at a Sunday afternoon jam session at Billy Berg's. I was underage, but L.A. was a free and easy town, and didn't demand IDs of minors. There were a few, not many, but a few white kids who wanted to hear more than the Andrews Sisters. So I went to a lot of joints, and that's where I met Mingus. The thing that sticks out in my mind is that L.A. was such a segregated town that we'd sit in the car and talk, and maybe after twenty minutes he'd say, "Move the car." He'd see, or imagine he saw, cops who were going to roust us. And I was naive. I had read a lot but had no firsthand experience. And I did not know many black people.

Charles was very interesting then. I remember the first thing he ever said to me was, "What are you?" Which in our day meant I could say I'm Irish and German. And he said, "I'm Irish, Indian, Mexican, and Nigger." True or not, I don't know; he always had a nonstop imagination going. At any rate, we launched right into talking about racism, on an adolescent level. But I can say from that first encounter, which I remember very well, that he was intensely driven to be a great musician. It made a profound effect on me, the intensity of this young man.

When eighteen-year-old Kate Mulholland first went to Lloyd Reese to "get the hang of improvising," the wealthy white girl was an anomaly, but not the only one, on the Central Avenue scene. Her grandfather was the Mulholland for whom Los Angeles's striking Mulholland Drive was named. Her family's history paralleled the growth and development of modern L.A.; it was distorted, though made famous, by Roman Polanski's film *Chinatown*. Young Catherine lived with her family on a ranch in the still-farmed San Fernando Valley. There, like little girls all across America, she had been classically trained on piano.

Her teachers, however, were far from average. Mulholland describes them as "part of the whole expatriate group on the eve of World War II. They were very sophisticated musically, and took a different attitude toward jazz than my folks." They recommended that she study with Reese. In the chancy ways of history, that completed a circle: Reese had helped point Mingus toward the music of expatriates like Arnold Schoenberg, who taught at UCLA.

For the nineteen-year-old from Watts, meeting Kate Mulholland confirmed that he could bridge worlds as Farwell Taylor and Reese had done, in the European-style world of salons where monied aristocrats met Bohemia. So he began a life-long friendship with Kate Mulholland. It was siblinglike, an attachment that foreshadowed many of his later male-female friendships. He and Kate shared perpetual weight problems, Romantic sensibilities that alienated them from their families and peers, and an obsession with music, especially jazz.

For while they hailed from opposite sides of the Los Angeles tracks, they never quite felt that they fit in anywhere they were—except in the land of jazz. There the promise of opportunity and equality touted by the American Dream was represented in musical form. And inside that world, at least some of the rules governing race in America seemed suspended.

KATE MULHOLLAND: Charles and I were like two strangers meeting someplace and being attracted and liking each other but not knowing, really, what to do about it. He didn't have a car. He had no money. He didn't hang out too much. He was a pretty good little boy. Not a wild man, other than temperamentally.

One day, because we got tired of sitting in cars talking, he took me down to his home in Watts. I met his stepmother, and we sat down and played some records. Years later he told me that, when I left, his stepmother said, "Never have that girl in this house again. She'll be your life." So he was being warned off from fraternizing with white girls by his stepmother, who was a brown-skinned distinctly Negro-looking lady. Charles, of course, wasn't—he had that Oriental-Mexican, very ambiguous racial look. But she was just a hausfrau, nice looking but not glamorous.

At any rate, he was not coming on to me sexually.

For Charles, Kate Mulholland represented a friendly point where several of his youthful desires ran together. For Kate, he was a fascinating close-up of the Other, a provocative mix of aggression and insecurity. She saw his unresolved vulnerabilities and yearnings from a perspective even his closest male friends couldn't have.

And she, like the many other female soulmates he'd find, dismisses the lurid stories he told, in person and later in his book *Beneath the Underdog*, about his sexual prowess, his recurrent bragging about his Jelly Roll Morton-wannabe days as a pimp.

Mingus was starting to work with bigger name musicians now, and for more than just pick-up gigs around L.A. His playing was developing rapidly—the rich and singing tone, the speed and melodic variation. So was his reputation for mouthing off, unpredictable behavior, and turbulent mood swings.

He was ambitious, though, and understood that unconventional behavior, especially in the jazz world, was often more help than hindrance. His hero Duke Ellington was known to have an endless string of women. Cab Calloway's antic stage act hyped up his audiences and sold lots of tickets and records.

Besides, jazz dealt in individuals; one of its implicit goals was the creation of musicians whose personal voices, like Duke's and Blanton's, stood out in the music. It was no accident that as he extended his control over the bass his personality developed.

His natural eclecticism had plenty to feed on. The same railroads that brought new, and often black, workers to power the increasing war plant capacity around the City of Angels also brought new sounds from deep rural bluesmen to European cosmopolites. And jazz was popping up all over L.A.

There were good-paying gigs in Hollywood and the West Side, at clubs for white audiences; only Billy Berg's consistently hosted mixed crowds. When they'd finished those, musicians would pile into cars and head over to Darktown, which housed near-constant after-hours jam sessions in the joints along Central Avenue, like Lovejoy's and the Ritz, the Memo and the Drugstore, Club Alabam and the Turban Room.

The Avenue was full of sharp-looking black men and women. There were wild-eyed jitterbuggers and quiet interracial couples, men making like pimps to come on to women and women making like hookers to snag men. It was called the Brown Broadway: there was no TV yet, and Central's entertainment was cheap enough for anyone.

The hovering wartime feeling, intensifying as the nation drew closer to the conflict engulfing Europe and Asia, enhanced the clubs' business. Before World War II, regular bars and clubs stayed open until 2:00 A.M. With the war, they shut down at midnight, and the after-hours spots picked up the slack.

Art Tatum, whom jazzers called God because of his endless invention and complex harmonic knowledge, who had played in The Streets of Paris in Hollywood, came to Lovejoy's. There he seduced the old battered upright piano into telling remarkable musical tales. Mingus was one of the many who played with him. But it was typical of the open oral tradition within jazz at that time that all the greats made that scene and shared their information with nearly all other comers.

KATE MULHOLLAND: I remember a jam session one night Tatum was at a dive —the Ritz, I think, a little off Central. The tenor men kept wandering in and playing I don't know how many choruses of "Lady Be Good." And there was Tatum at the piano exhorting them, "Go go go, one more time."

Tatum was universally revered as a master, despite his surly offstage manner and his egotism. Musicians overlooked his personality because of his stunning work. Tatum drew audacious harmonic ideas from the French Impressionist pallette. Debussy, Ravel—the same dense, chromatic chords that made their music so haunting and suggestive inspired him as they had Ellington, and made them Mingus's heroes.

Tatum, though, was systematically adapting those harmonies to jazz's blues-based vocabulary, using them as a basis for improvisation. His technique stunned classical as well as jazz musicians: Vladimir Horowitz was a Tatum fan. Watching Tatum astound, working with him in snatches, unveiled for Mingus yet another aspect of his vision of himself and his music.

But he had to develop a reputation before he'd be accepted as a composer.

And he had to earn a living. The bass was his vehicle. It was time to get started.

KATE MULHOLLAND: When I came home for vacation from Berkeley, he was all excited; he'd gotten what he considered his first important professional gig, with Alvino Rey. He told me, "Man, I was so proud of that gig. To think that somebody like that would hire me made me feel really good." It lasted no time at all. Next time I saw him, he said, "A couple of nights of that, it's just shit I don't want to play." There was always this double-edged nature; you have to say Charles was a mass of contradictions.

It shows in his music. It shows in his private life. It shows in the worlds he lived in. He could rage on one side, and two minutes later rage on the other. He was certainly an exciting person to be around.

And driven. Thanks to Reese, he was increasingly interested in jazz's ability to ingest new elements and evolve. Hadn't Gershwin vaulted into longer-form jazz hybrids with 1924's *Rhapsody in Blue*, and Ellington with *Reminiscing in Tempo* and *Black, Brown and Beige*? Hadn't Stravinsky used jazzy elements in *The Firebird*? And what about Tatum?

Charles's sharp ears led to relentless musical resourcefulness. Even at nineteen his compositions displayed powerful conceptual originality: hence, juvenalia like "Half-Mast Inhibition." Its punning title plays off his teenage sexual timidity—revealing in light of his later braggadocio—via a playful sense of self-deflation.

The prophets, he'd learned from Taylor, were holy fools, manifestations of the changeless reality behind the impermanent world. But their perceptions came from their lives, not dogmas. They fought to suppress their natures to unite their souls with the universal spirit animating the world. In that sense, "Half-Mast Inhibition" was the first glimmer of the ironic figure of the clown that would become an important motif in Charles Mingus's work.

On July 10, 1941, Duke Ellington opened *Jump for Joy* at the art deco deluxe Mayan Theater in downtown Los Angeles.[3] He had dreamed of writing a musical for an all-black cast for years and finally found backing in Hollywood. It was topical and antiracial in the elegantly matter-of-fact manner Ellington perfected. He wanted, Duke said, "to bury Uncle Tom." Indeed, one of the songs was called "Uncle Tom's Cabin Is a Drive-In Now"; another was "I've Got a Passport from Georgia," which drew death threats until it was cut.

The show ran until late September, for 101 performances. And the music was in constant rearrangement, as was Duke's usual mode.

Ellington's musicians hung around Watts between gigs. Billy Strayhorn, his arranger and musical alter ego, shared a room with Jimmy Blanton in a Watts private house—most L.A. hotels were racially restricted. It wasn't long before they showed up at Billy Berg's on Sunset and Vine, to check out the group led by Lester and Lee Young, saxist and drummer, and the nightly jam sessions.

Mingus, who worked with Lee, started running a bit with Blanton, who warmed to the frank idolatry of his not-so-junior colleague. Blanton encouraged him and told him tales of New York and a movement of younger, radical players who were working around Harlem, creating a new musical concept.

When Charles went to see *Jump*, he heard the tune "The Zoot Suits with the Reet Pleat" and raced to get that hip fashion gear. He also sat down and puzzled out the harmonies and voicings on the piano, and played them for an astounded Britt Woodman.

With his sharp new threads, Charlie Mingus figured he was done with his childish complexes.

Hollywood is only ten miles from Watts, and many movie industry people loved jazz, especially Duke Ellington and Billie Holiday. Some were left-leaning or communists, observing the oppression of ex-slaves by capitalists and inspired by the music's deathless spirit. Some were just real fans, free of cant or condescension.

Orson Welles was one of those, and he also happened to be one of Charles's heroes. Like Blanton, Welles was only a few years older than the Watts youth, but he was already hugely famous. His "War of the Worlds" broadcast on Halloween 1938 was indelibly etched into the nation's memory.

Thanks to relentless attacks and pressures from Hearst newspapers, his first movie, *Citizen Kane*, was a box office failure. Nevertheless, it validated Welles's status as creative wunderkind. Here was an outsider who learned how to shoot a movie from a homemade study guide in a few weeks. His shrewd genius allowed him to inhale technical ideas. Because he wasn't bound conceptually to the usual Hollywood shots and plots, he was hailed by critics as a visionary who had revolutionized film vocabulary. As indeed he had, by reaching back to silent movies for certain techniques even as he and his trusted cinematographer, Gregg Toland, pioneered others.

Darktowns across America knew and admired Welles. In the mid-1930s, while he was working for the Federal Theatre Project under FDR's New Deal, Welles built the Harlem Negro Theatre unit into a critically acclaimed dynamo. There he had premiered an acclaimed all-black *Macbeth*. Also, he editorialized on some of his many radio shows about the NAACP and Negro rights. In America, Welles felt, race was never beside the point. His Watts fans agreed.

That included one Watts fan who shared temperamental tendencies and weight problems with his new idol. An early publicity photo of Mingus from the 1940s makes his admiration for Welles self-evident. The hint of beefiness around Mingus's handsome face, the dapper mustache, the intelligent shining eyes, the wavy hair, and the brooding look—the entire pose alludes to Welles.

What fascinated Mingus most was the texture of Welles's films, marvels of editing that mixed and matched a riotous tumult of narrative and film techniques. It was as if Welles, who cowrote as well as directed *Citizen Kane*, were summarizing the history of film and pointing to its next directions.

Welles's offbeat shooting strategies mixed unusual camera angles, chiaroscuro shadows, long and carefully plotted single-shot scenes, and startling quick cuts. His scripts unfolded like mysteries: they probed the characters' psychology and context gradually, in layers, setting off deeper waves of understanding in the audience as the movie progressed.

Welles's virtuosity was overwhelming and meant to call attention to itself; that was part of the emotional response it sought from the viewers. It was how Charles wanted to write music.

As a musician, he was entranced by Welles's orotund voice. The cello and the trombone, his favorite horn, lived in the same sonorous timbre and range. And he knew that Welles's Mercury Theatre was a company of players, who worked together in many guises under the genius's guiding light. He thought of Welles and Ellington in similar ways.

In fact, his heroes planned to collaborate during this period. For three months, Welles paid Ellington a $1,000-a-week retainer to write music for a film project he was calling *It's All True*. This would be a history of jazz, but with a vicious twist. Foreshadowing much later movies like *Zelig* and *Reds*, it combined fact and fiction in deliberately obscured ways. Musicians and clubgoers along Central Avenue were recruited as extras. But like many another Welles project, it was lost in the studio recriminations that followed *Citizen Kane*.

Then the U.S. government sent Welles down to Rio de Janeiro in 1942; he was to make a movie emphasizing American friendship and to help blunt Axis attempts to woo disaffected Latin American governments. He filmed Rio carnivals and the city's wretched favelas, the black ghettos, and dreamed of splicing the footage into *It's All True*. When he returned, RKO had dramatically reedited *The Magnificent Ambersons*, his followup to *Kane*, meant to be his masterpiece. His contract was torn up.

Welles has often been accused of a lack of discipline, as Mingus would be later. But what looked like lack of follow-through was also a reaction to the hurtling pace of his ideas. At times both men took on too many projects at once, for creative and financial reasons.

Everyone on the Central Avenue scene knew the Welles story. Like many an exalted white figure in American history, Welles often hung out in Darktowns around the country. In Watts, along with stars like George Raft and Robert Benchley, he could meet black women.

Once the war started, the U.S. War Department exerted its muscle in Los Angeles to protect and discipline its growing numbers of workers and servicemen. Clubs closed earlier. Curfews were tightened. Segregation became even more rigid, especially in housing.

Writers like Raymond Chandler depicted Los Angeles as a place of almost nonchalant, if corrosive, racism. But the city, long run by a WASP elite, was fired into racist fever with the attack on Pearl Harbor by the Japanese on December 7, 1941. Around the country but especially in California, Japanese and Japanese-descended Americans were herded into "internment" camps, usually in the desert.

In Los Angeles, although 100,000 new black defense workers were pouring into the city, they couldn't find housing because of restrictive segregationist housing covenants—except in now-vacated Little Tokyo. Gradually, they filled out what became South Central L.A., tranforming Watts from a semirural multiculture into a suburban black enclave.

In his autobiography, Malcolm X looks at the World War II years, familiar in standard American history as an era of righteous blood, sweat, and tears, from a different perspective. He chronicles how the double consciousness of American blacks came home to roost in yet another moral dilemma: whether to serve and fight and die for a country that, nearly a century after emancipation, denied its freedmen basic rights. He portrays streetwise draft dodgers who knew how to manipulate a physical exam to ensure that they were given a 4-F rating, which would make them ineligible for the draft. He sees no need to scold or punish them for their lack of patriotism. His attitude represents one significant side of the dialog, spoken and unspoken, within the American black community at the time.

Like many young black Americans, Charles Mingus Jr. was torn about the war and his role in it. Many of his friends were enlisting or being drafted, now that Pearl Harbor had been bombed. But his father was an army lifer, a thought that left him ambivalent. Thousands of Japanese-Americans, including his friends the Okes, were being interned for the crime of having Japanese blood. The purely racial strategy—Germans were not being forced into camps—riled him, and painfully echoed white America's treatment of black America.

Nevertheless, in 1942, when Buddy Collette and another Watts pal took a

Greyhound bus to San Francisco to enlist in the navy, Charles insisted on coming with them. They'd enlist together to join one of the navy bands. But when
they got to the physical, Collette was dumbfounded. Charles started yelling
that he couldn't read music. He moaned that he had a bad heart. And he'd
prepped for the urine test: like many, he wedged sugar under his fingernails.
His tests said he was diabetic, which got him a 4-F classification. Buddy went,
and he stayed home.

His physical was real-life theater, an echo of Jordan High opening day when
he had faced down Coustie and the pants grabbers. He seized the initiative by
doing the unexpected, and doing it loudly. That crossed up people's reactions.
As long as he kept his cool, it also got him what he wanted.

And yet there's a heedless selfishness to his setting up Buddy, his closest
friend. That trait is shared by many artists. For them, what matters is what they
do; it's who they are, what they will become, the lines they draw on the sands of
time. Everything else is secondary. From the time he was small, his mystical
insights and dreams told Charles he was destined for greatness. Nothing could
be allowed to jeopardize that.

Everything was grist to Mingus's mill.

Like many from Watts, Buddy and Charles did extra work from the time
they could. In 1940, they were cut from *Road to Zanzibar*, with Bing Crosby
and Bob Hope. Chazz, as he sometimes called himself now, appeared in
Higher and Higher in 1943.[4] He drank it all in—the huge sound stages, the director's power, the scene blocking and flubs. A few stints like that taught him
plenty. By the 1960s, when he was being interviewed and filmed for TV internationally, he handled it like a pro. He worked to the camera without becoming
self-conscious. He knew when and how far the lens could follow his move-
ments. Few if any of his peers matched his apparent ease and professionalism.

Extra work was fun, but music was what counted. In early 1945, Lloyd
Reese sent him to film composer Dmitri Tiomkin. As Red Callender explained, "Sidelining paid good money, we all did it."[5] Like his peers, Tiomkin
used help to fill in parts of scores, to expand and arrange ideas. In Hollywood
studios, no one did everything; the work was parceled out and overseen by a
master, as in the arts studios of Renaissance Italy.

Tiomkin, no musical Leonardo da Vinci, created workmanlike scores full of
classical flourishes. For over a year, Charles learned about orchestration and
the grunt work of composition in hands-on fashion. The studio system left a
lifelong mark on him: he'd use members of his bands to flesh out or generate
music for him, sometimes from little more than a few chords. That would

cause disputes about authorship, responsibility, and pay that recalled arguments about those issues between some Ellington sidemen and Duke.

Pickup gigs were a musician's staple. A name comes to town and needs a backing band. The locals get the call; the headliner moves on with most of the money. The hook, besides the lure of any gig, was the potential spiral. Jazz networks, then even more than now, were oral. So-and-so heard such-and-such, and passed his name on. It took time, but Los Angeles was a major stop on the jazz circuit, and its scene had real snap.

Thanks to the draft, big-band personnel were harder to come by. So the spiral drew Charles in, out of local L.A. outfits led by the likes of Al Adams and Leonard Flennoy.

It was late 1941 when he got his break with steel guitarist Alvino Rey's orchestra. One thing led to another. Clarinetist Barney Bigard hired him. In August 1942, Louis Armstrong came to L.A. to film *Cabin in the Sky*, and his band broke up. He hired Charles. After sporadic touring and recording over a few months, by late 1943 Chazz was playing bass in his friend Lee Young's sextet. The drummer's brother Lester was now a sax star with Count Basie. Lee's band featured another Lloyd Reese alum influenced by Lester: Dexter Gordon.

The war limited recording, as did the musicians' strike in 1943. Early that year, Mingus made a few discs for Armed Forces Radio with Armstrong. In early 1945 he recorded with trumpeter Russell Jacquet, then with trumpeter Howard McGhee. That June, he made his debut as a bandleader for a local label, Excelsior, with the Charles Mingus Sextet. The four tunes he cut were steeped in the blues and proto-rhythm and blues, like "The Texas Hop." That summer, just before the atom bombs hit Japan, he recorded eleven tunes with Russell Jacquet; this time, the sessions were for Russell's now-famed brother Illinois.

Jacquet's honking and screaming sax solo on Lionel Hampton's 1942 smash hit, "Flying Home," had made him a national star. It also helped shape postwar rhythm and blues. Jacquet was one of the few jazzmen who knew of Mingus's new spiritual beliefs. Sympathetic, and impressed by his playing, Jacquet gave the young bassist a shot. At the end of "Merle's Mood," a sliding, double-stopped solo almost bursts out of its two bars. It was a proud echo of Blanton, and a preview of virtuosity to come.

As Mingus later explained, "I was open, I was learning. I went with them because everybody's music is an experience." And then, characteristically, he added, "I like Indian music as much as Charlie Parker, and Beethoven Quartets, especially 9 and 12."[6]

CHICO HAMILTON: He was a misunderstood young dude. People exaggerate things about him. He was highly sensitive, so he put on a front.

More and more, the guys passing through town just called him Mingus. He was getting a reputation for emotional volatility. Gerald Wiggins, in Los Angeles with the Les Hite Band in 1942, heard about it. So did Snooky Young, who played with Mingus in Hite's outfit. But neither saw him explode. Red Callender remembered leading a small combo around this time with two basses that included his ex-pupil; he too saw nothing.[7] Already Mingus had developed the art of having his reputation exceed the reality. It was self-protection, and it boosted his ego.

Besides, the more he delved into the jazz world, the more he had to be sensitive about. Black musicians could play in clubs, but aside from a few clubs along Central Avenue or those run by Billy Berg, black audiences couldn't see them. Some of these clubs were run by mobsters, who sold drinks and drugs and sex to the customers the musicians attracted. The white union, Local 47, which controlled the best-paying local jobs, was segregated and complacent about it. It often seemed like music was the least important part of the music business.

Still, he was working. In his impatient manner, he was perfecting his craft. He watched stars like Armstrong work the crowd and saw the reactions repeated over and over. He liked the emotional intensity of it—the wave of feeling riding out on the music, energizing the audience, then boomeranging back to the stage, augmented with their love and approval. It suited his self-dramatizing sense.

In many ways, he was more at home on stage than he was anywhere else. The only thing he liked better was ruminating at a piano.

Touring with a big band also meant thinking and talking about sex and women. A bus full of men on one-nighters couldn't help noticing that the war left a lot of women available, lonely, ripe. In his autobiography, Malcolm X recalled the white women hanging around black dance halls.

Mingus talked the talk, but he was thinking about the girl he left behind in Watts. In *Beneath the Underdog* he called her Barbara Jeanne Parks and wrote how he mistook her for his childhood love Mary Ellen Kelley, whom he called Lee-Marie, when they met at the McKinley Street playground.

CHICO HAMILTON: We all met our wives in high school, me, Buddy, Charlie. She was beautiful, Canilla Jeanne Gross. All the girls lived out in the more open spaces; it was a society thing. We wanted to be musicians. They all came from good families where musicians weren't necessarily cool. They were raised properly. We were considered bad guys; we played jazz. Canilla Jeanne's brother sang in the Delta Rhythm Boys. He was in the *Our Gang* series.

Jeanne Gross was Charles's first stab at bettering himself through marriage, though not the last. The Gross family lived on East 48th Street, their chicken farm in a neighborhood sandwiched between ethnic turfs. Like their neighbors, they were resolutely middle class. Jeanne's father Carl, a strict man like Sergeant Mingus, believed in self-help and education. His bookshelves were lined with tomes like H. G. Wells's *Outline of History*.

The Mingus family loved Jeanne and approved the match. Jeanne's father liked Charlie, but her mother was distant, a mother-in-law in waiting. In Santa Ana on January 3, 1944, he married Jeanne because it was the gentlemanly thing to do. She was pregnant.

His upbringing, his father's superego, left him no doubt what the rules were. But his father's image cut several ways. The old man barked orders and flared at any challenge to his authority. His rules never had to apply to him. What about his long-running affair with Miss Garrett? But hadn't Mamie driven him to it? Charles's father and stepmother weren't exactly poster children for the Christian morality they preached.

But inside, Charles also heard Baby, the incessant dreamer, the incurable romantic for whom women represented both sex and refuge. He loved Jeanne, and she loved him—adored is the word their friends use. But he was Charles. He was a musician. He was meant to become a great composer. Even his father now believed that. His sense of himself and his art eroded his sense of responsibility to her or their son Charles, who looked so like his daddy. His guilt washed away effortlessly, inevitably. It was like watching a hurricane sweep away a beach.

Charles and Jeanne fought almost from the first day of their marriage. Her pregnancy hastened the erosion of their relationship by robbing her of her one certain way of connecting to him—sex.

VIVIAN MINGUS: I'll tell you how determined he was about his music. When he first married Jeanne, he just sat around, all dressed up. She always wanted him to go get a job. He said, "I'm not no pick and shovel man." They argued so bad that one day she picked up the telephone and chipped his front tooth. He said, "I'm made to be a musician. I'm sticking to my music." And that's what he did. He wasn't making any money, so I guess she figured they needed some. But that's what he said.

He knew what he wanted, what he was supposed to have, what he would become. He avoided taking the post office test and made sure his navy physical got him a 4-F classification so he could follow his destiny. But money—a manifestation of his deeper insecurities—would always be an Achilles' heel. He'd spend like a Rockefeller as soon as he heard coins jingle in his pocket, and then he'd have to scramble or scrounge to make ends meet. And scrounging didn't come naturally to his father's son.

When they didn't fight about money, he and Jeanne fought about the baby. He yowled and complained and whimpered and cried and otherwise destroyed the concentration of an artist trying desperately to work. As flamboyant at home as on stage or in the street, Charles shut himself in the closet to practice his bass. He said that cut down the diaper stench and baby noise.

Their relationship was soon as tempestuous as the very public storms then surrounding Orson Welles and Rita Hayworth.

He didn't make much money, but he had enough places to play or hang that he didn't have to be home much either. He was playing with the Sweet N Hot basketball team, where he and Lee Young and another half-dozen musicians all wore T-shirts with the team name.[8] And Central Avenue beckoned almost twenty-four hours a day.

Around the time of his son's birth on September 12, 1944, he made his recording debut as a bandleader, for the local Excelsior label. He was working with a trio called Strings and Keys, which he'd later parody as Plink, Plank, and Plunk, and had a fling with the white wife of the owner of the Venetian Room in Long Beach, where the threesome worked.

His friend Eric Dolphy still lived at home, and his parents built him a practice room where he spent hours every day rehearsing his clarinet. Charles admired and envied that, especially during Jeanne's tirades about how he ought to hustle up work.

He was dressing sharp and was on the thinner side of his periodic weight swings. But despite his pegged pants and zoot suits and Mexican look, he missed out on the riots that erupted across L.A. in mid-1943.

The so-called Sleepy Lagoon murder had fired up the Chicano population. Six hundred young Mexican-Americans protested the police harassment of their community because twenty-three of them (and one Anglo) were accused (falsely, it turned out) of killing a young Chicano named José Diaz in a gang fight near a swimming hole on August 2, 1942. The L.A. papers sensationalized their coverage of the incident and trial, screaming for the police to stop the Chicano gangs and their alleged crime wave. The cops responded by harassing and rounding up Chicano youths.

These were children of the wave of Mexican immigrants who settled in L.A. during the 1920s, and some of their gangs dressed in zoot suits—high-waisted baggy pants, draped long coat, a dangling watch chain, and broad-brimmed flat hat atop a long duck-tailed haircut.

April and May 1943 brought skirmishes between zoot-suited gangs and military personnel stationed in Los Angeles. By June, these erupted in full-scale racially motivated riots that spread to Long Beach and Pasadena and even, that summer, to midwestern and eastern U.S. cities.

The riots began on June 3, when a gang of sailors searched Alpine Street for zoot-suiters. The sailors claimed other sailors had been beaten by gangs of Mexicans, and some sailors' wives raped. A few sailors went into the Carmen Theater and beat a youngster; a Chicano gang attacked eleven sailors just off North Main Street.

The next night, Friday, two hundred sailors formed a posse of about twenty cars and taxis to scout for zoot-suited Mexicans through downtown L.A. and the east side out to the suburbs. They beat four youths, who wound up hopitalized. Seventeen sailors were picked up, with no charges pressed; the rest were dispersed.

Saturday found soldiers and marines joining the sailors, linking arms as they walked through downtown L.A., warning zoot-suited young men they were targets. The cops watched and busted twenty-seven Chicano youngsters on suspicion. Several Chicanos were beaten when servicemen demanded they doff their zoot suits, and they refused.

Sunday, several carloads of sailors beat eight teenagers on Ramona Boulevard, then smashed up a bar on Indiana Street. Civilians began joining the frenzy, and the cops busted forty-four Chicanos that night.

Monday found 5,000 people, civilians and military, filling downtown near Main Street. They went on the prowl, even stopping streetcars, as they stripped anyone found in zoot suits and ripped or burned the clothes. They started going after blacks as well, as thousands of reserve cops called up on duty stood by.

By midnight, the military declared downtown Los Angeles off-limits to military personnel and sent the Military Police and Shore Patrol to end the riots.

In their wake, Los Angeles city and county officials stoutly declared the military personnel had acted strictly in self-defense, but most Angelenos, especially nonwhite ones, knew better. By the time the Sleepy Lagoon case's guilty verdict had been unanimously reversed by the court of appeals in October 1944, L.A. newspapers were routinely using racial epithets like *pachuco*.

The Zoot Suit Riots unmasked the racial prejudice riddling Los Angeles. Mexicans, blacks, Japanese, Italians—they were necessary evils, the help that took the jobs white men didn't want, or couldn't fill, because of the war.

Part of what culture does is create ideals, goals, and aspirations, the glue that binds society. So American culture often embodies what the American

Dream is supposed to contain, even when the distance between dream and reality seems unbridgeable. This helps explain why Orson Welles joined the Citizens Committee for the Defense of Mexican American Youth soon after the Zoot Suit Riots. Or why Peggy Lee got involved in supporting black musicians' attempts to end segregation in their unions.

Jazz has always represented some of the best of America. It was democratic: each individual was expected to develop a unique voice, then merge into ensembles. This mirrored the Madisonian dynamic tensions of the American body politic, where rugged individualists came together to form a democratic society. But jazz, unlike real politics, drew from all of America. If its rhythms were African and Cuban in origin, its melodies and harmonies were European. Like the mythic America, jazz was a melting pot. E pluribus unum, the motto on American money, meant more here than almost anywhere else.

For decades, black, white, and Hispanic musicians disguised their identities to work together on jazz recordings even when such combinations were taboo. By the war years, mixed-heritage bands had been accepted in public. Trombonist-vocalist Jack Teagarden worked with Louis Armstrong in the 1930s. Cuban musicians like Mario Bauza, who invented Afro-Cuban jazz, worked with Cab Calloway and Duke Ellington during the Depression. In 1938, jazz and blues impresario John Hammond talked his then-brother-in-law, Benny Goodman, into hiring Charlie Christian; they joined Lionel Hampton and Gene Krupa on the stage of Carnegie Hall.

It was in July 1944 that a young film editor at MGM named Norman Granz began hosting informal afternoon jam sessions at the Los Angeles Philharmonic Auditorium. He'd held benefits for those caught up in the Zoot Suit Riots. Now he had a bolder ploy. He opened the Philharmonic's doors to both white and black fans and let them sit without restrictions. It was the first time outside small enclaves like Central Avenue that American jazz audiences were integrated.

The excitement and crowds grew for his programs, so Granz set up a tour the following year. It leapfrogged briefly along the West Coast, then fell apart in Canada. No matter: Granz's idea—dubbed Jazz at the Philharmonic (JATP) after its original site—changed how the music was presented.

Granz conceived of jazz as drama in itself, the process of soloists battling for dominance. Illinois Jacquet became one of his biggest stars. Granz proved that jazz, even without swing dancers, had commercial potential. That insight would help shape the postwar era.

Besides heralding the end of segregation outside the South in a single dramatic gesture, Jazz at the Philharmonic showed Mingus he was right to think of jazz as drama. As a composer and performer, you could dramatize its inner workings as musical conversations.

Not long after the war, Mingus told Britt Woodman, "We don't need a vocalist. This band can have an argument with instruments." Sure, the JATP soloists sometimes thumped their chests like musical gladiators, forgetting their art in a contest of crowd-pleasing noise and fury. But what if a company of soloists could be more like the actors of Orson Welles's Mercury Theatre? Those actors knew each other's moves so well they could even improvise as a group and make it seem natural, organic.

And Mingus's bass would be in the thick of it. He wouldn't be relegated to glorified timekeeping. The ghost of Jimmy Blanton, dead of tuberculosis at twenty-four, stood at his shoulder. He'd play melodies in counterpoint to solos, ruffle the tempos with his triplet stutters and flamenco featherings of the thick, heavy strings. His sound these days was more cellolike but with heft and bottom. He loved the way the stage floors vibrated when he moved down the fingerboard and really nailed that beat.

So the voices in his outfits would be equal. No more frontline horns and backline bass and drums. He'd not only keep up but prod the reeds and brass, feed them unusual notes from the chords, shift around the beats. It would be a conversation, music that seemed like a natural interaction between real people —like the plays of the Mercury Theatre.

Naturally, for it to work best, it needed an artistic impresario at the center, the visionary who would provide direction and substance, the auteur.

It would be a decade before the bassist, relocated to New York, initiated his Jazz Workshop.

5 Portrait of the Artist

UNTIL LATE 1945, for L.A. jazz musicians, bebop was mostly hearsay. It was a New York thing, grown during the recording ban and the war, and it made little impact outside a small circle of musicians and intellectuals in the city jazz players had dubbed the Big Apple. So bop was far from twenty-three-year-old Mingus's mind.

He was gathering the reams of material he'd been writing around Lloyd Reese and Dmitri Tiomkin, music that drew from New Orleans, swing, proto-rhythm and blues, pop songs, film scores, Duke Ellington, classical models. He worked for Tiomkin for a year or so and did a flurry of record dates. There were a few mediocre tracks with vocalists for pianist-leaders Wilbert Baranco and Bob Moseley. On his originals as well as standards like "Ghost of a Chance," Mingus emphasized melody and Ellingtonian harmonies.

His taste didn't change much in December 1945, when the alto saxist Charlie "Bird" Parker, bop's best-known standard bearer and most virtuosic performer, hit town for the first time at Billy Berg's in Hollywood. By then, he'd heard some Parker recordings, but they hadn't moved him.

For eight weeks, Dizzy Gillespie headed an all-star, racially integrated bebop lineup featuring Bird that intended to plant bebop's flag in California. They wanted to wow the non-New Yorkers with the new sound's intellectual firepower and emotional rollercoaster ride, but Mingus found it chaotic and unlovely. He told everyone that Buddy Collette was a better player than Bird.

He was more lyrical, and his tone recalled Ellington's favorite alto saxist, Johnny Hodges. Buddy, he insisted, was the man.

In his autobiography, Gillespie wrote dryly, "They were much more interested in singers out in California."[1]

CHICO HAMILTON: When I came out of the army in 1945, L.A. was jumping. Mingus and Buddy and Lucky Thompson were there. Miles, Dizzy, Bird, Errol Garner, Howard McGhee were all there. When I left I was playing Papa Jones ding-ding things. When I came back it was bebop.

Bebop was the cry of a new generation, with new ideas and values to express in a new form of jazz. As Amiri Baraka (then LeRoi Jones) argues in his seminal book, *Blues People*, boppers saw themselves as self-consciousness artists, not entertainers. And they dressed and talked the parts, in a wily parody of European intellectuals. Reaching with deliberately mixed signals across racial lines, bop founders like Charlie Parker, Dizzy Gillespie, and Thelonious Monk established their claim: they were creating a new American art, the equal of the Old World's.

When they came out of Darktown, the embryonic postwar art scenes coalesced around their ideas.

Many of them confronted the color bar in art and life. Some refused to stay or play in segregated hotels and restaurants. In 1944 Billy Eckstine's orchestra, which included Gillespie and Parker, was threatened at the aptly named Plantation, a St. Louis club, for walking in the front door.[2] Onstage they struck older observers as arrogant; they refused to entertain. They insisted that the audience's job was to enter into their art.

It was a Romantic conception that suited the heightened complexity of their music and its small but fervent cult. And it heralded a change in postwar artistic forms—an emphasis on process. The "fourth wall" between artist and audience was coming down.

Bop combined dense, post-Impressionist harmonies with jagged melodies and rhythms that were more frenetic and unstable than those of swing. Its small groups foregrounded improvisation. They put the drummer and bassist on a par with the frontline horn and piano soloists.

To most older musicians and noncultists, bebop seemed cacophonous, sound and fury signifying nothing. But it reflected the feverish new rhythms and underlying discords of postwar American life.

For the next forty years, as prosperity and tensions percolated through American society, the culture heaved and buckled under the stress. Painfully, its dynamics gave birth to a postwar renaissance that spanned the arts. But in the late 1940s the voices of the new American individualism were fractional, underground, hardly more than a series of rumors.

The best known was Parker, and his following was limited largely to younger musicians and intellectuals and artists. His cult was small but fiercely devoted. Poets and painters and writers, most of them young and unknown, thronged his gigs. They thrilled to his spontaneous music, his freewheeling life, his wit and charm and unexpected depths. He reminded them of Existentialist antiheroes in books by Europeans like Celine and Sartre—except that he was black, and American. He was a Promethean figure.

In January, Norman Granz presented him at the Los Angeles Philharmonic, and sold out the house out.

Trombonist Jimmy Knepper was one Los Angeles musician who disagreed with Mingus. Later a stalwart member of several Mingus groups, Knepper was a devout Bird disciple. His friend Dean Benedetti, a sax player who devotedly taped countless Parker live sets, had a band. When their bassist didn't show up for a gig in San Pedro, Benedetti called Mingus.

JIMMY KNEPPER, *musician:* The rest of us were white. He didn't say a word all night long, just looked kinda mean and scowled. Mingus said it was the first time he'd played with all white guys. He later told me that because we all dug Bird so much, it made him go back and listen to Bird again.

The artist in Mingus, like the moralist, was anchored in a respect for tradition. His mentors had underlined the central importance of dedication and drill to technique. Art demanded order and discipline. Without structure, only chaos spoke. He was more interested in Tatum than Parker; they drew on overlapping harmonic ideas, but Tatum was more obviously rooted in fundamentals, from the classics to stride piano. And yet already Mingus's best music mingled styles. His complex life seemed to demand new forms for expression. He admired Beethoven, who stretched classical forms to suit his Romantic yearnings for self-assertion.

When nineteen-year-old Miles Davis came to Los Angeles a bit later, to join Benny Carter's big band and jam with Charlie Parker at Little Tokyo's after-hours Finale Club, he and Mingus felt an instant kinship.[3] Mingus showed up a lot to see the band.

Mingus and Davis shared an interest in composition and arranging for larger groups. They talked about using unusual instruments, like French horns and cellos, in jazz. Davis also adored Orson Welles, whose phrasing with that trademark voice helped shape his own on trumpet.

Besides, Miles had attitude. He was too cool even to talk. He was hell on women. He was so bad you'd never guess at first glance his father was a medical man with horses who was sending his son money, he thought to study at Juilliard. Miles didn't dig commercial music.

AL YOUNG, *writer and friend*: Dinah Washington had Mingus do commercial writing. "I wrote her charts," he said. And he said you could be artistic at whatever you did—just bring something special to it. That's what he tried to do when he wrote those. But he said he never liked the pressure of that business because the record companies always beat the artists.

Mingus's love for blues and pop forms made him well suited to be Washington's arranger, a Billie Holiday disciple finding her own voice. In mid-December, Washington insinuated her sexy way into "Chewin' Mama Blues," "Beggin' Woman Blues," and the like. The charts are clever but hardly revolutionary. They were attempts to make hit records. And he wanted to be a success —but on his own terms. For him, writing for singers put another arrow in his creative quiver. He was absorbing every style he tried, making it part of his own voice.

Tenor saxist Lucky Thompson, with whom Miles Davis was also hanging out, was the sessions' bandleader. He did another record date with Mingus where Dizzy Gillespie guested.

Dizzy and Mingus had a few basic things in common: violent fathers, a Methodist upbringing, kiddie tries at the trombone, an emphasis on self-reliance, a bent toward practical jokes and cat-and-mouse games, a love for "I Can't Get Started," an unshakeable belief that the piano was the crux of musical understanding, the overwhelming desire to compose and lead a band. Gillespie's father played bass. The pair had already become friends and colleagues.

Miles Davis had left for New York after a shouting match with Mingus, who accused him of abandoning Bird in Camarillo, but until then he and Thompson had been rehearsing with the bassist—mostly Mingus compositions. "He just wanted to hear his shit played all the time," is how Davis put it in his autobiography, adding, "It was some strange-sounding shit back then. But Mingus was just like Duke Ellington, ahead of his time."[4]

So Thompson joined the first of Mingus's cooperative composer-oriented groups, the Stars of Swing.

BUDDY COLLETTE: You've got to realize what's happening in this period. There's the bop thing coming in, and the categories along with it. Was it swing, or was it bebop? At this period we wanted to play music that was pretty.

"Laura," "Prelude to a Kiss"—these are the pretty tunes. There were a lot of ballads: "I Remember April." Our concept was four-part voicings. Mingus was playing with the bow. The things he'd written for the band—"This Subdues My Passion"—they were the pretty things. Dizzy and Bird weren't doing that. See, the reason Lucky Thompson got hired at Billy Berg's was because Billy Berg was very unhappy with the sound of what Diz and Bird were playing. He wanted it to be warmer. So Lucky came in and played some "Body and Soul."

When Buddy came back to Watts in late 1945, things had started to change, but it still had its garden plots and truck farms and neatly trimmed houses. Red Callender had been leading a push to integrate the musicians' locals, with some success. A lot of his peers, like Dexter Gordon, and his closest friends, like Mingus, had done some growing up. Mingus was thinner, and a father. He'd gotten a reputation for meanness and enhanced his reputation for emotional flareups. The rumor was that he was running around even though Buddy knew Charlie and Jeanne adored each other.

But Mingus was more self-assured now. He'd gotten some credits under his belt. And he was writing up a storm—a lot of different styles and ideas, almost cinematic. In "Chill of Death," which he'd soon try to record for Columbia, he combined poetry and music in a way that echoed hits by Orson Welles and Gordon Jenkins.

And Buddy was writing a lot too. What was more natural than two close friends and longtime colleagues joining to showcase their new musical wares? They'd be equal voices inside the music and out. Mingus could keep pace with the frontline soloists, bobbing and weaving on the bass's long neck and thick gut strings like it was an oversized guitar.

Thus was born Stars of Swing. The name must have sounded quaint to the boppers arriving in town, but Mingus always attributed near-magical powers to this septet. Later, he'd claim the band was formed in 1941.[5] That was a way to establish his originality, for in this band he tested musical strategies he'd employ more and more. There was pedal point—a bass note extended over measures and chord changes. There was polytonality—more than one key signature to a piece. There was striking counterpoint that wound two songs against each other, often ironically. And there was extended form, where measures were added and subtracted. Putting the band earlier was essential. His ploys had to be protected against competing claims.

It's often said New Orleans gave jazz had its first great improviser, Louis Armstrong, and its first great composer, Jelly Roll Morton. His time with Bigard and Armstrong reinforced Mingus's love of early jazz's jaunty two-beat parade rhythms. Morton became another Mingus hero. A Creole and self-proclaimed pimp, he composed jazz classics and organized the first big jazz bands before Mingus was born. The ambitious young man would always feel a wounded kinship with the sensitive, bragging Morton, who always felt under-rated and stolen from.

The Stars of Swing went unrecorded. But Mingus, Collette, and Woodman always remembered it glowingly.

BRITT WOODMAN: His writing was so much different. He was writing stuff like "Chill of Death." He had arrangements and lyrics. He was crazy about Orson Welles—Orson Welles was very popular at that time—and he wrote lyrics and music that almost sounded like Orson Welles.

We organized a band with Buddy Collette, Lucky Thompson, Spaulding Givens, and Les Hite's drummer and a trumpet player named John Anderson. Everybody was writing. We were sorry we never recorded, because that was a painful group.

BUDDY COLLETTE: There was a lot of rehearsing and experimenting with the new sonorities of chords. We started rehearsing at Mingus's house, which was around 43rd and McKinley. The band rehearsed about three weeks. Nobody had to go anywhere, so we'd get there at nine in the morning and go to five, we'd go have lunch together. We got so good in the material we were playing—smooth material, some of them fast tunes, but people realized they were real melodic, not like bop.

Harold Stanley, who managed the Rhum Boogie, and Black Dot McGee, who managed the Downbeat on Central Avenue, came to check the septet out. They signed the band for the Downbeat on the spot. They remembered the prewar local stardom of the Woodman Brothers. So did their friends and fans, who turned out and spent money. The sounds at the bar drove Mingus a little nuts already, but he kept himself in check. Buddy and Britt were in the pocket with him, grooving in a mellotone.

Then Lucky Thompson jumped the groove. The group's original sign gave everyone equal billing, but Thompson persuaded Black Dot to replace it. The new sign read Lucky Thompson and his All-Stars—the name of the group that had recorded with Dinah Washington. Thompson argued that would draw more people.

When the others saw it, they felt like they'd been kicked. They confronted Thompson in the dressing room after the first set. Collette recalls, "He said, 'I've got the biggest name, plus I'm the best player.' There could've been a killing there, with Mingus's temper." Thompson strode off confidently. The rest of them slid into Buddy's car and talked. One suggested that their original sign might still be in the back alley. They looked, and it was, so they took Thompson's sign down and put theirs up.

The tenorman was deflated, and his playing that night showed it. He was late the next night. After that, he didn't show up. Collette, as band spokesman, filed charges with the union, but nothing came of it. With Teddy Edwards on tenor replacing Thompson, the blend at the heart of the idea had shifted. After a month or so, the band drifted apart.

Woodman landed choice gigs. He joined Boyd Raeburn's Orchestra for *Boyd Meets Stravinsky*; the album was one of many attempts at the time to merge classical music and jazz. Then he worked with bandleader Benny Carter, who soon became the first black composer to pierce Hollywood's color bar. Meanwhile, Mingus did pickup dates. He soloed for forty-five minutes on "Body and Soul" on a tabletop stage one night, and played local joints like The Last Word with Collette and others. One night the band dared him to eat three hamburgers, fries, and malted milks in a single sitting, and he did.

But there were endless jam sessions at the Jungle Room, across from the Lincoln Theater. That was one joint where Tatum showed up when he hit L.A. People started having house parties again. Dexter Gordon, Chico Hamilton, and Mingus turned up at many. Mingus did scattered dates at Hollywood clubs, played a few dances. When Billy Eckstine sat in to sing "Old Man River" with Lee Young's group at the Oasis, Mingus kept inserting arco bass into what Eckstine wanted to be a capella.[6]

He kept looking for ways to make a vocal hit, but he wanted it Mingus-style.

BRITT WOODMAN: He rehearsed a big band with a popular vocalist named Damita Jo. I don't know how she could hear the melody, because there were all these different changes he had, so many. He did that, I think, because he was competing with Duke himself. He had to show what he could do.

That description fits much of Mingus's work during this period, but not all. He backed Ellington singer Ivie Anderson for the local, ironically named Black and White label. He rejoined Howard McGhee for four tracks. He worked with Darby Hicks and Gene Morris. He tried a big band session near Elysian Park that included both Knepper and Woodman on trombones, but nothing came of the demos. Most of this music that survives is undistinguished.

But near his twenty-fourth birthday, he found his voice as a composer. It was still embryonic, but its mode was eclectic. With Thompson that January he cut "Weird Nightmare," later retitled "Vassarlean"; it had a cantilevered structure and sounded like a German art song. And "This Subdues

My Passion" clearly echoes Ellingtonia like "Chelsea Bridge," with its gently discordant harmonies and moody atmosphere. To lead an octet that included Collette, he dubbed himself Baron Mingus. He was announcing his link to jazz royalty—Duke Ellington, Count Basie, King Oliver.

It probably wasn't coincidence that he also had a conceptual breakthrough on the bass. He later told critic Nat Hentoff, "I began playing and didn't stop for a long time. It was suddenly *me*; it wasn't the bass any more. Now I'm not conscious of the instrument as an instrument when I play."[7]

It was around August 1946 that Charlie Parker reappeared in Los Angeles. He was left behind (the reasons are unclear) when Gillespie and his other bandmates returned to New York and had gotten strung out on bad heroin and booze. Famously, he cracked on a July recording session during a painful rendition of Billie Holiday's hit "Lover Man." After a bit in the psychiatric wing of the L.A. county jail, he was sent to Camarillo State Prison for six months of rehabilitation. He was also subjected to electroshock treatments, and almost bit off his tongue during them.[8] Shock therapy, in which large voltages sizzled lobes and blotted out memories, was widely used on criminals, addicts, debutantes with rebellious tendencies, homosexuals, and other deviants.

Parker's heroin addiction was a crucial part of his myth and persona. His cult pointed to the long history of artists and religious figures like shamans using drugs for inspiration to get a deeper vision of reality. They believed that heroin shaped Bird's playing, so dramatically different from swing. Many "little Birds" aped his music and aped his drug habit, even though Bird warned them not to. "If you don't live it, it won't come out of your horn,"[9] a famed Bird maxim, could be understood different ways.

For some, heroin was also a form of revolt, of rejection. It allowed them to withdraw from a world they saw as unjust, or tightassed, or unchanging, or just uncool—a world with no use for many of them. Look at how the white man ran jazz, just like everything else—it was a plantation. Look at how the big labels in the record industry were shrugging off their new music. Too hip for the public, they said, and avoided recording it. But many boppers saw this as a conspiracy of silence, an effort to keep their revolt under wraps.

Heroin was a self-destructive way of saying Fuck You.

When Mingus saw Parker again, what struck him was Bird's presence, his self-possession and natural air of authority. He could talk about anything, it seemed, with ease—art, philosophy, race, music. He spoke like a widely read man, alluding to books and authors. He was a teacher. He reminded Mingus of Farwell Taylor.

BUDDY COLLETTE: Jam sessions were going on at Jack's Basket every night. When Bird came out of Camarillo, he was healthy. So there must've been twenty saxes or so lined up, starting at 1:00 or 2:00 A.M. Bird was very sharp and handsome then. Everyone was playing thirty or forty choruses to show him how great they were, but by 4:00 A.M. everyone knew Bird was getting ready to play. He played three choruses. It was a lesson. He didn't need more than three. It was complete.

Shortly after Bird left Los Angeles, a second son was born to Charles and Jeanne Mingus. She'd gone back to her mother more than once, but one of the peaceful interludes in their stormy marriage brought their son Eugene in September 1946. Soon their marriage was effectively over.

Mingus later told different stories to explain why it ended. He said Jeanne suffered from a condition that made sex painful; she'd had an operation that only made it worse. And he said she cheated on him with a friend, another bass player, which drove him to promiscuity and drugs.

During his life, Mingus fell in love repeatedly, each time almost innocently. That was the natural outgrowth of his dependence on women for sympathy and understanding. But he had to be the center. Children were competition. Besides, women hung around musicians; they liked the thrill of being different, the self-contained subculture, the way musicians' lives usually didn't run on standard time. The hippie chicks—a lot of them white—seemed thrilled to hear his stories and dreams. Was that his fault?

BRITT WOODMAN: He had this natural thing he didn't know he had. If I said to a chick the things he said, the chick would slap me, honestly. But the way he said it . . . he'd grown kind of handsome, with the little mustache and all—he looked kinda like Orson Welles. At that time, he started staying out late with chicks and things.

His personality was filling in its defining contours. He saw life as a series of dramas unfolding with torturous subplots and counterplots, like improvised jazz, like living theater. And he composed his life with the same complex audacity and breadth as his music. Usually, no matter how much he prowled, he had a primary woman he depended on, a physical and emotional tonal center.

Christmas 1946 found Charles Mingus in San Francisco, doing something he'd vowed he'd never do, and that he'd do more than once—working for the United States Post Office. He was shaken by the breakdown of his marriage. Then a white bandleader who was a friend of Farwell Taylor's offered him a gig, and the segregated union refused to let him keep it. Everything that haunted him when he first came to San Francisco seven years earlier was back. His world was collapsing. He hit another depression.

His escape was increasingly common. "In those days I didn't think too much of myself, and I got very paranoid on narcotics," he once told *Down Beat*.[10] It was the first time he'd done hard drugs. He was looking for another version of the out-of-body experiences he'd shared with Taylor.

Whenever he was hurt and confused, he turned back to Taylor. Taylor kept a loose and tolerant eye on Charlie, let him move in and out as needed. He fed his protégé cabbage juice and vegetables to clean out his system, then loaded him up on huge roasts and hash cookies. He reminded Charlie about his greatness, his gifts.

Taylor's breezily domineering attentiveness was, as always, a tonic. By summer 1947, Mingus was back in L.A. Among the few Central Avenue running buddies he confided in about Taylor and his religious beliefs was Jack Kelso.[11]

As Kelso and Mingus sat in Pershing Square one day, the bassist rambled enthusiastically through his psychic experiences, his search for answers to the questions he considered fundamental to human life. Kelso, familiar with Zen Buddhism and Eastern philosophies, suggested he read William James's *Varieties of Religious Experience*, which he'd read in the service. It opened a deeper bond. Mingus took Kelso back to the little house he shared with Jeanne and played rich, Ellingtonian harmonies while he sang poetic lyrics about the power of woman. Kelso was floored by his friend's growing musical maturity and power.

Meanwhile, Mingus was looking for work. He and Buddy were helping their friend Gerald Wiggins get a big band together. He snagged a short gig at the Million Dollar Theatre, playing in an otherwise all-white band behind Billy Eckstine. He complained to the other musicians, "You guys are prejudiced! You should have some more blacks. You could hire Buddy Collette."

Collette gives that reaction credit for starting him on his crusade to amalgamate the racially separate Los Angeles musicians' unions. He'd learned from white musicians about the extent of the racial disparity in pay for the same gigs and knew that the best calls—for that matter, most calls—went to the white local. He saw that without integration, blacks would always be stuck with leftovers.

In August 1947, Mingus's stepbrother Odell died of stomach cancer. Sergeant Mingus had never liked Odell, and the Mingus sisters recall his persistent sexual advances. Charles barely tolerated him, perhaps because he played guitar. Later, he told a mystic story of his brother coming to him as a bird while he was meditating and saving him from staying out of his body too long.

The funeral brought the Mingus family together. After months of self-flagellation, Charles wanted Jeanne back. He loved her. She adored him. They had two sons. What else mattered?

CHARLES MINGUS III, *artist and son*: I remember being three years old, and my mom and dad having one of their huge fights, rolling on the floor, him holding her by the shoulder and smacking her, like in a movie. I hit him in the nuts —it was the only place I could reach, I didn't really know what I was doing. He left. My mother took all his clothes and tore them up, cut them up, his suits and all. They reconciled that time, again.

In late 1947, Jeanne took her two sons back to her parents' farm for the last time. She worked as a domestic, then became a nurse. Much of the time, her parents or foster homes raised Charles and Eugene. Her friends say the heartache never left her.

Lionel Hampton led his popular big band into Los Angeles in the fall of 1947. He liked using two basses—it gave his band a defining heavy beat—and was looking for a second bassist who could solo. Britt Woodman, who'd joined the band at the Million Dollar Theatre in 1946, played one of Charles's records for Gladys Hampton and drummer Curley Hamner. Curley, Gladys's then-boyfriend, helped her run the band, including hiring and firing. The players learned choreographed routines and sported touches of sophistication, like white gloves, that contrasted with the free-swinging music. For his part, Lionel Hampton starred, collected an ample allowance, and had women visit him in his dressing room.

For Mingus, it was opportunity knocking louder than ever before. He'd been struggling to get bits and pieces of all the material he was writing, that seemed to sluice out of him, onto records. Hamp was big, and his band recorded all the time. In fact, that November brought Mingus into the studio with the band three times. At the second session, the band cut "Mingus Fingers."

BRITT WOODMAN: I warned him not to write, because he wouldn't get paid. Nobody who wrote for Hamp got paid. That's how Gladys worked it. So Charles said okay. But he wrote "Mingus Fingers" and they recorded it, and he had to get a lawyer to try to get paid.

The song was a vaguely chromatic, bop-flavored big band piece, edged with Ellingtonian touches. It became a local hit. Mingus's solo spot was the centerpiece, where he clearly announced his claims to Jimmy Blanton's mantle with virtuosity like his deft double-stops and melodic lines.

And he learned from Gladys Hampton's business tactics. The black woman had only done what endless male bandleaders and white record executives did before and since—target a neophyte, take a chance to make some money. It was a time-honored industry ploy. When Mingus left the band, he made sure to take the charts he'd written with him, including "Mingus Fingers," which he'd had to sign over to the Hamptons' publisher.

The lessons from this skirmish with the business side of music fit into his middle-class upbringing. Self-protection, he decided, was rooted in self-ownership. There had to be a way he could keep control of his ideas and material. Publishing companies, record labels, bandleaders, agents, club owners—they all got their piece of the artist and paid him chump change. The System seemed closed. But somehow he wanted to get some of his own action.

Although "Mingus Fingers" didn't make Mingus any money, it cemented his place in the band. So he joined the Hampton band for his first national tour. It brought him where he was starting to believe the real action was—New York.

Hampton's band hit all the big towns, like Chicago, Washington, Denver, and San Francisco, and all the one-nighters from Peoria to Geneva, New York, holdovers from the glory days of the Swing Era. The leader's brassy onstage showbiz shtick at times seemed like Uncle Tomming to the young bassist. But he also noted how Hamp held a crowd's attention with the force of his personality, as Louis Armstrong had. He spliced what he learned into his growing self-image, along with models like Orson Welles and Farwell Taylor.

Lucille (Celia) Gemanis was twenty-two years old and a jazz fan, and found herself drawn to Mingus, as so many women were. She was engaged to a young bebop trumpeter, Jon Nielsen. But when the slender five-foot, four-inch redhead caught an afternoon jam session at the Say When club on Bush Street, she felt drawn to the handsome twenty-seven-year-old bassist with the mobile, tortured face. He was strutting his unusual stuff, and she was intrigued.

That night, with a girlfriend, Celia went to see the Hampton band at Oakland Auditorium—and there he was again. He was doodling on the piano in the set break when she approached him. "I thought you played bass," she said. They talked, and he called her at her rooming house after she got home, at 2:00 A.M., and asked her to dinner the next night.

CELIA MINGUS ZAENTZ, *second wife*: The first night I met him he read me poetry. Then he took me to Farwell Taylor's apartment. Farwell made a big fuss over Mingus, and was kind of stand-offish to me. Very possessive of Mingus— and who was I?

He fell for her hard, and proposed to her. She was overwhelmed and more than a bit thrilled at his impetuous passion. Women loved that about him, its genuineness and intensity. Celia was no exception. But she was also raised a Catholic, and engaged. She explained the situation to Mingus. For once, in the face of a setback, he remained uncharacteristically calm.

That winter, it was in New York and in Hampton's band that he met trumpeter Fats Navarro, who helped get him more interested in bebop. Navarro didn't copy Dizzy or Bird directly, but he wove their insights into his own, more lyrical voice. Part Cuban and part black, he was the ideal soulmate for Mingus, who was still taken for Mexican. In Mingus's book, *Beneath the Underdog*, Navarro explains to the younger man how the music industry "owns" its black stars. Jazz, he notes, makes money for the gangsters and such who run it, but even stars like "King Spook" fork over the bigger chunk of their take to white management.[12] Navarro died in July 1950. But in six months, he filled Mingus's adolescent antiracism with significant detail and realism.

A mentor and friend to Mingus, Fats also dramatized heroin abuse. After snorting it once in San Francisco and getting physically ill, Mingus never touched heroin again. But all around him, the drug was the badge of the subterranean outlaw counterculture forming around bebop and Charlie Parker. In seedy Times Square coffeeshops, Columbia University hangers-on like William Burroughs scored uppers and downers and soon heroin itself for themselves and their friends. They were seeking new forms of consciousness, artistic and spiritual.

As Mingus plumbed the new scenes with their tang of danger, however, he kept one foot in familiar territory—family. His mother's sister Louise and brother-in-law, pianist Fess Williams, lived at 106-47 Waltham Street in Jamaica, Queens. The neighborhood was already home to the black middle class, which included entertainers and sports figures. Only a year earlier, Jackie Robinson had broken the color bar in the ritzier neighborhood next to Jamaica, St. Albans. Jazz stars like Illinois Jacquet soon followed him there.

Charles had last seen his cousins Estella and Rudy fifteen years before, when they visited his family in Los Angeles for a summer. But blood was thicker than water, and it was a place to stay, free room and board. Rudy, a solid sax man, was trying to break in as a pro musician. So he and Charles got pretty close, sleeping night after night on two small beds side by side in one small room. They'd make the scene and hang out, hitting sessions and clubs, looking for work. Mingus spent hours at the piano, often exchanging notes with Fess. With Fess's help, he polished a new arrangement of "Mingus Fingers." Soon he was sketching what became "Fables of Faubus."

He was beginning his lifelong rounds, his self-appointed task of making his way around the complex interconnected worlds of postwar New York. Its intensity fascinated him. He was meeting people faster, even, than in San Francisco.

Some of them, like Allen Ginsberg, he'd heard about in San Francisco. Ginsberg wanted to be a poet, but he was working as an ad agency copywriter. He was trying to dampen his homosexual yearnings by having a girlfriend. His mother, a communist sympathizer, had had a lobotomy and was confined to an asylum.

They talked about Ideas and Issues. Was The System heading toward emotional fascism, by forcing individuals to repress their personalities in order to conform? Was jazz proof that blacks were more in touch with the natural, spontaneous world than corporate America? Why should sex depend on marriage? Why were extramarital sex and homosexuality crimes? Were drugs a means to higher consciousness and insight?

One of their inspirations, he discovered, was Charlie Parker. "If you don't live it, it won't come out of your horn," Bird said. They took the maxim to heart, as they talked about renewing postwar American art to reflect the changes in society that many of them found threatening.

Like poet Walt Whitman, another of their heroes, they believed life itself was art in process, that all art was essentially autobiographical. They felt the postwar world was increasingly bureaucratic, faceless, hierarchical, conformist. So it was essential that art put a face on what it did, that it highlight how each individual's vision was personal and particular and different. They wanted no more poets like T. S. Eliot, carefully distanced from their work by irony and literary conventions. To counteract the faceless suburbs starting to sprawl, the corporate workers in uniform suits and work clothes, the standardizations they worried were permeating America, they wanted unmistakable human touches to differentiate their art.

Jazz, especially Bird's bebop, was a model. It highlighted the individual, yet depended on group communication. Its spontaneity and equal partnership on the bandstand opposed bureaucratic rulebooks and refuted segregation. And it was born in black America. Who had a more telling perspective on the brave new world?

The rough-and-tumble of ideas and personalities reminded Mingus of Farwell's parties, and he was fascinated. But he also had more pressing practical problems. He had to establish his jazz credentials. Coming from California, he was a rumor in New York, even though he later said he tumbled right into a party at the Band Box when he arrived.[13] The Hampton records gave him a calling card, as did his friendship with Miles Davis, but he had to make the scene to make his name. He wanted desperately to establish himself as a main man alongside Oscar Pettiford, who seemed to be every bopper's bassist of choice.

ESTELLA WILLIAMS: He used to leave our house every night to go to work—took the subway back and forth to New York. He came here in winter, and New York was colder then. My brother Rudy was slim, but when Charles needed a coat he had to borrow Rudy's, until he was able to get his own. It was a tight squeeze.

Even though he was making money, he still had financial problems. So he stayed with us for free, to help get him on his feet. When he lived with us, my mother cooked, and he'd have two or three plates when everyone else had maybe one and a half.

RUDY WILLIAMS, *first cousin*: He was a very studious guy, experimenting on the piano all the time. He went to jam sessions. Sometimes he'd sit in, sometimes not. He was very critical of who was playing. "Aw man, that ain't Jazz."

People think Mingus was mean but he was a comedian, telling jokes all the time. If you stayed with him long enough he'd put on a show for you, have you die laughing. He should have been an actor. Very friendly and very soft, not hard like people think. He loved to talk about women chasing, tell jokes.

He wasn't a pimp. He knew all those guys—all the musicians did. And you hung out with them. But he exaggerated all that. I hung out with him. He talked a lot, but he wasn't doing that much.

For the rest of his life, Mingus claimed that during this period he was a pimp. The women who knew him best—wives, lovers, friends—insist he never learned to do that. One, who first met him in spring 1949, says he was sexually shy then.

He had other reasons to adopt the role. Like his new acquaintance Allen Ginsberg, Mingus saw his personal life as symbolic. He already put himself at the center of most of his compositions, sometimes dramatically, as in "This Subdues My Passion." By the mid-1950s, when he began to work on his autobiography, books like *On the Road* and *Howl* had changed American literature, bent it toward confessional impulses.

But Mingus had learned the hard-earned value of biography from jazz. The best jazz musicians dedicate themselves to finding their individual musical voices—who they are on their instruments—and to pushing the envelope of technique and conception, rewriting the rules. That was the road to growth and maturity, part of what Charlie Parker's maxim meant. Art was a dialog, and its topic was change.

Besides, he was fascinated by New York's elaborate urban black demi-monde, even more elaborate than Central Avenue's. It sheltered musicians, hookers, pimps, gamblers—the motley lot that, as Malcolm X saw, were the capitalist princes of the local black economy. Like the Italian mafiosi, they were excluded from the white man's economy, so they created their own. They thumbed their noses at The Man just by living big-time. And if they lorded it over white women, so much the better. Didn't the white man treat them like property anyway?

Mingus had something else to prove—that he was as black as anybody. Other musicians, like Miles Davis and Max Roach, boasted that they even pimped white women.

Being a pimp meant living on the margins, being your own moral law. And besides, women loved the pimp stories Mingus told them.

Mingus got a friendly reception from his acquaintances in New York's bop precincts. The music had moved downtown, to bigger clubs with white and black clientele. It was being ignored by the major labels and large audiences, who were more drawn to singers and novelty hits. But it seemed that each time Mingus came back to town after a few tour dates with Hampton there were more jam sessions, more musicians hitting town and digging bebop, more people to meet.

He was growing in self-assurance, even arrogance, the more he mixed. And the more closely he watched the stand-up confidence, the self-assertion of the boppers, the more he chafed under the old-fashioned show-biz Hamp put on. Eight shows more or less by the numbers a day at palaces like the famed Apollo Theater irked him. Even a show at Carnegie Hall on April 10 and broadcasts over radio's Mutual Network couldn't buy his growing restlessness off.

By summer 1948, he'd clashed with Curley, Gladys, and Hampton too many times. One night during a show, he'd actually dumped Curley off his stool and into the audience. He left the band once it arrived back in Los Angeles, where Hampton was set to work on *A Song Is Born*, a movie about the Swing Era that also starred Hamp's old employer, Benny Goodman.

He asked Celia, the smart attractive redhead he'd met several months earlier, to write his letter of resignation, giving Hamp two weeks' notice.

For six months, before Celia left for New York after marrying Nielsen in October, he played mostly between San Francisco and Sacramento, and kept in near-constant touch with her. Then around New Year's, he sent her a copy of "Mingus Fingers" with a note wishing her "good luck in your new adventure (marriage)." He also wrote that "you will still have your first son by me."

Celia thought he was completely mad, but it wasn't the last time he'd fore-tell his future.

Mingus was sure he could capitalize on his new national visibility as a record-ing veteran with Hampton and Earl Hines, a gig he'd gotten through Hamner. Hadn't he placed in the top twenty on Metronome's 1948 poll? Short term, he looked right. He landed a steady gig almost immediately at Billy Berg's Holly-wood club and local hangouts like the Last Word. And he was hustling like he would from now on, recording for lots of local labels, trying to reach an audi-ence with the cinemascope of sounds in his head.

In early 1949, for Fentone's, a San Francisco-based label, he released one record as *Charles "Baron" Mingus Presents His Symphonic Airs.* "God's Portrait" (later "Self Portrait," then "Portrait") bore the marks of Farwell Taylor's beliefs. "The Story of Love" foreshadowed his use of multiple melodies within a single piece. He made his sole recording on cello, a quasi-classical rendition of the pop tune "He's Gone." Writing of the session, jazz critic Ralph Gleason said, "He has proven that there should be no segregation in music between classical and jazz. And that it is possible to make classical musicians swing by *writing* it correctly for them." [14]

For his more populist side, he changed the name to Baron Mingus and His Rhythm. "Lyon's Roar," dedicated to San Francisco disk jockey Jimmy Lyons, had a fast-paced bop edge. "Pennies from Heaven" illustrated his cunning mu-sical irony. He swaddled the naively optimistic tune in a funereal setting. It was the arranging equivalent of what jazzers from Louis Armstrong to Lester Young and Billie Holiday did: take banal pop tunes and imbue them with the complex, alienated understanding that was part of their daily living with racism.

The Baron and His Rhythm had different personnel to record in Los Ange-les that spring. With Buddy Collette for emotional and musical support, he recut "Mingus Fingers" for Dolphins of Hollywood, owned by Johnny Dol-phin, a jazz world fixture with underworld connections. It was a small irony that "These Foolish Things," its flip side, became a minor local hit, thanks partly to the electrifying section where Collette's reed work backed Mingus's bass solo—a startlingly effective role reversal.

But none of this was paying the rent. His musical ambitions had to out-weigh all others. But he didn't like eating canned spinach and mayonnaise as a steady diet. He had barely 165 pounds covering his five-foot, nine-inch frame, down from 185 pounds. Being thin never agreed with his temperament, and his reputation for meanness grew as he tried to cover the front tooth Jeanne had chipped. He smiled even more rarely because of it, and his scowl seemed worse. And he felt like he was getting nowhere fast.

EDDIE BERT, *musician*: I was in San Francisco in early 1949. (Bassist) Clyde Lombardi wanted to go hear this bass player he'd heard about. So we went down to the International Quarter, and there was Mingus, with four basses and a drummer; he was playing lead bass.

He was determined to break out of the molds jazz had atrophied into, to make it strange, to make it art, like Duke Ellington, like Charlie Parker, like Red Callender, even. But few wanted to see experimental art. Bebop's new language was taking musicians by storm, but not the public. The club scene was reeling under increased taxes, and the record industry faced another strike by the American Federation of Musicians. Times were bad for new music.

All his life, Mingus raged at people who he felt hadn't paid the dues he had. The trigger for the diatribe varied from moment to moment: racism, misunderstood art ahead of its time, personal vendettas, love spurned. He was an outsider, persecuted. That part of his self-image was now fixed, unyielding.

He spent a lot of time at Taylor's magnificent apartment looking for comfort. When he couldn't afford one of the cheap rooms San Francisco had so many of, he crashed in the artist's North Beach studio, as he had three years earlier.

By 1949, many big bands had disappeared. Two generations of musicians who were used to fairly steady work with big bands and theater bands were finding work harder to come by. Mingus was among them. So mid-1949, when Lionel Hampton hit San Francisco and needed a bass player, marked a rare moment when Charles Mingus Jr. ate some crow. He went for his old slot, and got it. That meant he could eat again, which eased a lot of the pain. Hamp was mostly touring locally for now, but the plan was to go to Europe later that year. Mingus wanted to check that out.

VIVIAN MINGUS: He had another child before he married Celia, and my dad would never own up to it. He was the type of person where, if you're not married, that's not my grandchild. They were real funny. Strict. Victorian.

After Celia left for New York with Nielsen, Mingus paradoxically got more self-confident. He'd met another of his dream girls, cute, direct, truthful, ripe but not an easy sexual target. She was white. She could talk music, and she played the piano. She understood the musician's life, not like Jeanne. And he knew they'd cross paths again—and soon.

Meanwhile, he was in San Francisco, which for a decade had been his second home. He appeared at places, and people were drawn to him. One was nineteen-year-old Shirley Holiday, who met him that spring. He was jamming with a female violinist at an after-hours place called Jackson's Nook. Some of Mingus's buddies from Los Angeles, like Dexter Gordon and Jerome Richardson, hung out there when they were in town.

Mingus didn't hang out, exactly. When he wasn't onstage, he sat in the back and wrote music.

When he saw Shirley the next night, he walked her home.

SHIRLEY HOLIDAY, *lover:* He was in turmoil. He reached out to some people, was very secluded with others. Our relationship . . . a lot of times, there weren't that many words exchanged. We did a lot of walking, and picking up leaves and looking at them and talking about them, if you can understand that. It was a period where he felt, "Get me away from whatever I'm thinking about." He needed a quiet time, and he found it.

Shirley already had a small child, Marva. Mingus felt at ease with the waiflike brown-skinned girl who was just over five feet tall. She didn't seem to want much except his company. And he needed someone besides Farwell to talk to about his confusion and pain over sex and morality. Even in his fifties, Mingus loved to talk almost like an advice columnist with women friends about tangled relationships and their dilemmas. With Shirley, he was unbuttoning some of his own defenses.

He'd had it again with Hampton's shtick. One night on stage, the star turned to use his mallets on the bass—a crowd pleaser to ham it up. Mingus pulled the bass away and turned his back. Offstage, Hampton got on him, insisting he had to contribute; everybody had to contribute. The next night, Hampton tried it again. Mingus started swinging the bass over his head. Hampton backed off, but he fumed. When Mingus dumped Curley Hamner off the drums again, complaining that he never could keep time, he sealed his fate. He was out, and so was Europe—for now.

He was broke again, but drinking in the tiny but lively new scene in his second hometown. A bar called 10 Adler Place—he'd later name a tune for it—attracted the nucleus of something aborning, poets like Philip Lamantia and Allen Ginsberg. Under Kenneth Rexroth's anarchistic mentorship, they were a highly self-conscious crowd.

Mingus was curious about the scene.

Sundays often found a group of sandaled, scruffy-looking young adults building a campfire above the Cliff House and picnicking as they overlooked the Pacific. They played music and talked about big topics like The System, sexuality, psychotherapy, and, of course, art and their role in its future. They worried about what they called Organization Man. They were sampling Buddhism and Eastern beliefs and all sorts of sexual setups.

They were reading Symbolist hero-poets like Rimbaud and the *Kinsey Report on Sexual Behavior in the Human Male*, which documented widespread, unacknowledged extramarital sex in the United States.

Like the others, Mingus wore handmade sandals. They corrected his pigeontoed walk.

Mingus developed an act with Shirley and pianist Richard Wyands that combined his retooled bebop with ballads and current hits. Walking the hills, he taught Shirley to sing "Body and Soul" in a way that sounded beyond the pale, except that Sarah Vaughan did it much that way in 1946. Vaughan was part of jazz's bebop wing, working with Billy Eskstine and Dizzy Gillespie and Charlie Parker, scatsinging like a horn soloist.

It was here, too, that Mingus unveiled his growing understanding of showbiz sleight-of-hand, his P. T. Barnum side. Outside the little club on Church Street stood a sandwich-board sign reading, the Why Not? Club presents Charles Mingus formerly with LIONEL HAMPTON, featuring vocalist Shirley HOLIDAY. It worked—for a while.

And there were moments when he felt in the thick of things.

SHIRLEY HOLIDAY: I remember a club on Post Street called Jack's, when Art Tatum was there. And Charles and I had just finished working at the Why Not? Club. So we went down, and closed the place up; he and Tatum played until 8:00 or 9:00 in the morning. They just played and appreciated each other. You could see and hear their minds click. Walter Bishop was a youngster then, and he just sat there and listened. And Jerome Richardson. And the little white kid: Paul Desmond. Somebody snuck him in. We all went over to Mills College to hear Dave Brubeck. Those were such beautiful days.

Mingus hooked up with Billie Holiday, and she ribbed him about hanging out with the big beboppers in New York. His response, characteristically, was to parry with an idea: he had material he wanted her to record. Still laughing, Billie agreed. Before the plans gelled, she was busted again for drugs.

Shirley was pregnant. He left San Francisco in August 1949 for Los Angeles, and she followed him in September.

Mingus felt trapped. There was little work and no recording in L.A. He and Shirley were living with his stepmother Mamie. Sergeant Mingus had moved in with Miss Garrett and stopped by weekly to drop off Mamie's allowance and the bill money. This he did sitting in his car in the driveway. His legs were swollen, purple, and ulcerated; the diabetes that soon led to the amputation of one leg was advanced.

Once again, Charles found himself at the post office, trying to cover bills. Mamie kept Shirley in bed, and when Yanine was born in October 1949, the baby slept in a dresser drawer. They found a small apartment in L.A., but when Mingus's December check was late, they were evicted, complete with their presents wrapped in paper bags and their tiny tree. Defeated, they took the bus back to Mamie's house.

In May, the Red Norvo trio hit Los Angeles and were playing a club on La Cienega when their bass player, Red Kelly, announced he wanted out. Pianist Jimmy Rowles reminded Norvo that he'd liked the bassist he'd used to back Billie Holiday in San Francisco. Norvo put the word out in San Francisco, and then several people, including Callender, told him Mingus was in Los Angeles working at the post office.

TAL FARLOW, *musician*: He came down and we rehearsed and he went to work right away. I don't remember anything like him crying or anything, like I've read. We were all pretty enthusiastic about him joining. The main thing we wanted to do was to keep working.

Mingus's virtuosity fit the trio's musical concept like a missing link. With vibes and guitar, they needed the bass to do a lot more than keep the beat. It was an equal voice, singing melodic lines in a dense conversation of interwoven parts. For weeks, they rehearsed two days a week at Norvo's Santa Monica house and worked every night. Norvo insisted that the music had to swing and stay accessible. After all, they were playing mostly restaurants and supper clubs. But Mingus could make it swing and sing harder than ever.

He felt like he'd escaped from prison, died and been reborn. He went on trial with the trio in San Diego for two weeks. When they came back, they recorded four tunes in a day. Norvo had a national tour lined up. Mingus wrote Celia excitedly that he was coming east, and Shirley proofread the letter for him; he was embarrassed about his poor spelling.

Shirley moved out of their apartment with Yanine. He found her, and gave her some money. He promised he'd send more. She didn't want it. Several times, when he came through L.A., he stopped by and saw her and her kids.

Jeanne brought the boys over to Mamie's to say goodbye. Sergeant Mingus was even there. He and his son drank ice water and ate chitlins, and threw rocks at pigeons they'd tied to stakes with kitestring. They'd try to fly, hit the ground, and get up dazed to try it again.

He got in the Ford convertible he bought on time, and headed toward the rest of his life.

Charles Mingus's mother, Harriet Phillips Mingus, and father, Charles Mingus Sr., around 1916. Courtesy: *Grace Mingus Washington.*

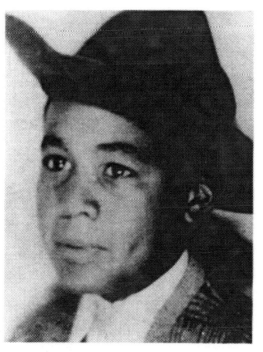

Mingus, about age six. *Courtesy: Grace Mingus Washington.*

Mingus, about age ten,
with his puppy.
Courtesy: Grace Mingus Washington.

Mingus graduating from junior high, age 14.
Courtesy: Grace Mingus Washington.

Mingus, about age eighteen.
Courtesy: Grace Mingus Washington.

Mingus in 1942, with Barney Bigard's band—his first big-time gig.
Bigard is holding clarinet. *Frank Driggs Archives.*

The "Baron," around 1946, with
visual echoes of Orson Welles.
Courtesy: Celia Mingus Zaentz.

The really big time—with Lionel Hampton (standing on drum) in 1948.
Frank Driggs Archives.

On the road with the
Red Norvo Trio, at
Fazio's Town Room in
Milwaukee, 1951.
Frank Driggs Archives.

At the 1953 Quintet concert, Massey Hall, Toronto, with Max Roach and Dizzy Gillespie. *Frank Driggs Archives.*

With Charlie "Bird" Parker at Birdland, around 1953. *Courtesy: Celia Mingus Zaentz.*

With Celia on the roof of the
Hotel Maryland, Fall 1951.
Courtesy: Celia Mingus Zaentz.

At home in late 1952 at 1594 Third Avenue, with the mural he painted in the background.
Courtesy: Celia Mingus Zaentz.

Mingus playing ping-pong at Camp Unity, 1952. *Courtesy Celia Mingus Zaentz.*

Big Kitty, the toilet-trained feline, around 1953. *Courtesy: Celia Mingus Zaentz.*

Charlie Mingus, bandleader and emerging star, 1956. *Frank Driggs Archives*.

The famed "Great Day in Harlem" photo, 1958. Mingus is four rows up on the right, with cigarette dangling. *Photo by Art Kane.*

Mingus in full dapper mode, 1959. *Frank Driggs Archives.*

Rebels reunited: Mingus and Max Roach at the 1962 Newport Jazz Festival.
Frank Driggs Archives.

Onstage at the great Town Hall debacle, 1962. *Photo by Chuck Stewart.*

Another new look for the changing times, 1963. *Frank Driggs Archives.*

Mingus and Miles Davis mug for the camera backstage at the Monterey Jazz Festival, 1964. *Photo by Grover Sales.*

At Central Park with
Keki, Eric, friends, and
cameras, around 1966.
*Courtesy: Judy Starkey
Mingus McGrath.*

Cowboy Charlie in Central Park
with Carolyn "Keki" Mingus,
around 1965. *Courtesy Judy
Starkey Mingus McGrath.*

Ex–New York cop/Mingus bodyguard Charles Wright
teaches karate kids Keki, Eric, and friends, around
1968. *Courtesy: Judy Starkey Mingus McGrath.*

Still on mellaril at the "Let My Children Hear Music" sessions, 1971. *Frank Driggs Archives.*

A rehearsal for *The Mingus Dances*: L. to r., Mingus, Sue, friend, Roberto Ungaro, Alvin Ailey. *Photo by Sy Johnson.*

Mingus meets arranger Gene Ramey at Lower East Side bank where Ramey worked, 1974. *Photo by Sy Johnson.*

Up on the roof, 1974. *Photo by Sy Johnson.*

6 The Big Apple, or On the Road

CHARLES MINGUS JR. was headed east. He was going to meet his true love, the woman who would bear his son. Work with the Red Norvo trio was non-stop. Between nightly gigs and recording in Chicago, they couldn't kick back.

Polished and even slick, the music descended from the Nat King Cole trio's relaxed, best-selling sound. Often fleet, it demanded split-second technical skill. Farlow and Mingus used aspects of bop. But it was a largely formatted harbinger of cool jazz. In part, cool jazz was a commercial reaction to bop. It drew young crowds with stars like the George Shearing trio, idealized by Jack Kerouac in *On the Road*.

Mingus thought Stars of Swing did it better. But nobody could sleepwalk through the fast-changing, episodic arrangements. Sometimes they had so many sections, they were like minifilm scores.

TAL FARLOW: We all pooled our tricks. I started playing harmonies with Red, and picking with my thumb to change the texture—you know, with that instrumentation you're sorta limited with your sound. You don't have a horn. Mingus used to bounce the bow and gave us a sorta string sound.

With no drummer, the bass had to keep the rhythms moving while parrying the others' lines. That give and take enlivened the music. Mingus was an equal. He liked rehearsals, where they jammed out the charts, and he conceived defiantly difficult parts, threading the others' lighter textures. He was making big waves on his tubby instrument.

The material was drawn from familiar old songs, reconceived but not unrecognizable. This wasn't the way bop worked. Charlie Parker's "Ornithology" sounded little like "How High the Moon," the popular song Bird had rearranged to make it. For most little Birds, solos were what jazz was about—the longer, the better. Compositions were vehicles for virtuosos. Composing meant taking a standard and reconstructing it, often radically. Change rhythms, alter chords, drop or add measures.

For bop's initiators, this was a way to make art from American pop the way Bartok made compositions from Hungarian gypsy melodies—an ironic blues inversion. It was payback. You made The Man's hit tunes vehicles for your voice. It was what happened to the slavemasters' hymns.

The trio was there to entertain, not confront. "I Get a Kick Out of You" lost its gliding swoon to become an eighth-note jog through altered chords. "Move" and "Godchild" demonstrated the threesome's grasp of bop. "September Song" and "Prelude to a Kiss," an Ellington favorite, showed off its balladry.

The best of their studio recordings have a crystalline, almost gemlike quality.

Mingus was making a lot of records fast, and the trio pulled in full houses. Red Norvo was a famous veteran, and they were getting rave reviews. But the music's static aspects started gnawing at Mingus. And he had other things to think about. Celia had never left his mind when he was with Shirley Holiday. She'd never leave it for long again.

The trio would play Buffalo for the Thanksgiving weekend. He wrote to ask if she and Jon could fly up from New York. She wrote back that they couldn't afford it. He sent her a single ticket, saying he could afford only one.

CELIA MINGUS ZAENTZ: It sounds very naïve, but Jon and I both believed at that time that I was just going to see a "friend"—the same as I would go to see my brother if he was in Toronto. But when I got there, he told me he'd had this conversation with God, who said if you want Celia, you have to clean up your life and keep improving yourself.

Storms delayed the rendezvous a few days. In Toronto, he proposed marriage. Celia said no. They faced hurdles as a mixed-race couple. She didn't want to be married again. Mingus was adamant. He loved her. She would bear his son. He wanted her to bear his name. He was his father's son, almost in spite of himself.

He wrote her from the road. There were satiric jabs at American hypocrisy and Nazis, gay sex in the YMCA across from his hotel, and ancient architecture. He wanted Grace to adopt Yanine, but Mamie was a problem. He just sent Jeanne a $140 check so he could claim his sons as income tax deductions.

He sketched a one-act play starring Fingers, New South, and Pinky to show he was faithful despite temptation on the road. He insisted that Celia meet him in Los Angeles, and brushed aside her worry about "cheapening" their love. They could get a place to stay together if "we . . . use your color," he said, and apologized: if they were discovered, they'd just be evicted. After he offered to pay for her divorce, he asked her to work out the budget for their cross-country travel.

He was dreading going home and sorting out his earlier life. He wanted to get on with his new one.

The trio headed to Los Angeles for Christmas, where Norvo's manager, a heavyweight industry figure named Joe Glaser, booked a long residency at the Haig, a small but popular restaurant-club on Wilshire Boulevard. For Mingus, coming home this time was utterly different. A year before, he was stuck working in the post office and was evicted with a baby on Christmas Eve. Now he had money, his first car, and a name. The spiral of success, it seemed, was drawing him in. And he had Celia.

So he could afford to be expansive, as he puffed on his new imported cherry briar pipe. He listened to Buddy Collette talk about the Amalgamation. Trained black musicians were playing classical literature every week, as an orchestra. Buddy and Britt Woodman and Red Callender and Milt Holland had started working on that in the late 1940s. Mingus didn't want to be involved, though he loudly supported the idea, because he only wanted to play his music.

But now they'd done it. Open rehearsals for Collette's sixty-five-piece Community Symphony Orchestra every Monday evening packed the crowds in.[1] It had white and black musicians playing classical scores together, and the expanded interracial contact was slowly broadening support for the blacks' desire to unite the segregated union locals. As Buddy saw it, the white musicians discovered that these black musicians could play any kind of music well. They could read music—a skill Hollywood studio contractors had doubted they had. Playing together would sharpen everyone's skills, even the pay scales, and open more jobs for blacks.

A few weeks after they'd started a Sunday afternoon jam session at Humanist Hall, Josephine Baker came. Five hundred people packed the hall, built for two hundred. She got onstage and asked, "I wonder why you have two unions. Well, I think it should be one, and I don't know why you people are wasting time." She called two little girls, one white, one black, up from the audience, and said, "These kids will show you how to do it." Then she walked off.

Other big stars, like Nat King Cole, publicly endorsed Collette's interracial push. But the NAACP refused to endorse the move.

Collette had run for president of the black Local 767 and had lost to Leo Davis by twenty out of 500 votes. Benny Carter ran in 1950, but lost by the same number. This time, however, Collette was elected to the union board, along with two of his compatriots.

They were on a long road. The unions weren't formally joined until March 1953.

Collette had not only been a leader in the move to integrate the L.A. musicians' unions. Thanks to Jerry Fielding, he had broken the TV-band barrier. Fielding was a political leftist, a believer in integration, and the musical director for the Groucho Marx hit TV show, *You Bet Your Life.* He heard Collette play a Bizet flute solo at a symphony rehearsal, learned he could play alto sax and clarinet, and hired him instantly.

Buddy was the Jackie Robinson of the TV networks.

Soon, Fielding hired Red Callender for *The Life of Riley.* He put together a TV jazz band with Collette, Callender, and pianist Gerald Wiggins, and got stacks of hate mail for it.

Collette came by to see the Norvo trio one night at The Haig. He brought a mixed party, including Fielding, a white woman, a white musician, and a black woman. When they sat down and tried to order, the waiter refused to serve them. Fielding demanded to know why. The reply: "It's mixed company."

Instantly Collette thought, "They probably don't know that Mingus, with his light complexion and wavy hair, is black." He didn't want to blow it for his pal, but he was angry about it. When Norvo came over during the break, Collette and Fielding were talking about taking the restaurant to court.

They backed off when it was clear to Buddy that Mingus went along with Norvo's pleas that they sue any other place. He figured Mingus needed the money. But he was surprised at his old friend's willingness to slide under the color bar instead of confronting it.

The Central Avenue scene was shutting down. The powers-that-be, as the musicians saw it, didn't like the interracial mixing so free and easy along the strip, the celebrities and movie stars, the white women looking for another side, a thrill. The cops routinely rousted mixed couples and whites to ask, "What are you doing on this side of town?" They'd go into the clubs and hassle people on the spot. Eventually, even real fans got tired of it and stopped coming.

This is the dark side of Los Angeles that Raymond Chandler pictured in books like *The Long Goodbye*, a world where money and power lure cops and district attorneys into cynical bargains, where blacks are ciphers whose murders aren't worth solving, and a private investigator named Philip Marlowe acts like an antihero knight with his own moral code. The law is corrupt. Only an outsider can see right and wrong, however imperfectly mingled in flawed human nature and the situations it weaves. This cloth fit Humphrey Bogart and his heirs in noir movie after noir movie.

The city fathers' official rationale for shutting Central Avenue was drugs, especially heroin. The postwar wave of addiction reached L.A., and it rode partly, maybe most conspicuously, on the musicians in constant transit. The musicians figured somebody with clout was shaking hands with the mob, which owned and operated the drug pipeline.

After all, the same thing was happening on 52nd Street, New York's postwar music capital where blacks and whites mingled freely. And was it coincidence that the postwar wave of heroin seemed to be washing over black urban neighborhoods almost exclusively?

Mamie angered her stepson. She harped at him about marrying a white woman. She wanted money. She was a hypocrite who drove his father off. When Mingus saw the old man, he was very ill with diabetes. But he liked his boy's road stories.

The trio kept moving. Mingus wrote the sound track for a film they did with Red Skelton, *Texas Carnival*, but he didn't perform in it with the others, who were dressed as Indians. Farlow thought this odd, since Mingus was always saying he was part Indian. In a short film, they performed a nightclub scene. And the touring came in bursts. In Boston that March, Celia and Mingus finalized their plans, and he dropped her off in Reno.

From L.A. a few days later, he wrote her at the Palomino Guest Ranch.[2] He addressed it, "Mrs. Charles Mingus Jr. c/o Mrs. Celia Nielsen." He suggested she go see *The Idiot*, a movie adapted from Dostoyevsky's novel about a Christ-like epileptic, by French director Georges Lampin. Despite Catholic Church censorship, he said, the film captured "certain too sacred vibrations that 90% of people liveing [sic] today deny and destroy." The director could touch ordinary people; he'd seen it happen.

She was filling out his income tax forms. On the back of the envelope, he scribbled a note not to claim Eugene as a deduction.

He wanted her to fly to Los Angeles. His waistline was expanding, but he wanted to show her off.

CELIA MINGUS ZAENTZ: Mingus was very proud, and he seemed very much at ease. It was the only time in my life we danced together. I was surprised: he can dance. But he also was talking to some of his friends about wanting to do something about segregation, trying to get a plan together to go to this place to eat. And I was very excited about going there with them. It was one of the first times I heard anybody wanting to do something like that.

It was happening all around them. Black Americans had prospered during World War II. President Franklin D. Roosevelt included blacks in the government. In 1939, singer Marian Anderson was refused the use of Constitution Hall for a concert, which drew national headlines; Eleanor Roosevelt helped set up a concert for her at the Lincoln Memorial that drew 75,000 integrated fans. It was a first.

In 1941, A. Phillip Randolph, head of the International Brotherhood, threatened a march on Washington if discrimination wasn't mitigated, and FDR established the Fair Employment Practices Commmission (FEPC). The FEPC didn't prevent racial discrimination in the war industries completely, but its creation taught black activists that threats of public action could have political results.

During the war, two-and-a-half million blacks moved out of the South to work in defense plants, until the soldiers came home and reclaimed their jobs. Pressures were building across the country. Something had to give.

The NAACP Legal Defense Fund, led by Thurgood Marshall, began to use lawsuits to overturn laws that all-white legislatures would never repeal. In 1944, all-white primaries were declared illegal. By the late 1940s, courts struck down discrimination in housing, education, and recreation. In 1948, President Harry Truman integrated the armed forces by executive order, after Congress rejected his civil rights proposals. The Korean War, which claimed 50,000-plus dead by its end in 1952, was the first war fought by integrated troops.

In 1943, the Congress of Racial Equality was formed and organized a sit-in at a Chicago restaurant to protest segregation.

Mingus was feeling the Zeitgeist again.

On April 2, 1951, Charles Mingus Jr. and Lucille Gemanis Nielsen were married in a friend's apartment in downtown San Francisco. Farwell orchestrated the party across the bay at the Palate. The groom and ushers wore white tie and tails and boutonnieres. The Trio had an extended gig at the Black Hawk, so for a honeymoon the newlyweds drove around the redwood forests of Marin and strolled the rocky beaches.

Celia knitted him socks in the car during all the hours they spent driving to and from rehearsals and gigs. She adored Charlie Parker and pushed Mingus to listen to Bird. He did. He now recognized Parker's thrilling virtuosity. He was starting to separate Bird from his imitators, and he was connecting bebop's language with Tatum and Stravinsky and even, via Debussy and Ravel, to Duke Ellington.

The attention bass players Oscar Pettiford and Ray Brown were getting in New York made him chafe at the trio's format. And Red would never play his stuff.

They went through the South—his first time, and with a white wife. A few times, Celia registered as Tal Farlow's wife. Her husband seemed amused about putting it over. Things were different in New York. There were a lot of white women, some of them rich, on the scene. Hell, Max Roach lived with a white hooker. New York was the Big Apple.

But he was starting to ride Tal about his southern drawl. He jumped on things Tal or Red said, hypersensitive to racial slurs. Tension was brewing. The white musicians were baffled. He could swing from friendly to sly to surly in a flash.

CELIA MINGUS ZAENTZ: When we were first married, he still had a fear of me. I used to say to him, if we had an argument, "You're still not sure that at the height of anger I'm not going to call you a black nigger or something." He'd never deny it. I used to say to him, "I wish we were both black or both white. Both our lives would be easier." And he would say, "Then the value of us being a mixed couple would be gone." And he was right, too. But I would say, "That's great, but I'd just as soon make it easier on us."

In New York, the Norvo trio settled into a long run at the Embers. In September 1951, singer Mel Tormé contacted Norvo. Near the time of the wedding, the trio did separate sessions with vocalist Ann Miller and Tormé. The Tormé material stayed in the can, but both Tormé and Norvo liked the musical fit.

And Tormé, the popular singer-drummer who wrote "The Christmas Song," had a hot deal. Television was entering American lives. People stayed home to watch the costly little blue screen, abandoning movies and concert halls and dance palaces. Hollywood panicked. It developed Technicolor and Cinemascope, which couldn't be reproduced in millions of living rooms. Early TV variety shows, like Milton Berle's or Sid Caesar's, were vaudeville—and they had live bands.

Tormé's show was testing the CBS color process, one of several designed to compete with Hollywood's counterattack. In the studio, a color wheel with six segments of gel colors rotated in front of a black and white camera. Each home needed another color wheel, twice the screen's diameter. It was costly and cumbersome. The Korean War ended the tests; the technicians were drafted.

The trio would be incorporated into a larger band; Tormé would play drums and sing. They'd back guests like singer Harry Belafonte, and they'd get their own spots.

For Mingus, it ended before it began. Even in Paradise, he was discovering, race mattered.

For Local 802, the New York musicians' union, TV was increasingly important. Radio was replacing live music with records. Television's live shows needed musicians. The shows were lucrative, but only members of the local were eligible for them. Its most powerful members and income-producing jobs were white. Musicians who once toured with swing bands and worked in theaters wanted TV's steady gigs.

The union dealt with jazz gigs, too, but not helpfully, as far as the musicians were concerned. When they monitored shows, they objected and threatened to shut things down if anyone joined to jam. They argued it was a contractual violation. Boppers saw it as infringement of artistic freedom.

Then there were the police, who licensed the musicians with a cabaret card. The card system was supposed to prevent mob involvement in booze by monitoring who worked in liquor-licensed spots. Instead, it became a Damoclean sword hanging over performers from Billie Holiday to Lenny Bruce. The cops could yank the card for anything; then you couldn't work. To get one took a year's residency.

Mingus was from Los Angeles, so he didn't belong to 802 or have a cabaret card. The union told Norvo to dump him or lose the Tormé job. Norvo argued they were a touring unit. That worked for clubs, but not for TV. He tried to use his clout to end-run the union, but the pressure stayed on. And so Mingus was out, and white bassist Clyde Lombardi was in.

The tensions within the band flared. Mingus had talked to Norvo like a father, about everything from his women to his writing. And he delivered, even if he was tired of the music. Norvo insisted he stay, just skip the TV show. In a rage, he quit. Norvo asked Fess Williams to convince him to come back. He wouldn't. He was going out on his own.

He went back to the Embers a couple of times, ostentatiously, to hang around. Lombardi was on the stand. Mingus didn't sit in.

Back in San Francisco, he'd been interviewed by *Down Beat* magazine's Ralph

Gleason, and didn't like the results. The letter he sent Gleason was so articulate the critic published it instead of his interview.[3]

It was the first of many Mingus missives. *Down Beat* was a forum. Most black jazzers thought it racist; its cover was reserved for white musicians. He used the letters pages to discuss himself, other musicians, race, atomic holocaust.

He was reading avidly, and Philip Wylie's *A Generation of Vipers* was a favorite. A widely popular writer, Wylie unloosed a vitriolic satiric diatribe, written in 1942, against American society that shared ideas and attitudes with postwar subcultures. He admired Taoism. He cited Freud and Jung, and railed about understanding human instincts. He hated hypocrisy, and saw it everywhere in America. Look at sex. Society said no sex outside marriage, yet half of all men and a third of women were not monogamous.

Mingus liked Wiley's slashing arguments and fed-up tone. He hated his own lack of formal education, but he could always read the first few pages of many books, then skip around, and get the gist. It was a gift.

He wanted to confront issues. He had to say what he thought. For a black man in America, jazz was his platform to address the world. And *Down Beat* was a place to start.

A week later, he was on the bandstand at Birdland, the boppers' mecca in the Big Apple, with Miles Davis. His old pal wanted to give him a boost. So with his bass strapped to his back like it was when he walked to Jordan High, he bent over the club's piano to learn the tunes. He didn't need a cabaret card for the off-night gig. Besides, Birdland's owners could fix things.

Opened in late 1949, Birdland was operated by Morris Levy—Moishe or Mo to everyone in the music business. Decades later, Levy died in prison for his part in 1980s mob scams. But he had a long history.

He looked and talked like a Hollywood thug, ran Birdland, and booked stars like Count Basie. He created the package tour to help big band bookings, an idea he'd later adapt to early rock and roll. He started labels like Roulette. In mob terms, he was a front, straight out of *GoodFellas*.

Most jazz clubs in New York dealt with the Mafia. They had to. Prohibition had made the mob booze overlords, and they'd never fully let go, police monitoring or no. Anyway, jazz had always been surrounded by gangsters and pimps and whores, and even its stars walked the edges of respectability. Who but other outcasts would deal with blacks? For a lucrative cash flow, the mob supplied them with drugs and booze and records, and numbers to play, and places to score and hear music.

Birth of the Cool, a more melodic, orchestrated reaction to bebop born partly of what he'd heard in Los Angeles, made Miles Davis a star in 1949. Now he was a junkie. His playing was erratic, his temper more unstable. And he talked even less.

Levy liked Mingus. They'd do business again.

But without his cabaret card, work was scarce. In October, he played some bass on "Conception" from Davis's album *Dig*, but he didn't get credited.[4]

Postwar New York was as ethnically subdivided as ever, but it wasn't yet polarized between rich and poor. Its suburbs were only starting to sap its middle classes, its financial and social cohesion. It was the home of Wall Street and Madison Avenue, the East Coast center of national communications media, headquarters for countless corporations. It embodied upward mobility, and it was open twenty-four hours a day.

But the city's substrata crackled with other energies. In the Jazz Age, the Harlem Renaissance made Harlem and black pride synonymous. White socialites and fans went uptown to see black jazz greats in clubs that were usually segregated and run by the mob.

The new Jazz Age was different. Charlie Parker moved downtown, to Times Square and the Lower East Side. He sought out his peers among white artists and hung out. He met composer Edgard Varese on the street. He was no faceless cog in the economy. He was no slave in his quarters. He conformed to nothing except the iron rule of heroin, and demanded freedom in his music.

It was a paradox worthy of a Zen master, an existential hero.

Bird's new companions were artists. But they worked as merchant seamen and day laborers. They dressed like hobos and lumberjacks and sailors. They drank and did drugs and talked about art and sex endlessly. They were hetero- and homo- and bisexual. They hung out with people they considered visionaries—criminals and drug addicts, the mentally ill and jazz musicians. Some of them called themselves Beat—short for beatitude, the blessed downtrodden in society.

They felt that those excluded from America could see into its secret heart.

Mingus broke in as a bop sideman. That winter, he worked with pianist Billy Taylor, who also admired Ellington. Most younger players thought Duke was out of it or a Tom. Besides, Taylor knew Cuban music, thanks to Dizzy Gillespie, a Latin-jazz pioneer. Taylor taught Mingus montuno—the open-ended, simply structured form for improvisation in Cuban music. Mingus energized the pulses in Taylor's trio with his bold bass.

In New York, he saw, style and allegiance counted. Cliques were defining. It looked like the Jordan High schoolyard.

Mingus filed a $500 grievance with Local 802: he'd had to leave Red Norvo without notice. The union gave it to him, and he used it to start Debut Records.

Dizzy Gillespie had started Dee Gee, and other musicians were considering the move. Why get ripped off in the white man's industry? Why let businessmen and mobsters tell you what to do with your art?

Bob Weinstock, head of Prestige Records, offered to record a Mingus trio for $10 apiece, and free lunch and drinks and cocaine. Mingus was infuriated and disgusted. The scene was being destroyed by Bird-imitating junkies. They'd put up with anything.

A year earlier, Mingus had recorded piano duos with his old Watts friend Spaulding Givens, and those sides ultimately became Debut's first release.

MAX ROACH, *musician and friend*: Nobody was beating down our doors to ask what we were doing. The only way to make records under our own names was to start our own company.

The big labels were pushing crooners and novelty acts and making money converting consumers from old 78s to LPs. And jazz wasn't classical music, which everyone agreed was art, and prestigious. Besides, the major labels shied away from bebop and bop-influenced sounds. They were leery of its arty assertiveness, its cult audiences.

Mingus was out on the margins, but it was his own show.

Debut would combine art music and pop music. It would give offbeat ideas and newcomers a shot. He used his apartment or out-of-the-way studios for cheap rehearsals. Like distributors, most recording studios then were owned by the major labels, so they found alternatives. And when he was on the road, he scanned for better contacts.

Debut was his ticket out of being another beat bebop junkie sideman.

For a year, Mingus and Celia were stuck at the Maryland Hotel on West 49th Street. They couldn't find a building that allowed interracial couples. Cabs wouldn't stop for him.

He worked around town in fits, and traveled in bursts. He stayed at YMCAs, but Y's and hotels both charged black musicians more—if they'd give them rooms at all. He ate frugally. He detailed expenses, less than $12 a day, and he apologized to Celia for costing so much.

Boston was a regular stop. He first went there with Billy Taylor, to a club called Storyville. In October 1952, a young disk jockey named Nat Hentoff invited him and white saxist Zoot Sims on radio station WMEX to talk. "I crossed my leggs [sic], lighted my cigar and spoke slowlye [sic]," he wrote. It

was his most Wellesian manner. Sims was nervous. He tried to calm the tenor
player during a break. When the light came on, Sims bashed pianist Lennie
Tristano and Stan Kenton. Bird, he said, was God.

Mingus was appalled. Tristano, white and blind, was building on bebop's
harmonic ideas. And he was a colleague. Hentoff asked Sims about contrapuntal harmony in jazz, one of the key ploys Tristano and Mingus shared.
Sims said, "Bird . . . " Mingus interrupted, repeating the question. He asked
about fugue and jazz. He made Sims admit he imitated the solos of Lester
Young, the Basie veteran who influenced Parker, but with a thicker tone borrowed from Coleman Hawkins, jazz's first great sax soloist. Young and
Hawkins were black.

Taylor's quartet had a weeklong date at Storyville. The club's owner, George
Wein, told Mingus he'd paid the Norvo trio $900 a week. Norvo always said
the trio was a cooperative, but Mingus had not been paid $300. Instantly he
crescendoed into a soliloquy about coop bands and white man's world and
slave labor, and hurled an ashtray at a wall.

It reopened the wound. He told Celia to call Norvo and read, word for word,
his threat to "fuck Red up."

Mingus wanted classical audiences to get hip to jazz. He was sure that would
bring more work and more discriminating audiences. He was sick of jazz clubland, its cliques and intrigues, its gangsters and drugs and ripoffs. In Boston
that October, he decided he'd quit. He wanted to study and write. That would
make him a better musician than playing derivative music with junkies. He
didn't want to become cynical like them.

CELIA MINGUS ZAENTZ: He wanted to take music in a different direction. He
was not going to be a slave to bebop. He could play it; he did it all the time. He
used to play Erroll Garner on the piano. He could do all that. He sat down one
time and figured out what Monk was doing, using all these old tunes. That was
the way Mingus's mind worked. He didn't want to copy. He wanted to figure out
what other people were doing, what he was doing, and be sure he didn't do what
somebody else was doing. He didn't want to listen to other people's music at all.
Ever. He didn't want to retain anything they did, even by accident, in his brain.

He was almost thirty, and the clock was running.

In early 1952, Mingus worked with a young saxist named Lee Konitz, a Tristano disciple who had Jack Kerouac for a fan. Konitz had a gig in Detroit, and
Debut had a distributor there that owed money.

After the first set, he rode drummer Al Leavitt about his stiff sense of time. Words passed. He slapped Leavitt's face. Konitz asked him to lay off, and for the rest of their two weeks, he did.

But he always had to establish himself.

On April 12, 1952, at Lennie Tristano Studios on East 32nd Street, Mingus recorded Konitz for Debut. The saxist had an unusual contract: he could improvise for only the label he was signed to. And so Mingus wrote a solo for him, on a tune called "Extrasensory Perception." The score pages were as cluttered as Beethoven's with attempts to capture every nuance, which made the music hard to decipher it and play with feeling.

He was trying to out-Ellington Ellington. Duke knew his soloists so well he could write parts just for them. So could Mingus. He was asserting his authority as a composer.

Konitz's reaction illustrated the recurrent problem many jazz players had with Mingus's notions about "writing it down correctly."

LEE KONITZ, *musician*: He had a lot of sixteenth notes written one sixteenth note before the downbeat. He was trying to get me to sound like I was playing a little bit back on the beat, which I was going to do anyway. He didn't have to intellectualize it. It was impossible for me to really feel what he had written, but I tried, and he seemed pleased enough.

Along with "Portrait," which he'd written in 1946, and "I Lost My Love," they recorded "Precognition."

CHARLES MINGUS: With the emphasis on psychiatry, the hidden recesses of the mind and their connection with the body and the scientific research being done to test the possibility of mind over matter as in the experiments done by Dr. Rhine at Duke University, I feel that this new field of development also has a place for expression in music.[5]

Nobody thought quite like he did.

Debut was formally incorporated in the Bronx on May 7, 1952. Celia's mom kicked in $600 she'd received after her own mother's death, so they had $1,100 in capital.

Celia did the books and typed out mailing labels and developed a list of distributors in the States and abroad. She wrote liner notes, designed record labels, got covers designed, and begged famed photographers like Herman

Leonard to sell them photos for album covers at ridiculously low rates. She ordered pressings from Kaltman Press, which shipped larger batches of discs directly to Debut's ramshackle regional distributor setup. Mingus was the resident artistic director, and packed discs and stuck the labels on boxes.

In 1952, they put out three recordings. The idea of musicians owning their own label to control and profit from their art and finances would grow, but slowly at first. There wasn't a lot of finance involved. It was mostly art.

Hentoff scrawled him a note to say he preferred "Portrait" to "Precognition," which he found "stiff." But he added, "What are your ideas on the twelve-tone scale in jazz?"[6]

Mingus worked in a quintet with Gillespie, Parker, Roach, and Taylor, and worked with Stan Getz. He and Max Roach played at Brandeis with Tristano and Konitz. He recorded more Jackie Paris. With Billy Taylor, he backed Oscar Pettiford on cello. He recorded with Tristano-ish pianist John Mehegan. He was trying things.

That summer, the Minguses moved to 1594 3rd Avenue. For $70 a month, they lived a year in the hotel-sized room with a kitchenette in one corner. It was next to the El, whose noise woke them up each day at 6:00 A.M.

He painted one wall with an abstract mural he'd laid out with masking tape. And he toilet-trained his cat.

Mingus found Big Kitty under a car outside a club. When the neighbors complained about the litter box on the fire escape, he remembered a Phoenix couple he'd stayed with on a Norvo trip. They had toilet-trained Siamese cats.

He knew exactly how to do it. He rigged a cardboard box on the toilet with ropes to lift it off, and cut a small hole in the bottom, spread a lot of paper, then cut the sides of the box down to that level. He gradually made the box disappear.

It was as ingenious as his shoeshine box.

Cheap window air-conditioners didn't exist, so in summer millions headed to movie theaters, which were chilled to meat-locker temperatures. It was one way the industry was counterattacking TV.

Charles and Celia went to the movies a lot. Art films like Jean Cocteau's *Blood of a Poet* and *Orphée* were among his favorites, because of the way they dealt with the trials of the Romantic artist.

In the middle of a heat wave, they went to Orchard Beach one night. He brought baloney and cheese and good bread and fruit and spread out a blanket. When the temperature suddenly plunged, they nearly froze.

Max Roach told them about Camp Unity, a spot upstate started by communists in the 1930s to help end segregation. The camp not only accepted racially mixed couples but was full of them. Mingus and Celia spent a few pleasant days walking and playing cards and Ping-Pong.

In September, Debut spent $400 recording vocalist Jackie Paris, an Italian-American singer in the Neapolitan crooner style. They broke even selling the record, then made some money. So they made another, and made a little money. And another. And another. By April 1953, Debut had released eight more discs.

Celia continued her studies in piano and composition with Lennie Tristano, and acting as a kind of spy, she reported Lennie's methods and her assignment to her husband: memorize Lester Young's solo on "She's Funny That Way." She also wrote out Joe Albany's piano intro to the tune, which was much admired by white boppers.

Tristano is usually described as downplaying jazz's rhythmic elements, but one of bop's most kinetic rhythm sections, Mingus and Max Roach, liked working with Lennie. They were intrigued by his contrapuntal harmonies, and respected his free improvisations. But there were limits.

One night, Mingus was driving to work at Birdland with Tristano and another black musician. Tristano asked why they didn't like the word *nigger*; blacks used it among themselves. "The way he asked," Mingus later told Hentoff, "showed he was just bugging us. . . . I knew how destructive Lennie could be."[7]

CELIA MINGUS ZAENTZ: Mingus took me everywhere because I think he felt some kind of completion in it. I think it solved the color thing for him. It was a way of trying to encompass all the hurt he felt, not a flaunting kind of thing, as white men take it, but a healing. And black musicians with white girls would often be putting down white as something or other. I never stood for that, even though the girls were doing it too. "I have no problem with the white race," I'd say; "my only problem with it is the same as yours, prejudice."

Dinah Washington and Ella Fitzgerald both gave Celia "the look" when she was introduced as his wife. When she traveled with him, they had to stay in black sections. One night in Philadelphia, their black waitress was rude to Celia. He told her, "There's no reason for you to treat my wife that way just because she's white."

Celia threw him a birthday party, and Miles Davis and Max Roach and a roomful of musicians came to eat birthday cake and talk music. Stravinsky and Bartok were on the record player.

By winter 1952, unemployment cascaded through live entertainment, and jazz clubs disappeared. For the last time, Charles Mingus Jr. found himself at the post office. His Local 802 card cost him $24 a year for nothing.

He got up every morning at six. When he came home, he and Celia had dinner, listened to the radio, played rummy. Celia had a system, and kept winning. They were in bed by ten, never went anywhere. He threw himself into the routine, just like he did with everything.

After all, he had Debut. He wasn't going to let himself off the hook by blaming The System. He was going to beat it, find his own way in.

Miles Davis showed up one night. He was in the depths of addiction, living off his girlfriends' largesse, playing erratically, getting stopped on the street and pulled offstage by cops looking for needle tracks. He pawned everything he owned. So for Mingus that night he did a Bird impersonation: he wanted a loan. Mingus offered him a $10 check. Miles put him down, demanded cash, took the check.[8] He was everything Mingus didn't want to become.

That December, Bird called. He and Mingus had played together and become friends. In the wee hours, he sometimes phoned Mingus to solo over sections of Stravinsky's *Firebird Suite*. This time he wanted Mingus in his band.

Parker's musical genius was now apparent to him. He told Celia he wanted to write a suite for Bird, but he still couldn't really respect a heroin addict.

Mingus hadn't counted on Parker's oversized personality, his gift of charming gab. Bird offered to pay Mingus $400 a week, a $125 boost over the post office. When he hesitated, Parker rolled his eyes back to show their whites, and insisted he'd lent Mingus $2,000 in California. "He said it with such conviction, I believed it, at least for a minute," Mingus later said.[9]

Bird was a teacher. Most of his self-proclaimed pupils were missing the point.

Mingus had other motives for joining Bird. The band's first stop was Philadelphia, where Debut's distributor owed money. When he showed up there, and was told there was no cash, he grabbed the adding machine, and asked how much it was worth: $400. "I'll settle for that," he said. He got his money.

Already Debut's files bulged with letters about unpaid bills to places like Al Smith's Record Bar and Dale Record Service and Florida Record and Appliance Company and Bilens Department Store.[10] Like every independent label, Debut was at the mercy of a patchwork of local and regional distributors, who took their records and paid late, if ever, for sales. There was practically no way for small labels to collect debts.

Two weeks after Mingus quit the post office, he was looking for a gig.

Birdland was off limits. He was walking past with Celia one night when a white guy was fighting Max Roach. Mingus hit the guy while two Birdland bouncers held Max. He told Britt Woodman, "I heard him say nigger." Woodman was startled; this was a Mafia club.

Mingus told Eddie Bert the white guy was a cop, when the trombonist asked him to sub one Monday night with Duke Jordan's group. He found Mingus at the Russian Tea Room. Mingus called Mo Levy in Florida and got permission.

That January, he worked with Duke Ellington. Ellington's regular bassist had taken a leave of absence,[11] so Mingus joined on at the Band Box, next to Birdland. He admired Duke's music, but he also wanted to outdo him.

He played bebop on the job, to show off. Ellington wanted him to play more like Jimmy Blanton. He brought in "Mingus Fingers," and Ellington had the band play it, but Woodman and the others saw Duke didn't like the brash new bassist.

They went to Boston, then came back to Harlem's Apollo Theater, where Mingus left the band on February 3. Duke was famed for his ability to tolerate erratic behavior, and as famed for his ability to get men to resign.

BRITT WOODMAN: They called us to go on. I was on my way when Charles came out of Juan's dressing room. "Hey Britt, man, Juan Tizol's plastered. He says blacks can't read music." Juan said, "Well, Britt, I wrote a number for him, eight bars, and I want him to play it the way it's written, but he always wants to play things high." "But you said that niggers can't read." I'm quite sure, knowing Juan, that he said that; it's the one thing Charles is going to be mad about. I said, "Man, forget about it."

Mingus couldn't. As they walked toward the bandstand, the stage curtains blocked them from the audience, and he kept arguing with Tizol all the way to the stage wings. Tizol reached into his coat pocket; everybody knew he carried a knife. Mingus pushed him with his left hand, and Tizol stumbled to the other side. There he stayed for the opening tunes of the set.

Afterward, Tizol went to Ellington and threatened to quit. Instead, Mingus resigned.

He played a few gigs with Bud Powell's trio. The pianist had just come out of Bellevue—the result of drugs, booze, and a white policeman's nightstick shots to his head in 1945. Electroshock didn't help.

Inevitably, social deviants like jazz musicians and artists—Jack Kerouac and Allen Ginsberg and William Burroughs, Bud Powell and Bird, Jackson Pollock and Mark Rothko—were among the hundreds of thousands caught in The System's psychological webs, so vividly depicted in contemporary movies like 1948's *The Snake Pit*, starring Olivia de Havilland. Some patients were basically held in custody on tranquilizers. Others drew heavier treatments.

In ironic hipster lingo, "crazy" came to mean the coolest, and became a staple of Beat prose and poetry. But it carried ironic shades of meaning, the kind of double vision you got from hearing "How High the Moon" and "Ornithology" in sequence.

You could use double consciousness to work for you.

Even at his wobbliest, Bud Powell had a cult nearly the equal of Bird's or Monk's. The New Jazz Society of Toronto wanted him to star in a gala concert, but couldn't find him. No wonder; he was in Bellevue. They couldn't find Dizzy Gillespie, so they called Mingus. He had Celia call Bird, Diz, Powell's manager Oscar Goodstein, and Max Roach.

On May 15, 1953, Bird and Diz were left behind at LaGuardia to catch a later flight; the Society only bought five tickets, and Goodstein, who was Powell's legal guardian, and Celia made seven. When the hornmen got to Toronto, Massey Hall wasn't full. The Society didn't make enough money to pay them and offered them tapes it made of the show.

When Charlie Parker tried to sell the Massey Hall tapes to Norman Granz, whose label had him under contract, for $100,000, Granz politely declined.

The musicians decided to release parts of the concert on Debut, as two ten-inch discs. The five band members—Bird, Dizzy, Powell, Roach, and Mingus —signed a contract on May 21, 1953. Debut got 10 percent; they split the rest equally. [12]

But a year after Debut's official incorporation, the company needed more cash, especially to handle the music and its marketing right. An all-star album like this could put them on the map, uniting the giants of an ending era.

Mingus and Celia had talked to musicians about buying shares in the company. For a few hundred dollars they'd be able to release their own and other projects. After Massey Hall, Max Roach and his girlfriend, a hooker named Margo Ferris, put up the cash, and Celia and Max signed the deal on June 1, 1953. A few days later, lawyer Harold Lovette got 2 1/2 percent of Debut's net profits in exchange for providing legal services, like dealing with mechanical licenses, publisher clearances, and royalties.

Debut was ready to deal with the quintet tapes. It wasn't just an idea, a statement. It was becoming a real record label.

Bird would be billed as Charlie Chan to avoid contractual hassles.

On June 26, 1953, Celia sent a letter to Local 149 of the American Federation of Musicians. Debut was notifying the local that Debut was using the tape to make records. The letter explained that the band had made the tapes "for our own personal use, but then musicians began urging us to release it on our label." It asked about procedures for sending a contract and a check for clearance. On July 21, Local 802 head James Petrillo sent a fierce memo to Lovette: "Warning: Under no circumstances use the tapes without my and the musicians' authorizations."

Quintet of the Year put Debut on the map, made it some cash, and guaranteed Mingus a place in bop history. It was solid and momentous work, and a historical document, the only time this unit recorded.

The concert had been taped from the public address system, which meant Mingus's bass's low frequencies were inaudible in spots. He couldn't stand the thought that the record would always sound that way, so he decided to overdub at jazz engineer Rudy Van Gelder's New Jersey studio.

Overdubbing means recording a part to take the place of or fit with a pretaped part. It had been used in primitive form as early as the days of Enrico Caruso, but it only became an artistic tool with guitarist Les Paul. On early 1950s hits like "How High the Moon," Paul stacked multiple tracks of guitar and wife Mary Ford's vocals, creating a radical new sound.

Recording was a timeless document. Live performance was an in-the-moment show. They had different functions. So with Billy Taylor doing bits of piano and Roach filling in drums for camouflage, Mingus overdubbed bass for "Perdido," "Salt Peanuts," "All the Things You Are," "52nd Street Theme," "Wee (Allen's Alley)," "Hot House," "A Night in Tunisia," and "Bass-ically Speaking."[13]

The process reminded him of Hollywood, where everything was done on soundstages and overdubbed afterward. He was using the studio as another instrument, a tool in composition. Over the next year, as Debut released additional pieces of the Massey Hall concert on 10-inch LPs, he edited them for home-listening impact. At one point, he was even "fixing crowd effect" for two-and-a-half hours. Cost: $20.[14]

At Birdland a few days after Toronto, Mingus rejoined Powell and Gillespie and a virtuosic Cuban percussionist named Candido. Then he recorded with saxist Sonny Stitt. But by summer 1953, the scene was collapsing.

Max Roach, Hank Mobley, John Lewis, Oscar Pettiford, Miles Davis, Thelonious Monk—a pantheon of postwar jazz—had no work. Spurred by Mingus and Roach, they looked to themselves.

Roach grew up in Brooklyn's Bedford-Stuyvesant district, a black neighborhood. He had a studio there, in a large building; upstairs, Debut had a room to store records. The ground floor had space they could use to perform in, so Max told Celia to call the place and set up a gig. The band was Roach, Mingus, Miles Davis, Monk, Oscar Pettiford, Hank Mobley, and Gigi Gryce; they made about $35 apiece. There was no time to get the word out, so few fans showed up.

Onstage, Mingus wanted to play "Memories of You." He liked soloing on it, but Monk said Davis didn't know the chords. Miles insisted he'd call out the changes on the bandstand, then deliberately mixed them up. Pettiford scolded him when the trumpeter came offstage. When they went back on, the pianist got his payback.

After Miles started playing, Monk came around the piano, behind Davis, reached into his shirt pocket and pulled out his cigarettes, then into his coat pocket for matches. He lit a cigarette, then returned everything to Miles's pockets.

CELIA MINGUS ZAENTZ: It was like a vaudeville act. And Miles—Miles wasn't going to give them the satisfaction of missing a note. God, that was funny. I had no idea at that time that they were so playful, because they would really get angry about stuff like that too.

Monk was asked to appear on the Steve Allen show with Mingus, Eddie Bert, Willie Jones, Teo Macero, and Art Farmer. They did two Monk tunes, and Allen, who was a bit of a hipster and interviewed other offbeat characters like Kerouac, interviewed Monk.

A young grad student in clinical psychology at New York University, Morris Eagle, wanted to produce jazz concerts. Trying to help, he found he was on trial. The musicians flared at the hint of race. At one meeting, he said, "Things are moving along, but we have to iron out the kinks." John Lewis, a light-skinned man from New Mexico, was insulted.

As Mingus later explained to Celia, "You get conditioned. If a black guy's standing far enough away when you say nickel, he can hear nigger."

Charlie Parker was having a drink at the bar. He wasn't involved in their project, but when he heard the antiwhite talk escalating he walked over and said, "Man, you've got to feel sorry for them, because they don't know what they're doing." The talk stopped dead. Bird was above it.

Mingus's respect for Parker grew a notch. Most of the people who came to his home were white, except for Max Roach and bassist Percy Heath, who was taking a few lessons on bass from Mingus. Sometimes Heath brought his wife over for dinner.

But Mingus never let Eagle fully off the hook, either. He punned on his name, dubbing him Eulenspiegel, from the Strauss symphonic tone poem. They tested Eagle but trusted him. So with Bill Coss, editor of *Metronome*, they incorporated Developments of Modern Jazz and staged a concert at Carnegie Recital Hall in 1954 that featured music by Mingus, Macero, and clarinetist John La Porta. The money, what there was of it, was equally divided.

Several concerts followed for what was becoming known as the Jazz Composers Workshop, at Carnegie Recital Hall and the 92nd Street YMHA. A rash of musicians participated, including Monk, Art Farmer, Don Butterfield, and Gunther Schuller. The musicians and Eagle split expenses. No one made any money.

Coss and his wife Roddie, both white, helped Celia and Mingus find their next apartment, in Flushing, across the street from their own.

Coss became a close friend. He was a hard drinker, one of the tortured sensibilities of postwar Bohemia. His liner notes for *Quintet of the Year* tell of "a crippled world," and the suffering it inflicted on the heroic yet tragically deformed figures onstage. He writes of drugs and twisted lives, artists debauched and corrupted by the stunted environment around them. Pointing out the contradictions of worshiping self-destructive behavior, he summarizes, one by one, how the men on this record had been bent by daily life.

"Charlie Mingus," he wrote, "is less disciplined and more restless, made, not hard, but suspicious by years of privation and insecurity."[15]

Mingus and Celia's new place at 138-29 68th Drive wasn't that much bigger than their Manhattan digs, with a large combined living room/dining room/bedroom and a tiny kitchen. It was seven blocks from Queens College, right behind the Mt. Hebron Cemetery. The graveyard was Mingus's favorite sight.

The neighborhood was white, largely Jewish. Mingus didn't want to move to St. Albans, the sector for black royalty, where Count Basie and heavyweight champ Joe Louis had moved into mansions, leading the way for Ella Fitzgerald and a host of other jazz stars. Illinois Jacquet, who'd made good money off Granz's extremely successful Jazz at the Philharmonic tours and recordings, bought himself a big house whose yard was fenced off by a brick wall. Later, rhythm and blues stars like James Brown moved in.

Mingus wanted everything in his life integrated. He was pushing the limits.

Celia signed their lease and told the landlord her husband was on the road. She didn't mention that he was black. It wasn't a secret for long. Once Mingus was spotted, they were told their two-year-lease would not be renewed.

The Cosses and Eagles were regular drop-ins. They discussed religion and listened to classical music, watched Mingus devour a hunk of chuck steak too large for four and swallow pickles after ice cream. He said the pickles dissolved the fat so he wouldn't gain weight.

One weekend, the Eagles and Minguses went up to Woodstock, to visit Morris's father-in-law, artist Julio de Diego. Morris and Julio got into a big row, so the two couples packed the huge steak they meant to barbecue upstate and headed home. They stopped under the George Washington Bridge, built a fire there and broiled the meat, and had their barbecue after all.

Mingus was very fat. He sometimes greeted musicians on the porch, in a cashmere scarf and a long housecoat. He started wearing dashikis. Friends like Roach and pianist Randy Weston were working with jazz's African roots, to reinvigorate pan-cultural awareness of black Americans. In the process, they wanted to reinvigorate jazz.

Race spurred Othello-like jealousies. He was fiercely possessive of Celia, and worried that Eagle, then Coss was having an affair with her, but he let her go everywhere with them because he fundamentally trusted them. But when any musicians came up to her, especially in a club, he went into a burn, and played warnings like "Dragnet" on the bass. He'd rant, then plead his love.

During one fight, he shoved his bass through their apartment's front bay window. It was mid-winter, but no one showed up to fix it. Finally, he put a sign in the broken pane so you could see it from the walk: "Manager Refuses to Replace This Window after 3 Weeks of Telephone Calls."

The window was fixed.

Paul Bley visited Flushing. The young white pianist first met Mingus in 1952. At the time, the Montreal native was running the Jazz Society of Greater New York, which counted Coss and Hentoff and Mingus as its mentors. Mingus liked the nineteen-year-old. In 1953, he called the young pianist back from Montreal to conduct a session with vocalist Janet Thurlow singing a version of "Weird Nightmare" called "Eclipse."

PAUL BLEY, *musician*: He was still trying to write his music down, step by step —and that was a problem. I was very lucky with him, though. In those days, it was permissible for a black jazz musician to take a young white musician under his wing and act as a mentor. It's very rare now.

In late 1953, Bley recorded with Mingus and drummer Art Blakey for Debut. It was part of a heterogeneous collection the label released that year and the next. There was a four-trombone choir with piano trio. There was a sextet

of French horn, tenor sax, piano, drums, bass by Mingus, and cello by Pettiford, arranged by a young Quincy Jones.

Mingus flipped over a young trumpeter from Detroit. Listening to Thad
Jones, he understood why writing it down correctly wasn't always satisfying. In
a letter that Coss excerpted for Jones's Debut album, Mingus wrote, "He uses
all the classical techniques, and is the first man to make them swing. . . .
He does the things . . . Diz heard Bird do, and Fats made us think were
possible."[16]

Debut's alumni went on to make big ripples. Trombonists J. J. Johnson and
Kai Winding continued their successful partnership. Teo Macero became
Columbia's star jazz producer, working with Davis and Monk and Mingus.
Thad Jones became a respected trumpeter and composer/arranger. Everyone
knows Quincy Jones.

Mingus and Max knew how to spot talent like nobody else.

But that didn't mean anyone made real money. By the end of 1953, DLP-2,
which featured "Perdido," "Salt Peanuts," and "All the Things You Are" from
the Massey Hall performance, had sold 1,415 copies. Each member of the quintet was getting quarterly royalties that ranged over the next few years from
$20.60 to $144.10.[17]

Decades later, Gillespie wrote, "Do you know that Charlie Mingus, who was
always being mistreated, took advantage of his position on the bandstand, tape
recorded that concert, went home, and put out a record? I ain't seen no royalties until recently."[18]

All around New York were drama workshops, like Lee Strasberg's famed Actors Studio, where Marlon Brando studied. Mingus had taken dramatics in
high school, which helped underlay a different direction he was formulating
for the Jazz Workshop. It would be a way to dramatize music, transpose the
jazz values of Method Acting back into music—you had to be in the moment.

He rehearsed the musicians a lot, often at Hartnet Studios near Times
Square, playing compositions by Macero, LaPorta, and Mingus that bent rules.
For one performance at the 92nd Street Y, Macero told trumpeter Art Farmer
to start the show playing up in the balcony. Farmer refused. Macero had ideas
the musicians thought were weird.

Art Tatum called Mingus in late January 1954 to play at Miami's Birdland.[19] He
had to miss a Jazz Composers Workshop at Carnegie Recital Hall, but he was
drifting from his coop partners anyway. Tatum helped nudge him further.

The old man knew how to steal the show, move the harmonies to keep you
at the edge. He was always revamping the standards he loved. It was like being

in school full time. And it wasn't written, and it was full of classicisms, and it swung like hell.

Mingus had had it with notating his music. Musicians couldn't play it right. They complained how hard or unnatural it was. He remembered all the pieces he'd faked his way through, relying on his ear. What could be more natural than to mimic what you heard?

And when you did, you inevitably changed what you remembered, to suit yourself.

They could learn to express themselves in his music better if they learned who they were for themselves. He'd sing or play them their parts. No music.

Mingus ran his open rehearsals at Cooper Union Hall like a school drill: mess it up, start from the top, written or not. He was relaxed. He knew what he wanted.

He liked a young Queens College student of composition, a black pianist named Mal Waldron. With trombonist Eddie Bert, Waldron was the core of his recreated Jazz Workshop.

MAL WALDRON, *musician*: He changed because the times changed, too. Everything was changing up in people. We were talking about freedom, and getting out of jails. Bar lines was like going to jail for us. So everyone wanted to escape from that. There was a general feeling that everyone wanted to be free. It was natural. It didn't happen one day.

That May, Max Roach wrote Celia and Mingus from California. He wanted to do some recording for Debut, and asked for $575. Celia wrote back that Debut had no money; could Max advance the amount, and Debut would repay him?

Roach canceled the sessions.[20]

Mingus went back to California in October, to work with Miles Davis and Max Roach at the Haig. In Max's new Cadillac, they picked up "fat hip Miles" who had just finished going cold turkey at his father's farm outside East St. Louis. They were flabbergasted at the huge Davis spread—prize pigs and horses, a maid and a cook and hired hands. They borrowed Davis's father's silk pajamas to sleep in. Davis had so much fun talking music and trash with them all night, it reminded him of New York, so he decided to ride with them to L.A. His father gave him some money, and the cook packed them a basket of chicken.

Miles trashed their ambitions, kept a bottle for the road, but stayed off heroin. He wrote in his autobiography that "Mingus was death on white people," how Mingus said he'd swerve a car to avoid hitting an animal but a white man wouldn't. Mingus wrote Celia, "He still worships the Black image of God."

When they ran out of chicken in Oklahoma, the others sent Mingus into a restaurant to buy them sandwiches and bring them back out, since he was the light-skinned one. They waited and got more and more nervous until he finally burst out yelling, "Them white motherfuckers won't let us eat in there; I'm gonna blow up their fucking place!"[21]

He had to prove something. The other two shut him up; a black man could be shot without question where they were.

They made it to Los Angeles, but Mamie ruined it for him. She claimed she had had a nervous breakdown; that's why she didn't ship his and Celia's things to New York like he'd asked. Each room in the empty house now had a picture of Jesus, and she walked around singing spirituals. She was disappointed when he told her the Cadillac they pulled up in was Roach's. He asked her if she'd take his money if he'd stolen it, or pimped it, like a friend of his did. She said if she didn't know where it came from, she would.

His old bitterness at her hypocrisy surfaced like bile. He wrote Celia, "It would make her happier if I had a Cadillac and no brains and no God.... For if my mother made one thing that deals with human understanding Then [sic] I'm a worshipper of the devil."

Home again for Halloween, he recorded the Charles Mingus Sextet for Savoy, his debut as a leader for a major New York jazz label. It was a recap, with heavy counterpoint and light, airy sound. But "Gregarian Chant" marked his first try at improvising from a few abstract ideas, like an acting exercise. Only Lennie Tristano had tried that earlier, in 1949.

For Debut, he recorded Julius Watkins on French horn—another artistic dare. Popular pianist Hazel Scott, wife of famed Harlem preacher Adam Clayton Powell, had a reputation for "jazzing the classics." Like the older ragtime and stride players, she'd improvise off a well-known chestnut. She recorded with Mingus and Max Roach. And they recorded a male soprano named Little Jimmy Scott.

Philadelphia pianist John Dennis teamed with Mingus, Roach, and Thad Jones, and then without Jones. For "All the Things You Are," a standard boppers often recomposed, Dennis played a baroque intro, explicitly connecting bop improvisation and fugue.

Mingus's own playing kept surging. He mastered playing two strings at once, one with each hand, and bluesy note bends, adapted from guitarist T-Bone Walker. Double-stops and pedal tones were regular punctuation amid octave jumps, partly to augment pedal tones, partly to agitate. His bass could sing: like Alvino Rey's steel guitar, it suggested a human voice in its flexible tones and timbres.

He and his instrument were one, just as Bird said they should be. And he was the man now. Bassists from all over the Big Apple took note. A number took lessons from him.

On March 4, 1955, six days before Mingus recorded Dennis, he did his last gig as Bird's bassist. With Art Blakey and Kenny Dorham, both junkies, he watched Bird and Bud Powell self-destruct on Birdland's fabled bandstand. Powell was drunk; he attacked Bird's playing. Parker lashed back. Powell smashed the keyboard and walked offstage. Bird called his name over and over in a dead voice—"a leaden tolling of the years," is how Nat Hentoff described it. While the others started Parker's "Now's the Time," Mingus grabbed a microphone and said, "Ladies and Gentlemen, please don't associate me with any of this. This is not jazz. These are sick people."

Backstage afterward, Thelonious Monk, who seemed the most eccentric of them all, scolded Powell and the rest. "I told you guys to act crazy," he said, "but I didn't tell you to fall in love with your act. You're really crazy now." No one said a word. It was the epitaph for an era. [22]

When Charlie Parker died of various complications resulting from his long heroin abuse on March 12, he was found in the hotel room of Baroness Pannonica de Konigswarter, part of the Rothschild family. Nica, as they all called the statuesque and imperious blonde, was an Old World–style patron of the arts with a new portfolio—jazz. She especially favored Bird and Monk. When Mingus saw her at the gigs, she reminded him of nights at Farwell Taylor's.

The coroner estimated Bird's age as late fifties; he was thirty-four. A Bird Lives frenzy immediately took hold. Everything he said was an axiom. His life was a model. His music was the final say. Mingus was revolted, more so when a wrangle ensued over possession of Parker's body between Doris, his white third wife, and Chan, his white common-law wife. Dizzy Gillespie, among others, sided with Doris, and the Reverend Adam Clayton Powell officiated at Bird's funeral at the Abyssinian Baptist Church.

The dead man's body wore a new blue suit, and its hands held a crucifix. He was shipped back to Kansas City and buried in his mother's plot.

Chan had wanted Mingus and Lennie Tristano to play at a simple funeral. "Bird," she said, "was irreligious." Instead they joined the Harlem ceremony. A woman named Maely Dufty began setting up a benefit for Bird's death expenses at Carnegie Hall and enlisted Mingus and Celia to schedule performers. On the board of the Charlie Parker Memorial Fund were Mingus, Nat

Hentoff, Maely's husband William Dufty who had co-written Billie Holiday's autobiography, and pianists Mary Lou Williams and Hazel Scott. [23] By the time of the all-star tribute on April 3, Mingus was disgusted. Everyone, he felt, wanted to play the gig for self-promotion, not because they gave a damn about Bird or his music.

The fiasco burned into him. It was a disastrous way to end a disastrous life. It would not happen to him.

Bud Powell had been committed again.

Miles Davis was sitting in the tank on Riker's Island, New York City's jail-house. He was in for nonpayment of alimony and child support until Harold Lovette—a friend of Max Roach, Debut's lawyer, and a huge fan—bailed him out.

Lovette told his Debut partners Davis needed cash badly, and that he was willing to record for Debut. Miles thought Debut was a crazy idea, bucking an unbuckable establishment, but he was in a corner. Debut recorded him at Audio Video Studios, a double session for union scale.

In the end, Davis didn't like the way the session turned out. "The playing didn't have any fire," he later wrote. [24]

In mid-July 1955, Mingus had his second afternoon shot at the Newport Jazz Festival. Started by George Wein in 1954 and backed by the wealthy Lorillards, the Newport Jazz Festival foretold things to come. It involved first wealthy patrons, then corporations, in promoting jazz concerts.

The festival began as a weekend in Freebody Park, a site overlooking the water. Old lions like Ellington filled the park in the evenings. Young turks like Mingus and the Jazz Composers Workshop had the afternoons. They were paid $35 apiece, plus $5 for travel.

The star of this Newport Festival, however, was Miles Davis, who had wowed the crowds so headily that suddenly Columbia Records wanted to sign him. It was the Cadillac of major labels, with the finest classical roster and an arty patrician image.

Davis did an interview with Nat Hentoff that ran in *Down Beat* that November. In it, he compared Mingus and Macero's writing to "tired modern paintings." Mingus replied swiftly in the first of his many open letters: "I play or write *me*, the way I feel. If someone has been escaping reality, I don't expect him to dig my music." [25]

That September, *Vogue* magazine ran a picture of Mingus bowing his bass, with a short accompanying piece. "Charlie Mingus," it said in part, "is the greatest bass player since the late Jimmy Blanton, who first took the bull fiddle out of the thumper class and made it a solo instrument. . . . Part of the Mingus technique depends on his revision of old fingering systems, a change comparable to Andres Segovia's broadening of the guitar's scope. In unconscious proof of jazz evolution, Mingus said recently: 'I could always hear everything Duke did.'"

He was beginning to make his mark. He was far from unconscious.

So was Buddy Collette, who saw Mingus in New York around this time. Buddy was recording and touring with their old comrade Chico Hamilton in 1955. With an unusual lineup that included Collette on flute, clarinet, and alto, Jim Hall on guitar, and Fred Katz on cello, the integrated quintet rivaled the Modern Jazz Quartet as the ultimate cool-jazz sound, and drew good crowds in upscale clubs.

Their smooth, silken sound reminded Mingus of the Stars of Swing.

Collette had a lot of tales to tell. He'd had the chance to watch the House Un-American Activities Committee (HUAC) at work close up: they'd grilled Jerry Fielding, and he'd been blacklisted. Collette and a few other musicians were helping him out financially.

So Buddy was in contact with the American Civil Liberties Union, and he was reading left wing newspapers, trying to place the struggles for integration in larger contexts like global politics and economics. Thanks to his status as a classical music teacher, he'd been asked to accompany Paul Robeson when the great black singer appeared in Los Angeles.

For black Americans, Robeson was both inspiration and cautionary tale. Mingus loved to tell how he'd once seen the great singer perform with a dead microphone, imitating the bass voice that boomed over the auditorium: "I don't need no microphone."

At Rutgers University in the early 1920s, Robeson had starred in four sports, was twice named All-American end in football, and graduated Phi Beta Kappa. He was class valedictorian and got a law degree at Columbia in 1923, but he dropped it all to become a widely acclaimed singer and actor, with countless records and plays and movies to his credit. And he hitched his political views to his art. Robeson thought Europe should free its African colonies, saw the American black man's plight hinged to Africa's, and approvingly toured Joseph Stalin's Soviet Union in the 1930s, intensifying his attacks on American racism.

In 1939, he spearheaded a drive to register black voters in Birmingham, Alabama. A year later, he cofounded the Negro Playwrights' Company. In 1942, he stopped a Kansas City concert to announce that because the audience was racially segregated, he was continuing under protest. Hundreds of whites walked out.

Robeson asked the commissioner of baseball to lift the ban against blacks in the major leagues. For his forty-eighth birthday, 8,000 fans and friends crammed into the New York Armory; another 4,000 were turned away. In August 1945, Robeson went on the first interracial USO tour for American troops in Europe. A year later, he testified before the House Un-American Activities Committee that he was an antifascist, not a communist, but was included on HUAC's list of 1,000 communists.

In 1948, the NAACP ousted W. E. B. Du Bois for attacking the anticommunist crusade. Called before HUAC, black leaders denounced Robeson. That August, rioters tore apart his concert at Peekskill, New York, smashing the stage, torching the seats, beating the fleeing audience.

In 1950, the government voided his passport. Paul Robeson couldn't work at home, and couldn't travel to work elsewhere. In 1953, the blacklisted performer founded his own record company.

Collette told Mingus about playing flute with a string quartet behind Robeson, in a classical program.

BUDDY COLLETTE: He had his side to tell, which was great; it was a whole different side. He'd talk about the attacks on him because of his statements on his trip to Russia. "All I said was that I got treated better there. They treated me like a king. And when I go home, they discriminate against my people." So he was a truthful man, and I was in awe of him. He was one of the first to speak out in that way, and that really did a lot for me to see that. And he wasn't afraid. Being around him, it was a turning period for me.

A lot of people don't realize the inspiration he was for a lot of the black people who were leaders, who were able to stand up. Because it can be costly if you stand up and say, "I believe in this." He was the kind of person who was true.

Early that fall, a young French horn player named David Amram turned up. He was out of the army, back from Europe, and fresh to New York. Dizzy Gillespie told him Mingus thought like a symphony composer too, that he was listening to Bartok and Stravinsky, that he was thinking about extended forms in jazz. Amram, who also played jazz, was intrigued.

Critic Leonard Feather introduced him to Mingus one night at Birdland, where he was playing with Bud Powell. Amram was struck by his independence: he was warping the tempo, playing solo lines against the piano's, commanding the performance. Mingus offered Amram a Workshop slot, $125 a week. Amram planned to go to school, he said. Mingus narrowed his eyes: "You'll learn more from me than from any music school."

A few days later Amram picked up saxist George Barrow and headed to

Flushing, where they'd learn the music at Mingus's apartment. The older stuff was written down; the rest was in his head.

EDDIE BERT: You'd just go up to his house and he'd play things, like "Jump Monk," and he'd say, "Learn it, because if I write it out, you're gonna play it different. If you learn it in your head, you play it like you want to play it." And that's what he wanted you to do. And that's the way it came out.

Mingus and Celia moved back to Manhattan. The apartment at 331 West 51st Street was home, rehearsal space, and Debut headquarters. Money was tight. Celia wrote their bank a letter about a twenty-cent account imbalance in their favor. They scrambled to cover the $20 a month payments to Maywood-Bell Ford, a car dealer in California.[26]

As he was painting the ceiling just after they moved in, Mingus couldn't forget Mamie walking from room to room, singing spirituals to pictures of Jesus. He thought about Bartok and the gypsy tunes he'd adapted. He thought about Weston and Roach. He got stuck on one spiritual, humming it, singing it, until he climbed down off the ladder and went to the piano. It became "Haitian Fight Song," a tribute to the island's slave revolt of 1801.

He told the musicians to forget about chord changes. Relate to each other and try to make a beautiful sound. Talk to each other on your instruments. The rhythms will come out naturally.

MAL WALDRON: With things like "Work Song," we were going into the area of traditional music. We were going into the background of black people in America, into their experiences in life. Mingus was trying to portray that in his music, so he chose worksongs and other things of that order. He would explain the feeling of a guy with a sledgehammer trying to hit a rock, trying to make little rocks out of big rocks. And we got into the mood of that, and just played it.

Mingus showed Waldron why sounds mattered more than chords, if they enriched the emotional color. He'd smash the keyboard with his elbow or fist. The nineteen-year-old watched it work. He admired Mingus, thought of him as a big brother.

Mingus hummed the horn players their parts, and they played them back, evolving their own phrasing within his guidelines. Slowly they assembled the arrangements in their heads. He tinkered constantly, so it was hard as hell, but they felt elated when it worked. He was giving them a kind of freedom they'd never had. He'd give them material, and they had to find themselves in his music. They had to believe their roles.

He'd found a unique way to compose, to formulate group improvisation. Duke Ellington often wrote tunes from phrases his soloists played, but Mingus went one better. He created a whole arrangement out of the way his musicians played what he gave them. They had to converse. Nobody else was reconceiving composition that way. He'd shape the performance on stage, edit it in the studio.

EDDIE BERT: He'd change the tunes. He'd be playing behind you, and you'd be playing and he'd be singing it, and then he'd be, "Play this." And as he's singing it, you're playing it. He was pushing us to different limits. Nothing wrong with that. That was the beginning of his style, that flamboyance.

Café Bohemia was a small bar on Barrow Street in Greenwich Village. It was a strip joint until its owner, a hood named Jimmy Garofalo, thought he had Charlie Parker, his favorite, booked. Bird owed Garofalo a tab and offered to play for it. It was his standard move. Even though he never performed there, Bird kept drinking there, with his downtown friends. The Bohemia became the center of a new Village scene.

Like Levy, Garofalo was a kind of mob *padrone*—a patron as well as boss. He always paid the musicians, even if the take was low. And he'd sometimes leap across the bar to silence talkers during sets.

Starting in the fall of 1955, Mingus's Jazz Workshop appeared there, sporadically and with different personnel, over two and a half months. Candido sat in. Randy Weston, then Herbie Nichols played piano at intermission. Max Roach, Miles Davis, Thelonious Monk, Art Blakey, Sonny Rollins, and pianist Cecil Taylor came to check the scene out. Kerouac and painter Larry Rivers were at the bar.

On December 23, 1955, Mingus recorded everything the Workshop did. Max Roach had a rare week off from touring with Clifford Brown and Sonny Rollins, so he sat in on "Drums," which drew on African and Latin rhythms, as well as on abstract but revealing pieces like "Percussion Discussion." (Mingus later overdubbed another line on three-quarter size bass.[27]) The long, braided, three-and-a-half-octave melody of "Jump Monk" distilled Monk's eccentricities without sounding like him.

CHARLES MINGUS: It's not supposed to sound like Monk. I liked him. It was a dedication to him. . . . The reason I called it "Jump" was because Monk was always moving around. We were working in a club in the Bronx one time, and there was a revolving door. He came in and out, in and out, for about five minutes.[28]

"Love Chant" prompted Miles Davis to taunt him, "How come your band can only play one chord, Mingus?" "A Foggy Day" nodded to musique concrete, as George Barrow and Eddie Bert blew foghorn tones. "Haitian Fight Song" was a canon, a call-and-response form of counterpoint: Bert's trombone repeated Barrow's sax phrases one measure later, then they punctuated their bluesy solos with double time and stop-time and martial beats.

Boppers thought of him as a bass player, but he was a composer. He was reimagining what that meant, right before their eyes. The range of material was a fist on the door.

Now, rehearsals by symphonic and pops orchestras are paid attractions, but in 1955, that notion was unheard of. The musicians made $60 apiece for the Debut recording. And the Workshop was mostly idle, despite critical praise.

That would change. Mingus was feeling the Zeitgeist again.

By 1955, Jack Kerouac had written one-and-a-half million words. Legend said he wrote *On the Road* in three weeks. But Kerouac understood Bird. He studied until he became one with his instrument. He could improvise words like jazz musicians did notes, and you'd know whose voice it was.

Allen Ginsberg transposed Kerouac's approach into poetry. On October 13, 1955, he read Howl at the Six Gallery in San Francisco, and created a huge and controversial sensation. He started taking his clothes off at performances. Often people came to see him and be outraged more than to hear his work, but there was no mistaking his voice and language. He was a celebrity.

So was artist Jackson Pollock. His abstract "drip" paintings were undulating abstractions he made by dancing over and around a horizontal canvas and flinging paint in a vocabulary of gestures he'd created from improvising. Pollock was soon the first artist of his generation to have a mid-career retrospective at the Museum of Modern Art.

American culture was shaking loose. The Korean War was over. The anticommunist hysteria peaked in 1954. Prosperity was spreading; people weren't so scared that it wouldn't last.

On December 1, Rosa Parks, a member of the Montgomery Alabama NAACP, refused to give up her seat on a public bus—the culmination of a year of small protests. Her action catalyzed antiracist forces, and 50,000 blacks boycotted Montgomery's bus system for a year, when federal courts ordered them desegregated. Dr. Martin Luther King Jr., a boycott leader, had his house bombed. King preached the idea of Satyagraha, or nonviolent resistance, he had learned from studying Gandhi. In 1957 the Southern Christian Leadership Council was formed, with King at its head.

Intellectuals like C. Wright Mills were publicly questioning postwar society

—its money-focused rat race, conformity, constricted morality, sexual silence, juvenile delinquency, drug and alcohol abuse, asylum horrors. TV quiz shows, which had riveted the country, exploded into scandals.

The cultural climate was changing, and Charles Mingus was reaching, very deliberately, to encompass its dreams and its nightmares and its needs and its pains in his work. He would make a world of his own in his art.

He had access to a major booking agency—Willard Alexander, where Celia was working as a secretary. Monte Kay, the well-connected manager of John Lewis's successful Modern Jazz Quartet, was his manager.

He stood on the cusp of greatness.

7 Pithecanthropus Erectus

CHARLIE MINGUS was three months shy of his thirty-fourth birthday in January 1956, when he led the Workshop into Audio-Video Studios in Manhattan. There they cut his first disc, *Pithecanthropus Erectus*, for Atlantic Records. Atlantic, an aggressive small label, became a big player in postwar cultural history.

Started by the Ertegun brothers, sons of a Turkish diplomat, Atlantic made a name by putting out innovative rhythm and blues and jazz. Nesuhi Ertegun, who had taught a jazz course in Los Angeles in the late 1940s, ran jazz, while brother Ahmet conferred first with Herb Abramson, then Jerry Wexler, on pop.

Mingus assembled a crew out of the Workshop's growing pool: saxists J. R. Monterose and Jackie McLean, pianist Mal Waldron, and drummer Willie Jones. The title track was born during the Workshop's Bohemia stint; it gelled early in 1956. That's when Barrow left, replaced by McLean. The young Harlem-born altoist with the slippery intonation and edgy tone inspired Mingus to push even harder at open improvisation.

DAVID AMRAM: He said to Jackie, "You know, this one, you've really got to stretch out. I want you to . . ." and he sang a long series of melodies, and Jackie would play them back. I said, "Aren't we going to practice it?" He said, "No, man. You practice at home. When you come here tonight, you create."

Mingus would turn around and kind of twist his elbow and spin at a certain point, and Jackie started making all these wailing sounds, and I started doing it along with him. Then we started getting into something where we were playing really complicated phrases that miraculously came out together—all night long, without saying anything, on stuff where there was no arrangement.

He called "Pithecanthropus Erectus" a jazz tone poem. The title came from so-called Java Man, the oldest fossil known until the later 1950s, when Louis and Mary Leakey pushed the time frame of human evolution farther back with their discoveries at Olduvai Gorge.

Taking off from an open-ended lope that suggests the vastness of the ancient world where Darwin said man evolved, the piece gradually gathered soloing instruments into a conversation, then a tribe. It is a moralist's fable, as he explained to the musicians and wrote in his liner notes.

CHARLES MINGUS: Overcome with self-esteem, he goes out to rule the world, if not the universe, but both his own failure to realize the inevitable emancipation of those he sought to enslave, and his greed in attempting to stand on a false security, deny him not only the right of ever being a man, but finally destroy him completely. [1]

The music was freely improvised around those themes. Each musician was given a set of phrases to start from, and used them as the basic vocabulary to portray his ideas. Improvisation was spontaneous composition. The eruptions of chaos and discord that closed the piece caught his feelings about man's self-destructive bent.

He liked using Latin for a jazz title. It made a claim.

The album recapped Bohemia-days material, like "Love Chant." "A Foggy Day" is subtitled "in San Francisco," and the saxmen brilliantly expanded the musique concrete effects—the foghorns and cars and background noises—introduced at the Bohemia.

Julio de Diego, Morris Eagle's father-in-law, did the cover art. De Diego was a man Mingus understood. The Madrid-born artist was the third husband of Gypsy Rose Lee. The couple toured with a carnival called Royal American Shows: Lee stripped, and de Diego did a Surrealist skit, "What Art Your Dreams?" [2]

De Diego's cover art set Mingus's music squarely in the mood of the times. Three small separate figures, black, red, and white, stand up and unify: a black outer man, white core man, red in-between. It's somewhere between Diego Rivera and Picasso, crossed with Henri Rousseau. It's surreally mythic.

It foreshadows the opening of Beneath the Underdog: "In other words, I am three."

One night, Mingus and Celia went to the Embers. Robert Preston came over to their table with Peggy Lee. After friendly chitchat, Preston asked Mingus what he was reading. He pulled out Plato's *Republic*.

The Workshop was never stable for long. Work wasn't steady. Ellington had the luxury of long-termers in his orchestra, but he paid for it by being on the road constantly. He subsidized the band with the royalties from his songs and compositions.

Universities like Columbia and Princeton housed composers like Milton Babbitt, but there were no subsidies in academia for jazz composers. For jazz there was no aristocracy of patronage, like the one that floated symphonic orchestras and opera companies.

Ironically, mainstream society's neo-Victorian mores were helping produce a new Jazz Age. Now it was coming aboveground, and money was finding it.

Mingus would mold his musicians, create a trained pool to draw from. He would make them find themselves in his music, and make his music elastic without losing his voice.

MAL WALDRON: The music changed as the musicians changed—who you were talking to. He was always excited when he hired somebody, like with Jackie McLean. In the beginning he'd say, "You should see this guy, he's fantastic, he can do everything." Then, once the guy was in the band, he'd start noticing what the guy lacked. Then he'd get down to correcting the cat to get the best results out of him. If the cat went along with it, it was okay. If he didn't, you had this ego thing going. Some of the egos would resent that and walk off, and then there'd be altercations.

At twenty-three, Jackie McLean was a Little Bird. Detractors thought him even more out-of-tune than Parker, thanks to his expanded use of piercing microtones. He'd studied with Bud Powell and worked with Monk. Charlie Parker himself sent the Harlem youngster to fill in for him at a gig when McLean was eighteen. The tough street kid started shooting heroin, like his friend Sonny Rollins, and made his record debut with Miles Davis.

Dizzy Gillespie once said that every sax player Mingus hired sounded like Bird, and every trumpet player like himself.[3] He had a real point. And it's true that, as a composer, Mingus used bop, as he did other musical idioms, and wrote tributes to both Bird and Diz.

But he wanted his sidemen to take it both ways: connect to the tradition, and be themselves.

JACKIE MCLEAN, *musician*: It was my first real taste of free improvisation. I was all bebop. I didn't believe what he was doing at first. But there wasn't prepared music. He'd say, "Forget about changes; all notes are right." He was serious about just being free. It was exciting for me. He kept saying, "I don't want Bird, man, I want Jackie."

Mingus was so thrilled with McLean's eccentric bluesy wail he wrote "Portrait of Jackie," one of his ongoing series of musical character studies, à la Ellington.

He faced off with McLean that March, in Philadelphia. At the bar, words between them escalated to shouts, and he lunged at McLean, swinging for his face.

To hit a horn player in the mouth is like breaking the fingers of a pianist. It can ruin his musical life. McLean slashed his knife at the 190-pound figure, but the bartender grabbed his arm. The action froze. Waldron kept his head down in his beer.

McLean was busted for drugs in 1957 and lost his cabaret card, with brief reprieves, for seven years. He was jailed twice and didn't return to the Workshop for two years.[4]

Celia was pregnant, and Mingus's jealousy intensified, even when it looked as though his prophecy about her was being fulfilled. She felt that she was losing her life. She couldn't have men friends, except for Bill Coss and Morris Eagle. Even men she worked with were suspect.

Mingus was endlessly, hydra-headedly demanding. Debut's business was a constant drain. They'd decided to reissue the Massey Hall concert on a 12-inch LP that June, and Celia wrote to Norman Granz to ask permission to use Bird's name on it, as a "favor." She added they'd pay him a royalty. Fifteen days later, on June 28, Granz's lawyers fired back a no, adding that Granz held Debut "accountable for the wrongful use of Bud Powell and Charlie Parker" at Massey Hall.[5]

She was beginning to feel worn out and trapped.

On July 5, 1956, Mingus returned to the successful Newport jazz festival. George Wein's series was drawing thousands of college kids, who packed Newport's bars. And the yachting set was showing up. Despite a downpour, 4,000 people thronged the park that holiday weekend.

The Workshop was churning personnel, so Mingus and Waldron rejoined Teo Macero in a sextet to play new extended pieces, "Tourist in Manhattan" and "Tonight at Noon."

He faced off with the Willard Alexander Agency, announcing he was hiring a new agent. Celia suggested Alexander let her manage her husband on her own.

Most club owners didn't like him. He was hard to handle. They endured harangues about stage size, the piano's condition, bathroom cleanliness. He was on diet pills and speed.

But he was getting a lot of press coverage, so Alexander agreed to Celia's proposal.

He bought himself a bandleader's car, a big, roomy 1956 Buick station wagon.[6]

His life with Celia was fracturing while his creative life focused. His jealousy turned to frenzy while he stayed out at night. The critics were coming around, big guns like Feather, Coss, and Hentoff.

For all his attitude, Miles Davis dug what his old colleague was up to. His new quintet with John Coltrane took standards like "Bye Bye Blackbird" and stretched them into new shapes. Trane admired Mingus, his push for open extended forms. And Max Roach's quintet with Clifford Brown and Sonny Rollins was pushing and pulling at musical formats.

Mingus was feeling the Zeitgeist again.

Celia felt she'd have to give up her own life to stay with him.

Allen Ginsberg was using amphetamines and coffee as a steady diet to write. The Beats and boppers were nearly all juggling drugs. Mingus was sure he himself was no junkie. But there were too many ideas, too many melodies to catch in too little time.

Pills weren't drugs. Housewives across America routinely took sleeping and diet pills. Heroin was a drug. Cocaine was a drug.

He needed to lose weight. He'd ballooned again. He was becoming a star, and he hated being fat. It was a drag with women. He remembered his father got so fat he had to reach down and cross his legs with his hands. It haunted him.

He went to Dr. Luther Cloud, whom he mentions in *Beneath the Underdog*. Cloud's office on Park Avenue offered counseling, vitamin shots, prescriptions, and pills. Thanks to Baroness Nica de Konigswarter, Cloud treated Lester Young and Billie Holiday and Max Roach and Thelonious Monk.

First Mingus got diet pills, then various uppers and downers. The fights with Celia escalated.

One running battle was about money. Mingus argued that the government should subsidize artists, but Celia saw that as an opening for wannabes and censorship.

She cut back work to three days a week, because of her pregnancy, and it intensified his usual gripes and worries about money. What if the gigs stopped?

He kept talking about the big money some people were making from the influx of new young fans. The Beat Generation had come aboveground, and it was hyped or attacked or belittled in newspapers and movies. Television had Dobie Gillis, with the addle-brained beatnik Maynard G. Krebs. It was the beginnings of "youth culture." In *Growing Up Absurd*, Paul Goodman surveyed the alienation of postwar American youth. "The importance of the Beats," he wrote, "is twofold: first, they act out a critique of the organized system that everybody in some sense agrees with. But second—and more important in the long run—they are a kind of major pilot study of the use of leisure in an economy of abundance."[7]

Jazz was the hip music for collegians, sounds to seduce by, to argue by, to think by. It was intellectual music, but without classical pretensions. It was created by outsiders, although cool white jazzers, from Gerry Mulligan to Chet Baker to Dave Brubeck, got big spreads in major magazines.

Newport was a magnet, and new converts were exploring the clubs. White college girls from Vassar and Barnard found jazz, and the proximity of black artists, thrilling. It was rebellious but not as dangerous as getting pregnant or using drugs. The girls' parents didn't discipline or institutionalize them just for going to jazz clubs, but hanging out bore the lure of the forbidden.

The musicians talked about rich white women patrons. Monk had Nica. It was like owning a flashy car. The more you had, the feeling went, the more The Man would pay you.

Waldron and the others came to the roomy Mingus apartment at 331 West 51st Street to learn new pieces and paint the walls and crate and ship Debut records. Mingus paid them. This was his version of Ellington; it kept the Workshop's core available.

Many of Debut's records didn't pay their own bills. Oscar Pettiford's sides sold ninety-six copies in 1954, sixty-seven in the first half of 1957. Debut advanced Peterson $288.75. By June 1957, Hazel Scott's sales still hadn't earned back $195.75 of her $279 advance.[8]

Debut's recordings were making a splash, but they weren't making money. The company was strung along by debtors, and pleaded poverty to creditors. Some musicians fumed about accounting in the Debut office.

In October, Mingus hired the drummer who stayed for twenty-two years. Dannie Richmond was twenty when saxist Lou Donaldson suggested him.

Mingus hated most drummers. His elastic sense of time threw them, and the Workshop's methods exacerbated the problems. He wanted tempos to breathe, to accelerate and decelerate organically. Even Willie Jones, who played with Monk, couldn't always do it.

And so Mingus took the young ex-tenor saxman and molded him into his kind of drummer. Max Roach was his key model. No one touched Roach's melodic percussion, his ability to interact. As Richmond learned to relax, to leaven his speed with dialogic timing, he and Mingus created a heartbeat that was rarely equaled and was utterly crucial to Mingus's extended pieces.

Dannie fast became his alter ego, Mingus's Sancho Panza inverted, the shorter skinny sidekick who smoothed his oversized boss's turbulent ways.

On a cross-country tour, Mingus took Richmond to Tijuana, where they downed tequila and stared at strippers and were followed by mariachi bands. He wondered about Celia. He had to retaliate for his dependence. He bought Dannie and himself some whores. He later wrote he screwed one each hour for a full day.[9]

After they came back around New Year's 1957, the fights with Celia heated up again.

Trombonist Willie Dennis was leaving the Workshop, so Mingus called Jimmy Knepper, who signed on for *The Clown*, Mingus's second Atlantic album. It captured how he pushed the band onstage, singing lines, shouting encouragement and instructions.

The title track tinged Pagliacci with P. T. Barnum, and featured a semi-improvised narration by Jean Shepherd, a hip radio personality. Shepherd and Mingus discussed plot turns and moods, but the satirist was free to tell the tale his way. He changed Mingus's finale; instead of shooting himself, the clown dies onstage by accident, to the audience's oblivious ovation.

For Mingus, the clown was richly symbolic. He'd seen paintings by Picasso and de Kooning, and read about lost innocents like Dostoyevsky's *Idiot*. Thanks to Vedanta, he thought of prophets like Christ as holy fools. Philip Wylie ended *Generation of Vipers* by calling himself a clown.

Clowns were seers who were rejected. To portray the figure, he picked one of his favorite instruments, the trombone. The intro and recurrent parts were written in waltz time, which made the musicians feel stiff, and he wrote out his bass solo. It felt like Kurt Weill at the circus.

Most of the other material was Bohemia vintage. Here "Haitian Fight Song" threw down the gauntlet to his accusers, the ones who said writing it correctly made his music stiff, unswinging. Nothing was written. Two pungent, four-bar phrases in canon sparked off fireworks for twelve minutes.

He was feeling the Zeitgeist again.

In January, a number of black ministers formed what they called the Southern Leaders Conference. A month later, Dr. Martin Luther King Jr. became its head. Soon the group was renamed the Southern Christian Leadership Conference and focused on getting voting rights.

J. Edgar Hoover, FBI director, believed that civil rights activists were communist-inspired. He soon had King and other leaders shadowed and wiretapped. From these days on, Mingus complained often and loud that he, too, was under FBI and CIA scrutiny.

For "Haitian Fight Song," Mingus reversed the canon sequence from the Bohemia days. Knepper, who prided himself on his precise articulation and speed, led off, shadowed by saxist Shafi Hadi.

Knepper was one of his ambivalent sidemen. He performed with Mingus whenever he could. But at times he'd say Mingus couldn't write in proper ranges for each horn, that he recycled old material shamelessly, that he wasn't the great bassist he thought. "His music was a mess," is one refrain.

Mingus never let anyone leave without a struggle. He never fully let go of people. He strode back into lives like he'd never left. And nearly everyone let him.

His fights with Celia continued to come in bouts. He was trapped in insomnia. He remembered how Bird used to call and play Stravinsky to improvise to. He started phoning friends like Hentoff in the middle of the night. First over the line came music, then that scratchy drawl. "I just wrote that; like it?" They'd talk. He was eager to explain his work—its forms, its goals. "What counts," he'd say, "is what stays in your head after you hear it."

He asked Hentoff, "Why would I want to be a classical bassist? What would I be doing playing somebody else's music?"

On February 2, Mingus was part of "Voice of Jazz," a Town Hall concert sponsored by the *Village Voice*. His friend Nat Hentoff was writing there.

At the Village Vanguard, jazz, folk, revues, and political satire all shared the stage. The scene was ready for Mingus.

That April, Celia left Willard Alexander to start Superior Artists Corporation. A month later, Mingus was at the Continental Lounge in Brooklyn. He told Gunther Schuller he decided to revive jazz dance, and hired dancers.

He was experimenting with multimedia. Poetry and music, theater and music and dance—these had once been joined. He refused to be stuffed into a compartment.

He made plans to meet avant-garde composer Edgard Varèse, as Bird had, and did shows with poets like Jack Micheline and Kenneth Patchen. The Living

Theater, an avant-drama collective, did a fund-raiser, and Mingus appeared. He and Julian Beck and Judith Malina, who had founded and run the innovative artistic group, were colleagues, and he liked their politics and their art.

That May in Mount Vernon, a New York suburb, he led a quintet with Knepper and Richmond. They tried out newer material plus reconceived versions of Bird's "Billie's Bounce" and Dizzy's "Night in Tunisia." Gillespie's Latin jazz conceptions always made him think.

For the 1957 Brandeis Festival that June, he got a commission from Schuller, who championed what he called "Third Stream," a fusion of classical music and jazz. Schuller conducted his piece, "Revelations," which was in the mode of "Half Mast Inhibition" and "Chill of Death." A lyrical young white pianist named Bill Evans was on the date. A year later, Evans joined the Miles Davis Quintet.

Mingus rejoined Schuller for a Duke Ellington tribute on the Steve Allen Show. He shared a bill at a Village moviehouse with Billie Holiday and the Modern Jazz Quartet; onstage, he wore Bermuda shorts. For Mo Levy's Roulette label, he recorded a piano trio playing his perennial favorite standard, "I Can't Get Started," and "Dizzy Moods."

On June 27, Celia wrote to Father Norman O'Connor that Mingus had gone on a diet, as the priest had suggested. In ten days, he went from 249 to 229 pounds.

He was using diet pills and uppers and couldn't sleep, and told Celia he'd taken a room across the street from his doctor's office.

In the 1940s, Dizzy Gillespie helped create Latin jazz, marrying bop's long lines and the fiery clave rhythms of Cuba. Mingus's Tijuana trip gave him some ideas. The strolling mariachi bands combined flamenco and light operatic vocals into a Mexican blues. He was gripped by the music's resilient sadness and wanted to transform it.

He had his first deal with a true major label, RCA, and on July 18, he went into RCA's Studio A to record *Tijuana Moods*. It was the first of two sessions, his first in stereo. But his deal developed snags.

Debut had an exclusive contract with Thad Jones. Mingus and Max Roach wanted to record Thad with his brothers and call it The Jones Boys. An RCA artists-and-repertoire (A&R) man stole the idea. Jones didn't realize he had broken his contract—or convinced Mingus he didn't. Celia sued RCA for Debut, and RCA held *Tijuana Moods* for five years. [10]

Mingus called Jones, whose wife answered the phone. He spent his rage on her. When Jones called him back, he warned his ex-boss that if he did anything like that again, he'd kill him. They didn't speak for twenty years.

Mingus was bitter. Everybody else was playing bebop and hard bop and funky jazz, but nobody was doing anything like this. The ensemble played opening figures in unison, then cinematically dissolved into simultaneous, extended improvisations, prefiguring the 1960s free-jazz movement. His juxtaposition of non-Cuban Latin beats and jazz was unique, neither bossa nova nor Afro-Cuban. And Ysabel Morel's dancing paralleled his multimedia uses of poetry and narration.

Debut's lawsuit led to a $1,200 settlement, but he'd lost his biggest shot to date. Years later, in an interview, he insisted that RCA had held his album for eleven years. When the reporter disagreed, he snarled, "How do you know when it was recorded?"

In the 1920s, Vachel Lindsay called his work jazz poetry, and Langston Hughes helped launch the Harlem Renaissance, a Jazz Age explosion of black artistic talent and demands for racial equality, by using lines from the blues, and phrasing like jazz's, to shape his supple free verse. In the mid-1950s, poets like Kenneth Rexroth and Kenneth Patchen and Lawrence Ferlinghetti, who ran a small hip bookstore-cum-publisher called City Lights Books, staged poetry readings with a jazz combo at the Cellar in San Francisco.

To celebrate the 1957 publication of On the Road, Jack Kerouac and David Amram and others packed the Brata Art Gallery on East 10th Street with a few xeroxed flyers. They did it again, at the Circle in the Square. Mingus showed up and growled at Amram, "They're stealing our music anyway and not doing it right. The cats that create this music should be part of the whole picture."

Notoriety was flooding over the scenes in New York and San Francisco. On the Road's publication coincided with the obscenity trial of City Lights Press for printing Ginsberg's Howl. U.S. Customs seized hundreds of copies of Howl because of its references to private parts and homosexuality. As the trial stretched through the summer, it became a cause celebre in magazines from Newsweek to The Nation. A conservative judge known for his Sunday School classes dismissed the case on October 3.

Hypocrisy was yielding to freedom.

Homosexuality, drug usage, and interracial romance were among the activities that earned the label fiend or deviant in 1950s America.

As Celia got more pregnant and their marriage further dissolved, Mingus was asked by John Cassavetes to do a sound track for a movie he was planning to improvise. It hinged on a black-white affair.

Cassevetes funded it with money from his early TV detective series, Johnny

Staccato. Like most, and the film noir idiom that spawned them, it had a jazzy sound track.

Shadows was shot over four months in 1957, on 16 mm film, for $40,000. Mingus visited the set, talked with the director and actors, and composed motifs. Cassavetes left him to do what he wanted.

Mingus was impressed with Cassavetes, the nature of his strategy. Cassevetes wrote a script, but he used it to force his actors to tap their own feelings for their roles. He'd give one actor lines for a scene but withhold them from others. That conjured natural surprise and shock.

It was what the Jazz Workshop was doing with music.

Most of the music, recorded in spring and summer 1958, was lost in the 1959 final version. Some was written. He and Dannie Richmond did effects separately. Shafi Hadi recorded a short piece as a solo, and Mingus fired him. The musicians were paid about $20 apiece for the sessions.

One part of his sound track became "Nostalgia in Times Square," a jaunty blues strut.

He was feeling the Zeitgeist again. David Amram was composing the soundtrack for *Pull My Daisy*, an improvised Beat classic starring Kerouac, Ginsberg, and Burroughs.

They were all trying everything. Larry Rivers played sax and wrote tributes to Monk. Kerouac painted and sang. Amram drew and wrote poetry. Ginsberg became a photographer.

Mingus wanted to write a book. He talked his history constantly, and it became mythic in his telling. He understood the autobiographical impulses firing the Beats. Sitting at the kitchen table at West 51st Street, he neatly printed hundreds of pages of stream of consciousness. Some of it was straight autobiography, and some was reimagined.

One early plot centered on Lynn, a white girl throwing money around at Billy Berg's club during the Stars of Swing gig there. She wants Mingus, and Buddy Collette tells him to play hard to get. Britt Woodman repeatedly plays wiseass under his breath—a Wellesian leitmotif. Mingus hangs tough, and scores $500 from Lynn.

During the next band break, drummer Oscar Bradley says he's balling Buddy's wife Lou. Buddy overhears, and, to the others' surprise, wants cash. Can't stop 'em from doing what they're gonna, he says, so might as well collect.[11]

In August 1957, Mingus cut *East Coasting*, the first of two Bethlehem albums, with Bill Evans. The session cost $1048.16.[12]

The title track, laced with a typical long-lined melody, was set in an unusual key, so the musicians couldn't play cliches. "West Coast Ghost" opened with layered, sparring riffs over a single chord, then shifted to a ballad section. "Conversation" pivoted on short instrumental exchanges.

Mingus opened the disc with a starkly plaintive "Memories of You" that featured a long bass solo. These days, Celia and he rarely spoke.

By fall, Diane Dorr-Dorynek, another five-foot four-inch white blonde, was taking care of his correspondence for Jazz Workshop Inc., which he'd set up that April. She was paid $40 a week.[13] Her father was a military man, but she was a talented painter in a largely male preserve. She also worked as a photographer and writer, although Mingus told Jimmy Knepper she was a high-class geisha, and told others he was going to turn her out.

She was part of the scene, and knew pianist Freddie Redd well, and lived in a place on East 25th Street that was covered with roaches. She became Mingus's assistant and picked up Celia's tasks, like writing his publicity and liner notes and typing up his lengthening autobiography.

Diane was very smart and very beautiful. At times she had a self-possessed air, although others found her vulnerable, delicate, nervous, uncomfortable around people. She had no girlfriends. She adored Stravinsky and Debussy, and she loved Mingus music.

Bethlehem paid him a 5 percent royalty on a three-year deal for three LPs. His first annual advance was $2,000, and each year added another $1,000 if the option was taken to record.[14]

He was separating himself from Celia and Debut, getting his outs ready.

Norman Mailer, author of the acclaimed novel *The Naked and the Dead*, published a controversial essay called "The White Negro." Mailer, no Beat, hung out on the jazz scene and was a Mingus fan.

Mailer's essay was grandiose and flawed and insightful. In it, the cultural inversion boppers had sought was complete. Blacks, no longer parodied as Stepin Fetchits, were the epitome of cool, of spontaneity, of what Mailer called "philosophical psychopaths," because they were outside society's values. They were the models for hipsters, what Mailer called White Negroes. They were "crazy."

It was heady and Romantic stuff, full of racial stereotypes no less condescending for being positive. It was in the European post-Enlightenment tradition of the Noble Savage, where the peoples "discovered" by explorers were thought more in tune with nature and life precisely because they weren't, as Huck Finn would say, "sivilised."

Mingus found attitudes like Mailer's insulting but revealing. He faced them again and again. He resented condescension but knew how to use guilt. It was a kind of fear, and it could give him the upper hand.

The civil rights movement was taking center stage in social debate. In 1957, Congress passed the first federal civil rights legislation since Reconstruction. It created the Civil Rights Division in the Justice Department and the Commission on Civil Rights. In 1954, the Supreme Court had ordered schools desegregated with all deliberate speed. This caused confrontations between several southern governors, who refused and called out National Guard troops, and the federal government, which sent in federal troops and Justice Department lawyers. Martin Luther King Jr. became the first president of the Southern Christian Leadership Conference, which catalyzed and coordinated nonviolent civil rights demonstrations across the South.

Mingus's family in Jamaica liked Celia, and they consoled him about the fights with his pregnant wife. He spent a lot of time at the piano with his Uncle Fess, working on a piece he tried at the Bohemia in September. It had a clunky, vaudeville intro and an oily B section. It was a parody, and he called it "Fables of Faubus."

He liked his history to be mythic. The legend says "Fables" was born on the bandstand, when Dannie Richmond improvised the name Orville Faubus to respond to Mingus's onstage query, "Who is it that's ridiculous?" Faubus was governor of Arkansas. An alumnus of the same blacklisted school as the witch-hunted Pete Seeger, he had stood symbolically in a schoolhouse door to bar black kids from entering.

Legend says Mingus went into an onstage tirade about what a drag it was to tour the South with a white guy, Jimmy Knepper, in the band. But the band hadn't been south of New Jersey and Pennsylvania.

Asked about that on a brief West Coast tour, he barked, "Don't mess with my act." He never forgot what Thelonious Monk said at Birdland when Bird and Bud Powell broke down onstage. Monk understood, with his prolonged silences and his spinning dances onstage and his crazy hats and his soul full of irony and blues.

Monk was a peer. He too was a large and imposing presence. He too was a composer, not a bopper. His music too was impossible to read, and his sidemen also complained bitterly. Monk, however, had Nica.

In October 1957, Mingus recorded his second Bethlehem album, entitled *A Modern Jazz Symposium of Music and Poetry with Charles Mingus*. It featured

"Scenes in the City," an ambitious piece with tempo changes and hand claps and narration by actor Melvin Stewart that spoke of black feelings in a hostile environment.

"Nuuroog" was written for one of the succession of blonde coeds and bohemians at his gigs.

The session cost $1,247.99.[15]

In November, he started the first of the Workshop stints at the Half Note, owned by Mike and Sonny Canterino. Later he'd write about it as the Fast Buck, and rename Mike Canterino Mr. Caligari, an allusion to the arty, breakthrough 1920 German expressionist film *The Cabinet of Dr. Caligari*, about an insane asylum.[16]

The Half Note, a small club on Hudson and Spring Streets, had just opened on the street floor of one of the commercial loft buildings that filled the neighborhood. It was an odd setup.

You entered the back room, where a riser held tables, and the kitchen and bathrooms were off the corridor. The front room was a little larger. The two rooms were separated by a bar across the club's middle. The stage was on a platform above the bar, so that if you were sitting at the bar or in the room behind it, you saw the band's backs. But you could see and hear from everywhere.

In Birdlike mode, Mingus went in and told Canterino he could fill the place for him. He opened with Jean Shepherd performing "The Clown." Pianist Horace Parlan, whose right hand was partly paralyzed from childhood polio, joined them. Shafi Hadi and Jimmy Knepper and Dannie Richmond filled the other chairs, although there was a rotating cast. Richmond got busted. Shafi Hadi had constant trouble with his cabaret card. Every night, it seemed, the cops would come in and demand to look at the club notebook where the cards were stored during a band's run. If they wanted, they could just yank a musician off the bandstand.

Some of it was about paying off the law. Hadi kept changing his name: Curtis Porter, Leon Rice.

The club was filled with pot smoking and varied drug use. Mingus didn't preach about it, but he didn't like the smell and periodically suggested the smokers take it outside. But he'd hire strung-out players if they were good for his music, even if he had to hassle them.

The Workshop stayed twelve weeks.

Here he met Maureen Meloy, who went to see him with a couple of girlfriends. Just out of school, she'd trained herself to listen to jazz by tuning into local radio station WNEW and disk jockey Martin Block, and she knew a lot about swing bands and Dixieland. And she fit Mingus's female profile: five-and-a-half feet, delicate features, sandy hair. He zeroed in on her, told her she reminded him of his beloved fourth-grade teacher, and after a quick sexual dalliance they became friends.

MAUREEN MELOY, *friend*: If he could have slowed down to put his life together, he could have had a Ph.D. in almost anything, because he was interested in so many different things. But he was also so undisciplined he never followed any of it through. He would read, but not really. He would listen to music, but not really. Because he was also busy trying to perform, to write, to have all these . . . interactions, periodically being a victim.

There were others obviously having parallel relationships with him. They could have been sitting at the next table, though, and you would never know it. I think it's obvious that every female who was involved with Mingus, whether it was one night or one week or whatever, a lot of them floated away, but the ones who really bought into the music—that was the most important thing. Everybody was available for the plucking. The sex, the flirtations, were sort of a rite of passage. Because he put it out, he emanated all of this. He would be playing for fifteen women in the same room at the same time, but never at the expense of the music.

When it was over, not that six weeks was true devotion, I remember thinking, "Oh my God, the music, I can't give that up." Then you show up, and it's a week since you've been with him, then four months, then seven years, then it didn't matter because you became part of this big rolling ball.

Melodies were pouring out of him, in the gospel-jazz mode of "Haitian Fight Song." "Better Get it In Your Soul" and "Wednesday Night Prayer Meeting" shared the ecstatic roots and a 6/8 rhythm that made them intoxicating.

He caught the ferocity of a Baptist church, its call and response, its canons, its rippling rhythms as the congregation strove for rough unison of individuals rather than unanimity. He remade those ingredients into improvised intensity.

The musicians complained that they got lost: the pieces all started with bass solos, and there was no way to tell them apart. Sometimes he'd deliberately cross them up.

Audiences adored the fervor, the slop, the human immediacy of it. They reacted to the drama. It was part of the act, but it was real. He could seize any platform, but this was his pulpit.

Mingus was in and out of San Francisco all the time. Ralph Gleason had a TV show called *Jazz Casual,* and he went on it. He visited Farwell and

Kate Mulholland, who'd moved to a huge house on a Berkeley hill. Kate and Gleason introduced him to Philip Elwood, a Pacifica Radio host. They spent afternoons listening to Elwood's 78s of Jelly Roll Morton.

He hit the Black Hawk with Bunky Green and Freddie Redd. A twenty-three-year-old saxist named John Handy borrowed a baritone and sat in. Mingus loved that particular horn, and liked the cocky young man. He told Handy to call when he got to the Apple.

After he returned before Christmas, Mingus and Celia, now nine months' pregnant, resumed fighting. So when her mother came in from California to be with her for her first child's birth, she left him. Mother and daughter moved into a hotel suite, without telling Mingus where.

She went into labor on December 30, and had Dorian the next day, at Flower and Fifth Avenue Hospital. Celia's mother, against her daughter's wishes, called Mingus, who showed up shortly after the baby was born at 5:00 P.M. When Celia was coming to in the recovery room, he strolled in nonchalantly. He'd already seen the baby.

MAUREEN MELOY: He and Celia were really disaffected at that point. I asked him the baby's name, and he said, "Ah, she's got some name for him, Darwin or something."

Still, he kept visiting mother and child in the hospital, and brought her a Japanese portable record player and some of his records. But when she was discharged, she took the baby and went to the Coss's Flushing apartment.

There were complications. One night Jimmy Knepper and his family visited the Coss's, and Celia hemorrhaged in the bathroom. She had to go back to the hospital for blood transfusions, which made Mingus frantic. For a few weeks, he called her daily and pleaded with her to come home with his son. She finally agreed to move back into their apartment, but she also had a separation agreement drawn up.

Friends of theirs and the Eagles, Marvin and Rhoda Karpatkin, were lawyers. He represented Mingus; she represented Celia. He was volatile, endlessly demanding. She was feeling cornered, with dim glimmers of doom hovering. Too much kept going wrong.

The Karpatkins set up such an airtight agreement that it could easily become a divorce settlement.

Max Gordon, short, feisty, acid-tongued, owned the Village Vanguard, the trapezoid-shaped club down a steep flight of stairs from its door on Seventh Avenue South and West 11th Street.

Gordon was a rarity—a New York club owner born in Lithuania, with a B.A. in literature from Reed College and dreams of being a writer.[17] In 1926 he came to New York to get a law degree from Columbia while teaching English to immigrants. Instead he moved to the Village, and hung out nights at Stewart's Cafeteria on Sheridan Square and clubs like Paul's Rendezvous on Wooster Street, where he got hooked on bohemians and poets and artists and the leftish political and social atmosphere.

In 1934, Gordon opened the Village Vanguard on Charles Street without a cabaret license. It cost $50 a year, and he figured poets taking turns onstage and in the seats didn't really need one. Besides, if he got one, the poets would all have to be fingerprinted in order to perform, and they wouldn't do it, he knew.

His first night open, two cops showed up to close the Vanguard. When Gordon went to court, he explained his club featured poetry, not entertainment, and the case was dismissed.

A year later, he moved the club to Seventh Avenue South, but kept the poets and the scene's leftist bohemian politics. In 1939, a blonde girl who worked the switchboard at Orson Welles's Mercury Theatre told Gordon about a play she'd been working on with a few pals. Her name was Judy Holliday, and her pals included Betty Comden and Adolph Green. In 1941, Gordon began booking folksingers like Huddie "Leadbelly" Ledbetter and Josh White, and became pals with Woody Guthrie. In the 1950s, he showcased Harry Belafonte. In 1961, Lenny Bruce opened there, climbing toward the peak of his popularity. The club was eclectic, like the Village at its best, which meant that jazz arrived on the Vanguard stage in the 1950s.

When Mingus first came into the Vanguard, Jimmy Giuffre, a leading figure of the 1950s cool-jazz movement, was leading a trio, playing what he called "Swamp Jazz." Mingus listened for half an hour, then propositioned Gordon: "Let me bring my band over next Sunday so you can hear some jazz."

MAX GORDON: He looked at the small, dedicated Swamp Jazz audience down in front, snorted, and gave the downbeat and let go with his first number. The volume, the intensity, the blistering attack of the music made me gasp. I'd never heard Mingus before.[18]

Early in 1958, the Workshop spent two weeks at the Vanguard, sharing the bill with monologist Professor Irwin Corey. Corey improvised routines, flights of verbal fancy laced with bad puns. Mingus lambasted him for repeating essentially the same routine over and over. "That's not real improvising," he told friends as well as Corey himself.

Elvin Jones was on drums, and Mingus picked up his thick drum sticks. "The ones Dannie uses are like pencils," he complained. But Richmond was hooked on heroin, and from now on, there were times he was busted or couldn't work. Mingus tolerated Dannie's addiction as he did few others. He needed him. He'd taught Richmond to be the perfect drummer, the other half of his heartbeat.

And yet there were times, even with Dannie, when he'd had it. Once, when Dannie got busted in Vancouver, Mingus said, "Fuck that, he did it, so he's in jail." He headed back to the Bay Area, and told Kate Mulholland about it.

KATE MULHOLLAND: Charles just walked away. He was totally disapproving. He became like his father, harsh and judgmental. A friend of mine bailed Dannie out instead.

In March 1958, Mingus recorded with Langston Hughes. They'd known each other since 1956, when Hughes saw the Workshop's set at Newport and wrote it up glowingly in the Chicago *Defender*. Celia sent him a copy of *Pithecanthropus Erectus* when it was released.

Hughes had just published *The Book of Negro Folklore*, which he edited with Arna Bontemps. Leonard Feather, a civil rights supporter, wanted to connect jazz with the movement. He would produce a record and write music for one side to accompany Hughes. He asked Mingus to write the other.

Hughes's light baritone voice is masterfully backed by the Workshop's urgent interactions on side two. Minus Richmond, the Workshop recorded as the Horace Parlan Quintet. But it was Mingus music.

He played a lot of arco bass, his voice conversing with Hughes's in countermelodies. The band segued through episodic pieces that recalled "Pithecanthropus Erectus" and "The Clown." Onomatopoeic effects and hand claps punctuate gospel feels. An alarm clock goes off during "Dream Montage."

"What happens to a dream deferred?" asked Hughes, in his most famous lines. "Does it shrivel like a raisin in the sun?"

Dr. Martin Luther King Jr. was stabbed and nearly killed on a speaking tour for his first book, *Stride toward Freedom*.

Trumpeter Gene Shaw, booked for the Mingus session, got the flu and tried to call him, but Mingus's phone was busy for hours. When Mingus called him, he threatened to have Shaw killed by the mob. The next day, Celia called Shaw back and told him Mingus had left the phone off the hook. Mingus cycled through the apologies and praise songs that usually followed his blowups. "I didn't mean any of those things," he said, as he would dozens of times. Shaw refused to rejoin the Workshop.

Shaw didn't know that Dorian had developed a throat abscess and a 105-degree fever. Mingus and Celia raced him across the street to New York Polyclinic. At first, the doctors thought the baby had meningitis, a potentially fatal condition for an infant, and the new parents were terrified.

Mingus made the papers on March 7, when columnist Dorothy Kilgallen reported in the New York *Post* that he'd slugged Alonzo Levister at the Bohemia.[19] He thought Lonnie was coming on to Celia. First they exchanged words, then they broke some chairs and glasses. Jimmy Garofalo called the cops, though Celia pleaded with him not to, because of Dorian's condition.

After a couple of weeks, the baby was well enough to come home, but almost immediately Celia was rushed to Polyclinic for an allergic reaction to the penicillin shot she'd received for a strep throat.

CELIA MINGUS ZAENTZ: I had all these harbingers of doom. I felt if I didn't leave New York immediately, something really terrible and final would occur.

So on their seventh anniversary, Celia left in the dead of night, while he was on a gig. Martha Glaser, who booked and managed prominent jazz musicians like Erroll Garner, suggested that the Eagles take Celia and Dorian to a hotel. She staked mother and child $35 for the hotel and a taxi to LaGuardia airport, where they took a 6:00 A.M. flight to San Francisco.

Celia swore them all to secrecy. She didn't want Mingus coming after her, didn't want to be persuaded to come back. She'd had enough of his jealous fantasies, his infidelities, his rages.

Without Celia, Debut ground almost instantly to a halt. The union claimed payments hadn't been made. Max Roach demanded an accounting, and Mingus didn't deliver one. Roach felt he'd been subsidizing the label from the successful Roach-Brown Quintet, and he wanted a statement. Then Mingus and Diane Dorr-Dorynek leased some sides by Jimmy Knepper to a Danish label also named Debut.[20]

Roach exploded. For a year or more they fought as much as they conspired.

Mingus seemed disdainful of Roach because Margo Ferris had supported him on her back through the lean years. But at the same time, he also seemed to admire Roach for it.

Mingus led the Workshop back into the Half Note, where the noise level approached bedlam and drowned out his music. One night, he used a record player onstage while the band read and played cards.

For $800, the Workshop performed with poet Kenneth Patchen at the Living Theater,[21] part of a series that preceded the off-Broadway troupe's premiere of *The Connection*, a probing look at drugs and jazz. They toured briefly with Patchen, weaving textures from the musical fragments he gave them, as they'd done on *The Clown*.

Mingus did a month of Sunday afternoons at the Vanguard, with Langston Hughes. Maureen Meloy salvaged one of the poems Hughes read, "Wait a Minute, River," from a typed sheet left at the club.

LANGSTON HUGHES, *poet*: Wait a minute, river/Wait a minute, steamboat of Time/Where are you going?/Where are you going?/Where have you gone? ... Hear my old piano on the way/Hear my barrelhouse horn down by the docks/Hear my trombone on a holiday/Hear that old bass man play.[22]

The musical cues were self-evident.

Mingus was unhappy with some of Hughes's poetry: it was too lyric, too old-fashioned. He was more intrigued by what Patchen and Kenneth Rexroth and other poets like them were doing. So in May, he returned to the Half Note with actor Melvin Stewart doing readings, till mid-June.

The college debutantes were coming out. He liked their attention, and they gave him willing ears. He talked to them about education and race, music and art and philosophy and religion, boyfriend problems. He held forth, and they sat in awe. Most he limited to between-sets meetings in the dressing room. Some he fantasized about. They were flirting with rebellion, though for most their trust funds ranked higher than a night with a black jazzman. But the cops still came around. At least one complained that Mingus encouraged miscegenation.[23]

He began making speeches attacking white liberals as racists. In Baltimore, he announced that a white club owner was ripping him off and played only ballads to punish him. Audiences loved the guilty pleasures of his racial thrusts. Their reactions were expected, part of the act, like Miles soloing with his back to the fans.

There were many nights at the subterranean Village Vanguard when the crowd got all it came for.

He demanded cash up front. When Gordon gave him less than he wanted, he threw it into the air and pulled a knife. "So what," said Gordon. He knew Mingus wouldn't use it. Dannie Richmond bent down and scooped up the bills.

There wasn't enough cash to pay him, so he chased Gordon, half his size, upstairs, brandishing a broom. Gordon immediately booked him back.

No one took it seriously. It was who he was. It was part of his act.

Once, he walked over to Gordon at the bar, deftly picked up his cigar, puffed, returned it, and said, "I love you, you bastard." [24]

MAX GORDON: Charlie was funny like that. He felt exploited. If he worked for you, you were exploiting him. The money you paid him was never enough. Maybe it wasn't. [25]

In July 1958, the Willard Alexander Agency dropped Mingus. Celia was gone, and they said he was too difficult. And so he was. They wanted to keep the band on the road, and build audiences. He wanted to play better clubs and halls. He didn't like hopping from Maryland to Chicago to Philadelphia; he wanted his tours better planned.

He found out that RCA was scrapping jazz, so hope evaporated for release of *Tijuana Moods*. Then Bethlehem dropped him; his first LP for them didn't earn its advance.

In August, the Workshop played the short-lived Great South Bay Fest on Long Island, and Whitney Balliett gave it a glowing write-up in the *New Yorker*. [26]

Right afterward, Diane Dorr-Dorynek wrote to Buddy Collette, suggesting that he buy Max Roach's share in Debut for $1,000. She mentioned the Great South Bay Festival, where the Workshop had appeared with poet/actor Melvin Stewart. Stewart read from his own work, *The Poet*, and did Mingus's recitative "Suite Freedom." The musicians got $200 apiece.

When their set ended, Mingus stood behind the tent's flap with his bass and played along with Duke Ellington's Orchestra, which had Britt Woodman on trombone. [27]

Mingus wasn't working enough to keep his musicians from taking other gigs. The Workshop went to Baltimore or Boston for a week, then nothing for a month. New York was sporadic. That year, Jimmy Knepper made less than $2,000 from Workshop jobs.

Dannie Richmond saw pictures of the thin Mingus, handsome and half-naked, posed with three half-naked women in a porn magazine. Mingus told him he took jobs as a male model when things were tight. [28]

That summer, Art Kane, a young photographer on his maiden voyage for *Esquire*, wanted to stage a mammoth group shot in Harlem of New York jazz musicians for a big feature celebrating the music's reemergence into the American cultural mainstream. So he put the word out, via scene makers like Nat Hentoff. What resulted was beyond anybody's expectations.

The roll call that day was a Who's Who: Count Basie, Willie "The Lion" Smith, Coleman Hawkins, Lester Young, Sonny Rollins, Dizzy Gillespie, Thelonious Monk, Mary Lou Williams, Hank Jones, Marian McPartland, Charlie Mingus, Art Blakey, Gerry Mulligan, Horace Silver—fifty-eight in all.

The photo shoot, however, was a comedy of errors that came out a triumph. Kane's neophyte assistant first loaded his film backward. The shutterbug tried for hours to get the attention of the slightly sleepy, happily milling throng he'd conjured up. Nobody had expected that many jazzers to show up at 10:00 A.M. As one eyewitness quips, "Most of them didn't realize there were two ten o'-clocks in the same day." [29]

Mingus had been hanging out with Peggy Hitchcock. The young blonde and her brother Billy loved jazz and were fascinated by the postwar demimonde. They were part of the monied Mellon family, with a Park Avenue address.

Mingus wrote "Peggy's Blue Skylight" for her on her piano, a yearning melody revamped from "Reincarnation of a Lovebird." He never used an idea only once.

Peggy Hitchcock wanted to use a blue fighter-plane cockpit shield for her skylight, so the sky would always be blue. The government wouldn't let her. He had a crush on her, but they stayed friends. She hosted soirees where artists like Allen Ginsberg mingled. A professor from Harvard named Timothy Leary, who was doing psychological research into drugs, showed up.

Mingus wanted more. He needed love.

ANN MCINTOSH, *friend*: It was fall 1958 that he met Sue Scott. She was a friend of mine from Vassar. I brought her to New York for the weekend, and he immediately fell wildly in love with her. Obsessively wildly. And this was not reciprocated. She knew he was a genius, but she was a WASP from Connecticut at Vassar. He always fell in love with these blonde WASP types. But she was seventeen and real straight.

His desperation about her would escalate.

In fall 1958 he signed himself into Bellevue Hospital on Manhattan's East Side. The System's psychiatric web didn't snare him; he walked into it. He told different versions of why, Rashomon-like, creating fables.

One story said he was avoiding Joey Gallo. Gallo wanted to record him, and he'd agreed, not knowing who "Crazy Joe" was—a killer mobster. He figured Gallo was another version of Mo Levy. Levy told him different, and he got scared.[30]

Another story ran that he wanted to be certified as crazy. That certificate could get you out of things. Bud and Bird each had one. It meant you weren't responsible.

Mingus needed help. He felt more vulnerable than ever. He stuffed bills into drawers. He was lean and mean. The drugs kept him going, but his mind was unraveling, and he had psychotic outbreaks. He had to get some sleep, and thought he could check himself in for a sedated rest. Degrees and lab coats spelled authority and calm.

They had him fill out forms and led him inside. Then he discovered he couldn't sign himself out. He was diagnosed a paranoid schizophrenic, like Kerouac and Ginsberg and Bud Powell and countless others. After all, he was black and potentially violent. He later told Knepper they threatened him with a lobotomy and electro-shock; he told others he was handcuffed when he entered.

He used the pay phone to call Hentoff, his family in Queens, Celia, the Karpatkins, Morris Eagle.

He tried to organize the patients into group activities. When he asked for blackboard and chalk, one doctor wrote, "May I comment that compulsive organization is one of the prime traits of paranoia."[31]

That group approach to therapy later became standard. Mingus was ahead of his time.

Hentoff called Dr. Pollock, and the psychologist went to Bellevue and assured them Mingus was over his violent outbursts. After they let him out, he shared an apartment with his cousin Phil for a while, to get back on his feet financially and emotionally. And he wrote "Hellview from Bellevue," a fiercely anguished piece he later retitled, "Lock 'em up."

For the next few years, he saw Pollock erratically. He'd show up for a few weeks, and they'd talk. These were not therapy sessions. Pollock just listened while Mingus poured out his soul. He was unloved, alone, in pain. His father and stepmother had never loved him. He was alienated from everyone. He wanted to be the center of attention. He was overlooked within his field and in the larger world. He never truly loved anyone.

Mingus wouldn't show up for months, then he'd call or drop by, and the conversations would pick up where they'd stopped.

In November 1958, he returned to the Half Note for five weeks. There he bailed Dannie Richmond out once, and hired Booker Ervin.

The tenor saxist was invaluable. His Rollins-inflected solos had crisp and

broad-reaching authority. He was sympathetic to Mingus's unwritten compositions, and his musical memory was so precise that he remembered everyone
else's parts too. He held things together in the Mingus hurricane.

The original Five Spot, a small room on Cooper Square between Fourth and
Fifth Streets, was a bit like the Café Bohemia. It was a five-minute walk from
the Cedar Tavern, meeting place for the writers and artists, who were being
forced out of Greenwich Village by rising rents and were moving to the Bowery
and what would be renamed the East Village.

The Termini family had run a neighborhood Bowery bar for twenty-five
years. Brothers Joe and Iggy Termini, back from World War II, took it over.
Gradually, the city tore down the old elevated trains and the neighborhood saw
daylight. Meanwhile came the waves of relocating artists, who eventually convinced the Terminis to book live jazz.

Bums still sometimes wandered in off the street to panhandle. But the walls
were covered with flyers for gallery shows and jazz gigs and poetry readings.

Mingus wasn't the first act in the Five Spot, but he moved in fast, Christ-
mas week 1958. The converted bar held eighty people. He packed in 110.
Eventually, his groups were paid as much as $1,500 a week, almost twice what
Monk's got.

The Five Spot gigs, starting with a summer 1957 run with a quartet that included the young John Coltrane, resuscitated Thelonious Monk's reputation.
For years, he'd been ignored or patronized; musicians and critics alike dismissed him as a primitive who could barely play. Now, it was clear, they
couldn't. Monk's audience grew, along with his fame for odd headgear and
weird glasses and gyring dances onstage, where he seemed somehow to be
conducting the band.

Willem de Kooning, Franz Kline, Kerouac, Ginsberg, Larry Rivers, Brendan
Behan, Orson Bean, Barney Rosset—these are just a few of the emergent underground figures who hung at the Five Spot.

Kerouac got tossed out for filling his wine glass from a bottle he brought in.
For weeks, every time he came back, Joe Termini glared at him and threw him
out, until he finally befriended the cowed writer. Ginsberg, famed in the pages
of *Newsweek*, stood alone in the rain until Termini waved him in and bought
him a beer.

Joe and Iggy weren't mobsters, although like Garofalo and Canterino and
Levy they knew who was who. But they were Italians, so boss also meant
padrone—patron. The Terminis loved Monk and Mingus, and admired their
music. They enjoyed jousting with eccentricity. They took care of their musicians. It was a dirty business with a human face.

Mingus was running his own show. People came to watch him erupt on stage, to see the band start and stop, to hear him recompose arrangments and even pieces on the spot.

Like Ginsberg, he became an attraction. He knew how to appeal to audiences. He'd shave his head, grow a beard, bring in props, dress for the stage in anything from Mexican sombreros and serapes to Chinese robes to African dashikis to bankers' suits to old checked shirts and jeans. But whatever he did, it was also real. He was totally on, completely in the moment. And he didn't like audiences interrupting his art.

That brought on a speech at the Five Spot.

CHARLES MINGUS: You, my audience, are all a bunch of poppaloppers. A bunch of tumbling weeds, tumbling 'round, running from your subconscious unconscious minds. . . . Minds? Minds that won't let you stop to listen to a word of artistic or meaningful truth. . . . So you come to me, you sit in the front row, as noisy as can be. I listen to your millions of conversations, sometimes pulling them all up together and writing a symphony. But you never hear that symphony. . . . You haven't been told before that you're phonies. You're here because jazz is popular, jazz has publicity and you like to associate yourself with this sort of thing. But it doesn't make you a connoisseur of the art because you follow it around. You're dilettantes of style. A blind man can go to an exhibition of Picasso and Kline and not even see what works. And comment behind dark glasses. Wow! They're the swingingest painters ever, crazy! Well, so can you. You've got your dark glasses and clogged-up ears. . . . You become the object you came to see, and you think you're important and digging jazz when all the time all you're doing is digging a blind, deaf scene that has nothing to do with any kind of music at all. [Editor's comment: Mingus's comments should be required reading for all jazz club audiences.][32]

Poppaloppers is not what he said. Diane Dorr-Dorynek copied down Mingus's full homily.

Painter Franz Kline was a good friend who worked to Mingus music. He used a house painter's brushes to wield thick bold lines, often stark black, that were his gestural language, his equivalent of Pollock's drips and de Kooning's sign painter's strokes. Like them, he was bringing new tools and materials into fine art. It was pragmatic improvisation.

One of his works, *Blue Center*, mirrored Mingus pieces like "Haitian Fight Song": it was structured around a handful of varied visual riffs that recalled the bridges and els of Kline's earlier work as an Ashcan School urban landscapist. His famed 1949 painting of Nijinsky portrayed the dancer as a clown.

Like his friend Mingus's music, Kline's art was abstract with its roots in realism, and his predominant dirty blacks and whites evoked the manufacturing
lofts many artists lived in.

Like the Beats, Kline and other New York School painters saw themselves
delving into the unconscious.

Diane Dorr-Dorynek and Mingus got a place together at 8 East 76th Street off
Fifth Ave. It was a chic and uppercrust part of town, a few blocks from the
Metropolitan Museum. The huge studio in a mansion had high ceilings and
gorgeous old carved marble fireplaces. He told everyone it had been Eleanor
Roosevelt's. In fact, it had been her cousin's, the site where FDR and Eleanor
married on March 17, 1905.

Mingus still had Big Kitty. He began piling his manuscripts and music
around. He stuffed bills and checks made out to him for less than $10 into
drawers and nooks, and moved in his piano.

DANNIE RICHMOND: In the early years, when we had to take gigs—any gig—
to keep going, it was always good to have a dame around who could bring in a
few bucks.[33]

That fall, John Handy roved the scene, jamming around, working with Randy
Weston. At the Five Spot in December 1958, he played in the break for Frank
Foster and Thad Jones. Mingus was standing at the bar. Handy got off. Noth-
ing happened; Jones hadn't arrived.

JOHN HANDY, *musician:* He started in: "Hey man, why don't y'all let this guy
play?" It was loud; everybody heard it. So Frank got nervous and said, "He can
play if he wants to." And I got up and played. Every time I took a solo Mingus
was jumping out of his seat. "Bird is back," he said. I was embarrassed, man. It
was positive but embarrassing. I'd heard about his antics, and he was doing it
to me. So he says, "Hey baby, you working anywhere?" I just shook my head. He
said, "Well, you open with me here, in two weeks." And we opened opposite
Sonny Rollins.

A week into the Five Spot gig, Dannie Richmond got busted. Drummer Roy
Haynes finished out the month. On piano was Horace Parlan. Mingus made
cracks like, "I only hired him because he's handicapped." Booker Ervin played
tenor, as did Handy for a while, although his usual ax was alto.

Rollins started showing up late for his sets, because Mingus was stretching
the Workshop's time longer and longer. Sometimes he didn't show up at all.

One night, John Coltrane sat in with Rollins's group. Another night, Mingus verbally pushed Handy into filling Rollins's chair.

He and Sonny were old friends. When Rollins kicked heroin, Mingus helped keep the younger man straight. He confronted junkies and told them to leave Sonny alone.

But Handy felt his boss was hogging the time. He was an unstable bully. One night, he tried to intimidate Handy, standing with his hands folded on top of his bass's head, appearing to rest all his weight on it, and thrusting his face into Handy's.

JOHN HANDY: It was like hitting me. I said, "Mingus, I can hit a lot faster with this saxophone than you can with that bass. And if something happens, you'll have to watch everywhere you go." He started laughing and said, "You're crazy." So we both laughed. And I'm not sure how serious I was, but I threw it out there, because I think that's what I would've done if somebody hit me in the mouth.

It wasn't that he was evil; he had a mental problem. He hadn't grown up, in some ways.

Sidemen from Britt Woodman to Mal Waldron to Jackie McLean agree.

It's an old saw that geniuses and artists are basically children. They can keep the sense of wonder that makes the world new when you're young, and translate it into something that makes their audiences wonder yet again.

One night, Mingus came running out of the Five Spot's kitchen with a cleaver at a group at a table right by the stage. They were talking during his set. The club was half-empty, but he chased them out.

Orson Welles had made *Touch of Evil*, his first try at a Hollywood feature in a decade. It opens brilliantly, with a lengthy tracking shot, a dazzling tour de force.

The movie is set in a Mexican border town, much like Mingus's still unissued RCA album. Welles himself plays Hank Quinlan, an American cop gone bad. He is disgustingly fat. His face makeup creates bags and pouches everywhere. Quinlan tries to frame Charlton Heston, a brown-skinned Mexican antinarcotics official, and his very white American wife, Janet Leigh, on a drug-and-bombing rap, in a tangled net of border racism and politics.

For Welles, Mingus, Jackson Pollock, Jack Kerouac, and other American artists then, Mexico represented the Other, North America's prickly Latin underbelly with a history of revolution and repression. Populist muralists like Diego Rivera who inspired Pollock arose in the Depression Era out of resurgent Mexican nationalism, and inspired other WPA artists. Kerouac saw Mexico as a place of near-natural purity and potential rebirth, where man wasn't isolated from himself, had to face his nature and nature itself. Welles saw it refracted in a border town as through a funhouse mirror, distorted and thus more deeply revealing.

For Mingus, Mexico was a musical release and challenge. He loved the Spanish guitars, the clipped rhythms, the yearning operatic voices. He was born on the border, and grew up near it. He had family from New Mexico that spoke Mexican, and often said he was Mexican himself.

Henry Mancini, master of jazz noir sound tracks, wrote the angular, atmospheric score for Welles's film. The way some of his ensemble voicings trail off comes straight out of Ellington via Mingus.

Mingus was thinner. He was perpetually in motion.

8 *Mingus Dynasty*

JANUARY 1959 brought snow.

One bitter night between sets at the Five Spot, Charles Mingus told his sidemen to pack their gear and follow him through the icy slush a few blocks, to the Nonagon Art Gallery. Joe Termini shrugged: Charlie was Charlie, and they loved him more than anybody but Monk.

Horace Parlan was out of town, so pianist Richard Wyands met them at an old row house off Second Avenue. The gallery was in a second-floor room filled with beams, heavy chandeliers, and a marble fireplace; it hosted a concert series that included composers like Milton Babbitt. The artwork, Whitney Balliett wrote, was full of unicorns and lions; he compared it to "a Hohenzollern hunting lodge."[1]

The musicians got $24.54 apiece.[2]

The show was recorded by MGM. They mixed new and old material: Ellington's "A Train," "Jelly Roll Jollies" (later renamed "My Jelly Roll Soul"), "Alice's Wonderland" (the long piece of contrapuntal melodies originally intended for *Shadows*), and "I Can't Get Started," one of Mingus's favorite standards since his teens. They rocked the staid gallery out with "Wednesday Night Prayer Meeting."

The program notes stated, "Specific works and order are contingent on the rapport between performers and audience and are thus not listed in advance. Both performers and audience will help shape the evening."[3]

Handy was in top form, his mercurial Bird-like lines darting fluidly, pecking out unusual notes in unpredictable rhythms, unleashing split tones that buzzed and burred. Ervin's own blend of rhythm-and-blues raunch and fleet bebop kicked.

And Mingus was on. On "Nostalgia in Times Square," his thrusting bass solo becomes almost pure abstraction in spots, then suddenly interpolates a quote—"Dixie" is one—that deliberately upends the mood. On "Started," he twists the rhythms into self-assured knots, dropping in phrases like "Nobody Knows the Trouble I've Seen."

He dubbed one tune "No Private Income Blues." That would get the up-scale crowd's attention.

Nat Hentoff wrote the liner notes, as he did for many Mingus albums. He's erroneously been credited as producer.

JOE TERMINI, *club owner*: Charlie kept running over an hour. We were really packed, line running around the block. So I finally signal to him, "Charlie, cut it." He says, "Ladies and gentlemen, in honor of Joe Termini, who's such a greedy guy, who wants to get more customers in here, I quit." And he walks off the stage.

Now, the week before I'd let him walk, because he had that concert to do. He says, "Give me my money from last week, I'm quitting." I said, "Come back and we'll talk about it." "No, I want my money right now." "Look Charlie," I said, "don't bother me. You quit, you quit. I let you off last week." We're arguing back and forth. So he says, "You don't give me my money, I'm gonna get my car and drive it right through your window." "Charlie," I says, "if you do that, one of us will be dead when this is through. 'Cause now I'm mad." We go back and forth. Finally he walked away, still mad.

An hour or two later, he knew what he'd done wrong. "Please forgive me, I'm sorry"; called up my brother Iggy at his house. He was that kinda guy.

Diane Dorr-Dorynek had closed their deal with a Danish company to distribute part of the U.S. catalog. That upset Debut's other shareholders. Mingus wanted to sell more shares to raise capital, and wanted Max Roach to sell his share. Celia refused to sell hers. Instead, she wanted to lease the Debut masters to raise money.

After working with Mingus on Debut from October 1957, Diane finally bought out Harold Lovette's share for $1,000.[4]

On February 4, the Workshop recorded for Atlantic. *Blues and Roots* became the first of three towering albums he'd record in 1959. He once again beefed up the recording band. Jackie McLean returned, and Parlan and Waldron split piano duties. Handy and Ervin were joined by Pepper Adams on baritone sax. Willie Dennis and Jimmy Knepper handled the trombones. The deep-toned horns he loved predominated. But they all had to deal with his erratic ways.

JOHN HANDY: You could never relax with Charles. There was always unnecessary tension, unnecessary intimidation. If he didn't like something you did, he'd threaten to call somebody else right in front of you. Worst of all was a lot of the music. I was right out of school, more academic about composition, but a lot of his stuff was raggedy, goddamn raggedy, not really put together. And that turned me off.

Nesuhi Ertegun suggested Mingus make a whole album like "Haitian Fight Song," to prove to detractors he could swing, that he wasn't hobbling his music any more by writing it correctly. He typically took the challenge in his own way, putting the musicians on edge to face the bluesy material laced with complex bop turns.

Nobody could say this record was too white, the way LeRoi Jones had about some earlier material, calling him a black Stan Kenton. Kenton was famed for not swinging.

"Tensions" was a powerful onomatopoiec representation of turmoil in musical form, largely improvised. The sliding bass intro for "E's Flat Ah's Flat Too," a characteristic punning title, begot Jimi Hendrix's guitar introduction to "Castles Made of Sand," among other later rock spinoffs. Mingus's propulsive bass lines from pieces like this became primers for Atlantic and Motown soul bassists.

Ray Charles was hitting with "I Got a Woman." Mingus was feeling the Zeitgeist again.

"My Jelly Roll Soul" was his tribute to Morton, his pre-Duke predecessor as a jazz composer. The multiracial Morton bragged of his pimping as well as his piano prowess, and he claimed to have invented jazz.

Mingus felt he and Morton shared grievances. They were not given their due by jazz critics and fans. Right now, the Adderley brothers, trumpeter Nat and saxist Julian "Cannonball," were among those getting credit for the gospel-soul-jazz resurgence he'd pioneered. They were still in an armed forces band when he was playing the Bohemia. Mingus felt slighted, abused, overlooked.

He would record "Jelly Roll" again shortly. Only it and "Tensions" were unedited when the album finally came out in April 1960. Miles Davis recorded *Kind of Blue* at around the same time, with Teo Macero as his producer. With Bill Evans and John Coltrane in his band, Davis utilized the modal and group improvisation ideas he'd once gibed at Mingus about.

Miles got credit for popularizing the trend, and Mingus seethed.

In mid-March, the pianoless Workshop got a month at Minton's, the birthplace of bebop. Mingus was playing more piano himself. He was the only one who knew what he wanted.

Handy quit for the first time. He got the usual phone call, pleading and cajoling. He finished the gig, then quit again when Mingus insulted a woman friend at the West Side YMCA April 5, where they shared the stage with the Tarriers, the Les Grinage Choir, and the Bill Rubenstein Trio.[5]

Lester "Prez" Young died in March 1959. The saxist who'd starred with Count Basie and Billie Holiday and inspired Charlie Parker was living in a cheap hotel near Birdland. One night, Mingus told Nat Hentoff, he visited Prez. Out the window, they saw Stan Getz in a gleaming car. Young said, "There's a guy who's driving a Cadillac on money from the way I play."[6]

The night Mingus heard Young had died, he was onstage at the Half Note with the Workshop.

MAUREEN MELOY: Somebody told Charlie, and he announced it. The club was fairly empty, and they started playing a blues. This was the Workshop, so they were always testing new ideas and discarding them. But this one was clearly a keeper, so over the next couple of weeks they refined and refined it.

Mingus took some of their solo lines and rewove the chords into denser harmonies, and it became "Goodbye Pork Pie Hat," a memorial to Young and his trademark headgear.

The Reverend John Garcia Gensel heard the piece and was deeply moved. The Lutheran minister had a radical idea: a jazz ministry. He took himself out to the clubs and bars to get to know his flock. He counseled musicians on family problems, drug abuse, emotional crises. After a while, they trusted him. He didn't want anything. He wasn't The Man.

Max Roach and Mingus became his good friends. Gensel talked to them about drugs and emotional instability. He used "Pork Pie Hat" and "Fables of Faubus" in his first sermons.

JOHN GARCIA GENSEL: He put his feelings about discrimination into his music, like Duke Ellington did. If you were to use one word to describe race in America, it's fable. Not truth. It's not the way we should treat one another. In other words, everything Faubus said wasn't true.

On April 9, Mingus signed a deal with Columbia records for two LPs of Jelly Roll Morton compositions, at a 4 percent royalty.[7] They were never recorded; he changed his mind.

Before April 15, income tax deadline, Mingus scrawled a note on yellow legal paper to Larry Chasen, his accountant. Apologizing for his small income in 1958, he explained that he'd survived largely on loans from the Baroness Nica de Konigswarter until he started collecting more substantial royalties from his records and TV work. "Trying to get famous enough to earn some real money," he wrote. His Prestige royalties for 1958 totaled $13.29.[8]

That May, the Workshop cut its first record for Columbia, *Mingus Ah Um*. He liked the pun on his Chinese ancestry and Latin declension. It was produced by his old friend Teo Macero.

He wanted each album to be a smorgasbord of sounds and styles. He was staking his turf.

The Workshop swung like a deliberately ragged but inspired sanctified church with an advanced music degree on "Better Get It in Your Soul." It was his latest 6/8 ecstatic, multipart demand for freedom in the "Wednesday Night Prayer Meeting" series. He shouted encouragement while the ensemble did unison one-note riffs, peeling off one at a time to solo. They navigated sections where Handy flew solo against hand claps, where the ensemble spoke in tongues, where the rhythms drove so hard they felt like a syncopated avalanche. One part anticipated the phase-shifting and imaging techniques that dominated 1960s psychedelic rock.

Mingus had raced to cut this track; Cannonball Adderley was interested in recording it, and he'd refused, which meant, he was sure, the Adderley brothers would come up with their own, and steal his credit once again.[9] Their single "This Here" beat his album to the market and began their string of gospel-jazz hits.

Mingus knew his music had more depth than any of its parts, and more versatility. His Workshop could revamp his eccentric look back at old New Orleans and Jelly Roll Morton on "Jelly Roll," the only surviving part of his original idea for Columbia. Mingus used horn voicings that, in their post-bop atonality, sounded like twelve-tone Ellington, yet evoked the antique sweet-and-sour Crescent City ensembles. He had each soloist do an old-style solo followed by a modern one.

Or there was the luminous braided melody and harmonies of the pointedly titled "Self-Portrait in Three Colors," the tributes that claimed mastery in "Bird Calls" and "Open Letter to Duke," a revamping of "Nouroog" that ran nine pages long, well over typical pop tune length.

He was claiming his place in jazz history.

Later, both Quincy Jones and Gil Evans would redo his "Boogie Stop Shuffle"; Jones revamped it as a bossa nova during that early 1960s craze, and Evans scored it to open *Absolute Beginners*, a movie starring rock icon David Bowie.

Mingus expanded "Nostalgia in Times Square" and renamed it "Strollin'." And he had the Workshop cut his dirgelike memorial for Prez.

JIMMY KNEPPER: He never had music for the band. And we never rehearsed before recording. So John Handy didn't know the chords for "Pork Pie Hat"; he didn't know about the flatted 10ths, I call 'em, beautiful chords. The song sounds like it's in a minor key, but it's not. But the effect of those chords was that you couldn't play a scale; you had to play blue notes. So John just played the blues, pretty much.

Handy was prickly enough already. He'd had it with Mingus's whole damn approach. He resented feeling like he didn't know what was going on. He was a highly schooled and sophisticated musician, and here he was being harrassed by this pretentious bully.

Handy was a formidable improviser with a thrilling tone—everyone said so. But he was humiliated time after time because he couldn't find out what it was he was supposed to be playing. Mingus laughed at him when he asked for chords or written music.

Handy's glowing tenor solo on "Pork Pie Hat" transmutes the color blue through its spectrum, culminating in his froggy split tones, a muted scream.

They cut "Fables of Faubus," but Columbia, Mingus said, wouldn't let them record the lyrics.

Diane wrote the liner notes. She said he now thought his Composers Workshop with Macero "got too far from jazz—spontaneity." [10]

Mingus took the album tapes and spliced solos in and cut them, juxtaposing and moving sections. Onstage, jazz was in the moment. A record was played over and over, for all time. It had to be the right representation of his music.

He went to bed at dawn and didn't get up until 4:00 P.M. He spent time at the piano, then he'd get dressed to go out. He spent nights talking to white coeds. He made beelines for tables of two and three, or for the bar if one was sitting there alone. He flirted with them mildly, but he mostly wanted to talk. He couldn't talk to most musicians about his ideas beyond music, and he trusted women. Over and over, he asked them to edit and type his manuscript. He would explain that he had no real education because of racism, and was embarrassed by his mistakes.

Roxanne Bethany worked at Katherine Gibbs Agency as a temp secretary. She liked jazz, so on weekends she and her girl friend Judy Starkey dressed up and left White Plains, a New York suburb, for downtown spots like the Village Barn to have a cocktail.

Roxanne heard about Mingus's show at the Half Note, where he'd start and stop the band and harangue the audiences, so she took Judy and another pal.

He stared at them from the bandstand. Judy was five foot seven and had reddish blonde hair. She had just finished nursing school. He said he thought at first she was someone else. He had a really wonderful smile, and was reading the Tibetan Book of the Dead, and said he was just ending a relationship.

He was only an inch or so taller than she was.

Judy and Roxanne came back to his gigs all through the fall of 1959.

He liked to mix media. Signing with Columbia Records got him get more access to CBS-TV, so he did a sound track for a TV show directed by Robert Herridge called *Camera Three*, a Sunday morning potpourri that featured all kinds of artistic forms.[11] The play featured "A Song with Orange in It," a ballad opening that segued into a shuffle blues with an unusual bridge. It starred Martin Balsam, and the three rehearsals used Mingus's bass prominently; the actors felt that the music was another stage presence.[12]

And he scored a ballet based on the Frankie and Johnny legend; it featured blues vocalist Jimmy Rushing and another gospel-laced composition called "Slop."

In spring 1959, Lenny Bruce opened at the Den in the Duane, on lower Madison Avenue in New York. Record producer Orrin Keepnews went to see him, urged by drummer Philly Joe Jones. Like a lot of jazz musicians, Jones was a big fan of Bruce's, not just because of the comedian's pointed material, but also for his jazzy delivery, his aura of improvisation.

Like jazz musicians, too, Bruce walked the tightrope between artist and entertainer.[13]

Mingus knew Bruce; he had first heard of him in San Francisco. "Sick" humor, Bruce's stock-in-trade, was a cultural aftershock of the Beats. With other satirists like Mort Sahl, Bruce used sarcasm and irony, hyperbolic logic and exaggeration to examine life in America from an iconoclastic outsider's perspective.

For a while, Bruce rocketed to big success, making best-selling albums, playing big-ticket venues, appearing on Steve Allen's TV show.

By late June 1959, when the annual Newport Jazz Festival rolled around, Mingus's recent albums still weren't out. For his third visit, he was scheduled with a quintet for an afternoon show. He brought a septet that became a sextet when Teddy Charles went sailing and his boat was becalmed. The rest of the band played Mingus's recent TV music.

He came in a new car, a 1959 Buick Invicta, an eight-cylinder convertible with power steering and brakes. He traded in his wagon for $1,100, put $200.78 down, and agreed to pay $95.69 a month on the $4,970.69 balance.[14]

He had arrived.

On the way back from Newport, Mingus was in an accident with a Chevy sedan and a Trailways bus. The right rear door and fender were smashed, the trunk was shoved in, and the other fenders and doors were grazed and bunged.

He took the car back to Royal Buick. Then he got his monthly payment book and wrote a two-page letter to Mr. Gould, the dealership's president, to lay out his case.[15]

He'd priced Elektra convertibles at other dealers, for $3,400. Then he visited Royal Buick's garage, where a black porter told him to see Mr. Angulia, who'd match the deal. When he went into the showroom, a short spectacled man pulled him by the arm into a back room. Mingus kept trying to explain he wanted an Elektra, but Specs shuffled him to an Invicta.

"I wanted a new car for the Newport Festival," Mingus wrote, "and if I couldn't have an Elektra an Invicta is close. I believed for once in my life I had a good deal."[16]

He registered shock at paying $5,000 for the car. He refused to make payments until his trade-in was deducted. He sent a copy to Marvin Karpatkin and the credit division, C.I.T.

A month later, he agreed to pay C.I.T.

CHARLES MINGUS: These payments . . . can in no way be construed to mean that the final purchase papers for the new car are in order. . . . May I suggest that it is also to your advantage to call Mr. Gould, president of Royal Buick, in the matter of repairing the damage done to the rear of "our" car . . . since the car is yours more than it is mine at the present moment. Originally they agreed to replace the damaged parts (fender etc.) with new ones; now they are speaking of "straightening out" the parts, and the car should *definitely* have new parts. Their change of heart may possibly be in response to my irritation at having been robbed.[17]

When *Mingus Ah Um* was released in fall 1959, it sold well, and "Better Get It" became a hit. Mingus later argued with Columbia about the sales figures. He said it sold 90,000 copies in nine months; they said no.[18]

The ad for the album showed him in a goatee and mustache. The copy exclaimed, "Working from a musical skeleton, Charlie Mingus spontaneously makes music related to the moment . . . a jazzophile's dream, experimental mile-high music that's solace for your soul." [19]

The October issue of *Harper's* ran a piece about him. "Mingus," it said, "has a hard earned reputation as the bad boy of jazz. He is outspoken to an extravagant degree." [20]

The Workshop's club dates still often read like a patch quilt. On September 12, they played the Plugged Nickel in Chicago. Ten days later, they did one night at the Half Note. Three days after that, they played the Hourglass in New Jersey. [21]

Then Mingus went out to the Coast, and pulled together a fourteen-piece big band to launch Farwell Taylor's newest venture.

For years, Farwell and Faye and Shelley rebuilt their two-level tumbledown structure on the Old Mill Stream in Mill Valley. They'd just added a deck to their restaurant, The Palate. Farwell's dream was to serve health food and host weekend jazz groups. They lived upstairs, and he had a studio in a small outbuilding, where he was painting a series of jazz portraits. On the best of them, the eyes seemed to move.

But his dream was $50,000 over budget. Faye hid in her room watching TV, and Farwell raved to whoever listened.

Charlie told him to get a Wellmar piano for the restaurant. Only twelve were made each year in Australia at $5,000 each. When the Workshop arrived, the piano was on the stage. But the electricians had problems, so the opening was delayed, and Mingus booked the band at the Black Hawk in San Francisco.

He went with Farwell to the Vedanta Temple, on 2963 Webster. Built in 1905, it mirrored the Vedantic faith that truth is universal in its startling mix of Colonial, Queen Anne, Moorish, and Hindu architecture and design.

It was there Farwell told him Shelley had to leave Mill Valley High School. Why, he asked. "Too damn many black people," cracked Farwell. Mingus flew into a fury, and went looking for Shelley, his mobile face gathering clouds. "What's this I hear?" he barked. She told him she was the only white girl in her year. The boys were hitting on her, and the girls were threatening to knife her.

He calmed down instantly. He told her she was looking too old for her age. She was sixteen, and nodded and ignored him, so she went to the Black Hawk that night in an evening gown and her grandmother Morgan's fox fur. He told her to leave. "You're underage, you're not supposed to be here, you're not supposed to dress like that," he said. "Even if your father doesn't care, I'm telling you now, it's not right."

He was really sweet and made her realize how wrapped up her parents were in themselves.

After she left, at the end of the set, Farwell charged the stage and smashed Mingus's bass. A few men came at Farwell. Mingus stopped them, and went home with Taylor.

SHELLEY TAYLOR: He knew it was because he had made a scene at the temple. He said he deserved it, and he was sorry. See, these kinds of things happened between them, and they didn't really care, either of them, what kinds of things they did in public. They had a kind of understanding.

The Workshop stayed in San Francisco for three weeks. Mingus loved play-ing the new piano. Thus was born "Far Wells, Mill Valley," written to open The Palate. It is a remarkable piece of music. Episodic and shape-shifting, it reca-pitulates different aspects of Charlie's vision of his mentor.

First the melody, an echo from "All These Beautiful Things," evokes Taylor's impact on his protégé. The orchestration and instrumentation, from piccolo to double bass, has a Beethovenesque reach. A characteristic loping, long-limbed melody then unwinds into a five-note phrase meant for the words "Farwell's Mill Valley." Next come harrumphing trombones, a wah-wah mute, a swirl of reeds and woodwinds and vibes. There's an Indian raga section, well before it was tried by John Coltrane, under the influence of sitar virtuoso Ravi Shankar.

A heated exchange between instruments takes off into that hard, springy jog Mingus had perfected in the Stars of Swing. Instruments pile in for loose call and response, layering motifs, a Dixieland band with far greater harmonic and rhythmic subtlety. Then a brief recap of motifs—a classical finish to an unclassifiable sound.

It was Mingus music.

He recorded it in November 1959, when the Workshop went into the studio for his second Columbia album, *Mingus Dynasty*.

Roland Hanna joined them on piano, and Jaki Byard's student Don Ellis, later famed as a composer/bandleader for time-signature and key shifts, played trumpet. Marvin Karpatkin bailed Dannie Richmond out of the tank and got his drug charges dropped, and charged Mingus $130. Mingus took the money out of Dannie's pay.[22]

"Slop" was another 6/8 gospel jazz outing; the title encapsulated its delib-erately bleary interwoven motifs, its human vocalizing sound. "Diane" was a retitled version of "Alice in Wonderland," now a portrait of Dorr-Dorynek. He wrote the notes.

CHARLES MINGUS: It may be the prettiest thing I ever wrote—a girl trying to make it in this big rough world, like I am. I try to show her sadness (the alto part on top) but also her strength in her art and her conviction in what she believes in (the tenor on the bottom) even if there are harsh, unresolved parts of her life. She was a painter I knew. It was written for her because I loved her at one time.[23]

Via near-constant rhythmic shakeups and richly Impressionstic voicings, "Diane" looked at romantic balladry with a sense of whimsy and irony and even touches of impatience that were hardly saccharine. They were Mingus at his toughest Romantic best.

Mingus explained "Song with Orange": "It's about a talented composer who meets a rich girl who tries to ruin his life. She doesn't have anything to offer him but money, so she asks him to write a song and dedicate it to her dress, which was orange."[24]

His whole life was a series of parables waiting for explication and music.

"Gunslinging Bird" was a tribute to Charlie Parker. Its full title was "If Charlie Parker Were a Gunslinger There'd Be a Whole Lot of Dead Copycats." There were two reworked Ellington pieces, "Things Ain't What They Used to Be," which had two cellos, and "Mood Indigo."

Mingus was claiming his place in the pantheon.

Diane edited the notes for him.

CHARLES MINGUS: I studied Bird's creative vein with the same passion and understanding with which I'd studied the scores of my favorite classical composers, because I found a purity in his music that until then I had only found in classical music. Bird was the cause of my realization that jazz improvisation, as well as jazz composition, is the equal of classical music if the performer is a creative person. Bird brought melodic development to a new point in jazz, as far as Bartok or Schoenberg or Hindemith had taken it in the classics. But he also brought to music a primitive, mystic supra-mind communication that I'd only heard in the late Beethoven quartets, and even more, in Stravinsky.[25]

The fights with Diane were increasing. In some emotional ways, she and Mingus were alike. To others he made harsh fun of her, or belittled her, but she usually tried to smile the conflict away. Sometimes their arguments got physical. She moved out but kept helping him, and he kept the apartment.

On November 28, 1959, the Workshop, now with Handy and Knepper, returned to the Half Note for a one-month stay.[26] Meanwhile, Ornette Coleman led his quartet into the Five Spot in November and became the biggest draw in town.

Self-taught, the alto saxist had both gone back to his Texas blues roots and taken a step beyond bebop. Like Mingus, he accepted atonality and polytonality. Like the Mingus Workshops, his bands could all solo simultaneously, without preset chord changes. Harmonic modulations came from the instrumentalists' quick ears and teamwork, and sheer chance.

It sounded familiar to Mingus—too familiar. *Blues and Roots* still wasn't out. He wasn't getting credit for something he started again. Coleman was an instant critics' darling, championed by Gunther Schuller and Martin Williams and Nesuhi Ertegun, who'd signed him to Atlantic.

Mingus was of two minds about the long-haired saxist.

He resented Coleman. He didn't like being upstaged, and he thought Coleman was a primitive who didn't fully understand his own intuitive musical revolt.

But he also recognized the younger man's discipline and focus. And he liked Coleman. He showed up at the Five Spot and played piano with Coleman's group a couple of times. But he also saw Coleman as an original thinker who, like Bird, would spawn a legion of imitators unable to maintain his vision, slackers looking for easy hooks to imitate, like Coleman's using a plastic alto.[27]

In scenes out of Thomas Pynchon's V, Mingus and Coleman would find themselves sharing the spotlight at Beat parties at LeRoi Jones's apartment on West 16th Street.

Mingus needed help to keep his life in order. He invited Roxanne and Judy and and their friend Marilou up to East 76th Street.

ROXANNE BETHANY: I would open a drawer and there were envelopes he'd never opened. If it was a small check under ten dollars, he wouldn't cash it. But there could have been seventy of them in there. And he had all this correspondence. I don't think he ever kept track of who owed him money or vice versa. I mean, he immediately trusted me with all his money and his checkbook. I think he felt women wouldn't rip him off that way.

He left them in the big room at the front of the brownstone. While Roxanne typed and filed and paid bills, Judy and Marilou snooped. They flipped through the records, the mounds of sheet music and scribbled sheets of manuscript. They goggled at instruments, and climbed up the stepladder into the huge closet.

He made them tea and hot chocolate with whipped cream and talked to them like a big brother. They thought he was a pussycat.

In December, the Workshop followed Lennie Tristano and Lee Konitz into the Showplace, a new club on the second floor of a West 3rd Street townhouse. They stayed in residence there into October 1960.

It was the peak of jazz's postwar popularity. Groups were playing concert halls, especially at colleges, where jazz societies thrived. In clubs, a few major figures could command long stays. Mingus was one.

The two-floor Showplace was started by a famed ex-model, Jim Paul Eilers, who lived on the top floor in the sumptuous apartment once inhabited by famed New York mayor Jimmy Walker. Eilers liked to sing. And so, on the ground floor, a few steps down from street level, was a piano bar called the Speakeasy, where the owner and his friends indulged their vocal fancies in between acts. Young up-and-comers like Joan Rivers and Woody Allen tested out routines. Barbra Streisand, then living over a fish store, sang. For a while, Warren Beatty played piano while he studied acting. The audience glittered with names like Lucille Ball and Broadway impresario Billy Rose, Anita Bryant and Edward Albee and Kennedy in-law Princess Lee Radziwill.

A staircase ran up the side wall to the parlor floor. At first, that level was home to revues, like the popular *In Your Hat*. Jerry Herman played piano and had his first show, *Nightcap*, showcased there. Ruth Buzzi worked as a hatcheck girl; Dom DeLuise was a waiter. The help spent a lot of time running between floors; there was no running water on the parlor floor, and so ice had to be hauled upstairs.

Eilers got the idea to turn the space, which held perhaps 100 people at little black cabaret tables and spidery little chairs, into a jazz club.

JIM PAUL EILERS, *club owner:* Jazz was all over the Village, and it seemed like a good idea. And besides, this was different: it was a proscenium presentation for jazz. The musicians liked it because it was theatrical; people actually sat and listened to the music.

The setup was a bit unwieldy, but distinctive. The bandstand was at the far end of the club, up over the bar. When you sat at the bar, it felt like you were practically onstage. It was an ideal way to present Mingus music—jazz as drama in the moment, in the making.

Near the upstairs door stood a player piano, nicknamed Invisible Irene. It provided musical backdrops for Eilers and his friends, and entertainment when there was no band. And Irene got the club big publicity, including splashes in Walter Winchell's column, when the union came down demanding Eilers pay dues for a player piano.

Maureen Meloy was hired as a barmaid downstairs, and Mingus had her watch the door receipts for him for a few weeks. He was working for a guarantee and a percentage of ticket sales, and he wanted to make sure he was paid his full share. Dapper Dannie Richmond came down often to chat up Maureen and grab a coke with grenadine, a junkie's sugar wet-dream.

MAUREEN MELOY: With those long gigs for months at a time and several sets a night, the audience got the chance to learn the music, to follow its growth and development. I did all the stuff that all the other women of that era did. I was trying to work during the day, then after the Showplace sets we'd all go down to Chinatown, and drag the Chinese waiter from the Showplace, whose father was with the UN, to order for us. You'd get home at 4:30 in the morning. Finally I just started working nights, so I could go out and party afterwards.

One night at the Showplace, Mingus pushed the tempos on pieces like "Lovebird" into hyperdrive. Workshop regulars called it being taken to the whipping post. If a pretty girl or a critic paid too much attention to anyone else on the bandstand, he'd change keys or shift tempos. This time, he went even farther.

That afternoon, with Dannie Richmond and Teddy Charles, he auditioned trumpet players. He wanted a different sound. He already had an alto player lined up. Chico Hamilton had broken up his band in New York to do ad jingles and sound tracks, which meant Eric Dolphy was free.

Dolphy was highly trained. He practiced hours a day, refused to accept conventions, and sounded like no one else. He loved bass clarinet, a horn no one had used in decades. So did Mingus, with his taste for lower-end sounds.

Having Eric Dolphy was the next best thing to having Buddy Collette. He could talk to Eric through their instruments, not like with Handy, who kept fighting him. The Dolphy-Mingus partnership would yield some of the finest work of the free-jazz upsurge.

That night, the phone rang in trumpeter Ted Curson's apartment: "Can you start now?" Curson ran into Dolphy on the stairway; he too had gotten the call. They walked to the club. When Mingus saw them, he gestured at the band on-stage and said, "Ladies and gentlemen, I have an announcement to make. These cats are fired!"

Dannie Richmond alone stayed onstage, and the new cats joined him. They played standards like "All the Things You Are," the shared idiom of mainstream jazz, to finish out the night. But Mingus altered or dropped chords, rearranged the structures, shifted tempos. And he wouldn't stand for copying. He told them he loved Duke, Bird, and Dizzy, and he didn't want to hear anybody trying to sound like them.

For ten months, Mingus tried all kinds of things. He had a quartet or quintet week nights, and guest stars on weekends. Mingus wanted a piano player who could mix Duke Ellington with Monk, the evocative clusters and shimmering harmonies his music demanded. A pianists' parade filed through the Showplace: Horace Parlan, Roland Hanna, Paul Bley, Nico Bunink, Sy Johnson, Kenny Drew, Barry Harris, Kenny Barron.

Sy Johnson later worked with Mingus as an arranger. But in early 1960, he was fresh in New York and came into the Showplace to see his college chum Bley, who'd just been fired. Baby Lawrence was tap dancing to his signature tunes like "Billie's Bounce," but there was no one on piano. Dannie Richmond learned to mimic Baby's routines and steps, including his tip-toe moves, with astounding grace.

Eric Dolphy was learning the band's book from Booker Ervin; it was his first week. Mingus asked Johnson to sit in. Baby Lawrence was doing two weeks, he explained, and Johnson could learn the music onstage, then join them for pay when the dancer left.

Johnson was elated. He'd memorized *Mingus Ah Um* and *Blues and Roots*. Dannie coached him from the drums, singing parts. "If I shake my head, stop playing," were the leader's instructions.

After a few nights, he let Johnson solo on the challenging variation on "All The Things You Are" he called "All The Things You Could Be by Now if Sigmund Freud's Wife Was Your Mother." He said he wrote it in Bellevue.

SY JOHNSON, *arranger:* He turns and says to me, "Pedal tones, pedal tones, play pedal tones." This thing changes keys every four bars. What kind of pedal tones does he want? I'm trying to find some pattern that works, and he's getting madder at me. "Pedal tones, pedal tones." Finally he throws the bass down. He comes rushing around behind Dannie and thrusts his nose into my nose. I see these maniacal eyes an inch away, and he's just glaring and making these funny breathing noises, he's enraged, and my life is flashing before my eyes. He's got his fists clenched. And suddenly he goes CRASH on the bass end of the piano, four times. Then he went running behind Dannie again and picked up the bass and started playing furiously.

I was humiliated. The club was half-full. I'm thinking, I don't need this shit. He was abusing everybody, of course, but it was usually from a distance; this was in my space. So I'm sitting there silently mouthing Fuck You and Dannie's saying, "Go ahead, man, play; he didn't mean nothing, he does that all the time." Finally I had it, so I made a fist and whacked the bottom end of the piano and Mingus looked up and his face broke into this wide smile, and he turned to the audience and said, "THE WHITE BOY CAN PLAY."

One night, when Johnson pushed the piano bench back too far, he fell off the tiny riser into the storage pit where the drum and bass cases were piled. He clambered and slipped to get out. When the set ended, Mingus said, "Hey, that was really great, man. Can you do that every night?"

At the end of two weeks, Johnson came in to find the band onstage early—a rarity—with Yusef Lateef. Mingus ignored him. When the set ended, he walked past Johnson, stopped, backed up, and leaned over to whisper, "If you had a chance to hire Yusef Lateef or you, who would you hire?"

Lateef, the six-foot-six saxist-composer who was probing world music, was a pal. They liked trading ideas. One night, when Mingus got mad at Lateef after a set, the big man picked Mingus up by the biceps and held him off the ground. He calmed down. Lateef stayed for three months.

Ben Webster was one of Mingus's heroes from his days with Duke during the Blanton wartime band. His brawny yet creamy sound and gutsy lyricism were a Swing Era standard for tenormen. Webster came down to play standards and the Ellington songbook, but Mingus provoked the quick-tempered, hard-drinking fifty-one-year-old, and Webster chased him around the block with a knife.

Tenorman Archie Shepp was testing his energy music excursions, his form of frenetic free jazz, and he too sat in. Mingus was open for anything.

On weekends, the place filled with tourists. Mingus got on the drums, and Richmond picked up the tenor and blew old-timey crowd-pleasers like "When the Saints Go Marching In."

In breaks, Mingus sat in the back and ate brandy snifters of ice cream, or simply spooned it out of the container. He was fat, but he was agile. He could still do the tumbles the Okes had taught him as a kid in Watts.

Mingus shepherded Judy and Roxanne and Marilou around town. He took them to Birdland, to the Half Note. They met Britt Woodman at the opening of the Terminis' new club, the Jazz Gallery, which held three hundred. The girls hung out and talked, then took the train home.

Judy was hanging out more and later than the others.

That January, Celia came back to New York. Debut was a mess. Since part of it was hers, she wanted to straighten it out. He acted like she'd come back to him, and was resentful of Dorian. Celia was involved with a young executive at Fantasy Records, named Saul Zaentz, and left after a day.

JUDY STARKEY MINGUS MCGRATH, *third wife*: There was a snowstorm one night, and he offered to drive me home. He drove all the way up to White Plains really really slowly, and we talked and talked.

There was one time, it was very late, that he wanted food. So he stopped at a place over on the West Side, and he went in a got a bagful of food, hamburgers and stuff. And we sat in the car and ate this food. Now he told me this, and I believed it: I was twenty-one. I believed it. He said, "My father always told me that if you meet a woman who's happy eating food out of a brown paper bag, marry her." So I bought it.

You know, he was fun.

We promised we wouldn't hurt each other. Which turned out not to be true.

Judy left work and moved down to the city with him. Her blue-collar parents were furious. She couldn't understand it. Her grandparents lived in a black White Plains neighborhood, and she'd always had black friends.

He went with her to visit and talk with them. They wanted her to spend a month without him. He said okay.

She slept on a sofabed in the living room. One morning her mother came in and started choking her. Judy fought her off and called him. He called Marvin Karpatkin, then he called back and told her to go to a hotel, write a really long letter explaining her feelings, and then come to the city.

That spring, she was pregnant. The trip to Europe she'd planned with Roxanne and Marilou was off.

They were married on March 25, 1960, at a Methodist church in the Village. Judy wasn't like the other women he'd fathered kids with, the several Charles and Charlene Mingus Juniors around the country. Judy was white and vulnerable. He felt her devotion, and wanted to do his duty. He was his father's son.

Two professional witnesses were their wedding party. They went out to dinner, at the steakhouse on the corner of West 8th and Sixth Avenue, where you could eat in the old wooden walk-in refrigerators. They had his favorite meal, steak and wine, and he went to work, and she went with him.

That February in North Carolina, four black college students sat in at a white-only lunch counter. They sparked the birth of the Student Nonviolent Coordinating Committee. Unlike the NAACP and Dr. King, SNCC emphasized voter-registration drives and local, not national, issues.

It marked the beginning of serious tensions within the civil rights movement.

In February 1960, Mingus got a check for $32.09 in royalties for *The Clown*. He still owed Bethlehem $5,304.04 on their advances. Over the first quarter,

Blues and Roots sold 2,510 copies. Atlantic Records paid him $2,336.19 in royalties.[28]

On holiday breaks, Ann McIntosh came into New York from Michigan, where she'd met Janet Coleman and Al Young. There was a clique of Mingus fans at Ann Arbor, partly because the prestigious university drew ethnic students from big cities.[29]

Coleman was a New Yorker who got involved in writing and radio and improvisation theater. She'd seen Mingus play in Detroit, where he stopped Booker Ervin from hitting on her, and afterward they exchanged letters. Young came from Detroit, where he'd followed Mingus since the early Debut days. Young wanted to be a folksinger, then an actor, then a poet.

Jazz was the collegiate sound track.

McIntosh brought Janet to see him that winter, and Al later that spring. They became his friends.

He talked to Al Young about heiress Sue Scott.

AL YOUNG: The night I first met him, he was madly in love. He was very avuncular about it. He said, "Man, put your hands next to mine. I touched her, man, sparks flew. That hasn't happened to me since the third grade."

He talked to Janet about Judy's pregnancy.

JANET COLEMAN: That was the first oddly intimate conversation, open in the way he could be—Here I am. There was a real sense of responsibility on his part. There wasn't a question of an abortion or him abandoning her. He did his manly duty, stood by her.

What a situation for her to be in: very lovely, innocent, a nurse, suddenly in the middle of this racial thing. To have children of color when you're a strawberry blonde. To be married to this person she might have loved, but barely knew.

Judy thought her children would be extra special because of the man she loved, and because they would be racially mixed. Most of the hip white women around Mingus condescended to her, when they noticed her at all.

One night early in her pregnancy, Judy felt really depressed. He put *Mingus Ah Um* on the hi-fi, and danced to make her smile.

In May, they moved to 2186 Fifth Avenue, the Lenox Terrace houses in East Harlem. In their roomy eleventh-floor apartment, he could rehearse the band, and the baby could have a room. Visitors admired the interracial couple's courage. Judy dealt with daily life, a white woman in a development for middle-class blacks, including the then-borough president of Manhattan, sur-rounded by a decaying neighborhood.

Mingus began using limousines like cabs, to ferry Judy and himself around town. Cabs wouldn't stop for him, and limos didn't cost much more. He told people her parents disowned her.

Just after they moved, Father Norman O'Connor, a columnist for the Boston *Globe*, approvingly reprinted Mingus's Five Spot speech. It was widely read.

In May 1960, Mingus connived to have a big-band session for Mercury Records.

Leonard Feather had just landed his dream job there as A&R man, respon-sible for signing and recording artists. It was a chance to practice what he'd preached in print, as a critic. Mingus was one of his first picks. Feather wanted to put the quintet into the studio, maybe change the pianist.

Mingus told Feather to come by the Showplace; he had something to show him. The next night, there were twenty-five people on the bandstand, includ-ing Lateef, Roach, Knepper, Eddie Bert, and Pepper Adams. He'd gathered the faithful.

Mingus had a box of yellowed music so crumbly the musicians could barely read it. Some of it was "Half Mast Inhibition," written in 1940 after he'd first visited Farwell Taylor.

JIMMY KNEPPER: I had the impression that Mingus wrote a lot of his music in his teens. Like Monk. Not that he finished it. Maybe he wrote four bars, then put it away, and later when he was famous he'd pull it out again and work with it.

Feather was a friend and booster, but he was taken aback by the sight on the tiny stage. He reminded Mingus he'd wanted to record the quintet. Mingus said, "You said you'd record my band. This is my band. You're always doing this to black people." And he stormed out of the club.

Feather talked to Mercury. The company balked. Mingus sent Feather and Local 802 telegrams threatening reprisals. He'd already taken a poke at a union official jazzers hated. He'd showed up at a union meeting dressed in a yellow hunting outfit with a bow and quiver of arrows. The union didn't want more trouble.

The sessions were on.

EDDIE BERT: For *Pre-Bird*, we rehearsed at his apartment first. He'd open the window and say, "You hear all the traffic? Get that in the music. The beeps and all."

He rehearsed in some funny places. There was one on Fourth Avenue. Little rooms. So there's a room over on one side with half the band, and a room on the other with half. And he's in the middle conducting.

A few days later, they were in the studio. Gunther Schuller conducted the twenty-five-piece orchestra in a variety of early revived Mingus music, including "Half Mast Inhibition" "Mingus Fingus No. 2," and "Bemoanable Lady."

"Prayer for Passive Resistance" was a blues nod to the strategy for social change adopted by Dr. Martin Luther King Jr. and Mahatma Gandhi. Its feisty assertiveness underlined the strength of the approach, and featured his patented double-stop sliding and triplets.

Lorraine Cousins weakly sang "Weird Nightmare" and "Eclipse," the overwrought ballad he'd written in 1948 for Billie Holiday.

He sent Mercury a bill for his arrangements that totaled several thousand dollars. [30]

He told Curson he reworked pieces from Debussy and Ravel and Gershwin for his compositions. Sometimes they compared women-chaser's notes. And sometimes Mingus chased the trumpeter around the block between sets at the Showplace.

Mingus signed a new deal with BMI, an agency that oversaw royalty distribution for radio play and sales. They would monitor some two hundred titles of his, which meant steady checks. [31]

In June, he appeared in a feature called "Stereo Shopping with Charlie Mingus." He was a hi-fi nut. For the road he had a Pilot Radio Encore phonograph, semiportable. At home he used a Garrard changer, GE cartridge, small push-pull amp, and eight-inch Jensen speaker. Knepper built him a small corner horn enclosure with a 12-inch coaxial University speaker—cost, $57. When he plugged it into his new stereo conversion kit, he had two-channel sound, the rage of the early 1960s. [32]

Stereo records cost more than mono discs. Arguments, especially among classical and jazz fans, the bulk of the listeners buying the new technology, turned on whether stereo was a step forward or backward.

His new apartment had elegant sound.

Mingus was enraged at George Wein. A lot of the musicians were. Wein had started booking folk acts and rock and rollers at the Newport festival. The crowds were swelling with collegians, who spent big bucks at the resort's bars.

But Wein kept non-Swing Era leaders in afternoon slots, which they considered demeaning. And the pay was far less than the evening gigs. Mingus was offered $700 to appear, and his name was listed in the early ads, but he complained loudly. He said he knew Benny Goodman was getting $5,000.[33] This was supposed to be his year. *Blues and Roots* had sold another 1,812 copies this quarter alone, two to one in higher-priced stereo.[34]

He pulled himself out of Wein's festival.

He sat down with Max Roach. They'd reconciled that winter, after Cloud and Gensel persuaded the drummer to spent time in Bellevue himself.

Inchoate anger was never far from either of them.

Max and his new wife Abbey Lincoln hung out with Mingus and Judy. They evolved a plan for a counterfestival, run by musicians—another cooperative. The Jazz Workshop gave Max a $50 advance, and Mingus $120.[35]

But the idea also seemed to have the clout of the new jazz patron class behind it. Peggy Hitchcock brought Elaine Lorillard and Doris Duke down to the Showplace.

JANET COLEMAN: Peggy Hitchock was part of the New York intellectual art scene. That doesn't exist in the same way any more, upper-class people acting as patrons and slumming. They're not that curious about black people any more, for one thing. And they're more nouveau. It was really old-money people. A lot of upper-class women, especially.

The Lorillards, Wein's main backers, were divorcing. Elaine wanted a piece of the nonprofit festival's take, and Mingus offered her a piece of the rebel festival if she'd help them.

She talked with Nick Cannarozzi, the Italian-American owner of Cliff Walk Manor, a hotel near Freebody Park in Newport. His huge lawn was their outdoor auditorium, and in return he'd get the bar profits and a piece of the gate.

The logistics were hasty and thrown together. Advertising was haphazard— some flyers, a couple of notices in newspapers. They relied on word-of-mouth. Mingus and Max Roach and Allen Eager, Peggy Hitchock's tenor-saxist-boyfriend, acted as musical directors.

They scanned the jazz spectrum for talent, lining up boppers like trumpeter Kenny Dorham, swing veterans like drummer Jo Jones, new stars like Ornette Coleman. Coltrane was supposed to show, but didn't.

They started on June 30, same as Wein's fest. The players were told they'd sleep in a Newport "cottage," as the mansions were called, but most of them wound up in pup tents.

Mingus rode around in his convertible, haranguing people to come. He walked the fences and collected money from folks listening for free. Opening day boasted the Workshop alternating with Coleman's quartet, and fifty people showed up.

Booker Ervin was back with the Workshop. When they came out from the wings, Hentoff introduced them, saying, "I've never seen a man try so hard to walk naked." As Mingus came onstage, he yelled, "That's not a problem, Nat," and proceeded to unzip his fly.

And then came the riot.

GEORGE WEIN: The riot wasn't at the festival; it was in the streets. At night, the city of Newport, which was very greedy, left the bars open all night long, instead of closing at 12:00 or 1:00 A.M. like state law says. So thousands of people showed up to ball. After years, the word was out. The police asked me to keep the concerts going until 2:00 A.M. so they could clean up the havoc outside. They put a lot of kids in jail. They were rich kids; one guy said they were throwing imported beer bottles. Next day, headlines: Riot at Newport Jazz Festival.

Wein's festival was shut down. Mingus was sure theirs would be too. It was a Wein plot. He headed toward Wein's hotel to threaten him, but Roach called Wein to warn him, and the promoter hid in the hotel's attic.

Although many fans saw the riots as a jazz tragedy, Mingus was elated. The musicians had struck a blow against commercializing jazz at the expense of its true artists. He said, "They did it themselves. They lost their identity with jazz."[36] Says Wein, "Charlie had a way with controversy."

By the Rebel Festival's last day, it drew several hundred fans.

Dorham walked off with what was left of the musicians' take, after others nibbled at the kitty. Some of them agreed to start the Jazz Artists Guild, another cooperative. That November, they recorded for Candid. One disc captured Mingus's tirade against cash registers in clubs.

On July 13, 1960, the Workshop went to France for the Antibes Jazz Festival. George Wein's idea was proliferating around the world. Leonard Feather, in his groundbreaking jazz encyclopedia, wrote that the festival changed the entire economic structure of jazz, and its audiences.

To fill the Workshop's difficult piano chair, Mingus tapped Bud Powell. Powell was often a wreck. Flashes of lucidity brightened an otherwise fractured consciousness. But he could still, at times, conjure the brilliance of his former glory, when his right hand runs struck fear and envy into pianists' hearts.

Bud only played one cut. For the rest, Mingus moved back and forth between bass and piano, as he would do more and more.

They recapped their preceding year's greatest hits, and his vision. When Atlantic finally issued the LP in 1979, critic Robert Palmer's liner notes credited the Workshop with influencing the key post-1960s avant-gardists.

Al Young and Mingus went to see Ornette Coleman's quartet at the Five Spot, and at the set's close he complimented the group.

Critics would make much of his rivalry with Coleman. And he'd bristle whenever contemporaries compared Coleman and Dolphy. He thought Coleman's compositions and attitude toward freedom more important than his playing.

In August, Dolphy recorded *Out There,* his debut as a leader. On it he played "Eclipse" and a piece dedicated to his Watts compatriot, "The Baron." Dolphy was one of the few who called Mingus that.

For two weeks, Britt Woodman played with an expanded Workshop at Pep's in Philadelphia. The dressing-room interplay between the boyhood pals was striking.

BRITT WOODMAN: We started reminiscing about when we were kids, and told some of our old jokes. The fellas in the band didn't know he had that side to him, his humor. They were surprised and started laughing, because he stayed so serious with his music, like Buddy Collette.

Most of the black musicians never knew him. When you'd go to his pad, there was nothing but white folks, white chicks. The black cats: "I'm scared he might hit me." They'd go along with the stuff people at the papers said. "Oh, that man's crazy."

But the white chicks, he'd lecture them like he was a god. And they believed him. Being great on the bass and his music, people were just astonished by this cat was talking about life, how you can use your mind, mind over matter, that kind of thing. When a person is that great, a lot of times there's something weird about them. They're different from ordinary people.

That was his outlet—talking to the chicks. Sitting on the floor, he'd talk and talk, and the chicks looked at him like, Whew, boy. But that happens, like with Duke. Any musician that has a style perfected like that, they just like to be around you.

When Charles played out in clubs, he was exciting to women. Living with him was a different story. It ain't the Mingus they saw on stage. He's so busy writing, he ain't got time for this and that. And they're disappointed.

Judy had no one to stop her, so she ate too much and gained forty pounds. She went with Mingus to Macy's to buy a wooden ice-cream maker. Nobody helped them. But when he hoisted it on his shoulder and started to walk out, a clerk appeared almost magically.

He called Mamie, and she gave Judy a recipe for peach ice cream.

That August's royalty statement from Columbia brought a $905.01 check. [38]

He was preparing for the first Candid recording of his Workshop. One rehearsal, he pulled up at a gas station with the band in his car, got one dollar's worth of gas, and asked for the special restroom key. He found the Brooklyn subway station he'd been told about. He parked and led the band down the wide stairway into one of the storage and electrical rooms that pock the subway system, behind steel doors. The key fit the lock. Somebody had transformed the room into a rehearsal and recording studio. But it wasn't soundproofed, so hell broke out every time a train rumbled past.

On September 4, 1960, the Workshop opened at the Showplace as a piano-less quartet. The band was in upheaval again, even as Mingus was getting ready to record. Dolphy and Curson wanted to leave, and they had offers. Mingus was furious, especially about Eric. He felt betrayed. He'd encouraged Eric's bass clarinet work, his eccentric note choices and angular lines when most others thought the young reedman was out of tune or crazy.

He paid Dolphy $175 a week, and the others $135. [39]

John Handy sat in two nights. Britt Woodman sat in one.

Yusef Lateef told Mingus about two kids from his Detroit hometown. Charles McPherson played alto like Bird; Lonnie Hillyer played trumpet like Dizzy. They were working afternoons with Booker Ervin at the Cafe Wha? up the street. Mingus came by, and told them to come down that night. They needed to understand his Duke Ellington side for his upcoming session. He talked to McPherson about bending notes like Ellington alto mainstay Johnny Hodges.

Instantly, he transformed the Workshop into a double quartet. That first night, Curson's mother and aunt came in from Philadelphia. When Mingus rode him onstage, Curson threw his horn down and lunged. Mingus grabbed the mike and announced that Curson was on drugs. The trumpeter froze, picked up his horn, and sat back down. He didn't play. After the set, his mother and wife talked him out of quitting.

Later that night, Mingus sat down at the Steinway grand piano.

JIM PAUL EILERS: He was a tempestuous man. I'd put up with a lot of anger to keep him there, although he never punched or threatened me. He'd been at the club for almost a year, and I wanted to present other things. He wanted to stay, forever, if possible. I'd told him I had another show coming in, that he had to leave, over a period of time. But one night he just got so upset, he started pulling out the piano's strings. That takes an incredible amount of strength. He didn't bleed at all; too many calluses on his hands, probably. But he just didn't want to leave. It was a beautiful piano, and everybody loved to play it. But I didn't hold it against him.

With that, the Workshop moved to the Half Note. The double quartet lasted less than a month. Ornette Coleman's double quartet, which included Dolphy, would record that December, to critical raves.

Like Duke Ellington and Jelly Roll Morton, Mingus was never part of any movement during his lifetime. He operated in parallel, sometimes intersecting other developments, sometimes not. Everything, however, was grist for his mill. He told a reporter, "Monk and I play similar music. Perhaps it's because we both dug Duke at the same time, and the old-time piano players, and we both like the use of 'pedal points' in compositions."[40]

In October and November the Workshop, in several forms, recorded for Candid, with Nat Hentoff as producer. With Dolphy and Curson and Dannie Richmond, Mingus recorded "Original Faubus Fables," a retitled "Fables of Faubus," complete with scathing, burlesquing vocals in call-and-response form with Richmond.

CHARLES MINGUS: Name me someone who's ridiculous, Dannie.
DANNIE RICHMOND: Governor Faubus.
CM: Why is he so sick and ridiculous?
DR: He won't permit us in the schools.
CM: Then he's a fool![41]

A later verse added Rockefeller and Eisenhower to the list of the ridiculous, because "they brainwash and teach you to hate."

He added Hillyer, McPherson, and Bunink for "Reincarnation of a Lovebird," another of his beautiful ballads with a glowing, lengthy melody, more than twice as long as Tin Pan Alley's thirty-two-bar pop format. With Bley replacing Bunink and Booker Ervin joining, they recorded "Lock 'em Up," originally titled "Hellview in Bellevue," a ferocious sonic representation of his time in the hospital.

"MDM," he said, combined Monk, Duke, and Mingus.

"Vassarlean" took musical revenge on heiress-hipster wannabes, a peek into his reaction to their patronizing. He told Nat Hentoff the piece was written for a barefoot, slender Vassarette who, he said, "was using me. I was just one of the props in the self-indulgent fantasy life she was trying to lead. I told her to get lost."[42] In fact, "Vassarlean" was "Weird Nightmare," itself based partly on "You Don't Know What Love Is."

He revived "What Love," his 1940s reworking of Cole Porter's "What Is This Thing Called Love," a bopper's favorite to recompose. His version was one of the most difficult. In 1955, when Max Roach had tried it out with his ace quintet with Clifford Brown and Sonny Rollins, they found the music too hard, too demanding.

Five cuts captured a few members of the Jazz Artists Guild, including trumpet elder statesman Roy Eldridge, who co-led the sessions.

Mingus was standing deliberately outside trends. He was going forward and backward at the same time.

The last week of October, the Workshop, with Booker Ervin back and getting a raise, went to Canada to record for the CBC. Dannie Richmond skipped out on his hotel bill.[43]

The Workshop went back to the Half Note around Thanksgiving.

Mingus began alternating Dolphy and Curson with McPherson and Hillyer for different gigs. Dolphy began working with Coleman, then Coltrane.

CHARLES McPHERSON: Aesthetically, he liked organized chaos. Now, that's a hard tightrope to walk. It's a hard tightrope to expect the other five, six people playing in the band to walk. Which is too much chaos and not enough organization, and vice versa? The subjectivity is incredible in this kind of concept, and even if you're the one in charge, you're not going to be consistent. And how are you going to get the other guys in the band to know exactly what you mean when you might not even mean the same thing tomorrow? On the same tune? It means a lot of the time you scare the hell out of yourself when you're almost falling. And sometimes you fall. It's that risk that's part of the attraction.

Mingus's quarterly royalty statement from Columbia showed he'd earned $790.13.[44]

Earlier in November, John Kennedy won the presidential election, beating Richard Nixon. There was a lot of speculation about the new era that might dawn now that Eisenhower's two terms were over. Kennedy was a war hero, a member of a new generation. He had money and charm. He and his wife had style.

Jaqueline Kennedy was expecting a baby. So was Judy Mingus. For Thanksgiving, Judy made a Thanksgiving feast, complete with giblet gravy. Somebody had warned Judy if she had any, she'd go into labor. She did, and she did. Mingus got her to Flower and Fifth Avenue Hospital.

While Judy was in labor overnight, eighteen-year-old Janet Coleman showed up at the Mingus apartment with a friend. [45] Mingus cooked them chicken and dumplings, and talked to them about his book, *Half Yaller Nigger* or *Half Yaller Schitt-Colored Nigger*. He figured white men wouldn't let him use those words, so he had a fallback: *Beneath the Underdog*.

Janet pored over the typescript and handwritten inserts until dawn, and he asked her to edit it for him. At seven, he told her to call her mother.

The next morning, after the baby was born, he showed up at the hospital with Max Roach. He was carrying his portable record player and a handful of his records. The nurses enjoyed the music.

A couple of weeks later, the Reverend Gensel baptized the latest Mingus, a daughter, Carolyn. But Mingus called her Keki.

JOHN GARCIA GENSEL: He was like a great big almost teddy bear, a child in many respects. Way beneath that veneer of being tough and getting into trouble with punching people in the mouth and so forth—underneath it all he was just a big boy. He craved acceptance, not in the sense of being paranoid, but he wanted affirmation. He knew that his music was not accepted by many, although some of the greatest moments I ever had in jazz were listening to him when his band was rolling.

Mingus had to go to San Francisco for three weeks at the Jazz Workshop. It was a cavernous place off Broadway with rows of chairs across the front and middle and tables at the back. The piano was a Steinway B—the best.

Every day, Judy got a present—jewelry, Ghirardelli chocolates. He bought her an Alaska seal fur coat, and dapper Dannie Richmond wore it back to New York City so his boss didn't have to declare buying it.

He sent Janet Coleman a note about the book: "Does the writer sound convincing? Has he been dead and alive?" He wanted "a chance to write about the true jazz scene that has made our *masters* millions and taken the most famed to their penniless graves they had awaited as the only escape from the invisible chains on black jazz as an art." [46]

The San Francisco *Examiner* called him "The Beethoven of Jazz Composers."[47] He was ebullient. He talked of how Bird had praised his writings when he first hit New York, then called him out of the post office.

When he met Kate Mulholland's husband during one intermission, he said, "You know, I never balled your wife, man. Not that I didn't want to. But it was against my religion."

He never edited himself. He said whatever he thought.

9 Camelot

CHARLES McPHERSON respected his volatile new boss. Mingus was forthright about money and paid his musicians fairly. He had a good heart and a sense of ethics and morality. He was constantly restless and goading them, but he wanted their best, all the time.

Others saw the younger man under near-constant siege. "You can't play all the instruments Eric did," they'd hear Mingus growl at him. The demands didn't have to be consistent: "You sound too much like Bird. You don't sound enough like Bird." But McPherson shed his fear as he sensed in Mingus the mind of a perfectionist turning endlessly on itself.

For New Year's 1961, the Workshop with McPherson and Hillyer played Copa City at 108-20 Merrick Boulevard in Jamaica, not far from Mingus's Uncle Fess Williams's house. During a series of dates there Mingus unveiled Rotary Perception, his latest label for how his bands made music by conversing onstage.

A few months later, he told an interviewer the name was a public relations gimmick.[1]

CHARLES MINGUS: Although the word was a gimmick the music wasn't. Swing proceeds in one direction only . . . Previously jazz has been held back by people who think that everything must be played in the "heard" or obvious pulse . . . With Rotary Perception you may imagine a circle around the beat.[2]

Bebop opened the basic rhythmic units of jazz, and drummers like Max Roach pioneered new ways to subdivide time. Mingus taught Dannie Richmond to approach his pieces by expanding his playing outward during them, like a spiral, then retracing the spiral back into a point.[3]

Those postwar insights into the nature of rhythm were now fueling the free-jazz movement that Mingus had helped create but stood apart from, as he had bop, hard bop, cool, Third Stream, and funky jazz.

He was not part of any movement. Like Groucho Marx, he would never join any club that would have him as a member. He made his own history. He was Charles Mingus.

He did a TV spot with the band and was interviewed about the elastic rhythms he and Dannie kept springing from. He described them as a railroad track, suggested by the beats they were actually playing, which were above and below and in front of the train. As he moved his hands to illustrate, he suddenly looked right into the camera and said, "Can you see this on camera?"[4]

Few in jazz were so conscious of cameras and placement and lighting, conscious enough to play to them.

He was a teacher.

The Workshop played Copa City several times over the next eighteen months. That April, Candid hosted a record release party there, and the invitations to music-biz VIPs mentioned Rotary Perception.[5]

Dan Morgenstern was newly in charge of *Metronome*, after Bill Coss left. He wrote a two-pronged article reviewing shows by Mingus and Louis Armstrong that discussed Rotary Perception.

Soon Morgenstern discovered Mingus was writing a book. The prickly bassist had read the *Metronome* piece and liked it, so Mingus, Coss, and Bob Altshuler of Candid Records met Morgenstern at the Copper Rail and brought the now-immense manuscript. Coss had edited and rewritten parts. They sat in a booth and leafed through it, then Morgenstern, intrigued, took the beginning home and was convinced it was a worthwhile project. But no matter how they tried, they couldn't find a publisher for the book.

Morgenstern was most struck by Mingus's caustic wit, his ready sense of humor. This wasn't the man he'd expected.

Mingus's Buick lemon had been in and out of the shop. That winter, a terrible snowstorm led to a ban on private cars in the streets. So when Peggy Lee, his old friend from Hollywood, was at Basin Street East, he took Judy to the show in a Cadillac limousine that cost seven dollars an hour.

Since her marriage, she was becoming another of his artistic creations.

JUDY STARKEY MINGUS McGRATH: See, one theory was that if people thought he was married to someone with money, they would want to give him more work and money. So he pretended that I had money. He took me to Bonwit Teller, and got me a personal shopper. I ended up with a black cocktail dress and suits and all these *things*. And I would have to dress up and go out.

It was the witching hour of Camelot, the Kennedy era that became glamorosly, instantly mythic. Kennedy charisma was a byword.

"The torch has been passed to a new generation" was one resonant line from the new President's January inaugural address. It was true. In business and politics and the arts, the generation born between world wars had come of age and was coming into power and influence and visibility.

A different sense of culture suffused the Kennedy White House. Writers, artists, musicians, scientists were regular high-profile guests. Pablo Casals performed. Robert Frost read. French cuisine was served. Frumpy Mamie Eisenhower was replaced by haute-couture Jackie Kennedy.

And civil rights, now center stage in American public debate, was at the heart of Kennedy's presidential agenda. It was time, he said, for the country to deliver on its promises. His brother Robert, now attorney general, vowed to use the Justice Department to ensure that black Americans got equal treatment. He aggressively enforced the Civil Rights Act of 1960, which allowed "referees" to help blacks register to vote.

The Kennedy brothers got Dr. Martin Luther King Jr. released when he was sentenced to a four-month jail term for sitting in at a restaurant.

Freedom Riders tested the new antisegregation court rulings in the South, putting their lives on the line as they rode into interstate travel bus stations. In Birmingham and Montgomery, they were beaten. One bus was burned. JFK's admininistration intervened to protect them. Black leaders realized again that adverse publicity for segregationist tactics was snowballing non-southern support for their movement.

The changes building since the 1940s were hitting critical mass. As Bird's title put it, "Now's the Time."

In early 1960s America, riding an unprecedented wave of prosperity, with the smart young Kennedy clan in charge, the good life seemed within reach for almost anyone, even a black jazz musician.

Miles Davis was making big money, dressing in European suits, collecting art and models, driving a Ferrari. One night, he pulled up to a club the Workshop was playing. The owner asked him if he was free in three weeks, and Davis sneered, "You can't pay me." He wanted $1,800 a week—for himself, band extra. The owner instantly agreed.

Mingus was dressing in sharp suits, bowlers, vests as he limoed around town. His favorite dinner was aged steak and fine Beaujolais. Sometimes he'd follow it, in between sets, with a Chinese dinner. If he went to a grungy joint, it was because the food was stellar.

He was fat. It had been a long time since the days in San Francisco, when he had eaten mayonnaise for the eggs. He wanted a piece of the good life.

At the end of March, Jazz Workshop filed its corporate tax returns for 1960. Gross receipts were listed as $18,445.74. Royalties totaled 4,103.57. Officers' compensation came to $7,213.95.[6]

Pastor John Garcia Gensel made a name for himself by seeing the Workshop fourteen nights in a row, including a few at Copa City.

Mingus came to a Good Friday service that April, at the Advent Lutheran Church on Broadway and 93rd Street. "I figured," said Gensel years later, "if he could come in on a Friday to a Good Friday service in the afternoon, I could go hear him that night at Copa City."

Later in 1961, the Workshop performed at Gensel's first jazz-worship service, with Doug Watkins on bass. Gensel continued to mix jazz with Lutheran services for thirty years. In 1965, when he moved crosstown from Advent to St. Peter's on East 53rd Street, St. Peter's became the church for marrying and burying and memorializing jazz musicians.

Gensel treated them with humor, irony, and respect. And they knew he loved the music.

Mingus's friend Kenneth Patchen, with whom he'd toured in 1958, had run up hospital bills for his spinal problems, which put him in a wheelchair until he died in 1972. A benefit was planned in Palo Alto, south of San Francisco, and Mingus brought the Workshop down from the city.

Patchen was Mingus's senior by eleven years. He'd lived in California and New York, and his first poetry collection was published in 1936. Patchen's work drew on religious symbols; his chewy language and striking, eccentric metaphors make him kind of a twentieth-century John Donne. But he wrote in the cadenced free verse the Beats had adapted from Walt Whitman and William Carlos Williams.

They were stretching and extending poetic forms, filling them with themselves, their voices, as Mingus was doing with music.

Patchen had also written a satirical novel in 1945, called *Memoirs of a Shy*

Pornographer. It was a a Candide-like story that foreshadowed parts of *Memoirs of a Half-Schitt-Colored Nigger*.

Before the benefit, Mingus told the band he couldn't pay them; all the money raised was for Patchen. They agreed to do it anyway. Then after the set, he started doling out five dollar bills: "This is my friend, but let me give you a little carfare or beer money."

He was touched they'd done it. He was more touched when McPherson told him to put his five back in the kitty. His eyes actually watered. From then on, McPherson could be late, but he never got yelled at.

McPherson instigated goofs on Gargantua, as the young band members called Mingus. They had to blow the tightrope pressure off; Gargantua was always serious. But McPherson could pull a straight face fast enough so his boss just shrugged.

Mingus wasn't writing as much new stuff these days. He'd poured out variations of his gospel-soul blowouts. He'd picked up and finished dozens of ideas he'd only sketched before, from the war era into the late 1950s.

It wasn't that his muse was slowing down, exactly. Besides, his extended works made his music mostly modular. The Workshop could take his pieces in different directions on any night.

Like the Nonagon program had warned, the audience played its part in his shows. They came to see him erupt onstage as much as to hear the music. Those in the know watched expectantly if conversations during a set grew audible, or the phone rang, or the cash register kept jingling. They could almost see his short fuse burning.

He had a kind of selective process, though it didn't always work. Inadvertent talkers got a glare or were told offhandedly to shut up. Usually they subsided. If they persisted or shrugged, he pushed the decibel level up, or got confrontational.

"Jivers"—fans who insisted on talking while he was playing—got to him worst. A tableful of hardware salesmen from Cleveland on expense accounts turned him into a grade-school teacher. He'd stop the set and poke a microphone into their faces, saying, "Okay, tell you what. I'm gonna let you have the show, so why don't you tell everyone else what you been talking about so loud?"

Self-styled hipsters got harangues that punctured their pretensions and were usually thrilled to be his target.

Race was always a wild card. Any action or slight could be reinterpreted at top volume from the stage as prejudice, and then things could escalate fast.

He was great copy, and the New York media loved him. For days after a write-up about some outrageous behavior, the crowds at his gigs swelled.

His music was multifaceted, a creative reflection of his complex personality and gifts. But his shows were never just about music. He was never just about music. Music was a distillation of life, and so he was his own show, acting in the moment. He never edited. He was the same onstage and off, always fully himself. Because few people ever are, that made him bigger than life, magnetic as hell.

And, a true master of existential paradox, he knew it.

Some of his sidemen never got it. Most of them did, some grudgingly, some with more understanding.

CHARLES McPHERSON: There were evenings when everything went a certain way and he was happy. But there were evenings when everything was great and I could tell he was uncomfortable, because it didn't give him a springboard to vent. It was very important for him to vent. Not just musically; verbally. It was weird. When something went wrong, when something was less than perfect, it was almost like, Now the fun is here again. He could be vocal, involve the audience now with something.

And people were expecting this. They didn't expect four hours of Mingus from 9:00 to 1:00. He's expected to have something to say politically in the moment, something to do, be mad, whatever.

You had to sweat every night, because otherwise Mingus would embarrass you. Because he just didn't care. He didn't care about embarrassing himself. There were times when he fired himself. He said, "I don't like the way we sound; we're fired." And he'd tell the club owner, "We quit, we're fired. I'M FIRED!!" Of course, he'd hire everybody back, including himself, by the end of the night. Or overnight. Next day, we'd be at the club again. But there'd be that moment. It's like taking someone and throwing them into the water, sink or swim. Five, six nights a week.

Some of the musicians who'd worked with him called the Workshop the Sweatshop.

The Connection, a play about racism and drugs that was first staged by the Living Theater, had become a hit. Director Shirley Clarke, who'd make a movie about Ornette Coleman, shot the play as an independently produced film, which was critically acclaimed for its searing social commentary. Ex-Workshop saxist Jackie McLean was in it.

Jazz was hot. Record sales were booming, and clubs and concert halls were thriving. Noir film sound tracks and TV detective themes had made stars out of composers like Henry Mancini, who incorporated jazzy touches into the scores. In 1959, Otto Preminger had directed the Oscar-winning *Anatomy of a Murder* with music by Duke Ellington, who had a cameo.

There was an audience to be tapped via jazz.

Nel King was an American jazz fan, a New York-based writer and editor who had seen Mingus and loved his show. She sensed he was a natural actor.

With echoes of Orson Welles and Paul Robeson in her head, she wanted to adapt Shakespeare's *Othello* to a jazz setting. The classic play spoke to America's contemporary racial conflicts. Jazz was an art forged mainly by black Americans. The music would be part of the drama, like it was in *The Connection*. It was a natural fit.

With Peter Jericho, King co-wrote a screenplay about a black jazz pianist and his white girlfriend Delia, a singer, with a white drummer as the Iago figure.

Interracial relationships were still a flash point for American media. For all its fame, John Cassavetes's *Shadows* was a tiny independent film, and few mainstream filmmakers were bold enough to risk alienating audiences for a social statement.

King and Jericho couldn't sell the script, so they took it to England, where in 1959 director Basil Dearden had made *Sapphire*, a thoughtful movie about a murdered black music student who'd passed for white. *All Night Long* suited him.

The writers redid the setting, replacing New York lofts with London flats. Patrick McGoohan, an actor known for his TV private-eye series *Danger Man*, signed on as the drummer. But Nel King also wanted Mingus in her movie.

He later claimed he was supposed to have had a bigger onscreen part. Even the music was relegated to occasional backdrop, and his camera time was a few minutes, barely in the frame, even if he was talking to Richard Attenborough.

He did one scene with Dave Brubeck, who otherwise fared no better with onscreen time. That didn't stop Mingus from seeing his being slighted as racially motivated, nor did it stop him for angling for more. He rehearsed a band on the set, to make a bid for writing or performing a bigger piece of the sound track. He squawked if his limousine was late, or smaller than somebody else's.[7]

With his Hollywood background, his uncanny sense of camera placement and musical cues, Mingus wanted to help the director, so he made suggestions. He wanted to retake his own shots until he was satisfied. Dearden humored him to a point, but didn't need his advice.

In the end, Mingus shot two numbers included in the movie. In one of them, he mimed a white British bassist's recorded part.[8]

The British were taken aback by the ways he came on to women. Restraint was hardly his forte; directness was. He had no trouble separating his duty to Judy from his extracurricular one-nighters. He was his own law.

Alexis Korner, a BBC disk jockey, interviewed Mingus, and was fascinated and appalled. He said Mingus was chasing a public relations representative named Diane, exploded into tantrums about crummy English restaurants, and talked race nonstop.[9]

Korner soon formed a band called Blues Incorporated, inspired by Mingus and Muddy Waters, and became a seminal figure in the London blues revival that yielded the Rolling Stones.

Mingus bought a German bass for 400 pounds. He took actress Betsy Blair to see Peggy Lee perform, and dropped 200 pounds at the supper club. He took cabs everywhere. It was then he discovered each pound was worth almost two-and-a-half dollars.[10]

But he was Mingus. He went to Paris with Diane on what he described as a tour of Paris clubs.

And back home, he decided to stop calling limousines and just buy one.

When he came home in August 1961, he took Judy out on the town. She hadn't been out with him much since the baby's birth. She was a full-time mother, took care of the apartment, cooked for the musicians. She'd become a housewife. He seemed to want a family and a home, and she wanted him to have it.

In mid-August, Mingus played piano with the Workshop for a one-night gig at the Village Vanguard, filling in for Art Tatum's foremost disciple, Jazz at the Philharmonic star pianist Oscar Peterson, who had softened the old man's angles. For almost a year, Mingus played piano in the Workshop and hired bassists.

He bought a stunning new Cadillac Fleetwood limousine, with burgundy exterior and fawn interior, for $13,000.[11] You could still park anywhere on the street in New York. He took Judy and Keki driving all over the city.

The annual insurance for his two cars cost $311.05.[12]

Joe Glaser's prestigious and powerful Associated Booking Corporation was handling him now. Glaser had managed Red Norvo when Mingus was in the trio, and he'd long managed big jazz stars like Louis Armstrong. He was a thuggish man with a widespread reputation for mob ties, and he commanded respect in the music business.

Glaser's agency booked the Workshop into the Coronet Club at 1200 Fulton Street for two weeks at $1,000 a week. The contractual stipulations included "two microphones, reasonable sound, and a piano tuned at 440 Hz western pitch."[13]

Mingus was living the good life.

That September, he got a long letter from his sister Grace.[14] Their cousin Phil told Vivian he'd quit working on his music, that he'd let his hair go nappy and was saying he was African.

Phil also said Mingus was writing his autobiography. Grace thinks nobody could tell about their lives as well as he could. He does it even in his letters.

Grace crashed her car; her head busted the windshield. But she's back at the post office, where she's almost a celebrity. Everybody knows who he is and asks if she's his sister, and she's so proud. But she doesn't have any of his albums. She can't afford to buy them, and he'd promised to send them, and please do!

She can't call him because she has too many bills, and it costs so much. She asks him to recommend a bass teacher for the grandson of the Sunday school teacher, who has all his records. Maybe he could teach the boy himself.

Mama, now living with her, and the rest send their love. They still haven't found his pictures and things. Vivian thinks they might have been lost in Mama's moving.

In September 1961, he played bass on an NBC Sunday morning religious program, with Max Roach and Randy Weston. The theme was religious expression in jazz.

They shot footage of the Reverend Gensel walking to the Village Gate, then sitting at the base of the three-foot-high stage platform. Just before they went on the air, Genz, as Mingus called him, said he had to pee. Mingus pointed his finger from on high at him and said, "You go. Jesus did."

Gensel loved Mingus's sense of humor, thought he was brilliant: "He captured the humanity of Jesus, a subject about which thousands of books have been written, in two words." Mingus told Gensel he liked him better than Father O'Connor in Boston, because "you go to bed with a woman."

On September 29, Lenny Bruce was busted in Philadelphia for possession of narcotics. Five days later, he was busted for obscenity at San Francisco's Jazz Workshop. But on November 19, 1961, Bruce made an appearance at the Curran Theater in San Francisco that was recorded. It became one of his finest albums, as he targeted his unyielding sense of rage and irony on America's web of racial, ethnic, and other unsolved dilemmas.

One night, a reedman named Ronald Kirk, who'd changed his name to Roland, showed up at Mingus's apartment. He'd been studying Mingus music. He too was a devotee of old gutbucket blues and raucous gospel churches. Like

Dolphy, he was trying to resuscitate antique instruments, but his were even more offbeat—older saxes like the manzello and the stritch.

And he played with the kind of disciplined but spontaneous abandon, the ecstatic possession, that Mingus wanted. Kirk would be his newest creation. He called the younger man "my Frankenstein."

They shared an obsession with pockets. Kirk wore overcoats and pants with more than the usual allotment, and Mingus was buying shirts with hidden pockets to stash cash.

Jimmy Knepper and Yusef Lateef bought Kirk his first dinner at Tad's Steak House, and David Amram went with Mingus to check out his playing at the 125 Club uptown, where painter Larry Rivers sat in regularly on sax.

In October, Kirk joined the Workshop at Birdland, and played Mingus's newest gospel-jazz piece, a hollering blowout slyly dubbed "Hog Callin' Blues." Kirk recorded the onomatopoeic tour de force a month later, when the Workshop went into the studio with Atlantic's Nesuhi Ertegun.

Mingus was talking about signing with Frank Sinatra's new label, Reprise, which in the late 1960s became home to rockers like Jimi Hendrix.

Even though he was playing piano almost full time onstage and had hired Doug Watkins and Henry Grimes to take the bass chair, he rarely let them find their way uncorrected through a set. It frustrated him to hear relatively predictable bass lines beneath the Workshop. But on the other hand, if he led from the piano, he could constantly prod the band just by wandering away from the tune. It was a Hobson's choice. He couldn't play two instruments at once, but he'd try it anyway from time to time, as they went on gigs in Philadelphia, San Francisco, and Los Angeles, as if to make sure.

He bumped into Kate Mulholland and her husband when they were browsing at Ferlinghetti's City Lights bookstore in San Francisco, and they went to see him play with Kirk at the Jazz Workshop.

The November Atlantic sessions for *Oh Yeah* were loose, and featured a beefed-up Workshop with Booker Ervin replacing Yusef Lateef next to Kirk for a bristling reed display.

"Ecclusiastics," a typically punning title, was another form of gospel drive, and they reworked "Peggy's Blue Skylight" and debuted a daring voice collage called "Passions of a Man," which swelled and burbled and mystified with the multitracked Mingus voices chasing through a torrent of assertions and ideas.

"Oh Lord, Don't Let Them Drop That Atomic Bomb on Me" was another of his acidly parodic blues-singing interludes, a "Faubus" aimed at the Cold War scenario of Mutual Assured Destruction. MAD was the military strategy keeping the United States and the Soviet Union hovering around the equilibrium of stalemate because, the rationale went, any upset to the status quo likely meant the end of the world.

When the record came out, *Down Beat*'s reviewer scoffed at Mingus's singing on "Devil Woman," and he shot back a characteristic note.

CHARLES MINGUS: My efforts at blues singing were not meant to challenge such diverse masters as Joe Turner, Ray Charles, or Big Bill Broonzy, and I don't think their singing was meant as a challenge to each other or to me.... No one could sing my blues but me (if you must call it singing), just as no one could holler for you if I decided to punch you in your mouth![15]

Mingus had a West Coast swing to make that spring, and he decided he'd get more money selling the Buick in Los Angeles than in New York. So he'd drive it cross-country and leave it with Buddy Collette. Dannie Richmond actually drove the wagon, filled with his drums. Doug Watkins was supposed to take the rest of the band in his Peugeot, but Kirk showed up with his wife, who was drunk or stoned and obnoxiously loud.

Mingus turned to Knepper: "I don't want to drive in the car with those niggers." The pair took the sharp new Cadillac limousine he'd just bought.

It was late afternoon when they finally got through the Lincoln Tunnel. Mingus drove all night, then all day. At dusk he said, "Jim, you got to drive. I gotta close my eyes." Knepper's license had expired. "Nobody," Mingus explained patiently, "stops a Caddy limo." Knepper drove.

They lost the others. Dannie copped drugs with the gas money, then called to New York and had more cash wired. Watkins peeled off somewhere. Knepper and Mingus drove for four more days. They stopped twice for food, picked up bags of fried chicken and ate on the road, and snacked on cookies and sweets Mingus stockpiled in the car. They stopped at a motel each night for precisely eight hours.

He was a black man with a white man in the middle of America. He didn't want to play Jim to Knepper's Huck Finn.

They stopped in Las Vegas, and literally ran backstage to see Sarah Vaughan, now a headliner, then ran back out to the car, and back on the road. Kerouac would have loved it.

Somehow, everybody wound up in San Francisco in time.

JIMMY KNEPPER: When we stopped to check into a hotel, Mingus sent me in to check in the band—and he knew what was going to happen. The guy says, "Who's with you?" He looks out, sees all these black guys: "We don't take colored in this place." Mingus just wanted to educate me, I suppose.

They stayed at Farwell's place instead.

Mingus wanted to make an impression like Miles Davis, so he started wearing sunglasses, even onstage. He wanted to lose weight, but being on the road didn't help.

He was rooming with Knepper and had an idea about how to get attention. He pulled out a gray and black wool tie that looked like what chauffeurs wore, and found a cap. He told Knepper to wear them, and taught him how to make a chauffeur's stop, gliding gently to a halt.

That night, Knepper drove him to the club, and jumped out to open the door for his boss. When Mingus edged his bulk out of the car, he found the sidewalk was empty.

Nobody had any money after the cross-country haul. Mingus cajoled the club owner for an advance and got $100. Next night, same dialog, but no cash, so he tried to grab some bottles from behind the bar.

He saw Dorian for the first time since 1958, with Celia, who'd married Saul Zaentz in 1960. They were at a sunset party for him, a buffet with a big ham, and fresh mayonnaise the hostess had made herself. Mingus was fat. He snarled at the embarrassed hostess that he was on a diet, took Dorian's hand, and went to buy raw vegetables.

When they came back, the Zaentzes had to leave. Saul suggested they talk about Debut. Maybe Fantasy could distribute Debut for him, make them all some money.

Mingus decided to leave too. The hostess wanted to call him a car. "No, it's all right," he said. "My wife and her husband will give me a ride."

Knepper gave him two-weeks notice. He decided he'd rather pay his own way back than spend another five days "driving back with this nut."

Meantime, they drove to Los Angeles and stayed at Knepper's mother's house. They were sharing a bill with Lenny Bruce on Sunset Boulevard. It was an intense back-to-back show. Acid as the Workshop's shows could be, Bruce was the king of existential absurdity. He turned racial and ethnic prejudices inside out, spewing slurs onstage to rip off the veneer of politeness that veiled the divisions crisscrossing the real America.

In May 1959, the *New York Times* had brought Bruce's huge underground reputation to wide public notice. Its reviewer primly wrote, "The newest and in some ways the most scarifyingly funny proponent of significance . . . is Lenny Bruce, a sort of abstract expressionist stand-up comedian paid $1,750 a week to vent his outrage on the clientele."[16]

A few months later, Bruce would begin a five-year-long series of busts for narcotics and obscenity. For a while his appearances at swanky clubs drew big crowds, and he made big money. But eventually, his NYC cabaret card was revoked, leaving him unable to work. He was banned from Australia and England. His act got increasingly stripped bare; he'd improvise onstage from a handful of themes. He was pushing his art's edge into the moment.

Like Mingus with music, Bruce felt comedy had dangerous real work to do in the world, that it was a calling and a craft, that it had to be able to encompass him, that he couldn't squeeze himself and what he had to say into its preexisting formats. Friends said if he hadn't been a comic, he would have been a preacher. It was exactly what Mingus's friends said of him.

One night during the Hollywood gig, Mingus started riding Knepper onstage in front of women friends. One of them was one of Duke Ellington's girlfriends, Mattie Comfort, wife of Mingus's Watts friend and fellow bassist Joe Comfort. Mattie looked like Lena Horne, and was sitting with Pat Willard, a white Duke fan, in the front row.

Mattie called out, "Hey, Mingus, leave that white boy alone, he loves you." He rasped, "You're not black enough to talk to me like that." She said coolly, "You're lighter than I am, Mingus."

JIMMY KNEPPER: So he plays eight bars of B-flat so fast, it was almost impossible. He'd do that every now and then, maybe to make the band realize he could play at the tempo and we couldn't—or at least, not all of us could. But we played a couple of choruses and boom, that was the end of the night.

Mingus spotted Knepper with the women in the lobby. When Mattie left to get her car, he followed her into the parking lot, then took out a thick pen fitted with a charge to shoot pepper. He had no pepper, just charges. He had taken to firing it off in the club during his shows, but now he shot it off in her face.

Mattie was still shaking when she picked up the other two. In the rearview mirror, she watched Mingus follow them up Sunset Boulevard in the Cadillac. She turned right on Vine, right on Hollywood, and headed for the police station. No cops, no cop cars, and Mingus was right behind them. So she made a right on N. Bronson and ran a red light at Sunset, where a police cruiser parked there stopped them.

To the puzzled cop, Mattie explained that Knepper worked for Charles Mingus, who was chasing them. When the cop looked up, the limo wheeled into a U-turn and sped off. The cop shrugged, and let Mattie off with a warning. Relieved, they drove to Pat Willard's house and listened to Ellington records.

On February 20, Local 802 entered a judgment against Jazz Workshop regarding Mingus's unpaid commissions to Shaw Artists Corporation, amounting to $300, for his work in Toronto. He was ordered to pay it off at $25 a week. He wrote back, "I will never get fair treatment in this asshole country."[17]

Her Majesty's Inspector of Taxes was interested in the problem as well: Mingus had booked $2,000 worth of dates in Britain on his own, while he was there filming *All Night Long,* and hadn't paid taxes on them. Inland Revenue was also interested.

He wrote and explained he'd had very heavy expenses in London, which should cut his taxes. Betsy Blair and Peggy Lee and his press agent, his misunderstanding about the value of the British pound, his new bass, his Gelusil capsules for his ulcer, and innumerable taxis all should cut his bill to near zero, he believed.[18]

In March 1962, the Workshop was back at Birdland. When Mingus hugged Eddie Bert, Bert felt like he was being enveloped in Jello. The duo went to see Count Basie, who featured Thad Jones in his big band. Mingus waved at his chauffeured limousine, and they climbed in and drove to the Village Gate, mingled, swapped road stories,

EDDIE BERT: And all of sudden he says, "I'm on the air in two minutes. Let's get outta here." So we get the chauffeur, and we're going uptown on Third Avenue. "Turn the radio on," he says. His group is playing. "Who the hell is playing my bass?" So he tears down the stairs at Birdland—and it's Paul Chambers. So that was all right.

Chambers played with Miles Davis and John Coltrane, and was one of Mingus's many ex-students.

Janet Coleman introduced Mingus to the Ninth Circle in the West Village. Sometimes he took Judy and Keki there; sometimes he came down alone.

The Circle was a stylish hangout at 139 West 10th Street, owned by Bob Krivit and Mickey Ruskin. It drew artists and celebrities and beatniks, an integrated crowd warmed by a jazz-filled jukebox and Ruskin's rich pumpernickel bread and sandwiches. The waves of talk rose over the under-foot crunch of empty peanut shells tossed onto the floor.

Krivit, another large man, had dealings with the mob and cashed Mingus's small royalty checks for him. He handled cash payrolls for Mingus's club gigs too; Mingus carried the money around in his socks.

Roxanne and Janet Coleman hung out there. A lot of people did. Roxanne was going out with Bruce Bethany, who managed the Circle's dining room.

One night, Mingus got upset because Lenny Bruce, sharing a back booth with Janet and him, was saying "cunt" so much in front of her.[19] He told her to drop a black boyfriend; she wasn't rich enough to afford the hardships that a mixed-race relationship would inevitably bring.

Every night, as soon as Mingus got off a gig, he'd go out, anywhere from the Cafe Figaro on Bleecker to Birdland. He'd head home at five or six in the morning.

The Man Who Never Sleeps was all over town.

In early 1962, Sun Ra and his Arkestra were living in New York, and had finally found a place to play: the Café Bizarre on West 3rd Street, a Beat hangout with sawdust floors and a potbellied stove.

Ra, born Herman Blount, was an iconoclastic pianist, bandleader, composer, and mystic. He claimed he was from Saturn, spoke in long philological-mystical sentences about the true inner meanings of language, wrote music that spanned jazz history from ragtime through swing and into the contemporary avant-garde. His bands were strictly disciplined vehicles for his music, which could be wild and woolly, on the edge of chaos but spinning with powerful attractive energies. Ra maintained total control, firing musicians at will. Onstage they wore outrageous costumes and put on a freewheeling show.

While Ra was breaking ground in jazz, he only sometimes intersected with other pioneers. He was a prophet, an avatar, predicting where the next wave of avantists would head while he reclaimed and rewrote musical pieces of jazz's history. He and Mingus had much in common.

Mingus came down to the Café Bizarre and liked what he heard, defended Ra's Arkestra against their detractors, introduced Ra to his friend, choreographer Katharine Dunham.

Later, when Ra returned the favor, showing up at the Five Spot, Mingus asked him what he was doing there. "I come down to the Village a lot," said Ra. "No," Mingus replied, "I mean what are you doing here on *Earth*."[20]

Mingus had started using pianists again, but he was fighting with Jaki Byard, so at Birdland he used a young pianist named Toshiko Akiyoshi. He met her when she played intermissions at the Five Spot.

Few, if any, other bandleaders would have hired a Japanese woman. She heard the comments: "How is he gonna hit *her*?" He never did, despite stories that he slammed the keyboard cover on her hands.

His reputation was mythic. It gave birth to its own stories now.

Akiyoshi wanted to be a composer herself, and loved his music and approach.

TOSHIKO AKIYOSHI: I asked him, "Why me?" He said, "It's true there are a lot of players who play as good as you, others better than you, but you are a new face, a new name. That's good for the group. Whenever there's a new name, people ask about it." I really thought that was extraordinary. He could have said to me, "It would be good for you, playing with me will get you recognition, what have you." But he didn't. He was honest, straight-ahead honest. That impressed me so much I joined the group.

Booker Ervin helped her with the band's book. With Richard Williams on trumpet, they played his haunts: Birdland, Pep's Showbar in Philadelphia. Akiyoshi liked the rehearsals at Mingus's Fifth Avenue apartment best. There was no paper, no cushion. Essential music, she felt, could be lost by only using paper.

Mingus was getting drawn deeper into the links between New York mobsters and jazz. The Ninth Circle, where he cashed the checks BMI sent him from monitoring performance rights, was just another portal.

Mo Levy offered to have Debut distributed by Brunswick Records.[21] Like Levy, Brunswick owner Nat Tarnopol was connected to the mob. He'd made a fortune off black singing star Jackie Wilson, and booked shows with legendary disk jockey Alan Freed.

Mingus said no, he wanted his company. Levy said he could get a lot more out of Debut, for a small percentage.[22]

He was dealing with Joe Glaser, who had handled Red Norvo and big stars like Basie and Miles. Glaser sent him several letters about booking arrangements during 1962.[23] But what worried Mingus was that Glaser seemed connected too. Rumors swirled that whenever Miles hit a town where there was trumpet competition, Glaser made sure the competition disappeared. Word was that sometimes lips got cut.

On his way to see Glaser, Mingus stopped a few times to see Roxanne Bethany. Her office was below Glaser's. She felt Mingus was nervous; it wasn't like him.

Later, Mingus told a story about an attorney named Max Kauffman, who offered him a big salary guarantee whether he was working or not. Basie, Duke, they all did that. They all work for us, Kaufman said. You'll be booked by the Joe Glaser office.

Mingus told Kauffman he'd agreed to record for Levy. Kauffman said he'd speak with him. According to Mingus, Kauffman said, "Do you know who you're with now? Joe Gallo."[24]

In 1957, Gallo had engineered the death of kingpin Albert Anastasia in a Manhattan barbershop. He was a throwback to the mob's precorporate days. The mob bosses didn't like him, and for good reason. They had enough headaches. Bobby Kennedy had declared war on them, and they didn't need an attention- and headline-grabbing loose cannon like Crazy Joe running loose. Besides, Gallo wanted to poach on their carefully carved-up duchies, or else blow them out of his way.

Mingus had no idea who Joe Gallo was. He thought Gallo was another Mo Levy. He knew Mo was connected, and he knew Mo was tough. He'd seen him pull tickets off cars of favored customers parked illegally in front of Birdland, and slap the cop who put them there.[25] Levy had an understanding with the NYPD.

Levy owned Patricia Music, named after his wife. He owned the biggest piece of "Lullaby of Birdland," the hugely successful tune he'd asked George Shearing to write about his club. Everyone recorded it, and it sold millions.

Levy warned Mingus, "These people, they'll kill your wife, they'll kill your mother, they'll kill your babies. They're not like us. We don't do things like that."[26]

Mingus wrote Janet Coleman a letter that was part of his growing book.

CHARLES MINGUS: Perhaps someday the musicians will profit as well as their barterers, barkers, and sacred professional friends that crap up the scene intentionally to confuse the profit where they think best, their pockets; and the few toms [sic] who this far have been satisfied with their picture in their magazines and less than fifty percent of their salaries in their pockets.[27]

Fantasy began reissuing Debut material soon after the Workshop's swing through San Francisco, and Mingus began getting more little checks. He'd carry them to the Ninth Circle in a briefcase, and walk out with cash.

That May, Joe Glaser wrote to Dominick Monea, one of Mingus's many nominal managers of the period. Glaser apologized for Charlie's feeling ignored, explaining he'd been sidelined for five months by an accident. Now he was back, though. Charlie wanted to accept his Italian Grand Prix on newsman Mike Wallace's TV show PM East. Glaser would put his men onto making it happen.

Eleven days later, Glaser's associate Jack Green wrote to Monea, offering Mingus a gig for the week of July 12 at $1,350 for the band. Mingus had wanted

$2,500, but, Green explained, he couldn't draw that well. Besides, Green added, it was a raise from the $1,250 he usually got there.[28]

Mingus just wasn't a star on the order of Basie or Duke or Miles.

Glaser wanted to put Mingus on the road like Ellington, set him on constant tour and draw royalties from record sales as well as road income, to expand the whole operation.

Mingus wasn't sure he wanted the deal. He didn't want to have to travel all the time. Ellington spent his life in hotels and cars and trains, and spent night after night in crummy out-of-the-way joints just to keep the salaried band in work. It was his instrument.

Mingus couldn't decide if he was up for the tradeoff. He'd string Glaser along for a while. It was dangerous, but he'd be sly, careful. He had to be. He was getting in deeper. He had his reputation as an unpredictable outsider, a volatile character to help. But Glaser's power and friends made him nervous.

That's the main reason he and Judy created Monea, as they did a few other "managers" of Italian descent who, in this period, sent and received letters and offers. The name was like the name of a kid Judy grew up with. Mingus needed leverage with Glaser. He was afraid of the mob.

In spring 1962, *Tijuana Moods* came out to praises, five years after it was recorded. It sold 1,795 copies in three months, 2,099 the next quarter, 3,079 the next. For this Mingus was paid additional royalties of $640.04.[29]

He gave one copy to Maureen Meloy, and inscribed it.

CHARLES MINGUS: Dear Friend, I hope someday that, [sic] those dreams, [sic] and hopes that so often appear as fantasies of conscious sleepless nightmarish, day and night sleep, are uncovered to to [sic] that they truly are, exercises of the unconscious seeking to truely [sic] express what is you . . . that we both know would be contant [sic] beauty, but that the world we live in has little place for truth, or love, or whatever, unless it has a market price. So just to remind you the ways of the world is far from truth, lover, but the mind in search of what it has found in it self [sic] to be good, is holy and irreplaceable..Chazz.. P.S. Chazz with love that is . . . [30]

To the press, Mingus had been talking up his book, now swollen into a stack of more than 1,000 typewritten pages. He was creating interest. He signed with editor Louis Lomax at McGraw-Hill, one of New York's largest publishers. He told people he got a $15,000 advance. It was actually $5,500.[31]

Still, he didn't want to stay on the road so hard. He could stay in the public eye without that.

David Amram wrote the score for a movie that was a sign of the changing times. *The Manchurian Candidate* was released in 1962. The plot turned on brainwashing. During the Korean War, the Communists were said to have perfected turning people into automata via hypnosis and Pavlovian conditioning. The fears in part reflected the spread of post-Freudian psychological ideas across American culture, as well as front page scandals over shock treatments, lobotomies, and the like.

The movie's credits were thick with people blacklisted during the McCarthy/House Un-American Activities Committee era. The main character was a brainwashed GI, a commmunist dupe helping prepare a takeover of the U.S. government by his power-hungry mother and bumbling stepfather, the jowly far-right Senator Iselin. The movie thoughtfully turned cold-war hysteria inside out, and portrayed rabid postwar anticommunists as the true anti-Americans. Frank Sinatra, fresh from championing the Kennedy campaign, played the Army Intelligence hero who deciphers the convoluted plot in Richard Condon's biting screenplay.

That spring, Mingus went to Toronto for the premiere of *All Night Long*, and took limousines around town for a couple of days. The Rank Organization, which produced the movie, reimbursed him for $160 in expenses. When he got back to New York, he had Judy send a letter to them. He was still getting installments of the $9,000 fee for his work on *All Night Long*, and hadn't received his last two payments. By August, he had.[32]

In early 1962, Allen Ginsberg's friend Timothy Leary, a professor at Harvard, was called before a university committee for conducting psychological experiments with LSD.

Leary grew up in an Irish Catholic family abandoned by his alcoholic father. Trained by Jesuits, he was expelled after a year at West Point, but wound up in the army as a psychologist, then was hired at Harvard.

On a 1960 vacation in Mexico, Leary tried psilocybin mushrooms, a psychedelic used in Indian rituals. He talked Harvard into letting him set up experiments about psilocybin's therapeutic effects. Then a British philosophy student showed up with a mayonnaise jar full of sugar laced with LSD, a hallucinogen discovered in the 1940s by Swiss scientist Dr. Albert Hoffman. Leary took it, and it changed his life.

At Cambridge, he met Allen Ginsberg, who'd heard about his Mexico trip, and Aldous Huxley, who'd written the dystopian novel *Brave New World* about drugs and perception. Leary turned them on to LSD, and then, via Ginsberg, expanded the circle to include Jack Kerouac, William Burroughs, and Thelonious Monk. Huxley suggested artists were best suited to take and use psychedelics, and Leary initially agreed, and hired an assistant, Richard Alpert.

Harvard was getting uneasy about his drug experiments, but Leary refused to allow more supervisory control. Suddenly the Bureau of Narcotics got involved, rumors of CIA penetration began, and Leary saw the writing on the wall.

Ginsberg introduced him to Peggy and Billy Hitchcock, who offered him the family's estate, called Millbrook, on the Hudson River's gently rolling eastern side. The old main house looked like a gingerbread mansion, with turrets and towers and elaborately sawn shingles. Peggy had a slightly smaller modern house, called the Bungalow, off to the side.

The big house had a bowling alley. There were smaller outboard buildings and cottages, and acres of orchards and meadows for solitude. It was the perfect setting for Leary and Alpert to adapt the new drug into cult sacrament. Free your mind, and the rest will follow. Leary's meditative, Buddhist-inspired use of LSD led, in 1967, to the League for Spiritual Discovery.

After Toronto, Mingus got in the limousine and took Judy and Carolyn to Millbrook. LSD scared him. He didn't take it, but he went there frequently, often alone, mostly because of his friendship with Peggy Hitchcock. He'd join the other artists and musicians and writers at the big dining hall banquet table, eating and drinking and talking.

Satori by pharmaceutical. Leary was as American as a patent-medicine salesman, but he and Mingus shared beliefs. Born two years apart, they had imbibed pop versions of Eastern religions that had been widespread during the Roaring Twenties and Depression among the cultural elites and were now resurgent in the postwar era.

TIM LEARY: When the individual's behavior and consciousness get hooked to a routine sequence of external actions, he is a dead robot, it is time for him to die and be reborn. Time for him to "Drop-out," "Turn-on," and "Tune-in."[33]

Mingus at Millbrook spent nonmealtimes outdoors. He loved the spreading apple orchards surrounded by stone walls made from clearing the meadows of rocks and boulders. As a kid, he had liked helping Mamie prune their peach trees. It was a careful job: clean cuts, no tearing, painting the smaller cuts, tarring the big ones to protect the tree from pests and frosts.

He drove into town and got the supplies he needed, then spent days pruning the apple orchard. He was as focused as if he were writing a new piece, or coming on to a woman.

Once when he went there by himself, Judy asked him to bring back some lilacs. He sawed off branches and branches, and stuffed them into the limousine. There were almost enough to assemble a lilac bush in their Manhattan living room.

On April 4, 1962, Mingus wrote a multipage letter with a list of gripes to Cadillac Motor Car Division.[34] It cost $3,000 to fly his band to and from California. He bought the Cadillac to save; instead, it was costing him in cash and prestige.

CHARLES MINGUS: My plans were to have at least two chauffeur-driven limousines parked in front of the clubs or theaters I appear at. I felt it would be good for business. In fact, so do the club owners, but not when I have to send for a garage attendant to get it started or tow me off the Hollywood Freeway.[35]

Four months later his insurance policy was canceled for being nearly $100 overdue, and he threatened to report his harrassment to the FBI.[36]

Mingus was the first one hired for the June 1962 Newport Festival, reopened after a year hiatus. Both Wein and he knew how to make hay from their 1960 face-off. On the former site of his Rebel Festival, Mingus played mostly piano, although Akiyoshi sat in. The Workshop had Booker Ervin, Richard Williams, Charles McPherson, and Dannie Richmond.

Judy brought eighteen-month-old Carolyn, in a blue dress, to see the show. Someone reached out to touch her, and he snarled from onstage, "Get your hands off my daughter."

In late August, he began the last gig at the old Five Spot, which closed August 27. Joe and Iggy Termini were moving to the Bowery and St. Mark's Place.

McPherson and Dolphy stood side by side in the expanded Workshop that included Pepper Adams, trombonist Julian Priester, and tuba player Don Butterfield—Mingus's favorite low-end horns.

One night Mingus came in late and threw an athletic bag with dumbbells on the stage. The audience was chattering, and he snarled at them, "Drink or listen, but shut up."

These days, he often stopped by to see Sonny Rollins, who was living on the Lower East Side. Rollins adopted a rigorous physical and spiritual regime after kicking his drug addiction and had a lot of exercise equipment. Sonny respected him. They talked about spirituality and racism, how their music wasn't being appreciated.

SONNY ROLLINS, *musician and friend*: We discussed how angry we both were about social conditions. It was the natural reaction to the societal ills we had to deal with, that the music had to deal with; those were givens. He knew I felt like he did. His "Fables of Faubus" and my *Freedom Suite*—the point is, we were both thinking along those lines. Mingus, me, Max Roach—activists trying to address some of these social ills through the promoters. Max had a lot of problems with George Wein. So did I. So did Mingus.

Rollins had twenty-four-hour access to RCA's studios on East 24th Street, and they went there to play ideas at each other. Mingus stopped gaining weight.

That August, he got a rave review in the American Record Guide from a young saxist-critic named Don Heckman.

The roundup took in five albums, from *Pre-Bird* to *Mingus Ah Um*. Heckman noted his rise to the top of the composer/arranger category in jazz magazine polls. He pointed out, "Mingus gets a great deal from a large group that many composers do not. All his personal touches remain—warm, moving textures, polyrhythms that twist and turn through the basic meter of the music and, most characteristically, a timbral density which always seems to be present in Mingus' music."

Heckman thought the unedited "Original Faubus Fables" "a classic Negro put-down in which satire becomes a deadly rapier-thrust. Faubus emerges in a glare of ridicule as a mock-villain whom no one really takes seriously. This kind of commentary, brimful of feeling, bitingly direct and harshly satiric, appears far too rarely in jazz."[37]

Mingus got a $10,000 advance to record for Impulse!, an aggressive young label that was home to avant-gardists like John Coltrane. Producer Bob Thiele set it up so that he got the advance in weekly installments, like a salary.[38]

It was what he'd always wanted. This was the big leagues, paying enough money to stay home and write.

Typically, he had another deal going with United Artists (UA). Naturally, he wanted to lead a big band. But he wanted to record it live, before an audience. That would take his Workshop shows one step further. People could see a recorded document being made in real time.

It was a daring idea. Even straightforward live albums were still rare.

His first deadline was November 15, then it got moved to October 12. He lost five weeks, thanks to UA. He was overwhelmed with ideas, but he didn't have any time. Anyway, musicians hated to play what he wrote down. Could he run a big band like a Workshop? He thought back to Leonard Feather and Candid.

Onstage, the Workshop started to grow. Pepper Adams was in, and Julian Priester signed on, and he called McPherson and Hillyer back. He was trying different combinations, made up of graduates of his Workshop. They could all make the chemistry he needed to create, and he'd plug the holes with good session sight-readers.

He was sifting through his boxes of yellowing music.

On September 17, Mingus went into the studio with Duke Ellington and Max Roach for a United Artists deal. They had one day's rehearsal, then two days for recording.

When Roach and Mingus showed up the first day, Ellington was already in the studio, writing. He smiled at them, and said in his gracious way, "Think of me as the poor man's Bud Powell." As they ran through the pieces, he told them a story that fit each. For "La Fleurette Africaine," he said, "Think of a beautiful flower in a forest that's been untouched by human hands."

MAX ROACH: We were supposed to be the hot young guys, but we were scrambling. Duke had that left-hand stride thing going, his real sharp sense of time. That was covering up the bass, and I was just playing broken time, because it was so strong.

Everybody from the jazz world, all the critics, came to see this particular session, so the pressure was on—really on, if you were as sensitive as Mingus. And there was a lot of booze, everybody drinking. Mingus got so unsettled he started cussing us all out, and he decided to pick up the bass and leave, just dragged it out of the studio.

Ellington looked at Roach and said smoothly, "I guess this is now a duo." Roach, thinking of how Ellington's band often started sets with most of its personnel still at the venue's bar, stared back blankly. Then the producers came out of the booth and begged Duke to talk to his disciple, so the courtly composer went into the foyer where Mingus was holding his bass and ranting to the dismayed spectators. Duke lit up his famous smile and whispered in Mingus's ear, "Charles, you sound wonderful." Mingus started crying, but he came back inside, and they finished the sessions.

The multiple tensions of this Oedipal meeting show musically on the title track, "Money Jungle," where the bass and piano duel for dominance. Still, the album underlines Ellington's timelessness, his ability to absorb even musical formats, like bebop, that he didn't participate in. And it reenforced the versatility and power of one of bop's great rhythm sections. It's a jazz landmark.

Frank Mabry was a tall thin black man Mingus often introduced as a pimp and a race car driver. Mabry had a flashy handmade "pimpmobile," all leather and chrome. A big corporation supposedly gave it to him for services rendered.

Mabry was a fixer, a jack of all trades, a special-forces veteran who some-times watched their backs for Max Roach and Miles Davis. His long leather dusters and coiled presence said street. He spun tales of his deeds, knew how to handle situations. He was a trickster, and lived in the same building as the Reverend Gensel.

He and Mingus gave Janet Coleman advice about her love life. "Tell him fuck you," Frank urged about a pushy boyfriend. "Send him a telegram." She was fascinated, and she did it.

Mingus wasn't sure just what he'd gotten into with Joe Gallo and Joe Glaser. He badly needed backup, and Mabry was it.

Judy was pregnant again. She was going to a black doctor in Lenox Terrace. Late in the pregnancy, the baby suddenly stopped moving, but the doctor did no tests, just told her to wait and deliver the infant normally. She had dreams that the baby was alive.

Mingus was taking Doridan every night to sleep.

Jaki Byard had first played with Mingus in 1960, at the old Five Spot, when the parade of musical guests included Clifford Jordan. Byard was nearly Mingus's age, which was rare in the Workshop. Like Ervin and Dolphy, Byard was an equal, or as near as possible, within the band.

And Byard was an original. Like Mingus, the pianist had made his own way back through jazz history. He was adept at stride-piano voicings and rhythms, which most boppers found irrelevant. He knew classical music, and he com-posed by mixing genres and ideas from wherever he wanted.

The pair first met in 1959, when Mingus came to hear Byard at Club 82 back-ing female impersonators, and they quickly discovered they both loved to eat.

In the fall of 1962, Byard was back, and alternated with Akiyoshi. He wrote out lead sheets for Workshop neophytes, and Richmond sang their parts from the drums to help guide them.

The group did a broadcast from Birdland, and Mingus pulled a knife out on the producer, who started whimpering. Byard mouthed, "Don't worry." Mingus wheeled. "What?" "I told the guy, Don't worry." "You're right," he said, and threw the knife down.

Byard liked him, saw the gentleness and hurt underneath the rage.

That Labor Day, Jimmy Knepper was working in a parade band when he stopped by Mingus's Fifth Avenue apartment. He was hired back: the boss wanted him to copy some music for his upcoming concert recording.

Almost daily for the next six weeks, Knepper shuttled by bus, ferry, and train two hours each way between between his new Staten Island house and Mingus's uptown apartment, to pick up and drop off sheet music. He worked on his new dining room table, on the ferry and the subway using a clipboard. That way he kept pace with what Mingus and his arrangers were writing.

Gargantua was volatile. He was surrounded by music paper, piles of it, some yellow and cracked. He wasn't writing new stuff as much as researching his past. He couldn't get music together fast enough, so he hired Gene Roland and a couple of other arrangers. They orchestrated his ideas and sketches for the growing orchestra.

It was like what Hollywood film composers did.

Jerome Richardson would be concertmaster. Buddy Collette and Britt Woodman, Eddie Bert and Teddy Charles, Zoot Sims and Booker Ervin, Lonnie Hillyer and Charles McPherson, Toshiko Akiyoshi and Jaki Byard, Richard Williams and Snooky Young and Clark Terry, Milt Hinton on bass with him, so he could solo and conduct more freely—many people from his past would play their parts in this magnum opus, this living orchestral theater.

His uncle Fess Williams would open the second half, putting Mingus music into historical perspective, linking it to early days of jazz. The music and the players would be an onstage, documented summary of his life.

Later, he would try to rework some of the pieces and the overarching idea, and call it *Epitaph*.

In October 1962, the Cuban Missile Crisis riveted the world. Kennedy and Soviet premier Nikita Khruschev walked to the brink of thermonuclear holocaust over the issue of Soviet missiles in communist Cuba, ninety miles off the American coast. For forty-eight hours, the world waited to find out who would blink. Khruschev pulled the missiles out, and Kennedy unleashed a series of CIA assassination plots aimed at Cuban leader Fidel Castro.

Columbus Day loomed nearer. Mingus rehearsed Workshop alumni, the core for the big orchestra, in his apartment and on New York stages like Birdland's. For the first week of October he took them to Pep's Showbar in Philadelphia, and picked up $1,750 for the band.[39]

He wanted the musicians to be ready to leave the music when he led them out of the scores. A lot of the material was old, and written in his forbidding Beethovenesque manner. The musicians looked at it, nonplussed. They only had three full rehearsals. How were they supposed to navigate it?

He didn't care about what musicians considered the natural ranges and limits of their particular instruments. He pushed them on paper the same way he pushed them with his voice: play THIS! Going for what he wanted and missing it was better than playing it safe.

He fell farther behind his workload each day, each hour. He was a slow writer and reader.

He told the *New York Times* he was thinking about leaving the country permanently. The United States was no place for a black jazz musician. Europe was better and fairer. [40]

For the first time, he asked Dr. Pollock to come over to his apartment. The arrangers were holding up his music, he complained, and he was losing his greatest opportunity. He wept.

Judy cooked endless chicken as musicians trooped in and out. Mingus was up all night playing the piano, so she tried to keep Carolyn out of the way during the day.

He argued with the record company and the union about bringing Buddy Collette in from Los Angeles. "No Buddy, no record," he yelled. Finally Collette got his round-trip ticket.

By the second week of October, dozens of scores for pieces and parts of pieces were pouring in, and Knepper was coordinating a four-man copying service to keep up with the torrent of diverse music from a crew of arrangers working from old complex arrangements or a single polytonal chord.

The night before the show, Mingus scheduled a midnight rehearsal, the band's second, in Town Hall's basement. It was more new music. Workshop veterans had played most of it in other forms, but the staggering amount and the band's sheer size changed everything.

By the time Collette arrived at the apartment the day before the concert, Mingus had finally exploded. He'd called Knepper at the copyists' office, and when the trombonist got to his apartment he said, "Jim, you've gotta help me. I want you to write some backgrounds for solos." Knepper said, "This is your music. You should write the backgrounds."

The Bull saw red. He turned and half-slapped Knepper in the mouth, and broke a cap and its tooth stub. Knepper fell down and waited out the storm. Mingus raged at the white faggot and traitor, brandished a kitchen chair. He was still yelling when Knepper finally got up and walked out, but Mingus didn't try to stop him.

When Collette and Britt Woodman saw Mingus at the apartment before the midnight rehearsal, he was shooting off emotional sparks. He told them Knepper called him a nigger and refused to help him.

The midnight rehearsal was a mess. Mingus sang new backing riffs, tried to get soloists to interact, but he tightened the musicians up even more. He couldn't understand why they couldn't follow him, see how important this was. The music was his life.

Collette, the longtime Hollywood studio veteran, understood his pal was compounding the musicians' problems with the demanding, unfinished scores. Mingus needed these people more than they needed him. Buddy told him, "They have to want to play your music."

Knepper, his mouth closed so air wouldn't hit his exposed nerve and ripple it with pain, dropped off his last copying at the rehearsals.

That afternoon, they tried one last rehearsal. The music still wasn't finished. Jerome Richardson told them all to wear tuxedos that night.

For the performance at Town Hall, Mingus showed up in dungarees and a T-shirt and sneakers, and almost immediately started yelling at George Wein backstage. The promoter warned him about time limits and costs, and said the orchestra couldn't do endless stops and starts and retakes. Union charges went into overtime at 11:00 P.M.

Thirty pieces filled the stage, which was bristling with microphones as technicians scurried around and the audience filled the house.

Mingus stormed onstage, annnouncing, "George Wein didn't give us enough time to rehearse." He'd been "mousetrapped" into the show, and anyone who didn't like what he was doing could get their money back. Then he stormed off to change.

The audience expected him to be Mingus, so most of them just shrugged.

Wein had nothing to do with rehearsal time or budgets. Art Talmadge, UA's head, told him to keep the show tight: the night was costing $35,000.

Melba Liston, a fine composer-arranger and another Watts-bred musician, had tables set up on the side of the stage, to oversee copyists still working. They'd run to pass music out during the show.

Mingus came back out in a tuxedo and immediately took his coat off.

The evening rapidly became a musical train wreck. As the music piled up, and the orchestra fell farther behind the program, the musicians got more and more frustrated and Mingus got more volatile. He was desperately trying to forge them into a small and supple Workshop, confronting them with music that was dense and often brand-new to them. The audience was increasingly bewildered.

Before the intermission, Mingus called for Dr. Pollock, who came backstage during the break. Mingus was inconsolable, crying and raging.

Never before could anyone in jazz remember Joe Glaser going onstage and offering an audience their money back. That Columbus Day, he did.

By intermission, the 1,500-seat venue was emptying out. Mounted police arrived to handle the fracas at the box office, then Mingus's uncle Fess Williams played.

When the stagehands dropped the curtain at the show's 11:00 P.M. overtime deadline, the band, sparked by Clark Terry's trumpet, ironically ushered out the stragglers with Ellington's "In a Mellotone." Eddie Bert had left his jacket on, to make a quick escape. He finished the Duke tune with a sarcastic *waahhh* from his plunger mute that's on the recording *Town Hall Concert.*

Back at Britt Woodman's house with Buddy Collette, Mingus was furious and hurt while they cooked and ate. Collette had helped him assemble session players, he complained, and he blamed Buddy for their lackluster performances. "You said they could play anything," he yelled. Buddy repeated that he had to make musicians want to play his music instead of bullying them into it. Mingus sneered that everyone he grew up with had given up trying to do their own music. He was the only one really doing anything.

There were bouts of silence between his tirades. They could see how crushed he was.

The day of the concert, Knepper's dentist pulled the tooth stump. He needed a bridge. He lost an octave of range on the trombone and some mobility. And he started a civil lawsuit against Mingus.

United Artists asked Wein to secretly edit the two hours or so of tapes into a record for release. Wein had no music, no outline, no clue about structure or intention. He didn't dare ask Mingus, who terrified him. So in a single session that ran from 2:00 to 6:00 A.M., Wein cut the music by 50 percent, and in the process jumbled pieces and titles. The album got five stars when it was reviewed in *Down Beat.*

A week afterward, Mingus was quoted about racism in jazz in *Time* magazine, along with Max Roach and Billy Taylor and Mary Lou Williams. White jazz stars made big bucks while black pioneers went unsung. Even great black bandleaders like Ellington earned less than a mediocre white. [41]

He brought a septet to Birdland for two weeks, which included Town Hall orchestra members baritone saxist Pepper Adams and tubaman Don Butterfield. He loved the low-end horns, their Ellingtonian textures that suggested sexy power. Byard was back in full-time and started doing solo introductions to open Workshop shows.

Judy gave birth. The doctor told Mingus in the waiting room, "You have a beautiful little girl, but she's dead." The umbilical cord had gotten wrapped around the baby's neck. Judy was sick for weeks afterward, and Roxanne Bethany's family took care of Keki while Judy recovered.

On December 10, 1962, in a issue whose cover screamed "War in Vietnam," *Newsweek* ran a feature about Charles Mingus. He'd opened with a ten-piece Workshop at the Village Vanguard the week before, his first time onstage since Town Hall.

"'Hump, hump, hump,'" he chanted to the three saxophones in the front row, and they humped back at him, the instruments taking the beat and even the tone from his voice," the article said. "[He] is usually called 'Jazz' Angry Man.' But he is capable of joy in his music and warmth toward his fellow musicians. He is also capable of extraordinary music-making. He is, along with Charlie 'Yardbird' Parker, Lester Young, and Thelonius [*sic*] Monk, one of the towering figures of modern jazz.

The piece included lines from "Suite Freedom," a recitative the Workshop performed at the club: "This mule's not from Moscow/This mule ain't from the South/But this mule's got some learnin'/Mostly mouth to mouth."[42]

Some nights he led them through old hits from Duke Ellington and the like. Other nights the group winged it through snatches of new music he said was inspired by El Greco's charged atmospheric paintings.

They did a couple of the club's Sunday matinees. At one, he had his daughter Carolyn and Charles Moffett's son and Jaki Byard's son playing with instruments behind a curtain while the Workshop mimed onstage. He was parodying the rising avant-garde. They didn't have enough training, he insisted, enough background. You have to know the rules to break them.

At another, the Workshop was double-billed with Coleman Hawkins and Roy Eldridge. Hawkins was one of his heroes, but the sax star, on the skids from booze, started laughing loudly at a table during the Workshop's set. So Mingus stopped the Workshop and chewed Hawkins out. The club went silent with embarrassment.

When he stormed offstage at the set's end, piano great Earl Hines had joined Hawkins and Eldridge in the Vanguard's kitchen. Mingus strode in complaining about old niggers, and Hines got offended, but the two hornmen laughed it off. When they went onstage for their own set, Eldridge announced they were starting with "Blues for Old Ns."

When the Vanguard stint was over, Mingus took Judy to California. He needed to see Farwell Taylor. He had bleeding ulcers and was fatter than ever, and his heart was breaking. For three weeks, Farwell fed him cabbage juice every two hours. Bottles of vitamins. No food.

Under Taylor's hovering, he cleared his body of toxins. He felt rejuvenated, twenty pounds lighter. He was going to keep to his regimen, like Sonny Rollins did.

Shelley Taylor baby-sat Carolyn while Judy and Charlie went into San Francisco for dinner, and drove around Marin County. Mingus was blaming Judy for their child's death, saying she was too naïve. She said she'd try to be more questioning.

He talked with Farwell about an idea for a school that would combine music and art and martial arts, physical fitness and history. He had no real education himself, but he wanted to pass on what he and others like him had learned as they knocked around.

When they got back to New York, he got himself an Acme juicer and began scouting possible school locations. He even went a few times to the Vedanta temple at 94th Street and Fifth Avenue.

He didn't want to perform constantly, like a trained monkey.

He brought United Artists before Local 802, claiming $18,000 in unpaid expenses and $5,000 in lost royalties from his Town Hall concert. At one point, Frank Mabry sent a ten-page telegram, filled with assertions and innuendoes about racism, claiming 802 had decided in favor of his client.[43]

Mingus tried lining up more advances so he could stay home and write. He started pulling together material for Impulse Records.

JUDY STARKEY MINGUS MCGRATH: "Myself When I Am Real" was one of the things he composed in my living room. It made me feel ecstatic. You know, whenever I was feeling in pain, this music would come on and I could get really happy from it. And that was a great gift.

He was an artist. He could transmute the tangled emotions of his life into powerful music that drew listeners in, at times almost assaulted them with the sheer force of his personality.

"Myself When I Am Real" was a kaleidoscope. The swirling sounds alternately seduce and seize. A hammered two-note motif opens with surprising gentleness into a Romantic waltz-time fantasia. Moods overlap, collide, elide, layer, and linger, creating an emotional palimpsest as the piece's variegated sections unfold. It was pieces of time metamorphosed into music, each section a different aspect of him, and yet all suggested his coherence and contradictions, his volatility, his sweetness, his irony, his swagger, his frustration, his humor and charm and childlike wonder, his dreams.

Mingus music was autobiography in sound. Everyone in his life had a role. His portraits, his musical tributes, his insistence on forcing his sidemen to find themselves in what he imagined, his clamor for recognition, his emphasis on his originality, his refusal to settle into a predictable mode, his restless unwillingness to leave the sounds and shows as is—these were more than stylistic trademarks.

They were the essence of who he was.

10 The Black Saint and the Sinner Lady

FOR THE NEXT two years—1963 and 1964—Charles Mingus would ride at the apogee of his popular recognition. He was in and out of the local papers all the time, a man about town familiar to tabloids like the New York *Daily News* and New York *Post*. He was articulate, outrageous, good copy. And he was everywhere.

His music, as diverse as ever, maintained its high-stakes gambles, its ambitious reach and daring execution. He made yet another entrepreneurial stab at owning and distributing his own albums. And he played and toured and recorded, if not quite as nonstop as he had in the late 1950s, steadily and well.

Around him, America had survived the Cold War and its latest threats, and the economy had recovered from a brief recession to continue the longest upbeat expansion in its history. As some of the more conformist and repressive aspects of the 1950s were undermined, jettisoned, rerouted, long-standing issues, spearheaded by the black civil rights movement, became central social concerns.

The first generation to have grown up absurd was now old enough to spend real money and create its own arts, subcultures, marketplaces. The country faced dramatic changes, some so liberating and some so wrenching that their consequences would haunt and divide American society for decades.

Mingus was getting lean—as lean as he ever was. He was writing prolifically. He was living the good life. He was an artist, a duly recognized if controversial member of the jazz elite. But he always had bigger ambitions, and he was feeling the Zeitgeist again.

The December dates at the Vanguard unveiled a new ten-piece edition of the Workshop that Mingus would sometimes call the New Folk Band. On January 20, he led them into the studio to record his Impulse! Records debut, *The Black Saint and the Sinner Lady*. The title was, in part, a reference to his father's father and mother.

Producer Bob Thiele had heard the Town Hall concert and wanted him to do something like it for Impulse! Mingus wouldn't let that debacle crush him. He had an apparently endless capacity to keep coming back when he was knocked down.

For the new record, he created a hearty smorgasbord of sound. Tempos speed up and slow down as the mournful horn section plays backing riffs and sliding voicings. Flamenco guitar filigrees in and out. A dirge yields to a snorting baritone sax as Ellington crosses with bebop. Multiple solos flower against a kaleidoscopic wall of sound.

In some ways, the album was his most Ellingtonian. The ensemble work woven from separate lines rather than blocked chords, the luminous harmonies, the predominance of deep-toned horns, the lovely winding melodies, the extended format all deliberately evoked Duke.

But none of Mingus's interdisciplinary web of influences ever overwhelmed his voice. They shone through it, like light through a prism shimmering into color bands. It was as if his music reversed the prismic effect, reintegrated a rainbow of inputs.

Originally, he'd conceived *Black Saint* as a single sweeping piece to be choreographed, but the marketing people at the record label wanted it segmented, for radio play.[1] It was ambitiously edited and overdubbed. His time at Columbia with Teo Macero, who was doing such far-reaching editing with Miles Davis, sharpened his pioneer's interest. For Mingus, the studio was another instrument. He had altoist Charlie Mariano overdub his parts—that yearning alto meant to echo and update Duke's famed sideman Johnny Hodges—a week after the band sessions.

Thiele told associates, "There are dozens of splices in Charlie's head." In the moment was where you stood right now. A live recording could be less real.

Mingus asked Dr. Pollock to write liner notes, saying, "I never pay you, so at least this way you can make $200." It was another Mingus jazz first: a shrink's-eye view of the music. Pollock described it as a manifestation of Mingus's tortured selves. "There can be no question," he wrote, "that he is the Black Saint who suffers for his sins."[2]

As he often liked to do, Mingus wrote notes too. His albums were multipronged manifestos, and he was the most articulate, self-conscious promoter of his own positions. He described the music and his struggles to be original, the influence of Jelly Roll Morton, his lack of recognition for earlier achievements, his distaste for critics. He was stung by the passion many jazz critics had for the growing avant-garde inspired by Ornette Coleman and now spearheaded by the crossover popularity of John Coltrane.[3]

At first, he had resented Charlie Parker, too. He had to protect his historic firsts, his artistic legacy. He wanted recognition as the avatar who'd encompassed all the dizzying scenes a-borning around his music.

He claimed the Stars of Swing played Central Avenue in 1940. It didn't matter how much good press he'd gotten. He lambasted Dirty Faucet, his name for Leonard Feather.

CHARLES MINGUS:... he gets paid to play records to brainwash innocent little people who don't know that if you're going to like something that's beautiful no one can tell you how if it doesn't just happen. If it doesn't just happen, you're already brainwashed and instead of hiring someone to tell you what's beautiful for you, and you're past five years old, this means you need an analyst.[4]

Immediacy was his mode of creation. It should be the listener's mode of perception.

That didn't stop him from discussing technical aspects, like the microphone placement for his sax section, a V-shape with alto and baritone closer than tenor. He wanted the section to seem bigger: "an illusion of sound—overtones coming through between the baritone and alto."[5]

He pointed out that his pedal-point compositions allowed soloists to use three keys for their "spontaneous composition"[6]—improvisation.

The music was a tour de force. Like Duke, he managed to use his players' individual voices to create Mingus music. He fought with Jaki Byard in the studio and did a couple of piano solos himself. They made up. He knew how hard it was for Byard, a recognized composer and leader, to subsume himself, but Mingus had to demand it.

Any Mingus Workshop blended his charismatic, headlong leadership with an insistence on disciplined individuality. He asked his musicians to find themselves in his sketches and formats and theater, to complete the architecture in the moment with their voices.

Brilliant as it was, *Black Saint* sold fewer than 10,000 copies. Two decades later, an Italian who set out to record avant-gardists named his small, pivotal label Black Saint.

Mingus and Janet Coleman went to a Stan Brakhage movie at a Bleecker Street Cinema festival. Brakhage, an abstract filmmaker, dealt in flickering subliminal images. Mingus saw no discipline, no structure. Improvisation without structure was only chaos. He got up and yelled "Fraud," over and over at the screen.

In early January, Saul Zaentz suggested Mingus record one LP per year for Fantasy, and one for Debut. Later that year, the band recorded live at San Francisco's Jazz Workshop, and released *Right Now* on Zaentz's label.

One night, during a stint with Peggy Lee at Basin Street East, Jimmy Knepper came home about 6:00 A.M. His wife was readying their kids for school when the doorbell rang. The postman needed his signature, so he staggered downstairs in his pajamas. Two men leapt out of the bushes by his front door.

They were Treasury agents following a phone tip. Knepper's package contained a glassine envelope with about five dollars' worth of heroin. The return address was fake.

He was sure it came from Mingus. So were the feds, who took him to the Federal Building in Manhattan. A few musicians suggested Knepper could get Mingus whacked for $100. Others knew where to pick up guns cheap. Cooler heads suggested a lawyer. First criminal, then civil charges, they suggested.

On February 6, at 100 Centre Street, Part 2B, Room 400 Mingus faced charges of third-degree assault, for knocking Knepper's tooth out. His attorney, Marvin Karpatkin's partner, was Manfred Ohrenstein, a powerful state legislator.[7] Britt Woodman and Buddy Collette and Pastor Gensel were Mingus's character witnesses.

BRITT WOODMAN: Now, I knew Jimmy Knepper very well. He understood, I guess. I felt bad, because I knew that Charles was always hitting somebody, that he kept losing his temper. But we said to the court, "Yeah, he's meek and mild. He would never hurt anybody. He wouldn't hurt a fly." Buddy and I, we sure hated to get up there and do that. But it was one of those things we had to do for him.

Two days before St. Patrick's Day, Mingus got a suspended sentence. He insisted that Knepper had come to his apartment drunk and fell down. He repeated that Knepper had called him a nigger. The black judge scowled at him and said, "That's got nothing to do with it."

Knepper dropped his civil suit.

Mingus berated Ohrenstein for calling him a jazz musician, a badge of second-class citizenship. Then he stayed in the courtroom to wait for the next case, which involved a CORE sit-in.[8]

Eugene Callender, a cousin of Red's, ran Sunday night services at Church of the Master uptown. He invited Mingus to participate that spring.

After his sentencing, the Workshop played at a Carnegie Hall benefit for the Student Nonviolent Coordinating Committee. SNCC was a sign that, racially speaking, the tenor of the times was playing the tune of a new generation.

Not since the post-Reconstruction split between Du Bois and Washington had the civil rights movement seen such a schism. Stokely Carmichael, the SNCC's fiery head, later introduced Black Power, which demanded, rather than asked for, equality.

It was a linear descendant of bebop's attitude.

Black nationalism was getting hip. Blacks should live and shop and work within black communities, to prevent whites from skimming profits, manipulating their culture. Black nationalists emphasized self-achievement, racial pride, independence. Many, like Malcolm X, followed Du Bois and Franz Fanon in linking their struggle in America with struggles around the globe.

On Good Friday, the SCLC began protests against school segregation in Birmingham, getting children and teens to march. Police commissioner Eugene "Bull" Connor arrested Dr. Martin Luther King Jr. and ordered the police to use attack dogs and firehoses to disperse crowds of nonviolent protesters. The violence spilled into living rooms coast to coast via TV, and the national recoil pushed Kennedy, and many white Americans, closer to the civil rights movement agendas.

It was the turning point in the civil rights movement.

When George Wallace stood in the schoolhouse door a little later, JFK sent the U.S. Army into Alabama to protect the grade school integrationists.

The die was cast.

Celia and Saul Zaentz booked the Workshop for a West Coast swing. They played the Berkeley Jazz Festival for two days, two days after Mingus's forty-first birthday, did two weeks at the Jazz Workshop in San Francisco in May, then headed to Los Angeles.

That summer, Mingus's firstborn son wanted to come to New York, and at first his father was excited. Charles Mingus III had just graduated from high school, wanted to be an artist, and had a portfolio of abstract paintings. He found his father at a huge, bare space on 386 Third Avenue.

His father looked at his work, and told him to learn to paint an apple. You had to know the rules to break them. The teenager slept in a corner of the cold, bare loft in a sleeping bag, warmed by the space heater.

Mingus put him to work in his 5,000-square-foot space. He had plans and could use the tall boy who looked like a skinny version of him.

Mingus was working out with Sonny Rollins, getting ready for the new holistic school he'd talked about with Farwell Taylor. Physical and mental fitness were crucial. Jazz Workshop Inc. had a ten-year-lease on the loft. He was calling the school Music, Art, and Health.

His son and two bums he hired from the street hauled sacks of cement, exercise equipment, paint, furniture, and whatever else they needed up five floors of stairs. Charles Jr., as he was called, strung below-code electrical wiring, and poured a cement floor.

There would be a corner for the juice bar, a recording studio. The huge main room housed chrome exercise equipment from a workout chain gone bankrupt, knickknacks, books, LPs, tapes, posters, scribbled notes on scraps, Mingus's pipe collection, an oversized chess set, his electric typewriter, some pinups, the suitcases with his ever-growing autobiography, and his basses and a piano.

There was a pay phone to prevent spongers.

He had great teachers lined up. Katharine Dunham would teach witchcraft and dance. Charles Wright, an ex-cop who was one of his new bodyguards, would teach karate. The Reverend Gensel would lecture on religion. He was thinking about Richard Alpert to teach Zen.

The semi-finished loft had constant traffic, including his fans from Michigan. He was always a teacher.[9]

DAVID AMRAM: He came by my apartment with a whole bunch of students from Ann Arbor. And he said, "Dave, I want to play you this piece of mine, then I want you to play these students one of your classical pieces." So he played *Black Saint*. Then I put on an air check from Yale of the Marlboro Trio playing *Dershian's Variations for Cello, Violin, and Piano*. Then we sat down at the little piano I had and just made something up, four-handed, no plan. He wanted them to see how someone who was an improviser could be a composer and vice versa—that there wasn't a big wall between the two musics.

Ann Arbor was a seat of student revolt. The core of Students for a Democratic Society (SDS), founded in 1962, came from the huge public multiversity there, which drew heavily on New York for students. By the late 1960s, SDS would become the backbone of campus uprisings across the nation.

Mingus often took his Michigan-grad circle of artist-wannabes to a Third Avenue diner, and to Grand Central Station, where they whispered names in certain corners, and could hear them echo in others. He'd played the game with Susan Scott.

After a few months, fire department inspectors called a halt to construction in his loft. They wanted the floor reinforced, which would cost six to eight thousand dollars. The neighbors complained about noise. The landlord refused his rent check. Mingus refused to pay off the inspectors.

He found a storefront at 303 East 26th Street,[10] and piled his stuff up in there. There was no shower or tub, just a toilet and sink. It was another in his long string of homes away from home.

Mingus was popping pills, uppers and downers and diet pills. He started using vitamin shots. He told Judy he was going to lose weight. "I'm warning you," he said, "that after that, women won't be able to leave me alone." She shrugged.

He was up every night, playing the piano. He told Bob Thiele he wanted to record a solo piano disc, but he was nervous. It wasn't like being onstage, or at home.

On July 30, he recorded eleven tunes at RCA Studios. The first was "Myself When I Am Real."

He got royalty statements from Impulse! about *Black Saint*, which had come out only that summer. He was astounded. No other record label had ever been so prompt.

That summer, Rahsaan Roland Kirk recorded a big band version of "Ecclusiastics," his old Workshop showcase, arranged by saxist-composer Benny Golson.

Six years after whacking mob kingpin Albert Anastasia, Joe Gallo was sentenced to eight years for extortion.

FRANK MABRY: I helped when the Mafia guys, the club owners and the agents, didn't want to pay the artists. Being a genius has its limits; it don't pay the rent. I'm an ex-Marine, so I don't give a fuck. It's like a private war we all had to fight. They'd scare the musicians, fuck with them. "Fuck with me, we'll put your hand in a car door." Okay, then we will fill your car full of holes. It was like that. We fought back.

Mabry was a street Houdini. Sweeping into a club, he kept his hands under his overcoat, draped like a cape. When one of his clients needed pressure to get paid, he got Anthony Maynard and another bodyguard and spread out in the offending venue. They'd stand up, one at a time, hands under their overcoats, and converge on the bar. If no cash was forthcoming, they knocked all the glasses off it, then demanded drinks.

It was great theater. And it worked.

In August, Mingus brought a tentet to Village Gate for ten days. He and Jaki Byard were fighting, so Joe Albany filled in on piano. Eric Dolphy and Booker Ervin and Pepper Adams played reeds.

In September, he went into the studio for a session nominally led by Adams. Motown, Detroit's hit soul music label, had started a Workshop Jazz series, and signed the baritone saxist. Teddy Charles was his producer, Dannie Richmond played drums, and Charles McPherson played alto.

Mingus was one of soul music's jazz godfathers. A historical circle was being closed.

It was the first album of his material Mingus didn't record himself. He was credited as director, and he stalked the studio, humming new parts for the players, shifting dynamics and tempos on pieces like "Portrait, "Diane," "Dark Light," and "Haitian Fight Song." Motown paid him $298.08 for fifty-four pages of sheet music.[11]

Later that month, he recorded *Mingus Mingus Mingus Mingus Mingus*, his last Impulse! disc. Drummer Walter Perkins replaced Dannie Richmond for all but two tracks. Richmond's drug habit was remarkably controlled, but it still got to him, or got him busted, from time to time.

As often happened in the studio, the Workshop grew, becoming a tentet again, augmented by some veterans, like trumpeter Richard Williams and Booker Ervin.

Mingus reworked old pieces; more musicians meant more cinematic effects. Bob Hammer's arrangements created contrapuntal ghosts to familiar melodies like "Better Get It" and "Celia" and "II BS," really "Haitian Fight Song."

The renamed "Better Get Hit" broke out into ten-part glossolalia for its finale, then into an old-timey coda that lovingly parodied early New Orleans ensemble jazz. On "II BS" and "Celia," Byard scattered slightly dissonant whole-tone chords like bangles. Charlie Mariano, the Italian saxist, was back for two aching solos over the luminous harmonies of "I X Love," a remake of "Nouroog," and on "Celia," in which "The Lady in Red" becomes a second theme.

Mariano was his current Johnny Hodges, his lyrical heartbreak balladeer. His soaring cadenzas echoed Bird's slippery lines on his recordings with strings.

The album formally saluted Ellington with "Mood Indigo." Mingus limned a jaggedly beautiful counterpoint to the familiar melody, then soloed from the fingerboard's bottom through gentle harmonics, bending notes blue like T-Bone Walker.

He retitled "E's Flat, Ah's Flat Too" "Hora Decubitus." He liked punning in other languages. Judy said it meant something like "hour of sleeping" or bed-time, which was the feel he wanted, he said.

He always reused old material, reworked and renamed it. Even this simple format, the round, he used countless times. He loved the overlap, the slop, the schizzy delay effect, a bit like a strobe light, that the form induced.

In the studio, he worked like Jackson Pollock layering paintings. Any composition, any arrangement was only a draft for how he'd express himself in the moment.

On August 28, 1963, came one of the last sweeping shows of civil rights movement consensus. Dr. King and others led a march on Washington, like the one planned in 1941 by A. Phillip Randolph. The old man was among the leaders on the dais, as King delivered his famed oration, "I Have a Dream," in front of the Lincoln Memorial to 250,000 demonstrators.

The thirty-five-year-old King would soon be *Time* magazine's "Man of the Year" and be awarded the Nobel Peace Prize. He was at the peak of his influence. The time was coming when the civil rights old guard would be pushed aside by new waves they'd made possible.

That summer, King would be stoned by Black Muslims in Harlem.

Thelonious Monk opened the new Five Spot on St. Mark's Place and Third Avenue, and stayed for seven months. The Workshop followed him in September, staying on and off for months as well.

The new club was twice the old club's size, and held 223 customers. The Terminis combined an old cigar store and a cafeteria into an odd-shaped room. Customers entered a small hallway, then the wall-length bar, moved from the original club, stretched to their right. To their left was the stage, and behind the stage were arches that led to a patio, where audience overflow could find seats. The musicians had to walk through the kitchen to get to the stage from their dressing room.

The new Five Spot had red walls, but like the old its walls were covered with flyers for gallery shows and jazz gigs.

Eric Dolphy was back and musically sharp but restless. A run of mainstreamers like Clifford Jordan sat in, mostly on weekends. Sonny Rollins replaced Dolphy a few times, to help his friend Charles keep him in check. Dolphy was talking about leaving again, going to Europe.

The core Workshop developed "Meditations."

Like Jackson Pollock, Mingus named his work only after it was done. Like Pollock and Kerouac, he disliked or resented many of those who followed his blazed trails. They lacked his vision, his discipline, his depth of understanding, the breadth undergirding his reaches into multimedia art.

"Meditations" was multisectional, like "Far Wells, Mill Valley." It opened into complex meters and melodies that stretched into long solo sections. He told them to capture the feel of the slave ships and relate that to civil rights, the same sort of dramatic instructions he'd given Mal Waldron and Jackie McLean a decade earlier.

Starting with his mournful bowed bass, "Meditations" erupted into sections billowing with agitated conversational gusts. Sometimes sheer noise streaked across like a jagged bolt opening up a lowering sky.

Valerie Porr was five foot three and platinum blonde and stunning. By day, she was a substitute teacher in New York's public schools. By night, she roamed the jazz club scene until the wee hours and beyond.

Mingus had met Valerie at City College of New York (CCNY) in the late 1950s, after playing at Townsend Harris Hall there. With a group of Beat-wannabe friends, she listened to his monologues about politics and current events. Then she got married, moved to the Bronx, put her new husband through medical school, got divorced, went to Europe, stayed there a couple of years, and came back to the United States.

After weeks of trying, she talked her father into letting her drive his car into Manhattan, and showed up at the Five Spot.

Mingus made a beeline for her. She heard his voice before she saw him: "I know you. City College." She was floored; how could he remember her from one brief encounter seven or eight years earlier?

He retold her the whole story. He did remember her.

Soon, she moved down from the Bronx to a small three-room railroad-style apartment off Lexington and East 26th Street that housed her and, later, her French boyfriend, a designer. Most nights, she walked down to the Five Spot, watched Monk play and the Baroness Nica de Konigswarter come in like a storm trooper on patrol.

VALERIE PORR: I would sit with Mingus until four in the morning, sleep two hours, and go teach school. He would just talk about all these things. Classical music. Politics. The state of the world. Cultures. Class. Racism. Nobody talked about racism then, just talked about it, the black experience. And here was this man telling me he couldn't play in a classical orchestra because he was black.

He was always talking about his book, all these things in his book. But what I'm trying to get across to you is this: Now, I can go home at night and turn on Charlie Rose and have the world in my bedroom, intellectuals talking about topics that, in those years, you had no access to information about. You just didn't have those kinds of conversations. He talked about the Kennedy assassination, how Kennedy was killed by the Mafia and the CIA. Here was this man talking about what the government was doing, and he sounded crazy, yet he fascinated me. I felt he was tutoring me. But in those days, jazz musicians didn't get socially accepted in the intellectual world.

He was a very intelligent person who had a low tolerance of stress, rage attacks. But he was very engaging, very charming. That raised eyebrow, that twinkle in his eye: there was a very, very adorable boyish thing about it.

One night, after the club closed, he was still talking to her. "You don't know anything, anything about what's really going on out there, do you?" he demanded. He told her he was taking her up to Times Square; she should do just what he said, and go along with whatever he did.

The nice Jewish girl from the Bronx got introduced to a pimp and some high-priced hookers, and discovered the seedy underworld jazz musicians traditionally moved in.

He was always a teacher.

That fall, Mingus's autobiography was rejected. The publisher found it too dirty, too rich with potential libel suits. He named names in the music industry, called gangsters and mobsters what they were.

He'd told McGraw-Hill he wanted the book bound in white buckram with the title in gold. He wanted extensive editorial support but was unwilling to change anything. They saw a costly nightmare. He tried and failed to sell it to Random House.[12]

In November, the Workshop played the Village Gate to promote the Impulse discs. John Wilson wrote in the New York *Times*, "He's deepened but can't mold his work."[13]

On November 22, 1963, John Kennedy was assassinated in Dallas. The country went into shock—the shooting was replayed endlessly on nationwide TV. The new president, Texas-born Lyndon Johnson, pledged to pass civil rights legislation, stalled in Congress by southern barons.

Malcolm X announced that the killing was "chickens coming home to roost."

Across the nation, people disbelieved official explanations for the assassination and found conspiracy. Mingus was one of the millions who was sure Kennedy was murdered by a cabal.

CHARLES MINGUS: To get one man, you gotta have more than one marksman there, right? ... It takes about twenty guys to hit a guy like Kennedy. For society to sit by and say Johnson killed Kennedy, he had it done with some hoods ... that's cool.[14]

Mingus was sure the country's intelligence agencies routinely operated beyond the law. Most people had this media-made reality they accepted, but he could see through that, into what was really going on. He thrived on conspiracies and loved to talk about them, play with them like a piece of music, weave different elements in and out to see how they looked.

At the end of 1963, Mingus's advance from Impulse was supposed to be raised to $15,000. He hadn't sold enough records, the bookkeeper explained. Bob Thiele agreed.

Impulse was about to release *Mingus Mingus Mingus Mingus Mingus*. The next day, when Thiele came to work, he found a knife with a note stuck in the back of his chair. The note read, "Where the fuck is my money? MINGUS."[15]

Mingus was hopping between the Gotham Hotel and the Earle Hotel, where people who played the Five Spot stayed. Judy was pregnant again. He wasn't sure what he thought about that. She insisted Carolyn needed a companion. He just stopped coming back all the time to their new apartment at 1160 Fifth Avenue.

He liked the locale and called it "Jackie Kennedy's neighborhood." JFK's widow lived a couple of blocks away.

One worried night, Mingus gave his son Charles a shotgun, and told him to keep it under his overcoat outside the Five Spot, on the corner of Bowery and St. Mark's. He was expecting a visit from Joe Gallo's boys. He wanted warning. Young Charles thought he was being sent to die.

Ann McIntosh spent New Year's with them.

ANN MCINTOSH: What is this timid nurse doing with this big black genius? She seemed calm, mothering. With him standing around, how could you tell if she was interesting? I met her many many times, always as his attachment.

He was Charles Mingus. He always had others.

On one snowy winter night, a tall thin Englishwoman with a cockney accent waited for him in a cab as he bought a case of Chateau Neuf-du-pape at the liquor store across from Birdland. She rolled down the cab window to taunt the horseback cop stationed there. The cop headed toward the cab, ready to bust her. Suddenly Mo Levy appeared, as if out of a secret door, and said, "What do you think you're doing?" The cop stopped dead.

At the Five Spot in early 1964, the Workshop was playing with a succession of guest stars: Ben Webster, Illinois Jacquet, Sonny Rollins, Coleman Hawkins, Cat Anderson. Clifford Jordan was now a regular.

Jazz was facing a generational changing of the guard as younger jazz players embraced free ideas. So Mingus would be different, reposition himself by using older stars. It was about marketing, and instinct, and being Charles Mingus. He was never part of a crowd.

He started calling people out at the club. Sometimes it was street jive. When Webster sat in one night, he challenged the rotund saxist, who chased the cab Mingus leapt into once he got outside.

Sometimes it was real, a forum to play out other issues.

MAX ROACH: Amiri Baraka was the only guy who could beat him. One night, Ming invited Amiri out, and Amiri knew karate; he was using his feet, but Ming kept coming at him anyway, and we finally broke it up. We could hear his feet thudding into Ming's chest.

Baraka disparaged him as a black Stan Kenton. Baraka pushed for black musical separatism as early as 1961, arguing that with so many avenues closed to blacks, jazz should remain their province. Black Americans needed pride in themselves. Black boys needed black mentors. White men just creamed the fame and big money off jazz.

Mingus had talked about these issues for years. From his teens he'd focused on unequal pay scales and opportunities for black musicians, and especially jazzers. Now was the time. Maybe the country was catching up.

In one of the historical ironies it set in motion, Black Power helped end integrated bands in jazz for a decade.

Mingus was living his life in the Village. He didn't care about musicians' colors, just their voices. Many of his closest friends were white. He was a walking emblem of integration and wanted to be a great synthesizer. And so he'd become, but his world was starting to crack.

At the Five Spot, Mingus met a stunning five-foot-four strawberry blonde with prominent cheekbones, a Smith College degree in American history, and a wealthy inventor-father.

She reminded him of Susan Scott. She was married to an Italian sculptor named Alberto Ungaro, whom she'd met on her post-collegiate year abroad, working for the *International Herald Tribune* in Paris. She had a near-teen daughter and a young son. Her name was Susan Graham Ungaro.

He was looking for help to start another independent label. She was looking for New York excitement in the jazz scene.

The year before, she'd starred in an experimental movie by Robert Frank, called *OK, End Here*. Ornette Coleman wrote the score. She'd known Allen

Ginsberg and other Beats since college; one of her college mates had married poet Kenneth Koch. She had her own scene.

They fell quickly into torrid love.

One night, she went down the block with him when he took a dinner break between sets and ordered three steaks. Jack Micheline showed up. Micheline was a true street poet, a genuine Beat. He'd walked back and forth from California to New York. He dressed like a bum. He lived in hobo squats and run-down hotels, and he talked like Mo Levy, and his spoken poetry rang with the rhythms of postwar jazz.

He asked Mingus for some food. Mingus refused.

SUSAN GRAHAM UNGARO MINGUS: You know that Chaplin film where he runs into this multimillionaire when they're drunk and they're buddies, then they wake up in the palace and the millionaire kicks Chaplin? There's a scene where they're sitting at this fantastic banquet table and Chaplin has a cup of coffee and he takes lump after lump of sugar, then he breaks the last one in half. Charles had his own sense of measure. He was a man of excess.

Mingus had performed with Micheline and hung out with him at the Ninth Circle and Cedar Tavern. In fact, Mingus's writer friends sent him their newly published work. The books lined his studio's shelves. Ferlinghetti, Micheline, Patchen, Rexroth, Ginsberg, Corso—the Who's Who of the Beat Generation.

Mingus liked talking about ideas. When he read something new, he couldn't wait to ask questions. He floated through art galleries, artists' lofts, bars, parties. He was an American bohemian, a self-made intellectual.

He was posing again as a pimp wannabe, living his autobiographical fantasies, what he was weaving through his book. It teased the white girls, got their juices going. It was revolt for them. For him, it was more complicated. It was one way to bridge his black and white worlds.

He offered to turn Janet Coleman out when she was working at the *New York Review of Books*, and he took her to Trude Heller's on the corner of Sixth Avenue and West 9th Street—another portal into the New York underworld.

Coleman saw pimpdom as a key part of his private symbolology: "It was the road not taken, of easy money and camaraderie and street approval and flash that a young man from a ghetto gives up when he commits himself to being, as Mingus was, relentlessly, an artist."[16]

Mingus sometimes walked around town in a yellow hunter's outfit. Once he wore it to a union meeting. He'd organized Frank Mabry and Tony Maynard and a couple of other bodyguards to write ballots about union contracts, which discriminated against jazz musicians. The men then accompanied him to the vote-count.

FRANK MABRY: The union guys said they had only 150 ballots. Ming started yelling, 'cause he knew there were more than 150. He put this shotgun on the table. That changed things. See, he was making a statement against the union's racism.

Mingus patrolled the Village streets like a bohemian dandy in nineteenth-century Paris. He stopped by the Figaro on Bleecker almost nightly, then headed east toward the Annex, over on Avenue B and 10th, down the block from Ginsberg, where Bird lived his last years. He'd pass the building plaque honoring W. H. Auden. The neighborhood was rich in New York artistic history.

Even if much of it was negative and demeaning, the wave of attention engulfing Beat culture from the late 1950s produced a new Village-centered artistic heyday. To Mingus, most folkies and protest musicians couldn't really play. But the little downstairs clubs that new stars like Bob Dylan haunted lined streets like Macdougal.

Dylan was the center of a group that was wedding a new poetry in their charged lyrics, with music, creating their own post-Beat synthesis of the personal and political. They saw themselves as outlaws, as modern troubadours in the folk-hero tradition of Woody Guthrie. They used benzedrine and grass and hash, and some tried heroin. It was part of being a creative bohemian.

Allen Ginsberg, maybe inevitably, was drawn to that scene, and they saw themselves as Ginsberg's heirs. They loved him because of his outspokenness about The System, The Bomb, war, racism, sexual repression. They loved the way he took his life and wrote it large, went global with his obsessions and concerns. He was the modern spirit of Walt Whitman: "I am vast; I contain multitudes."

At the core of Ginsberg's relationship with Mingus was a shared insatiable, roving curiosity and the artistic egoists' ability to see themselves reflected everywhere, and everything refracted through themselves. That was part of what kept their work from devolving into brilliant pastiche. They were both Romantics, cynical about the world yet very much plugged in. They were outrageously who they were, no matter where they were. They were too much themselves to do anything else. They were haloed with a magnetic charisma. And they both knew it, and knew how to use it when they wanted to.

Among the fans Mingus drew to the Five Spot were Ryan O'Neal, Peter and Jane Fonda, Godfrey Cambridge, so thin he looked like a black Bogart, Chuck

Norris, and Barney Rosset, head of Grove Press, which fought censorship battles for Beat and post-Beat books.

In April 1964, Mingus put $10,000 into Edison Savings and Loan, a trust account for his daughter.[18] He adored her and saw her regularly, played with her, read to her, talked music and politics and things she couldn't understand.

On April 4, the Workshop joined an NAACP benefit held at Carnegie Hall. His father had belonged to the NAACP and he believed in integration. But he saw the reality of who made big money in music. The cards were stacked. So he understood black nationalism's emphasis on self-help. After all, he was his father's son: he didn't believe in handouts.

But he distrusted the Black Muslims, whose visibility, thanks to Malcolm X's firebrand speechifying, was rising. Malcolm, too, was yellow.

Mingus was disgusted by the black hookers off Time Square, taking the easy way out. He lectured black panhandlers about self-reliance and education and offered a few odd jobs. He told friends, "I'm a stone capitalist."

He was skeptical of racial divisions, although he was well armed to exploit them. He had to be. There was no racial explanation for him.

On April 4, for the first time outside a club, the Workshop played "Meditations" at Carnegie Hall. It was now the set's pivotal and defining moment. It was open-ended, about conversation in music, its structure shaped by Mingus's exchanges with Eric Dolphy and Clifford Jordan.

Whenever "Meditations" started, Dolphy contemplated his bass clarinet, his flute, his alto sax on their stands. First he moved toward one, stopped, turned toward another, paused, finally made a selection.

Mingus waited Dolphy out and never said a word. They'd talk and fight and squall and seduce and make love on their instruments, a full range of onomatopoeic emotions from Dolphy's edgy flute, with its breathy interval leaps, and his bass clarinet, with its hiccupping, snaky lines.

They fired each other up.

Jaki Byard had known Dolphy since 1959, when the younger man came to New York with Chico Hamilton, and could see his need for independence. A decade older and established, the pianist could feel it too, and periodically left Mingus.

The dynamic tensions fueling his high-octane Workshop created a powerful musical dialog of equals where there was only one chief. It had to fracture. But losing Dolphy would hit the Workshop. It would hit Mingus even harder. He pleaded, persuaded, argued, threatened, cajoled. He did it onstage in the music, offstage in words.

The next day, the Monterey Jazz Festival's press release noted the fall lineup. It called Mingus "a major figure in contemporary music" and "the Segovia of the bass." He shared a Sunday afternoon program with "another preeminent composer-performer, Thelonious Monk." Tickets were $4 and $3.[19]

Monk beat Mingus to Europe. George Wein was handling the new European circuit, a natural outgrowth of his festival contacts. First Monk, then Max Roach, then Mingus went to Europe, with Jordan, Dolphy, Byard, trumpeter Johnny Coles, and Richmond.

In Oslo on April 13, 1964, Dolphy finalized his leaving. He would stay in Europe after the tour. The Charles Mingus Sextet was taped for NRK, Norwegian TV that night[20] in a salon setting, the walls embellished with frescos, the stage all gleaming blonde wood.

"Low stools," Mingus mutters as he slides onto one after removing his sport coat. He has trouble settling in with the bass. Just after he launches into a bass solo to kick off, the bass slips. Immediately he stands up and says, "Can you splice that up, the tape, know what I mean?"

The audience, all skinny ties and black-rimmed glasses, mostly younger Scandinavian Beat wannabes, gasps, then titters, then laughs as he stabs his bass pegleg into the blonde wood to anchor it, then screws it from side to side to make sure it stays.

"You have slippery floors here," he explains, as the laughs grow, so he adds, "You know, I could slip and break a shoulder, or even my neck. I could sue you."

Then Coles fires up an increasingly dissonant, atonal blues haloed by echoes of Miles and Jaki Byard's thick harmonies, punctuated by Jordan and Dolphy's backing drones. Byard takes over, crossing swelling, sophisticated chords with gospel and barrelhouse rolls. Clifford Jordan, in granny glasses and a three-piece suit, starts squealing his solo, and the volume drops precipitously. Triplets and time changes insinuate themselves. Finally Mingus bobs his head, cuing Richmond and Byard into his solo, laced with ballad quotes and slides and hammer-ons and pull-offs worthy of a blues guitarist.

Dolphy finishes the piece out, entering very softly, gradually upping the volume and the jagged chromatic leaps fundamental to his attack and sound.

At the end, Mingus says, "Goodbye Eric, and hurry back. He's gonna stay over here someplace."

Mingus adjusts his bass peg, hammered out of its setting by his slamming it into the floor. Then, turning to stage right, he asks Wein, "How much time we got left, George?" "One tune." "One minute?" "One tune." "One tune," replies Mingus, with a sweetly ironic smile. "Well, I was thinking about running for a while."

They play "Ow" by Charlie Parker, and thread it with themes from dozens of bop standards.

Four days later in France, Coles, recovering from surgery, fell off the bandstand during "Orange was the Color of Her Dress."

JAKI BYARD: He had to go the hospital for stitches, an operation. Hazel Scott and Bud Powell were standing behind the stage when it happened. Mingus said, "Man, what the hell happened." Ran backstage to see, and came back. Dolphy said, "Come on man, let's blow. They're taking him to the hospital, but we got a gig to play." So we went on the stand, and did the rest of the tour without Johnny. But that was Dolphy. "C'mon, man, blow. These people come here to see us."

Mingus bought Byard's wife a ticket to meet them for the Byards' anniversary, then threw the couple a party and walked off with half the champagne.

He discovered chitlins were a delicacy in France, and ordered them everywhere.

The Workshop was sensationally received, and taped and filmed all over Europe for radio and TV. It drove him crazy to look out over an audience and see all the cameras and microphones. His life's blood was being stolen.

The international jazz circuit was young, shaky, jerry-built, low budget and low personnel. Tour logistics were a mess. The band traveled hours a day, then hit the stage that night. There were no rest layovers, so the musicians got exhausted and routinely showed up late for performances. French and Italian crowds didn't care much, but German crowds did.

Mingus always checked the piano. If it wasn't good or properly tuned, he'd growl, "How do you expect Jaki there to play this shitbox—excuse me, piano?" The promoters took care that the pianos were good, and Byard was grateful. He was opening their concerts solo, with ragtime, Ellington, jazzed-up Chopin à la Hazel Scott, Fats Waller and stride classics. The crowds loved it, and Mingus gave him a raise.

Sometimes Byard, an accomplished multi-instrumentalist, played bass while Mingus played piano. Byard enjoyed that, and was developing some real chops when one night Mingus rose from the piano stool and said, "That's enough." Byard figured he'd gotten too good at it. He never played bass in the Workshop again.

But the pianist was pleased that Mingus told everyone this was the best band he ever had. He liked the volatile leader, and his own easygoing nature let him absorb the usual shocks and ruptures. He understood that the only way to shut Mingus up was to play at the top of your game, and that that didn't always work either, since Mingus was the center of the show. Even to uncomprehending Europeans, his diatribes and shtick were part of the act.

As a regular feature the Workshop played "Peggy's Blue Skylight." They transformed "Fables of Faubus" into a spectacular open-ended triumph that could run nearly an hour, with long solo sections freely romping out of tempo and in, and the melody of "Lift Every Voice and Sing," the Negro National Anthem, twining through parts of it. And then they wailed on "Meditations." It was aggressive, finely honed, utterly without boundaries, yet ingeniously disciplined. It was Mingus's latest statement on how freedom allowed organic structure with people who knew how to use it.

On April 20, RTB, the Belgian TV network, taped a special devoted solely to Mingus.[21]

Many musicians felt Europeans treated jazz with respect, as the art form it was. Kenny Clarke and Bud Powell moved there, as had many others, and now Dolphy. European jazz fans seemed free of American racism, though after a while abroad many black musicians chafed under the Europeans' semiconsciously patronizing respect.

Still, the same Europeans who went to the opera and the Louvre and Monte Carlo came to jazz concerts. Black Americans who couldn't eat with whites in parts of the United States rubbed elbows with titled and wealthy Old World patrons.

The Workshop went to Italy, and Mingus bought a bass in Milan for $2,200. He and Byard got stuck belly to belly in a train corridor, as passengers grinned.

He preferred to be paid in cash, and European promoters were funny about that. In Munich, the promoter didn't have cash, so Mingus tore off the dressing room door and carried it onstage. The promoter warned they'd never work there again, but after the show, he begged them to come back.

In Hamburg, someone painted a big swastika on Dolphy's door. Mingus kicked in a few doors at the hotel, broke a couple of microphones in front of the stage, and started waving a knife. The German police came to restrain him. He announced the show was over; the audience didn't understand his music.

He'd done the same in Bremen. The Germans were Nazis. They hated and incinerated blacks.

The tour ended at Biel, where the audience filed in as the musicians left for dinner. When they returned over an hour later, Mingus kicked a fan's tape deck to pieces. He grabbed a boy's camera, claiming to police the boy was secretly filming him for German TV.

Down Beat devoutly reported his outbreaks. His image was growing constantly, absorbing and overshadowing more complicated facts.

GEORGE WEIN: The volatility was always there. If everything was right, he was looking for something wrong, because he knew it focused attention on himself. I don't know if it was calculated or not, but he loved to be the center of attention. And by finding out something was wrong—there was some prejudice—it would become a cause celebre.

In Copenhagen, he wanted to buy some shirts. Ben Webster told him he'd been ripped off because he was black. He went back with Frank Mabry to demand a better deal. Next thing Wein knew, the incident was in the papers.

When Dolphy finalized staying in Europe, Mingus announced onstage that "Meditations" would be renamed "So Long Eric." He was sure Dolphy would come home.

Mingus got to London and met British pop scenemakers, including Brian Epstein, the manager of the Beatles. He had his perpetual brown bag of pills, each bottle labeled neatly and held in place by thick rubber bands. A photographer snapped him with it open, sitting next to Epstein in a backstage room.[22]

By the time the Workshop played Ronnie Scott's in London, the Copenhagen incident was widely reprinted. Mingus had lined up a gig on a transatlantic ocean liner leaving from England at the end of the tour—something he'd always wanted to do. But ship's owners canceled the gig when they read about his shirt-shopping expedition.

The Workshop finally went home in early May.

Dizzy Gillespie was running for president—a lampoon candidacy with a serious point in a three-way field that included segregationist Alabama governor George Wallace, war hawk Senator Barry Goldwater, and John Kennedy's successor, Lyndon Johnson. Gillespie's platform included changing the name White House to Blues House, disbanding the FBI and Senate Internal Security committee, legalizing the numbers racket that paid the mob so well in black neighborhoods, and forcing job applicants to wear sheets so potential employers couldn't tell their race.

He named Miles Davis his future CIA head, Max Roach his Minister of Defense, and Charlie Mingus his Minister of Peace. "He'll take a piece of your head," Gillespie explained, "faster than anybody I know."[23]

Mingus had to talk to Farwell Taylor. He was torqued up, needed to recoup. Conveniently, he had a gig at San Francisco's Jazz Workshop. Byard didn't want to leave New York after just getting home, so Jerome Richardson suggested a sixteen-year-old pianist who'd just arrived in town.

Jane Getz played like a cross between McCoy Tyner and Bill Evans. And the five-foot-two white blonde was stacked and stunning. She'd make a great stage impact, set off by the large Clifford Jordan and the Big Dog, as she called the boss.[24]

She went to his place on East 26th Street and auditioned. He wanted her to play like Ellington.

On the plane, he told her to sit next to him; he sensed she was nervous. Charles Wright, on his other side, carried his old brown leather briefcase, with his dozens of prescription drugs. Mingus took a handful or two before ordering a rare filet mignon, and lectured her about vegetarianism.

Mingus was still thinking about Dolphy.

Onstage, he yelled at her, "Think Duke Ellington, Ellington, baby," and thundered his big hands on the keys to demonstrate. She was stunned. He kept yelling at her. When they started "Meditations," he shoved her off the bench with his hip, and began to play. Dapper Dannie Richmond wouldn't look at her.

The next set was the same.

The next day, she listened to Ellington records. That night, she played lots of flat fives and nines, the slightly discordant, luminous harmonies Duke shared with the Impressionists. Everything seemed fine until the middle of the second set, when Mingus stormed off the stage to the dressing room. The Workshop kept playing to a backdrop of tearing sounds, until he emerged with long strips of terrycloth—a torn-up towel. He pushed her off the bench, crawled below, and tied the piano pedals up.

He wiped his forehead dry of sweat, and told her she used the pedals too much. She told him, "Fuck you, man," sat down in the audience, and stared at him. He ignored her, and she figured she was fired.

Dannie Richmond took her out for coffee and told her to see Madame Rose, a Sausalito spiritualist. The next afternoon, Rose fed her tea and told her to visualize Mingus surrounded by white light and peaceful. When Getz got back to the hotel, he'd called her three times and left word for her to meet him at the gig.

Mingus spent the afternoon with Magda Lewis, mother of pop star Huey Lewis and an old pal of Farwell. They drove through the Broadway Tunnel, and Magda hit the horn. He loved the swelling echo and the Doppler effect so much, they had to do it again twice.

That night, when Getz came to work, Mingus grinned and pulled two boxes of strawberrries, a bright red lipstick, and a pair of pantyhose out of a shopping bag. "We're recording tonight," he beamed, "and I want you on the record." John Handy sat in. "Meditations" and "Fables" surged and bucked with power and wit. Fantasy, buoyed by the sales of Debut reissues, released the set as *Right Now.*

A table of blacks muttered about his pianist. He paid their tab and announced, "They can leave right now."

The Autobiography of Malcolm X was published to instant controversy. Black Power was an increasingly familiar slogan since the 1959 TV special, *The Hate That Hate Produced,* brought the Muslims to mainstream America.

Many whites grew fearful of racial backlash. Malcolm's book was a fierce indictment of white racism but ended with what was for him a new, more modulated tone.

Malcolm had broken with the Black Muslims and gone to Mecca, and, in a profound epiphany, renounced black separatism during the multiracial hajj. He ceased attacking Martin Luther King Jr. and integrationist leaders, and pledged to work with others, white and black, for his newly broadened goals.

Mingus asked Saul Zaentz to use his Debut earnings to pay some monthly expenses, like garaging his car. It was like getting a salary, but he never touched the money.

He returned to the Five Spot. The *New Yorker* ran an article that called his music "ruthlessly honest,"[25] and described his dramatic physical transformation over the last year, his clean-shaven face and 180-pound figure.

JANET COLEMAN: He was really, really thin and handsome. He was very very naked. Al Young has also commented he couldn't stand his own beauty. He got shyer, more withdrawn. He was so sensitive, you could see his face naked with feeling.

He sometimes made the reedmen hide in the cloakroom and then appear playing a Bird medley, a theatrical flourish, an echo of Hamlet's Ghost, another experiment.

Two weeks later, on June 29, Eric Dolphy died in Europe, and rumors swirled. It was a heart attack, brain tumor, Nazis, drugs, diabetes, malnutrition.

Mingus broke down. Only Dannie Richmond rivaled Dolphy's musical and personal link with him. Only Buddy Collette and Britt Woodman went as far back. Jaki Byard felt there was something unresolved between the two. When

Mingus went to Los Angeles for the July 9 funeral, he stood at the graveside and yelled, "I'm sorry, Eric."

The day before, Judy bore a son, and he named the baby Eric Dolphy Mingus.

For a while, Mingus spent a lot of time with Judy, Carolyn, and the new baby. The New York World's Fair was on, a celebration of worldwide progress, American achievement, the unlimited future of technology and man. He went over and over, by himself and with them. He was enthralled.

He was thinking about San Francisco twenty-five years earlier. He was dreaming of the future, and he was lost in the present.

Outside San Francisco, Ken Kesey was planning his own trip to the Fair.[26]

An heir to Kerouac's attitudes, Kesey wrote *One Flew over the Cuckoo's Nest*, a fable of asylum life after scandals compelled changes in postwar mental institutions. The book showed how little asylum-staff attitudes toward patients had actually shifted. A best-seller, it became a Broadway smash by July 1964, when Kesey's next novel, *Sometimes a Great Notion*, was due to be published.

So to New York came the West Coast's version of Tim Leary: Kesey was California's chief LSD honcho. He'd assembled disciples, the Merry Pranksters, prototype hippies with wild-colored and velvet clothing and painted Day-Glo mask-faces. They believed LSD opened the doors of perception to creativity, to living totally in the moment, the Eternal Recurrent Present.

Satori by pharmaceutical.

For the trip east, the Pranksters clambered into an old yellow school bus with bunks and a kitchen, splashed with Day-Glo designs, rigged up with electronics, recording equipment, instruments, tape loops. Neal Cassady, close friend of and inspiration for Kerouac and Ginsberg, was the driver, as he was in *On the Road*. Cassady was the Beats' holy primitive in whiteface; for him there was no separation between thought and deed. He acted totally in the moment.

After the Fair, the Pranksters went to Millbrook. But their loopy California circus clashed with the East Coast's monastic seriousness. Peggy Guggenheim tried to entertain them in salon fashion, but they were too trippy.

Leary sent word he couldn't meet them; he was on a three-day acid voyage. They piled on the Bus to head back to California.

Mingus was starting to think about Monterey. Duke Ellington and Dizzy Gillespie and Thelonious Monk were on the bill. He was in the company he deserved, in a setting he'd long craved.

And it meant pressure.

Present during the first week of September at the Five Spot was a young journalist named Bill Whitworth, from the *Herald Tribune*'s Sunday magazine, founded by Clay Felker; it evolved into *New York* magazine. Whitworth later became a *New Yorker* editor, then editor of the *Atlantic Monthly*.

His assignment: spend a few days with Mingus and sketch his character through his behavior—the New Journalism that Felker and Tom Wolfe, who was writing about Kesey, made famous, that was the stylistic identification of counterculture, outsider journalism.[27]

Whitworth watched Mingus throw the $2,200 bass from Milan out of the Five Spot's kitchen door. It smashed into pieces near an obnoxious groupie, and he stomped what was left. Iggy Termini had the cook, Chan, rustle up a bloody steak. Mingus calmed down as he chewed, and apologized to Iggy for wanting the audience to listen to the music. He gave his son Charles the wooden shards to paint on.

The woman was heckling him, he said, because Sonny Rollins rejected her. Whitworth was only a few feet away. Mingus was not above grabbing attention.

He stopped at Timothy Leary's table to toast Jesus, Rama Krishna, and the Devil. He reported that Susan was married to a rich artist, and he would pimp her as soon as he got her broken tooth fixed. He said gangsters were threatening him, and he might have to leave the country.

He replaced his banker's suits and bowler hat with a black leather vest, T-shirt, corduroy slacks, and sandals, and told friends ruefully, "Susan likes me to dress scruffy."

His mantelpiece at the studio at 26th and Second held eight bottles of good wine and dirty glasses. He had books by H. G. Wells, D. H. Lawrence, Rainer Maria Rilke, Jean-Paul Sartre, and Winston Churchill. His manuscript was scattered in piles across the sofa. His letters were routinely carbon copied to LBJ, the U.S. Labor Party, Malcolm X, the Black Muslims, the FBI, Charles De Gaulle, even J. Edgar Hoover.

He said he was more or less separated from Judy, who found out when she read Whitworth's article that November.

JUDY STARKEY MINGUS McGRATH: There must have been a confrontation. I remember throwing my wedding ring across the street in the Village. For a long while, he was trying to tell me that Susan was this woman Susan Scott, and she was back and on the scene. But I later met Susan Scott, and she was a different woman. Of course, I met Susan too. I didn't hate her. I just felt really jealous and threatened.

Things just sort of slid. One time I went out to mail a letter, in front of my apartment on Fifth Avenue. And he's out there, leaning against the mailbox, talking to Susan. And she's wearing a black leather coat and has blonde hair. And I had on a housedress. A housedress. Can you imagine? I felt like such a jerk.

I would see her. We met a couple of times around the Village. And we got along great. You know, women do that. You meet another woman you think is a threat, but you can still relate at some level.

The night Mingus smashed his bass, in the audience was an English rock band called the Animals, part of the British Invasion spearheaded by the Beatles. A new generation was fired up by American music, especially black rhythm and blues and blues, which they valued for its emotional authenticity and power—an antidote to bland white teen pop.

The Animals were huge Mingus fans. They wanted to make a movie like *Shadows.* Their bassist later became Jimi Hendrix's manager and producer. They were stunned when Mingus destoyed his bass, but not long afterward Hendrix and The Who's Pete Townshend were destroying their guitars onstage after performances. It became rock theater.

On September 20, 1964, the Workshop appeared at Monterey.

Mingus drove cross-country with Byard. They were friends who loved to pig out, who had once inhaled a leg of lamb together and ordered multiple courses in Chinatown restaurants as snacks. Jaki brought him garden-grown beefsteak tomatoes; they reminded Mingus of Mamie's produce.

But they fought during the trip. Byard was writing arrangements. He'd always tried to write down lead sheets for the musicians, explaining to Mingus, "This is very important music. Bach used to write his music down. Beethoven. Even Byard. Why can't you do it?" Mingus laughed and left Jaki alone until their drive, when he hovered over Byard while he arranged "Meditations" for an augmented band.

At Monterey, rehearsals were the usual grueling start-and-stop affair. There wasn't much time. Byard suggested Mingus conduct the band and let Red Callender play bass instead of tuba. No response. He suggested Mingus let him rehearse the band. No response. He suggested they get a meal. Mingus vanished for nearly two hours. The band hit the music again, without him.

Five thousand people showed up on a beautiful, crisply cool, coastal California Sunday afternoon. It was Mingus's Monterey debut, and he and Monk were legends now.

Buddy Collette hired studio veterans to augment the Workshop's core quintet and old pals like Callender and John Handy. They had to fill in for Dolphy. Collette played flute and piccolo; Jack Nimitz played bass clarinet. They hit the stage twelve strong.

Mingus weighed 190 pounds, and his Fu Manchu mustache was accentuated by his onstage shades. He bowed a long, achingly lyrical solo take of Ellington's "I've Got It Bad," punctuated with darting runs and flamenco picking. It was a highly unorthodox concert opener.

Charles McPherson took Birdlike arcing swoops and darts over the ensemble for "In a Sentimental Mood." Jaki Byard tinged "All Too Soon" with flecks of stride and dissonance. Red Callender soloed on "Mood Indigo," seconded by Buddy Collette's alto.

Mingus was staging the history of his life and music inside an Ellington ballad medley. They ended with a long, powerful string of solos on "Take the A Train."

He was claiming his due. He was Duke's true heir. He had found ways to organize postwar jazz into compositional form, ways that no one could duplicate.

After "Orange" and intermission came "Meditations," billed as a Monterey Festival commission. He'd started calling it "Meditations on Integration." The opening was full of odd meters and counterpoint, and the written sections alternated with improvisations based on a range of notes. Each individual had a different mix of written and improvised sections.

Mingus introduced the piece onstage.

CHARLES MINGUS: Eric Dolphy explained to me that there was something similar to the concentration camps once in Germany now down South . . . and the only difference between the barbed wire is that they don't have gas chambers and hot stoves to cook us in yet. So I wrote a piece called "Meditations," as to how to get some wire cutters—before someone else gets some guns to us.[28]

Mingus dropped his bow and bobbed around the bass as he plucked thick, dissonant chords and Richmond built threatening rhythms. "The music was thunder," Newsweek's reporter wrote. "It was Dante's Hell opened up, and Mingus was dancing, exhorting, shouting, roaring laughter, like a man before a hurricane he had conjured up himself."[29]

He wasn't Huck Finn's Jim. He was Prospero.

He thwacked the bass, and all was silence. The crowd sat for a moment, breathless. Then they rose in a standing ovation. He kept his back to them. He told Newsweek, "I was scared, man."[30]

He recorded it to launch his new record label. No one but him would own Charles Mingus Enterprises.

Perceptions onstage, as often with him, were like Rashomon in jazz time. Everyone had a different slant on what happened.

Buddy Collette thought Mingus hated the album. "It's studio white playing," he sneered onstage. "It's boring." Buddy winced. He knew his pal's bands worked off his voice. That was impossible with so many players and so little time.

Charles McPherson felt the core quintet was tight, and made the music great. Mingus was high from the crowd's reaction, and loved everybody. He knew he was a success.

John Handy played two choruses on "A Train" instead of the feature he was promised, and the boss cut him off with a drum solo. But he extravagantly praised Handy's solo, massaging the altoist's delicate ego.

The critics shouted hosannas. In the *New York Times*, John Wilson wrote that Mingus was the missing link who bridged the stylistic gap between Ellington and Monk. The photo showed him in a derby.[31]

In *Time*, Mingus explained his music was chaos, but organized chaos.[32] He was an avant-garde formalist.

Newsweek's cover on October 2 had Lee Harvey Oswald's picture: the Warren Commission had rendered its verdict on the Kennedy assassination. Inside, it ran a large feature on Mingus, which began, "Charlie Mingus is a short, hulking, brooding man who for years has been recognized as the greatest jazz virtuoso ever to thump a bass fiddle. At the Monterey Festival last week, his 'Meditations for a Pair of Wire Cutters' demonstrated that he must be ranked among the greatest of jazz composers."[33]

The story described the concert and his bass virtuosity, then said, "Mingus is an angry man, sensitive about his color, and the fact that his skin is 'high yellow' only makes him more intense about being a Negro. He broods, he gulps red wine by the gallon, he brawls in bars." It toted up his marriages and divorces and children, and noted that Judy was white.

It continued: "Perpetually bitter, usually unkempt, he rants against racial discrimination and society in general. . . . 'The word jazz means nigger, discrimination, second-class citizenship, the back-of-the-bus bit,' he shouts. . . . A former mental patient at Manhattan's Bellevue Hospital, Mingus tells anyone willing to listen, 'They say I'm crazy, and I really am.'"

His complex contradictions, the ironies propelling his life and music, were now more directly in the public eye than ever. Like his music, he was always in danger of being reduced.

That fall, a harbinger of the future was unfolding 200-odd miles to the north, in Berkeley, where Mingus listened to Jelly Roll Morton 78s with Phil Elwood and visited Kate Mulholland while the Free Speech Movement was rousing students to defy the University of California-Berkeley administration.

Traditionally, the area in front of the campus off Telegraph Avenue was a haven of student political activity, buzzing with tables and leafletteers, fundraising and speakers. That September, the dean of students shut it down. Thus was born FSM, a coalition of CORE, the Young Socialists Alliance, SNCC, the W. E. B. Du Bois Club, and Women for Peace, among others.

The Movement had instant heroes, like Mario Savio, who addressed 3,000 students from the top of the police car holding Jack Weinberg, the CORE table's representative busted for violating university rules. The students surged around the car; the cops went nowhere.

Some had learned their craft in the civil rights movement, with SNCC or the fledgling Students for a Democratic Society. They forged the template for the decade's college confrontations. Initially they believed in nonviolence, à la Thoreau, Gandhi, and King. Besides its ethical rightness, it was effective: meeting violence with passive resistance created victims who appealed to American consciences, even politically unsympathetic ones.

Street Theater was going more and more white.

That October, Mingus had a gig for the Charles McPherson–Lonnie Hillyer quintet lined up at the Five Spot. They did an extended piece built around recapping various musicians and styles. Jaki Byard went from Joplin to free jazz. Hillyer played Miles Davis in the piece's development, and turned his back on the audience while playing muted quotes from Miles chestnuts like "Bye Bye Blackbird." One night, Miles himself walked in during the solo, and came up onstage. Hillyer handed him the trumpet, and the audience went nuts.[34]

From the Five Spot, Mingus went to Birdland, where he fielded an expanded outfit. It included trumpeters Hobart Dotson and Jimmy Owens, who doubled on flugelhorn, Eddie Bert, Julius Watkins, and a young tuba player named Howard Johnson that Byard knew. Mingus had put Johnson through a grueling onstage audition at the Five Spot. He needed a tuba player, but Red Callender had CBS-TV commitments, and he didn't want to use Don Butterfield.

Richmond cued Johnson, singing the tuba parts. He too loved deep-throated horns. He was Mingus's alter ego, his buffer and his conduit, and he made the wheels go round.

They rehearsed a lot, but Mingus right now was supportive, not confrontational. He was coming off a high. When a couple of hornmen said they couldn't do their parts, he told them he'd work with them on material like "Meditations" and *Mingus Mingus Mingus Mingus Mingus*.

He and Hillyer did a duet; he played piano. The trumpeter was beyond bebop, under his guided prodding, and they dialoged freely.

Frank Mabry was their paymaster. Bert found him aggravating. The musicians had to ask to get paid, and the thin black man always seemed startled when they did.

The opening act at Birdland was a little-known comedian named Flip Wilson. Sharing the bill was the John Coltrane Quartet, at the peak of its power and fame.

Earlier in 1964, Birdland started booking rock acts. Mo Levy saw the money hovering over the rebirth of rock. Suddenly major labels were interested, because kids were buying it in huge numbers. He'd had his fingers in that pie from the 1950s, and he just stuck them in deeper.

It was a sign. Soon jazz was no longer the sound-track for hip collegians, and its popular audience began to fade. The residue fractured into true believers in Dixieland, swing, bop, cool, gospel, and free jazz.

The days of jazz's overarching umbrella, sheltering many dialects, were dwindling.

That had helped make Mingus possible. He was one of the last great modernists. He believed he could know and say it all, in his voice, from his soul. He could only have happened in his moment, and in some ways his moment, at its zenith, was already drawing to a close.

In the meantime, he was on top of the world. An editor from *Playboy* asked for the manuscript of his autobiography; he was sure his superiors would love it, once they read it.[35]

Janet Coleman and Susan and assorted others helped with Charles Mingus Enterprises. Some, in the Beat tradition, drew cartoons for ads and the album cover. But Charles and Susan ran it. Mingus wanted to sell only by mail order, so he couldn't be ripped off by distributors or retailers. He wouldn't lug stock and collect checks. It would be straightforward. It was his.

He planned to put ads in the burgeoning counterculture papers, many, like the *Village Voice*, started by Beats. He wanted the ads to look homemade.

The coupon read, "Jazz Workshop pays all postage, foreign add $1. Warning: This album will not be sold at record stores! This album can be purchased only by mail . . . or at an authorized booth set up on the Monterey Jazz Festival fair grounds during the 1965 concert. Any other form of sale is unauthorized.

"Legal Notice: $500.00 Reward for evidence which secures conviction of any person for selling these records."[36]

Mingus excerpted the *Newsweek* feature in the liner notes.

The two-record set could be had for $10 sent to Charles Mingus Enterprises at 128 East 50th Street, New York City, 10022. It was the address of Bernard Geis Associates.

A young woman named Letty Cottin Pogrebin worked with Geis and had first met Mingus in 1961, when dancer Katharine Dunham introduced them at the Ninth Circle. She was a jazz fan, so she started checking his shows out.

LETTY COTTIN POGREBIN: I was young and innocent and naïve, but he never hit on me. He was more like an uncle figure. I was living just around the corner from the Circle, and he'd come over and just hang out and talk. When my now-husband came over to pick me up for one of our first dates, Charlie was in the shower, because he couldn't shower where he was living then.

He was the kind of person you took risks in front of. I remember dancing for him at his loft; it was the first time I'd done anything like that since college.

In the run-up to Monterey, he asked her if her boss would be interested in collaborating with him on a new independent label. He fumed at her about how he'd been cheated consistently by every label he'd ever dealt with. He had to own himself. There was no other way to guarantee that his art and his income matched.

When Pogrebin brought the idea up, Geis jumped on it. Geis figured the record business was more lucrative than books, and was eager to get into it, especially with a star the magnitude of Charlie Mingus.

The deal was done. Bernard Geis Associates took over the design and shipping of what would become Mingus at Monterey. Mingus would sign the first 5,000 copies. His total advance, including reimbursed Workshop expenses for the Monterey concert itself, came to $10,000.[37]

Mingus was pleased. He had a friend on the inside, big bucks in his pocket, glowing press, and his own business again.

On December 11, Letty ordered the first 1,000 sets of Mingus at Monterey from RCA Custom Records.[38]

FRANK MABRY: One time we were bullshitting in his studio. The discs he'd put out were all piled up in boxes. He was saying, "They can't cheat us this time. The records are all numbered." He got mad, and kicked one of the boxes, and somehow got the scissors sticking out of it in his foot. "Okay, okay, man," he said, and he starts to play the bass. He was playing all these little kids' stories, these songs. You knew which ones because you understood the words. The words were THERE. He was playing the words.

Mingus's words about the industry got increasingly pointed, despite or because of his increasing visibility.

In early October, he sent a long letter to Bill Chance, a union rep. He claimed the union had been telling record companies not to record him, since he was big trouble to deal with. The unsettled United Artists judgment hung over him and Local 802, and he lashed out with rambling gibes like, "We feel that the black heirs to this country need fear no more the fakers in high positions in musicians' unions who neglect their duty when it suits them best to the black men in honest business with the white men."[39]

Late October found Mingus in Toronto, where a seven-man Workshop, McPherson and Hillyer and the others, augmented by seven Canadians, prepared to film "Meditations" for the CBC program *Other Voices*. They taped a long day's rehearsal, and the producers picked additional music for the final Halloween taping.

In the half-hour film,[40] Mingus wears his black leather vest and T-shirt and sandals; the others wear suits.

The Halloween Toronto *Daily Star* ran a story under the headline "Negro Artists Exploited; Mingus Urges Investigation." It said he "loosed a bitter blast yesterday against the record business and indirectly against the white race."

He accused several record labels of releasing his discs without paying him. He said a New York agent was constricting his bookings and threatening his wife and child with death because he demanded equal pay with whites. He'd hired his own strongmen for protection. He wanted a congressional investigation of racially motivated disparities in pay. Negroes were confined to nightclub work. Ed Sullivan hired virtually no black musicians for his popular variety show, which had helped launch Elvis and the Beatles and Rolling Stones. Cruise ships never hired Negro bands. He said, "These people can dance to Negro music, can't they? They used to." To friends he had often complained that jazz had been shoved out of the dance-halls and into nightclubs because it was too helpful to racial integration.

He told the reporter that McGraw-Hill paid him $7,000 for *Beneath the Underdog*, then dropped it because it was too dirty.

On November 2, the Toronto *Telegram* ran a similar story. He told them, "You have to be a gangster to survive. If I have to get killed to expose certain people in the booking business, I'll do it."

At a party, Frank Mabry pulled one of his street-magic moves. He said he could beat the rest of them downstairs without taking the elevator. They got in on the eighth floor, and he was waiting for them when they got out in the lobby.

On November 6, 1964, Mingus wrote to Goddard Lieberson, the aristocratic head of Columbia Records.[41] He wanted to lease his Columbia albums and reissue them on Charles Mingus Enterprises. He explained that his company would become a division of Columbia, and both would benefit. Between the lines, he complained about being underpaid. He was initially told he had sold 90,000 copies of *Mingus Ah Um*, but then was told it wasn't more than 3,000.

The ploy went nowhere.

The year ended with Mingus's school in motion again.

In December, he got a letter from Herman Badillo, commissioner of the Department of Relocation, about a meeting at Carmelite School Hall on December 7 at 7:30 P.M. concerning the Bellevue South Urban Renewal Plan. The city took title to the building he lived in.[42]

Urban renewal, a widespread effort to rebuild crumbling housing for poorer residents, was in vogue across America, with longer-term mixed effects. Too often it replaced old decrepit buildings with new ones that became ghettos. It became a symbol of the age—misguided hopes and dreams based on misunderstandings of gritty reality, a parable of good intentions gone awry, thanks to the tangle of interests in real estate and racism.

Robert Kennedy, just elected senator from New York, had won partly on his vows to clean up the degradation of urban poverty, exacerbated by racial bias. He kept the Kennedy legend alive among black believers.

For Mingus, there was an up side to being moved yet again: the city would pay to relocate his school.

His relationship with Susan was intensity itself. He called her from all over the country. He moaned about her and bitched about her and worshiped her.

She let him be himself, let him find his own levels, and accepted them. But she wasn't passive. He'd test her like he tested everyone. Sometimes she'd shrug and say, "Oh Charles, cut the bullshit," and he'd grumble to a halt. Sometimes there were fireworks.

One night at his studio, Whitworth watched a fight escalate. One of her high heels came off, and they scrambled to hit each other with it. A few times she showed up at friends' apartments after a fight, looking for a place to roost.

He was never easy. He was wounded by emotion, always ready to be hurt. He was jealous as Othello. He wanted his women to be his alone, though he was never totally theirs. He had his own sense of measure, and the charm to make women love that in him—that big spreading smile when he was glad to see you, the one that lit up his eyes while they crinkled. Almost everyone melted in the warmth.

He and Susan went to the Ninth Circle regularly. He ordered his steaks double-cut and raw, bloody. He'd carry in his crocheted bag with a few bottles of first-rate French wines, like Chateau Lafitte Rothschild.

That quarter, his royalties from Impulse Records totaled $1,883.72. His royalties from overseas for the second half of 1964 came to $432.05; the first half of 1965 would bring $972.71. His Columbia quarterly payments had dipped to $100 or less. His Candid records were out of print. His BMI performance royalties fluctuated between $50 and $200 per quarter.[43]

He was living the good life. He was in love and in pain, caught in an unfurling melodrama perfect for a wounded Romantic. He owned his music again. He was a star. He wanted to hire dancers to perform a concert of *Black Saint*.

He was on top of the world.

11 One Flew over the Cuckoo's Nest

FOR MONTHS after Monterey, Charles Mingus got big positive press. He was sure the recording would put Charles Mingus Enterprises in the black from the git-go. He was a Village artist-celebrity. He had arrived.

But he was standing at the edge of a series of cliffs. His personal life was more fractured than ever. Like his valise of prescription bottles, everyone in his realm was supposed to have a place. He was a composer, in life as in music.

Life around him, however, was changing, partly thanks to many of the circles he'd frequented over the last twenty-five years. A series of revolts, seismic cultural shifts, displacements was shuddering through American society, many of them the results of bebop attitudes.

Mingus marched in demonstrations against racism and the Vietnam war. He often didn't plan to, and didn't have to. There were plenty to choose from. He'd be on his rounds and one would pass him, and off he'd go. It was natural. He talked endlessly about the people who really ran things. He was convinced that a secret order lurked behind the TV reality that everyone else saw, and knew it was bent on power, and he couldn't just stand by. He was deeply affected by a poem by a German Lutheran pastor named Niemöller, who wrote of the successive waves of Nazi sweeps and arrests in World War II, as people who didn't protest the earlier waves disappeared in later ones. Mingus figured you had to stand for something. The powers that be would come for you anyway.

He was busted a few times with other marchers and spent time in the Tombs, New York's downtown holding tank.

Playboy's top brass turned out to be uninterested in his autobiography.[1]

Mingus's life was about to pivot and lurch into ruts of confusion and depression. He would become desperate, financially and emotionally, until he almost shattered. When these times came and he would wander around the Village streets, he would often seemed distracted, distant, muttering. And yet he had days when he was himself, where the fires of musical creativity stoked the core of his being, and he spent hours at the piano, sometimes scribbling on score paper.

He would discover again that even Prospero had limits.

The next few years would change his life, after taking him through the outer precincts of living hells.

Before the 1960s were over, America's increasingly stridently divided society would shatter into fragments. Even its counter- and subcultures fractured, as their identities and goals diverged and government agencies infiltrated, undermined, and played them off each other.

The era would become a byword for anarchy, rebellion, and revolution. But in 1965 America's antiwar and antiracist movmements still could forge a broad consensus.

Another long and bloody unpopular Asian war, this one in Vietnam, not Korea, was met by an upsurge of riots, usually student directed. Blacks served in disproportionate numbers in the military, and it showed as the casualties mounted on TV screens across America each night. The SDS—Students for a Democratic Society—had a slogan: Democracy is in the streets. As what was happening in the streets washed across people's living rooms, as riots erupted across American cities into millions of homes after dinner, many worried that it looked more like anarchy.

Art, however, sometimes thrives on disorder. Having things in upheaval sanctions experimention. So the Psychedelic Age was also the incubator of an interdisciplinary artistic explosion.

Jazz and the "chance" music of John Cage inspired rockers to stretch out, try improvisation, whether they were musically tutored or not. They used cocaine, marijuana, LSD, even heroin for inspiration. It was a funhouse-mirror reflection of the boppers and heroin, another confirmation that many artists have always used drugs.

Andy Warhol created a rock band, the Velvet Underground, and a psychedelic light show called the Exploding Plastic Inevitable. Their music was about drugs and sex, but the drug was heroin, not LSD. They listened to Ornette Coleman. The Grateful Dead listened to Coleman and John Coltrane and Roland Kirk. Jimi Hendrix adapted Trane's sound and extended solo style. Jazz ideas reorganized American pop music, as they had during the sophisticated heydays of the Gershwins and Cole Porter.

All this was bound together by the heady sense of experimentation and the feeling of being in opposition on the right side, in an era of prosperity.

Paul Goodman's ideas in *Growing Up Absurd* were among the many about to be severely tested by history.

Mingus brought his core quintet—Lonnie Hillyer, Charles McPherson, Jaki Byard, Dannie Richmond—into the Village Vanguard in February 1965, and they stayed for two months. Things were rocky. He'd shaved his head. He broke a light fixture and took a fireax to the club's door and battered it off its hinges.

JAKI BYARD: I was taking medication for hives, and passing out. So I walked off the bandstand at the Vanguard. He came into the kitchen after me. "What do you mean walking off my set?" "I'm ill." He grabbed an ax. Bam-bam-bam. "What do you mean walking off?" I said, "Man, put the ax down." "What?" So I grabbed the fire extinguisher. I said, "Go ahead." He threw the ax down and said, "Come on, man, let's go play some blues." Boy, I was shaking. That's when I left the group. We were tight before that.

Byard stayed for a handful of one-night stands. They passed through Minneapolis on May 13, where they recorded *My Favorite Quintet* at the famed Tyrone Guthrie Theatre. Then Byard just drifted away.

Dolphy was dead. Byard was gone. The molten core of Mingus's most triumphant group, the equals who torqued his music up, was spent. Only Dannie Richmond was left, and even he was spending more and more time holed in up Greensboro, North Carolina, trying to shake his addiction.

Whatever was riding the whirlwind, Mingus would go through it by himself.

On February 2, Martin Luther King Jr. was arrested in Selma, Alabama. Mounted police beat and tear-gassed the demonstrators at the city's edge, and "Bloody Sunday," as it became known, poured into living rooms on TV. The moment cemented broad national support for the Voting Rights Act, which was then passed into law.

King considered that part of his work done, and moved to Chicago to confront economic inequality. His efforts there turned to failure.

On February 21, 1965, Malcolm X was murdered at the Audubon Ballroom in Harlem. His widow and friends suspected the Black Muslims assassinated him, though it was never proved. Malcolm became the latest in the 1960s lengthening list of political deaths in America.

As the Vietnam War escalated under President Johnson, there would be dozens more leaders killed at home, and 50,000-plus dead American soldiers abroad.

The antiwar movement grew in many ways from the civil rights movement, but Black Power advocates were voicing increasingly shrill options, from black secession to establishing black segregated areas of the country. White college students, who had been crucial to the media coverage of SNCC and the Freedom Riders, were increasingly consumed with the military draft and the war's mounting tolls as well as its politics. Black students pushed for the development of Black Studies programs.

The focus of the emerging psychedelic counterculture was on self-improvement and realization. Drugs became sacramental. These "hippies"—the word itself came, ironically, from jazz slang—jettisoned the feeling that black culture was primary in America, the very feeling that had given bebop and the civil rights movement their ironic cutting edge.

TOM WOLFE: The fabled North Beach, the old fatherland bohemia of the West Coast, always full of... long-haired little WASP and Jewish buds balling spade cats—and now North Beach was dying. North Beach was nothing but tit shows... But it was not just North Beach that was dying. The whole old-style hip life—jazz, coffee houses, civil rights, invite a spade for dinner, Vietnam—it was all suddenly dying... It had even gotten to the point that Negroes were no longer in the hip scene, not even as totem figures. It was unbelievable. Spades, the very soul figures of Hip, of jazz, of the hip vocabulary itself.[2]

Soul music, the pop music coefficient of gospel jazz, filled the pop charts of the early to mid-1960s with cultural dreams of real racial integration.

Soon soul music would atrophy, psychedelia would be parodied and pilloried, and the broad-based coalition that had made the Civil Rights Bill of 1965 possible would fracture into smaller self-interested units.

There would be no one to sum it all up. The age of modernism would be in smoking ruins, and with it, much of the American dream.

In March, Bruce and Roxanne Bethany were married by the Reverend Al Carmines at Judson Memorial Church, site of antiwar and civil rights activism. Carmines was an increasingly political advocate, and an artists' friend.

Mingus came to the wedding with Judy, who was Roxanne's witness, and poet Joel Oppenheimer and a few close friends. The Bethanys knew the arty Village circles. They watched Mingus and a French filmmaker pal burn themselves with cigarettes to show who was more macho. They saw them race cars with sculptor John Chamberlain and painter Neil Williams up and down Park Avenue at 3:00 A.M. to see how many green lights they could hit—12, 13, 14, 15.

In April, the New York City Department of Real Estate, Bureau of Urban Renewal sent Mingus a dunning letter for his previous month's rent at the 26th Street storefront. He claimed his check was lost in the mail. [3]

The New York State tax people and the feds starting wondering about his business. It never made any money, and there were complaints about unfulfilled orders and cashed checks.

Mingus took his copy of Edmund Shaftesbury's *Cultivation of Personal Magnetism in Seven Steps* and carved out the mid-section, so he could stash a handgun in it. He collected picture postcards and a Tarot deck. He had a lock of hair from Eric's first visit to the barber. [4]

In May 1965, Mingus bought himself a Corvette Sting Ray at Don Allen Chevrolet, a big dealership on West 57th Street. He listed his occupation as composer. [5]

The 'Vette was the hottest and sleekest and most prestigious American sports car of the time. His was dark green, with 400-plus fuel-injected horsepower under the hood. It cost a bundle, but he felt compelled to buy it. It suited his stature, his need for speed and power, his competitiveness.

The sales manager sent a congratulatory note to G. Mingus. C. Mingus wouldn't let Judy or Susan drive it.

He couldn't stand being in public without being in the public eye. When he went to see Miles Davis at the Village Vanguard one night, he started shifting in his seat, and after a while began singing along with the music onstage, as if he were cuing the Workshop. Miles shaded his eyes from the spotlights, spotted him, and croaked, "Quit Tommin'."

Mingus didn't like being merely a civilian.

His friend Bill Whitworth went to a concert where an extended Ellington piece was performed. The next night, Mingus asked him what he'd thought. Whitworth said casually it reminded him of a movie score. They kept talking.

At four that morning, Whitworth's phone rang. Mingus was screaming and cursing over it: "How dare you say something like that about Duke Ellington?"

You couldn't make small talk around him. You never knew when he was going to pivot, or on what.

In April, Nat Hentoff praised Mingus's two-LP Monterey album in *HiFi/Stereo Review*, and in May, Martin Williams wrote a long, glowing piece in *Saturday Review*. "Mingus's musical personality," it said in part, "is so exaltingly forceful that he can uplift almost any musician and transmute almost any material, and this aspect of his talent is captured on these records as I've not heard it before."

He owed the Kaybank Recording Corporation of Minneapolis $388.90 overdue for recording *My Favorite Quintet*.[6]

The British Invasion fired rock back up, and America was dotted with teen garage bands learning hits and obscurities. Ken Kesey was throwing "acid tests" around San Francisco and the Bay. Bands like the Grateful Dead were emerging from this heady combination of LSD-laced crowds and musicians to in-the-moment flights of Jungian synchronicity, thanks to the evolving light shows, strobes and projectors throwing liquid colors globuling across a big screen.

The line between audience and performer was deliberately blurred. Each show was unpredictable.

By Mingus's standards, none of these people were serious musicians. He had the same argument with Leary. Drugs didn't make you creative. All the junkie boppers weren't worth a shit, and LSD wasn't any different. You had to work to be creative. Inspiration was a great and holy gift, but you had to push and pull and work to shape it.

An artist had to be able to deal with the real world, and it was an unfriendly place, man.

Jazz clubs were beginning to empty and shut down. Only a couple still presented jazz all the time; most mixed it up. The glory days were gone. Few leaders could command extended gigs, the way Mingus and Thelonious Monk and Miles Davis had done only an eyeblink earlier.

But for the moment, those three still could.

That spring, Mingus led a pianoless octet for two weeks at the Village Vanguard, opposite the Les McCann trio one week and Monk's quartet the next. Then he hooked a three-month date at the Village Gate, co-billed with Monk, then Herbie Mann.

He had a new piece for a bigger Workshop. Trumpeters Jimmy Owens and Eddie Preston, tuba player Howard Johnson, and French hornist Julius Watkins joined with the rump Workshop quartet. The lineup recalled Miles Davis's *Birth of the Cool* octet.

The new work was intended, he said, as a ballet, and opened with circusy vaudeville flourishes that recalled Kurt Weill. It was dense, rippling with subsections. He called it, "Once There Was a Holding Corporation Called Old America."

The last week of June 1965, when they opened at the Gate, Dannie Richmond got married and took a honeymoon, despite a severe talking-to. Mingus couldn't believe Dannie would leave him flat. It was too late for a sub, so the band played drummerless.

Art D'Lugoff hired a middle-aged woman to run the downstairs club—the Gate had three floors. She lectured the musicians before the set about keeping it to forty-five minutes. She wagged her finger in Mingus's face and told him she'd turn on a clicking red light toward the club's rear when his time was up.

Monk's drummer, Ben Riley, planned to play Richmond's drums, which weren't there, so he had to race back home and get his own.

Forty-five minutes into the opening set, the woman turned the red light on, with its click-click-click. Forty minutes later, Mingus ended the set when he saw Ben Riley come in.

In the dressing room, Monk and Mingus embraced, grinning.

HOWARD JOHNSON, *musician*: Monk says, "Hey Mingus, you want to get high?" Mingus says, "Yeah, yeah." Monk says, "Yeah, me too." So he opened his cigar box. It had a variety of pills of all kinds, colors, sizes. Monk grabbed a handful of pills and threw them in his mouth, whatever they were. He didn't even look, and said, "Yeah, go ahead, Ming." Mingus was looking at the box and trying to figure out what he wanted. And Monk said, "Come on, go ahead." Mingus: "Oh yeah, okay." So he grabbed a handful and threw them in his mouth. Later he whispered to me, "Gee, I don't know what that shit was."

Later that week, his big, fat, red steak wasn't ready when it was set time. He was upset, and told the waiter to bring it to him as soon as it was done, whether he was onstage or not. He wouldn't eat it if they put it under a warming lamp.

He was bowing a solo when the waiter brought a little square table onstage, put a flower and service on it, then laid out the meal. Mingus stopped immediately, brought the mike to the table, and said, "In the spirit of the Jazz Workshop, we're gonna show you what our individual soloists can do. I know you've never heard anything like this."

He ate, and introduced each soloist through a mouthful of food. Most of the audience thought it was part of the show.

Mingus rehearsed the pianoless Workshop at the apartment at 1160 Fifth Avenue he still nominally shared with Judy. One day during a session, Judy answered the phone. It was Billy Strayhorn, Duke Ellington's alter ego and shadow composer. Her husband dropped everything, said different forms of "Yeah" into the receiver, then hung up.

Strayhorn had caught the band at the Gate and was attracted by its unusual lineup. He wanted Mingus to arrange his signature tune, "Lush Life," now widely used as a solo piano tour de force, highly ornamented, full of out-of-tempo curlicues and displays. But, Strayhorn explained, he originally wrote "Lush Life" in straight tempo with far simpler harmonies—the melody, a bass line, and a voice-leading line. He asked if the Workshop wanted to play off his original lead sheets.

As soon as the messenger brought the envelope, Mingus ripped it open. His eyes got big, and he immediately ended the rehearsal. He spent the night spreading the notes around six horns and his bass, moving the melody from one instrument to another, doubling and tripling each note.

He was a master at creating complexity from simplicity, and now duly recognized by another. Strayhorn came to the Gate again and was impressed by the Workshop's version.

Jazz fans raved about the chart's rich and complex harmonies and textures.

Mingus kept popping up at the Fifth Avenue apartment. That summer, Judy rented a car and a bungalow on Cape Cod. He drove up there, and they tooled around in the Corvette and went out to dinner. He reappeared later, and drove back to the city with them.

He wanted Judy and the kids. He wanted Susan. He wanted it all. Why shouldn't he?

He was eating like a horse and gaining weight.

FRANK MABRY: Ming didn't like to have to pay off people to get gigs, and that led to a lot of violent arguments. But I knew that's how it had to work. Why, the first time I got him over $20,000 was at Monterey. Told the guy he was getting a percentage anyway, so he should jack up the price. And then Susan nearly blew it, when I sent her out there with the promoter's $3,700.

On the books, Mingus was paid $2,500 for his 1965 festival appearance.[7]

Mingus was torn between worlds as the worlds he bridged moved apart, sped into retrograde. Mabry, his black street pimp sidekick and alterego, kept Baby the wannabe from Watts at conscious bay and the mob off his back. Susan believed in art and culture and the fineness of things. She thought of him as a serious composer, and wore the power of white money.

He was both. He was neither. He was Charles Mingus. He needed his white women to handle his career, like Celia. And Judy couldn't and didn't want to do it.

In August, the worst racial riots in decades exploded in Mingus's hometown. Watts had run down, like many ghettoized neighborhoods left behind by white flight. The tinderbox ignited into a horror show of rioting and robbery and burning that the nation watched on TV, as thirty-four people died.

Bobby Kennedy went to Watts, trying to focus attention on the disaster rather than the violence.

Mingus remembered what it was like growing up absurd. He knew too well what made people mad enough, and stupid enough, to burn down their own neighborhoods, especially one left to decay.

On September 10, 1965, before they left for Monterey, the Workshop gathered once more at the Village Gate. The TV cameras of NET were set up there; this was the precursor of the Public Broadcasting System, which ran a program called *Music USA*.[8] This show was called "The Experimenters." The half-hour was divided between Cecil Taylor's quartet and the Workshop; Ralph Ellison, jazz fan and famed author of *Invisible Man*, hosted the Workshop segment; critic Martin Williams, the Taylor segment.

Ellison's complex novel chronicling and critiquing the racial and political divisions across America, from the South to Harlem, from lynchings to communist rallies, had become an instant classic. Its hero was invisible partly because he was struggling to be an independent, thinking human being in a world where labels and tags and loyalties and skin color were defining. When the book was published as a paperback in 1952, Mingus was among the millions who bought it and read it.

Ellison saw jazz as the quintessential American art form, a cultural realization of the nation's potential for color-blind creativity. In his introduction to the Workshop's set, he speaks of jazz as the equal of classical music, alludes to the Third Stream school. The casually dressed Mingus, his eyes looking haunted, leads the suited Workshop through "The Arts of Tatum and Freddie Webster" and his pungently narrated "Don't Let It Happen Here," an adaptation of the poem by Pastor Niemöller that had so affected him.

On camera, he has the same professional ease and ability to play to the lens that always marked him off from virtually all other jazz musicians. He knew his cues and his angles, like an actor. Sidelining years back had taught him in subtle ways.

A few days later, the Jazz Workshop was on the way to California. Susan left them in New York at the airport, and beat them to San Francisco. Then they drove over the Coastal Range and wound down Highway 1 to Monterey.

They hung out for a few days. Naturally, fans took his picture. He grabbed at their cameras or threatened them, because he went everywhere with Susan, and he was sure there were detectives from New York following him.

At 8:00 A.M. one morning, the phone rang in the suite Jimmy Owens and Howard Johnson shared. Johnson had just rolled in, and picked it up. It was Judy. She said, "So Howard, is Susan out there?" Johnson stammered. She said, "Yeah, that's what I thought." She packed up the kids and took the next flight to San Francisco.

JUDY STARKEY MINGUS McGRATH: I was willing to stay. I was willing to let him do whatever he did and still be there. But I guess I must have reached my limit. Showed up at the hotel with the kids. I don't remember much more than that, except I probably made it uncomfortable for a few people. But that's okay.

Susan wasn't in the hotel room—or if she was, she was hiding. I didn't confront the two of them. Charlie wasn't yelling at me or anything. He moved from that hotel to another hotel, where we were, one with a kitchenette. He was probably just going back and forth. But I guess it had reached a point where I wanted to know what was going on.

That night, he told the band Judy had demanded his room key, and stormed in while he and Susan were in bed.

Saturday afternoon, before the Workshop took the stage, he discovered there was no booth to sell his new record. Seven thousand copies of *Mingus at Monterey* were sitting on pallets at 1016 North Sycamore Avenue in Los Angeles.[9]

Jimmy Lyons, the festival director, ex-disk jockey and longtime Mingus acquaintance, was drunk, so he didn't tell Mingus the records hadn't arrived yet. That would have been bad enough, but instead he said nothing. Mingus demanded to headline Saturday night; it was his right, after last year's triumph. Lyons shrugged.

The Workshop played a bit, then Mingus ranted into the mike about Lyons and his record. He cued the band into "When the Saints Go Marching In," and they marched off the stage after barely half an hour.

The audience thought it was a put-on, and waited for him to come back.

This Workshop was recorded a week later, on September 25, at UCLA's Royce Hall. As he usually did, Mingus wrote new music for this new lineup, to suit its particular sound. So there was the ambitious tone poem "Holding Corporation," and a multifaceted piece called "They Trespass the Land of the Sacred Sioux." The typical punning title, originally "The Taming of the Sioux," meant to underline the music's depiction of Susan Graham's ascendancy in his life.

He was calling her several times a day from Buddy Collette's house, where he stayed, leaving his pal with a $200 phone bill.

Mingus mythology spawns itself rapidly, so much has been made of his sending half the octet offstage during the performance to practice the tricky introduction to "Holding Corporation." But this was his Workshop. He'd started and stopped and cued and berated his players onstage, goosed them on record, since the 1950s.

In fact, he liked this outfit. He'd been talking to them about their responsibility as black musicians, encouraging them to get into studio work, to expand the opportunities for blacks. Most of them found him supportive, encouraging. He was always a teacher.

At Royce Hall, he and Dannie Richmond had already screwed up the ending to the latest of his "Meditations" pieces, this one aptly titled "Meditations on Inner Peace." So when the band bobbled "Holding Corporation," he told them, "If we can't play together, who's gonna play with us?" In stark contrast to Monterey's, this set ran eighty-seven minutes. While half the octet practiced, Hillyer and McPherson shone on their showcase, the rapid-fire tour-de-force suite of bebop classics called "Ode to Bird and Dizzy."

Mingus sat at the piano for his duet with Hillyer, his current dialog partner. Neither of them had a map. Mingus did what he did at the piano—improvisational flights of fancy, unprogrammed shifts and zigzags connecting the dots of tunes, and Lonnie knew how to respond. In the midst of it, Mingus breathes into the microphone, "Love."

At full power, the Workshop then tackled "The Arts of Tatum and Freddy Webster," a version of the Satchmo classic "Muskrat Ramble," and "Don't Let It Happen Here."

His adaptation of Martin Niemöller's anti-Nazi poem was stark. "They" came for the communists, the Jews, the unionists, and the speaker stood by because he was not one of them. When "they" burned Catholic churches, the Protestant narrator was silent. Finally, inevitably, "they" came for him: "And I could say nothing, because I was as guilty as they were, for not speaking out and saying all men have a right to freedom."[10]

He kept telling the musicians, "I wish Buddy Collette was here."

He'd found a whipping boy in the band. Hobart Dotson, who'd replaced Eddie Preston, was easily riled and flustered. He was vulnerable, and he wasn't dangerous, like feisty little Jimmy Owens.

After two weeks at Shelley's Manne-Hole in Los Angeles, they headed back to San Francisco for a two-week stint at the Jazz Workshop. He was paying them out of pocket; he said his accountant in New York had screwed up the pay schedule. So he'd peel money off his roll and hand it out when asked.

Nobody complained but Dotson.

At the Workshop, Dotson and Mingus went at it. Dotson, a fine lead trumpeter who shaped the ensemble sections on knotty pieces like "The Clown," wanted more solos despite his relatively limited improvisational skills. He started bitching on the bandstand.

One night, Mingus pulled up his mike from behind the bass and said, "Well, we have a couple of other great trumpet soloists here. What can you contribute that's really original?" Dotson offered to demonstrate, and Mingus and Richmond started playing. Dotson blew a couple of notes. "No, no, that's Clifford Brown," said Mingus into the mike. Another phrase. "No, no, that's Miles. Play something original, man." Another phrase. "Now that's Harry James."

It was like watching a cat with a mouse.

A couple of nights later, Dizzy Gillespie dropped by. He was drunk, and mean because of it. He knew Ming well, how to push his buttons. He peered over his glasses and teased Dotson about money and solos and prodded Mingus: "Are you gonna take that?" Owens hustled Dizzy out, but not before his mice exchanged punches.

They both missed.

Mingus offered Dotson forty bucks. Dotson demanded his entire back pay. Mingus pulled a wad from one of his secret pants pockets. He peeled off a hundred bucks for Johnson, for Watkins, for Owens. He put the rest back in his pocket and patted it and said, "Your money is here. Try and get it." Then he turned and walked out of the dressing room.

At the end of the set's time, Jimmy Chan, the bartender-manager, turned the lights up as warning. He accidentally bumped into the turntable used to play between-sets music, and the needle fell onto a Jazz Crusaders record just as Mingus was bowing to finish his solo on "Meditations."

He yelled into the mike that he would kill Jimmy. Chan didn't move; he had a martial arts degree. Mingus started lecturing about how the black man and the Chinaman ought to stand together.

It was Dotson's last night with the Workshop. Back in New York, he would take his case about pay to the union.

Mingus showed up the next night in a kimono and headband, carrying a briefcase. He put it on a stool and pulled out a bullwhip, and started flicking it wildly around the room while he continued his tirade from the night before. Fans at front tables dived under them, and the band kept ducking. He was out of control.

When Judy brought the kids home, she dusted off her nursing diploma and got a job at Mt. Sinai Hospital, down the block from their apartment. One day, walking the children across 96th Street, she decided to make her own life. She'd move them all out. She found a smaller, dingier apartment at 24 East 97th Street, for $97 a month. "I'll take care of these kids," she thought, "and the hell with you."

He called her regularly, to touch base. He told her he loved her. And after he got back in November she brought the children to visit, or he came and took them on outings.

He got a letter dated December 13 at the studio from the Housing and Redevelopment Board. There were temporary holding areas for commercial tenants within the new project that would demolish his building.[11] He did nothing about it.

A few days later, the Workshop returned to the Five Spot, where it stayed until the end of April 1966.

One night Max Roach sneaked in and stood in the vestibule, where Mingus couldn't see him. As he segued into a bass solo, Mingus said, "I don't see him, but I know Max is here tonight."

Mingus was always plugged in.

Once at 4:00 A.M., he called his neighbor and fan Valerie Porr from the storefront. "It's all over. I'm killing myself," he said. "I have something for you. Come over and get it."

She ran down the street, and found him sitting on a throne-like chair surrounded by huge lit votive candles. "I'm killing myself," he said. "No, you're not," she said. "You're coming to my apartment." He handed her a package of records, her favorites and his: Debussy, Rachmaninoff, some of Mingus's own.

He moved into her apartment, with her French animation-artist boyfriend. Cases of Beaujolais started arriving soon after, along with pounds of double-cut steaks that he spit out after chewing them. Valerie cooked him the steaks, and she and her boyfriend slept on the couch in the living room while Mingus slept in her bed.

They had a quick sexual fling, and reverted to being friends. He took her to see John Coltrane's new mystical group, with its Indian influences and tenor saxist Pharoah Sanders, and dropped in on Miles Davis shows.

He told her Susan's husband was in the Mafia and that they had to hide from him, and she let them use her apartment to get together. He told her it was the first time they'd slept together.

Too many jazz musicians died young: Bird, Bud Powell, Dolphy. Before his comeback at Newport in 1956, Ellington was playing mambos at aqua-shows. Jack Kerouac drank himself to death by 1969. Jackson Pollock died, after repeated suicide attempts, at barely forty. Bird was dead at thirty-four. Mingus was forty-four. He was getting fat, and popping pills, and using speed and vitamin shots, a well-organized drug cocktail.

He wasn't an addict. He never touched heroin.

He owed the IRS $650 in back taxes, New York State $84. He owed back rent on his East 26th Street storefront. [12]

Mingus didn't get many debutantes at his gigs these days. The kids were gone. He didn't know if he cared. Musically, they owed their rock thing to black rhythm and blues. And the psychedelic stuff . . . well, he'd been using open forms, much more sophisticated than these young thrashers, for over a decade.

Out in San Francisco, Ken Kesey and his Pranksters joined the first Trips Festival, coordinated by a twenty-six-year-old named Stewart Brand, who'd later start The Whole Earth Catalog. The festival was billed as an acid test without acid, and all the paraphernalia—the trippy strobe and blobby light shows, the undulating jams and edge-city feedback and tape loops—were meant to put the uninitiated as close to an LSD trip as possible.

A member of the San Francisco Mime Troupe named Bill Graham helped produce the show. Two weeks later, he'd set up shop at the Fillmore Auditorium and was putting on a Trips Festival every weekend. He booked increasingly eclectic musical acts, put up posters in the Art Nouveau style popular among acid heads, and surrounded them with acid-test hoopla, and sold phenomenal tickets.

It was the seismic shift of another scene.

Mingus heard the convoluted bass lines pumping energy into one Motown and Atlantic soul hit after another, one psychedelic underground favorite after another, and ruefully, sometimes angrily, recognized his influence. The moment that had made him possible was turning.

He was certain the eyes and ears of The System were on him. FBI, CIA, NYPD: somebody would show up sooner or later.

He joined in a February benefit concert for the striking faculty at St. John's University in Queens. He had to speak out on what he believed. He was Charles Mingus.

In spring 1966, the city transported his belongings from the East 26th Street studio to a loft at 5 Great Jones Street. He found it through a friend of Susan's. She knew Judith Nathanson, who had two large lofts on the main floor.

Nathanson wanted two thousand dollars in key money—a custom still current at the time in New York, where tenants often "sold" their leases to lofts, especially commercial lofts, plus a surcharge for improvements or simply for saving real estate broker fees.

Mingus still had cash. He'd been paid almost entirely in cash for years, and had spent it as soon as it flowed in. He forked over the key money. It was a good space, big enough for the school. He was tired of hassling, tired of the road, tired of seeing the scene do a slow motion, accelerating collapse.

He wanted a place to rest, to live, to compose, to find the intermittent equilibrium he felt slipping away with his wallet's heft. He'd talked about the project from every angle, even the idea of loading a bus or flatbed truck with a band to tour around the city, one neighborhood at a time.

It was his last best shot at passing on what he knew, extend his Workshop to nonmusicians, kids who wanted to be musicians, show them how to create the holistic life that would let them tap into those inner voices only the determined and gifted few learned to hear.

He would recreate the studio atmosphere of Lloyd Reese and Farwell Taylor in his own image.

He heard there'd been break-ins in the building, so he set traps. Electric eyes turned the lights on if the windows were touched from the outside. The doorknob zapped the unwary with an electric shock. He had a rifle aimed at the door, rigged to fire at intruders.

He moved in his trinkets, the cigar boxes full of American coins, the trick Hollywood rope that broke when you pulled it. He set up his piano. The movers piled the boxes all over, and he left them mostly alone.

Mingus didn't know the landlord planned to void Nathanson's lease and take the lofts back, that he'd lose his cash. He had no place else to go, and the cash was running out. So he moved in.

A decade later, landlords would evict artists all over New York's Soho once the artists had fixed up the old commercial lofts and they could be rented or sold to lawyers and admen. Unfortunately for Mingus, he was ahead of his time again.

The financial snowballs rolling downhill at him were becoming an avalanche.

On March 18, he got a letter from RCA Custom Discs, which had taken over distributing Charles Mingus Enterprises recordings after his scene with Bernard Geis. There were still 7,000 LPs in their LA warehouse, and the tax bill from Los Angeles County now totaled $1,751.31.

Mingus shot back that the tax problem only existed because the records never made it to the 1965 Monterey festival, where the 7,000 attendees would have snapped them up. He threatened to sue RCA for his estimated $20,000 loss. He added, "I feel someone there at RCA is aware of their wrong doing to me—and trying to take my records from me. If so ... [sic] that man should take out a good insurance policy. Thieves of horses get hung."[13]

Once the Five Spot gig ended, he played sporadically. Late May 1966 found him joining flautist Jeremy Steig for a Downtown Community School scholarship benefit fund.[14]

Education was his focus. So was business.

From his shoeshine stand on, he always had entrepreneurial schemes. He was a stone capitalist. With the help of Susan and others, he sent out spring mailers for Charles Mingus Enterprises. He was seeking subscriptions for the records the label would be releasing: the NAACP benefit at Town Hall, *My Favorite Quintet*, and *Special Music Written For (and not heard at) Monterey*.

The albums had pictures of him taken by his son Charles, and the liner notes were excerpts from his still-unpublished autobiography. He made fun of legendary Columbia A&R head John Hammond, a Vanderbilt scion who'd recorded a host of jazz greats since Bessie Smith. Hammond had also discovered Charlie Christian, Jimmy Blanton's guitar-soloing counterpart, and insisted that his brother-in-law Benny Goodman use the black kid in his band.

Mingus called him John Ham-head and spoofed him as "a main investor for one of those major record-labels" and "a liberal tongued beast of high finance."[15] He complained Hammond and Columbia had lied to him about record sales.

Mingus was still very visible on the Village streets, making his rounds. He was eating constantly, swelling in size, becoming Gargantua. His appetites were mastering him.

He took friends to eat in out-of-the-way ethnic restaurants around the Lower East Side and Harlem, and dared them to plunge into unknown dishes. He prided himself on fearless eating.

He had no luck with cars. His prized Corvette was acting up all the time. He was shuttling it back to the dealer constantly, and it was driving him nuts. They weren't fixing it, but he kept paying them.

They were ripping him off because he was black. He called Mabry, and they concocted some street theater.

One afternoon, a stretch limousine pulled up in front of the West 57th Street dealer. One at a time, out stepped half a dozen leggy models draped suggestively, and then Mabry emerged, dressed like an exotic foreign potentate, all turban and flowing robes. He swept into the dealership offices, and hunkered down to deal with the big honcho.

Ming's car's gotta get fixed right.

Mingus sat across the street. Mabry was supposed to give him a high sign if the deal went down. Before Mabry could signal him, he revved the Corvette and drove it through the dealership's huge plate glass windows.

Sue says this never happened, that they were sitting in the showroom talking to the salesman when Mabry drove up.

Whatever happened, the dealership gave him another car, a Corvair, the rear-motor car with a tendency to fishtail that prompted Ralph Nader to write the best-selling book *Unsafe at Any Speed*, and helped launch the consumer-activist movement.

He added to the list of Charles Mingus Enterprises the Charles Mingus Cat-a-Log for toilet training your cat. The mail-order ad said, "Don't be surprised if you hear the toilet flush in the middle of the night. A cat can learn to do it, spurred by his instinct to cover up."[16]

He released 200 copies of the recording done at UCLA, and titled the double disc, *Music Written for Monterey, 1965: Not Heard . . . Played in Its Entirety, at U.C.L.A.* No one was going to mistake his aims.

The Black Power Movement was formally launched when James Meredith, the first black student at the University of Mississippi, was shot by a sniper during a civil rights march. Stokely Carmichael, H. Rap Brown, and the other leaders of SNCC decided they had proof of white duplicity regarding civil rights.

They saw a white America unwilling to give up its racism without violence. They saw a white America unwilling to loosen its economic stranglehold on black communities. Like the Muslims, they began agitating for black self-sufficiency. They wanted education for black children to reflect black values and history.

"Black is beautiful" was their slogan.

It was the beginning of Black Studies programs across America, a double-edged sword that further segregated students and tracked them out of job possibilities.

In July 1966, poet Frank O'Hara was hit by a jeep and died. O'Hara bridged scenes. He wrote jazzy poetry, most famously about Billie Holiday. He'd written enthusiastic art criticism that spanned the diverse schools popping up on the postwar New York art scene and had become a curator at the Museum of Modern Art. Larry Rivers painted him nude; Franz Kline was a close pal. Rivers eulogized him at the funeral.

That summer, Mingus and Susan got married. Neither of them was divorced. He sent Eric and Keki $100 each to buy new outfits for the wedding. Susan forgot to invite them.

The chanting ceremony took place at Peggy Hitchcock's Manhattan penthouse at 829 Park Avenue; Allen Ginsberg officiated.

SUSAN GRAHAM UNGARO MINGUS: Allen and Charles were friends. Charles had a kind of macho attitude: he was troubled by homosexuality. He didn't like it, but he liked Allen. That was his division, because he liked Allen as a human being, and Allen liked him. It was a funny kind of relationship. But they always hugged, they cared about each other, they laughed and told stories. They respected each other. Allen would ask him things about music or what was going on with militant blacks like the Panthers. Allen was very interested in that.

The Black Panther Party was founded in Oakland, California, in 1966 by Bobby G. Seale and Huey P. Newton, who were inspired by Malcolm X. It started as a self-defense organization for black communities and got progressively more outspoken about the need for violent revolution to overthrow The Establishment—the now-common term from the Beat Era.

The Panther Minister of Information was a fan and came to hear the Workshop. Panthers buzzed around. Mingus was known to be outspoken. He liked guns, believed in self-defense, knew The Man was out to get him. He loved the Panthers' outfits and street theater. He liked playing street.

That September, Mingus returned to the Village Gate for a couple of weeks, with a thrown-together group that included Britt Woodman and Walter Bishop. Dannie Richmond came back from Greensboro, North Carolina.

The band was now always in flux and did mostly medleys. At one point, Mingus hired Ronald Shannon Jackson, who he had ignored and even shoved out of his way until he heard the drummer sit in with Toshiko Akiyoshi at the Gate.

Herbie Mann was co-billed. The white flautist was building a college following for his African-esque music, a popularization of what Randy Weston, for one, had been forging for a decade.

Mann grated on Mingus. He was another white guy creaming off the work of black artists. One night, Dr. Cloud and Pastor Gensel came together to see the Workshop.

JOHN GENSEL: When he came out, he took his tambourine and threw it out into the audience, just spinned it out. That burned me up. So at the intermission I went back to his dressing room with Dr. Luther Cloud and said, "Mingus, why don't you do what you can do so well and forget about what anybody else is doing?" He said, "You're shouting at me." I said, "Damn right I am." And I put my hand on his shoulder and said, "Remember, I can lick you." He said, "Okay."

The Reichman family were friends and fans. Dr. Thomas Reichman and his two sons loved Mingus, and he reciprocated. Young Tom had a brainstorm: he'd make a documentary about the bassist-composer.

It was the heyday of garage art. Thanks to the long-filtering influence of the Beats, the art of the counterculture looked homemade, natural, organic, personal, amateur. Sometimes it was amateur. Sometimes it was a look, an aesthetic, a political statement.

Tom Reichman got technical helpers, some of whom went on to Hollywood features and *Saturday Night Live*. He decided to shoot his movie largely improvised, following Mingus around, trying to capture as much of the torrential flow of monologues as possible, forgetting continuity, editing footage later to create it.

It was not that far from Mingus's studio approach.

Mingus assembled the Workshop to play at Lennie's outside Boston. McPherson and Hillyer did it willingly; Byard wanted pay extra to be in a movie; Mingus shrugged.

A college journalist tried to interview him while he was talking at the bar with the musicians. He spun around and snarled, "Can't you see I'm rehearsing?"

Mingus had a new attorney for his case with Rosemarie Holding Company, the Great Jones loft-building owners. He was Bruce Wright, a high-powered black activist lawyer who was friends with all the jazz musicians. On October 7, 1966, the day after Wright took over, attorney Joseph Warde drafted a sublease between Mingus and "Frank Maybry." Mabry was subletting the rear part of his Loft #3 on the second floor "as a studio for music, painting, sculpture, and other art purposes."[17]

It was a last-minute try to avoid eviction for commercial-only lease violation. The rider states, "Lessor will vacate the leased premises and remove therefrom all items of personal property and/or belongings with the sole exception of one (1) Bass Violin which lessee will permit to remain in said premises."[18]

The rent was $100 a month.

From Mabry, Rosemarie received a duplicate of the lease and a letter dated October 18. It said in part, "Please be sure that Mr. Mingus has cleaned out the rear studio so I can move in with the rest of my belongings. I am very anxious to get to work."[19]

The loft was a shambles. Mingus never really unpacked anywhere, but he'd pulled out bits and pieces of whatever he needed from wherever it was, and then left it wherever he left it. Despite the warning notices, he decided to shoot part of his movie with Reichman there.

It was a real-life tragedy, starring himself. People would see not just the music, but the up-against-the-wall nature of life for the black artist in America.

CHARLES MINGUS: I pledge allegiance to the flag, the white flag. I pledge allegiance to the flag of America. When they say black or Negro it means you're not an American. I pledge allegiance to your flag—not that I want to, but for the hell of it, I pledge allegiance. I pledge allegiance to the flag of the United States of America, the white flag, with no stripes, no stars. It is a prestige badge worn by a profitable minority.[20]

He called Judy and demanded she bring the kids down for the shooting. They'd add to the movie's pathos. She refused, but six-year-old Carolyn wanted to see her daddy, so Judy relented. He talked to Keki on camera, as she dangled her legs from the piano stool, about love and politics in America. "Remember Fifth Avenue?" he asked her. "The Cadillac and the chauffeured limousines? Do you miss it?"[21]

He knew how to work a camera and a scene better than almost anyone in jazz.

He fired a rifle blast ("This is the same kind of gun that killed Kennedy") at the ceiling. He wanted to be street. "We're just acting, right?" he said to Reichman.

He barely knew how to load the rifle. He thrashed the bullwhip with no technique, coaxed Carolyn into splitting his trick Hollywood rope, delivered diatribes about American racism, quoted his parody of "My Country Tis of Thee," slugged from the jug of CK Mondavi wine on the piano, chomped on his pipe, and ricocheted from the sublime to the ridiculous without missing a breath.

He wrote FBI head J. Edgar Hoover about his eviction, he explained, because "I've always written him. If anything goes wrong, I wanna tell all the fellas, all the white folks, I'm trying to be a good boy. . . . I'm all for the FBI. Basically, I'm a cop. All kids are." With no education, he said, he was just a kid. What else could he be?

He'd written Governor Nelson Rockefeller and President Lyndon Johnson too. He insisted the city should be paying to move him, not evicting him, because they approved his move from East 27th Street to Great Jones Street, and thus were liable for his faulty sublet.

CHARLES MINGUS: I'm Charles Mingus. Half black man, yellow man, half yellow, not even yellow, not even white enough to pass for nothing but black, and not too light to be called white. I claim that I am a Negro. Charles Mingus is a musician, mongrel musician who plays beautiful, who plays ugly, who plays lovely, who plays masculine, who plays feminine, who plays music, who plays off sounds, sounds, solid sounds, sounds, sounds, sounds…a musician who loves to play with sound.[22]

Reichman returned with his camera for the eviction the next morning.

Three years to the day after JFK's assassination, the city marshals, cops, and sanitation workers congregated outside his building early in the morning. He'd just come back from walking his German shepherd—useful protection.

Not in this case. The marshals slapped the eviction notice on his door. The sanitation workers began hauling his stuff down the stairs and into their trucks, to take it to the storage facilities at 134 Madison Street, where the Department stored evicted tenants' belongings for thirty days.

For Mingus, being evicted was living theater, a surreality of the absurd. He made his points. He wooed the camera, and even in his most outrageous free associations, brought to bear much of his looming personality. When he walked with his dog into the eviction in process, he started crying. "My whole life since I was a baby," he said, "is in those boxes." His eyes were still wet when he tried explaining to the TV reporters about his school.

And he lost music from the 1940s so yellow it crumbled when it was touched. His turn-of-the-century German bass was hauled to the pound. His life's possessions, the haphazard record of where he'd been and what had grabbed him and who he was, were a shambles.

The cops found hypodermics and the rifle, so they took Mingus to the station. He was severely rattled. He knew what drug busts historically meant to black jazz musicians. When a TV reporter asked him if it was true the cops had found heroin, he almost jumped with fear, then quickly claimed "my wife" Judy had gotten him a prescription for Vitamin B injections, although she hadn't. He claimed Judy was so light she was passing. He was jeopardizing her credentials and her job.

When one reporter asked him if he was being persecuted because he was a jazz musician, he shot back, "I think I'm being helped. People get to see what's going on in a so-called jazz musician's life."[23]

When the cops let him out of the holding cells the next day, he quipped to reporters, "It isn't every day you see a Negro walk out of a police station with a box of hypodermic needles and a shotgun."[24]

A week later, he got a notice from Helmsley-Spear, important New York land-lords, about a 2,000-square-foot loft he might be interested in. By then, he was hoarding cash.[25]

One of the ideas his ad hoc brain trust had hatched for a cartoon to sell his mail-order records was reworked and published in the *Village Voice* that December.

The plot: a beautiful woman helped him ferret out bootleg record dealers by going into shops and asking for his records, which were going out of print. He appeared with her, to urge readers to buy his stuff only through the mail. He was drawn wearing his khaki army shirt with many pockets and a snapbrim fedora.[26]

In the panel, he was shorter than the babe. He told everyone he was five-foot-ten, but he missed by almost two inches.

Mingus was losing his internal balance.

Susan was keeping a warier distance, unnerved by his growing incoherence, nervous about her husband. Judy was finished with him; when he called her, she was friendly, but she was struggling with two kids and a job and no time.

For the first time he had no woman to live with, to take care of him and his work.

For the next two years, he would wander in a desert at least partly of his own devising. He doodled with music for a ballet called "My Arrest."

In California, Ken Kesey was arrested on the freeway sneaking back into the States from Mexico, where he'd gone as a fugitive from two pot busts. In Texas, Tim Leary was busted for marijuana.

The Vietnam War was spawning demonstrations and counterdemonstrations, and dividing families, friends, the entire country as the death toll mounted and the horror pictures multiplied on nightly TV.

On January 9, 1967, the State Insurance Fund sent a registered letter to Jazz Workshop, which owed $76.27 on its policy. Effective that date, his insurance was canceled. He scribbled a memo across the top: "This came *registered* [underscored twice]—they seem to mean business."[27]

Mingus's eviction was more than a metaphor. He was lost in America, and his sense of helplessness was choking him in ways it hadn't since he was seventeen.

He took a plane to the West Coast and went out to Farwell Taylor's place in Mill Valley, where lawyers for NYC's Urban Renewal program sent him mail dunning him for the rent he still owed on his East 26th Street storefront.[28]

For the next six months, he crashed at hotels like the Earle when he was in New York—which was rarely.

He was eating constantly, drinking jugs of cheap red wine. He wasn't writing anything, although he still spent nights at the piano. He was noodling; he didn't have anyone to write for. The Workshop basically wound down, coalescing only occasionally over the next three years.

For his whole life, music had been the center of gravity that prevented his ever-growing enthusiasms from pulling him apart. He lived music. He poured his massive will and discipline into it. It was his way of understanding the world and relating to it.

He was a composer in life and in music, but he was unable to shape all the minidramas and narrative themes he'd woven as his existence.

Judy wouldn't take him back. Susan wouldn't leave her family. He was cornered. The pressure would ratchet up on him for the next three years, producing a series of breakdowns that punctuated his life and undermined his will to create music—the linchpin of his complicated, fractured personality.

He had nowhere to go. He and Sue had a big fight. She moved in with her brother, which Mingus gave as one of his mailing addresses that winter. He cut his hand open and wrote "I love you" in blood on the door. For $700, he bought her a fur coat from Judy, who needed the cash. He told friends Sue threw it in the middle of the street.

CAROLYN (KEKI) MINGUS, *daughter:* He wanted to be vulnerable, he wanted to be emotional. Some of the worst fights I ever saw were between Sue and my father. As much as he was guarded, he wanted to be vulnerable to these women, to feel that pain. It was a conscious thing. He wanted to set himself up for suffering, and he picked the women who could do it best. Three redheads who could cause him grief and tear him apart.

Mostly he went back and forth to home, to California. He missed it. He craved acceptance and attention. He crashed with old friends like Taylor, Kate Mulholland, and Buddy Collette.

Kate Mulholland and her husband had an enormous villa in Berkeley, once owned by Eugene O'Neill, up by the Claremont Hotel, so it overlooked the bay with stunning detail. It reminded him of Farwell's apartment long ago, the parties and head-turning guests and endless talk and food, the hopes and dreams.

He was eating constantly. He was fat as a pig. When Kate picked him up at the airport, he was wearing a safari suit that barely fit around his middle.

He'd fought with Susan and took off, dialed Kate and told her he was coming. Flying coast-to-coast was like walking to the kitchen for him.

The Mulhollands gave him his own bedroom and bath, and there he sat most mornings, writing scraps of music and new bits for his autobiography, now the size of two suitcases. Afternoons he played their grand piano in the parlor, improvising to Debussy and Ravel.

He helped tutor Kate's son on the viola, and said the boy read music better than he did. He charmed Kate's daughter with an oversized lollipop.

He went down to the creamery to buy gallons of pineapple ice cream, and ate them himself. He didn't bother keeping track of his Wells Fargo account balance. That should be the bank's job, not his, so it was their fault when his checks bounced.

He had a little black suitcase full of pills. Kate suspected Leary as a source. She knew him from graduate school and thought he was a celebrity hound.

KATE MULHOLLAND: [Mingus] was having this turbulent relationship with Sue. A kind of love-hate thing, phone calls going back and forth, fulminating, "That bitch," and then going out and buying some expensive present for her. He was in full conflict. He just totally flipped for her.

One day I asked, "What the hell is so great about her?" And he said, "She can cross her legs like Jacqueline Kennedy." He went to see *A Man and a Woman* with Anouk Aimee every other day, it seemed, because Aimee reminded him of Sue. She was his society lady, she was international—somehow, she was it. Then the other side. We were in Chinatown one day shopping, and those stiff prickly blowfish...well, he said, "I'm gonna send one of these to that bitch. It looks like just what she is."

It was almost unerringly right of him to zero in on her, as if he perceived that she was going to take care of business for him. That was my feeling around this period, that she was going to be the one, the controlling person, and do the things he was unable to do.

He wanted to resolve his tangle with Judy and the children and Sue. He was feeling nostalgic. He could go from being surly to mocking himself: he asked Kate more than once if she wanted to just get in the car drive to Mexico and leave it all behind.

He told her it was the first vacation he'd ever had. The Mulhollands didn't want anything from him. Almost everybody else seemed to.

A couple of weeks after he got there, he took off to meet Ginsberg and Leary. It was January 14th, 1967, the first Human Be-In. Thousands of "heads," the psychedelic counterculture's self-description, converged on San Francisco's Golden Gate Park dressed in velvet and denim and stovepipe hats and motorcycle boots.

Mingus wandered through the crowd, fat and old and black and prickly. He listened to Allen Ginsberg lead the crowd in an "Om" chant, something the wily poet, this self-professed priest, was doing more and more.

Only a few people recognized Mingus.

In mid-April, he started a stint at the Half Note with Hillyer, McPherson, and Richmond, but a week later moved across the street to a new joint called Pookie's Pub. He was tired of the Half Note. He liked opening new rooms, like Bird had, and cut a deal.

The Workshop stayed at Pookie's through June.

In May 1967, a group of Black Panthers invaded the California Legislature to protest a gun-control bill. The party began talking about armed rebellion. It spilled into people's living rooms. Nonviolence was squeezed between the war in Vietnam and the guerilla-theater tactics at home.

The Panthers claimed a membership of 5,000. They became the targets of highly successful government infiltration campaigns, and agents provocateurs successfully fomented conflicts between the Panthers and other radical violence-oriented groups, right and left.

The System was chewing people up and spitting them out, killing off promising leaders and ideas. It was snuffing out change.

Mingus watched the growing waves of separatism, of what would later be dubbed ethnic or identity politics, with wariness. They held no hope for him. There was no place for him in organized violence.

On May 5, following almost eighteen months of warnings, he was notified he'd been removed again from the rolls of Local 802 for failing to pay Hobart Dotson $400 plus $112.36 in transportation expense. In 1966, he had failed to pay his union dues and was dropped, so the new notice meant little.

On June 30, ABC Records notified him that he'd sold 2,957 LPs that quarter, for a royalty of $84.64.[29]

Everything was collapsing.

On July 17, he signed a lease for a 1 1/2-room apartment at 512 East 5th Street, under the name Charles M. Holdings, as in holding company. It was a professional address. He claimed to have been living with Sue at 340 West 87th Street for the previous three years. He said his previous landlords were "Mama and Pappa Mingus" and included Peggy Hitchcock as a reference. The apartment cost $130 a month. He paid the broker $520 for his fee and the security deposit.[30]

He scribbled Tom Reichman's phone number and address on the back of an envelope. He was always scribbling on scraps, and losing them. Bits of paper just wafted away, bearing lost information, like the rush of ideas that still sometimes circulated through the pill rushes and hazes and crashes that exaggerated his already manic character.

He was constantly giving off vibes, like the San Andreas fault system running through his hometown, jostling, jiggling, torqued tighter by the friction of its architectonic plates day by day until it suddenly slipped, and the land along it heaved with a force that ripped cities apart in minutes.

HOWARD JOHNSON, *musician*: He had lots of locks on the door. The windows were barred and boarded. There was music all over the place. "Man, why don't you catalog this?" I wanted to help him a little. But he kept saying, "I've got to go through this myself. I've got to go through this myself."

NAT HENTOFF: He was depressed. It was classical clinical depression.

CHARLES MINGUS: For about three years, I thought I was finished. Sometimes I couldn't even get out of bed. I wasn't asleep; I just lay there. But living where I do, on East Fifth and Avenue A, I began to learn about people, and that started me coming back. In that neighborhood they didn't know me from the man in the moon, but they took an interest in me. I'd go into a bar, sit by myself, and I'd hear someone say, "There's something wrong with this guy. He doesn't come out of his house for four or five days at a time." And they'd invite me to join them. I got to know what friends are. Ukrainians, blacks, Puerto Ricans—a house painter, a tailor, a woman who owns a bar, her bartender, a maintenance man who says, "I'll walk you home tonight if you get drunk. And if I get drunk, you walk me home." Sure, in a way it's hell down there. I've been robbed four times. They stole almost everything I had. All that's left are a Steinway and my basses. So now I've got locks on my doors, bars on my windows, and a baseball bat near at hand. But I'm not going to move. Even with the danger, I want to stay because it's family. We all look out for each other. Not just against muggers and robbers. There was a time when I had no money left at all, but the tailor on the block made sure I had enough to eat. I don't know if I could have come out of the graveyard had it not been for them.[31]

The bar catty-corner from his dive was called Chic Choc, a local dump where no one knew who he was. That's what he wanted. He'd had it with the spotlight. His life was drifting into pieces on a rapids. He didn't need the focus of attention he got in the jazz world; it did nothing to help him. It only distracted him. At Chic Choc, he was no celebrity.

His cash-only payment system and his spending habits drained his savings for what was supposed to be a Sonny Rollins-type period of self-retrenchment. But he lived as he had, in the moment. Fly to California? Dial up a ticket. What cost? Who cares? Want a new English bike? A new Rolleiflex camera? A new handful of cameras, because doing it means really doing it, big time?

He never added up the stubs in the checkbook.

He thought about the great jazzers who'd lived in poverty, including his heroes Art Tatum and Bird and Lester Young. He had enough, with the Fantasy sales and his royalties, not to have to keep trying to sing for his supper—yet.

At Chic Choc, he made friends among the regulars, and became one. There he was Charlie, not Charles, like he'd been telling everyone everywhere else to call him. There he found loyal drinking buddies. One day, when his son Charles came in with him, the pair had an argument. When the son wagged his finger at his father, one regular barfly bit it into the knuckle.

And there was plenty of action on Avenue B. Drugs were rampant, sold on the streets if he needed cheap stuff. And there were a string of bars, many gay, like Sweets, where name acts like Dick Gregory played.

Money was no object, because he didn't have much, so he just didn't pay bills.

In 1967–68, the Banque de Bruxelles dunned him. He owed the Park Crescent Hotel on Riverside Drive almost $100. Bill collectors for the Fairmont Hotel in San Francisco tried to get almost $1,300. Western Union wanted their money. Savoy Garages wanted their money. The appraised value of the 7,000 records moldering in an L.A. warehouse dropped to $1,160. Con Ed wanted $166.92 of "considerably overdue" electric and gas charges.

He wrote, in big print along the bottom of the notice, "I owe $10. I used X. Ordered no gas. Will pay for lights. C.M.H."[32]

He always had an angle. Even now.

His records slipped gradually out of print, out of circulation. Musical styles were mutating as rapidly as politics. He'd predicted many of them in his own music, set the patterns, opened the possibilities. But he sat out the flowering, commercial and artistic, he'd helped create, self-exiled to the margins of a poor ethnic New York neighborhood, avoiding the stage.

The Zeitgeist was rolling past him.

He spent time practicing looking at himself in the mirror and wishing he could die. He practiced seeing himself leave his body.

He was seventeen again. He was clinically depressed.

Mingus called Judy to collect his children, and got Charles and Dorian lined up too. He was going to take them all to Disneyland. They stayed at the Mickey Mouse Hotel, in the penthouse, with a grand piano.

It was the first significant time Dorian spent with Mingus after discovering that he was his father, not a friend of the family's. They sat on opposite sides of the kingsize bed and compared the fact that each of them had three nipples.

Mingus stayed up all night playing the piano, so the next morning Charles had to take care of the kids during the day, and he took them to the shooting gallery. They went on almost no rides.

When they came back, Keki and Eric ordered vats of food from the menu. When their father woke up that evening, and saw they hadn't eaten all of it, he whipped them with his money belt—not for ordering all the food but for not eating it all. It was the only time he hit them.

CELIA MINGUS ZAENTZ: In fall 1967, he wanted me to find him a house, and schools for Carolyn and Eric. He had taken them for the weekend and flown them to California. I asked him if Judy knew what he was planning. He said no. I was horrified. I refused to help him, and told him not to call me any more—and he didn't, for a while. When he did I handed the phone to Saul.

He was being very irrational, taking things into his own hands. And he was always going off on a big long tirade. He was taking uppers and downers. It was a bad time for him. His thinking was skewed. He was being outrageous just for the sake of it, less than any logic it had.

Shortly after, he showed up at his old Half Note friend Maureen Meloy's New York apartment in the wee hours. He told her he wanted to snatch his kids and take them to Mexico, and she spent hours trying to talk him out of it. She gave him her full-sized bed to sleep in, and crashed on her sofa; he was too fat to fit on it. When the phone rang that morning, he jumped up and snatched it. It was her boyfriend.

Mingus headed up to the Hitchcock mansion at Millbrook that October, and Leary's endless experiment: how does LSD affect the creative process? Janet Coleman's boyfriend, another actor-writer named David Dozer, had a surrealistic script for an improvisatory movie called *Indiangivers*, about the Taking of the West—a politically apt theme of the period.[33]

Mingus, open as ever to other art forms, was cast as Pancho Villa, and brought his serape, his sombrero, and his bullwhip. He'd shaved his head again. Allen Ginsberg got involved. Andy Warhol superstars Ultra Violet and Wavy Gravy joined in. Dozer played Dracula. Coleman was painted silver to play Joan of Arc. They painted the horses green, and a Dalmatian pink: it was the heyday of psychedelia.

The shooting was fun and inspired. Then Leary intervened and called a meeting in the kitchen while he cooked chicken. He wanted to throw the script out completely.

Mingus said simply, "You can't improvise on nothing, man."

He saw Leary as part guru, part fake, part celebrity hound. He deferred to Leary's formal education, and told friends he was appalled by what Leary was doing, the way the famed ex-professor, whose slogan "Turn on, tune in, drop out" rippled across America's media, thought drugs were the mainspring of artistic creation.

ROBERTO UNGARO, *friend*: We'd all go to Millbrook and see the Learys. In fact, he'd go there and kinda upset everything. Tim Leary would be giving a religious speech, and Charles would be waving fly spray and smacking himself. I'd kill some frogs in the pond, we'd go in the kitchen, and everyone would be freaking out: "What are they killing frogs for?" We'd cook them, they'd be delicious, and we'd have our little victory.

He took benzedrine and demerol, and he was drinking a lot of wine and snorting cocaine. But he wasn't a junkie, and he didn't take acid. What he saw at Millbrook was younger people, many rich, destroying valuable property, wasting time, learning little. He was a puritan. He pointed out to Leary regularly that Milbrook was a cocoon, that little could come of it outside.

There were no short cuts. If you don't live it, it won't come out of your horn.

Leary saw chains cast away. Mingus saw childish self-indulgence. And art was a sacred thing.

Leary had made records with Jimi Hendrix, Stephen Stills, and Buddy Miles. He wanted to make one with Mingus, who shrugged it off politely. And Ginsberg asked him to play music to his reading of William Blake's "Songs of Innocence and Experience," but he turned that down too.

While artists of all sorts blew their minds, he was carrying a brown satchel and composition paper, and noodling at the grand piano in the main house. He was trying to write again.

Flower Power held little for him, or people like him. He was almost forty-six years old.

David Amram had been composer-in-residence at the New York Philharmonic for the 1966–67 season. When he bumped into Mingus, his old boss said almost sheepishly, "I guess you can't hang around with me any more." Amram was taken aback.

Toshiko Akiyoshi had her own big band debut at Town Hall, almost five years to the day after his debacle there. Mayor John Lindsey had earlier declared that same day New York Jazz Day, and so there was a free concert in Central Park and a black-tie event at the Metropolitan Opera House.

Mingus showed up to hear her band, with a camera, and took pictures. Aside from the *New York Times* critic, he was the only jazz VIP there.

Saul Zaentz had taken over Fantasy Records from its founders, the Weiss brothers. He struck a deal with Mingus; in return for "one dollar and other considerations," he bought the rights to deal directly with BMI and distributors about Chazz-Mar music and Jazz Workshop publishing. Fantasy also reissued the Monterey live album with an open letter from Mingus.

CHARLES MINGUS: Saul Zaentz, who is an honest person and who is now distributing my records for the first time in public stores, has consented to include this letter in my album. Anyone who cares to alter my deplorable financial condition which has resulted from the misfortunes I have suffered may send a contribution.[34]

He listed his post office box, which had been discontinued for lack of payment.

That April, the Better Business Bureau of New York notified Jazz Workshop of a number of complaints BBB had received about unfilled orders on *Mingus at Monterey*.[35]

On April 4, 1968, at sunset, Dr. Martin Luther King Jr. was assassinated on the balcony of his Memphis hotel. Across the country, 130 cities erupted into riots and civil disturbances. Twenty thousand people, overwhelmingly black, were arrested.

Dignitaries from around the world came for the funeral.

Allen Ginsberg's *Planet News*, a collection of poetry he wrote between 1961 and 1967, was published, and helped solidify his influence as poet and counterculture guru. His work was showing up in academic anthologies, and he was being taught in college courses. He was being accepted into The System, with his own demands largely intact.

In May, Sue sent a letter to the Pilobolus dance company about Mingus's commission from them. They'd changed the musical direction originally agreed on, which left the music to Mingus's discretion. Now they had more specific things they wanted. Plus the $4,000 fee he'd agreed to accept was now said to be contingent on further grants. Mingus had already written and rehearsed and taped the music at his own expense.[36]

On June 6, Robert Kennedy was assassinated in Los Angeles. Sirhan Sirhan was a Israel-born Jordanian, what the official sources described as yet another lone, pathological gunman, in the Lee Harvey Oswald mold.

Mingus didn't believe in lone gunmen. He believed in conspiracies, and he was far from alone.

On July 1, 1968, Mingus signed a new deal with BMI that gave him a thousand-dollar advance with each annual renewal.[37]

That same month, Tom Reichman's *Mingus* premiered in theaters. The man himself was taking public relations shots as a photographer for the La Mama theater group. He was shooting antiwar protests, as he marched in them with Sue. In her calf-high leather boots, she was nearly his height.

He was busted and tossed in the Tombs for taking pictures from atop a parked car. He made friends with some of the inmates. He liked hanging out. He knew somebody would make bail.

He backed poet Sayed Hussein for four Thursday nights at a place called Joey Archer's.

At the Democratic convention in Chicago, the growing antiwar movement had gathered to derail Lyndon Johnson's heir apparent, Hubert Humphrey, after Robert Kennedy's assassination. Thousands gathered to take on the scripted convention bosses, including Chicago mayor Richard Daley.

The Chicago police, under Daley's orders, brutalized the thousands of American youths filling the streets, and the horrified delegates, along with millions of Americans, watched it on TV inside the convention.

SUSAN GRAHAM UNGARO MINGUS: Everything was coming to a head. He was tired of dealing with white America, living in this culture with the gift, the talent that he wasn't able to utilize fully in the way he would have liked.

During that fall's Indian summer, he called Judy and told her he was coming uptown to take the kids to the park.

He needed to be around people. He needed someone to help him. He needed attention. He wanted love. He couldn't find his center of gravity, the inner certainty that let him fly off on tangents without pinwheeling or exploding.

Like the San Andreas fault, he'd given off small tremors for three years. The Big One was coming.

There's a meadow and a small playground in Central Park right opposite Mt. Sinai hospital, one block north of Judy's apartment. She often took the children and their friends there. He met them, and took the kids off to the meadow's far side while Judy sat on a boulder in the sun.

Eric noticed his father's cigarette bent back into his mouth, and a startlingly goofy look on his face when he gasped, "Did you see that? Did you see that witch prick me with a needle?"

CAROLYN (KEKI) MINGUS: All of a sudden, my father takes his pants off and starts throwing his money all over the lawn. I couldn't figure out why. Because I knew my father was crazy, but I mean, why would he do this to me? The person he had never done anything crazy in front of?

Eric ran to Judy, who tried to calm Mingus, failed, and called the cops. A motorcycle cop, then a car, then an ambulance showed up, and Judy accompanied her legal husband across the street to the place she worked.

JUDY STARKEY MINGUS McGRATH: In his mind it had to do with money, because he was just throwing money away. Everything seemed to revolve around money: he wasn't getting what he was worth, and it was a constant battle. He had all this beautiful music inside, and that's what he should have been doing —writing and performing music, and getting paid so he could live.

It would just tear your heart out if you could picture this man who was a great presence in one of those striped hospital robes and medicated. It's like there's this person inside who can't get out. It was awful. He told me they had him on a lot of thorazine. Back then it was standard; they'd think he was a violent black guy, and want to keep him immobilized. But he was like a zombie.

Mingus was on mellaril, a thorazine-like medication, an antipsychotic with unpredictable side effects that included confusion, disorientation, and restlessness, as well as physical risks like retinitis pigmentosa and painful priapism. He would be on it, more or less heavily, for the next couple of years. Sue would exhaust doctors trying to wean him from it, with temporary successes and relapses until finally he moved in with her.

Thorazine-type drugs can backfire when used consistently, and can set off manic episodes.

But even at this nadir there were flashes of his powerful personality. When Britt Woodman visited him in Mt. Sinai, after Judy called to tell him what happened, Mingus unloaded complaints: "They're treating me like a dayworker or something. They don't realize who I am."

Mingus was almost docile with Nel King. He'd tried and fired editor after editor over the years, complaining that most of them had tried to whitewash his book. With Nel, he was amenable, almost meek. He needed the book published. He needed the money. He needed the fame, the notoriety even.

He was fat. To Toshiko Akiyoshi visiting him at the hospital, he looked almost feminine.

Keki thought he was happy. He needed time off from his brains. The Man Who Never Sleeps thought too much.

He was in the hospital for almost a month. When he came out, he went back to his juicer and bags of carrots on East 5th Street.

Eric and Keki saw their father almost every weekend. Sometimes Judy brought them to his apartment, and tried to clean the place up a bit. He muttered darkly about conspiracy theories. He was a broken person. His usual diatribes trailed off into mumbles, incoherence. The CIA and FBI were watching him.

The kids slept in a loft bed while he played piano into the wee hours, and amused themselves making shadow puppets on the walls all morning while he slept.

His cats and kids used the toilet but he didn't. The walls were lined with Tropicana juice bottles filled with his urine. He was sure the usual agencies were monitoring his waste for clues.

Then he'd take the kids to the bar, where there were bowls of peanuts on the countertop and a shuffle-bowling game. He'd buy them endless Cokes and sit and talk.

He had Charles Wright, the ex-NYPD karate instructor, pick up the kids and drop them off at a martial arts school.

Sometimes he met the children at Judy's apartment and they all went to Central Park. He'd give them rides on the back of his multispeed English bike, and they'd laugh happily, hugging his huge body.

Sometimes he took them walking around the Bowery, to look at the bums. He'd say, "If I had that guy's skin, I'd be in Carnegie Hall, respected like Beethoven." If the kids misbehaved, he would snarl at them, "You're gonna end up like that bum over there."

He bought fifty bubble-umbrella America flags and gave them out to everyone he met.

12 Beneath the Underdog

SHORTLY AFTER New Year's 1969, David Amram was eating at a little restaurant where Marilyn Sokol, soon a famed comedienne, was the waitress when suddenly somebody came up behind him and put his hands over his eyes. It was Mingus. He looked drained and puffy, but not too bad. He was drinking his carrot juice, trying to eat right. He was losing his blubber.

The pair went back to Amram's place, where they noodled around on his Baldwin piano. He asked where Amram performed. Colleges mostly, was the response. The clubs were tight; only a couple had full-time jazz. But you could jam at this little joint called Casey's, where pianists Freddie Redd and Nico Bunink played. Amram often sat in on French horn.

That January, Mingus came by a few times with what he called his electric pocket bass. There were only a handful of people. He'd sit at the piano with Amram after midnight, and they'd improvise four-handed pieces, the way they'd done for a decade plus.

He needed to get back to the music.

A week after New Year's 1969, he was publicly reunited with Sue after their long split.

The New York *Free Press*, which she worked on, was one of the countless underground papers that had bobbed up in cities and towns across America from the mid-1960s on. They usually blended sex and off-center politics that ran the gamut from SDS-style leftist activism to psychedelic self-liberation and the street theater of the Yippies. Their journalists routinely employed the Beats' first-person perspective, made mainstream by Tom Wolfe and the New Journalism, the mix of reportage and self-examination and rhetorical flights that marked Norman Mailer's nonfiction, like the recently published *Miami and the Siege of Chicago*, his panoramic, passionate take on the Democrats' 1968 Chicago convention debacle.

The *Free Press* staged a benefit at the Fillmore East, the old vaudeville theater that impresario Bill Graham had refurbished into a rock venue. Graham's New York site signaled the march from small clubs to bigger arenas that found rock stars like the Rolling Stones headlining at Madison Square Garden by the early 1970s. Clubland began to thin out, and the venues that were left would house mostly second-tier and below acts, and folkies, and jazzers who couldn't fill concert halls the way Ellington and Miles Davis did or cross over to the new rock-based audience.

Like the best aspects of the psychedelic era, Graham's Fillmores were musically nondenominational. In an ironic historical echo of George Wein's non-jazz-purist approach—a sin that had prompted the 1960 anti-Newport fest—Graham put artists like Miles Davis and the Grateful Dead on the same bill. That was part of the point. There were only two kinds of music, as Duke Ellington said, good and bad.

For Mingus, the downside to that whole world was hedonism for its own sake, and a lack of formal discipline and training. He was his father's son, even if he didn't apply the rules to himself with the same zeal he did to others. He could bend them because he knew them. He was exempt from his own judgments. He was Charles.

Sue was coming around to accepting him. Alberto Ungaro, her husband, was dead. She was drawn by the need for an artist in her life. He had a life and a life's work he needed someone to run.

She'd made sure at first he had little to do with her children, and he rarely interfered in their lives. She wanted them educated where she wanted, raised the way she wanted. She tried to keep her jealousy down.

As these years went on, they gradually fashioned an old-school relationship, male-female division of labor from their irresistible mutual attraction. They still often fought like cats and dogs. He wanted her. He needed a woman in the center of his life.

Mingus was volatile and uncentered. He was trying to recalibrate his focus, but his old certainties seemed gone. He wanted her help, was pulled in and repelled by her tendency toward control.

He saw Sue's work in the alternative press mostly as an endless round of dinners and deadlines with some interesting people. He wanted her focused on him.

She was living a few blocks away, on the east edge of Tompkins Square Park, next store to the building Bird had lived in before he died. The apartment had been Diane Arbus's.

The *Free Press* was a smart but typical counterculture organ. Al Goldstein was hanging out around the office, and soon, with typesetter Jim Buckley, founded *Screw* magazine. It was a harbinger. Sex had always been part of the alternative critique, although the trumpeted sexual freedom created hippie madonnas as well as nascent feminists.

Everything was collapsing.

The 1960s American cultural revolution was inexorably undermining itself, separating into conflicting interest groups huddled with increasing unease under the antiwar/antiracism umbrella. The inheritance of FDR's New Deal, his grand synthesis of disenfranchised groups, working classes, and wealthy progressives was breaking down.

In another small harbinger of things to come in the 1970s, the New York *Free Press* became the *New York Review of Sex and Politics*.

The Fillmore East benefit was Sue's first go at reintroducing Mingus to the world of musical performance, and it came, characteristically, in an offbeat setting. The lineup included Peter Yarrow (of the folk group Peter, Paul & Mary), the Fugs (a satirical band that included Beat poets Ed Sanders and Tuli Kupferberg), Norman Mailer, David Amram, and Jeremy Steig, an early fusion flutist.

Mingus played upright electric bass for half an hour with Dannie Richmond, who came up from Greensboro, North Carolina, for the set. Then he joined Steig, who whistled abstractions on the flute while Mingus played balloon.

On March 6, 1969, Mingus got a letter from the New York City Department of Social Services—welfare. He'd applied for medical assistance payments on Mt. Sinai file #140972 in February, once he got out of the hospital. But, said the letter signed by a supervisor, he was not over sixty-five or medically incapacitated, so he was not eligible for financial help.[1]

Sue started to reintroduce him to the scene, the very different scene, and vice versa. He had to start playing again, or disintegrate. He had no money left.

In April, she gave him a birthday supper, and invited all the children. Her birthday was also in April, and that began a tradition of co-celebrating them. In May, he paid his respects to sax great Coleman Hawkins, who was buried with a now-typical jazz funeral out of Pastor Gensel's church in midtown Manhattan.

In June, he had a gig at the Village Vanguard with a band of Workshop veterans: Charles McPherson, Bill Hardman, and Richmond, along with new-comer Billy Robinson, a Texas tenor in the Illinois Jacquet mode.

The Milbrook crew descended on the Vanguard. One of them had con-vinced Max Gordon to let them to rig up one of their light machines on the bar top and run a light show during Mingus's sets.

Dick Alpert opened a show one night, telling extemporaneous stories. He was scared stiff. Mingus had shared the stage with Lenny Bruce. Before going on, Alpert took Sue to a diner across from the club and begged her to tell him if Mingus was going to heckle him.

Mingus was still carrying pepper in a tissue, to defend himself. He got into an argument with a heckler, and called him outside. Sue trailed them. When he pulled out his tissue, the pepper got blown into her face, and when she could see again, Mingus and his foe were in a bear hug.

In July 1969, the Jazz and People's Movement, spearheaded by Roland Kirk, revived the 1960 anti-Wein protests at Cliff Walk Manor. Mingus showed up with the Vanguard outfit. It was billed as his comeback. He smiled but said almost nothing onstage. He played like an introvert while Dannie Richmond introduced the pieces and gave them their propulsive life.

He wasn't all there. He was forgotten, almost a legend. Sales of Debut al-bums were infinitesimal, and he got few royalties. One critic wrote "his records were a rumor."[2] He had to work.

He was tired, just tired. He wanted to dream, to write, to teach, not to be an organ grinder's monkey on endless tour. But he needed cash. And he needed a vehicle, a reason to write. Music on paper was nothing until you heard it. It had to get out into the world to matter.

After the last three years, his soul was shredded by intimations of mortality. He was an elder statesman without portfolio.

He stopped in at the Village Vanguard to see Thad Jones's big band; Jimmy Knepper was playing with them. He tried to make up, came over to Knepper and sat down next to him, behind the pillar blocking part of the small stage. Jones came over immediately. He said to Mingus, "This is my boy. If you hurt him, I'll clobber you." Mingus said nothing.

In summer 1969, the Chicago police killed two Black Panther party leaders under circumstances that remain obscure. Several other confrontations led to shoot-outs and deaths. The two founders, as well as the party's chief propagan-dist, Eldridge Cleaver, were charged with murder at different times.

Richard Nixon, the new president, was a staunch old friend of J. Edgar Hoover and the FBI from the 1950s. He called Hoover one spring night to brood about the surge of anarchy across the land, especially on campuses. The Berkeley and SDS student sit-ins had escalated across the land in a motley display of antiwar opposition. ROTC and CIA and FBI recruiters were the targets of student-led campaigns to oust them from colleges.

Hoover compared the outbreak to the 1917 Bolshevik Revolution in Russia. Nixon agreed. The result was the expansion of COINTELPRO, originally set up in 1956 to infiltrate communist and red-dominated organizations, often with agents provocateurs. Now COINTELPRO would target the New Left, from the mainstream antiwar Mobilization Committee to SDS and the Yippies to more radical splinter groups.

A decade later, army sources would tell the TV newsmagazine 60 Minutes that about one demonstrator in six was a government agent of one sort or another.

Everything was collapsing.

Mingus led the band into the Village Gate for the last two weeks of August 1969, at $3,000 per week. They got $2,000 a week for the first two weeks of September at Chicago's Plugged Nickel. For $1,300, they performed the following week at Baker's Keyboard Lounge in Detroit.[3]

The music was still tentative, but he was feeling his commercial way back.

The end of September brought a two-day tribute at Berkeley for Duke Ellington's seventieth birthday year. There were lectures, recordings, films, discussions. Among the speakers were John Handy, Gunther Schuller, John Lewis, and critic Stanley Dance.

Mingus was asked to perform as part of the tribute on September 28 and 29, and Sue dogged him to do it. It kept his crescendo back into music going. And the band would earn $1,000 for one set.[4]

Down Beat reported that his set sounded like a jam session at the Bohemia a dozen years earlier, bebop material with agitated solos and some organized ensembles. And he led the Duke tribute medley that had wowed Monterey five years earlier, but this time his bass solo on "Sophisticated Lady" was jarringly out of tune.

He never practiced the bass any more, hadn't really touched it for years. His fingers bled when he played too long. The spirit was uncertain and the flesh was undisciplined.

Like everyone in jazz, Ellington was aware of Mingus's wandering in the wilderness. Elegant and self-possessed, he thought it befitting his role as elder statesman to offer his self-described disciple a hand. He decided to play Mingus's "The Clown."

Mingus didn't have a copy of the music, so Sue called radio stations trying to locate a copy of the recording, and found one through a fan. She passed it to Ellington, who had someone copy the arrangement off the disc and adapt it to his band's instrumentation.

Mingus didn't really want them to play it. Not even Duke could do what his music needed. And he was sure it was too hard for Ellington's band, that some of them hated him, that they'd screw it up on purpose or because they couldn't play it right. He didn't want to face them onstage. Ellington thought Mingus would conduct the piece, but he'd already made up his mind not to.

And so, after playing trademark tunes like "Take the A Train" and "Creole Love Song," Ellington introduced "The Clown" and called for "Mingus, Mr. Mingus, Mr. Charles Mingus." He sat in the top row of the balcony with Sue and Kate Mulholland and her son and John Lewis. He was reduced to total silence. He was overwhelmed. He could let himself go because he was with people he trusted.

He was honored, truly, even if the performance, under Ellington's game leadership, turned out mediocre.

The relaunch of Charles Mingus was shifting into steadier gear, but he wasn't, not really. He and the band now played from lead sheets, which was unsettling for Mingus fans who saw him.

The rumors about his breakdowns and the movie about his eviction must be true. Here was Jazz's Angry Man subdued, sometimes somnambulant, never seizing the moment onstage in the ways that had made him famous, and a draw.

Music was the core of his soul, and he'd only been noodling with it for two years. Without it, he was a smashed kaleidoscope, tossing off bits of brilliant but busted glass as he whirled pointlessly.

Sue began acting as his manager and booking agent. That fall, he led the Workshop sextet with Billy Robinson at Los Angeles's Troubadour, Monterey's Cotton Club (two nights for $650), the Plugged Nickel in Chicago, the Both/And in San Francisco (two weeks for $4,000), Keystone Korner in Berkeley, and the Village Vanguard at the end of October (a week for $1,350). In November, he returned to Lennie's outside Boston. He came back to New York that December for a gig at Slugs and pair of two-night stands at the Village Gate, at $500 per night.[5]

In 1970, he was back on the road.

February brought a bass solo spot opposite Kenny Dorham's band at Town Hall in New York. He was listless. In March he played Slug's with McPherson, Hardman, altoist Jimmy Vass, and Richmond; a fan recorded them doing fair versions of pieces like "So Long Eric," "Peggy's Blue Skylight," "Better Get It," and "Orange Was the Color of Her Dress." In April he went to Berkeley.[6]

He did a bass solo gig at the Great American Music Hall, a Gay Nineties-style venue near the Tenderloin, where the streets were home to whores, drug dealers, transvestites. The Hall showcased a broad array of entertainers, like Robin Williams and the Grateful Dead's Jerry Garcia.

Mingus was fat. He mumbled, wasn't always lucid. He was back on musical track, but not really. He was torn. He didn't really like being on the road any more. He wanted to settle things with Judy. He had to get back to work. He was a black jazzman haunted by images of all those who'd died broke and broken. He needed the money.

His huge personality was an alternating electric current flashing like lightning between poles.

Gerald Wilson, an L.A.-based bandleader and composer-arranger, had a radio show, and gathered Buddy Collette, Red Callender, Britt Woodman, and Mingus to reminisce about the Central Avenue glory days. Mingus said almost nothing. He had always done most of the talking, so everybody else fell silent, instinctively. This time he was monosyllabic. It was eerie.

After twenty years of drug use, Charles Mingus's body chemistry resembled a research experiment.

In 1969, Jack Kerouac died of alcoholism, bitter about his legacy being connected to the antiwar and hippie scenes.

In 1970, Allen Ginsberg and his assistant, Anne Waldman, set up the Jack Kerouac School of Disembodied Poetics at Naropa Institute, run by Tibetan guru Chogyam Trungpa Rinpoche. The Institute was sited in Boulder, Colorado, a node in the countercultural grid across America.

On February 16, 1970, Mingus was served with divorce papers. Judy had a court date with her Legal Aid lawyer in June; she claimed abandonment for more than two years. He would have a chance to defend himself against the charge in September.

She didn't want or expect to get anything from him. She'd changed nursing jobs, from Mt. Sinai to Columbia University Student Health Service, and wanted her life and her children's lives out of perpetual legal limbo.

. He wasn't about to contest it. But Sue wasn't about to take him on, either. Not full time. Not yet. He couldn't understand it. Her husband was dead, and now he was getting clear.

He was a wreck. And she was very protective of her kids.

After New York *Free Press*, Sue started a magazine about radical-chic politics and culture, called *Changes*. It launched writers like satirist Fran Lebowitz. In

Volume 1, issue number 3, *Changes* published an excerpt from Mingus's autobiography, the first of several.

Sue was helping him bid for a publisher. He'd been carting the thing around in suitcases and boxes for years. He had started with his handwritten scenes and free associations in the mid-1950s, expanded and reworked and expanded, the way he often did with his music. He'd incorporated scathing critiques of the music business, a panoply of musical characters and tough street types, lots of explicit sex meant to be outrageous alongside adolescently romantic talk about love, insistent musings on the divine and spiritual sides of life, and some James Joycean verbal strategies. Over a decade and a half, the book was transformed and retransformed. Judy had typed and retyped a few versions herself. And countless other hands had passed over it, editing, rewriting, cutting, pasting.

It was a tribute to the force of his ideas and personality that, despite all that and the repeated obstacles to its publication, the best of what came to be called *Beneath the Underdog* kept the vital urgency, the searching and scarred and relentless humanity of his voice, his tumultuous being.

He'd made some of it up, embroidered much of it, often with help from Britt Woodman and Buddy Collette. He put a lot of sex in to sell, he told them, to titillate the stereotype. He liked puttin' on ol' massa.

Nel King, who'd co-scripted *All Night Long*, enthusiastically enlisted as his editor and helped in the search for a publisher. Regina Ryan, an editor at Knopf, bought it for $5,500.

On April 24 and 25, 1970, he performed at Berkeley's Greek Theatre. The band was paid $3,500. He signed a deal with George Wein's Festival Productions to go on European tour, with provisos. "You will never work more than five concerts in a seven-day period," the contract stated, then listed various reasons that agreement could be voided. He would go to Oslo, Belgrade, and Stockholm, with more to follow.

On May 25, his $250 check bounced—the one he had written to pay off part of Hobart Dotson's grievance, which had gotten Mingus expelled from Local 802 for his failure to comply.[8]

On May 4, there was an antiwar demonstration at Kent State University in Ohio. It was just one of the increasing American antiwar uprisings, this time protesting President Nixon's invasion of Cambodia in April to destroy Viet Cong supplies and support, a widening of the unpopular and divisive war.

The protest at Kent State was one of hundreds across the country, but it was there that National Guard troops fired on the college students, leaving four dead and nine wounded and plunging the nation deeper into self-laceration.

Mingus waded back into the blur of the road, but he still seemed to have nothing to prove. His shows were far from performance art.

His own essence still eluded him. He wanted something else now. He'd earned it: concert hall dates, ballets, museum chamber-music series, unclassifiable music he wanted to write. The road with its endless club dates couldn't give him that, but it was one way to get there, to build his reputation and his audience back up after so long off the scene, and in such a changed cultural environment.

So onstage he worked and plodded his way through the music, leaving the heavy solo labors to everyone else. He was a legend. Rumors of his breakdown circulated and accelerated. The enemies he'd made in jazz's incestuous world, knowingly and not, grinned and sharpened their knives and waited for him to stumble.

He could feel it out there. He never got credit. He'd created an enduring set of myths from his turbulent self, but he wasn't sure any more exactly what that meant, where the payoff was. Still, Sue had set bookings in motion, and Mingus followed them out.

In June 1970, he got a pencil-written note from Sarge, in the Queens House of Detention. They met "in the bullpen when you got arrested and were falsely accused of assalting [sic] a police officer." Sarge was in England trying to write a good book but got broke, and wanted to sponge $50 for bail.

In September, Booker Tillery, #145999, wrote him in real friendly fashion, mentioning Sue and his kids. Mentioning his own wife and kids, he said Irene would make sure Mingus ate his meals regularly.[9]

These were some of the friends he made in his times in the Tombs and jail and Chic Choc. The notion of outlaw was always close to him. He always wanted to be street. It was the side of him that Max Roach and Frank Mabry and even Buddy Collette were part of.

For Sue, it was romantic only at a distance. She was no streetfighter, and sometimes when he was talking or acting street with Mabry or the others she didn't plug in at all, didn't understand what was going on.

That summer, Judy rented a chalet-style house on a hill in Waitsfield, Vermont. Mingus hopped a puddle-jumper prop-plane flight from Boston to Burlington, where she picked him up. He looked really queasy coming down the walkway, but he wasn't letting go of the two containers of live lobsters he was carrying. They spent a couple of days together as a family, in their intermittent way.

That summer and fall the Workshop played brief stints at Slugs, the Village Vanguard, the Village Gate. The new horn lineup featured trumpeter Eddie Preston, who had some piercing moments. Mingus asked Jaki Byard back, and got him.

In jazz's down-sized world, the name Charles Mingus still brought gigs, and word was out his book was finally being published, that he was really coming back. Despite all the hassles he'd instigated over the years, people remembered him. Most of the old-timers in the jazz-business world were glad to see him come back. If nothing else, he'd once made them all money.

Only a few old-timers were left anyway, after the deluge of rock and roll.

It was at the Gate that Mingus hired Bobby Jones. Jones reminded him of Clifford Jordan—same big blustery rhythm and blues tone with bebop fleetness. The young white tenorman with the shoulder-length hair and beard showed up in mid-August and asked to sit in. Mingus's then-tenor player, Carlos Garnett, left when Jones took the stand. After the last set, Mingus told Jones to come back the next night. And so on, through the week, until Jones got paid and realized he was in the band.

Byard and Jones both sketched charts of his music, and so, for the first time since the early 1950s, the musicians had all the ensemble parts to read. It was a good band, but Mingus wasn't really leading it.

Mingus didn't call his bands Jazz Workshops any more. Jazz Workshop was the name of one of his companies.

At the end of August, 1970, Booker Ervin died. He was one of Mingus's most understanding and powerful sidemen, a solo voice and a mentor to younger Workshop musicians, a keeper of charts and a smoother of waters whose soaring musical spirit helped give the Atlantic-era Workshop its bite.

Muffled by mellaril, Mingus numbly added Booker's name to the list of friends and colleagues he'd outlived.

A few days later, he played on the Jazzmobile, a roving truck that presented free jazz on the streets of Harlem—an idea he'd talked about for years. Pianist Billy Taylor, who'd taught Mingus Latin jazz's montuno twenty years earlier, was its founder and guiding spirit.

One of Mingus's sidemen warned him he shouldn't do his usual set; this was a strictly rhythm and blues street crowd. But much of his stuff spoke directly to that feel.

CHARLES MINGUS: I took the music as far out as I could, and they still liked it. All those kids, following the truck, wanting more. Of course they wanted to hear it. It's their music, man. It's their lives. It goes back so far, and has so much farther to go.[10]

Bowed and bent and dazed and foggy and very nearly broken, he was coming out of it, still a teacher. If you don't live it, it won't come out of your horn.

He was interviewed on TV by critic Chris Albertson, who asked him about the recognition denied jazz, or black music. Mingus looked startled. "Where'd that come from, man?" he shot back. "Why not call it American music?"[11]

At the Village Vanguard on September 14, he premiered a piece called "Us Is Two," also called "Us Is Too." Depending on who he was talking to, he said the piece reflected the United States' polarized divisions, like black/white ("Two"), or about blacks like himself demanding civil rights ("Too"), or a tribute to Duke Ellington.[12]

He told Sy Johnson he'd inverted a few bars in the middle from a Mozart horn concerto. His music's skeletal structures reached in every direction, from ape-men on up.

On September 28, 1970, he didn't show up at court, and his marriage to Judy was dissolved. She was given custody of Keki and Eric, and Family Court kept jurisdiction over the question of his alimony and child support.

He was never very good about money. He liked to give his children presents, take them places, do things for them. The attention came in bursts, when it was good for him. But when it came it was engulfing, reassuring, total.

From October through November, Sue had him booked in Europe. There jazz was concert music. He could cash in, and edge toward his other ambitions.

She already had a few irons in the fire about those. She had to draw him back out of himself, out of the haze, without rekindling the rage that fired him into a Roman candle.

The tricky part was that rage was at the molten core of his layered personality.

Mingus was on autopilot—which meant notches above the usual thing, but far from what aficionados expected. He wore a suit and spoke rarely onstage. Dannie provided the music's pulse; Mingus kept time, artfully but basically, and told interviewers if he didn't need the money he wouldn't be there.

One of the pieces they played was called "The Man Who Never Sleeps," an obviously autobiographical title.

The Workshop recorded for Musidisc in Paris. They did a few of his classics like "Pithecanthropus Erectus" and "Reincarnation of a Lovebird," and did a version of "I Left My Heart in San Francisco."

Critic Gary Giddins later praised the album, called *Reincarnation of a Lovebird* when it was released in the United States. He credited the simplified charts with being "jaunty," said, "The improvisations sparkle," and described the mood as "less ominous" than the originals.

"If Charles Mingus didn't actually introduce fear and trembling into jazz," wrote Giddins, "he has been its most persistently apocalyptic voice. He can be generous in communicating joy as any practitioner of what is generally thought of as joyous music, but he often asks us to run the gauntlet with him before emerging triumphant on the mountaintop. For all his technical innovations, I think Mingus's greatest achievement has been to put the emotional scope of jazz on a footing with that of European music."[13]

By the time the European swing ended, Dannie Richmond left to join the Mark-Almond blues-rock band, and Jaki Byard pulled out again. Mingus was fighting with Sue, and she came home halfway through the tour.

His biography was now titled *Beneath the Underdog*, and the advance and the money from touring helped pay for his medical bills. Hospitals and drugs didn't come cheap, even then, and the union wasn't much help.

Psychiatric problems weren't real medical claims yet in America. Drug usage, however, was booming.

Alongside government-prosecuted gurus like Ken Kesey and Timothy Leary, the armed forces were producing thousands of heroin addicts and more casual drug users with each tour of duty for the hundreds of thousands of Americans who served in Vietnam. They came home to spill across the streets and TV screens of America, ever more threatening.

The returning vets got no victory parades. Some met abuse from antiwar groups, who routinely called cops and soldiers "pigs." Some were radicalized by the war they'd seen up close, its covered-up massacres and incompetence and thievery, its stalemate. Others tried to fit quietly back into The System, or society.

The "Vietnam veteran syndrome" came to describe an ex-soldier on a hair-trigger. Drug-addicted veterans, trained in weapons and killing, turned to crime to support their habits, to exact revenge on a system that sent them to die and left them to rot, because unemployment was rising fast and jobs were harder to find all the time.

Watching TV night after night, steeped with flickering but vivid images of war, campus revolt, street fighting, rioting, and crime, many Americans felt threatened.

This atmosphere had enabled Richard Nixon to come back from political death. Nixon took a cue from the charismatic Kennedys, whom he hated, and built a more extensive crew of media handlers than earlier election campaigns or the presidency had ever seen. To avoid alienating people with his abrasive, shifty personality and rabidly anticommunist past, "Tricky Dick" was repackaged into "the New Nixon."

The new Nixon had forged a new constituency from the collapsing New Deal: blue-collar workers who cut union-driven liberalism loose to vote Republican, white-collar suburbanites, the growing black middle class scared of and scarred by the specters of sex and drugs and crime.

The revolt piloted by the boppers and Beats, with its glorification of outlaws operating outside The System, was now fully loosed on America, and fueling an inevitable reaction. Part of that came in tightening criminal penalties. The System was said to be "soft on crime, tough on victims." Too many protections had been granted by the Chief Justice Earl Warren-era Supreme Court, the liberal-minded issuers of the 1954 school desegregation order.

In 1971, Clint Eastwood starred in *Dirty Harry*, a movie about a cop caught between pinko judges and prosecutors, rogue right-wing cops, and long-haired criminals and killers who mouth 1960s political slogans like "Power to the people." It was the first film of a successful trilogy that reflected shifts in American perceptions after the 1960s.

Eastwood's movies were set in San Francisco, Mingus's second home and the headquarters, in many eyes, for the 1960s countercultures of drugs, sex, and politics.

Lalo Schiffrin wrote the sound tracks for the first two, but Jerry Fielding signed on for *The Enforcer* in 1976. Fielding had been musical director for Groucho Marx's 1950s TV show, *You Bet Your Life*, where he'd hired Buddy Collette. Then he was blacklisted by the House Un-American Activities Committee and forced to resign, before being rehabilitated in the early 1960s, like author Dalton Trumbo and other lucky survivors.

Mingus didn't like Nixon, but he liked Eastwood's movies, beginning with his breakthrough spaghetti Westerns, filmed in Italy in the mid-1960s and endowed with jagged, startling noir-jazzy sound tracks. The shooting was highly stylized yet full of deliberately disorienting editing; the material was often violent.

The Westerns reminded Mingus of the Japanese movies he loved. The lurid gunplay in them and the cop movies appealed to him as bourgeois street punk. There were no easy explanations for him.

When Mingus came back from Europe, he had a couple of club bookings in New York, then headed to Japan for a couple of weeks in January 1971. There a revamped Workshop—Bobby Jones, Eddie Preston, drummer Al Hicks—recorded with a Japanese big band modeled on Woody Herman's swaggering Herd. He used Jaki Byard's arrangements and tentatively soloed on *Charles Mingus with Orchestra*, a largely disposable disc.

He came home and did a couple of nights at Slugs, his new regular home. A lot of the young crowd that hung there hadn't seen his Workshops, and the music had enough visceral power to hit them in their souls.

For at least the third time, he was notified that he'd been dropped from the rolls of Local 802 for nonpayment of dues.

He got his most recent statement from Fantasy Records. Between 1968 and 1970, Fantasy paid GMAC $1,204.82 for his car, $904 for the Polo Grounds Warehouse, $105.14 to tax collectors, and $4,316 to Davidson Management, his landlord.[14]

On January 24, 1971, Mingus joined his old sideman Roland Kirk to celebrate victory for part of what they called the Jazz and People's Movement (JAPM) protests. Tenorist Archie Shepp, a champion of free jazz as a vehicle for black power, was the ringleader. One participant in the demonstrations was white trombonist Roswell Rudd.

The arguments sounded familiar to Mingus: that TV ignored black jazz musicians. That night, he appeared on *The Ed Sullivan Show* with Kirk and Shepp and a few others, doing a version of "Haitian Fight Song."

On March 30, JAPM picketed outside the Guggenheim Foundation. A month later, Charles Mingus was awarded a Guggenheim Foundation Fellowship, only the seventh jazz artist so honored. He was duly recognized as a composer.

The System had nodded to him and to the traditions he represented and culminated—at last.

DAVID AMRAM: When he went with Rahsaan Roland Kirk to the television station to insist that they have more jazz, he wasn't doing it for himself. "I'm already there," he said. "I'm doing it for the younger cats who wonder whether they should keep this music going or not." He felt that jazz was a great continuing music, that you had to be conscious of the history. It's very unusual, especially in New York City, to have anyone known as an innovator acknowledge anyone else. Mingus would acknowledge not only the giants of the past but his contemporaries. Fats Navarro. Howard McGhee. Jimmy Blanton.

His life was falling into place one puzzle piece at a time.

On April 1, 1971, Saul Zaentz received a letter from Musidisc-Europe, guaranteeing a $10,000 advance for Mingus.

On April 19, his divorce became official. That same day, he played two sets solo at SUNY Buffalo for $400 plus 70 percent of the gate receipts.

He still had the 1964 Caddy limo stowed in a garage. He was ready to let Grace have it. He told her to claim he was living with her to speed up the paperwork.[15]

He was forty-nine years old.

He felt the new generation was encapsulated in his son Charles, the painter turned playwright turned dilettante, undisciplined but desperate to be creative in the moment, feeling that their lives were big, baggy, natural ongoing metaphors that gave the universe meaning.

The difference between them and him was his artistic nature, his seer's abilities. He felt the same thing, but credited the eternal vibrations underlying human reality, and his own artistic nature. He could see through the veil. They couldn't.

He was his father's son.

Beneath the Underdog was published in May 1971. It was like beginning a new life. He wanted a best-seller, and told Buddy Collette and Britt Woodman that the overblown sex scenes would move it like hotcakes. He was most like himself when he was mau-mauing the flakcatcher again.

Like Malcolm X, he loved to titillate white readers with what white middle- and upper-class women did to get to forbidden black men for their secret thrill of revolt, the joy of sex with the Other.

Maybe it was because mostly white women had edited it. Maybe it was because of fears of libel, or the mob, or the sheer sprawling size of the manuscript. The book had a lot of swagger and soap opera, both parts of his interactive repertoire, but somehow it had fewer of his satirical, pointed scenes about the music business.

Those that were left, however, suggested the sweeping, if sometimes trite and reductive, indictment he'd originally planned, before the book was cut by more than half.

Besides, sex sold. Partly, he was playing off sensationalized best-selling autobiographies like Jelly Roll Morton's and Billie Holiday's. But *Beneath the Underdog* also used sex to explore parts of his character—as cynical suitor and pimp, as wounded lover and yearning Romantic, as a "schitt-colored nigger" artist caught in the racial tangles of American daily life. Even though the story's chronological order was scrambled in some places, the early chapters maintained his uniquely careening, epiphanic voice. After that, the text was mostly honed too finely, like the band charts for the Musidisc album, for his multiplicitous selves to find space.

Most of his friends felt it was silly, or demeaning, that it reduced him, that it didn't capture all the moods that once flickered across his face as fleet as thought. Some asked to be left out of it and were. Many characters' names were changed. Some saw it as a sell-out. They knew he needed the money.

Its penultimate chapter was, ironically, a paean of sorts to Judy, telling of her meeting him at the Half Note, of his mouthing off about wanting to be a hardass pimp and sundry other things, and her reaction: "The girl Judy laughs. She's entertained and amused and she doesn't believe a word of it, otherwise she would never have married him and borne his two youngest children, would she?"[16]

The party for the book's publication showed some of his old élan: refreshments included lobster and Pouilly Fuisse. His sextet was playing his music loud while Nesuhi Ertegun, Nat Hentoff, Ornette Coleman, and Murray Kempton talked shop. Mingus fingered his Fu Manchu mustache and beard while he told stories of being busted with hippies, and said he was supposed to have played the huge peace demonstration in D.C. the preceding weekend.[17]

He introduced Sue to everyone as his manager.

But he was barely audible when he talked to Down Beat's correspondent. He muttered about Jaki Byard leaving because of money. The writer described him as "a sagging Buddha."[18] "Buddha" became a recurrent way friends started to describe him around this time. It suited his inward gaze.

There were more blacks than whites at the blowout. He left with Sue to head to a favorite East Village Japanese restaurant. His son Charles brushed off the New Yorker reporter there, telling him he was too busy writing a play to read his father's book. They were barely talking to each other now.

Right after the party, he called Judy. He was hurt that she hadn't come to the party. People were asking for her. She'd typed the whole book. Why didn't she come?

Sue "forgot" to send her an invitation.

Joe Gallo got out of prison two weeks after Beneath the Underdog was published. Mingus shuddered, even under mellaril's soothing grayness. Was Crazy Joe was still looking for him?

Mingus showed his son Charles a photograph, taken in Central Park by what looked like a Polaroid camera with a telephoto lens. It showed Judy and the children, and was flecked with knife cuts. On the back was written in red pen, "This could happen."

He would later tell people he went crazy and was hospitalized several times to get his certificate to avoid Gallo. Even if it were true, the scheme wouldn't have worked. No loony-bin would've stopped Crazy Joe. But Gallo had bigger fish than a moolinyan jazz musician to fry, and bigger vengeance to wreak. He was fighting for control of the Colombo family. Just out of the pen, he ordered a hit on Joe Colombo, and left him, in Crazy Joe's phrase, "vegetabled."

Colombo had started the Italian-American Civil Rights League. The name deliberately echoed the black civil rights movement. The League existed to combat media stereotypes of Italian Americans. Colombo poured scorn on movies and TV for picturing his ethnic group as mobsters and pizza makers and organ grinders.

Gallo wanted to bring blacks into the mob, to broaden its base and range, just as Lucky Luciano had linked up with the Jews to control New York rackets and politics. For most mob bosses, the idea was an *infamia*.

Richard Nixon made white ethnic identity politics a key to his political coalition. But he also wooed the black middle class, increasingly disaffected by the violent wings of black nationalism, with affirmative action programs.

Lionel Hampton loved Nixon. He was a stone Republican.

That spring, Charles Mingus Jr. received his prestigious Guggenheim grant, worth $15,000. It was for his proposed composition for the Robert Joffrey Ballet, to be choreographed by Alvin Ailey. It would be called "The Mingus Dances."

George Wein lost no time in booking Mingus into the 1971 Newport Jazz Festival—the last to be held on the site of its birth. *Beneath the Underdog* was getting huge press.

GEOFFREY WOLFF: It is directed by three narrative conceits: by the conventional first-person voice of autobiography; by the third-person voice of a disengaged Charles Mingus judging the hazardous progress of his alter ego; by a patient's confessions to his analyst. The book is meant to be read as a calculated composition and as an ongoing act of therapeutic self-investigation. ...[Its] great value lies in its most casual virtues. It is a lexicon of inventive language, the seldom-read because seldom-written slang from the '30s, '40s, and '50s...used by hookers and hustlers and pimps and jazz musicians....For my taste, there's too little here about his life as a musician, because what there is...is first-rate cultural history and music criticism.[19]

JONATHAN YARDLEY: Though *Beneath the Underdog* is only incidentally a book about Mingus's music, it makes clear that his music is as much a vehicle for personal release as for artistic expression, if not more. Beneath the Underdog is part of that same process of intimate revelation, and though it has great weaknesses it possesses much the same wild fascination as his music. . . . Mingus's sexual extravagances, his incessant assertions that black is best in bed, are part of his larger search for self-discovery and self-justification. . . . Mingus adds nothing of real moment to the chronicle of black suffering, save where he portrays the unique agonies of a "mongrel" such as he calls himself. . . . He feels he has gone beyond prejudice, that he occupies a "colorless island." Odd that a man who has raged so violently against a white man's world should say that, but some of *Beneath the Underdog* makes you believe him.[20]

BURT KORALL: . . . a shaped outpouring, much of it in the third person, sometimes flawed by overstatement and overwhelming self-concern. The picture drawn is that of a creative black man—turning on a spit, cooking in his own juice over a fire provided by the so-called Establishment. . . . Music provides a center for Mingus. It answers the pressing need to accomplish. . . . The hyperactive Mingus descriptions approximate a sex manual in content and the preening of a schoolboy in manner. It would have been preferable if Mingus had concentrated on the music, its makers, and the business. . . . The scenes with musicians . . . have about them a distinct, informing, almost visual character. . . . A highly moral man in his own way, he finds redemption in music. It challenges and keeps him from the ultra-lower depths of depression and . . . junk.[21]

Mingus called his current sextet into session for the festival and performed old pieces from his Japanese album. He was supposed to be writing on his Guggenheim grant. But there wasn't time, and his focus was still blurred, and his muse was still numb and heartbroken, so work was sporadic.

He shipped Grace his Caddy limo just before Newport. She'd had an accident, and been laid up, and needed a car but couldn't afford it.[22] He paid AAACON $245 to cart it cross country. She was his sister, after all.

On July 4, 1971, Mingus picked up $600 in cash from Ann McIntosh, who had set up a concert at Music Inn's courtyard amphitheater. He gave her, he said, a 40 percent discount because it was on the band's way back to New York. He told her he'd do it for free, but he had to pay the guys.

Besides, there was a photo exhibit dedicated to Eric Dolphy at the Thembi Arts Center nearby. He was distracted by an ample white caftan, trimmed in gold, that he saw in a shop window. It was his size, so he bought it.

These days, it seemed like his life was sometimes more past than present.

It seemed like he'd accumulated baggage, karma enough for more than himself.

He smoked a little pot to relax after Ann McIntosh's gig. He was trying to lay off cocaine, mellaril. Sue cajoled him into going to several doctors to try to wean him, but he'd sooner or later slide back into the drug's protective haze.

They fought about it steadily.

Around this time he asked Janet Coleman, "Were you there at the old Five Spot? We used to have dancers come down. Artists would come and paint. Sketches of people posin' and musicians playin'. I should have waited ten years. Before I got any ideas. I was too soon." [23]

In August, he got a check from the Westinghouse Broadcasting Co—$31.20. [24]

At SUNY Buffalo that September, he was given an honorary degree and asked to take a one-term turn at the Slee chair. [25]

Mingus wanted to be a composer, not a performer. He was dividing the functions more. He wanted his work in concert halls and artistic surroundings, not jazz clubs, whenever possible. He was too tired to pull things into shape in the moment the way he had. He wondered what would happen to his music after he died.

The cauldron was on a low flame.

He flew up to go to the first meeting of the music department, and fell asleep at the conference table.

Famed black choreographer Alvin Ailey, who had founded one of the nation's first black dance companies in 1958, had approached Sue the year before about choreographing Mingus music for the Robert Joffrey Ballet. [26] He used Byard's arrangement of "Myself When I Am Real" for a centerpiece of "The Mingus Dances." The material was renamed, but old: "Haitian Fight Song," "O.P.," "Pithecanthropus Erectus," "Dizzy's Moods," "Ysabel's Table Dance," "Diane."

The reviews were mixed, but it was another rung on Mingus's ladder back to prominence, his redefined self as composer on paper.

In some ways, he was coming full circle, back to the 1940s and early 1950s. He was writing it down, localizing the role of spontaneous conversation within his music.

On November 20, 1971, he played at a benefit at Slugs. Two weeks later, he played St. John the Divine Cathedral in New York with Barry Harris, Clifford Jordan, Lonnie Hillyer, and Al Leavitt.

December brought more acknowledgment of his return, his reputation, his long shadow. He was voted into the *Down Beat* Hall of Fame. He shrugged, although he was also glad. He wanted the world to acknowledge his greatness. He deserved the honors he was getting. He'd worked for them, against the odds—and until he couldn't do it any more, until he'd just worn out.

In December, he went with Sue to a Black Panther fund-raising party in a gutted Brooklyn warehouse.[27] The Panthers were a focus of Radical Chic, as Tom Wolfe dubbed the phenomenon of rich white people adopting often violent revolutionary groups. Leonard Bernstein had them over to his house, and Wolfe wrote about it.

Mingus was less impressed with the Panthers than Sue, and he was no political joiner.

Through the strobe lights, the black women eyed him and his blonde. He'd sparred with their Afro-ed likes before. He was tired of it.

He thought of Mamie and his sisters.

13 Let My Children Hear Music

AT THE END OF 1971, Charles Mingus Jr. was leading an outfit that was sub-bing for Thad Jones's big band at the Vanguard Monday nights. He kept shuffling the personnel. He was going to record for Columbia, with Teo Macero producing. The album would be called *Let My Children Hear Music*, another multiple-meaning title.

Mingus was back on the major label map and closing some circles of his sprawling life. History was propelling him toward legend, and he could swallow his diatribes about John Hammond, Columbia's eminence grise, for the money.

Ellington's longtime baritone soloist, Harry Carney, had agreed to play on the record. Mingus was excited but was still heavily medicated. He seemed hal-lucinatory at times. He couldn't decide things. He didn't have his old sense of certainty. Everything seemed under a mist.

Thad Jones was supposed to be writing and arranging material for his album, but had done nothing. Mingus needed help. After his swing on Jimmy Knepper in 1962, no established copyists or arrangers wanted to work with him.

It turned out that Carney was out of town for the dates, and Mingus was heartbroken. The recording had to be postponed. He had to find an arranger and a baritone sax.

While he was at the Village Vanguard, he added Howard Johnson on bari-tone and Bob Stewart on tuba. He wanted the lovely deep voices to predomi-nate again.

And he bumped into ex-Workshop pianist Sy Johnson, now an arranger, and fed him material to chart. Some of it was pieces he'd written recently, most was old stuff, redone. He always had multiple ways to realize any piece. He could always hear its potential echoes.

He was going back to his roots, back to when he was seventeen, when he first met Farwell Taylor and got encouragement and concern about his music and himself, and the world seemed to open up again. The piece dictating the band's huge size and varied instrumentation was "Chill of Death."

It was a Mingus kind of rebirth.

He gave Johnson the 1965 UCLA album so he could transcribe "Don't Be Afraid, the Clown's Afraid Too" and "Holding Corporation." The latter was re-named "The Shoes of the Fisherman's Wife Are Some Jiveass Slippers." A few years earlier, the religious novel *Shoes of the Fisherman* had been a runaway best-seller.

His sense of humor and wordplay was coming back, but he was still dosed up. He told Johnson, "You fix it, man. If it's wrong, I'll tell you in the studio."

Johnson had admired Mingus music for more than a decade. He loved the way Mingus avoided the section-by-section clichés of big bands, the way he wanted everyone to have a unique line to play, like Duke Ellington did. So Johnson worked hard at orchestrating the music so he'd preserve its organic clarity.

When Mingus heard the taped sessions, he scheduled another overdubbing session, and called Johnson.

SY JOHNSON: Men were there with sound effects records and overdubbing solos and muddying the whole context up, deliberately. When I complained to Charles, what he said was very revealing: "Nobody should be seeing the bones of this music." I think in effect he was saying that he was disguising what he felt were his influences—and in some cases downright steals. He was voracious. He'd steal from himself and from anything he thought was interesting. It would always come out Mingus, but he didn't want anyone to be able to tell. So I did that on "The I of Hurricane Sue"—the storm and thunder stuff.

When they mixed the album, Johnson experienced the recurrent sore issue of credit firsthand. Mingus had been passive and agreeable about naming Johnson his arranger, until it was time to print the album jacket. He announced in the mixing room he wasn't giving Johnson arranger credit. A fight erupted, and they sent a gofer to look up "arranger" and "orchestrator" in the dictionary.

Teo Macero just rolled his eyes. Johnson had written most of the charts. He deserved the credit.

Dannie Richmond and Sue mediated for Mingus, with Johnson and Macero and whoever else needed the treatment.

Mingus was thinking of Dmitri Tiomkin. He had trouble focusing for very long. He hadn't made a real record for a major label in almost ten years. But he was ready to come back, to make some money, to snare more recognition.

They sorted out the credits so Johnson got some, if not all he thought he was due. They said he conducted "Hobo Ho," which was another major splice job. That's when Mingus and Macero really got working. They loved editing tape. Mixing put Mingus to sleep.

One night, when Mingus fell asleep in the mixing room, Macero prankishly left him there. When the producer walked in the following day, Mingus was still there. Suddenly he pulled a gun on Macero, pointed it, and squeezed the trigger. Macero heard the hammer click, then saw a flame sprout. The "gun" was a lighter.

Mingus was going to be fifty years old. He was still so fat he sometimes had to pick his leg up with his hand and put it across his knee, if he wanted to cross his legs, like his father.

SY JOHNSON: I was taking a picture of him on the roof at 10th Street. I was attaching my Rolleiflex to its tripod via a quick clamp, sitting in the stairwell with a skylight overhead, the light was soft. He was really out of it—on medication. He looked half-dead. Suddenly the camera slipped, and he turned—pppooofff! —and caught it flush as it started to fall. His reflexes were astonishing.

His creative resurrection demanded a concerted effort. Fantasy issued a press release stating that Mingus had studied with Rheinschagen, that he was an extra in *Higher and Higher*, a Sinatra movie, and *Road to Zanzibar*, and that he appeared on the first CBS color TV show with Mel Torme.

One indisputable assertion was that he was then working with Lee Konitz at the Vanguard preparing for a big February concert at Philharmonic Hall.

Columbia would release *Let My Children Hear Music* the week of the concert and take out a full-page ad in the program that night.

Everything was coming together.

As they were mixing the disc, Julie Lokin and Art Weiner heard a rough tape of it. They'd earlier approached Mingus about doing something when they were college kids, fledgling promoters. Now they were trying to establish themselves in jazz's Big Apple as adults, although they kept their day jobs.

The once mighty New York live jazz scene was a shriveled corpse. Only the Village Vanguard presented jazz all the time; the other clubs mixed in other formats. There were few concerts in halls. Lokin and Weiner wanted to change that.

So they formed New Audiences, and went to Brooklyn to see Sonny Rollins, who was once more "retired" and off the scene. They couldn't convince him to come back yet, even offering Abbey Lincoln as a special guest.

Then they thought of Mingus. His book was out and highly visible, and the Ailey pieces and his deal with Columbia validated his resurgent marketability. They contacted Nel King, who told them he was on medication, so he was calmer, easier to deal with. She put them in touch with Sue, and they heard the tapes of *Let My Children Hear Music*.

They put a $500 deposit down with Lincoln Center, to reserve Philharmonic Hall for February 4, 1972. Everybody thought they were nuts. He'd go out on them, or they'd lose money, or both.

Mingus wanted to host his friends from several generations. It would be a reflection of his life and times and music, the first of his attempts to resummarize his life and meaning.

So with Sue's input and help, he went to Columbia to propose an idea: he would front a big band, and the label would partly subsidize the show and record it. A young marketing executive named Bruce Lundvall facilitated matters, suggesting that Mingus get brawny tenor man Gene Ammons, who'd just gotten out of jail after several years. The old hard bopper, son of piano legend Albert Ammons, even refused to call what he played jazz. He said it was rhythm and blues.

From some perspectives, so were Mingus classics like "Better Get It in Your Soul." He wanted Ammons for that big, screaming, male-sex sound.

Mingus also wrote a piece for "Little Jazz," trumpet great Roy Eldridge. The sixty-one-year-old was Lester Young's contemporary, a veteran of Norman Granz's Jazz at the Philharmonic, and the inspiration for postwar pioneers like Dizzy Gillespie. But Eldridge was sick. Mingus asked Snooky Young. He couldn't make it and recommended an eighteen-year-old wunderkind the grapevine said was apprenticing to Dizzy Gillespie, Jon Faddis.

Eldridge was Dizzy's forebear. Dizzy himself was in the hospital near death. Faddis was Dizzy's musical heir. Mingus hired him, even though Young hadn't actually heard the young trumpeter play. Faddis went to Mingus's apartment and looked at the music for the piece. "Don't you want to practice it?" Mingus asked. "No, it'll be okay,' said Faddis; it was a lot of improvising, but the written music wasn't that hard.

Mingus thought he was cocky. He was actually scared. Most Mingus stories among musicians revolved around his violent outbreaks, and the teenager wanted to keep their first meeting short and to the point.

The deal struck between Mingus and New Audiences carried a whiff of cooperative deja-vu. They were partners. New Audiences paid for advertising and the hall and other promotional and set-up expenses. Ticket-sale proceeds were split once those expenses were covered. The musicians were paid $148.50 apiece for rehearsal.[1]

The word on the street grew quickly from a murmur: Mingus was really back. He was leading a twenty-four-piece band. Then the ads hit. The tickets started to move fast.

A couple of weeks before Philharmonic Hall, Nat Hentoff showed up in the Columbia editing studio while they were finishing work on *Let My Children Hear Music*. Mingus was smoking cigarettes made of lettuce, and was expansive, even excited.

NAT HENTOFF: I knew immediately that Mingus had somehow regenerated himself. Long, boldly arching melodies ... swelling, deeply textured designs ... sinewy interplay ... pulsing beat changed cadences like speech—gathering momentum in exuberant passages, slowing down for reflection, disappearing briefly, leaving a shock of groundlessness.[2]

Mingus complained about critics not understanding his compulsion toward stylistic restlessness. "I don't want to be caught in any one groove," he told Hentoff. "Everything I do is Mingus. That's why I don't like to use the word 'jazz' for my work. I write what I think is classical music too. Of course, there always has to be improvisation in it."[3]

He said "Adagio Non Troppo" was the first part of a large symphony he was contemplating, one that would change each time it was played, via the improvised parts. "Adagio" was actually "Myself When I Am Real," arranged by Jaki Byard. The symphony would tell the story of his life, like a book.

CHARLES MINGUS: But to have that kind of symphony played as it ought to be, [sic] requires more so-called jazz players who actually compose as they improvise. Most of the time, after the average jazz musician takes the first eight bars of his solo, there's not much of value left. The rest becomes repetitive. They fall into familiar riffs and patterns. They're not really creating. So I've been working on developing new kinds of lines—foundations for improvising inside a composition—that will make it impossible for a musician to slip back into playing something he's used to in order to fill the time. I want to get to the point where everyone playing something of mine will be able to think in terms of creating a whole, will be able to improvise compositionally so that it will be hard to tell where the writing ends and the improvisation begins.[4]

Word was out that Ornette Coleman was writing a large-scale work he was calling a symphony. He, not Ornette, should be doing that. He had the training, the background, the sophistication, the long-standing desire. In formal terms, Coleman was deliberately primitive; his symphony was more like a suite. Mingus, by contrast, wanted to remake the symphony from inside, entwine thematic expositions and solo and group improvisations, as classical music had done even into Mozart's day. He wanted to rewire the symphony's theme-and-development structures and light them with jazz.

His rhapsodic arco solo in "Adagio" came on over the speakers while he was talking with Hentoff. "Yeah, I got that back too," he said.[5] It was the first solo he'd taken worth a damn since 1967.

He didn't like calling his music jazz, or classical, or anything else. It was Mingus music.

They were still recording and mixing when he put Sy Johnson to work writing charts for the Philharmonic Hall concert. He didn't have anything for the orchestration he wanted to use. This was another special event, meant to remind everyone of Monterey in 1964. It was Philharmonic Hall, so it was big, his real comeback.

Johnson rode his bike from his West Village apartment over to the East 5th Street dump. He was startled by the bars on the windows, by the number of locks on the door. Mingus was literally locked in.

The top bunk bed was piled high with music. Open boxes of sheet music lined the room. Mingus was going through what he hadn't lost.

His grand piano and drafting table took up the center of the room. He ate on the drafting table. He had his juicer and a huge bag of unwashed carrots, and a pot of soup bubbling on the stove virtually all the time now. He liked to keep tasting it, adding bits of seasoning. Sometimes he'd chop an onion and toss it in. He was trying to eat better. He was trying to get straight.

This concert was important.

Mingus wrote even more slowly than usual, which meant a glacial pace. He'd spend days on the same page. He'd ask Johnson about using more hats, meaning rests. He was nervous. He was rewriting old stuff. He was chewing dozens of pencils up in the electric pencil sharpener Sue bought him along with a tape recorder, so he could hum melodies and ideas into it at any time. Johnson told him to get an IBM pencil, and left him one. By the time Johnson pedaled back to Jane Street, the phone was already ringing off the hook. He raced upstairs and picked it up, and heard Mingus yelling, "The music writes itself! The music writes itself!"

Mingus bought boxes and boxes of IBM pencils.

He played Johnson a single complex polytonal chord. It had major and minor sevenths, major and minor thirds, flatted fifths, a potpourri of clashing, ambivalent notes. "That's the chord I want," he said. Johnson asked if he had a melody for the piece. "No," he said, "but you can figure something out."

Trying to get his scores copied was no piece of cake, since he'd been blacklisted by all the major copying services. Johnson was orchestrating and arranging, but how was he going to get all those parts done for the musicians to read?

At the time, a young black musician named Paul Jeffrey was copying scores for Gil Evans. Evans told him Mingus needed a copyist, and he went up to Harlequin studio to meet with the man himself. There was a lot of music, so Jeffrey went up to Sam Herman's, one of the bigger copying services, where he also worked, looking for help. Herman shrugged, and reminded Jeffrey about Knepper.

So Jeffrey was on his own. Once he started work, he knew he couldn't possibly finish by himself. He had a plan: instead of the usual procedure of copying each part from beginning to end, he'd copy for all the musicians up to the same point. That way, at least they could all rehearse a chunk of the night's music.

He needed Mingus's okay, so he called the two phone numbers he'd been given: one for Mingus's apartment, and one for Chic Choc.

Jeffrey found him at the bar. Mingus was gruff but agreed to the plan. Ten minutes later, he called Jeffrey back.

PAUL JEFFREY, *arranger and musician*: He says, "Look at bar number so-and-so." Then it sounds like Mingus fell on his piano. "I just heard these chords—put that in there." "But Charles, I have no idea what you're playing." He starts telling me notes; I wrote them down. Fifteen minutes later, the phone rings again. It's Mingus. "Go to bar so-and-so. I want some clarinets in there, and I want some Middle Eastern sounds." So I wrote some.

Rehearsals started the next day. Gerry Mulligan, Lee Konitz, Johnson, Faddis, Eddie Bert on bass trombone, and the core Workshop with Charles McPherson and Lonnie Hillyer and Bobby Jones and pianist John Foster, augmented by some ace New York session musicians, were all there. Aside from some bickering between Johnson and Jeffrey, things went well—much more smoothly than if he hadn't been on mellaril.

Gene Ammons turned out to be a sharp sight-reader; he picked up his difficult parts with ease.

Jeffrey finished copying the score, working nights, during the next four days. They'd see the rest of it for the first time while they rehearsed or onstage.

LEE KONITZ: At the rehearsal there were about eight saxes, very impressive bunch, and he brought out this arrangement by Sy Johnson. At some point the saxes were all over the place with this phrase in sixteenth notes—just like I felt in 1952—and Mingus said, "Follow Konitz." And I was more confused than I was originally, only now with seven guys on my ass. At least when I was playing it alone, I could fake it. But I'm good-natured. I appreciated it.

Faddis was late for the rehearsal; he was stuck in cross-town traffic in a cab. When he raced in, Mingus looked up and yelled, "You fucked up my rehearsal." He was really scared and explained and apologized all he could, under a withering glare.

After the sound-check at Philharmonic Hall on February 4, Mingus strolled back into the lush dressing room and announced everyone was fired. "You can take me to the union," he scowled. "Milt and me, we're gonna play this concert ourselves."

He was almost his old self. He was carrying around several pocketknives and a switchblade.

Nobody was fired, except the conductor. Macero thought Mingus was heading for total disaster, a reprise of Town Hall in 1962. "Why," he thought, "do you fire a conductor on the day of a concert?"

Macero volunteered to conduct.

That night, before the concert started, he was backstage wearing headphones. Mingus came in with his scores. None of them were bound, and they tumbled out of his arms all over the floor. As people scurried to gather up the pages, Mingus said to Macero, "I need an opening for the trumpet concerto. Can you write one?"

Macero had known Mingus for two decades. He grumbled, "God, Mingus, I've only got fifteen minutes." He wrote the intro. When Mingus insisted he had to rehearse it in the few minutes left before the concert started, Macero and comedian Bill Cosby, who was going to emcee the show, talked him out of it.

The show started almost on time, and the audience was full of younger people —a rare and welcome sign in jazz at this point. The book was crucial in bringing them out, the reputation he'd forged, the mythic Mingus, the manifold

Mingus, the unpredictable outbursting Mingus. Ammons's raw-boned tenor would get to them if nothing else did.

And it did, especially on the raucous, improvised "Mingus Blues."

That night, his big band filled the hall with a retrospective of Mingus music that ran hard on adrenaline even if it lacked the depth and variety of his classic outings. Often boisterous and spirited, the show certainly was laced with eloquent and fire-breathing solos. It was an Event, an announcement. He was back.

The program had its full-page ad for *Let My Children Hear Music*, heralding his first album in eight years.[6]

He had recreated the old Jazz at the Philharmonic in his own image, using his own history as the structure. He'd sold out the Hall, even if the music was sort of baggy and shapeless, nowhere as probing as his old Workshops.

Macero conducted the scores, and Cosby, a huge jazz fan and friend of Max Roach and Dizzy Gillespie, hosted, combining rambling intros and off-the-cuff remarks in his characteristic fashion. Dizzy himself, barely out of the hospital, did some weak scatting sheerly out of love and respect for one of his few surviving peers and friends. Randy Weston did a cameo, as did James Moody. Milt Hinton doubled Mingus on bass so he could solo.

Mingus was remembering Red Callender.

In the dressing room, Mingus carted Eric around on his shoulders like a trophy. He'd given the boy a shoeshine box, and Eric brought it, hoping to shine Bill Cosby's shoes: the comedian's character Fat Albert was his hero. Cosby showed up in suede, and Eric was crushed. He held onto the dressing room door and screamed even after his father hoisted him up.

The show was a sellout. *Down Beat*'s reviewer gave the thumbs-up, astonished at the age of the audience.[7]

Afterward, family and friends headed downtown to the Ninth Circle for an impromptu post mortem of "Charles Mingus and Friends." He looked up from his food long enough to drawl, "Too many friends."[8]

Lokin and Weiner immediately booked halls in Boston and Washington. Mingus played Friday night in Boston. Saturday morning, he and Weiner took the plane to Washington, D.C., where Lokin picked them up.

Sales in Boston were poor, and he apologized to them both about it. They were struck by that even more since he also lost money on it.

The Washington performance was at the Kennedy Center, so they went to the hotel. He told Lokin and Weiner the rubber boot on the end of his bass peg was worn out, and he needed a new one. It was Saturday, 5:00 P.M. Lokin and Weiner ran around to music stores, but the couple they found were either closed or didn't have it. Finally they took it to a shoemaker, who made a round rubber heel to fit.

When they got back to the hotel, Mingus grinned. They'd made big points. He'd wanted to see what they'd do.

Jeffrey, too, was surprised by Mingus's fairness in paying and supportiveness, since he'd heard so many stories about him. Mingus paid him three times union scale for his laborious copying effort. Columbia was footing the bill, anyway. And when they recorded the concert, Jeffrey was paid again. He became Mingus's copyist, then arranger, for much of the last period of his life.

PAUL JEFFREY: You know, Charles McPherson says something I think is true: Mingus made up his mind about a person right away. If he likes you, nothing can change that. But if he meets you and something happens he doesn't like, he wouldn't change his mind. I mean, I was scuffling. Mingus used to call me up and say, "Look man, I've got some music here, I'm thinking about doing something, come over to the house." He'd call all hours of the night: "Take a cab, I'll pay for it." But I'd get on the subway, because I lived in Staten Island. He was just extremely kind to me. When I was broke, he'd call me up: "Come and have dinner." And dinner with Mingus was DINNER. He had an appetite, and always the Cuban cigars. I always had to tell him, "Mingus, I don't smoke." But I had to have these cigars and Benedictine brandy.

Not among Mingus's first-rank recorded works, the Philharmonic Hall concert did effectively mark his full return to his music. For it was after the show that he finally shook mellaril, and his fogginess lifted, and his hydra-headed personality reasserted itself.

It was around this time that Dizzy Gillespie told Janet Coleman: "Mingus is a super bebopper.... I think one of his main contributions is administration of the music, of putting it together. He reminds me of a young Duke. As a matter of fact, his music sounds like Duke Ellington. I think that's the main thing: his organizational genius."[9]

After Philharmonic Hall and its outpouring of attention, he led the huge outfit with the seven-man sax section into the Village Vanguard, to replace Thad Jones's big band as a Monday night fixture there into May. It was like rehearsing after the show. The big band got more aggressive and tighter, and the soloists felt more at home in the panoramic music. He brought out "Strollin'" for them that April—the last time he'd play it.

Mingus too was coming out of himself more, which was a mixed blessing to some of his sidemen. But to the crowds who lined up outside the Vanguard's Seventh Avenue South door, heavily leavened with younger faces that weren't seen at most other jazz shows, Mingus was a legend on a comeback.

The steady flow of live work, as it had always done, prompted him to write more.

Paul Jeffrey found himself heading toward Mingus's 5th Street dump almost daily to pick up works in progress. The Boss was working on a lot of different music for the first time in years. He handed Jeffrey "Little Royal Suite," with its chewy chord clusters, to copy. He was finishing a piece called "Number 29" that never got recorded, and fleshing out another autobiographical piece, "Taurus in the Arena of Life."

Astrology, constantly floating near and through twentieth-century Bohemian worlds, had made a big impact on the 1960s countercultures. Mingus himself believed in an almost animist universe, where power, invisible and not, exerted pulls, directed forces, moved mountains.

Taurus is the Bull, determined, fixated, driven, yet charming in order to get his way. The astrological sign fit. He shared it with Duke Ellington and Mary Lou Williams.

Jeffrey copied music day by day, and on the Village Vanguard bandstand Mingus handed it out week after week for his big music machine to sight-read. He called Hale Smith to conduct the band; Smith came down with a two-foot-long baton and his ever-present cigar. The first Monday, the band ran out of music before the first set was up, and ground to a halt. The packed club emptied out. Smith cornered Mingus, and insisted the band had to rehearse the music.

"Fine," said Mingus. "Let 'em come in before the show." So every Monday night before their sets, the band spent hours onstage wrestling with new charts.

The next week, the line of eager young Mingus fans ringed the Vanguard's block. He was outdrawing Thad Jones.

Money was coming in. Mingus was wearing his funny shirts and pants with the special pockets again.

In January, he got a $3,700 check from the Guggenheim Foundation. By June, he had more than one bank account; one at the Bank of Commerce had over $15,000 in it.[10] He was working steadily on college campuses and a mix of clubs and concert halls. He was recording for a big label again, and reaping the financial rewards of their promotional and marketing power, even in an era that was minimizing or ignoring acoustic jazz.

Jazz-rock fusion was inevitable, given the artistic convergences of the postwar era that culminated in the 1960s. As rockers pushed at improvisation and jazzers took up electric instruments and more contemporary backbeats, Miles Davis came to the forefront of fusion's popularizers.

He hardly invented the idea. Jimi Hendrix, the Grateful Dead, and others like them developed the free-form jam into a rocker's vocabulary. Blues bands like Paul Butterfield's and the Blues Project stretched and prodded the formats into jazzy shapes; Butterfield recorded Nat Adderley's "Work Song," and soloed on harmonica.

Miles Davis loved Jimi Hendrix and wanted to record with him. He loved the aggressive black edge, the wash of hyperspace sounds and wah-wahs and globular atmospherics and sheer beautiful certainty. Alan Douglas, one of United Artists' men who'd been involved in Mingus's Town Hall 1962 fiasco, was trying to put the duo together.

Davis would increasingly incorporate touches of Hendrix, Sly and the Family Stone, and other crossover black rockers into his fusion vocabulary. His fan base at the Bill Graham's Fillmore rock palaces soared. In his wake, and via his metamorphosing bands, came the Fusion Era, almost as gloomy for many older jazzers as the post-British Invasion days.

But not for Mingus—at least not now. He was making money. He was coming back.

The country around him was groping toward reaction to the 1950s and 1960s, some sort of closure or cease-fire or counteroffensive. Much of pop culture became more conservative and commercial. Party-downs replaced politics as the 1970s wore on into the disco era.

Mingus was feeling the Zeitgeist again. He would reorient himself and his life's work. He'd spent a lot of thinking on death and immortality during the last few years. He wanted his artistic legacy bulletproofed. His liner notes for *Let My Children Hear Music* and writings elsewhere made that clear. He wanted his role in history nailed down.

He was bourgeois as well as bohemian. He never resolved the division. He didn't have to. It was a source of his energy, his power, his self-ness.

Mingus and Davis were going in different directions. Mingus craved legitimate acceptance; he wanted the people with degrees and power conferring greater authority on him and his art.

That spring, a competition was held at the Whitney Museum, part of a series, and he decided to enter it by setting a Frank O'Hara poem to a string quartet with vocalist.

Mingus called Paul Jeffrey and told him to bring a tape recorder to the apartment. Once Jeffrey arrived, Mingus sat down at the piano, and started playing and singing for hours. He sketched two versions of the gnarled, demanding music he asked Jeffrey to transcribe.

It took Jeffrey days to get it right. He raised the key up a fourth from the tape; the singer was a mezzo-soprano, unlike Mingus. There were some scuffles, but the rehearsal went well. Mingus invited David Amram and a few pals to come to the performance. Amram showed up, and loved the piece; the jazz musicians didn't bother to make it.

Jimmy Giuffre, whose "Swamp Jazz" he'd replaced at the Village Vanguard years before, was also in the competition. He came in and led a jam session, and won first prize. Mingus was beside himself with rage.

He was becoming his old self again.

Thanks to Sue, he picked up the pace.

In March, he did a solo performance-lecture at Rutgers for $300. That May, he played at the University of Hartford, where Jackie McLean was now working. He brought up his standing group of the period—Bobby Jones, Charles McPherson, Lonnie Hillyer, Roy Brooks. They were paid $1,500. In June, he taped comments for a Duke Ellington tribute the Educational Broadcasting Company, a forerunner of PBS, was putting together, and was paid $141.90.[11]

He worked at the Mercer Arts Center in late June and early July, breaking only for two Newport in New York Festival gigs. The Newport Festival had relocated to New York, and producer George Wein booked big halls around town, including Radio City Music Hall and Carnegie Hall and Philharmonic Hall. Wein planned to present several days of concentrated all-star jazz and related sounds from rhythn and blues, like Ray Charles. He hoped it would appeal to New York's rush of tourists and conventioneers as well as fans.

Wein planned to premier Ornette Coleman's *Skies of America*. Coleman called it a symphony and recorded it for RCA. Mingus led a twenty-four-piece band that reprised pieces of *Tijuana Moods*. New Audiences stage-managed the gig at Philharmonic Hall.

It was a financial disaster. Wein later said, "I should have thrown the money up a creek." Jazz's foremost impresario, whose own tastes were fashioned in the pre-bop era, was struggling to find combinations to appeal to hard-core fans and critics as well as to create events to lure new ticket buyers. He was trying to bridge the music's schizophrenic nature: jazz as art music versus jazz as popular music. As jazz became a niche market, the tensions between traditionalists and emerging fusioneers accelerated the breakdown of the jazz audience into ever-smaller, often mutually exclusive and even antagonistic stylistic schools.

Mingus also played two Newport in New York jam sessions at Radio City, with Cat Anderson, Charles McPherson, Jimmy Owens, and others. One was recorded by a fan and released as a bootleg. The session with ex-Ellingtonian trumpeter Anderson burned, fired up by the squealing high notes on "Lo-Slo-Bluze." The jams were benefits, held at midnight, and the Urban League got 50 percent of the gate. Mingus was paid $150. [12]

His new accountant, Gwendolyn Jackson, was trying to straighten out his income taxes from 1969 through 1971. [13]

A week later, Mingus was in Chicago with McPherson, Bobby Jones, drummer Roy Brooks, pianist John Foster, and young Faddis, who'd answered Mingus's call for summertime work. Mingus was staying at the Croyden Hotel and becoming more and more himself.

He got a telegram from Sue: "As you say don't do anything you wouldn't do. The phone is out of order but I wasn't." [14] They were fighting again. He needed her in the center of his life. She was handling his business, but he still wasn't living with her. He was consumed by jealous fits, and so was she, though she tried to stay calmer.

He spent a lot of time at her Avenue B apartment, but it felt like they kept circling around living together. Something had to give.

Faddis liked and admired Mingus, and the older man, knowing his friend Dizzy Gillespie's connection to the young trumpeter, kept a pleasant attitude on for him. He liked Faddis's bad-pun sense of humor; it reminded him of part of himself. "Young Faddis, tell me a joke," he'd say.

JON FADDIS, *musician*: For me, he was always pushing the limits. He'd write stuff from the bottom to the top of the horn, and say, "Is that possible to do?" And I'd say, "Yeah, it's possible, but I don't know if I can do it." Then we practiced it, and somehow it would get done, because that's what he was hearing at the time.

Following the Chicago stint, Sue had lined up dates across Europe, following the festival circuit and ending up at London's jazz mecca, Ronnie Scott's, where he had always drawn well.

Sue came along, with her daughter Susanna. Mingus's son Eugene, now twenty-five and known as Sonny, was road manager. Faddis thought, "How interracial can you get?"

Their concert in Milan was a rocky start. When they came onstage, they looked out over a sea of microphones, and Mingus, recalling his earlier incidents with tapers, refused to play. There was almost a riot. The promoter accused him of not really wanting to play, and he shrugged and said, "Man, you're crazy." That hiked the promoter's blood pressure; he thought Mingus meant all Italians were crazy.

Mingus simply turned and walked off stage. Later that night, he wrote a cunning, punning piece called "A Mind Readers' Convention in Milano."

Roy Brooks, his drummer while Richmond played the rock circuit for two years, doubled on musical saw. He bent it and played on it with mallets, making a keening tone that came out of old-timey blues and hoedowns. Audiences loved it.

This 1972 tour marked Mingus's real reemergence. He was all over the bass, playing with an edge he'd lacked for years. He took charge of the band onstage, cued them verbally, forced them away from the sheet music. Onstage and off, he let loose impromptu blasts about politics and music and racism, all his hobbyhorses. And he was carrying a small briefcase of pills.

At the festival in Nice on July 20, Gillespie sat in, scatsinging some blues and soloing.

CHARLES MINGUS: I was some distance away, and his back was turned. I was looking at him, thinking how important he was and how I hoped he'd live forever. Suddenly Dizzy turned around and said, "Where's all this love coming from?" He looked at me. "You really do love me, don't you?" I felt like I was in heaven.[15]

At the Chateauvallon jazz festival, they ran into Max Roach and his M'Boom, a unusual collection of percussionists. The volatile drummer nearly smashed Mingus with a drum stool because he was talking to the press about how he'd started Debut, been the first to do this or that. Roach thought of jazz as a collective historical effort, a kind of Baconian scientific pursuit. Ming wanted too much individual credit for the group historical enterprise.

Gillespie pried them apart.

Mingus was fighting with Sue about living together full time. He was pushing his sidemen in ways the newer guys, like Foster and Jones, had never experienced.

He was almost his old self.

By the time they got to London in mid-August, he was wired up pretty tight. Sue had left with Susanna. Bobby Jones was feeling cornered; Mingus had grabbed his mouthpiece away on a couple of occasions.

Ronnie Scott's, named for the erstwhile British jazz fan who owned it, was England's Village Vanguard. Mingus felt at home there. He liked London. He had himself ferried around town in a Daimler limousine, taking young Faddis with him one night to Omar Khayiam's, a high-class belly-dance venue with women so beautiful the teenager's eyes bugged.

He was hanging out a bit with the band, and even bought them gifts.

In London, Jones erupted. He was drinking heavily, and one night he walked off stage and tripped on his way to the dressing room, hurting his leg. Faddis was behind him; no one else was there. A couple of days later, they read in the papers that Jones accused Mingus of pushing him down a flight of stairs.

There was an inevitable shouting match, and Jones called him a nigger.

The tour got extended to Eastern Europe and Scandinavia, and the band started to dissolve. Jones wanted out. McPherson wanted to get back to Los Angeles. Faddis's father wanted him to start his studies at Manhattan School of Music.

Mingus told Faddis his band was the best college he could go to. Faddis shrugged. Two months later, he dropped out of school and went back on the road, this time with Dizzy Gillespie.

When Mingus came back in September for the tour break, he transacted a flurry of business. He deposited nearly $3,700 worth of guilders, French francs, and Belgian and Danish currency. Two weeks later, he withdrew $10,000.[16]

He moved into Sue's new apartment, on the fourth floor at 39 East 10th Street, a huge, rambling space.

Sue hosted endless dinners that were part social, part editorial conference, with a whirlwind of up-and-coming and established writers. One wing of the apartment housed *Changes'* editorial staff, and there were always five or six or seven people floating around, and more dropping in.

SUSAN GRAHAM UNGARO MINGUS: He participated in my career, but I don't know that I would say he was supportive of it, or even interested in it, particularly. My career was very much a part of our home life, because I had dinners all the time, and he sat at the head of the table, enjoyed himself, and put up with us. But I don't think of him as being particularly supportive or entering into my publishing world at all. He had his music world.

Mingus was no women's libber. He and Sue coexisted in separate, overlapping spheres of influence. *Changes* published for seven years and put out a number of things he wrote. One was "Open Letter to the Avant-Garde," which was published in June 1973.

He reiterated, in rawer form, the points he had made about discipline in the liner notes to *Let My Children Hear Music*. He said he'd like to hear Cecil Taylor play "Lush Life." Taylor was one of the Black Power jazzmen, and gay besides. Mingus was sure he, Duke Ellington, Clark Terry, and a few others were far more technically versed and farther out than any so-called avant-garde.

There was "Open Letter to John Ass Wilson," attacking the *Times'* reviewer's lukewarm notice for the Philharmonic Hall concert. Wilson had complained Mingus didn't solo, and Mingus retorted that he wrote the music. Wilson wrote reviews, but did he sell the paper at the newsstand too?

Mingus was reclaiming his spirit, his place in history. He was half a century old.

Buddha-like, he seemed calmer, more centered, more himself but with less of an edge. He'd gotten what he wanted.

He saw less and less of his old friends—Britt Woodman, Buddy Collette, even Kate Mulholland, the whole Los Angeles gang. He hadn't seen Frank Mabry and he'd fought with Max Roach and Miles Davis. Thelonious Monk was living in New Jersey, in retirement; he'd withdrawn into silence.

Mingus's life became entwined more with Sue's.

Over the next couple of years, there'd be periodic blowouts between the two of them, and he had his eruptions out in the world as well. He couldn't have another strong personality around without tangles. But he needed Sue's strength and direction to complement his own, to deal with his grievances and free his mind for his art.

Once, he pulled a pocket knife out on her, for what Janet Coleman calls "some imagined and Othelloesque betrayal." He backed her into a corner and said, "What was the name of the guy who stabbed his wife? The writer. It was in the paper, years ago." "Norman Mailer," she answered, eyes on the blade. "That's the one," he said, forgetting the quarrel, "the guy who sat in the back one time when I was playing the Half Note."[17]

The ten-room apartment had an upright piano, and he composed on that. He kept the East 5th Street place until 1977, though, and the grand piano at its core.

On October 6, he was one of nearly forty major jazz figures, including Dizzy Gillespie, who were invested as Duke Ellington Fellows at Yale University. Professor Willie Ruff was the ceremony's instigator. There was a huge jam session on "How High the Moon," which included several bassists and hornmen, including Faddis and Gillespie.

The Groves of Academe were opening to jazz. A year earlier, Max Roach had been named a professor at the University of Massachussetts at Amherst. Yusef Lateef would soon teach there as well. Jaki Byard had been teaching at the New England Conservatory. Mingus's friends and associates were beginning to infiltrate the white power structures of education, even if his school had never come to be.

Yale reimbursed him for $62 in travel expenses for the weekend.[18]

He had to collect a new band for the rest of his European tour, and he kept thinking about updating Harry Carney's baritone sound, the deep-toned Ellingtonian mix he'd always loved. A young baritone man recommended by Paul Jeffrey, Hamiet Bluiett, came down to the club and got the nod, along with trumpeter Joe Gardiner. And Cat Anderson, Ellington's last high-note trumpeter, took a break from his intense schedule of studio work to hit the road.

Bluiett doubled on clarinet, and could do the raucous, old-timey pieces Mingus always loved to play with loving parody, as living history tableaux. An avant-gardist with leanings toward blues and free form, Bluiett also felt the exuberant pull of traditional jazz from early New Orleans, like other free-jazz artists.

Mingus was their avatar, overtly straddling jazz history from before Duke to after himself.

In two weeks, the band crisscrossed the continent. In Berlin and Warsaw, fans sneaked in microphones and taped portions of the shows. Anderson wailed with Brooks on the wonderfully relaxed "Blues for Roy's Saw." Mingus was reaching deliberately into the past. Young fusioneers like Mahavishnu Orchestra and Weather Report were packing houses across Europe.

Sue cabled him at the Carlton Hotel in Sweden, and he printed, in careful capital letters on the back, "WHY WERE YOU RUSHING ME OFF THE PHONE AND WHAT MALE VOICE KEPT ECHOING, WHILE I TALKED TO YOU."

By the time he reached Oslo's Hotel Continental, she lined up a date with Atlantic Records with a good payday—$5,000 for him alone.[19]

He was back in the big time, and the black. He was closing some of the circles in his life.

The liner notes for *Let My Children Hear Music* were nominated for a Grammy award. It was the only nomination he'd ever get, and it wasn't for his music. But the notes were pure Mingus. He poured out his soul in rigorous terms, simultaneously taking on the mantle of tradition and insisting on his own radical credentials.

CHARLES MINGUS: Each jazz musician...when he begins to ad lib on a given composition with a title and improvise a new creative melody, this man is taking the place of a composer....I, myself, came to enjoy the players who didn't only just swing but who invented new rhythmic patterns, along with new melodic concepts. And those people are Art Tatum, Bud Powell, Max Roach, Sonny Rollins, Lester Young, Dizzy Gillespie and Charles Parker, who is the greatest genius of all to me because he changed the whole era around. But there is no need to compare composers. If you like Beethoven, Bach or Brahms, that's okay. They were all pencil composers. I always wanted to be a spontaneous composer. I thought I was, although no one's mentioned that. I mean critics or musicians.[20]

He railed about over-long solos, noting that after a couple of choruses most jazzers lapsed into "repetition, riffs and patterns, instead of spontaneous creativity." To clinch his case, he lied: "I could never get Bird to play over two choruses."[21]

He complained, without naming it, about free jazz, where "everything is supposed to be invented, the guys never repeat anything at all and probably couldn't." He scoffed that "there can be originality in stupidity." Emotional outpourings weren't enough; discipline and structure counted. It was the same argument he'd had with Timothy Leary and the boppers and so many others, including his oldest son. "I know and hear what they are doing. But the validity remains to be seen—what comes, what is left, after you hear the melody and after you hear the solo. Unless you just want to hear the feeling, as they say."[22]

Contemporary jazz's simplistic structures ignored bop's revolution, its insistence on jazz as high art. "It's as if people came to Manhattan and acted like it was still full of trees and grass and Indians instead of concrete and tall buildings," he gibed, adding, "What's worse is that critics take a guy who only plays in the key of C and call him a genius, when they should say those guys are a bitch in C-natural."[23]

He used his improvised bass solo on "Adagio Ma Non Troppo" to explicate how variations on a theme must remain integrated with the composition, griped that his command of the bass had never been appreciated, then added, "I have never struggled to be accepted as a great bassist—I imagine I could have been if I had seen my available musical goal there." He was more than an instrumental whiz. And there were lots of them in jazz, even though the critics and polls only allotted one top spot for each instrument.

CHARLES MINGUS: Had I been born in a different country or had I been born white, I am sure I would have expressed my ideas long ago. Maybe they wouldn't have been as good because when people are born free—I can't imagine it, but I've got a feeling that if it's so easy for you, the struggle and the initiative are not as strong as they are for a person who has to struggle and therefore has more to say.[24]

He gave Lloyd Reese credit for helping make him a composer, and told of watching him transcribe Stravinsky harmonies from a recording. When Mingus was growing up, classical music for white people dominated record stores, with a few hillbilly and rhythm and blues records. People didn't know what it took a black man, a jazz musician, to become his trained spontaneous self. His answer: classical music and the church choir. "I wasn't raised," he said, "in a night club. I wasn't raised in a whore house [sic]."[25]

He'd learned about harmonic movement and substitution from Art Tatum, but Bud Powell and Charlie Parker were composers. "Their solos are new classical compositions within the structured form they used. It is too bad for us that they didn't compose the whole piece instead of using other people's tunes to work within. . . . If they had, they would have been put in the same class as Bartok and Debussy—to anyone who knows."[26]

Mingus had done what they hadn't.

He told the story of Bird's improvising to a record of the "Berceuse" from Stravinsky's *Firebird Suite* over the phone.

CHARLES MINGUS: It gave me an idea about what is wrong with present-day symphonies: they don't have anything going on that captures what the symphony is itself, after its written. I'd like to write a symphony, myself, on this form —the old western form of classical music—I'd like to write a suite of three or four hours and have a solo in spots that is like Charlie Parker, with Bird in mind, playing ad lib.[27]

He urged jazzmen to think beyond their usual horns-and-rhythm-section lineups, to annex classical horns and reeds and strings. "If we so-called jazz musicians who are the composers, the spontaneous composers, started including these instruments in our music, it would open everything up, it would get rid of prejudice because the musicianship would be so high in caliber that the symphony couldn't refuse us."

Mingus was thinking of Buddy Collette and the Amalgamation. He'd said these things before, from the time he was a teenager. He reminded his readers that jazz musicians extended what instruments could do beyond the dreams of

European composers, and cited Louis Armstrong, Dizzy Gillespie, Tommy Dorsey, Britt Woodman, Jimmy Knepper. "Who," he asked with a flourish, "wants to be in a symphony anyway, nowadays?"

The notes ended, "Let my children have music! Let them hear live music. Not noise. My children! You do what you want with your own!"[29]

He would not be written out of history. With *Beneath the Underdog* and his liner notes and his letters and his pieces in *Changes*, he staked his own claims. He culminated some developments, originated others. He was summing up, taking his stand, claiming his role as elder statesman.

The liner notes were a remarkable verbal tour de force, a spontaneous, edited-in-the-studio performance that fulfilled the conditions he'd laid out for his music. They were unmistakably his voice, rich complexities and paradoxes and insights and ironies and contradictions and all. But they didn't win the Grammy.

Mingus and New Audiences planned a second concert—with only a sextet, but with Dizzy Gillespie as special guest. It was set for January 19, 1973, at Carnegie Hall. Roy Brooks suggested he hire a young pianist-organist with an avant-garde and rhythm-and-blues pedigree, and so Don Pullen came into the outfit. He stayed two years—longer than most Mingus keyboardists.

Max Gordon let them rehearse at the Village Vanguard one afternoon a week before the show. Bluiett didn't show up. He'd been feeling rubbed the wrong way by some of his bandmates and the Boss.

Mingus turned to Lokin and Weiner and said, "How much does it cost to cancel the show?" They were startled. "Well, I can't have a rehearsal if my band's not here, and if the band's not here, we can't have a show." Weiner gulped and said, "It'd cost around thirty or forty thousand dollars." Mingus nodded and said, "All right then, let's rehearse."

Bluiett showed up for the press conference that doubled as public rehearsal before the concert. Mingus made fun of him onstage, and then replaced him with Howard Johnson.

Mingus had lost weight. He was fairly engaged with the music, and the band had fun.

HOWARD JOHNSON: When Roy Brooks played the saw, he held it between his knees and hit it with a hammer. So he had to bend his knees, and he already had a big butt, right? I'd never seen anything like it before in concert. At the end, he had breaks, and he'd be rocking back and forth. It was such a crackup, Don Pullen asked me to move off the piano where I was leaning, so he could see it.

Gillespie came out and soloed on "Profiles of Dizzy," a new Mingus portrait based on Gillespie's riffs, and the sextet did revised versions of "Pithecanthropus Erectus" and "Fables of Faubus," now retitled "Fables of Nixon" with new lyrics.

In January 1973, Richard Nixon was about to be sworn in for his second term as president. In the November elections, he swamped his Democratic opponent, antiwar Senator George McGovern, who'd picked up Robert Kennedy's mantle and following.

Nixon's henchmen had tried to clinch an election no one thought could be lost. McGovern was widely seen as a fringe candidate. His running mate, Thomas Eagleton, was forced to quit the race when Nixon's reelection committee leaked word he'd had electro-shock treatments for depression.

The Committee to Re-elect the President, CREP, was widely called CREEP by those on Nixon's extensive "enemies list," compiled with the help of the FBI and the CIA and the IRS and other government agencies and wings. His lieutenants engineered a third-rate burglary on the Democratic party headquarters at the Watergate complex, and rifled and burgled files.

There were no lampoon candidacies like Dizzy Gillespie's or Pat Paulsen's this time out. Social dialog in America was shifting. Inflation and unemployment were building. The Vietnam War was dividing even its opponents.

This election was the overture to a slow-building national drama, the start of a long reaction to what the boppers and Beats and their heirs had unloosed. The pendulum was swinging back.

Mingus didn't like Nixon. He was still living in California in 1950 when Nixon had defeated Congresswoman Helen Gahagan Douglas for the Senate. He'd watched Nixon make his reputation at the House Un-American Activities Committee, seen him ride close behind Senator Joe McCarthy during the 1950s anticommunist hysteria. He knew the New Nixon was the shape of things to come, part of the new Zeitgeist.

Mingus and Roberto, Sue's son, got along great. He never tried to act like Roberto's father. Instead, they were friends. He liked the boy's stubborn independence, his love for hunting rabbits and squirrels and catching frogs and snakes. He wished his own boys were more like that. Only Eugene, who lived as a hustler on the edges of Los Angeles's show-biz whirl, had that sort of élan, but he was more street. Roberto was tough without the mean streak.

The pair loved Westerns and cop movies. They'd sit side by side, wearing T-shirts and rapt expressions and drinking wine and smoking cigars, while they watched them until two or three in the morning on the late-night movie reruns that filled pre-cable TV: *The Good, the Bad, the Ugly*; *The Magnificent Seven*; Clint Eastwood's spaghetti Westerns; pioneering Japanese movies like *Rashomon*, one of Mingus's favorites; *Omega Man*, an apocalyptic sci-fi thriller starring Charlton Heston; and a noirish allegorical tale of innocence stalked by evil and hypocrisy, *The Night of the Hunter*, starring Robert Mitchum, Shelley Winters, and Lillian Gish and directed by the eccentric, pudgy actor Charles Laughton.

And whenever Mingus was around for it, they'd tune in the weekly TV series *All in the Family*. Carroll O'Connor starred as Archie Bunker, a blue-collar bigot from Queens who used words like *nigger* and *kike* and *mick* and *wop*, who called his hippie son-in-law Meathead, who saw the world almost exclusively in reductive stereotypes. His creators said he was a parody. Many of his fans weren't so sure.

Mingus loved it. He was his father's son.

One night, he and Sue went out to dinner, and left the annoyed Roberto at home. They brought him back food, but he'd already eaten and pretended he hadn't and didn't want to. Mingus shrugged and said, "Well, you should study then." "No," sneered Roberto, "school should be burned." Mingus said, "Turn off the TV." When Roberto said no again, Mingus put his foot through the screen.

The boy knew he deserved it. He thought it was cool that this black sorta bohemian was so into cop shows.

CAROLYN (KEKI) MINGUS: Roberto and my father would take my brother and me to the horror movies. We'd be walking home from them in Woodstock—walking because my father didn't drive then. And they'd be scaring the hell out of us. I remember *Omega Man*, this Charlton Heston movie where everybody died, and I was scared for weeks and weeks.

Keki and Eric adored Roberto and often hung out with him, first on East 10th Street, then at the place Sue had bought in Woodstock, the longtime artist colony ninety miles north of New York. The nine-room house on Witchtree Road needed insulation and wallboards and finished flooring, but it was cheap and big and had a huge fireplace and thirteen acres of rolling woodland, so the nearest neighbor was a quarter-mile away. The hamlet was almost two miles down the road.

It reminded Mingus of Mill Valley, his refuge in Northern California.

The house never got cluttered, but Mingus and Sue lined it with thousands of books and records. The grand piano dominated the living room's country furnishings. Their bedroom boasted a low-slung Japanese bed. All around were gourds and stringed and percussion instruments from around the globe, especially Africa and South America.

Mingus had been interested in music from all over the planet since he first met Farwell Taylor, nearly forty years earlier. He'd been a consistently original and wide-ranging annexer to jazz, expanding its vocabulary with sounds from elsewhere. And the walls bore witness to his history.

Judy moved with the children to Rosendale, just down the Hudson Valley from Woodstock. Mingus gave her $20,000; she used some of it for a down payment on a house. The kids gathered at Witchtree Road for holidays and weekends, and then summer visits. He showered presents on them while they were around, and Roberto felt a bit jealous. Sue hired Judy's new husband, a ponytailed carpenter artist, to finish off the house and do odd jobs.

CAROLYN (KEKI) MINGUS: My mother would have to call him to get child support, and they'd yell, and he'd still tell her, I could hear that he was saying, "I love you." My stepfather would hear my mother saying, "I still care about you too, Charles, I love you too." It was a little tense.

Eric had learned to play cello at P.S. 198 in Manhattan and wanted to continue after he moved upstate, so Judy got a teacher. His dad was thrilled. Hadn't he played cello at the same age? He decided to buy his son a cello. So he sent the boy a round-trip ticket on a two-prop plane out of Kingston airport and met him at LaGuardia.

They went to a music store where the upstairs area was nothing but cellos. They were behind the service counter, so Mingus said, "If you don't mind, I'm going to look at them." The salesman retorted, "These are very expensive instruments." Eric thought, "What's wrong with these guys?"

ERIC MINGUS, son: He started looking them over, and plucking the strings. And these guys are looking at him like, "Yeah, right." Then he started playing one. It was very strange. You should have seen their mouths open: "Whoaaa, man." Then he bought it.

Spending a day with him was like a week, and spending a week was like a month, a year. A month was eternity. It wasn't boring.

The sax chair in Mingus's band rotated, and among those who sat there was John Stubblefield, an old pal of Don Pullen. Stubblefield fit Mingus's bill: someone fluent in bebop, rhythm and blues, Latin, and free jazz. The brawny young tenor played with the group long enough to have Mingus bully him on a plane ride. He told Mingus he'd take him out if he didn't stop. Mingus calmed down and grinned and said, "I'm just messing with you, man."

He had to have somebody in the band to pick on.

By the time Mingus led the band into the Village Gate in March, he'd found the sax voice and personality he needed. George Adams combined blues roots with hyperexpressive screams and squalls, and he could sing, in a gravelly authentic rasp. The saxman was big and bluff, and immediately locked in with pianist Don Pullen to create textures that could go from church to free jazz.

They could give Mingus plenty to think about.

Mingus was closing circles from his life, finishing out themes.

The Half Note had reopened on West 54th Street and he did a couple of weeks there. One payroll night, he pulled a hundred-dollar bill out of one of the pockets of his jumpsuit, and gave it to the cabbie; it was the smallest he had. The cab driver gave him change for a ten. He exploded. The cabbie tried to drive off, and he clung to the car. When the cops came, he told them what happened.

They looked at him and grinned, "What the fuck are you doing with a hundred-dollar bill?" They carted him downtown, and forgot to give him his legal phone call. Nobody knew where he was for hours. He didn't show up at the club.

The next morning, he was arraigned. He told his story, and the judge asked him where he got a hundred-dollar bill. He started unzipping pockets and pulling out wads of money, all hundred-dollar bills. There was a long silence in the courtroom. The judge picked up his gavel and dismissed the case. Mingus got back his belongings, including the switchblade he carried all the time now.

The Terminis had punningly renamed the Five Spot Two Saints, inspired by the address at 2 Saint Mark's Place. This had been a center of psychedelia. Warhol's Exploding Plastic Inevitable and his rock band, the Velvet Underground, had spawned the Electric Circus, ultimate hip psychedelic club, down the block.

After six years, the two saints of jazz had decided to reopen part time to the music they loved, for the people they loved. And they loved Mingus.

He canceled the rest of his summertime gig at the Village Vanguard to reopen his old haunt with sets of mostly Mingus classics. Adams and Pullen starting his mind going, but he was focused on his legacy. He was coming back from the dead. He knew now what that meant.

Lonnie Hillyer had rejoined him. John Handy was in New York and sat in with him. Mingus kept telling the musicians, "If only my drummer came back." He meant Dannie Richmond.

By 1974 Mingus switched record labels again, from Columbia back to Atlantic, the home of his first big hits, storehouse of many of his finest recorded moments. Atlantic wanted to announce his return by putting out a two-record set of selected cuts from those glory days. It was a popular format for repackaging out-of-print material, priced relatively cheaply to lure new fans. In the 1970s, Fantasy Records would outdo everyone in the field with a torrent of such "twofers."

Mingus wanted more money for the reissue, and Sue was tenacious about getting better royalty rates than the original years-old contracts offered. The album would be called *The Art of Charles Mingus*.

At Two Saints, *Times* critic John Wilson described his performance: "Mingus is more like a mother hen these days, placidly plucking his bass, supporting soloists."[30]

Two months later, *Village Voice* reviewer Victor Stein caught the band, this time with trumpeter Ron Hampton, and wrote, "Mingus seemed to be controlling the music to some extent by projecting thought waves to the other musicians. (No, I'm not crazy.)"[31]

Mingus rode the new and growing circuit of colleges and jazz festivals relentlessly. George Wein's Newport Jazz festivals had proliferated across America and Europe; eventually he'd operate nearly two dozen. And the college kids loved Mingus music, its gutsy immediacy and melodic yearning, and they knew something about his reputation.

Sometimes he lived up to it, and sometimes he didn't. He had his satchel full of pills, as did Roy Brooks, which made unpredictability inevitable. Sometimes the pills calmed him down to a placid grin. Sometimes they wired him up like a Christmas tree.

When they played at the Boston Jazz Workshop, he had to be led on and off the stage.

That Christmas 1973 season, when the band appeared at the Village Vanguard, they had an unexpected visitor.

A pianist pal told Dannie Richmond about Mingus's gig, and Dannie decided to show up. He went down the familiar narrow stairs and turned left to go to the dressing room, which doubled as a kitchen where Max Gordon rustled up burgers. At the doorway, he met Mingus, who shouted, "I had a dream last night my drummer was coming back, and here he is."

He liked to go to Woodstock to compose. It reminded him of Mill Valley. All that fall and Christmas, his children gathered there. As usual, Roberto went hunting for rabbits and squirrels. He'd taught Eric to shoot, so the boys happily disappeared for hours.

Mingus wasn't interested in tramping through the woods, but he'd get involved when they brought something back, and he'd spot Roberto cleaning the catch in the kitchen sink. He liked to cook what they had, especially if it was rabbit or grouse. He was a gourmet cook as well as a gourmet diner.

He gave the kids each a hundred dollar bill for Christmas but didn't get anything for Sue. She got upset, so he went into town and bought her an entire kitchen plus washer and dryer.

Sue was the domestic center of his orbit now, home base. He had slowed his infidelities way down. But sometimes he still, Keki felt, treated her like a slut. He had to do that to all his women.

Mingus was always telling Keki that he was stupid, that he had no education, although the kids could sense his incredible quick intelligence, his breadth of subjects, his apparent command of facts and arguments in monologues that echoed Farwell Taylor's or Philip Wylie's.

Education, he thought, gave you armor against the world. It was self-protection. Over and over, he insisted they read Rudyard Kipling. He wanted them to understand imperialism and racism at the root.

Dannie Richmond recorded with the band after Christmas, on their first new album for Atlantic.

Mingus Moves had new material, but lacked spirit. Richmond claimed he had had only two days to learn the music, but Mingus himself sounds dulled, plays out of tune.

He was too self-conscious. He was reiterating some of his 1950s ideas about classical music and jazz, using some of the music from then. It didn't always meld into more than pastiche, and the performances seem unfocused.

Titles like "Opus 4" were complex without his characteristic drive. "Opus 3" put a new melody to "Pithecanthropus Erectus" with less fire. The band sounded better on Pullen's pieces, like the clave-beat "Big Alice." And Hampton just wasn't cutting it on trumpet.

Mingus needed something else.

He was going to perform at Carnegie Hall again, on January 19, 1974. He sketched out the ideas to Sue. They'd record live, when the nervous energy feeding back from the audience was on max. It would be a different take on his post-comeback concept. He wanted a complete spread of saxophones, from so-prano to baritone, and he wanted to include Ellington tributes. The saxists should come from different periods, different bands he led.

It would be his personal history, a roundup of firepower to rival the old Jazz at the Philharmonic showstoppers.

Sue started lining up guests to augment the band. He was wrapping him-self in his rightful mantle. He was reinventing himself, using his own past, one more time.

He was closing circles everywhere.

14 Changes

ON JANUARY 19, 1974, Charles Mingus led his third large-scale concert at a class-A concert hall in as many years. New York had been his home for nearly twenty-five years, and finally some dreams he'd come with were being realized.

He was reinventing himself yet again, as a different kind of composer, one suited for the concert hall opportunities that were slowly opening in jazz. His legends loomed larger, and the thought of his musical legacy was never far from him. He was operating more from written-down scores than he had since the early 1950s, but his music was hard to write down, hard to play from what was written, and he had always been its animating spirit, onstage, in the moment. What would happen when his spirit had left?

What happened to Monk's music during the long silence and retirement he began in 1972? It had withered from view.

Mingus felt he'd had another resurrection, like the one he'd had at Farwell Taylor's when he was seventeen.

He was Charles Mingus. He had to keep pushing. He was driven.

Mingus followed his recent tradition of warming up at the Village Vanguard for the big show to follow. Roland Kirk, Charles McPherson, George Adams, Hamiet Bluiett, Jon Faddis, Don Pullen, and Dannie Richmond made an octet. His newest self-referring version of the old Jazz at the Philharmonic was billed as "An Evening with Charles Mingus and Old Friends," and sold out, with tickets ranging from $4.50 to $6.50.[1]

On January 19, they hit Carnegie Hall. For the first half, he led his quintet. Then the guests joined in for long solos on "Perdido" and Ellington's "C Jam Blues," and a free-jazz blowout.

Four days later, John S. Wilson cut the concert dead in the *New York Times*.[2]

Late in February, Mingus showed up with a band at Max's Kansas City, sharing the bill for the weekend with Manhattan Transfer. They were a white vocal quartet in the mode of Lambert Hendricks & Ross, an integrated bop vocal trio that in the 1950s had penned lyrics to bop classics, scatting solo lines a la Ella Fitzgerald and Sarah Vaughan.

He was feeling the Zeitgeist again.

Max's Kansas City was owned by Mickey Ruskin, who had sold his share of the Ninth Circle in the late 1960s. Contractually prohibited from opening a new place in the Village, he found an old coffee shop on Park Avenue South and East 17th Street, just off Union Square, where hip photographers and artists like Andy Warhol had moved into the huge, vacant old manufacturing lofts lining the neighborhood. When the original Cedar Tavern closed, the clientele headed across the Square to Max's, and another cultural crossroads was born.

Most of the bohemian crowd thronging the place didn't have much money, and almost all of them knew Mickey well enough to run a tab.

In 1972, Ruskin had started the music policy in the club's upstairs room to draw a paying crowd. It was a huge success. The venue's stage was wide open stylistically, and the bookings included early New York dates by punk stars like Patti Smith and Blondie, by rock superstar Bruce Springsteen, by a troop of garage bands that helped spawn the 1970s punk/New Wave regeneration of rock.

Mingus told Dannie Richmond he was sad. He was tired of other people getting the credit for things he did. When they listened to the radio Mingus would shrug or grimace and say, "Oh, I did that," and name a date, a time, and the sidemen.[3]

The night of his fifty-second birthday, they did a concert that included "Fables of Nixon," "Goodbye Porkpie Hat," "Celia," and "Peggy's Blue Skylight" in Toronto and got a rave review that underscored how he'd bridged postwar jazz history.

On February 4, 1974, Patty Hearst, heiress to the Hearst newspaper fortune, was captured by a self-proclaimed revolutionary group called the Symbionese Liberation Army. That April, the SLA released a tape on which she announced that she'd joined them, then she participated in an SLA bank robbery in San Francisco.

Patty Hearst changed her name to Tania, and the country was rife with speculation. Was she brainwashed? Or had she crossed the radical-chic line from vicarious thrill to real-life fantasy?

On May 24, 1974, Duke Ellington died. He'd been sick with lung cancer but stayed on the road till three months before the end, when he checked into Columbia Presbyterian Hospital. The funeral home stayed open around the clock; 65,000 people trooped through. On Memorial Day, the body lay in state at the Cathedral of St. John the Divine. Inside were 10,000 people; the cops held 2,500 more outside.

The officiating ministers included Duke's old friend Father Norman O'Connor. There were musical tributes by Ella Fitzgerald and others, including Charles Mingus.

That spring, Mingus returned to the Village Gate, where he debuted "Sue's Changes." The piece is complex and multisectioned. Its gently yearning opening melody unwinds on muted trumpet and sax, followed by a series of shifts in tempo that finish up-tempo and perky, with a sprightly turnaround that opens into raucous overlapping riffs. Don Pullen's piano solo starts at a slower pace that returns the piece to its initial contemplative setting, then builds brightly through the rest with splashy dissonant chords and percussive slams. George Adams's sax followed, launched softly with trills and darting lines, by the end riding rhythm and blues squalls through Pullen's piano waves.

Mingus explained, "It's about how changeable her moods are."[4]

One late afternoon around this time, Mingus took Sue to the Top of the Mark, a famous bar that rotated as it overlooked San Francisco. He had developed a liking for the Ramos fizz, a rum-based drink that was a complicated recipe bartenders hated.

Mingus ordered a Ramos fizz, and the bartender said, "We only make them in quantity." Mingus asked how many. The bartender's eyes narrowed. "Twenty-two," he said. Mingus ordered twenty-four.

SUE MINGUS: He drank all of them. We sat there for hours. I remember not knowing whether the room was moving, or I was moving, or the skyline was moving.

Mingus was tired a lot. The road was hard. He had all his music written out, and spread it out across three music stands, and he'd play his way through them. He rarely soloed, but the European crowds didn't seem to care. They just wanted to see Charles Mingus.

He played Ravenna on July 27, 1974, where the band premiered "Remember Rockefeller at Attica."

It was another of his political signs-of-the-times. Nelson Rockefeller, longtime governor of New York and a leader of the liberal Republican party wing, had ordered Attica Prison stormed by National Guardsmen when the overwhelming numbers of black prisoners rioted and took guards hostage. The resulting pitched battle ended in forty-three deaths.

What could be more natural and inevitable than Mingus commenting on it with a title, his music? Even if the music itself was almost breezy, its long-limbed melody sporting the kind of humor that marked "Fables of Faubus"?

The band moved on to Eastern Europe. In Yugoslavia, when they played "Fables of Faubus" and "Remember Rockefeller at Attica," an attache from the U.S. embassy came running to the stage. He told the band they shouldn't play songs that reflected poorly on America.

CHARLES MINGUS: I told him, "You know, man, we're from a free country. We're supposed to show people over here how great our country is by telling them we're able to talk about the wrongs and the rights of our country, whereas they're not allowed to." He wasn't nasty, but he sounded like he forgot he was from America.[5]

It was no accident Mingus joined demonstrations as they wove through New York streets.

One night that summer, Janet Coleman was visiting the East 10th Street apartment.[6] Mingus was talkative. "Most of the classical soloists," he began, "they live good, they ride around in Rolls Royces. Most of 'em marry very wealthy women. Or have a sponsor."

Mingus complained about jazz's would-be patrons. The society types hired jazz musicians only for parties; they didn't help in any sustained way. He shifted gears to Bird, inevitably, with the grace of a solo in full unfolding. The Baronness Nica's patronage, he pointed out, was basically money for Bird's drug habit. Why, he asked, didn't she build him a nightclub to play in?

Bird, he said, was self-educated and could talk about anything from isotopes to frontal lobotomies, and was very religious, a mystic, like himself.

Coleman and Mingus listened to his 1964 Monterey album. He complained his bass solo was sharp and that the flute parts were out of tune. He loved Buddy Collette's work, and Byard's yelling, "Chazz!"

Many of his closest musical associates were dead, or on the road, or living abroad, or still in Los Angeles. His older friends were disappearing out of his life, now that Sue had taken charge as he seemed to want. The process didn't appear malevolent. It was more like inevitable. She'd make way when old Watts pals like Buddy Collette or Britt Woodman visited, but others felt uncomfortable, even if they couldn't put their fingers on exactly why.

Mingus was starting to make real money again, more than he'd ever made. Income was growing from his publishing rights.

SY JOHNSON: He was a businessman too. He kept his own publishing, and had pride in being able to provide for his family, to take care of his needs. He spent a lot of money but he made a lot of money, and he made sure there weren't too many deals where anybody got the best of him.

Outside the apartment, Mingus wore his special zippered shirts and jumpsuits and jackets, sometimes carrying thousands of dollars along with his knives. He had shirts that had pockets hidden beneath his fat upper arms. He got paid in cash whenever he could and paid for everything in cash. He didn't trust banks. They didn't do their jobs right.

Besides, he never knew what he'd want to eat, or when, or where.

Now one of his regular companions was an artist and political satirist named J. C. Suares. They'd met in 1969, but only drew closer once Mingus felt settled with Sue.

With J. C. he could really eat. Suares was rotund, and a gourmet—quality and quantity. They shared a passion for fine Cuban cigars. And they talked trash about women.

Suares was smart and savvy, the perfect hedonistic co-conspirator. He turned Mingus, who was smoking cheaper Grenadiers, on to fine and costly Cuban cigars, banned from the United States because of a long-standing anti-Castro boycott, one legacy of John F. Kennedy's Bay of Pigs and October 1962 missile crisis. J. C. carried a big switchblade he'd bought in Paris to cut cigar tips with.

Mingus loved cigars. Naturally, he had to get an expensive humidor to store them properly, and experimented with flavoring them. Then he had to get lots more. So that spring, he went to the French side of the island of St. Martin's in the Caribbean. Fantasy had a condominium there, so he called Celia and Saul Zaentz, who let company artists and employees use it regularly, and asked for time there.

He went down once with Suares.

J. C. SUARES: We only went down there because he'd heard we could get Cuban cigars. Somebody said, "When you're down here, you really should get some sun. Get in a bathing suit"—because we were just walking around in our clothes, smoking cigars in this tropical paradise. So in response, we took our shoes off and went to the kiddie pool, where the water went up to our ankles, and stood there for four hours. We're smoking cigars, talking about food and cigars and what's for dinner. And the babies are wading around us in this pool, trying to figure out what the hell is going on.

Mingus developed a plan.

The next time he came down with Eric and Keki and Sue and her children, he scouted for Cuban cigars. Sue got fed up and packed Roberto and Susanna back to New York. Mingus blew money on bribes and found them, and snapped up boxes of them. The kids spent hours changing labels from Cohiba and Montecristo, two of Cuba's best, to Te Amo, a cheap brand. He'd had a special overcoat made for Eric with secret pockets like his dad's—enough to hold four or five boxes of cigars. He had special sweaters for Keki and lined her underwear with them. Her suitcase was full of them. She was the girl; Customs wouldn't look there.

The kids thought they reeked, but they sailed through Customs without a notice. And he walked through with them, puffing on one of his smuggled treasures in full view.

All spring, the drama of Watergate riveted the nation. Richard Nixon was being accused, by a growing chorus, of high crimes and misdemeanors—impeachable offenses. The third-rate burglary at Democratic headquarters during the 1972 campaign had been only one part of a skein of dirty tricks, plumbers' squads, enemies lists, and other abuses of power being traced directly back to Nixon's Oval Office and his closet confederates.

The televised hearings of the Senate committee investigating Watergate riveted the country in the summer of 1973. Then from October to July 1974, the House Judiciary Committee held hearings, ultimately voting to recommend three articles of impeachment.

On August 7, Nixon resigned, the only president in American history to do so.

On many afternoons, Mingus and Suares exchanged notes to ask the day's key question: where do we eat tonight? They could end up in Chinatown or Paris. It was nothing to cross the ocean for the right meal.

The boon companions greeted each other by bumping their protruding bellies together. Once, Mingus went to a Suares show in Paris, saw J. C. bump bellies with a stout French artist, and left. Susan called Suares the next day. "Mingus is very upset," she said. "He thought he was the only person you bumped stomachs with."

Local listener-sponsored, leftist radio station WBAI wanted to interview Mingus, and he brought Suares with him. The interviewer asked, "Why isn't jazz more popular?" Suares jumped in and talked about people in board rooms making decisions about neglected artists. The interviewer turned to Mingus: "Why doesn't John Wilson cover more jazz?" Mingus said tersely, "Because he's a faggot."

WBAI had programs devoted to homosexual topics and political interests. The interviewer replied, "I'm sorry, but you can't talk that way on the air. And you shouldn't use that word." He replied, "I don't mean a faggot like he takes it up the ass. I mean a faggot. Understand? A faggot."

He was always being misunderstood.

Mingus took Suares to see Sarah Vaughan at La Maisonette and got stuck at a bad table. He took the $20,000 he had in his special underarm pocket to count it showily. At the set's end, he handed the waiter a thousand dollar bill, and said, "I want hundreds back. Don't go giving me no tens and twenties." He didn't leave a tip to teach them a lesson.

Suares watched Mingus act like a little boy with Sarah Vaughan, kowtow to her. He suddenly realized Mingus was awed.

Mingus's sister Grace needed money. She'd had a no-good husband and had to draw money from her post office pension fund to raise their daughter. To pay it back, the money was taken from her paycheck directly. He asked her, "What would it take for you to retire?" He repaid the amount she'd taken out, and she got her full weekly salary again.

Over the next two years, Mingus spent time in "fat farms," weight-reduction centers set in bucolic upstate New York settings where he'd eat vegetarian food, salads, special cuisines. Somehow, each spa was opposite a pancake house or a steak house. Sue shrugged, resigned. It was fate, he told her, completely out of his hands.

He kept trying spas with his usual focus. Sometimes when he came back, he'd actually lost weight. He soon made it up, with steak and ice cream and several Mingus-sized meals a day. He tried chewing steak without swallowing it again. Then he'd go back to a farm, and have the kids smuggle food in for him.

Each time he came back, he was thinner, unchanged, or even fatter.

Late that fall, he was staying for a few weeks at a fat farm where he had a bungalow with a piano. He called Paul Jeffrey to pick him up. When Jeffrey got there, he said, "You've gotta hear this, man." He tried to call Sarah Vaughan from the farm: "She's really gotta hear this." He didn't get through.

Jeffrey drove him back to New York, with the bass and Mingus and himself stuffed into his tiny Volkswagen bug. The bass's neck stuck out the window, and it started to rain. They stopped and got out and improvised a cover while they got soaked.

Hamiet Bluiett left the band in October 1974. Mingus wanted something else, and he found it with young white trumpeter Jack Walrath.

Walrath had moved to New York for the chance to play with Mingus, and Paul Jeffrey endorsed him. Walrath worked in Jeffrey's octet, as well as Latin gigs. He'd played free jazz, bop, Motown. He studied at Berklee School of Music, played with Ray Charles, and had that Gillespie tinge Mingus loved.

Walrath sat in with the quartet at the Village Gate, The band was playing things like "Free Cell Block F, 'Tis Nazi USA" and "Remember Rockefeller at Attica." Mingus told Nat Hentoff, "I ought to give titles to my music that make people think."[7] Then there were Don Pullen's tune, "Big Alice," and a complex piece, never recorded, called "Opus 32."

"Free" was written after he read an *Ebony* magazine article about electrocutions in southern prisons; he first played it on his European swing in summer 1974.[8] It featured a classically Mingus melody, long and tumbling and winking. From that perspective, it was cousin to other pieces like "Jump, Monk." But its lilt, and a bossa-nova-style section, undercut any sense of rage the title might conjure.

He gave pieces political titles, but he never sacrificed his sense of his music to his need for a political pulpit.

On the road, Walrath inevitably became Mingus's target.

JACK WALRATH, *musician:* He didn't say anything to me for about a week. Then, "Sounds like an exercise book." To get on the new guy in the band, that was part of his show. He used to pull it on me, then on Ricky Ford. Then he started in on me again.

He would apologize, not like some people I know. He was smart enough to know when he'd gone over the edge, even if he did it from some kind of psychological problem. Britt Woodman told me some of Mingus's childhood stories. People who were slapped around a lot as kids often turn into bullies. He could tell, though, when he was too tough, when he'd pushed too hard and it affected the music. He wasn't stupid. Just a little bit nuts.

With a stint at the Village Vanguard following the run at the Village Gate, the band worked up enough material live for almost three albums. They premiered "Duke Ellington's Sound of Love" at the Vanguard.

George Adams felt that the key difference in the band's newly energized shows was Walrath. The kid could take Mingus's personality because he knew he was good, and he adored Mingus's music. Walrath's avant touches and Latin tinges enhanced his post-bop versatility and complimented Adams's gut-bucket-free attack. Mingus was sure he could be molded into a dialog partner.

For Mingus wanted to spar onstage again, and he conducted "Orange Was the Color of Her Dress" from the bass, cuing dramatic shifts and changes of theme and mood and tempo in the characteristic way of multipart Mingus works. But he was having trouble remembering the music, had to keep lead sheets in front of him. He could play with verve and gusto, though, and his willingness to stretch more into risk onstage grew when this band began to really click.

First, there was the Atlantic recording date, now set for right after Christmas.

Sue threw a Christmas party for *Changes*, and the guest list filled the spacious apartment with cultural glitter.

Mingus said he lost fifty pounds, he was eating vegetables, he was off eggs, which were unhealthy. There was no eggnog—a long tradition broken. They had glog instead.

The party was, Janet Coleman would write, "an ode to beatnik history."[9] Allen Ginsberg and his lover Peter Orlovsky, Gregory Corso, William Burroughs's secretary/companion James Lauerquist, who was writing for *Changes*, Village Gate owner Art D'Lugoff and Village Vanguard owner Max Gordon were all there.

Mingus went to Bradley's with Sue and Coleman and a crew afterward. He was tight with owner Bradley Cunningham, who'd taken a bar on University Place around the corner from Sue's apartment, on the cusp of the East and West Villages, and turned it into the unofficial headquarters for the Big Apple's late-night jazz. Mingus would come around with his German shepherd, Duke, and hang, or sit at the piano and play impromptu concerts. Eventually, he wrote a tune for Cunningham based on the old spiritual, "Nobody Knows The Trouble I've Seen."

Sooner or later, everyone passed through Bradley's, to play or to hang out. Once Thelonious Monk came in, and passed by the table on the way to the bathroom, and again on the way out. Mingus and Monk only exchanged a few words, but everyone felt the echoes.

Two days after Christmas 1974, Mingus went into the studio with an augmented group.

At the Village Gate, he'd brought in trumpeter Marcus Belgrave, an old colleague, but kept Walrath. It was an endurance trial, a test. In the studio, he announced that Walrath would play the written parts, but Belgrave would solo. Then he cut a lot of Walrath in the editing stage.

But he included on the album the young trumpeter's composition "Black Bats and Poles," which had a contemporary funky feel somewhere between Mingus music and Miles Davis's.

Mingus soloed on "Devil Blues," with playful and elastic rhythms and harmonies, yielding to George Adams's throaty down-home vocalizing. Blues guitar great Gatemouth Brown wrote the lyrics when the band first started to work this tune out at Max's Kansas City.[10]

They recorded Sy Johnson's elegy, "For Harry Carney," in honor of Duke Ellington's great baritone saxist, one of Mingus's heroes. And they recorded "Duke Ellington's Sound of Love," partly inspired by Billy Strayhorn's "Lush Life" and penned as a tribute after the great man's death, not once but twice for the double album, as an instrumental and with vocalist Jackie Paris. It was another set of recapitulations.

Mingus was closing circles, reweaving loose ends, getting ready for history.

Changes One and Two, the name of the new double-album, made a powerful statement. The band was rich in possibilities; it could manuever through and master and remake his daunting tempo shifts and chord changes. It gave his music the edge he always looked for. And now he was vital again, reaching out, collecting new and old sounds for his mix. He was writing Mingus music.

Despite the treatment he got during the *Changes* sessions, Walrath was learning more about how Mingus worked. Things that were theoretically wrong, like major sevenths on dominant chords and major thirds on minor chords, were consistent, part of Mingus's vocabulary. It wasn't just bebop voice-leading, anticipating the next chord change. He was hearing polytonality, multiple keys, tone rows.

JACK WALRATH: The other older guys too, a lot of them, had all this weird stuff. They were playing by ear. That's how they got the ideas.

With Mingus there were always little pieces of things stolen, a lot of things. But he put them together his way; it seemed different.

And he was very precise about his chords. He'd write chords with twelfths and twenty-firsts, instead of writing out a voicing; the chord symbols were the voicings. It's an ear-training thing. He taught me to use my ear more.

The album was being edited and mixed when they had a big New Year's Eve gathering of family and friends at the Five Spot. J. C. Suares, Janet Coleman, the kids, Judy, Charles III, Sue and her kids were among the throng.

It was late when something crucial happened, although everyone saw it differently, like in *Citizen Kane* or *Rashomon*, where bystanders and intimates alike describe only aspects of the situation, sometimes misleadingly.

Janet Coleman remembers Charles III calling Sue something like "white whore," which caused Roberto to grab a chair. Then Dannie Richmond intervened, telling Mingus he was too hard on his son. Janet saw a clear racial divide.

The son with his name was jealous. He'd come to New York to have a father and felt he'd been shortchanged.

J. C. Suares says the air was heavy and brutal but there were no names called. Charles III was complaining that he hadn't been invited to the party, that he wasn't being treated fairly as a person, that the rest of the family didn't respect him, that Roberto was a scumbag. Suares says Mingus refused to take sides, that his attitude was that eating chicken was more important. Chicken was his favorite dish. When the fight broke out, he picked up his chicken, holding a chair for protection with the other hand, moved out of range and resumed eating, unconcerned.

Roberto says Charles III was drunk and saying unflattering things about his mother. The skinny teenager walked up to the broadening thirty-year-old and said, "What did you say about my mother?" Charles knocked his cigarette out of his hand. Roberto punched him in the face and broke Charles' glasses, sending him sprawling. Everyone in the place applauded. Mingus picked up a chair, and said to his son, "You black motherfucker, get outta here."

Mingus gained back all the weight he lost that spring. He was back on the binge.

One evening before 6:00 P.M., he met J. C. Suares in Chinatown and they dropped $50 apiece in a spot where $10 stuffed two people. They went back to the East 10th Street apartment and settled in front of the TV. He decided he wanted to watch a Jack Palance movie, but none was on, so he dialed until he found a Western.

It was nearly 8:00 P.M. He was hungry, and as he settled in front of the TV with J. C. he yelled to Sue's daughter, without turning around, "Hey Susanna, make me some spaghetti." She went into the kitchen, and came out twenty minutes later with a huge bowlful and handed it to him. His eyes barely left the TV, and he polished off the bowl in under half an hour.

J. C. SUARES: Five minutes later, he mumbles something. I say, "What?" He says, "The spaghetti was no good." I don't want to offend him, but I say,

"Charles, why did you eat it then?" He finally turns around and looks at me and says, "You got to eat."

He made a deal with J. C.: they'd both go to a fat farm.

Suares got cold feet; he found the idea humiliating. So he went on a stringent diet and dropped forty pounds. He talked to Mingus at the fat farm on the phone: "What are they feeding you?" "Salad." "Have you lost weight?" "Don't know."

When Mingus got back to the city, Suares went right over to see him. He hadn't lost a pound. Suares thought the spa was a scam, then Mingus explained. He'd bribed the cabby who picked him up at the airport to pick him up at the spa at seven every night for five weeks, and bring him to a nearby cooking school, where he sampled every dish.

During this time, Mingus played Boston's Jazz Workshop while Sonny Rollins was playing next store at Paul's Mall. Mingus came over to Rollins's dressing room, and Sonny said, "Thanks for the beautiful birds of paradise you sent to my apartment." Mingus shot back, "I bought 'em for Dizzy, but he was out of town."

When Rollins led a New Audiences concert at Carnegie Hall, trumpeter Freddie Hubbard didn't show up, and promoters Lokin and Weiner called Mingus and Gillespie, hoping one or the other would pull them out of a disaster. They both showed, and seemed annoyed at first, then pitched in to help save the show.

Vibist Milt Jackson, whom Gillespie had given his big break almost three decades earlier, joined the core quintet at Carnegie Hall. The Modern Jazz Quartet, which he co-led with pianist John Lewis, had gone into a hiatus after running longer than any small jazz group in history.

In February 1975, Mingus and Sue celebrated Janet Coleman and David Dozer's sixth anniversary with them, then they went to the posh St. Regis Maisonette to see Sarah Vaughan.

Mingus wanted her to sing "Duke Ellington's Sound of Love." He'd sent her the lead sheets and overripe lyrics. But Vaughan didn't do it. He got on the house phone, and after going through the usual phalanx of managers and doorkeepers, he asked Vaughan plaintively, "Hey Mama, how come you don't sing my song?"[11]

Mingus's band did another European round. First it was March in Italy, including Bergamo, where the Communist party subsidized arts performances.

When they came back, Mingus began unleashing the band more, though they still had to stick pretty close to the standard set list.

Dannie Richmond's parents died, and so the band played without a drummer. Once, Mingus hired a conga player. He kept putting the band in slightly altered situations. He was sampling their skills, and compiling their voices, almost like he used to in the Workshops. Dannie Richmond told an interviewer this was the second band in jazz—the first being the 1964 Workshop with Dolphy, Clifford Jordan, Johnny Coles, and Jaki Byard.

George Adams said, "Jack [Walrath] . . . was more secure in what he was playing. Therefore Charles felt free to write. He trusted our musical ability to bring things out." [12]

But Mingus was getting on Pullen's case some.

They often played Sy Johnson's chart of "For Harry Carney," a beautiful simple blues. During each solo, Mingus laid out and let the soloist and Dannie Richmond interact. Pullen would play the melody, start strumming the strings inside the piano to get a shimmering background, embroider the themes and chords, strum, then break out into hard-rollicking gospel piano, the style that had made Ramsey Lewis a crossover smash.

But Pullen threw the tune's twelve-bar form out the window with what he was doing. So when he went to end his solo with a big flourish, the rest of the band was caught flat-footed, because he'd lost his place in the music.

This went on night after night. Finally, Mingus called Pullen on it on the onstage microphone: "I don't care what you do, but keep the form."

You can't improvise on nothing.

Pullen quickly shot back, "It's my solo, I'm gonna do what I want."

It was the same tension between soloist and composer Mingus had been wrestling into art for thirty years.

He was fifty-three years old.

He told Pullen, "You know, you're gonna get fired."

They went from big joint to big joint. The next night they were at Jilly's, a famed spot in Dayton, Ohio. A few years later, New Wave rocker Elvis Costello would call Ray Charles a nigger from the stage there.

Mingus led them into "For Harry Carney," and when it came time, Pullen ended in the wrong place yet again. Mingus took his own part and ripped it into little pieces and threw them up in the air.

Everybody was cool. They finished the gig.

On to the next town, and the next gig. The band figured "For Harry Carney" was history, since Mingus never learned his own tunes any more and had torn up the score. He was lazy, needed the sheet music.

Mingus opened his satchel and pulled out the part, taped back together like

337

a jigsaw puzzle. He put it on the music stand. The band just stared at him. He tried to glare at them, then broke into a wide grin.

He started to loosen up and talk to Walrath, almost always about music. But sometimes he'd talk about growing up, how his father beat him and his sisters, how his father passed for white, how once a guy who sounded like Joe Gallo held a gun to his head and pulled the trigger, but it didn't go off. And he talked about sex and women, about his own exploits and what he'd seen other men do.

He liked to talk trash.

In early June 1975, the quintet played Teddy's, in Milwaukee, for four days, and was paid $2,000 or 65 percent of the ticket sales, whichever was greater. [13]

From June 24 to August 3, the quintet did eleven concerts and eleven club dates. [14] They ran the growing gauntlet of European jazz festivals, including Montreux and Antibes, and jazz venues.

On July 20, the band, expanded by the presence of Gerry Mulligan and Benny Bailey, taped a show at Montreux, including a moving version of "Pork Pie Hat." Mingus looked worn, aged, despite his hair being conked and piled like James Brown's. The Europeans usually paid better than Americans, but the logistics were still brutal.

He felt like he was always on the road and was tired a lot. He had an electric pickup on his bass and was using an amplifier Paul Jeffrey got him. It made it easier to play. He didn't have to work as hard to project volume and tone. Legato touches came easier.

His body was like an extended chemistry experiment, agents and reagents and catalysts swirling in a dense, cumulative mix. Anything could be happening.

He wanted Duke Ellington's mantle, but he didn't want to spend his life on the road. He made a lot of money and he spent a lot of money.

When the band came back from the brutal tour of one-night stands in Europe, Mingus went into the neurological wing of Columbia Presbyterian Hospital. Some days when he woke up, he was tingly or numb in his hands and feet. Dannie Richmond sometimes rubbed his feet so the feeling came back.

Mingus told friends he had gotten a slipped disc from a bad bed in Germany. Sue didn't believe him. He was fat as a house.

Roberto's girlfriend's mother knew the doctor who treated the Kennedys, and he was asked to check on Mingus's back. An intern came for preliminary tests, and stuck three needles into his spine—and missed. Mingus glared at him: "If you do that again, I'm gonna pull your balls off." The next time, the intern didn't miss.

Sonny Rollins came by, and Mingus complained bitterly about the nonstop European grind.

Norman Mailer recommended Dr. Soltanoff, who had an office on Route 28 near Woodstock. Soltanoff was a holistic chiropractor, adding herbal treatments and dietary supplements to the usual bone manipulation. In fact, the doctor was a local natural-medicine guru, in one of the self-conscious natural-medicine capitals of the United States.

From then on, whenever Mingus had back problems or needed to be under dietary supervision, Soltanoff was the medical man on the case.

The two-week hospital stay and back pains meant Mingus blew off the plans Sue had made for their wedding.

SUSAN GRAHAM UNGARO MINGUS: We were going to get married up in Woodstock, we were going to have a pageant. A rented bus was going to bring all the people who were involved with *Changes* up there, and all the kids, who were going to wear costumes. We had it choreographed. It was going to be an Event, and then we had to call it off.

Sue says they were married later, at City Hall, with no fanfare.

In August 1975, the New York *Daily News* wrote up Mingus's upcoming five-week stint at the Village Gate. He was back big time, and tabloid-ready.

He liked the people who owned Joyous Lake in Woodstock; they had good food, so he played there. Keki took a few friends over from Rosendale. They were into Queen, the popular glam-rock band. Mingus was fat, sloppy. She was mortified.

Mingus was having trouble walking. He didn't want to end up like his father. He told Jack Walrath one doctor threatened to cut off his legs because he was so fat.

At the end of August, Dick Gregory came to visit for two days, to talk with him about a new dietary regimen.

Gregory was a decade younger and had interwoven his callings as comedian, antiracist crusader, and political commentator. He had the platforms Mingus always felt were rightly his, or any prominent black man's with brains.

Gregory had earned his visibility. In 1961, he opened the Playboy Club—and became the first black comedian to crack to big-time white-audiences circuit. The next year, he popped up on TV shows like Jack Paar's late-night talk show, and stretched his pointed social commentary in albums like *Dick Gregory: The Light Side—Dark Side* and his first book, *The Back of the Bus. Nigger*, written with journalist Robert Lipsyte, followed two years later.

In 1966 he made a movie, *Sweet Love, Bitter*, about a Charlie Parker-type jazz saxist nicknamed Eagle and the interracial tensions and romances around him. The film was scored by Mal Waldron; the Bird-like sax was dubbed by Charles McPherson.

A devotee of nonviolence and 1968 candidate for president on the Peace and Freedom party ticket, Gregory followed Mohandas Gandhi's lead in using fasting—self-starvation—as a pacifist tactic to call attention to social ills. His hunger strikes against the war and racist outbreaks earned him headlines and brickbats. Ironically, it was only a short step from political fasting to vegetarianism and holistic, healthful eating. In 1973, he wrote *Dick Gregory's Natural Diet for Folks Who Eat.*

Which is why he was visiting Sue and Charles. He and Mingus had a few things in common. One of these was a problem with weight. Gregory had always been plump, or fat, until he started his hunger strikes.

On September 2, 1975, Sue sent the diet guru a note saying Mingus was following Gregory's regimen and was on his way back to health.

Five days later, Mingus sent a note in a tiny scrawl scarred with crossed-out words and phrases: "Tried to call you. Have cancelled bookings frm Sept 25 through Oct 25. Can I come to your place Sept 26? Will doctor be in town? Have lost 15 lbs so far [blur] mailing [blur] to colonic irrigation lady as I can't make it this Tuesday. Peace & love Mingus."[16]

A week later, Sue sent Gregory another note. Art D'Lugoff was interested in the idea of a health food restaurant at the Village Gate. Mingus was booking a few nights at the Bottom Line later in the year; did Dick want to do a double bill? The problem was that Gregory didn't want alcohol served where he performed, and Allen Pepper, the Line's owner, wasn't enthusiastic about dropping his bar profits to zero.[17]

Mingus never kept his enthusiasms to himself. Everyone had to share them. Immediately, if not sooner.

The band went to London. At the airport, Dannie Richmond saw Charlie get on a scale; he weighed 307 pounds. Richmond told him, "You can't eat a half-gallon of ice cream at every meal." "I've got to do something about it," he said.[18]

He went to Gregory's new spa and followed the strict regimen, and came back to New York a new man. Or so he said.

On October 30, he sent Gregory a note: "Thanks for everything. . . . Anytime you want to give a benefit for your purposes in life, I'm with you with my band. Take care of those kids. Love, Mingus."[19]

He used the blank back of one of Sue's form letters:

"Dear Music Lover, If you are interested in having the great composer, bassist and jazz musician Charles Mingus perform with his quintet at your college this year, please contact me.

"Mingus has represented the avant-garde in music for almost twenty years. Jazz's Angry Man not only pioneered many of the changes in music today, but recently voiced his outrages in the controversial biography "Beneath The Underdog" [sic] . . . "[20]

The phone number for East 10th Street was below.

JACK WALRATH: He would do things like go up to Dick Gregory's and fast for forty days, lose forty pounds, come back, and gain sixty in two weeks. It's an attention-getting device. For fat people it draws them attention, but when you get it you get hurt, in a way. It's very complex.

When we were in Montreal, he ordered four lamb chops. Jesus. So we're eating, and they whisper to Mingus. Mingus repeats loudly, "It's being paid for?" So George Adams came up and quipped, "Yeah? Then bring me four more lamb chops." Mingus was hurt by that. He was easily hurt, you know.

I had a contest with him one night. I could keep up with him. At Umberto's. A whole table of chicken. "Anything you want." I was right up his butt. I only weighed 155.

Mingus sometimes saw his son Charles. He couldn't let the kid jeopardize his relationship with Sue. He wasn't paternal anyway, and the thirty-year-old frequently annoyed him. To Mingus, his son seemed to want to claim mastery over things he barely understood, from art to politics. He'd tried his hand at painting and drama and photography, and he had gotten a work selected for a Museum of Modern Art Christmas card, and had written and directed a play at Joseph Papp's downtown cheap-chic Shakespeare Public Theater, a big exploratory venue that had launched, among many, Mingus III's ex-roommate Sam Shepard.

But Mingus thought his son was scuffling aimlessly. It was like watching himself disintegrate into entropy, like he did when he couldn't find the music that was his gravitational center, the molten core of his complex and often contradictory personality.

He didn't think his son, the one with his name and his father's, had that center, that anchor, that focus, that discipline. Dealing with him was like looking into a funhouse mirror. He saw ghastly echoes of Sergeant Mingus, Jeanne, her parents.

He was his father's son.

He almost never hit his kids and he never fully let them go, even when he rarely saw them.

Charles carved him the first of a series of canes, when he told his son he had phlebitis. Sometimes he called Charles, who lived down the block from his East 5th Street apartment, and picked him up in his car. They'd pull around the block, cut the lights, and see who was sitting in the parked cars that they believed were watching Mingus's old pad.

Roberto was going to Bard College when he caught on that something was wrong with Charles's legs. An official school function brought Mingus and Sue across the Hudson from Woodstock. Everyone was dressed up and meeting and greeting. Things went fine.

Then Mingus and Sue headed back toward the new Chevrolet Blazer he'd bought. "We need a vehicle for the snow up here," Mingus had said, and the Blazer was a man-sized toy, a big rugged set of wheels, the kind later called sport utility vehicles, high off the ground. A small knot of admirers walked the pair back to the truck.

When they got to it, Mingus couldn't lift his leg high enough to put his foot on the running board. Roberto moved to cover his back. Standing behind the much larger man, he inserted his knee into the back of Mingus's, and lifted it so unobtrusively no one noticed.

ROBERTO UNGARO: He thought his foot was numb because he'd kicked the TV to break it. Dr. Soltanoff gave Charles these brushes; he was supposed to brush his skin and it would bring up the circulation. I remember one night Charles had a horrible stomachache. I'd read this somewhere, so I told him to get into bed, raise his knees, put four pillows under them. That raises the blood level to your stomach, and the pain goes away. He did it, we were real quiet, and it worked.

Starting October 30, 1975, Mingus began another series of European concerts booked through George Wein. He wasn't happy.

In Berlin, he picked a fight backstage because he discovered the band was being taped for TV. He compared it to the Nazis gassing the Jews.[21] The whole band saw the racism in Germany; it was rife in the hotels and restaurants.

At Wuppertal, where the band rode the famed monorail, there was a club run by an American as part of a community arts center. They had a big lawn party where everybody got drunk on schnapps. Mingus was holding court in a crowd when Walrath spied him from across the yard.

Walrath yelled, "I can hear you from all the way over here, motherfucker, so shut up, goddamn it." As he walked toward Mingus, people moved out of his way like it was high noon in a Western. When Walrath reached him, Mingus said simply, "Jack, you're fired."

Walrath came to the next day and asked Dannie Richmond if he was really fired. Richmond shrugged. For two weeks, Mingus said nothing about the incident to Walrath. Then, when they were in an Italian train station, Mingus suddenly walked up to him and said, "Look Jack. You don't call me a motherfucker, and I won't call you a motherfucker."

Mingus kept the band happy with his usual extra bonuses, but Pullen was getting restless. Mingus was hard on pianists, and Pullen was still butting heads with him.

Crossing the Franco-Swiss border on the Orient Express, Walrath stayed with the equipment while the others went to eat. When the check came, they insisted the waiter had padded it. An argument ensued.

Suddenly they realized the dining car had been decoupled from the train. At precisely that moment, Walrath was trying not to be tossed out of the baggage car. Like auditioners for the Keystone Kops, the rest of the band tumbled out of the dining car and started running for the slowly disappearing Express.

George Adams the athlete led the pack, and leaped aboard. Pullen was puffing hard as he closed in and yelled, "Pull the cord." Adams yanked the emergency-brake cord, and the train screeched to a halt.

Dannie Richmond had fallen over trying to run. Mingus had barely pulled away from the dining car. Then the train started up again, and Adams yanked the cord again.

When they got to the first Swiss station, they were all tossed off the train, and their baggage was searched. Mingus's bag had barbeque chicken in it.

Mingus called Eric and Keki from the road. He seemed to want to teach them lessons. He'd ask them questions, tell them tales, soliloquize about Nazis and racists and the music business. He told Eric, "You're the man in the family now. Take care of your sister."

He started pulling Eric aside at gatherings to talk with him. It was as if he was making up for all he hadn't done with his kids.

He gave his youngest son advice about life and women, and usually finished saying, "You're gonna ignore all this and do what I told you not to anyway."

Like Marlon Brando in *The Godfather*, he told Eric, "Keep your friends close, and your enemies even closer." He loved Mafia sagas. The boy thought the words reflected how his dad dealt with some of the people at Sue's parties.

Mingus was his father's son. He was a teacher.

George Adams later told Eric, "We played with your father out of love."

That fall, Don Pullen left the band, and Mingus plugged in Danny Mixon who could also double on piano and organ. He'd need that for some of the projects he had brewing.

But he was bummed out. It was a disappointing end to an underappreciated band. He'd worked hard, staying on the road, overcoming his rash of physical annoyances and complaints, losing weight and ballooning back up.

With all the work and the touring and the press coverage, none of his Atlantic albums sold more than some 15,000 copies. Atlantic's East Coast a&r head, Raymond Silva, said even the people at the label weren't listening to them. [22]

Thanks to Atlantic jazz head Nesuhi Ertegun, one of Mingus's many patrons, he and Silva would soon sit down and do business.

Mingus spoke less and was quieter around the apartment these days. He'd settled in. He was in his kind of domestic routine, and he ignored things that before would have set him flaring.

He was telling people he descended from Abraham Lincoln. In North Carolina a lot of people, white and black, told that story, since Lincoln's family came from those parts.

He was thinking about Sergeant Mingus.

In December 1975, Mingus played the Bottom Line. The club was a record-industry showcase, a hotspot where anyone could play, regardless of musical label. He tapped Paul Jeffrey for the gig, and winked at the saxist every time he was about to do some stage shtick. Jeffrey knew he wanted the crowd to listen to the music, but they had to get hooked in.

For Christmas Eve, James Lauerquist invited Mingus and Sue to a party. Full of wrapping paper and ribbon and last-minute purchases, they showed up at 11:00 P.M., and there were a half-dozen men: Allen Ginsberg and his current lover, Lauerquist and William Burroughs, and another duo. Mingus parked himself and said nothing.

SUSAN GRAHAM UNGARO MINGUS: It was the most excruciatingly awkward half an hour. We had stepped in and interrupted whatever fun was going on; it was an awful feeling. So we finally left and picked up our own Christmas tree.

Mingus had made $135,000 in 1975. Jazz Workshop, his publishing company, pulled in $25,000. Sue made $19,600. He put $7,500 into a Keogh account, which they estimated would be worth $400,000 by 1983.

They listed assets. Chase Manhattan Bank Savings, $38,076. Bowery Savings Time Deposit, $29,941. Edison Savings and Loan savings account, $5,276. Bank of Commerce Savings, $10,102. Chase Manhattan Checking, $6,000.

Then there were real estate assets. The seven-room apartment on East 10th Street cost $24,000, with a fair market value of $45,000; they paid $300 a month. The nine-room house with thirteen acres at 100 Witchtree Road cost $29,000, had a mortgage outstanding for $11,000, and a fair market value of $85,000.

They had 100 shares of NCR common stock, valued at $2,625. There were two Italian bass violins and a grand piano, valued at $10,000, and twenty-five original music scores estimated to be worth $1,000 apiece.[23]

He made a lot of money and he spent a lot of money.

He listed his occupation as composer. Sue listed hers as manager. He was president of Jazz Workshop. She was secretary-treasurer.

They were compiling their accounting because they were scouting a new place to live, at 205 West 57th Street. The Osborne was a prestigious building. Bobby Short lived there. Mingus and Sue were interested in buying apartment 8D, which was selling for $55,000 plus a monthly maintenance fee of $1,278.70.[24]

The apartment needed at least $100,000 worth of work and modernizing, but it was huge and high class and, Sue felt sure, worth it. It was the last flat in the Osborne that wasn't subdivided, a triplex with different wings. She'd already planned to sublet part of it to one of her artist friends, cartoonist Will Eisner. The jump in monthly maintenance from $300 for the apartment on 10th Street to nearly $1,300 for this place scared her some, but she figured with Eisner covering part of it, and her writing part of it off as workspace for herself and Mingus, they'd cover the rest.

In spring 1976, Mingus and Sue were sitting in the East 10th Street apartment listening to records. One was by rock guitarist Jeff Beck, a version of "Pork Pie Hat." Beck, a 1960s rock guitar god, had crossed into jazz-rock fusion. He'd simplified the dirge's complex chords, and flown a solo mostly, as Beck did, on emotion.

Unlike the jazz avant-garde, Beck sold lots of records. Asked what he thought it sounded like, Mingus said, "Money."[25]

On March 31, the band started a two-day recording session in Italy for *Todo Modo*, the sound track for a new movie by Elia Petri. The Italian director's 1970 Oscar-winning film, *Investigation of a Citizen Above Suspicion*, told of a politically powerful police chief who slit his mistress's throat and waited to see if he'd get caught. The eerie noirish score was by Ennio Morricone.

Mingus relished the chance to work with Petri. Daniel Senatore, an old friend of the Ungaros, had made the introductions.

There were Italian horns to augment the quintet. Danny Mixon played organ, and Walrath was knocked out by the parts Mingus had written. When he told him that, Mingus seemed oddly touched, and open to questions about it. He said people didn't ask him about his music much.

An a cappella trumpet theme that recalled *The Godfather*'s opened the piece, was soon embroidered with counterpoint, then gave way to sonorous brass chords flecked with dissonance. George Adams soloed with his vocalizing effects, then Danny Mixon worked a churchy organ leading into more thick chords and drones.

It made a big classically tinged sound, and yielded to a bluesy, swinging section whose solos embroidered and reworked the opening themes.

You could improvise on anything, but you can't improvise on nothing.

Mingus's bass was brilliant. His slurs and interval leaps were as strong and evocative as ever, and his arco work during a duet with flute sounded solid and melodic with a whiff of microtones.

The movie had deadline problems, and didn't get an American distributor.[26] Mingus's music sat on the shelf.

When Mingus came back from Italy, he faced the initial meeting with the Osborne's cooperative board, who had the power to veto their application to buy.

He fell asleep.

He'd just gotten back from Italy a few hours earlier. A strike at Rome's airport kept him there ten hours, and he landed exhausted.

Several elderly ladies on the board examined him rather closely. He was snoring.

SUSAN GRAHAM UNGARO MINGUS: It didn't go over too well. They asked things like when he would be coming home, and about playing only between certain hours. It was so stupid. I said he plays when the music strikes. It might be at four in the morning. They scowled. But there was no point in telling them something that wasn't true, because Charles played the piano at all hours.

On April 14, 1976, the co-op attorney notified them they'd been rejected.

Sue desperately drafted a letter to Naomi Graffman, the board president, asking for another discussion, or a face-to-face talk. She explained the exhausting circumstances, adding that they were "not our most clear thinking and cordial selves."

She suggested a suitable place could be found for the piano, noting "Mr. Mingus tours a good 9 or 10 months out of the year, so there shouldn't be a music or noise problem."

She concluded that they needed a space appropriate for his stature and the producers, publishers, record company heads, critics he met with, "without bumping into children or having to type a letter on the dining room table."[27]

Later in April, Mingus led the band down to New Orleans, where they played George Wein's Jazz and Heritage Festival in the town where, according to legend, jazz was born. Later that month, he did a solo performance for Duke Ellington's birthday at the cathedral of St. John the Divine, near Columbia University in Harlem. The cathedral was a bastion of political and social outspokenness, and had begun a long series of cultural offerings meant to broaden its impact in the surrounding communities, divided by race and money and academic power.

Mingus's storied reputation preceded him wherever he went, and interpreted his complexities to his newly expanding following.

On one of their whirlwind tours, the band—Walrath, Adams, Mixon, Richmond—stopped at the Pioneer Banque in Seattle, a place, according to Robert Gwynne, run by the Greek mob. Gwynne, a fan, watched the door to make sure the band wasn't cheated—something Gwynne didn't know Mingus did regularly. The deal was $250 up front, $250 cash at each night's end. When the bartender refused to pay him until he'd done a final cash-register tally for the night, Mingus said he'd sit there. "I'm a great artist and I deserve to be paid."

A barmaid tried to calm him down, and he turned on her. Gwynne was disgusted when she started crying after he called her a white bitch and told her he had a gun and would use it. Gwynne couldn't understand how Mingus's sidemen were unperturbed by his mean treatment. When Walrath couldn't find music for a piece and said he couldn't play without it, Mingus shot back, "If you don't have it memorized by now, you ought to hang yourself."[28]

Gwynne knew plenty of standard-issue Mingus stories, and it fit. That was one reason Mingus was wary of his fans. They didn't know him, but they thought they did. Celebrity had its vices as well as virtues. And he'd created an overwhelming image and myth for himself. It wasn't exactly Ellingtonian. It was more like anti-Duke.

George Adams left to join Don Pullen in a long-running group of their own. A young tenorman named Ricky Ford filled the slot. Ford had a big, lunging tone that recalled Paul Gonsalves's, his hero and an Ellington mainstay who set Duke's big band on fire with a long, burning blues at the Newport Jazz Festival in 1956.

In May, the band and Sue went to Berkeley, where they played a festival. Kate Mulholland saw them and thought they seemed pretty domesticated and comfortable. Over the next three years, she only heard from him once or twice, by postcard.

The people from his pre-Sue past kept dropping out.

When the couple got back to New York, Sue and her friend Myra Friedman, who had written a best-selling biography of psychedelic rock-blues singer Janis Joplin called *Buried Alive*, decided to rent a house in the Hamptons. The Long Island beachfront was the hip summer site for the New York artistic community as well as for the rich.

They took the two-hour-plus jitney bus ride out to Ammagansett and rented a house, at $3,000 for three months, on Louse Point Road: two small bedrooms, modern kitchen and bath, a big main room, and a glass wall opening onto a sun deck 20-odd feet from the bay.[29] Just across the road was a bigger waveless bay. Their neighbors included Larry Rivers and Robert Motherwell.

The first weekend Mingus and Sue and Roberto and Friedman went out there, the Mingus dogs attacked and killed the neighbors' cat.

SUSAN GRAHAM UNGARO MINGUS: I took the side of the cat, I stood up for truth and justice, I was going to tell the architect what had happened. And Charles said, "Put it in the road. It was hit by a car." It was his idea to buy another cat—just replace it. And so we ended up putting the dead cat in the salad compartment of our refrigerator, because it was very hot out, and we didn't want it to decompose.

Myra was screaming, "How am I going to get coffee in the morning with a dead cat in the refrigerator?"

When the famous architect who owned the cat returned, Sue told him of his pet's death. He raised his arm as if to strike her with Zeus's thunderbolt. She raced ahead of him to their rental house, thinking they might not be amused to find their cat stored like lettuce. Its body was a frozen mess: Roberto had tried to revive it under water.

The neighbors were upset, took the body, and keened and wailed over it throughout the night.

They sublet the house from mid-August to mid-September, and rented out the house on Witchtree Road, because Sue decided to go to Europe and then Japan with the band. There was no point in paying rent.

That November, they got a bill from the Hamptons rental's realtor for $80 worth of furnishings the dogs had chewed up.[30]

In late June, as part of the 1976 Newport Jazz Festival, Mingus led a live version of *Tijuana Moods* at Carnegie Hall.

Sy Johnson was arranging the music for the big orchestra when Mingus called him up: "Come on, we're auditioning dancers." They went to an old Spanish restaurant on West 14th Street and Seventh Avenue, and ordered a huge paella. Everybody dug in.

It was only the beginning. They clubhopped further east, then further west again. Every place had a minimum for tables, and every place Mingus ordered enough food for two. "What we don't eat, we'll just take with us," he shrugged. While the rest of the party took tinier and tinier portions, he attacked it all with undiminished gusto. And he paid for the whole outing.

They found good flamenco dancers, and Ysabel Morel, who'd played castanets on the record, contacted the dancers for them.

Flamenco dancers have fixed steps; they are not improvisers, jazz dancers. So Jimmy Knepper copied the music off the record, and Sy Johnson rearranged it.

The concert was a huge success, and Mingus was so carried away by the music that he danced with his bass onstage.

A few days later, he led a big band at Radio City Music Hall to raise money for Roland Kirk. The brilliant multi-instrumental alumnus of his Workshops had had a severe stroke in 1975 and could use only one arm. Game and determined to ignore adversity, Kirk learned to play one-handed and made his comeback.

In August 1976, the core band headed to Europe for six weeks.

Mingus looked worn much of the time. He was using his electrified bass and amplifier. He was playing the same handful of pieces—like "Song for Harry Carney," "Fables of Faubus," "Remember Rockefeller at Attica," "Sue's Changes"—over and over from sheet music. The pictures from the tour show the tired and lined face, his bone-deep weariness.

His body was showing the long years of abuse. And other things were coming up in his face.

During a plane hop to Germany, he came over to Walrath's seat and put his arm around the young trumpeter: "You and me, we're gonna defeat these Nazis." He was thinking of Eric Dolphy.

In Rome, they had four days off, a rare gift. Mingus had always wanted to go to Africa, and so it seemed like another gift when a representative of a Nigerian music festival asked him to fly down for it. He added, "You must leave the white guy in Rome." Mingus turned him down, saying, "We're gonna wait 'til you're ready."

On September 11, they played a Communist party rally Archie Shepp had organized. The local press tried to interview him about his politics, and he said, "I used to be a member of the Communist party when I was nineteen, because their place had pool tables and pictures of movie actresses all over the walls." It wasn't what they wanted to hear.

He backed out of a similar rally in Italy soon afterward. He told Max Roach it was because Mao Tse-tung had died, and he'd signed a new contract with Atlantic.

Raymond Silva from Atlantic Records had approached him slowly, indirectly, trying to build up trust. He sat while Mingus sliced an apple, giving some to Dannie Richmond, ignoring Silva. He found a way into the monologue, made a remark Mingus considered intelligent, and was offered an apple slice. [31]

Silva seemed to understand how to handle Mingus. And Mingus was ready to deal on somebody else's terms. Everything he'd built, he feared, could slip away if he didn't make the right moves.

Mingus was still making the scene. When the Bethanys opened Café Loup on East 13th Street, he dropped by often, sometimes with friends like Dexter Gordon in tow. Once he showed up with ex-fooball hero and movie star Jim Brown.

Eric was singing classical music in high school, and gave his father the medal he won for his recital. Mingus was elated: "My son's mastering the white man's music." Eric, so light he looked Irish, was the black percentage of his rural upstate school and was regularly beaten up for it. When Eric got into trouble, as he regularly did, the school staff complained that his mother was such a lovely person, a nurse, but his father was a jazz musician. What could you expect?

Every summer, Eric was sent to a secular Jewish summer camp for eight weeks, where he felt totally out of place. It was an echo of Camp Unity, where Mingus and Celia had gone.

On November 11, 1976, the band came back to New York's Town Hall for part of a series called Interludes. Produced by Marilyn Egol, each hour-long 5:45 P.M. concert show was preceded by 5:00 P.M. cocktails, and cost three dollars. [32]

The Man Who Never Sleeps felt tired all the time. His feet were tingly, losing sensation. He'd walk on marbles when he got up, have someone massage the soles of his feet, use Dr. Soltanoff's brushes. He couldn't play bass any longer without amplification. He needed recognition as a composer. He'd always wanted it, but now, as he felt his body rebelling, his audiences regrowing, his ability to lead his bands onstage diminishing, it became more urgent than ever that his music be recognized separately from him, survive him.

Everyone thought he just needed to lose weight, clean up again, eat right, take care.

They would soon find out how wrong they were.

15 Don't Be Afraid, the Clown's Afraid, Too

NOT LONG AFTER New Year's 1977, Janet Coleman saw Charles Mingus. He was excited, almost like a kid. Uncharacteristically, he blurted out that he'd made over a quarter-million dollars the year before.

She was taken aback. He'd always talked about ripoffs and scandals and how much money the black jazz creators had lost, had skimmed off the results of their labors by white record label honchos, white club owners and agents and managers, white imitators. She'd never heard him boast about his earnings before. Ever.

Stagflation, the economic mirror-image of the Great Depression, was raging across America, so it actually meant less that Mingus had doubled his income. Stagflation combined double-digit price inflation with flat wages. The prices of supermarket staples could change almost every week. Banks paid 15 percent to 20 percent interest rates on year-long certificates of deposit. This was largely the legacy of Lyndon Johnson's decision during the Vietnam War to run the economy full tilt. He didn't want to cut back on consumer goods for war supplies and thus increase opposition to the war. But it was inevitable that the American economy would overheat under the strain and create stresses, exacerbated by the steep oil price jumps of the 1970s, that took years to work through the system.

Stagflation helped seal the historical fate of the era Mingus and his peers had helped shape, already seen by many Americans as destabilizing, heedless, immoral. The stage was set for a reaction. Ronald Reagan, an ex-California governor and ex-movie actor who led the 1950s anticommunist crusade as president of Hollywood's Screen Actors Guild, made his second stab at the Republican nomination for president in the primary run-up to the fall 1976 elections.

Historical circles were being closed all around Mingus.

On March 9, 1977, Mingus led a vastly augmented band into the studio to record the fusion crossover disc Raymond Silva at Atlantic wanted.

Mingus had wanted to rerecord *Todo Modo* for Atlantic. One night while he and Sue went out to dinner, he had Paul Jeffrey transcribe it from the Italian recording, which was a half-step off true pitch. When they returned, Jeffrey had finished. But a strike halted that idea, and Silva countered with a demand for fusion guitars.

Mingus was increasingly remote from the whole recording process. He didn't even show up for all the rehearsals. He called Paul Jeffrey and complained, "They want me to record with guitars." The label said he needed to get radio play to sell records, and fusion was the ticket.

Mingus's favorite jazz guitarist was Jimmy Raney, whose classical touches and deep harmonic knowledge didn't have a lot in common with the post-Coltrane/Jimi Hendrix wailings of fusion hero Larry Coryell. But Coryell and Phillip Catherine, a Belgian touted as the fusion heir of Django Reinhardt, and John Scofield, who would later work with Miles Davis, threaded the popular sound of jazz-rock guitar through the album dubbed *Three or Four Shades of Blues*.

Jeffrey rewrote Mingus's music to fit the new sound while the composer and his band were on the road. The musicians didn't like producer Ilhan Mimaroglu, a classical musician who liked takes that were safe and clean and without clams. He'd pull a track for one flub, even if the solos were ferocious and music rocked. It was very un-Mingus. And Silva was rarely around during the sessions.

Saxist George Coleman, a Memphis native who played with B. B. King in his early days, slid into the traditional Mingus-band brawny tenor slot where blues meets bop, the slot that Booker Ervin and Clifford Jordan had filled years earlier. Another Bradley's regular, Coleman had taken Sonny Rollins's vacated spot in Max Roach's late-1950s band, then moved into Miles Davis's group between John Coltrane and Wayne Shorter, later working with Elvin Jones and Charles McPherson. He never became a star, but his 1970s octet drew a lot of critical acclaim.

Whenever the big, tight-lipped Coleman joined the looming Cunningham and Mingus at a table in Bradley's, the trio overwhelmed everyone in the room.

George Mraz played bass, to buttress Mingus's weakening efforts and give him room to solo without having to hold down the bottom. Ron Carter took over for one track.

Mingus used the Yamaha amplifier all the time now. He virtually always used a cane when he walked. He shrugged it off when people asked him what was wrong, and he and Sue managed to keep gossip about his physical condition down. It was his back. It was his weight. It was too much touring.

He didn't want anybody messing with his earnings, or his legacy.

By the end of their first day in the studio, the group recorded the remakes of "Better Get Hit in Your Soul" and "Goodbye Porkpie Hat" and "Noddin Ya Head Blues." Jeffrey's charts tried to weave fusion guitar through Mingus music.

Coryell's blistering solo on "Better Get Hit in Your Soul" led into Ford's sinewy tenor, and Jeffrey scored the guitars to back Ford with riffs like horns would. It was a novel Mingus touch, although the mix often buried the piano and horns behind the guitars, pushed the basses way up front like a rock recording.

"Goodbye Porkpie Hat" opened with Mraz's bowed introduction. It was a tacit admission of loss of ability from Mingus, always so proud of his arco playing. Coryell and Catherine sped around on acoustic guitars in the macho fashion of many fusioneers, an attitude that had something in common with the postwar flock of Bird imitators and their strutting derivative solos. The guitars sandwiched a subtly muscular solo from Coleman.

"Noddin" was the kind of slow blues widely favored in rock and jazz at the time, but graced with an affectionately tongue-in-cheek old-timey melody of the type Mingus loved. Coryell lit his solo with homages to the string-bending skills of B. B. and Albert and Freddie King as well as the space-blues of Jimi Hendrix. Mingus's bass was brief, full of the revolutionary note-bending skills he'd introduced to the bass thirty years earlier.

He was reclaiming his own history for a new generation. He was almost fifty-five years old.

Few record company people outplayed him at negotiating for long.

On March 10, the day after the initial recordings for the new album, Atlantic wanted him to come up with three-minute tunes for radio play. He brought in a different large band to play a long piece he'd been working on, called "Cumbia and Jazz Fusion."

The piece marked the first time Jimmy Knepper had played with Mingus in years. When he was writing "Cumbia and Jazz Fusion," Mingus called him: "I wrote this part for you. You're my trombonist, man."

He was closing circles everywhere.

"Cumbia and Jazz Fusion" was one of the strongest works he'd written in years, inspired by another non-Cuban Latin music. He never liked to tread the beaten path. He told the musicians he'd gone to Colombia and heard the raucous, loping music that had come down from the rural hills and into the cities. Called cumbia, it was Colombia's national music, like bossa nova in Brazil.

Mingus loved the rhythms rippling from clave's three-against-two insistence, bought a bunch of records, and started sketching ideas based around the sound. He came up with this extended piece to play off his band's strengths, let them stretch but keep them in the pocket, push them but discipline them. It was episodic and multithemed. Once again, he was suggesting a new Latin jazz synthesis alongside the dominant Afro-Cuban-jazz pioneered by Dizzy Gillespie in the 1940s.

A couple of weeks before the early March session, Mingus had Jeffrey come up to Woodstock, and they listened to his Colombian records a lot.

PAUL JEFFREY: He'd say, "Hear that sound there? That's what I want." He messed around for a while trying to get his thoughts together, how he'd like it. All of a sudden it clicked. He stayed up for almost a week making his music. I remember well, because I was doing the orchestrating. He'd stay up, and I'd be so tired. He'd tell me, "Go and lay down. When you wake up, come on back." The sheer energy of the guy. He did all that in almost one sitting.

The piece opened with bird and animal effects ricocheting off a battery of South American percussion instruments and congas. An augmented fifteen-piece band that included Knepper and Jeffrey played call-and-response with short, pithy Latin melodies. Jazzier interludes and ensemble sections appeared and alternated, opening into solos over Mingus's relentless six-note bass pattern.

It seemed natural for Mingus to hire his bar-owning pal Bradley Cunningham as part of a big percussion section that included the famed Cuban conga master Candido. They loved each other. They were both outsized, with huge appetites. And they'd shared dentists and psychiatrists.

Walrath's Latin-tinged hornwork iced the cake. In its range, the piece even incorporated contemporary disco beats. The band wasn't surprised. They knew Mingus showed up at rock showcase clubs like the Bottom Line and at rock concerts by stars like Stevie Wonder at arenas like Madison Square Garden. He was always checking out other scenes, was open to sounds from anywhere if he could use them for his needs.

In the midst of "Cumbia and Jazz Fusion" was a gutbucket blues section. Near the piece's end, the second time the segment appeared, Mingus sang a parody of the old darky song "Shortnin' Bread" in a thickened guttural voice.

CHARLES MINGUS: Who said Mama's little baby liked shortnin' bread?/That's some lie some white man up and said/Mama's little baby don't like no shortnin' bread/Mama's little baby likes truffles/Mama's little baby likes caviar/Mama's little baby likes all the finer things of life/All the things that a real good person should have/Mama's little baby likes African gold mines . . . ./Mama's little baby likes schools.[1]

Live, "Cumbia" became a showstopping set piece. But recording, as always, had its own Mingusy demands.

When Mingus brought the music into the studio, the Atlantic brass were not amused. The label wanted something short and radio-ready, not too challenging.

He stonewalled the producers. "This," he said, "is it, what we've been doing live, and I haven't recorded it here yet." He wanted to recut "Todo Modo" as well, so they'd have an album with two pieces, each a full side's length.

They were reduced to quibbling about duration: twenty-three to twenty-five minutes was the ideal length for an LP side, to maximize fidelity. In its original form, "Todo Modo" was just shy of twenty-eight minutes, and he wouldn't cut a note, a phrase, a solo.

It was payback time for the pressure to do fusion.

Playing back the session tapes from "Cumbia and Jazz Fusion" for Mingus, Jeffrey was once more astonished by how acutely he could listen.

At one point in the piece, a pedal-point F is doubled at length by trombone, bassoon, baritone, and other instruments. Bassoonist Gene Scholes, one of the crew Jeffrey brought over from Juilliard to fill out the fifteen-piece recording outfit, had a squeaky reed. Every time he played, Mingus grunted, "Uh, uh, uh."

Each instrument had its own recording track, so Jeffrey, when he mixed the piece later that day, thought, "We can't get the squeak out, so better to drop the track. It's doubled up anyway." That's what he and the producers did.

Then he brought the tape to Mingus at the East 10th Street apartment, as he did for all the recordings during this time. Mingus never went to mixing sessions.

At the apartment, Mingus listened, then started shooting odd looks at his arranger. Finally he said, "Where's the concert bassoon?" Jeffrey was shocked: "He had a squeak." "I don't care, you're messing with my music."

Jeffrey returned to the studio, put the bassoon back in, and went back to the boss with the new tape. Mingus listened to the squeak, was satisfied, and said, "We're gonna leave that out."

Nobody made the final call but him.

He wanted a rattlesnake for part of the track. The producers overdubbed maracas instead. At the apartment he yelled, "What's that? That ain't no rattlesnake. I was born in Arizona, and I know what the hell a rattlesnake sounds like." They went up to a game preserve in upstate New York, and taped a rattlesnake's shakes, and Mingus was satisfied.

The day after the "Cumbia and Jazz Fusion" sessions, they were back in Atlantic's studios to record "Nobody Knows," a ten-minute cut for *Three or Four Shades of Blues* that featured young guitarist John Scofield, with altoist Sonny Fortune and bassist Ron Carter replacing George Coleman and George Mraz. Its jaunty bop-inflected melody reworked "Nobody Knows the Trouble I've Seen," with allusions to "Down by the Riverside" and "Alexander's Ragtime Band." It was a typically Mingus melange. The twin basses, both amplified, jostled for position, sometimes effectively, sometimes as an amplified muddle.

They took a flyer at the complex, multisectioned title track Mingus had fashioned. He transformed Silva's prodding toward fusion into a thematic conception for the piece, which traced a few strands in the history of blues development. Different sections referred to music by Duke Ellington and Count Basie, Latin-jazz and what he called "super bebop." Playing one section of that music, Coryell remarked, "Hey Mingus, that's the Caucasian blues." He used that as that section's title.

When the playback got to that part, though, Mingus got upset. Pianist Bob Neloms used diminished chords in his solo. "There's no diminished chords in my music," he raged, as he had at pianists over four decades.

Musically, diminished chords are modes of transit from one key or tonal center to another. Mingus didn't like to make transitions, musically or otherwise. He didn't see the need. Just do it. When Miles Davis had asked him thirty years earlier why he didn't modulate, just went blam from this key to that, Mingus smiled sweetly and said, "Miles, just play the shit like I wrote it."[2]

Neloms didn't. The solo had to be fixed. Mingus withheld final approval for the track.

The band went back on the road for a few days, and the producers had a brainstorm. They put tacks on the hammers of an upright piano, so Mingus could recut the piano solo like it was an old honky-tonk. At the end of March, when

Mingus walked back into the studio, he hit the ceiling and started yelling, "What is THIS?" He wasn't born in a whorehouse. What did they think he was? The studio technicians tore down the setup fast.

Jimmy Rowles, another buddy from Bradley's, got the call to overdub the solo. Only Mingus, Sue, Jeffrey, and Mimaroglu were there when he unfurled a beautiful, thoughtful story across the "Caucasian Blues." Rowles was a performing fixture at Bradley's because of the same virtues Mingus treasured in him: he respected the architecture of the music he played, didn't reduce it to a vehicle for his blowing.

Younger players came to Bradley's to jam with Rowles and his compatriots in order to learn the ropes. This informal club was a center of the old oral tradition in jazz, the big band incubators and jam sessions that had nurtured and educated Mingus's generation, the on-the-bandstand training that made them jazz-literate and musical individuals.

When Rowles finished, there was utter silence in the studio. Everyone waited for Mingus to speak. He looked up and said, "That's it." One take. They spliced it in.

Interviewing Mingus before the disc's release, *Down Beat* interviewer Arnold Jay Smith asked him why he made it, given his often-stated dislike of fusion.

CHARLES MINGUS: Because that's what the public wants. Rock music is taking over what I was doing twenty years ago. This is a way of saying, "Look what I've done." "Pork Pie Hat" was recorded by Jeff Beck, so I wanted to hear the way Larry Coryell would play it. Jeff Beck didn't play the chord changes, just the melody. So many people have recorded it—like Rahsaan Roland Kirk, John McLaughlin, Bertram Turetsky, so I just wanted to hear it myself—and get others to hear it as well.[3]

He was reclaiming his legacy.

Producer Ilhan Mimaroglu agreed in his liner notes, an uncomfortable stab at mixing pseudo-hip attitudes ("This is 1977 A.D., man! Indeed it is, and A.D. stands for Anno Disorientato") and ponderous explication. He defended Mingus's taking on electric guitars despite his dislike of rock, and claimed Mingus especially enjoyed Phillip Catherine's work. "Let's adopt his restrained way with accolades," he wrote, "and say he was satisfied."[4]

Mingus said Mimaroglu behaved like a German producer. He wrote like a cross between a low-rent Tom Wolfe and a dusty academic.

Three or Four Shades of Blues sold 50,000 copies in a couple of months.[5] Mingus told people he didn't like the album, at least at first; it sounded too commercial. But he took the money happily. He rarely used material from it onstage.

Around their scattered March days in the studio, the band was on the road almost nonstop, as it had been for most of the preceding four years. Mingus had never wanted to tour endlessly, like Ellington, but like Duke, he had to keep the band together to make big money.

The itinerary for spring 1977 that Sue, as his manager and booker, created for him, listed tens of thousands of dollars' worth of dates. He scrawled along its side, "This is how Nixon does it and don't go to jail."[6]

For a six-night stint at Seattle's Pioneer Banque, the band got $6,000.[7] He was using an amplifier all the time now. It was written into his contracts that the clubs had to provide it.

With the same will he'd always focused on what he wanted, he overrode his now-constant disabilities and nagging problems and toured North America, South America, Europe, North Africa. Starting May 21, the band played São Paulo, Rio de Janeiro, Belo Horizonte, Porto Alegre, Montevideo, Buenos Aires, Lima, and Mexico City before they landed back in the United States for a one-nighter in Santa Fe on June 10. Twelve days later, they performed at a benefit for feminist-writer-politician Bella Abzug at the Village Gate. On July 5, the band went to Europe, where they played Nice, Italy, Sicily, San Sebastian.[8]

They were running hard.

But Mingus did no soloing. Dannie Richmond and the band covered the holes. People came to see him, just to see him. He got ovations spontaneously, sometimes, like in San Francisco, just for walking onstage to put his bass there. He loved it.

Three or Four Shades of Blues was selling better than anything else he'd done. He was generating a new generation of fans. He was a legend fully reborn. Kids were coming to see him, the way they had in the golden days.

Mingus told an interviewer that "Cumbia and Jazz Fusion" was a sound track for a movie about Colombian drug dealers smuggling cocaine.[9] The upturn in American cocaine use was part of the time, the disco era. The hot clubs, like Studio 54 in New York, were full of well-heeled heads and transactions. The pipelines from Colombia to the American market involved governments, armies, secret services, and various mafias in its internationally tangled cash flow, culminating years later in the Iran-Contragate scandal, under then-President Ronald Reagan.

That June, as he'd done for twenty-plus years, Mingus was set to perform at the Newport Jazz Festival. He was taking a fifteen-piece band into the Bottom Line to test-drive "Cumbia and Jazz Fusion" onstage.

At Avery Fisher (formerly Philharmonic) Hall, he wowed the crowd. In the *New York Times*, critic Robert Palmer claimed enthusiastically that the piece fused Latin street music with Mingus's impressions of a Colombian village.[10]

Mingus liked Palmer and let the young writer hang out. It didn't bother him that Palmer was an Ornette Coleman champion, that he liked a good deal of fusion, that he covered rock and blues with the same intensity he followed jazz. Mingus was always looking for minds, especially younger ones, that didn't run along precut channels.

Mingus's old colleague David Amram was organizing a children's concert at New York University, as part of George Wein's festival, and the two bands wound up rehearsing at the same space, so the leaders bumped into each other.

He was closing circles everywhere.

Mingus told Amram he was proud to have had him as a sideman and glad they'd been able to keep hanging out and exchanging ideas, even after Amram's 1966 composer-in-residency at the New York Philharmonic. Amram retorted, "If it wasn't for hanging out with you, Mingus, I'd probably be trying to get a job."

Later that summer, Keki, on school vacation, Eugene, and Sue all came on the tour through Europe and North Africa.

Keki was elated at first. It was a big treat to be on the road with her dad, even if she was really into a Rolling Stones–knockoff band called Aerosmith. But she quickly realized she was a big drag for the musicians. They had to behave better, clean up their talk, even though she saw the girls going in and out of their rooms, her father's room.

When Mingus got paid, the musicians gathered in his room, and he had Keki dole out the money.

CAROLYN (KEKI) MINGUS: I was embarrassed by him a lot of the time then. He was different on the road, very animated, telling exaggerated stories, elaborate, grandiose stories that weren't true. He didn't usually do that stuff in front of me. All the guys were doing it, one-upping each other, being macho.

In the lobby of the huge Hyatt hotel in Tunis, a man came up to her and said, "You shouldn't be with this man. He's dark." She said, "He's my father."

He said, "We don't do that here. You're light-skinned." She wanted to protect him. She knew how it hurt, made him ache like a little kid.

Mingus complained all the time across Europe about racism causing bad service. A few times he hurled plates of food through doors and windows. He'd order one of everything off the menu, eat it, lie on the floor, and deliver a lecture to his daughter about learning to drink so she could never be taken advantage of.

Bringing him drinks, she felt somewhere between mascot and manager.

He was happy, she thought. He was playing, and the crowds were big and appreciative. But she was sure he was dying, and sure that he knew it too.

Just before Sue joined them in Tunisia, Keki tried to persuade Walrath and Ford that her dad was sick. They shrugged. But she knew he wouldn't use a wheelchair at every airport, show that kind of weakness in front of her time after time, unless something was desperately wrong.

Just then, his voice came out his windows: "Carolyn! Carolyn!" She raced to the elevator. When she got to his room, he was stuck in bed: he couldn't turn over. He cried, and she cried, as she helped him roll.

After the tour, he didn't see her as much.

In Tunisia, Mingus began formulating the follow-up album to *Three or Four Shades of Blues*. The Atlantic brass wanted another crossover record. He wasn't sure yet what he wanted.

In Tunis, he took the whole band out to a fancy restaurant, where he ate an entire bass himself. He'd picked up more North African records, and was listening intently.

Two years earlier, Ornette Coleman had gone to Morocco with writer Robert Palmer and recorded part of his album *Dancing in Your Head* with the Master Musicians of Joujouka, who drummed and went into ecstatic trances. Rock musicians like Rolling Stones founder Brian Jones were fascinated by their music. So were writers Paul Bowles and William Burroughs.

The vogue for bringing African culture into Western culture had accelerated during the 1960s, as it had in the 1920s, across the cultural front, from rock and jazz to the visual arts.

Mingus knew Stravinsky's dictum: "Lesser artists borrow. Great artists steal." The Russian composer meant, in part, that all artists work from previous ideas. What matters is how deeply they make those ideas their own. Great artists transform their sources into their own art completely enough to subsume them.

The seeds of one of the last Mingus extended pieces, "Three Worlds of Drums," were sown here. It was another work of synthesis, melding African, Latin, and American drumming. Integration in all forms was at his core.

The end of August 1977 brought one last review from John S. Wilson at the *New York Times*. The critic described Mingus's "slow steady revitalization" between his time off the scene and his early, tentative comeback. Wilson saw him "approaching the creative generating role of twenty years earlier." And he noted that the live shows were more Mingus than *Three or Four Shades of Blues*.

The band covered his encroaching inabilities with extended solos, with fuguelike lines between horns, with drum solos instead of encores, with shtick. And they stayed on the road until he finally wore out.

The quintet pulled into Tempe, Arizona, not far from where he'd been born more than fifty-five years earlier. The World Series was in full swing, and the New York Yankees were once more in the thick of it.

Mingus didn't care about baseball, but Walrath and Ford did. The young guys were watching the series on TV during the band's breaks. When they came back for the second set, Mingus said simply, "I can't go on." They got him into the car, back to the hotel, and then, the next day, back home.

Sue and Mingus headed up to Woodstock for a couple of weeks' breather, and Mingus had a plan.

He and Sue had talked about moving up to Woodstock eventually. If his friend Sonny Rollins living across the river could have a private rehearsal space on his farm, why couldn't he have a studio on his land?

So he sketched one, looking at architecture books. It had an air about it of Fallingwater, the famed Frank Lloyd Wright house: about it: he pictured it hanging off a glacial outcropping behind the house at Witchtree Road.

They hired architect Robert Young, and paid him $960 to draw Mingus's design according to proper specifications. Young himself lived on Manhattan's Upper West Side but had a weekend place in Bearsville, just west of Woodstock. Three days later, Mingus asked Young for an estimate for construction costs. For the new deck connecting the studio and house, and a new driveway road and parking, the total was $67,532.07, including a $7,000 architect's fee.[11]

Mingus was making big money. He thought he was coming back once the numbness lifted again.

He wanted to go to India. He didn't want to have happen to him what happened to Charlie Parker when he died, the ego clashes, the wrangles over the body, the competing claims.

Sue contacted Lucille Rollins, Sonny's wife and manager, about his trip there to play the first Indian jazz festival.[12] She wanted to see if there was some way Mingus could tag along, or do something similar.

Mingus believed in reincarnation. He was thinking about Vedanta more and more. Farwell Taylor had died, and he called the artist's wife and daughter a day after he'd died, and said simply, "He's gone, isn't he?"

One part of him knew he was dying. He refused to believe it, or get it confirmed or denied.

CELIA MINGUS ZAENTZ: I was in Woodstock, and I went over to meet Sue for the first time and see Mingus, and I was shocked when I saw how unwell he was. I was furious, too. They were talking about going out on tour, and I said, "That's ridiculous, you're in no condition." And Sue said, "Well, he wants to keep the band together, and we need some money coming in to do that." I asked Mingus how much he'd make on the tour, and he said about $12,000. See, it didn't seem like he wanted to go out. It seemed more like Sue was pushing for the tour. I was upset enough that when I got back to California I said to Saul, "You've got to give him some money, whether he has royalties coming or not." So Saul wrote the check. They hadn't done accounting for a while, and Mingus did have money coming.

He was closing circles everywhere he could.

On November 6, 1977, Mingus had a date to record with Lionel Hampton. Hamp was going to present Mingus music, a reverse tribute to his former sideman. Baritone saxist Gerry Mulligan was joining them, and Paul Jeffrey played tenor sax, which made the group an octet.

Rumors about his health were eddying slowly around the jazz world. Mingus had slipped discs. Mingus was overweight. Mingus was strung out.

The eddies would slowly widen, as did the intrigues around him.

He asked Jeffrey to arrange the music for the album and show it to Hampton. Jeffrey showed up at the vibist's apartment opposite Lincoln Center. Hampton, a stone Republican, got to "Remember Rockefeller at Attica" and said to the young black man, "No, Gates, we are not going to play that." Rockefeller and Hampton were close, Attica or no. Mingus shrugged and said, "Change the title." Hamp never knew.

Mingus played one solo, on "Just for Laughs, Saps," his new title for "Remember Rockefeller at Attica."

PAUL JEFFREY: By the end of that date, Mingus said, "My hands, man, they're stiff." Everyone said, "Gee, it sounded beautiful." He didn't want to play solos at the date. And it was the last recording he played bass on, that one solo too. Then I remember going to his house and him saying, "I can't play this piano no

more." I thought he was being Mingus, being dissatisfied with his piano playing. I didn't realize he was at the beginning of Lou Gehrig's disease.

The day before Thanksgiving, November 23, 1977, Charles Mingus Jr. entered Columbia Presbyterian Neurological Institute. Jody DeVito's mother had
given him the name of the neurologist who had operated on Robert Kennedy
after his assassination by Sirhan Sirhan in Los Angeles in 1968.

Mingus was grossly overweight. He couldn't walk. The tests began: an elec-
tromyocardiogram (EMG), where needles are inserted into the muscles to
record their electrical activity, spinal column X-rays, tests of sensation, reflexes,
heart and lungs. The verdict was finally rendered: amyotrophic lateral sclero-
sis, or ALS. [13]

ALS is better known as Lou Gehrig's disease, after the famed 1930s New
York Yankee first baseman, Babe Ruth's teammate and pal. In 1939, ALS cut
off the Iron Man's record streak of playing in 2,130 consecutive games—a
record that stood until 1995. A soap-opera version of his life, *Pride of the Yankees*, starred Gary Cooper.

ALS is a fatal neurological disorder, mostly found in people between the
ages of forty and seventy. It attacks the nerve cells and pathways in the brain to
the spinal cord. It kills the motor neurons that reach from the brain to the
spinal cord and thus to the muscles throughout the body. In the process, it de-
stroys the brain's web of circuitry for muscle nourishment and control.

Early symptoms include twitching and cramping of muscles in the hands
and feet, reduced use of arms and legs, thickened and slurred speech, weak-
ened vocal projection, shortness of breath. The muscles atrophy as the nerves
degenerate and die, and the brain's ability to start and control muscle movement throughout the body diminishes and finally halts.

The area of the body affected and the rate of progressive decline vary from
patient to patient, but the result is virtually always the same: progressive paralysis, usually ending in death within five years from one or another type of res-
piratory failure.

Throughout all the disease's stages, the mind remains fully alive. The
senses remain intact. The eye muscles are unaffected. Sexual functions remain. The patient watches himself die, slowly and inevitably buried alive in his
decaying body.

The disease with Gehrig's name is not rare—each year, nearly 5,000 people in
the United States are diagnosed with it. But doctors in 1977 thought it was
rarer. And it was, and is, extremely difficult to diagnose accurately. Patients are

typically 20 percent to 50 percent into the disease when a neurologist finally makes the call.

There is no known cause. There is no known cure. There is nothing to do besides keep the patient well fed and as healthy and happy as possible. Maximize the quality of life, while the victim slides toward death.

Charles Mingus had refused to be a victim ever since he'd learned to vanquish Coustie, the bully of his Watts childhood. As often as he cast himself in the role to play agent provocateur, he refused, in his life and his music, to play the part. He'd always reared up and fought, overcome and come back over whatever obstacles he had to, and if he bitched about having to do it—well, he was a genius, and the fact that he was black, even shit-colored like him, meant he couldn't get his genius properly recognized without fighting.

He wasn't a victim. He wasn't taking their bullshit lying down. He had too many things still undone.

They told Sue that Mingus had three to six months to live. She couldn't believe it. She was numb and stunned. She'd seen the Gary Cooper movie. But what did that have to do with the fact that suddenly Charles was going to die?

But she could see he couldn't do the European tour with electric guitarists to promote *Three of Four Shades of Blues* in Europe, so she canceled it. And she began wrestling with the first of the near-endless stream of problems, demands, needs, and hopes that would engulf them during the last year of Mingus's life.

ALS meant a lot of immediate changes. He couldn't climb the four-floor staircase to get to their East 10th Street apartment. They had to find a new place to live, with an elevator. Meanwhile, they had to stay somewhere. And he'd need intensive nursing care. Somehow he had to keep creative. And of course his music had to be organized, tended, pushed.

The tenacity that he'd recognized in her, that was one of the lures she had for him, focused on him entirely now.

One of the most vitally intense people who'd ever walked the planet was on an inexorable trajectory to a living death, and she not only had to watch but had to help him maintain some dignity, self-possession, creativity.

Sue didn't tell him the diagnosis right away. "How," she asked herself, "can you tell a fighting man he doesn't have half a chance?"

Mingus was delirious from medication and stress. The flickering shadows of numbness and paralysis and doubt that had been lurking around him for two years, that he'd been brushing aside and away, wondering about all those pills he'd taken, all those things he'd done, had now come around from trailing doggedly behind him to face him head-on.

Sue had to get him out of the hospital. There was nothing else the doctors could do, and they wanted to keep him there. Sue was determined. As many people would, they underestimated her, and Mingus.

Roberto Ungaro knew Mingus was always finding allies everywhere. A black elevator operator helped Sue walk Mingus out in a wheelchair, past the doctors.

Sue was racing to research the disease, treatments and alternative treatments and sources and sites they might need. First they flew to Switzerland, where he was injected with sheep placentas.

He didn't accept the verdict. He was Charles Mingus. He had never accepted a verdict on him in his entire life. He would not go gentle into that good night. He wasn't finished with his work. His legacy was still in the making. The symphony he'd started sketching in the laborious detail that always crabbed his written music, with the names of the players he wanted for each part, wasn't done. It was mostly old pieces he'd played for twenty and thirty years.

Later, Sue and Gunther Schuller and a young musicologist named Andrew Homzy would try to fit the pieces, old and new, back together like a jigsaw puzzle, and call the results *Epitaph*.

The injections heightened Mingus's hallucinations.

Sue and Roberto brought him back to a suite at the Plaza Hotel, a gorgeous landmark on Central Park South. They manuevered him onto the king-size bed. There he imagined he was on the beach, stretched out in the sun on the sand. Like the dying King Lear, he went through a period of madness, bouts of hallucinogenic irrationality intercut with scenes of apparent lucidity, as the core members of his brain trust came through the hotel.

He refused to believe the diagnosis. Sue didn't want anyone to know what it was until the marks of the disease were undeniable. She couldn't stand the thought of his humiliation. She worried about money. She scrambled to bring some in, whatever it took.

She had been doing her homework. She knew how much it cost to maintain an ALS patient: full-time nursing care, massages, drugs, alternate treatments. She knew Mingus didn't trust Western medicine. She interviewed doctors and found their confusion frustrating.

She wondered whether mellaril hastened the progress of ALS, since it lowers the white corpuscle count, the body's first-line defense system. She called Dr. Alden, who'd prescribed it, and he hung up on her.

The East Coast medical establishment thought ALS was a virus attacking the nervous system. The West Coast thought it was the defense system turned against itself.

She was getting the drift—an implacable verdict rendered from a dimly lit room. She knew Mingus wouldn't lie down on the doctors' say-so.

Mingus started to cover his bets the best he could. Among those he summoned to the Plaza was the Reverend Gensel, his old Lutheran pal/sparring partner/chaplain.

THE REVEREND JOHN GARCIA GENSEL: Charlie could barely get out of bed. When he was alone with me, he brought out and gave me two of his bankbooks. He said, "Here, here." I looked at him. One of them had $40,000. The other had about $20,000. I didn't want to say, "Well, no Charlie"—I didn't want to offend him. "Gee, thanks, Charlie." And I took them. Then he gave me a $500 bill. He said, "Here, give that to the church." I stuck it in my pocket. Afterward, when I was with Sue alone, I said, "Sue, Charlie gave me these books, but of course they're not for me." So I gave her the two bankbooks. Then I said, "He also gave me $500. What should I do with it?" She said, "Well, keep it. He wanted it to go to the church?" I said yes. "Then give it to the church." Isn't that something? Given his dislike of organized religion and being suspicious and all, he gave me those two bankbooks.

Mingus was staring into the abyss, and looking for a handhold. The waves of delirium washed over him like gentle, rocking surf.

When Gensel visited, Sue's son Roberto was playing under the covers in the next room with Jody DeVito. It was Roberto who broke delirium's wall of mirrors around Mingus.

The twenty-one-year-old watched the others fret about how to get Mingus off his beach and out of the hotel. "We're gonna need a boat to get outta here," Roberto heard him say, and thought, "We'll turn the bed into a boat." Roberto sat down and told Charles to pretend, while he was at the beach, that he was at a hotel, and he needed to get into a wheelchair, which was really a boat, to roll out of it. Mingus started laughing, as if he'd sighted the humorous outlines of his madness, and it began to lift.

And so he climbed into his irreal boat of Ra.

Once Sue found a new apartment in Manhattan Plaza, the madness subsided.

The new apartment was in artists' housing, a subsidized project overlooking the Hudson River on West 43rd Street. They got a spacious two-bedroom with dining room, work kitchen, living room, and a spacious balcony where the westward views along the river shone spectacularly.

It was a fine place to die.

"If you have only a few months to live," says Sue, "you don't go to pieces. You try to do something as pleasurable as possible."

His regime stabilized: the daily round of injections, the shift nurses coming and going, the man in the wheelchair with the increasingly unhooded eyes, powerful beacons wired to the unyielding will within. His eyes in these last months could make clear what he wanted, even when speaking became difficult or impossible.

It was a ritual to get him clean and dressed and into his wheelchair and out around noon. The rest of the day was filled with planning for his evening outing. Dinner was the main event. What good restaurant that had duck with sherry sauce—his current passion—could accommodate him? Where could they get the invalid coach to pick them up?

They doggedly worked their way up and down Restaurant Row, some of the finest and most expensive eateries in New York. People would recognize him. Sometimes he wanted to be known, sometimes he didn't.

JODY DEVITO ALSOP, *assistant*: He got emotional. I saw him cry a lot. When you have an illness, it humbles you. He had to be doing a lot of thinking, he was so trapped in his body. You have to understand, this was one of the most powerful people in the world, who can't move, who's frozen. He was losing his speech, it got very slurred, and he would dribble. Sometimes that mattered to him, and sometimes I don't think he gave a shit. That's who he was. It depended on the mood.

They would fight ALS up to the very end, and keep the diagnosis secret from the world as long as they could.

SUSAN GRAHAM UNGARO MINGUS: When Charles was dying, Roberto would come just to keep up his spirits. Called him misery—"Hey, misery." It was refreshing because when people are dying, no one knows how to deal with it. Bradley used to invite us down and worry about whether Charles could pee. Straightahead thing, but most people are hands off. The first time we sort of made a public appearance after the shit hit the fan and we knew Charles was going to die, we went to a rehearsal. Very poignant. We opened the door and this blast of sound and music came at us as I was wheeling Charles. Afterwards, they came over and grabbed his hands, which were already pretty motionless. But there was no distance. Most people weren't like that. There is a big distance with illness. A terrible thing happens, the fear that's associated with it, the lack of knowledge if you haven't been around it.

Days after they moved into Manhattan Plaza, Sue sent a note to one of the officials at the Guggenheim Foundation, along with a copy of John Wilson's laudatory *New York Times* piece from that summer and other materials. She wanted a follow-up grant for Mingus.[14]

Meantime, life had to go on. The dogs grew even more protective of him, sitting close to his wheelchair, hovering, alert and ready to lunge when anyone drew too near.

The procession of family and close friends continued while rumors circulated about his condition. They went up to Woodstock, and Roberto came across the river from Bard every weekend. He and Jody would clown around, prancing in front of Mingus's wheelchair sharing a pair of his billowing shorts like a vaudeville team. Judy brought Eric over. He didn't want to see Carolyn. He didn't want to see his son Charles. Dannie Richmond, Sonny Rollins and Lucille, Sy Johnson and his wife Lois, Janet Coleman—only a handful saw him the way he was.

JUDY STARKEY MINGUS MCGRATH: The last time I saw him, I went to 43rd Street to drop Eric to visit for the weekend. He was already in the wheelchair, and Joni Mitchell was there talking to him. I remember stroking his arm. His diagnosis was pretty dismal. I was a private duty nurse then, and I took care of a man who had ALS. At some point, it arrested and he'd had some mobility. I hoped for that. But Charlie—he couldn't move. He was in the chair.

He had a recording session scheduled for *Me Myself an Eye*, the album slated to follow *Three or Four Shades of Blues*. He had to delegate even more music than usual, which made crossed lines of power and responsibility inevitable.

When the king is dying, the intrigue among the courtiers intensifies. And that is precisely what happened around Mingus's last sessions.

He asked Jack Walrath to arrange "Something Like a Bird" and "Three Worlds of Drums." The hornman came up to Woodstock, and he and Mingus were up around the clock for days. He'd give Walrath a tape of him noodling at the piano, and say, "Make a tune out of this." Or he'd hand him a lead sheet and ask him to orchestrate. Sometimes Walrath supplied parts of the melody, or wrote a bridge, or infused counterpoint, or created chord changes—what he saw as the work of an arranger. It was a collaborative effort in classic Mingus mode.

JACK WALRATH: It was intense. He'd give me some guides. "Why don't you try this?" I'd write all this out, and be checking it on the piano. He'd be glowering:

"What are you doing to my music?" Most of the stuff he didn't like was stuff he wrote. I wanted to kill him. Jimmy Knepper told me that happened with him too. But he was one extreme or the other—extremely positive or negative.

Mingus kept focusing on coming back again. He told Walrath to write the charts so that the band could play them. But Atlantic had other ideas. The label lined up a host of special guests to enlarge the group, including the Brecker Brothers, fusion stars who played sax and trumpet.

Then Paul Jeffrey became a flashpoint.

Walrath thought Jeffrey, his friend and mentor, was jealous of his relationship with Mingus. The trumpeter felt offended. For this session, Mingus didn't want to use Jeffrey, and Walrath had changed the sick man's mind. Then at the rehearsals Jeffrey treated him like a jerk. Rumors began spreading that Walrath was telling people he wrote all the music for the record. Nothing could be more calculated to fire up Mingus's temperature.

Sy Johnson thought Jeffrey played the race card heavy-handedly with Mingus, hovering around him, keeping him separated from his other musical cohorts. He was disgusted Mingus would go for it.

Jeffrey thought otherwise. He talked Mingus into rehearsing the band, which had grown from the core quintet to various lineups embracing thirty-odd players. He brought in some friends from Juilliard again, and added in more of Mingus's own history, like George Coleman, Slide Hampton, Jimmy Knepper, and Pepper Adams.

Eddie Gomez played bass. Mingus couldn't even pretend to. Mercifully, that quelled Atlantic's other commercial plan: a collaboration on electric bass with fusion star Stanley Clarke.

Sitting in the chair, Mingus was still furious about that. The label spent a year trying to talk him into it, insisting it would help him sell records. To Jeffrey and others he snorted, "The guy can't even play 'A Train.' And what he plays isn't a bass, it's a bass guitar. Do you see any frets on my bass?"

During the rehearsals for *Me Myself an Eye*, a few musicians bailed out, complaining about the music, the politics, the tensions.

On January 18, 19, and 23, Charles Mingus went into the studio for the last time. He sat in his wheelchair, wearing a neck brace and a Stetson hat and usually smoking one of his Cuban cigars. The musicians say his presence was palpable, that he managed to direct the recording even though he said little and could play nothing.

The first two days, work was slow. The ensemble was massive, the charts were difficult, and there was an air of death hanging over the session. He told them he'd be back, but he looked like hell, even behind the shades and hat. And the wheelchair was undeniable.

Lee Konitz smoked a cigar with him, and felt that they had great communication. Randy Brecker felt like Mingus ran the whole session with his eyes. Walrath and Ford felt like the session had been taken away from them.

The music was a muddle, poorly recorded, mediocrely arranged, but well intentioned, and with some glowing moments. Dannie Richmond wondered why they paid so many great jazz players so much to read music. [15]

Listening in his wheelchair, watching the pile of mixes to choose from and correct, left him exhausted. Jeffrey hovered in attendance, but Mingus felt frustrated. He had to do everything himself, and now he wasn't able to. He'd always had others involved in his arranging and composing, but never before was he forced to abdicate so much control over the final product.

He thought of Hollywood, of Dmitri Tiomkin.

When he came back and listened to the mixed tapes, he sent a note over to Walrath. The trumpeter had written a brass solo for "Something Like a Bird." Mingus asked him to come to West 43rd Street and sign a statement saying that Mingus himself wrote it. Walrath was stunned. It was the first time Mingus had ever asked for anything like that.

JACK WALRATH: Mingus would always say, "Pass the melody around," which is like Ellington. A guy plays four bars of a melody, and another guy would finish it, write it down.

In *Rolling Stone*, the countercultural bible that arose in late 1960s San Francisco, Ben Sidran quoted Silva saying, "There's a new interest in him over here at Atlantic. They are interested in pushing him with ads. Everybody's concerned now about when the new album's coming out and how great the cover looks, things like that. Even if he, God forbid, passes away, Mingus will still be here." [16]

He had Sue get an ambulance one Sunday, and they loaded his chair to go cross-town to one of the Reverend Gensel's Jazz Vespers services. A hush settled over the church as he was wheeled in.

Roberto's girlfriend Jody was now working with Sue, managing the office, filling her days with phone calls to places to eat, searches for alternative treatments, and amusing distractions for the restless spirit looming from the wheelchair.

When they couldn't go out, they had dinners at home, on the long table set with gourmet dishes on beautiful Moroccan plates. He sat at its head, ruling the intellectuals as his nurse fed him or, after dinner, held his cigar while he puffed. Mingus music played in the candlelit apartment as guests like writer-photographer-filmmaker Gordon Parks feasted and talked.

Sue kept digging up projects to keep Mingus going.

The Brain Trust, as Roberto dubbed his friends, continued to troop into the apartment. Sonny Rollins helped steady Mingus and Sue with advice and sympathy and his calming attitude. Morris Eagle visited, as did Dannie Richmond. Sy Johnson grew closer to them than he'd been for a while, spending hours talking with Mingus, holding the phone for him so he could talk his sisters in California and friends around the world. Johnson was amazed how Mingus's presence seemed undiminished by his physical confinement.

Mingus's sister Vivian flew in from California, with her daughter. He gave her one of several wills he'd scrawled for people over the last few years.

Sue got Mingus a new tape recorder, so he could keep composing, at least hum or sing melodies into it. He used it constantly.

Down at Bradley's, the proprietor made sure he had a table waiting, and the clientele was cool as Mingus and Sue denied rumors of his illness. Even Jeffrey, sitting next to him at the table by the door one night, didn't realize how mortally ill Mingus was until the male nurse leaned over to him one night and said, "You'd better pray for him."

It was April 1978, and Sue decided to continue their tradition of throwing themselves a big joint birthday party. Things had to stay as normal as possible.

SUSAN GRAHAM UNGARO MINGUS: One of the regulars from Bradley's came over and was standing kind of uncertainly in front of Charles and Charles said, "What's the matter? Aren't you going to pick up my hand and say hello?" It's hard. Unless you've been around illness, it's distancing. Some good friends disappeared into the woodwork when Charles got sick because they couldn't handle it.

Keki saw him paralyzed in the wheelchair for the first time. She could see the life draining, but couldn't conceive of him dying. He was too alive, his force too strong. She was sure the party wasn't what he wanted, that it was embarrassing and demeaning for him.

Eric agreed. He'd spent the afternoon with his dad watching Steven Spielberg's *The Duel*—a movie about a driverless diabolical vehicle chasing people down California freeways. They were dialing around when they stumbled onto a special about Paul Robeson, who had died in 1976. Mingus pulled himself up in his chair and said, "Do you know who that is?" Eric said yes, but got a full-blown Robeson lecture anyway.

It was inevitable, necessary. Paul Robeson—singer, actor, political activist, scapegoat—was one of his favorites among the cautionary tales popular among black Americans.

Mingus told Eric he would always be considered black by the world around him, no matter what color his skin was.

ERIC MINGUS: Anyway, we get to share this intense father-son thing, and the door swings open, and in comes a throng of people. Some of the people who surrounded my dad were Sue's friends and people he didn't like. They were people who had him as a sort of ornament. They looked at him as an eccentric black jazz musician who you invited to a party because it was a great thing to do.

For her birthday, he presented Sue with a complete twenty-eight-volume Oxford English Dictionary, with a note that said, "To my best friend Sue." She burst into tears, and the party ground to an embarrassed halt for a while.

Johnson played the piano while Sue and his wife Lois sang "Happy Birthday," with Charles clearly in the background. They recorded it for posterity.

His hands got swollen, puffy. He had bouts of terrific pain, spasms when he could almost feel the nerves dying, his muscles shriveling. He'd stiffen and jerk, and then slump. If it happened when he was out, they had to load him into the van quickly. He was incontinent, which prevented him more and more from leaving home.

Sue pushed herself and Jody and the rest even harder. Find this doctor. Get that information. Order this wine. She was dogged, and she made impossible things happen, and she rarely slept long.

Mingus had a couple of major blowouts with her, even now. While she was screaming at him, he wheeled away into his room, and simply refused to talk to her. Silence was almost the only power he had left, but he knew how to wield it.

Inevitably, he went further into himself as he passed through the stages of dying.

A few months earlier, Daniel Senatore had played music by Joni Mitchell, the pop-folk diva, for Mingus and Sue. He thought they'd be interested in the mix of literate lyrics and jazzy vocal flourishes she'd developed. Mitchell's introspective, complex songwriting was highly regarded by rock critics and fans, and she cited jazz singers as her inspiration.

Besides, the record company wanted him to try collaborating with her. It was good visibility, a new audience.

Mitchell wanted to work with a jazz master who had a sensibility fit for poetry. Mingus had a long history of just that. The first time she was supposed to come by to see him, she sent a tape instead. He listened to it and told Paul Jeffrey, "She's trying to copy Billie Holiday a little, so maybe she can do something with me."

He had an idea: a full-scale work based on T.S. Eliot's "Four Quartets," a dense modernist poem about the decline of Western civilization. [17]

He wanted a symphony playing one sort of music and a small group, with Mitchell on acoustic guitar, doing a musical overlay. There would be a formal literary voice reading Eliot; Mitchell would be the vernacular voice. It was, he explained, in the tradition of the Baptist church, where one reader presents the Bible in the original and another glosses it colloquially.

Mitchell scotched the idea, and assumed that was the end of that. A call came from Mingus: he'd written several melodies, and he wanted her to set words to them. She flew from Los Angeles to New York to meet him and hear them.

JONI MITCHELL: He has a reputation for being a very violent and ornery person, but I seem to like those kind of people. I always suspect that there's a heart beating under there that's very sensitive, which turned out to be true. He has a wide emotional spectrum. Our relationship has been very sweet. [18]

Mingus called her the Hillbilly. "Is the Hillbilly coming over today?" he'd ask, eager when she made a series of visits over a few weeks.

She came to him like a student, and listened diligently to his short speeches, asking questions, paraphrasing and interpolating his faltering observations. He knew she was talented and famous, and she was warm and respectful and seemed open with him. He liked her.

She was another poetic white girl sitting at his feet, another key to keeping his legacy alive.

Mingus called Paul Jeffrey to have him transcribe and arrange the Mitchell material. Jeffrey demurred, "I can't think of how you'd do it, man."

As the money coming in slowed, and the medical expenses escalated, and the record company pushed harder, he had few options, little real control. The music for Mitchell was parceled out for arrangements among musicians, like Jimmy Rowles, living in Manhattan Plaza.

When Jimmy Knepper called Mingus from the street one afternoon to wish him happy birthday, the wheelchair-bound man whispered, "Please, Jimmy, you gotta come over here and help me, man. They're ruining my music."

JIMMY KNEPPER: He was half-paralyzed by that time; he could lift his hands but couldn't do anything with them, so he couldn't play the piano. So Susan had set up a metronome and turned a tape recorder on, and he sang, about five different pieces. One of those pieces, "Sketch Number Five," became "Chair in the Sky." He was right—the arrangers were ruining his music. They'd figured he was a strange writer, so they gave it the strangest harmonies they could come up with. But he wasn't *that* strange a writer. Anyway, I did one of the pieces right there, and I took the other one home, then delivered it back to him.

Four or five of the arrangements Mingus had done were recorded, at Electric Lady, the studio built by Jimi Hendrix. The initial tracks laid down had Dannie Richmond reading parts of *Beneath the Underdog* to bass and drums accompaniment, then the big band overdubbed. Mingus used to listen to the tapes over and over.

Apparently they've disappeared or were erased. The album Mitchell ultimately released paired her with Weather Report, fusion swashbucklers, who boasted Mingus devotee Jaco Pastorius on bass. It didn't sell as well as hoped, and got mediocre to negative press. Its contents were far from Mingus's conception, though Mitchell later blamed her time with Mingus, and her flights as a pop-jazz singer, as the ruin of her commercial career.

Mingus needed the money. They had to put it out.

Paul Jeffrey led a tribute at the Newport Festival in Saratoga, New York, the old resort. Jack Walrath and Ricky Ford were cut out of the gig, but Jimmy Knepper was included. Gunther Schuller conducted a big band, reprising Mingus music he'd led at Brandeis in 1957.

Mingus was turning into ghostly legend, even though his illness was not yet public. When *Rolling Stone* sent a reporter to interview him about the collaboration with Joni Mitchell, Sue said he was vacationing and unavailable.

Nat Hentoff stopped by, and they reminisced. Mingus told of how Lennie Tristano one night announced, "There is no God." Charlie Parker looked at him and said, "Is the job open, Lennie? I'll take it." Mingus stopped smiling, adding, "Bird, you know, believed in God."

Then Mingus recalled how John Coltrane came to hear the Workshop in the late 1950s, and asked, "Mingus, where do we go from here?" Mingus was astonished: "Who is we? Charlie Parker would never have asked me that. He'd have just gone on to something else."

Hentoff thought, "The one thing Mingus never wanted to become was placid—which also means any bunch of people who sound alike. He was no more capable of placidity than dissembling."[19]

They spoke, inevitably, of racism.

CHARLES MINGUS: It's not only a question of color any more. It's getting deeper than that. I mean it's getting more and more difficult for a man and a woman to just love. People are getting so fragmented, and part of that is that fewer and fewer people are making a real effort any more to find out exactly who they are and to build on that knowledge. Most people are forced to do things they don't want to most of the time, and so they get to the point where they feel they no longer have any choice about anything important, including who they are. We create our own slavery.[20]

Hentoff reflected, "What makes his music so exhilarating is the unbendingly free spirit at its core."[21]

Each month, Mingus got a check for $149.50 from Fantasy.[22] In a tiny way, one of his life's dreams had come true at last.

Sue refused to let the music languish despite his illness. She sent a letter to Leonard Bernstein on April 27, 1978, informing the maestro that Mingus would like to compose a large-scale work for symphony orchestra, and would like Bernstein to conduct it.[23]

The next day, she sent the score of his String Quartet No. 1 and a tape of its premiere at the Whitney Museum to the Lincoln Center Chamber Music Society.[24]

That weekend, Gunther Schuller conducted Mingus's "Revelations" with the New York Philharmonic.

His legend was overshadowing his life and work.

In *Rolling Stone*, Ben Sidran wrote of Mingus's work with Joni Mitchell: "Mingus' reputation in the music world is based not only on his musical virtuosity but also on his unrelenting criticism of whites. He hasn't simply been voluble on the subject; he has been volcanic. To think now, so late in Mingus' life, his music will be heard in hundreds of thousands of homes interpreted by a leading white female pop singer is perhaps the ultimate twist in an extremely stormy career. . . . [He has] a volatile personal style that often seemed more noteworthy than the music itself."[25]

Sue and Mingus started planning for his death.

A friend in Vancouver asked the Indian consul general about transporting a body there. He explained that usually only the ashes were brought there by a family member "for the sake of convenience." They would have to find facilities to cremate a non-Hindu.

Sue's friend detailed what was needed: visas, death certificate, a document from the New York Police Department for customs in India. And she said the consul suggested Haridwar, 150 miles from New Delhi, as the best spot, an ashram called Varanasi #2. She enclosed the card of Devander Singh in the American embassy in New Delhi.[26]

A week later, Sue and Mingus and Roberto took the train to Washington D.C., with TV talk show host Dick Cavett and a raftload of celebrities.

President Jimmy Carter planned a celebration on the south lawn of the White House, to honor George Wein and the twenty-fifth anniversary of the Newport Jazz Festival.

Mingus complained bitterly that morning. He had cramps in his legs. He didn't feel good. He didn't want to go. Sonny Rollins came over to give Sue a hand calming him down.

At the gathering of stars and music industry and political VIPs, Ornette Coleman duetted with his drummer-son Denardo for a few minutes. Then Cecil Taylor played for six minutes, probing the interstices between free jazz and classical composition, lacing his percussive hammerings with filigrees of expansive melody. Carter listened intently to the avant-gardist. Taylor finished, then immediately jumped up and dove into the shrubbery behind the bandstand—in back of it was the tent serving as the musicians' dressing room. Carter leapt up to chase Taylor to congratulate him. The secret service agents on duty, momentarily stunned, snapped into action, and took off after the president.

It looked like a Max Sennett movie.

Wein asked Carter to go over and shake hands with Mingus. The president did, and put his arm around the slumping figure in the wheelchair as tears rolled down Mingus's cheeks. Dozens of cameras went off, and the scene became famed.

Some say Mingus cried because of the moment's emotional impact. Some say Wein called him Charlie and asked him to stand for the president. Some say Mingus wept because Wein called him the world's greatest living jazz composer and asked for an ovation for him.

One symptom of ALS is heightened emotional swings completely unconnected to any particular stimulus.

But under such public glare at such a painful time, such a sensitive, private person would have to crumble.

Years earlier, his psychiatrist had asked him, "Why are you obsessed with proving you're a man? Is it because you cry?"

He couldn't close all his circles.

MAX ROACH: When Mingus died, we were in the throes of a dispute about Debut—money, fucking money. At the White House, Sue came over to me and said, "Charles wants to say hello." I didn't do it, because I was so mad at him about the money. It fucked me up for a long time, because he died soon after, and we never made it up.

That afternoon set the course of his remaining months. Gerry Mulligan, a longtime devotee of natural healing, told Mingus and Sue of a Mexican healer named Pachita who lived in Cuernavaca. A friend of his, he said, had ALS, and she'd cured him.

They'd run out of herbs and teas and embryo treatments from Switzerland and biofeedback technicians and hypnotists and masseuses and what little hope they'd had. They had nothing to lose. So they went back to New York, and Sue began to unsnarl the logistics of moving to Mexico.

ROBERTO UNGARO: My mother's philosophy was, give Charles some light of hope. So they got this huge villa for $1,200 a month. We had two swimming pools, maids, gardeners, people we didn't even know what they did. One of them stole my mother's wedding ring.

She stuck by him. Turned her house into a hospital. Changed whatever had to be changed. They had a real loyalty. Money was going out. Charles had this insurance policy he'd gotten through the union, and whatever my mother had done didn't meet their scrutiny. After they pay a certain amount, they investigate. I think they'd gotten to the point of $27,000 when they cut it off. They didn't go for the back amount, just said, "We're not going to cover you any more." And they were spending a lot of money, because Charles needed twenty-four-hour-a-day help.

SUE MINGUS: Particularly with someone as physical as Mingus. And he never lost that physicality. He had more energy than ninety people running down the block when he was frozen in a wheelchair. He dominated everyone in Mexico. We rode to the tops of mountains and the bottoms of valleys, went all over Mexico. We would spend all night driving to keep him happy, get home at the break of dawn. It was a marathon, an incredible marathon. But he never cursed the

379

gods, never whined or complained. He was miraculous. I just say, that last year was like a show of who he was in the most profound fashion. Try to stay alive, beat the rap, get out all this music that he must have had in his head—that was the last year.

JODY DeVito Alsop: It kept him going. He would wake up in the morning and there'd be his tea. And he loved mangos. We were always going to the market to get mangos. He taught me how to cut a mango the proper way. He was most articulate about it. And his eyes were powerful. He didn't have to say anything, he really conducted everything with his eyes.

Jody stayed in the West 43rd Street apartment, their New York office, and tried to keep the three-way Mingus business dealings between Mexico, New York, and the rest of the planet flowing reasonably well. They were booking musicians now, like Cecil Taylor, besides handling Mingus music and the details of dying.

Jody and Sue used codes to save money on the high-priced Mexican phone calls. They could claim it was a wrong number, and not be billed. It was the way it was when Mingus and Sue were courting in the mid-1960s.

What photograph to use for the album cover? Sue called New York, and when Jody picked up, she asked for Mister Not-the-one-with-the-Flowers.

In the van they rigged to hold his wheelchair in position with straps, Mingus, Sue, his gay male nurse Mr. Mackey and his helpers, his son Eugene, who was also helping tend him, and a stream of visitors toured Mexico. They sought out Aztec and Mayan ruins, rode daily to the chattering open-air markets and endless restaurants. They had birthday parties for the cook, the gardeners. Sue shipped the dogs from New York and back. Something was always happening. It was better to keep moving.

Eugene spent time in jail for drug-related charges, and circled around the Los Angeles entertainment industry, an erstwhile promoter and singer. He was a daredevil who scared virtually all the other kids. Here his job was to move his father—which meant if Mingus got an itch at 2:00 A.M. or if it was time to eat at noon.

Mackey sometimes gave back as good as he got from the man in the chair. After a barrage of demands for tea, massages, being turned over, his tape recorder, Mingus listened as the nurse bitched, and said in his frail voice, "Hey man, I got a gun under here. And if you don't straighten up I'm gonna shoot you right in the cunt."

Mingus endured two operations, massages, exercises. After the first of Pachita's "operations," an apparently mystical affair which involved no cutting, he felt better for a month, and ate a lot of crushed pineapple ice cream puffs. He was supposed to eat specially grown snails, which were housed and multiplied across the walls and ceilings and floors of the villa's bathrooms. Pachita gave him mud baths in the courtyard, hauling bags of dirt to the teeny fountain at its center, then soaking him in it, then hosing him down. He drank iguana blood. When he got boils, Pachita wrapped them in cow manure, to dry out and detoxify them. She boiled potatoes and put them up his rectum. She pronounced words over him.

The treatments gave him something to live for, something for his massive and focused will to cling to. They were the rituals of his daily life as it ebbed, part of the incipient spiritualism that became more overt while he desperately fought Death.

He now wore a medallion with symbols from all the great religions. He believed in ghosts, in spirits and hauntings. He was his father's and stepmother's son. He was hedging his bets. He was slowly acquiescing to his inevitable fate.

Visitors trooped through. Joni Mitchell flew down, and painted Sue and Mingus, as well as some of the paintings she'd use for the album of their collaborations, Mingus, which was being readied for January 1979 release.

He sent for Roberto and Eric. Jody DeVito flew down. He didn't want Charles or Keki to come. Celia went down from California; she was talking to Sue every few weeks, helping them with a nursing service in Los Angeles to replace aides.

By this point Mingus could only turn his head, and speak in a very hoarse, broken whisper.

For several hours, Eric sat in a room with his ear close to his father's mouth so he could hear him, as he wheezed out a few words at a time, trying to talk to Eric away from Sue and Eugene. He told Eric he'd been ripped off for Beneath the Underdog. "It wasn't the book I wanted," he said. He reminded Eric that as a black man he faced constant battles.

Roberto saw acceptance and resignation creeping into his face. He croaked at Jody, with tears brimming, "Tell your mother I said hello." Celia thought he was coming to terms with his death.

He'd argue about which piece of mango should go into his mouth first, which direction he should be turned. His world of obsessions shrank as his body seized up.

For a while, they discussed suicide, euthanasia, letting him go. He wanted them to kill him, to get drugs for him, but finally quashed the idea. Sue was afraid what would happen if the authorities did an autopsy. They could all get hit with a murder rap.

He couldn't even kill himself. Somebody had to help him.

Eugene pushed his wheelchair up and down cliffside trails, rolling fast, thrilling Mingus with the sensation of movement, fixing him with the chilly nearness of death.

Sometimes he'd suddenly hum a melody or fragment, and his eyes would twinkle, and he'd croak, "Whaddya think?"

He was going down fast, and Sue called Jody in New York to start making arrangements for India. Jody went to Queens and interviewed the Brahmins there about procedures for a Hindu funeral, without divulging Mingus's name.

She discovered transporting the body intact could cost nearly $75,000, mostly because of the several special coffins needed, since the body wouldn't be embalmed. Then there were the papers from Washington, D.C.

So that was out, and back to Queens she went. Jody discovered that Hindu cremation requires a low flame, which would leave chunks of bone, unlike modern Western cremation.

She passed the information to Sue, in code, along the U.S.-Mexico phone lines.

When Buddy Collette came down from Los Angeles over the Christmas holidays, he had an agenda. Mingus's family and friends wanted him to come home to die, and he was going to broach it to Sue and Charles.

The two old friends had an emotionally painful reunion. Buddy was horrified at how bad Mingus looked, at the treatments he was getting. They talked about Mingus coming back to Watts. When Collette was leaving, his childhood pal managed to get out, "Take me with you. I want to come home."

As Sue drove Buddy to the airport, he told her of the conversation. She seemed flustered: they had a lease on the house they couldn't break, they had the apartment in New York they were paying for, the medical bills that weren't being covered, the nurses. They didn't have the money to do it. Collette shrugged, irritated but understanding what she faced dealing with Mingus twenty-four hours a day, even with help.

On New Year's Day, Collette got a call from Sue. She'd talked it over with Charles. They were coming to Los Angeles, as soon as they could find a house. Buddy passed the word around the old Watts community.

On January 5, 1979, Sue left Mingus with his son Eugene while she headed to the American consulate to update their passports and visas for the trip to

Los Angeles. Mingus was grumpy and draining until she made the call to Buddy, then he'd calmed down.

When Sue got back, Charles Mingus Jr. was gone. He'd died in his son's arms, while Eugene was moving him from his wheelchair to his bed.

She called Collette, and he announced to the press in Los Angeles, and the world, that Mingus was dead.

In the liner notes for Joni Mitchell's album *Mingus*, she reprinted a piece from a Mexican newspaper about fifty-six whales beaching themselves on the Mexican coast the day Mingus died. His legend would only grow. He was just shy of fifty-seven years old.

SUE MINGUS: When Charles died, I sat in the garden with the sun streaming down, and I thought what a relief that he's flying off and not hovering around here, being released into the whole spiritual center of the universe where he belonged. As he once said, Music is his presence on earth. I think he felt that having his ashes distributed over the Ganges, on the other side of the globe, would probably ease his passage from one life to the other without a lot of gangster club owners and promoters messing with his spirit back in New York. And he hated the hoopla that surrounded a lot of jazz funerals he'd attended, like Bird's. In his eyes, they became forums for self-serving musicians. He didn't want any part of that.

JUDY STARKEY MINGUS MCGRATH: When he died, I was living in Rosendale. That was the house I'd put the money down on. And Eric was down in Mexico, and headed back. For some reason, I felt I had to lie down. I didn't know anything had happened. I just had to go lie down on the couch in the living room. And I got into one of those altered states. I don't do drugs or anything, but I wasn't asleep and I wasn't awake. I couldn't move. I was just lying there, and I saw his face, and it was scared. It almost looked like snakes were coming out of it—green snakes. And he looked very scared. And then shortly after that I had the call from Sue that he had died.

CELIA MINGUS ZAENTZ: He got irritable but not anything like what you'd expect. I felt, this is going to be impossible for him to handle. He's dependent on everyone for everything. But something else was going on. I think he was coming to terms with the whole thing.

CAROLYN (KEKI) MINGUS: My mother's into metaphysical stuff, but when he died, we didn't know. No one called to tell us. We found out about it on TV. I was watching Nancy Drew with my brother, and all of a sudden Chuck Scarborough comes on and tells me my father is dead. The thing about it is, I knew. Two days earlier, I was dreaming that my father was in my room. He was saying, "I'm going now." He was getting on a bus to Woodstock. I was saying, "Well, I'm coming too." He said, "No, you can't come this time. You cannot come." And finally we said our goodbyes, and that was that. Two days later, I find out from Chuck Scarborough that he died two days before.

JODY DEVITO ALSOP: He'd made his whole life into a work of art. He made dying into an art, too.

Notes

All quotes are taken from the author's interviews, unless otherwise noted.

CHAPTER 1

1 Key Mingus family documents courtesy of Grace Mingus.
2 Priestley, 1; Grace Mingus thinks it might have been chronic gastritis instead.
3 Du Bois, 3.
4 This historical background on the Mingus clan is drawn from archival materials provided by Great Smoky Mountains National Park: the Edward C. Conner manuscript, a detailed 121-page unpublished local history; sheets from the census of 1800 to 1880; and the Mingus Mill Historic Structures Report.
5 As he would with many others, Mingus recast these events in his fictionalized autobiography, *Beneath the Underdog*.
6 Gitler, "Mingus

Speaks . . . and Bluntly," *Down Beat*, January 21, 1960, 29ff.
7 Hentoff, "Mingus Ah Um," Village Voice, March 5, 1979.
8 DeLillo, 276–77.
9 Du Bois, 10.

CHAPTER 2

1 Bryant, 169.
2 Mingus recast many events in this chapter in *Beneath the Underdog*.
3 Coustie is renamed Feisty in *Beneath the Underdog*.
4 Mingus, *Beneath the Underdog*, 61.
5 Ibid, 64.

CHAPTER 3

1 Gitler, "Mingus Speaks . . . and Bluntly," *Down Beat*, January 21, 1960, 29ff.
2 Gioia, 334.
3 Feather, "Mingus and

the Music of Chaos," Los Angeles *Times*, January 14, 1979.
4 Bryant, 175.
5 Gitler, "Mingus Speaks . . . "
6 Ibid.
7 Ibid.
8 Ibid.
9 Ibid.

CHAPTER 4

1 Dance, "Mingus Speaks," *Jazz*, November-December 1963, 11ff.
2 Bryant, 198–99.
3 Some key material in these paragraphs is drawn from Hasse, 246ff.
4 Coleman and Young, 192.
5 Ibid., 102.
6 Hentoff, "Mingus Dynasties," *Village Voice*, March 12, 1979, 34–35.
7 Feather, "Mingus and the Music of Chaos,"

385

Los Angeles *Times*,
January 14, 1979.

8 Otis, 9

CHAPTER 5

1 Gillespie, 244.
2 Ibid., 188.
3 Davis, 92, 270.
4 Ibid., 92–93.
5 Smith, "Charles Mingus: Developmental Changes," *Down Beat*, January 12, 1978, 22ff.
6 Bryant, 71.
7 Hentoff, *Jazz Life*, 161.
8 Davis, 93.
9 "Jazz on Upswing; Keep It There," *Down Beat*, September 9, 1949, 10.
10 Gitler, "Mingus Speaks . . . and Bluntly," *Down Beat*, January 21, 1960, 29ff.
11 Bryant, 222–23.
12 Mingus, *Beneath the Underdog*, 185 ff, 313ff.
13 Ibid., 293ff.
14 Gleason "Charlie Mingus: A Thinking Musician," *Down Beat*, June 1, 1951, 7.

CHAPTER 6

1 Some material in these paragraphs is drawn from Bryant, 132ff.
2 Letters courtesy Celia Mingus Zaentz.
3 Gleason, "Charles Mingus: A Thinking Musician," *Down Beat*, June 1, 1951, 7.
4 Davis, 147.
5 Barry Ulanov, *Metronome*, May 9, 1952.
6 Mingus Archives, Library of Congress.
7 Hentoff, "Mingus Ah Um," *Village Voice*, March 5, 1979.
8 Unpublished interview, courtesy Celia Mingus Zaentz.

9 *Triumph of the Underdog* (film)
10 Mingus Archives, Library of Congress.
11 Rutgers Institute for Jazz Studies.
12 Mingus Archives, Library of Congress.
13 Gitler, liner notes, *Complete Debut Recordings*.
14 Mingus Archives, Library of Congress.
15 Liner notes, *Jazz at Massey Hall*.
16 Liner notes, *The Fabulous Thad Jones*.
17 Mingus Archives, Library of Congress.
18 Gillespie, 375.
19 Priestley, 55.
20 Mingus Archives, Library of Congress.
21 Davis, 165–66.
22 Hentoff, "Mingus Ah Um," *Village Voice*, March 5, 1979.
23 Mingus Archives, Library of Congress.
24 Davis, 192.
25 Mingus, "An Open Letter to Miles Davis," *Down Beat*, November 30, 1955, 12–13.
26 Mingus Archives, Library of Congress.
27 Gitler, liner notes, *Complete Debut Recordings*.
28 Mingus, *More Than a Fake Book*, 75.

CHAPTER 7

1 Mingus, liner notes, *Pithecanthropus Erectus*.
2 Archives of American Art web site.
3 Coleman and Young, 19.
4 Spellman, 225.
5 Mingus Archives, Library of Congress.
6 Ibid.
7 Goodman, 170.
8 Mingus Archives, Library of Congress.

9 Mingus, *Beneath the Underdog*, 4.
10 Unpublished interview, courtesy Celia Mingus Zaentz.
11 Original autograph ms., courtesy Celia Mingus Zaentz.
12 Mingus Archives, Library of Congress.
13 Ibid.
14 Ibid.
15 Ibid
16 Mingus, *Beneath the Underdog*, 348.
17 Some material in these paragraphs is drawn from Gordon, 1–54.
18 Gordon, 106.
19 Kilgallen, "Kilgallen's World," New York *Post*, March 7, 1958.
20 Mingus Archives, Library of Congress.
21 Ibid.
22 Original mss., courtesy Maureen Meloy.
23 Hentoff, *Jazz Life*, 60. Priestley also notes this.
24 Gordon, 106–7.
25 Ibid. 106.
26 Balliett, "Jazz Concerts," *New Yorker*, August 16, 1958, 179–81.
27 Mingus Archives, Library of Congress.
28 Gordon, 107.
29 *A Great Day in Harlem* (film).
30 Unpublished interview, courtesy Celia Mingus Zaentz.
31 Coleman and Young, 22.
32 Cerulli, 16–17.
33 Gordon, 107.

CHAPTER 8

1 Balliett, "Jazz Concerts," *New Yorker*, January 24, 1959, 103–5.
2 Mingus Archives, Library of Congress.
3 Rutgers Institute for Jazz Studies.

4 Mingus Archives, Library of Congress.
5 Rutgers Institute for Jazz Studies.
6 Hentoff, "Mingus Dynasties," *Village Voice*, March 12, 1979, 34–35.
7 Mingus Archives, Library of Congress.
8 Ibid.
9 Unpublished interview, courtesy Celia Mingus Zaentz.
10 Liner notes, *Mingus Ah Um.*
11 Mingus Archives, Library of Congress.
12 Priestley, 105.
13 Keepnews, 146–48.
14 Mingus Archives, Library of Congress.
15 Ibid.
16 Ibid.
17 Ibid.
18 Gitler, "Mingus Speaks ... and Bluntly," *Down Beat*, January 21, 1960, 29ff.
19 Rutgers Institute for Jazz Studies.
20 Ibid.
21 Mingus Archives, Library of Congress.
22 Ibid.
23 Liner notes, *Mingus Dynasty.*
24 Mingus Archives, Library of Congress.
25 Liner notes, *Mingus Dynasty.*
26 Mingus Archives, Library of Congress.
27 Liner notes, *Mingus Dynasty.*
28 Mingus Archives, Library of Congress.
29 Key material in these paragraphs is drawn from Coleman and Young.
30 Mingus Archives, Library of Congress.
31 Ibid.
32 Rutgers Institute for Jazz Studies.

33 Goldblatt, 72.
34 Mingus Archives, Library of Congress.
35 Ibid.
36 Lees, "Newport, the Trouble," *Down Beat*, August 18, 1960, 20ff. See also Goldblatt, 80.
37 Key material in these paragraphs is drawn from Coleman and Young, 82–83, 76–77.
38 Mingus Archives, Library of Congress.
39 Ibid.
40 *Jazz News*, July 19, 1961.
41 Lyrics to "Original Faubus Fables," Candid.
42 Liner notes, Candid box set.
43 Mingus Archives, Library of Congress.
44 Ibid.
45 Key material in these paragraphs is drawn from Coleman and Young, 3–5.
46 Coleman and Young, 5–6.
47 San Francisco *Examiner*, December 11, 1960.

CHAPTER 9

1 *Jazz News*, July 19/26, 1961, quoted in Priestley, 292.
2 Ibid.
3 *Triumph of the Underdog.* (film).
4 Ibid.
5 Rutgers Institute for Jazz Studies.
6 Mingus Archives, Library of Congress.
7 Priestley, 126–27.
8 Ibid., 127.
9 Ibid., 128–29.
10 Mingus Archives, Library of Congress.
11 Ibid.
12 Ibid.
13 Ibid.
14 Ibid.

15 Letter, *Down Beat*, August 16, 1962, 10.
16 *New York Times*, May 3, 1959.
17 Mingus Archives, Library of Congress.
18 Ibid.
19 *Mingus/Mingus*, 19.
20 Szwed, 190.
21 Unpublished interview, courtesy Celia Mingus Zaentz.
22 Ibid.
23 Mingus Archives, Library of Congress.
24 Unpublished interview, courtesy Celia Mingus Zaentz.
25 Ibid.
26 Ibid.
27 Coleman and Young, 54.
28 Mingus Archives, Library of Congress.
30 Ibid.
31 Courtesy Maureen Meloy.
32 Mingus Archives, Library of Congress.
33 Ibid.
34 Official Leary website.
35 Mingus Archives, Library of Congress.
36 Ibid.
37 Ibid.
38 Heckman, "About Charles Mingus," *American Record Guide*, 18ff.
39 Priestley, 144–45.
40 Mingus Archives, Library of Congress.
41 Priestley, 135.
42 "Crow Jim," *Time*, October 19, 1962, 58–60.
43 Lyrics to "Suite Freedom."
44 Mingus Archives, Library of Congress.

CHAPTER 10

1 Priestley, 146.
2 Liner notes, *Black Saint.*
3 Ibid.
4 Ibid.
5 Ibid.

6 Ibid.
7 Levin, "Court Frees Mingus," New York *Post*, March 17, 1963.
8 Ibid.
9 Coleman and Young, 21.
10 Mingus Archives, Library of Congress.
11 Ibid.
12 Coleman and Young, 38–39.
13 Wilson, "Concert Review," *New York Times*, November 3, 1963.
14 *Mingus* (film).
15 Thiele, 132.
16 Coleman and Young, 28.
17 Ibid., 66–67.
18 Mingus Archives, Library of Congress.
19 Flyer, Rutgers Institute for Jazz Studies.
20 *Charles Mingus Sextet* (film).
21 Priestley, 157
22 Photos, Charles Mingus, *More Than A Fake Book*. The bag is at the Mingus Archives, Library of Congress.
23 Gillespie, 375.
24 Key material in these paragraphs is drawn from an unpublished ms., courtesy Jane Getz.
25 Balliett, "Jazz," *New Yorker*, June 13, 1964, 133–35.
26 Key material in these paragraphs is drawn from Wolfe, 93–96.
27 Key material in these paragraphs is drawn from Whitworth, "The Rich, Full Life of Charlie Mingus," New York *Herald Tribune*, November 1, 1964, 13ff.
28 Introduction to "Meditations," *Mingus at Monterey*.
29 "M+M at Monterey," *Newsweek*, October 5, 1964, 120ff.

30 Ibid.
31 Wilson, "Mingus at Monterey Jazz Festival," *New York Times*, October 4, 1964.
32 "Beneath the Underdog," *Time*, October 2, 1964, 88–89
33 "M+M at Monterey."
34 Berliner, 138.
35 Mingus Archives, Library of Congress.
36 Ibid.
37 Ibid.
38 Ibid.
39 Ibid.
40 *Triumph of the Underdog* has footage from this program.
41 Mingus Archives, Library of Congress.
42 Ibid.
43 Ibid.

CHAPTER 11

1 Mingus Archives, Library of Congress.
2 Wolfe, 9.
3 Mingus Archives, Library of Congress.
4 Ibid.
5 Ibid.
6 Ibid.
7 Ibid.
8 Video Archives, Library of Congress.
9 Mingus Archives, Library of Congress.
10 Lyrics, "Don't Let It Happen Here," on *Mingus at Monterey*.
11 Mingus Archives, Library of Congress.
12 Ibid.
13 Ibid.
14 Rutgers Institute for Jazz Studies.
15 Liner notes, *Mingus at Monterey*.
16 Mingus Archives, Library of Congress.
17 Ibid.
18 Ibid.
19 Ibid.

20 *Mingus* (film)
21 Ibid.
22 Ibid.
23 Ibid.
24 Ibid.
25 Mingus Archives, Library of Congress.
26 Rutgers Institute for Jazz Studies.
27 Mingus Archives, Library of Congress.
28 Ibid.
29 Ibid.
30 Ibid.
31 Hentoff, "Mingus: I Thought I was Finished," *New York Times*, January 30, 1972, 17.
32 Mingus Archives, Library of Congress.
33 Key material in the following paragraphs is drawn from Coleman and Young, 34–36.
34 Liner notes, *Mingus at Monterey*.
35 Mingus Archives, Library of Congress.
36 Ibid.
37 Ibid.

CHAPTER 12

1 Mingus Archives, Library of Congress.
2 Sidran, *Rolling Stone*, December 28, 1978, 33ff.
3 Mingus Archives, Library of Congress.
4 Ibid.
5 Ibid.
6 Ibid.
7 Key material in the following paragraphs is drawn from Coleman and Young, 89ff.
8 Mingus Archives, Library of Congress.
9 Ibid.
10 Hentoff, "Mingus: I Thought I Was Finished," *New York Times*, January 30, 1972, p. 17.

11 *Triumph of the Underdog* (film).
12 Mingus, *More Than a Fake Book*, 145.
13 Giddins, "Three or Four Shades of Mingus," *Village Voice*, July 3, 1978, 53ff.
14 Mingus Archives, Library of Congress.
15 Ibid.
16 Mingus, *Beneath the Underdog*, 354.
17 Balliett, "Reporter at Large," *New Yorker*, May 29, 1971, 42–44.
18 Hennessey, "Charles Mingus: Changed Man?," *Down Beat*, May 13, 1971, 14ff.
19 Wolff, "Man with a Bass," *Newsweek*, May 17, 1971, 110.
20 Yardley, "Agonies of a Mongrel," *New Republic*, July 3, 1971, 29.
21 Korall, "Mingus on Mingus," *Saturday Review*, July 31, 1971, 42.
22 Mingus Archives, Library of Congress.
23 Coleman and Young, 64.
24 Mingus Archives, Library of Congress.
25 Mingus, *More Than a Fake Book*, 5.
26 Mingus Archives, Library of Congress.
27 Coleman and Young, 41–42.

CHAPTER 13

1 Mingus Archives, Library of Congress.
2 Hentoff, "Mingus: I Thought I Was Finished," *New York Times*, January 30, 1972, 17.
3 Ibid.
4 Ibid.
5 Ibid.
6 Rutgers Institute for Jazz Studies.

7 "Stars Spark SRO Mingus concert," *Down Beat*, March 16, 1972, 10.
8 Coleman and Young, 43–44.
9 Ibid., 19.
10 Mingus Archives, Library of Congress.
11 Ibid.
12 Ibid.
13 Ibid.
14 Ibid.
15 Hentoff, "Mingus Ah Um," *Village Voice*, March 5, 1979, 34–35.
16 Mingus Archives, Library of Congress.
17 Coleman and Young, 31–32.
18 Mingus Archives, Library of Congress.
19 Ibid.
20 Liner notes, *Let My Children Hear Music*.
21 Ibid.
22 Ibid.
23 Ibid.
24 Ibid.
25 Ibid.
26 Ibid.
27 Ibid.
28 Ibid.
29 Ibid.
30 Wilson, "Bassist Charles Mingus Performance at Five Spot," *New York Times*, April 16, 1973, 49.
31 Stein, "Mingus in Concert," *Village Voice*, June 28, 1973.

CHAPTER 14

1 Rutgers Institute for Jazz Studies.
2 Wilson, "Charles Mingus Concert," *New York Times*, January 23, 1974, 35.
3 Sidran, "Charles Mingus Finds a New Voice," *Rolling Stone*, December 28, 1978, 33ff.

4 Liner notes, *Changes One*.
5 Mingus, *More Than a Fake Book*, 48.
6 The following paragraphs are drawn from Coleman and Young, 10–16.
7 Hentoff, "Mingus Dynasties," *Village Voice*, March 12, 1979, 34–35.
8 Mingus, *More Than a Fake Book*, p. 57.
9 Key material in these paragraphs is drawn from Coleman and Young, 49–51.
10 Liner notes, *Changes One*.
11 Coleman and Young, 51–52.
12 *Triumph of the Underdog* (film).
13 Mingus Archives, Library of Congress.
14 Ibid.
15 Coleman and Young, 52–53.
16 Mingus Archives, Library of Congress.
17 Ibid.
18 Gordon, 108.
19 Mingus Archives, Library of Congress.
20 Ibid.
21 Lindenberger, "Die Faszination des Rhythms," *Hi Fi Stereophonie*, January 1976, 26–29.
22 Sidran, "Charles Mingus Finds a New Voice."
23 Mingus Archives, Library of Congress.
24 Ibid.
25 Coleman and Young, 44.
26 Liner notes, *Changes One*.
27 Mingus Archives, Library of Congress.
28 Robert Gwynne website.
29 Mingus Archives, Library of Congress.
30 Ibid.
31 Sidran, "Charles Mingus Finds a New Voice."

32 Rutgers Institute for Jazz Studies.

CHAPTER 15

1 Lyrics, "Cumbia and Jazz Fusion," on *Cumbia & Jazz Fusion* (album).

2 Davis, 93.

3 Smith, "Charles Mingus: Developmental Changes," *Down Beat*, January 12, 1978, 22ff.

4 Liner notes, *Three or Four Shades of Blues*.

5 Priestley, 210.

6 Mingus Archives, Library of Congress.

7 Ibid.

8 Ibid.

9 Smith, "Charles Mingus: developmental changes."

10 Palmer, "Charles Mingus and Azucena y Edo," *New York Times*, June 23, 1976, 23.

11 Mingus Archives, Library of Congress.

12 Ibid.

13 ALS information here and below is drawn from ALS Association materials.

14 Mingus Archives, Library of Congress.

15 Priestley, 218–19.

16 Sidran, "Charles Mingus Finds a New Voice," *Rolling Stone*, December 28, 1978, 33ff.

17 The following paragraphs draw on Sidran, "Charles Mingus Finds a Voice."

18 Sidran, "Charles Mingus Finds a New Voice."

19 Hentoff, "Charles Mingus 1922–79, " *Rolling Stone*, February 22, 1979, 16–17.

20 Hentoff, "Mingus: You'd Be Playing, and He'd Yell, Get into Yourself," *The Progressive*, August 1981, 52–53.

21 Ibid.

22 Mingus Archives, Library of Congress.

23 Ibid.

24 Ibid.

25 Sidran, "Charles Mingus Finds a New Voice."

26 Mingus Archives, Library of Congress.

27. Mingus, *Beneath the Underdog*, 4.

Bibliography

REFERENCE

Berendt, Joachim E. *The Jazz Book.* Brooklyn: Lawrence Hill Books, 1992.

Burke, W. J., and Will D. Howe. *American Authors and Books: 1640 to the Present Day.* New York: Crown, 1972.

Carr, Ian, et al. *Jazz: The Essential Companion.* New York: Prentice Hall, 1988.

Chilton, John. *Who's Who of Jazz.* New York: Da Capo, 1986.

Cook, Richard, and Brian Morton. *The Penguin Guide to Jazz on CD, LP & Cassette.* London: Penguin, 1994.

Erlewine, Michael, et al. *All Music Guide to Jazz.* San Francisco: Miller Freeman, 1998.

Feather, Leonard. *The Encyclopedia of Jazz.* New York: Da Capo, 1984.

———. *The Encyclopedia Yearbooks of Jazz.* New York: Da Capo, 1993.

Hardy, Phil, and Dave Laing. *The Da Capo Companion to 20th Century Popular Music.* New York: Da Capo, 1995.

Hart, James D. *The Oxford Companion to American Literature.* New York: Oxford University Press, 1980.

Heffner, Richard D. *A Documentary History of the United States.* New York: Mentor, 1963.

Hitchcock, H. Wiley, and Stanley Sadie, eds. *The New Grove Dictionary of American Music.* New York: Macmillan, 1986.

Hughes, Langston, and Milton Meltzer. *Black Magic: A Pictorial History of the African-American in the Performing Arts.* New York: Da Capo, 1990.

Jackson, Kenneth T., ed. *The Enyclopedia of New York City.* New Haven, Conn.: Yale University Press, 1995.

Katz, Ephraim. *The Film Encyclopedia.* New York: Perigee, 1982.

Kernfield, Barry, ed. *The New Grove Dictionary of Jazz.* New York: Macmillan, 1988.

Lax, Roger, and Frederick Smith. *The Great Song Thesaurus.* New York: Oxford University Press, 1989.

Maltin, Leonard. *TV Movies and Video Guide*. New York: Signet, 1986.

Miller, Jim, ed. *The Rolling Stone Illustrated History of Rock & Roll*. New York: Random House, 1980.

Mingus, Charles. *More Than a Fake Book*. New York: Hal Leonard, 1991.

Monaco, James. *How to Read a Film: The Art, Technology, Language, History, and Theory of Film and Media*. New York: Oxford University Press, 1986.

Presidential Transcripts: The Complete Transcripts of the Nixon Tapes. New York: Dell, 1974.

Rachlin, Harvey. *The Encyclopedia of the Music Business*. New York: Harper & Row, 1981.

Report of the National Advisory Commission on Civil Disorders. New York: Bantam, 1968.

Scholes, Percy. *The Oxford Companion to Music*. London: Oxford University Press, 1978.

Schuller, Gunther. *Early Jazz*. New York: Oxford University Press, 1968.

———. *The Swing Era*. New York: Oxford University Press, 1988.

Shaw, Arnold. *Dictionary of American Pop/Rock*. New York: Schirmer Books, 1982.

Stambler, Irwin, and Grelun Landon. *Encyclopedia of Pop, Rock and Soul*. New York: St. Martin's Press, 1977.

Steinberg, Corbett. *Film Facts*. New York: Facts on File, 1980.

———. *TV Facts*. New York: Facts on File, 1980.

Thomson, David. *A Biographical Dictionary of Film*. New York: Morrow Quill, 1981.

Weiler, Uwe. *The Debut Label: A Discography*. Norderstedt, Germany: private edition, 1994.

Whitburn, Joel. *The Billboard Book of Top 40 Hits*. New York: Billboard Publications, 1983.

BOOKS OF MORE GENERAL INTEREST

Baldwin, James. *The Fire Next Time*. New York: Dell, 1964.

Barthes, Roland. *The Pleasure of the Text*. New York: Hill & Wang, 1971.

Berliner, Paul. *Thinking in Jazz*. Chicago: University of Chicago Press, 1994.

Blake, William. *The Poetry and Prose of William Blake*. New York: Doubleday Anchor, 1970.

Bloom, Harold. *The Anxiety of Influence*. New York: Oxford University Press, 1973.

Brown, H. Rap. *Die, Nigger, Die*. New York: Dial, 1969.

Brown, Norman O. *Life Against Death: The Psychoanalytical Meaning of History*. New York: Vintage, 1959.

Bryant, Clora et al. *Central Avenue Sounds*. Berkeley: University of California Press, 1998.

Bullard, Sara. *Free at Last: A History of the Civil Rights Movement and Those Who Died in the Struggle*. New York: Oxford University Press, 1994.

Burroughs, William. *Naked Lunch*. New York: Grove, 1959.

Caughey, John Walton, and Laree Caughey, eds. *Los Angeles: Biography of a City*. Berkeley: University of California Press, 1977.

Canon, Cornelius Baird. "The Federal Music Project of the Works Progress Administration: Music in a democracy." Ph.D. dissertation, University of Minnesota, 1963.

Caro, Robert. *The Power Broker: Robert Moses and the Fall of New York*. New York: Random House, 1975.

Cerulli, Dom, et al., eds. *The Jazz Word*. New York: Da Capo, 1987.

Chambers, Jack. *Milestones*. 2 vols. New York: Beech Tree Books, 1983.

Chandler, Raymond. *The Big Sleep*. New York: Vintage, 1976.

———. *Farewell, My Lovely*. New York: Vintage, 1976.

————. *The High Window*. New York: Ballantine, 1971.

————. *The Lady in the Lake*. New York: Vintage, 1976.

————. *The Long Goodbye*. New York: Ballantine, 1971.

Charters, Ann, ed. *The Portable Beat Reader*. New York: Penguin, 1992.

Charters, Samuel. *The Blues Makers*. New York: Da Capo, 1991.

Clarke, Donald. *The Rise and Fall of Popular Music*. New York: St. Martin's Press, 1995.

Cole, Bill. *John Coltrane*. New York: Da Capo, 1993.

Coleman, Janet, and Al Young. *Mingus/Mingus: Two Memoirs*. Berkeley, California: Creative Arts Book Company, 1989.

Collier, James Lincoln. *Duke Ellington*. New York: Oxford University Press, 1987.

Dannen, Frederic. *Hit Men: Power Brokers and Fast Money Inside the Music Business*. New York: Times Books, 1990.

Davis, Miles, with Quincy Troupe. *Miles: The Autobiography*. New York: Simon & Schuster, 1989.

DeLillo, Don. *Libra*. New York: Viking, 1988.

————. *Underworld*. New York: Scribner, 1997.

Dickstein, Morris. *Gates of Eden: American Culture in the Sixties*. New York: Basic Books, 1977.

Doctorow, E.L. *Ragtime*. New York: Random House, 1975.

Dolce & Gabbana, and Harry F. Gaugh. *Franz Kline: The Vital Gesture*. New York: Abbeville Press, 1994.

Douglas, Ann *Terrible Honesty: Mongrel Manhattan in the 1920s*. New York: Farrar, Straus & Giroux, 1995.

Du Bois, W.E.B. *The Souls of Black Folk*. New York: Bantam, 1989.

Edsell, Thomas Byrne, with Mary D. Edsell. *Chain Reaction: The Impact of Race, Rights, and Taxes on American Politics*. New York: W. W. Norton, 1991.

Eisenberg, Evan. *The Recording Angel: Explorations in Phonography*. New York: McGraw-Hill, 1987.

Ellison, Ralph. *Invisible Man*. New York: Vintage, 1995.

Ellroy, James. *American Tabloid*. New York: Ballantine, 1996.

————. *L.A. Confidential*. New York: Ballantine, 1991.

————. *White Jazz*. New York: Ballantine, 1993.

Fanon, Frantz. *The Wretched of the Earth*. New York: Grove, 1968.

Ferlinghetti, Lawrence, and Nancy J. Peters. *Literary San Francisco*. New York: Harper & Row, 1980.

Finkelstein, Sidney. *Jazz: A People's Music*. New York: International Publishers, 1988.

Foucault, Michel. *The Order of Things: An Archaeology of the Human Sciences*. New York: Vintage, 1973.

Galbraith, John Kenneth. *The Affluent Society*. Boston: Houghton Mifflin, 1958.

Gambino, Richard. *Blood of My Blood: The Dilemma of the Italian-Americans*. New York: Buccaneer Books, 1991.

Gid Powers, Richard. *Secrecy and Power: The Life of J. Edgar Hoover*. New York: Free Press, 1988.

Giddins, Gary. *Celebrating Bird: The Triumph of Charlie Parker*. New York: Beech Tree Books, 1987.

————. *Rhythm-a-ning*. New York: Oxford University Press, 1985.

————. *Riding on a Blue Note*. New York: Oxford University Press, 1981.

Gillespie, Dizzy, and Al Fraser. *To Be or Not to Bop*. New York: Da Capo, 1988.

Ginsberg, Allen. *Collected Poems, 1947–1980*. New York: Harper and Row, 1988.

Gioia, Ted. *West Coast Jazz*. New York: Oxford University Press, 1992.

Gitler, Ira. *Swing to Bop: An Oral History of the Transition in Jazz in the 1940s.* New York: Oxford University Press, 1986.

Gleason, Ralph. *Celebrating the Duke.* New York: Da Capo, 1995.

Goldblatt, Burt. *Newport Jazz Festival.* New York: Dial, 1977.

Goodman, Paul. *Growing Up Absurd.* New York: Random House, 1960.

Gordon, Max. *Live at the Village Vanguard.* New York: St. Martin's Press, 1980.

Graham, Bill, and Robert Greenfield. *Bill Graham Presents.* New York: Doubleday, 1992.

Gray, Herman. *Producing Jazz: The Experience of an Independent Record Company.* Philadelphia: Temple University Press, 1988.

Guralnick, Peter. *Feel Like Going Home: Portraits in Blues & Rock'n'Roll.* London: Omnibus Press, 1978

———. *Last Train to Memphis: The Rise of Elvis Presley.* Boston: Little, Brown, 1994.

———. *Sweet Soul Music: Rhythm and Blues and the Southern Dream of Freedom.* New York: Harper & Row, 1986.

Hadju, David. *Lush Life: A Biography of Billy Strayhorn.* New York: Farrar, Straus & Giroux, 1996.

Halberstam, David. *The Best and the Brightest.* New York: Random House, 1972.

———. *The Fifties.* New York: Ballantine, 1994.

Hampton, Lionel, with James Haskins. *Hamp.* New York: Amistad Press, 1993.

Harris, William, ed. *LeRoi Jones/Amiri Baraka Reader.* New York: Thunder's Mouth Press, 1991.

Hasse, John Edward. *Beyond Category: The Life and Genius of Duke Ellington.* New York: Simon & Schuster, 1993.

Hentoff, Nat. *Jazz Is.* New York: Limelight, 1984.

Hentoff, Nat, and Nat Shapiro, eds. *Hear Me Talkin' to Ya: The Story of Jazz by the Men Who Made It.* New York: Dover, 1990.

———. *The Jazz Life.* New York: Da Capo, 1978.

———. *Listen to the Stories.* New York: HarperCollins, 1995.

Heilbut, Anthony. *The Gospel Sound.* New York: Limelight Editions, 1985.

Himes, Chester. *If He Hollers Let Him Go: A Novel.* New York: Thunder's Mouth Press, 1995.

Hobsbawm, Eric. *The Jazz Scene.* New York: Pantheon Books, 1993.

Hofstadter, Richard. *The Age of Reform: From Bryan to F.D.R.* New York: Vintage, 1976.

———. *The American Political Tradition.* New York: Vintage, n.d.

———. *Anti-intellectualism in American Life.* New York: Vintage, 1972.

———. *The Paranoid Style in American Politics.* New York: Vintage, 1967.

Johnson, James Weldon. *The Autobiography of an Ex-Coloured Man.* New York: Vintage, 1989.

———. *Black Manhattan.* New York: Da Capo, 1991.

Jones, Leroi (Amiri Baraka). *Blues People: The Negro Experience in White America and the Music That Developed from It.* New York: William Morrow, 1963.

Keepnews, Orrin. *The View from Within: Jazz Writings 1948–1987.* New York: Oxford University Press, 1988.

Kerouac, Jack. *The Dharma Bums.* New York: Penguin, 1971.

———. *On the Road.* New York: Penguin, 1976.

Kesey, Ken. *One Flew over the Cuckoo's Nest.* New York, Viking, 1962.

King, Martin Luther Jr. *Why We Can't Wait.* New York: Harper & Row, 1963.

Knight, Arthur. *The Liveliest Art: A Panoramic History of the Movies.* New York: Mentor, 1959.

Knoedelseder, William. *Stiffed: A True Story of MCA, the Music Business, and the Mafia*. New York: Harper Collins, 1991.

Leaming, Barbara. *Orson Welles*. New York: Viking, 1985.

Levine, Lawrence. *Black Culture and Black Consciousness*. New York: Oxford University Press, 1981.

Litweiler, John. *Ornette Coleman: A Harmolodic Life*. New York: William Morrow, 1992.

McShine, Kynaston. *Andy Warhol: A Retrospective*. New York: Museum of Modern Art, 1989.

Mailer, Norman. *Advertisements for Myself*. Berkeley: University of California, 1976.

———. *Miami and the Siege of Chicago: An Informal History of the Republican and Democratic Conventions of 1968*. New York: Signet, 1968.

Marling, Karal Ann. *As Seen on TV: The Visual Culture of Everyday Life in the 1950s*. Cambridge: Harvard University Press, 1994.

Miles, Barry. *Ginsberg*. New York: Simon & Schuster, 1989.

Miller, James. *Democracy Is in the Streets: From Port Huron to the Siege of Chicago*. New York: Touchstone, 1988.

Miller, Marc H. *Louis Armstrong: A Cultural Legacy*. New York: Queens Museum of Art in association with University of Washington Press, 1994.

Mills, C. Wright. *The Power Elite*. New York: Oxford University Press, 1976.

Mingus, Charles. *Beneath the Underdog*. New York: Vintage, 1991.

Mosley, Walter. *Devil With a Blue Dress On*. New York: Norton, 1990.

Murray, Albert. *The Omni-Americans*. New York: Da Capo, 1990.

———. *Stomping the Blues*. New York: Da Capo, 1989.

Osofsky, Gilbert. *Puttin' on Ole Massa: The Slave Narratives of Henry Bibb, William Wells Brown, and Solomon Northup*. New York: Harper Torchbooks, 1969.

Otis, Johnny. *Upside Your Head! Rhythm and Blues on Central Avenue*. Hanover, N.H.: University Press of New England, 1993.

Padgett, Ron, and David Shapiro. *An Anthology of New York Poets*. New York: Vintage, 1970.

Palmer, Robert. *Deep Blues*. New York: Viking, 1981.

Patchen, Kenneth. *The Memoirs of a Shy Pornographer*. New York: New Directions, 1999.

———. *Selected Poems*. New York: New Directions, 1972.

Phillips, Lisa, ed. *Beat Culture and the New America 1950–1965*. New York: Whitney Museum/Flammarion, 1995.

Porter, Lewis, ed. *A Lester Young Reader*. Washington, D.C.: Smithsonian Institution Press, 1991.

Priestley, Brian. *Mingus: A Critical Biography*. New York: Da Capo, 1984.

Pynchon, Thomas. *V.* New York: Bantam, 1968.

Rexroth, Kenneth. *American Poetry in the Twentieth Century*. New York: Herder and Herder, 1971.

Robeson, Paul. *Here I Stand*. Boston: Beacon, 1988.

Robinson, David. *The History of World Cinema*. New York: Stein and Day, 1974.

Roszak, Theodore. *The Making of a Counter Culture*. New York: Doubleday, 1969.

Sanjek, Russell, and David Sanjek. *The American Popular Music Business in the 20th Century*. New York: Oxford University Press, 1991.

Sayre, Henry M. *The Object of Performance: The American Avant-Garde since 1970*. Chicago: University of Chicago Press, 1989.

Schlesinger, Arthur. *The Age of Roosevelt*. 3 vols. Boston: Houghton Mifflin, 1957–60.

Sidran, Ben. *Talking Jazz: An Oral History*. New York: Da Capo, 1995.

Smith, Anthony, and Richard Paterson, eds. *Television: An International History*. New York: Oxford University Press, 1998.

Stampp, Kenneth. *The Era of Reconstruction, 1865–1877*. New York: Vintage, 1967.

Stearns, Marshall. *The Story of Jazz*. New York: Oxford University Press, 1972.

Szwed, John. *Space Is the Place*. New York: Pantheon, 1997.

Taylor, Arthur. *Notes and Tones: Musician to Musician Interviews*. New York: Da Capo, 1993.

Thiele, Bob, as told to Bob Golden. *What a Wonderful World*. New York: Oxford University Press, 1995.

Thompson, Hunter. *Fear and Loathing in Las Vegas*. New York: Vintage, 1998.

———. *Hell's Angels*. New York: Random House, 1996.

Tocqueville, Alexis de. *Democracy in America*. New York: Random House, 1970.

Tucker, Mark, ed. *The Duke Ellington Reader*. New York: Oxford University Press, 1993.

Turkel, Studs. *Working*. New York: Norton, 1997.

Tytell, John. *Naked Angels*. New York: Grove, 1976.

Varnedoe, Kirk, with Pepe Carmel. *Jackson Pollock*. New York: The Museum of Modern Art, 1998.

Welles, Orson, and Peter Bogdanovich. *This Is Orson Welles*. New York: HarperCollins, 1992.

White, Timothy. *Catch a Fire: The Life of Bob Marley*. New York: Henry Holt, 1989.

Whyte, William Allen. *Street Corner Society: The Social Structure of an Italian Slum*. Chicago: University of Chicago Press, 1981.

Williams, Martin. *Jazz in Its Time*. New York: Oxford University Press, 1989.

———. *The Jazz Tradition*. New York: Oxford University Press, 1983.

Wolfe, Tom. *The Electric Kool-Aid Acid Test*. New York: Bantam, 1969.

Wright, Richard. *Black Boy*. New York: Harper and Brothers, 1945.

———. *Native Son*. New York: Harper and Brothers, 1940.

Wylie, Philip. *Generation of Vipers*. Illinois: Dalkey Archive Press, 1996.

X, Malcolm, with Alex Haley. *The Autobiography of Malcolm X*. New York: Grove, 1966.

NEWSPAPER AND MAGAZINE ARTICLES

Balliett, Whitney. "Jazz Concerts." *New Yorker*, August 3, 1957.

———. "Jazz Concerts." *New Yorker*, August 16, 1958, 179–81.

———. "Jazz Concerts." *New Yorker*, January 24, 1959, 103–5.

———. "Eighth Annual Monterey Jazz Festival." *New Yorker*, October 2, 1965, 185–90.

———. "Reporter at Large." *New Yorker*, May 29, 1971, 42–44.

Barnes, Clive. "Ailey Review." *New York Times*, fall 1971.

"Charles Mingus, Methodical Maniac." *Jazz Journal*, June 1963, 12–13.

Dance, Stanley. "Mingus Speaks." *Jazz*, November-December 1963, 11–14.

Feather, Leonard. "The Blindfold Test (Charles Mingus)." *Down Beat*, May 12, 1960, 39.

———. "Mingus and the Music of Chaos." *Los Angeles Times*, January 14, 1979.

Giddins, Gary. "Three or Four Shades of Mingus." *Village Voice*, July 3, 1978, 53.

———. "Charles Mingus, 1922–1979." *Village Voice*, February 12, 1979.

Gitler, Ira. "Mingus Speaks . . . and Bluntly." *Down Beat*, January 21, 1960, 29ff.

Gleason, Ralph. "Charles Mingus: A Thinking Musician." *Down Beat*, March 9, 1951, 7.

Hadlock, Dick. "Review: Mingus at Berkeley." *Down Beat*, November 27, 1969.

Heckman, Don. "About Charles Mingus." *American Record Guide*, August 1962, 916–18.

Hennessey, Mike. "Charles Mingus: Changed Man?" *Down Beat*, May 13, 1971, 14ff.

Hentoff, Nat. "Mingus in Job Dilemma, Vows No Compromise." *Down Beat*, May 6, 1953, 21.

———. "Interview with Mingus." *Down Beat*, November 2, 1955.

———. "Charles Mingus." *Down Beat*, January 11, 1956, 8.

———. "Newport." *Down Beat*, August 8, 1956.

———. "Mingus: I Thought I Was Finished." *New York Times*, January 30, 1972.

———. "Charles Mingus 1922–79." *Rolling Stone*, February 22, 1979, 16–17.

———. "Mingus Ah Um." *Village Voice*, March 5, 1979.

———. "Mingus Dynasties." *Village Voice*, March 12, 1979, 34–35.

———. "Mingus: You'd Be Playing, and He'd Yell 'Get into Yourself'." *The Progressive*, August 1981, 52–53.

"Interview with Lenny Bruce." *New York Times*, May 3, 1959, 28.

"Jazz on Upswing, Keep It There." *Down Beat*, September 9, 1949, 10.

Kilgallen, Dorothy. "Kilgallen's World." New York *Post*, March 7, 1958.

Korall, Burt. "Mingus on Mingus." *Saturday Review*, July 31, 1971, 42.

Lees, Gene. "Caught in the Act (Charles Mingus)." *Down Beat*, March 31, 1960, 34–35.

Levin, Alan. "Court Frees Mingus; He Sits in on a Sit-in." New York *Post*, March 17, 1963.

Lindenberger, Herbert. "Die Faszination des rhythmus." *Hi Fi Stereophonie*, January 1975.

Locke, Don. "Black Saint Review." *Jazz Monthly*, November 1965.

"M + M at Monterey." *Newsweek*, October 5, 1964, 120ff.

Mingus, Charles. "In Defense of Duke." *Down Beat*, June 18, 1952.

———. "An Open Letter to Miles Davis." *Down Beat*, November 30, 1955, 12–13.

"Mingus Arrested." *Down Beat*, January 12, 1967.

"Mingus in Bay Area," San Francisco *Examiner*, December 11, 1960

"Mingus in Mill Valley." *Down Beat*, February 23, 1967.

"Mingus Moves." *Jazz*, June 1963, 16.

"Monterey Jazz Festival." *Time*, October 19, 1962.

Palmer, Robert. "Charles Mingus Ain't No Jive Bassist." *Rolling Stone*, January 20, 1972, 11.

———. "Slim Pickings for the World's Greatest Bassist." *Rolling Stone*, July 18, 1974, 24.

———. "Charles Mingus and Azucena y Edo." *New York Times*, June 23, 1976.

Santoro, Gene. "Pithecanthropus Erectus: Mingus on Atlantic." *Fi*, March 1998, 132ff.

Sidran, Ben. "Charles Mingus Finds a New Voice: The Underdog Meets Joni Mitchell." *Rolling Stone*, December 28, 1978, 33ff.

Smith, Arnold Jay. "Charles Mingus: Developmental Changes." *Down Beat*, January 12, 1978, 22ff.

"Stars Spark SRO Mingus NY Concert." *Down Beat*, March 17, 1972.

Stein, Victor. "Mingus in Concert." *Village Voice*, June 28, 1973.

Whitworth, Bill. "The Rich Full Life of Charlie Mingus." New York *Herald Tribune*, November 1, 1964, 13ff.

Wilson, John. "Mingus at Monterey Festival." *New York Times*, October 4, 1964.

———. "Bassist Charles Mingus Performance at Five Spot." *New York Times*, April 16, 1973, 49.

———. "Charles Mingus Concert Reviewed." *New York Times*, January 23, 1974, 16–17.

———. "Mingus Dynasty (portrait Dannie Richmond)." *Jazz Magazine*, May/June 1975, 24–25.

Ulanov, Barry. "Are We Cantankerous? An Examination of Some Criticism of Criticism." *Metronome*, April 1949, 15ff.

———. "The Function of the Critic in Jazz." *Metronome*, August 1949, 16–17.

Wolff, Geoffrey. "Man with a Bass." *Newsweek*, May 17, 1971, 110.

Yardley, Jonathan. "Agonies of a Mongrel." *New Republic*, July 3, 1971, 29.

MUSIC VIDEOS

Mingus Performances

Bryn, Bjorn (director). *Charles Mingus Sextet* (Shanachie).

McGlynn, Don (director). *Triumph of the Underdog* (Shanachie).

Reichman, Tom (director). *Mingus* (Rhapsody Films).

Kirchheimer, Manny (director). *Stations of the Elevated*: music by Charlie Mingus (Rhapsody Films).

Non-Mingus Musical Performances

Jackie McLean on Mars (Rhapsody).

Last Date: Eric Dolphy (Rhapsody).

Made in America: The Life and Music of Ornette Coleman (Caravan of Dreams).

Mystery, Mr. Ra: Sun Ra and His Arkestra (Rhapsody).

Rahsaan Roland Kirk, the One-man Twins (Rhino).

Sonny Rollins in Saxophone Colossus (Sony).

Sound?? starring Rahsaan Roland Kirk and John Cage (Rhapsody).

Texas Tenor: The Illinois Jacquet Story (Rhapsody).

FILMS

Cassavetes, John. *Shadows.*

Dansak, Herbert. *Sweet Love, Bitter.*

Dearden, Basil. *All Night Long.*
> *Sapphire.*

Eastwood, Clint. *Play Misty For Me.*
> *High Plains Drifter.*

Frankenheimer, John. *The Manchurian Candidate.*

Kurosawa, Akira. *Rashoman.*
> *Seven Samurai.*
> *Throne of Blood.*
> *Yojimbo.*

Laughton, Charles. *The Night of the Hunter.*

Leone, Sergio. *A Fistful of Dollars.*
> *For a Few Dollars More.*
> *The Good, The Bad, and the Ugly.*

Post, Ted. *Hang 'em High.*

Siegel, Don. *Dirty Harry.*
> *The Enforcer.*

Magnum Force.

Sudden Impact.

Welles, Orson. *Chimes at Midnight.*

Citizen Kane.

Macbeth.

The Magnificent Ambersons.

Othello.

The Stranger.

Touch of Evil.

WEBSITES

AAA Collections: Sketchbooks for the Archives of American Art (www.si.edu/artarchives/wharnett.htm)

Bay Area history in the 1960s (www.diggers.org)

The Disinformation Site: compendium of alternative publications and viewpoints (www.disinfo.com)

Fillmore Museum (www.amacord.com/fillmore/museum)

Fine Arts Museums of San Francisco (www.famsf.org)

Martin Luther King Jr. timeline/biography (www.indigo.lib.lsu.edu)

Tim Leary Home Page (www.leary.com)

The Real Mingus Website (www.mingusmingusmingus.com)

The Unofficial Charles Mingus Home Page (www.siba.fi/%eonttone/mingus)

Mingus in Seattle: Robert Gwynne on The Unofficial Charles Mingus Home Page.

Museum of the City of San Francisco (www.sfmuseum.org)

Discography

This discography, adapted with permission from Esa Onttonen's excellent discography at the Charles Mingus Home Page on the World Wide Web, is based on CDs. LPs are included if the same material is not available on CD. All compositions are by Charles Mingus unless otherwise noted.

MINGUS AS LEADER

1. unknown titles (1945, unknown) PERSONNEL: Britt Woodman (tb); Buddy Collette (as); Spaulding Givens (p); Charles Mingus (b); Roy Porter (d) DATE AND LOCATION: ca. early 1945, Los Angeles UNISSUED.

2. Charles Mingus Sextet (1945, Excelsior) TRACKS: 1. The Texas Hop 2. Baby Take a Chance With Me 3. Lonesome Woman Blues 4. Swinging an Echo PERSONNEL: N.R. Bates (t); Maxwell Davis, William Woodman Jr. (ts); Robert Mosley (p); Charles Mingus (b); Roy Porter (d); Oradell Mitchell (voc on 1, 3); Everett Pettis (voc on 2) DATE AND LOCATION: ca. June 1945, Los Angeles ORIGINALLY ISSUED in September 1945 as Excelsior CM132/CM133 (1, 2) and CM134/CM135 (3, 4). Reissued as *Mingus in California* by Smithsonian Institution.

3. Charles Mingus Sextette (1946, Excelsior) TRACKS: 1. Ain't Jivin' Blues 2. Baby Take a Chance With Me 3. Shuffle Bass Boogie 4. Weird Nightmare PERSONNEL: Karl George, John Plonsky (t); Henry Coker (tb); Jewel Grant, Willie Smith (as); Lucky Thompson (ts); Gene Porter (bars, cl); Wilbert Baranco (p); Buddy Harper (g); Charles Mingus (b); Lee Young (d); Claude Trenier (voc except 3) DATE AND LOCATION: January 1946, Los Angeles ORIGINALLY ISSUED as Excelsior 162 (1, 2) and Excelsior 163 (3, 4).

4. Baron Mingus and His Octet (1946, 4 Star) TRACKS: 1. Ashby De La Zouch 2. Love on a Greyhound Bus 3. After Hours 4. Make Believe 5. Honey Take a Chance With Me 6. Bedspread 7. This Subdues My Passion 8. Pipe Dream PERSONNEL: Buddy Collette (as); Lady Will Carr (p); Charles Mingus (b) plus unknown t, tb, ts, bars, g, d, and voc DATE AND LOCATION: April 26 (1-3) and May 6 (4-8), 1946, Los Angeles ORIGINALLY ISSUED as 4 Star 1105 (1, 2); 1106 (3, 8); 1107 (4, 6); and 1108 (5, 7).

5. *Charles "Baron" Mingus Presents His Symphonic Airs* (1946, Fentone) TRACKS: 1. He's Gone [O-189] 2. Story of Love [O-190] 3. God's Portrait 4. unknown title PERSONNEL: According to Priestley: Vern Carlson, 4 unknown (t); Henry Coker, 3 unknown (tb); 5 unknown reeds; Dante Profumato (fl); Richard Wyands (p); unknown g, b; Charles Mingus (b, cello); unknown d, tamb; Herb Gayle (voc on 1, 3). According to Lohmann: Vern Carlson, Miles Davis (possibly), 3 unknown (t); Henry Coker, 3 unknown (tb); Danto Perfuro (fl); Lucky Thompson (probably) (ts); 4 unknown (reeds); Richard Wyands (p); unknown (g); Charles Mingus (b, cello); unknown (b); unknown (dr); unknown (perc); Herb Gayle (voc on 1) DATE AND LOCATION: ca. March 1946, Los Angeles (Lohmann); ca. January 1949, San Francisco (Priestley) ORIGINALLY ISSUED 1, 2: Fentone 2002; 3, 4: Fentone 2001 (unissued?).

6. *Baron Mingus and His Rhythm* (1946, Fentone/Dolphins Of Hollywood) TRACKS: 1. Pennies from Heaven 2. Lyon's Roar 3. Mingus Fingers (DH-200) 4. These Foolish Things (Strachey/Link) (DH-200) 5. Say It Isn't So (DH-300-A) 6. Boppin 'n Boston (DH-300-B) PERSONNEL: 1, 2: Herb Caro (bars); Buzz Wheeler (p); Charles Mingus (b); Warren Thompson (d); Herb Gayle (voc on 1); 3, 4: According to Lohmann: Miles Davis (t); Britt Woodman (possibly)(tb); Buddy Collette (ts); Wilbert Baranco (p); Charles Mingus (b); unknown (d); according to Priestley: Buddy Collette (as, cl); unknown (p); Charles Mingus (b); unknown (d); 5, 6: Miles Davis (t); Britt Woodman (possibly)(tb); Buddy Collette (ts); Wilbert Baranco (p); Charles Mingus (b); unknown (d); Helen Carr (voc on 5); unknown (voc on 6) DATE AND LOCATION: 1, 2: ca. January 1949, San Francisco (Priestley); 3-6: Spring 1947, Los Angeles (Priestley); 3-6: March 1946, Los Angeles (Lohmann) ORIGINALLY ISSUED: 1, 2: Fentone 2003; 3, 4: Dolphins of Hollywood 2001 5, 6: Dolphins of Hollywood 300.

7. *Charles Mingus and His Orchestra* (1946, Rex Hollywood) TRACKS: 1. The Story of Love (REX 28002-A) 2. Inspiration pt. 1 (REX 28014-A) 3. Inspiration pt. 2 (REX 28014-B) PERSONNEL: Charles Mingus (b) with unknown big band possibly including; Miles Davis (t); Lucky Thompson (ts) DATE AND LOCATION: ca. March 1946, Los Angeles (Lohmann); Spring 1947, Los Angeles (Priestley) ORIGINALLY ISSUED: 1: Rex Hollywood 28002; 2, 3: Rex Hollywood 28014.

8. *The Chill of Death* (1947) TRACKS: 1. The Chill of Death 2. unknown titles PERSONNEL: 1. unknown large orchestra including; Buddy Collette, Ted Nash (reeds); Red Callender, Billy Hadnott, Artie Bernstein, Art Shapiro (b); unknown cond; Charles Mingus (narr); 2. unknown big band including; Jimmy Knepper (tb); Charles Mingus (b) DATE AND LOCATION: 1: February 1947, Los Angeles; 2: spring 1947, Los Angeles UNISSUED, recorded by Columbia.

9. *Central Avenue Sounds: Jazz in Los Angeles (1921-1956)* (1946/49, Rhino) TRACKS: Disc 2: 21. Bedspread (3:00) (Buddy Collette) 22. Pipe Dream (3:12); Disc 3: 22. Mingus Fingers (2:56) 23. These Foolish Things (3:15) (Strachey-Link) PERSONNEL: Karl George (t)(Disc 2 only); John Anderson (t) (Disc 2 only); Britt Woodman (tb) (Disc 2 only); Buddy Collette (cl, as); William Woodman Jr. (ts) (Disc 2 only); Lady Will Carr (p) (Disc 2 only); Charles Mingus (b); Eugene Porter (b) (Disc 2 only); Lee Young or Oscar Bradley (d) (Disc 2 only); unknown p and d (Disc 3 only) DATE AND LOCATION: Bedspread, Pipe Dream: June 5, 1946, Los Angeles; Mingus Fingers, These Foolish Things: spring 1949, Los Angeles ORIGINAL ISSUE: Bedspread: 4 Star 1107; Pipe Dream: 4 Star 1106; Mingus Fingers, These Foolish Things: Dolphin's of Hollywood 200.

10. *The Young Rebel* (1946-52, Swingtime) LP TRACKS: 1. This Subdues My Passion (2:50) 2. Honey Take a Chance With Me (3:12) 3. Story of Love (2:52) 4. He's Gone (3:31) (Manza/Stevens) 5. Precognition (2:45) 6. Portrait (3:13) 7. Cello Again (2:37) (Pettiford) [R1102] 8. Ah Dee Dong Blues (2:30) (Pettiford) [R1103] 9. Sonny Boy (2:52) (De Sylva/Henderson/Brown) [R1104] 10. I'm Beginning to See the Light (2:50) (Ellington) [R1105] 11. No Good Woman Blues (3:03) (Hines/Evans) 12. Bow Legged Woman (3:08) (Hines/Evans) 13. Bama Lama Lam (2:52) (Hampton) 14. Spooky Boogie (3:05) (Hines/Evans) PERSONNEL: 1, 2: Baron Mingus and His Octet: probably, Buddy Collette (as); Lady Will Carr (p); Charles Mingus (b); unknown t, tb, ts, bs, g, d, and vocals; 3, 4: Charles "Baron" Mingus Presents His Symphonic Airs: Vern Carlson (t); Miles Davis (t); Henry Coker (tb); Dante Profumato (Priestley) / Danto Perfuro (Lohmann) (fl); Richard Wyands (p); Charles Mingus (b, cello); Herb Gayle (voc); unknown 3 (t), 3 (tb), 5 reeds, g, d, tambourine; 5, 6: Lee Konitz (as); Phyllis Pinkerton (p); George Koutzen (cello); Charles Mingus (b); Al Levitt (d); Jackie Paris (vocals

on 6); 7-10: Oscar Pettiford Quartet: Billy Taylor (p); Oscar Pettiford (cello); Charles Mingus (b); Charlie Smith (d); 11-14: Earl Hines and His Orchestra / Curley Hamner and His Orchestra: Duke Garrette (t); Bobby Plater (as); Morris Lane (ts); Charles Fowlkes (bs); Bill Dougherty (v); Earl Hines (p); Billy Mackel (g); Charles Mingus (b); Curley Hamner (d); Wini Brown (voc) DATES AND LOCATIONS: Original issue 1, 2 May 6, 1946, Los Angeles 4 Star 1108; 3, 4 ca. January 1949, San Francisco Fentone 2002; 5, 6 April 12, 1952, NYC Debut M-101; 7, 9 October 16, 1952, NYC Roost 546; 8, 10 October 16, 1952, NYC Roost 561; 11, 12 December 31, 1947, Chicago Pickwick PR127; 13, 14 December 31, 1947, Chicago Sunrise 2115

11. *Debut Rarities Volume 4* (1952/53, OJC) TRACKS: 1. Portrait (take 1) (3:11) 2. Portrait (take 2) (3:10) 3. I've Lost My Love (take 1) (3:01) 4. I've Lost My Love (take 2) (3:01) 5. Extrasensory Perception (2:48) 6. Extrasensory Perception (alternate version) (2:42) 7. Precognition (2:43) 8. Make Believe (3:04) 9. Paris in Blue (3:12) 10. Montage (2:54) 11. You Go To My Head (2:42) (Coots/Gillespie) 12. Can You Blame Me (2:48) (Gordon/Leonard) 13. You and Me (2:47) (Gordon/Leonard) 14. Bebopper (2:40) (Gordon/Leonard) 15. Cupid (2:46) (Gordon/Leonard) PERSONNEL: 1-7: Lee Konitz (as); Phyllis Pinkerton (p) ; George Koutzen (cello); Charles Mingus (b); Al Levitt (d); Jackie Paris (voc on 1, 2); Bob Benton (voc on 3, 4); 8-10: Paige Brook (as, fl); John Mehegan (p); Jackson Wiley (cello); Charles Mingus (b); Max Roach (d); Jackie Paris (voc); 11-15: Hank Jones (p); Charles Mingus (b); Max Roach (d); The Gordons: Honey Gordon, George Gordon, George Gordon Jr., Richard Gordon (voc on 12-15) DATE AND LOCATION: 1-7: April 12, 1952, NYC; 8-10: September 16, 1952, NYC; 11-15: April 29, 1953, NYC ORIGINAL ISSUES: 2, 7: Debut M-101; 8, 9: Debut M-102; 5, 10: Debut M-103; 11: Debut DEB198 (issued as *Hank Jones Trio*; 12, 14: Debut M-110; 13, 15: Debut M-111; all others first issued on The Complete Debut Recordings

12. *Jazzical Moods* (1954, Period) TRACKS: 1. What Is This Thing Called Love? (8:08) (Cole Porter) 2. Stormy Weather (3:18) (Arlen) 3. Minor Intrusion (10:13) 4. Abstractions (4:12) (Teo Macero) 5. Thrice Upon a Theme (6:40) 6. Four Hands (8:50) (Charles Mingus, John LaPorta) 7. The Spur of the Moment/Echonitus (8:36) PERSONNEL: Charles Mingus (b, p); John LaPorta (cl on 1-5; as on 1-4, 6, 7); Teo Macero (ts on 1, 3, 4, 6, 7; bs on 5); Thad Jones aka "Oliver King" (t, except 6 and Echonitus); Jackson Wiley (cello, except 6 and Spur of the Moment); Clem DeRosa (d, tambourine) DATE AND LOCATION: December 1954, NYC ORIGINAL ISSUE: 1-4: Period SPL-1107 as *Jazzical Moods*, vol. 1; 5-7: Period SPL-1111 as *Jazzical Moods*, vol. 2 REISSUES (most of these are unauthorized): Affinity AFF 135 (1985, LP); Affinity CD AFF 750 (*Abstractions*, CD); Drive Archive (*Intrusions*, CD)—no Abstractions and Stormy Weather; Everest Records Archive of Folk & Jazz Music FS-235 (*Charlie Mingus*, LP)—no Abstractions or Stormy Weather; Fresh Sound Records FSR-CD 62 (*Jazzical Moods*, CD)—no Abstractions; Koch Records 321 974 D1 (*Welcome to Jazz*, CD)—no Abstractions; 5-7: Black Bird (*East Coasting*, CD, Spain?)

13. *Jazz Composers Workshop* (1954/55, Savoy) TRACKS: 1. Purple Heart (5:33) 2. Gregarian Chant (2:48) 3. Eulogy for Rudy Williams (6:19) 4. Tea for Two (6:16) (Vincent Youmans, Irving Caesar) 5. Smog L.A. (3:10) (Wally Cirillo) 6. Level Seven (4:14) (Cirillo) 7. Transeason (4:19) (Cirillo) 8. Rose Geranium (4:09) (Cirillo) 9. Getting Together (4:27) PERSONNEL: 1-4,9: John LaPorta (cl on 1, 2, 4, 9; as on 3; Teo Macero (ts on 2, 3, 4, 9; bs on 1; George Barrow (ts on 1; bs on 2, 3, 4, 9); Mal Waldron (p except 1); Charles Mingus (b); Rudy Nichols (d); 5-8: Teo Macero (ts); Wally Cirillo (p); Charles Mingus (b); Kenny Clarke (d) DATE AND LOCATION: 1-4, 9: October 31, 1954, Rudy Van Gelder's studio, Hackensack, N.J.; 5-8: January 30, 1955, Rudy Van Gelder's studio, Hackensack, N.J. ORIGINAL ISSUE: Savoy MG-12059 (1956) as *Jazz Composers Workshop No. 2*

14. *Debut Rarities Volume 2* (1951/53, OJC) TRACKS: 1. What Is This Thing Called Love (3:02) (Porter) 2. Darn That Dream (3:38) (Van Heusen) 3. Yesterdays (3:05) (Kern) 4. Body And Soul (3:34) (Green) 5. Blue Moon (3:33) (Rodgers) 6. Blue Tide (3:10) (Givens) 7. Darn That Dream (3:37) (Van Heusen) 8. Jeepers Creepers (3:37) (Warren) 9. Jeepers Creepers (3:03) 10. Day Dream (3:42) (Ellington/Strayhorn) 11. Day Dream (2:38) 12. Theme From "Rhapsody in Blue" (3:24) (Gershwin) 13. Theme From "Rhapsody in Blue" (2:39) 14. Jet (2:44) (Benjamin/Weiss/Revel) 15. Jet (2:35) PERSONNEL: 1-7: Spaulding Givens (p); Charles Mingus (b); 8-15: Spaulding Givens (p); Charles Mingus (b); Max Roach (d) DATE AND LOCATION: 1-7: April 1951, Los Angeles; 8-15: April 14, 1953 ORIGINAL ISSUES: 1-6: Debut DLP-1 (Charles Mingus/Spaulding Givens: *Strings and Keys*); all others first issued on The Complete Debut Recordings

15. *Newport, Rhode Island* (1955, VOA) 1. The Emperor 2. Sounds of April 3. Minor Intrusion 4. Non-Sectarian PERSONNEL: Art Farmer (t); Britt Woodman, Eddie Bert (tb); John LaPorta (as, cl); Teo Macero (ts); Teddy Charles (vib); Mal Waldron (p); Charles Mingus (b); Elvin Jones (d) DATE AND LOCATION: July 17, 1955, Newport UNISSUED

16. [December 23, 1955, Cafe Bohemia, NYC— Charles Mingus Jazz Workshop] *a. Mingus at the Bohemia* (OJC) TRACKS: 1. Jump Monk (6:44) 2. Serenade in Blue (5:57) (Gordon/Warren) 3. Percussion Discussion (8:25) 4. Work Song (6:16) 5. Septemberly (6:55) (Warren/Dubin and Lawrence/Gross) 6. All the Things You C# (6:47) (Kern) 7. Jump Monk (11:38) 8. All the Things You C# (9:50) (Kern) PERSONNEL: Eddie Bert (tb); George Barrow (ts); Mal Waldron (p); Charles Mingus (b); Willie Jones (d); Max Roach (d on 2, 5) DATE AND LOCATION: December 23, 1955, Cafe Bohemia, NYC ORIGINAL ISSUE: Debut DLP-123 REISSUES: Prestige P 24010 (*Charles Mingus* with *Charles Mingus Quintet Plus Max Roach*, 2 LP); Fantasy DEB-123 (1983, LP); (*Mingus at the Bohemia*, Japanese, 2 CD with *Charles Mingus Quintet Plus Max Roach*) *b. Charles Mingus Quintet Plus Max Roach* (OJC) TRACKS: 1. A Foggy Day (5:35) (Gershwin) 2. Drums (5:25) 3. Haitian Fight Song (5:20) 4. Lady Bird (6:00) (Dameron) 5. I'll Remember April (13:20) (Raye/DePaul/Johnston) 6. Love Chant (7:35) PERSONNEL: Eddie Bert (tb); George Barrow (ts); Mal Waldron (p); Charles Mingus (b); Willie Jones (d); Max Roach (d on 2, 5) DATE AND LOCATION: December 23, 1955, Cafe Bohemia, NYC ORIGINAL ISSUE: Debut DLP-6009 (1956, later retitled *Chazz!*) REISSUES: Prestige P 24010 (*Charles Mingus* with *Mingus at the Bohemia*); (*Mingus at the Bohemia*, Japanese, 2CD with *Charles Mingus*)

17. *Pithecanthropus Erectus* (1956, Atlantic) TRACKS: 1. Pithecanthropus Erectus (10:33) 2. A Foggy Day (7:47) (Gershwin) 3. Profile of Jackie (3:07) 4. Love Chant (14:56) PERSONNEL: Jackie McLean (as); J.R. Monterose (ts); Mal Waldron (p); Charles Mingus (b); Willie Jones (d) DATE AND LOCATION: January 30, 1956, NYC ORIGINAL ISSUE: Atlantic #1237 (1956) REISSUES: Atlantic SD 8809 - Jazzlore 2 (1981, LP)

18. *Freebody Park* (1956, VOA) 1. Tonight at Noon 2. Tourist in Manhattan PERSONNEL: Bill Hardman (tp); Ernie Henry (as); Teo Macero (ts); Mal Waldron (p); Charles Mingus (b); Al Dreares (d) DATE AND LOCATION: July 5, 1956, Freebody Park, Newport, R.I. UNISSUED

19. *Cafe Bohemia* (1956) 1. Confirmation (Purple Heart) 2. Bohemia 3. Laura 4. Jump, Monk PERSONNEL: 1, 2: Bill Hardman (tp); Jackie McLean (as); Mal Waldron (p); Charles Mingus (b); Al Dreares (d); 3, 4: possibly, Tommy Turrentine (tp); Willie Dennis (tb); George Barrow/Shafi Hadi (ts); Mal Waldron (p); Charles Mingus (b); Al Dreares (d) DATE AND LOCATION: August 18, 1956 (1, 2) and Autumn 1956 (3, 4), Cafe Bohemia, NYC UNISSUED broadcasts

20. *The Clown* (1957, Atlantic) TRACKS: 1. Haitian Fight Song (11:57) 2. Blue Cee (7:48) 3. Reincarnation of a Lovebird (8:31) 4. The Clown (12:29) PERSONNEL: Shafi Hadi (as, ts); Jimmy Knepper (tb); Wade Legge (p); Charles Mingus (b); Dannie Richmond (d); Jean Shepherd (narration on The Clown (4) DATE AND LOCATION: 1-3: March 12, 1957, NYC; 4: February 13, 1957, NYC ORIGINAL ISSUE: Atlantic #1260 (195?)

21. *Charles Mingus Trios* (1953/57, Jazz Door) TRACKS: Disc 1: 1. Back Home Blues (5:25) (Mingus) 2. Yesterdays (4:08) (Kern) 3. I Can't Get Started (6:25) (Duke) 4. Hamp's New Blues (3:45) (Hawes) 5. Summertime (4:28) (Gershwin) 6. Dizzy Moods (6:40) (Mingus/Gillespie) 7. Laura (6:30) (Raksin) • Disc 2: 1. How High the Moon (Lewis) 2. Budo 3. Hallelujah 4. I've Got You Under My Skin (Porter) 5. Embraceable You (Gershwin) 6. I Want To Be Happy 7. I've Got You Under My Skin (Porter) 8. Sure Thing 9. Embraceable You (Gershwin) 10. Woodyn You (Gillespie) 11. Salt Peanuts (Gillespie) PERSONNEL: Disc 1: Hampton Hawes (p); Charles Mingus (b); Dannie Richmond (d); Disc 2: Bud Powell (p); Charles Mingus (b); Roy Haynes (d) DATE AND LOCATION: Disc 1: July 9, 1957, NYC; Disc 2: March 21, 1953, Birdland, NYC and/or April 5, 1953, Club Kavakos, Washington, D.C. ORIGINAL ISSUE: Disc 1 as Jubilee JLP 1054 REISSUES: Disc 1: Trip TX-5040 (*Trio and Sextet*); Disc 2: partly as *Inner Fires* (Elektra E1-60030) under Powell's name. This same set of recordings appear on Jazz Door 1204 as part of a Bud Powell 3-CD box *The Legacy of Bud Powell*.

22. Mingus Three (1957, Roulette) TRACKS: 1. Yesterdays (4:13) (Kern) 2. Back Home Blues (5:29) 3. I Can't Get Started (6:28) (Duke) 4. Hamp's New Blues (3:52) (Hawes) 5. Summertime (4:28) (Gershwin) 6. Dizzy Moods (6:51) (Mingus) 7. Laura (6:33) (Raksin) PERSONNEL: Hampton Hawes (p); Charles Mingus (b); Dannie Richmond (d) DATE AND LOCATION: July 9, 1957, NYC ORIGINAL ISSUE: Jubilee JLP 1054 REISSUES: Trip TX-5040 (*Trio and Sextet*, LP); Jazz Door (disc 1 of *Charles Mingus Trios*, 2 CD); Drive Archive 3529 ("I Can't Get Started" without "Yesterdays," CD); Fresh Sound FSR-CD 81 (1989, unauthorized CD)

23. Debut Rarities Volume 1 (1953/57, OJC) TRACKS: 1. Pink Topsy (3:03) 2. Miss Bliss (3:03) 3. Blue Tide (3:08) (Givens) 4. Pink Topsy (alternate) (3:38) 5. Eclipse (2:54) 6. Eclipse (alternate) (2:57) 7. Latter Day Saint (4:00) (Knepper) 8. Cunningbird (4:45) (Knepper) 9. The Jumpin' Blues (Jump The Blues Away) (4:52) (Gordon) 10. The Masher (3:33) (Knepper) 11. Latter Day Saint (alternate 1) (5:22) (Knepper) 12. Latter Day Saint (alternate 2) (3:46) 13. Latter Day Saint (alternate #?) (3:51) 14. The Masher (alternate) (4:15) (Knepper) PERSONNEL: 1-6: Ernie Royal (t); Willie Dennis (tb); Eddie Caine (as, fl); Teo Macero (ts); Danny Bank (bs); John Lewis (p); Jackson Wiley (cello); Charles Mingus (b); Kenny Clarke (d); Spaulding Givens (arranger); Janet Thurlow (voc on 3, 5, 6); 7-14: Jimmy Knepper (tb); Joe Maini (as); Bill Triglia (p); Charles Mingus (b); Dannie Richmond (d) DATE AND LOCATION: 1-6: October 28, 1953, NYC; 7-14: June 10, 1957, NYC ORIGINAL ISSUE: 1-3, 5: Debut EP-450 (*Charles Mingus Octet*, EP); 7-10: Danish Debut DLP 101

24. Tijuana Moods (1957, Bluebird) TRACKS: 1. Dizzy Moods (5:47) (Mingus, Dizzy Gillespie) 2. Ysabel's Table Dance (10:24) 3. Tijuana Gift Shop (3:44) 4. Los Mariachis (The Street Musicians) (10:18) 5. Flamingo (5:31) (Ted Grouya) 6. Dizzy Moods (alternate take) (8:17) (Mingus, Gillespie) 7. Tijuana Gift Shop (alternate take) (4:39) 8. Los Mariachis (alternate take) (12:23) 9. Flamingo (alternate take) (6:37) (Grouya) PERSONNEL: Clarence Shaw (t); Shafi Hadi aka Curtis Porter (as); Jimmy Knepper (tb); Bill Triglia (p); Charles Mingus (b); Dannie Richmond (d); Frankie Dunlop (percussion); Ysabel Morel (castanets); Lonnie Elder (voices) DATE AND LOCATION: 1, 2, 4, 6, 8: July 18, 1957, RCA Victor's Studio A, NYC; 3, 5, 7, 9: August 6, 1957, RCA Victor's Studio A, NYC ORIGINAL ISSUE: 1-5: RCA Victor LSP2533 (1962). REISSUES (as *New Tijuana Moods*): RCA Bluebird 5635-RB-1 (1986, 2 LP, including all alternates and an alternate of "Ysabel Table Dance," which was excluded from the CD because of total time limitation); RCA/Ariola International Bluebird 5644-2-RB (1986, CD)

25. Great River, Long Island (1957, VOA) 1. Dizzy Moods 2. Tijuana Table Dance 3. Woody 'N You (Gillespie) 4. Haitian Fight Song PERSONNEL: Clarence Shaw (t); Shafi Hadi (as, ts); Jimmy Knepper (tb); Bill Triglia (p); Charles Mingus (b); Dannie Richmond (d) DATE AND LOCATION: July 20, 1957 (1, 2) and July 21, 1957 (3, 4), Great River, Long Island, N.Y. UNISSUED

26. East Coasting (1957, Bethlehem) TRACKS: 1. Memories of You (4:23) (Blake) 2. East Coasting (5:10) 3. West Coast Ghost (10:29) 4. Celia (7:50) 5. Conversation (5:25) 6. Fifty-First Street Blues (5:45) PERSONNEL: Clarence Shaw (t); Shafi Hadi aka Curtis Porter (as, ts); Jimmy Knepper (tb); Bill Evans (p); Charles Mingus (b); Dannie Richmond (d) DATE AND LOCATION: August 1957, NYC ORIGINAL ISSUE: Bethlehem BCP 6019 (1958) REISSUES: International Polydor Production 623215 (*Charlie Mingus Sextet*, pre-1969, LP); Affinity CD Charly 19 (*New York Sketchbook*, 1986, unauthorized, CD); Black Bird (matrix: Tecval 01 Jazz 100-41 CD 54) (*East Coasting*, CD, Spain?); Bethlehem 30022 (1995?, USA)

27. Debut Rarities Volume 3 (1957, OJC) TRACKS: 1. Untitled Original Blues (take 1) (3:55) (Hadi) 2. Stella by Starlight (take 4) (3:57) (Young) 3. Stella by Starlight (take 5) (3:53) 4. Untitled Original Composition (take 3) (5:17) (Hadi) 5. Untitled Original Composition (take 5) (4:34) 6. Autumn in New York (take 1) (5:29) (Vernon Duke) 7. Autumn in New York (take 2) (5:05) 8. Long Ago and Far Away (take 2) (3:24) (Kern) 9. Long Ago and Far Away (take 4) (3:11) 10. Long Ago and Far Away (take 5) (3:17) 11. Untitled Original Blues (take 2) (Hadi) 12. Joldi (take 4) (5:24) (Hadi) 13. Joldi (take 5) (5:08) PERSONNEL: Clarence Shaw (t); Shafi Hadi (ts); Pepper Adams (bs); Wade Legge or Wynton Kelly (p); Charles Mingus or Henry Grimes (b); Dannie Richmond (d) DATE AND LOCATION: September (?) 1957, NYC ORIGINAL ISSUE: *The Complete Debut Recordings*

28. *A Modern Jazz Symposium of Music and Poetry* (1957, Bethlehem) TRACKS: 1. Scenes in the City (11:20/11:49) 2. Nouroog (5:01/4:49) 3. New York Sketchbook (8:29/8:51) 4. Duke's Choice (6:25) 5. Slippers (3:27) 6. Wouldn't You (unreleased) (8:42) 7. Bounce (unreleased) (9:20) 8. Slippers (alt. take) (3:49) PERSONNEL: Shafi Hadi aka Curtis Porter (as, ts); Jimmy Knepper (tb); Horace Parlan (p, left hand on 1 and 3); Charles Mingus (b); Dannie Richmond (d) with; Clarence Shaw (t) on 1, 3, 4; Bob Hammer (p on 1, 3); Melvin Stewart (narration on 1; Bill Hardman (t on 2) DATE AND LOCATION: October 1957, NYC ORIGINAL ISSUE:Bethlehem BCP 6026 (1958) REISSUES: 1, 3, 4: Affinity CD Charly 19 (*New York Sketchbook*, 1986, unauthorized CD); 4: Jazz Masterworks-Intermezzo CJZLP 10 (*Mingus & Duke*, 1985, Italy, LP); Bethlehem #20-40092 (USA, includes tracks 6-8) COMMENTS: Weiler notes many edits on each track, combining mono and stereo takes.

29. *The Complete Debut Recordings* (1951-58) TRACKS: Disc 1: 1. What Is This Thing Called Love (3:02) (Porter) 2. Darn That Dream (3:38) (Van Heusen) 3. Yesterdays (3:05) (Kern) 4. Body and Soul (3:34) (Green) 5. Blue Moon (3:33) (Rodgers) 6. Blue Tide (3:10) (Givens) 7. Darn That Dream (3:37) (Van Heusen)** 8. Jeepers Creepers (take 1) (3:37) (Warren)* 9. Jeepers Creepers (take 2) (3:03)* 10. Portrait (take 1) (3:11)** 11. Portrait (take 2) (3:10) 12. I've Lost My Love (take 1) (3:01)* 13. I've Lost My Love (take 2) (3:01)* 14. Extrasensory Perception (2:48) 15. Extrasensory Perception (2:42)** 16. Precognition (2:43) 17. Make Believe (3:04) 18. Paris in Blue (3:12) 19. Montage (2:54) 20. Day Dream (take 1) (3:42) (Ellington/Strayhorn)* 21. Day Dream (take 2) (2:38)* 22. Theme from "Rhapsody in Blue" (take 1) (3:24) (Gershwin)* 23. Theme from "Rhapsody in Blue" (take 2) (2:39)* • Disc 2: 1. Jet (take 1) (2:44) (Benjamin/Weiss/Revel)* 2. Jet (take 2) (2:35)* 3. (Medley) You Go To My Head (2:42) (Coots/Gillespie) 4. Can You Blame Me (2:48) (Gordon/Leonard) 5. You and Me (2:47) (Gordon/Leonard) 6. Bebopper (2:40) (Gordon/Leonard) 7. Cupid (2:46) (Gordon/Leonard) 8. Drum Conversation (4:02) (Roach) 9. I've Got You Under My Skin (2:49) (Porter) 10. Embraceable You (4:18) (Gershwin) 11. Sure Thing (2:03) (Powell) 12. Cherokee (4:48) (Noble) 13. (Jubilee) Hallelujah (3:51) (Youmans/Robin/Grey) 14. Lullaby Of Birdland (2:29) (Shearing/Weiss) 15. Wee (Allen's Alley) (6:40) (Best)* 16. Hot House (8:58) (Dameron)* 17. A Night in Tunisia (7:22)* (Gillespie) • Disc 3: 1. Perdido (8:10) (Tizol)* 2. Salt Peanuts (7:18) (Gillespie/Clarke)* 3. All the Things You Are (7:12) (Kern)* 4. 52nd Street Theme (0:38) (Monk)* 5. Perdido (7:24) (Tizol) 6. Salt Peanuts (7:20) (Gillespie/Clarke) 7. All the Things You Are (7:10) (Kern) 8. 52nd Street Theme (0:35) (Monk) 9. Wee (Allen's Alley) (6:36) (Best) 10. Hot House (9:01) (Dameron) 11. A Night in Tunisia (7:22) (Gillespie) • Disc 4: 1. Bass-ically Speaking (take 1) (3:58)** 2. Bass-ically Speaking (take 2) (3:50)** 3. Bass-ically Speaking (take 3) (3:51)** 4. Bass-ically Speaking (3:52) 5. Untitled Blues (2:35) 6. Wee Dot (Blues for Some Bones) (14:17) (Johnson) 7. Stardust (4:52) (Carmichael) 8. Move (6:48) (Best) 9. I'll Remember April (11:04) (Raye/DePaul/Johnston) 10. Now's the Time (14:22) (Parker) • Disc 5: 1. Trombosphere (3:24) (Givens) 2. Owl! (15:11) (Gillespie) 3. Chazzanova (4:54) 4. Yesterdays (10:04) (Kern) 5. Kai's Day (5:22) (Winding) 6. Pink Topsy (3:03) 7. Miss Bliss (3:03) 8. Blue Tide (3:08) (Givens) 9. Pink Topsy (3:38)** 10. Eclipse (2:57)** 11. Eclipse (2:54) 12. Opus 1 (3:21) (Bley)** 13. Opus 1 (4:08) 14. (Teapot) Walkin' (4:28) (Carpenter) • Disc 6: 1. Like Someone in Love (4:03) (Van Heusen) 2. I Can't Get Started (3:37) (Duke) 3. Spontaneous Combustion (4:15) (Bley) 4. The Theme (3:40) (unknown) 5. Split Kick (3:05) (Silver) 6. This Time the Dream's on Me (3:07) (Mercer)* 7. Zootcase (2:33) (Sims)* 8. Santa Claus Is Coming to Town (3:22) (Coots/Gillespie) 9. The Pendulum at Falcon's Lair (4:40) (Pettiford) 10. Jack the Fieldstalker (4:30) (Pettiford) 11. Stockholm Sweetnin' (4:11) (Jones) 12. Low and Behold (3:26) (Pettiford) 13. Bitty Ditty (5:12) (Jones) 14. Chazzanova (3:41) 15. I'll Remember April (3:48) (Raye/DePaul/Johnston) 16. Elusive (Illusive) (4:50) (Jones) 17. Sombre Intrusion (2:46) (Jones) 18. You Don't Know What Love Is (3:29) (Raye/DePaul) • Disc 7: 1. Like Someone in Love (3:47) (Van Heusen) 2. Peace of Mind (4:02) (Scott) 3. Lament (4:43) (Johnson) 4. The Jeep Is Jumpin' (3:56) (Ellington/Strayhorn) 5. Git Up from There (4:26) (Scott) 6. A Foggy Day (6:04) (Gershwin) 7. Mountain Greenery (4:44) (Rodgers)* 8. Git Up from There (3:56) (Scott)** 9. Lament (4:56) (Johnson)** 10. More One (7:28) (Jones) 11. I Can't Get Started (6:05) (Duke) 12. More Of The Same (5:12) (Jones) 13. Get Out of Town (8:43) (Porter) 14. One More (3:59) (Jones)** • Disc 8: 1. Get Out of Town (7:28) (Porter)** 2. Ensenada (5:25) (Dennis) 3. Machajo (4:02) (Dennis/Roach/Mingus) 4. Cherokee (4:17) (Noble) 5. Seven Moons (4:03) (Dennis) 6. Seven Moons (4:19)** 7. All the Things You Are (take 1) (5:27) (Kern)* 8. All the Things You Are (take 2) (4:12)* 9. Cherokee (5:11) (Noble)** 10. Nature Boy (6:12) (Ahbez) 11. Alone Together (7:13) (Dietz/Schwartz) 12. There's No You (8:01) (Adair/Hopper) 13. Easy Living (5:02) (Robin/Rainger) • Disc 9: 1. The Edge of Love (2:48) (Baker/Ables/Goode) 2. Makin' Whoopee (2:38) (Donald-

son/Kahn) 3. Fanny (3:01) (Rome) 4. Portrait (2:47) 5. Jump Monk (6:44) 6. Serenade in Blue (5:56) (Gordon/Warren) 7. Percussion Discussion (8:26) 8. Work Song (6:16) 9. Septemberly (6:55) (Warren/Dubin-Lawrence/Gross) 10. All the Things You C# (6:47) (Kern) 11. I'll Remember April (13:03) (Raye/DePaul/Johnston) • Disc 10: 1. Love Chant (7:20) 2. A Foggy Day (5:22) (Gershwin) 3. Drums (5:20) 4. Haitian Fight Song (5:16) 5. Lady Bird (5:51) (Dameron) 6. Jump Monk (11:38)** 7. All the Things You C# (9:45) (Kern)** 8. Drums (take 1) (6:17)** 9. Drums (take 2) (5:23)** • Disc 11: 1. I'll Remember April (13:07) (Raye/DePaul/Johnston)** 2. A Foggy Day (5:23) (Gershwin)** 3. A Portrait of Bud Powell (4:09) (Waldron)* 4. Haitian Fight Song (5:17)** 5. Love Chant (8:12)** 6. Lady Bird (5:35) (Dameron)** 7. What Is This Thing Called Love (fragment) (2:30) (Porter)* 8. Latter Day Saint (4:00) (Knepper) 9. Cunningbird (4:45) (Knepper) 10. The Jumpin' Blues (Jump The Blues Away) (4:52) (Gordon) 11. The Masher (3:33) (Knepper) 12. Latter Day Saint (take 1) (5:22) Knepper** 13. Latter Day Saint (take 2) (3:46)** • Disc 12: 1. The Masher (4:15) (Knepper)** 2. Latter Day Saint (take #?) (3:51) (Knepper)** 3. Untitled Original Blues (take 1) (3:55) (Hadi)* 4. Stella by Starlight (take 4) (3:57) (Young)* 5. Stella by Starlight (take 5) (3:53)* 6. Untitled Original Composition (take 3) (5:17) (Hadi)* 7. Untitled Original Composition (take 5) (4:34)* 8. Autumn in New York (take 1) (5:29) (Duke)* 9. Autumn in New York (take 2) (5:05)* 10. Long Ago and Far Away (take 2) (3:24) (Kern)* 11. Long Ago and Far Away (take 4) (3:11)* 12. Long Ago and Far Away (take 5) (3:17)* 13. Untitled Original Blues (take 2) (4:00) (Hadi)* 14. Joldi (take 4) (5:24) (Hadi)* 15. Joldi (take 5) (5:08)* 16. Untitled Percussion Composition (7:18)* PERSONNEL: Disc 1, 1-9: Spaulding Givens (Nadi Qamar) (p); Charles Mingus (b); Disc 1, 10-16: Jackie Paris (voc on 10, 11); Bob Benton (voc on 12, 13); Lee Konitz (as); Phyllis Pinkerton (p); George Koutzen (cello); Charles Mingus (b); Al Levitt (d); Disc 1, 17-19: Jackie Paris (voc); Paige Brook (fl, as); John Mehegan (p); Jackson Wiley (cello); Charles Mingus (b); Max Roach (d); Disc 1, 20-23 • Disc 2, 1-2: Spaulding Givens (Nadi Qamar) (p); Charles Mingus (b); Max Roach (d); Disc 2, 3: Hank Jones (p); Charles Mingus (b); Max Roach (d); Disc 2, 4-7: Hank Jones (p); Charles Mingus (b); Max Roach (d); Honey Gordon (voc); Richard Gordon, George Gordon, George Gordon jr. (voc on 5, 6); Disc 2, 8: Max Roach (d); Disc 2, 9-14: Bud Powell (p); Charles Mingus (b); Max Roach (d); Disc 2, 15-17 • Disc 3: Dizzy Gillespie (tp), Charlie Parker (as Charlie Chan on original issue)(as); Bud Powell (p); Charles Mingus (b); Max Roach (d) • Disc 4, 1-5: Billy Taylor (p); Charles Mingus (b); unknown (d); Disc 4, 6-10; Disc 5, 1-5: J.J. Johnson, Kai Winding, Bennie Green, Willie Dennis (tb); John Lewis (p); Charles Mingus (b); Art Taylor (d) • Disc 5, 6-11: Ernie Royal (tp); Willie Dennis (tb); Eddie Caine (as, fl); Teo Macero (ts, cl); [Danny Bank (bars?)]; John Lewis (p); Jackson Wiley (cello); Charles Mingus (b); Kenny Clarke (d); Janet Thurlow (voc on 8, 10, 11); Spaulding Givens (Nadi Qamar) (arr); Disc 5, 12-14; Disc 6, 1-8: Paul Bley (p); Charles Mingus (b); Art Blakey (d); Walter Bishop Jr. (p); Oscar Pettiford (cello); Charles Mingus (b); Percy Brice (d) • Disc 6, 13-18: Thad Jones (tp); Frank Wess (ts, fl); Hank Jones (p); Charles Mingus (b); Kenny Clarke (d) • Disc 7, 1-9: Hazel Scott (p); Charles Mingus (b); Max Roach (d); Disc 7, 10-14; Disc 8, 1: Thad Jones (tp); John Dennis (p); Charles Mingus (b); Max Roach (d) • Disc 8, 2-9: John Dennis (p); Charles Mingus (b); Max Roach (d); Disc 8, 10-13: Miles Davis (tp); Britt Woodman (tb); Teddy Charles (vib); Charles Mingus (b); Elvin Jones (d) • Disc 9, 1-3: Don Senay (voc); Thad Jones, Louis Mucci (tp); unknown (brass); John LaPorta, Julius Baker (woodwinds); Billy Taylor (p); unknown (harp); Jackson Wiley (cello); unknown (strings); Milt Hinton, Fred Zimmerman [Charles Mingus?] (b); Joe Morello (d, perc) or; unknown (perc); Alonzo Levister (arr); Disc 9, 4: Thad Jones (tp) overdubbed onto instrumental track (without vocal) from preceding session; Disc 9, 5-11; Disc 10; Disc 11, 1-7: Eddie Bert (tb); George Barrow (ts); Mal Waldron (p); Charles Mingus (b); Willie Jones (d except on Disc 9, #7, 11; Disc 10, #3, 8, 9; Disc 11, #1); Max Roach (d on Disc 9, #7, 11; Disc 10, #3, 8, 9; Disc 11, #1) • Disc 11, 8-13; Disc 12, 1-2: Jimmy Knepper (tb); Joe Maini (as); Bill Triglia (p); Charles Mingus (b); Dannie Richmond (d) • Disc 12, 3-15: Clarence Shaw (tp); Shafi Hadi (ts); Pepper Adams (bars); Wade Legge or Wynton Kelly (p); Charles Mingus or Henry Grimes (b); Dannie Richmond (d); Disc 12, 16: unknown (fl) (Shafi Hadi?); Charles Mingus (miscellaneous perc including piano perc); Dannie Richmond (d); unidentified others (probably including Jimmy Knepper, Clarence Shaw, Horace Parlan or Phineas Newborn) (miscellaneous perc) DATE AND LOCATION: Disc 1, 1-9: April 1951, Los Angeles; Disc 1, 10-16: April 12, 1952, Lennie Tristano Studio, NYC; Disc 1, 17-19: September 16, 1952, NYC; Disc 1, 20-23. Disc 2, 1-2: April 14, 1953, NYC; Disc 2, 3-7: April 29, 1953, NYC; Disc 2, 8-17. Disc 3: May 15, 1953, Massey Hall, Toronto. Disc 4, 1-5: Summer 1953, NYC; Disc 4, 6-10. Disc 5, 1-5: September 18, 1953, Putnam Central Club, Brooklyn, N.Y.; Disc 5, 6-11: October 28, 1953, NYC; Disc 5, 12-14; Disc 6, 1-8: November 30, 1953, NYC; Disc 6, 9-12: December 29, 1953, NYC; Disc 6, 13-18: August 11, 1964, Van Gelder Recording, Hackensack, N.J. Disc 7, 1-9: January 21, 1955, Van Gelder Recording, Hackensack, N.J.; Disc 7, 10-14; Disc 8, 1-9: March 10, 1955, Van Gelder Recording, Hackensack, N.J.; Disc 8, 10-13: July 9, 1955, Van Gelder Recording, Hackensack, N.J. Disc 9, 1-3: September 19, 1955, NYC; Disc 9, 4: probably September 26, 1955, NYC; Disc 9, 5-11: Disc 10: Disc 11, 1-7: December 23, 1955, Cafe Bohemia, NYC; Disc 11, 8-13; Disc 12, 1-2: June 10, 1957, NYC; Disc 12, 3-15: September (?) 1957, NYC; Disc 12, 16: Late 1957 or (?) 1958, NYC ORIGINAL ISSUE: Disc 1, 1-6: on Debut DLP-1 (10") as Spaulding Givens/Charles Mingus—*Strings and Keys*; Disc 1, 11 and 16: on Debut M-101 (78rpm); Disc 1, 14 and 19: on Debut M-103 (78rpm); Disc 1, 17 and 18: on Debut M-102 (78rpm); Disc 2, 4 and 6: on Debut M-110 (78rpm); Disc 2, 5 and 7: on Debut M-111 (78rpm); Disc 2, 10-14 and Disc 4, 4: on Debut DLP-3 (10") as *The Amazing Bud Powell—Jazz at Massey Hall*, volume two/trio; Disc 3, 5-8: on Debut DLP-2 (10") as *The Quintet—Jazz at Massey Hall*, volume one; Disc 3, 9-11: on Debut DLP-4 (10") as *The Quintet—Jazz at Massey Hall*, volume three

Volumes one and three were combined on Debut DEB-124 (12") as *The Quintet—Jazz at Massey Hall*; Disc 4, 6 and 9: on Debut DLP-14 (10") as J.J. Johnson, Kai Winding, Benny Green, Willie Dennis—Jazz Workshop—*Trombone Rapport*, volume 2; Disc 4, 7 and 8; Disc 5, 4: on Debut DLP-5 (10") as J.J. Johnson, Kai Winding, Benny Green, Willie Dennis—Jazz Workshop—*Trombone Rapport*, volume 1; Disc 4, 10; Disc 5, 1-3: on Debut DEB-126 (12") as J.J. Johnson, Kai Winding, Benny Green, Willie Dennis—*4 Trombones*; Disc 5, 6-8 and 11: on Debut EP-450 (7") as *Charles Mingus Octet* - see cover; Disc 5, 13-14; Disc 6, 1-3 and 5: on Debut DLP-7 (10") as *Introducing Paul Bley with Charlie Mingus, Art Blakey*; Disc 6, 9-12: on Debut DLP-8 (10") as *The New Oscar Pettiford Sextet*; Disc 6, 13-18: on Debut DLP-12 (10") and Disc 7, 10-13: on Debut DLP-17 (10") both combined on Debut DEB-127 (12") as *Thad Jones*; Disc 7, 1-6: on Debut DLP-16 (10") as *Hazel Scott—Relaxed Piano Moods*; Disc 8, 2-5: on Debut DEB-121 (12") as *John Dennis—New Piano Expressions*; Disc 8, 10-13: on Debut DEB-120 (12") as *Miles Davis—Blue Moods*; Disc 9, 1 and 3: on Debut M-112 (78rpm); Disc 9, 5-10: on Debut DEB-123 (12") as *Mingus at the Bohemia*; Disc 9, 11; Disc 10, 1-5: on Fantasy (Debut Series) F-86009 (12") as *The Charles Mingus Quintet + Max Roach*; Disc 11, 8-11: on Danish Jazz Worshop DL-101 as *Jimmy Knepper*; Disc 1, 14 and 18; Disc 2, 3, 4, 6, 8 and 9; Disc 5, 5 and 11; Disc 6, 8; Disc 9, 2 and 4: on Debut DEB-198 (12") as *Various Artists - Autobiography in Jazz* All other tracks first issued in this box set. * previously unissued ** previously unissued alternate take

30. Shadows (1958) 1. Nostalgia in Times Square 2. unknown titles PERSONNEL: Jimmy Knepper (tb); Shafi Hadi (ts); Horace Parlan (p); Phineas Newborn (p); Charles Mingus (b); Dannie Richmond (d); unknown trumpet, flute, alto sax DATE AND LOCATION: Spring 1958, NYC UNISSUED

31. Jazz Portraits—Mingus in Wonderland (1959, United Artists) TRACKS: 1. Nostalgia In Times Square (12:18) 2. I Can't Get Started (10:08) (Duke) 3. No Private Income Blues (12:51) 4. Alice's Wonderland (8:54) PERSONNEL: Booker Ervin (ts); John Handy (as); Richard Wyands (p)o; Charles Mingus (b); Dannie Richmond (d) DATE AND LOCATION: January 16, 1959, Nonagon Art Gallery, NYC ORIGINAL ISSUE: United Artists UAS 5063 (*Jazz Portraits*) REISSUES: United Artists UAJS 15005 (*Mingus in Wonderland*); United Artists UAS 5637 (*Wonderland*)

32. Blues & Roots (1959, Atlantic) TRACKS: 1. Wednesday Night Prayer Meeting (5:39) 2. Cryin' Blues (4:58) 3. Moanin' (7:57) 4. Tensions (6:27) 5. My Jelly Roll Soul (6:47) 6. E's Flat, Ah's Flat Too (6:37) PERSONNEL: Jackie McLean (as); John Handy (as); Booker Ervin (ts); Pepper Adams (bs); Jimmy Knepper (tb); Willie Dennis (tb); Horace Parlan (p); Mal Waldron (p); Charles Mingus (b); Dannie Richmond (d) DATE AND LOCATION: February 4, 1959, NYC ORIGINAL ISSUE: Atlantic #1305 (April 4, 1960) REISSUES: Atlantic ATL 50 232—*That's Jazz 2* (1976, gatefold silver cover, LP); Atlantic KSD 1305 (in *That's Jazz* series, 1976, LP)

33. Mingus Ah Um (1959, CBS) TRACKS: 1. Better Git It in Your Soul (7:22) 2. Goodbye Pork Pie Hat (4:46) 3. Boogie Stop Shuffle (3:41) 4. Self-Portrait in Three Colors (3:05) 5. Open Letter to Duke (4:56) 6. Bird Calls (3:12) 7. Fables of Faubus (8:12) 8. Pussy Cat Dues (6:27) 9. Jelly Roll (4:01) PERSONNEL: John Handy (as on 1, 6, 7, 9; cl on 8; ts on 2); Booker Ervin (ts); Shafi Hadi (ts except 2); Willie Dennis (tb on 3-5); Jimmy Knepper (tb on 1 and 7-9); Horace Parlan (p); Charles Mingus (b); Dannie Richmond (d) DATE AND LOCATION: 1, 6-9: May 5, 1959, Columbia 30th Street Studio, NYC; 2-5: May 12, 1959, Columbia 30th Street Studio, NYC ORIGINAL ISSUE:

Columbia CS 8171   REISSUES: Columbia CG 30628 (197?, 2LP) as half of *Better Git It In Your Soul;* Columbia CK 40648 (CD, USA)

34. Mingus Dynasty (1959, CBS)   TRACKS: I. Slop (4:39) 2. Diane (7:31) 3. Song with Orange (4:14) 4. Gunslinging Bird (3:58) 5. Things Ain't What They Used To Be (4:25) (Mercer Ellington) 6. Far Wells, Mill Valley (6:14) 7. New Now, Know How (3:01) 8. Mood Indigo (8:15) (Duke Ellington, Barney Bigard) 9. Put Me in That Dungeon (2:53)   PERSONNEL: John Handy (as); Booker Ervin (ts); Jimmy Knepper (tb); Roland Hanna (p); Charles Mingus (b); Dannie Richmond (d) with (on 1, 5, 8, 9): Don Ellis (t); Maurice Brown (cello); Seymour Barab (cello); (on 2-4, 6, 7: Richard Williams (t); Benny Golson (ts); Jerome Richardson (bs, fl); Teddy Charles (v); Nico Bunink (p)   DATE AND LOCATION: 1, 5, 8, 9: November 13, 1959, NYC; 2-4, 6, 7: November 1, 1959, NYC   ORIGINAL ISSUE: CS 8236 (1960)   REISSUES: Columbia CG 30628 (197?, 2LP) as half of *Better Git It in Your Soul;* Columbia CK 52922 (CD, USA)

35. The Complete 1959 Columbia Recordings (1959, Columbia)   TRACKS: Disc One: *Mingus Ah Um* 1. Better Git It in Your Soul (7:21) 2. Goodbye Pork Pie Hat (5:42)* 3. Boogie Stop Shuffle (4:59)* 4. Self-Portrait in Three Colors (3:08) 5. Open Letter to Duke (5:49)* 6. Bird Calls (6:18)* 7. Fables Of Faubus (8:13) 8. Pussy Cat Dues (9:13)* 9. Jelly Roll (6:15)* 10. Pedal Point Blues (6:28)+ 11. GGTrain (4:37)+ 12. Girl of My Dreams (4:08)+ (Sonny Clapp) • Disc Two:*Mingus Dynasty* 1. Slop (6:14)* 2. Diane (7:28) 3. Song with Orange (6:47)* 4. Gunslinging Bird (5:12)* 5. Things Ain't What They Used To Be (7:35)* (Mercer Ellington) 6. Far Wells, Mill Valley (6:11) 7. New Now Know How (4:12) 8. Mood Indigo (8:12) (Duke Ellington) 9. Put Me in That Dungeon (2:51) 10. Strollin' (4:33)+ (Mingus, George Gordon) • Disc Three: *Alternate Takes* 1. Better Git It in Your Soul (Alternate) (8:30) 2. Bird Calls (Alternate) (4:53) 3. Jelly Roll (Alternate) (6:41) 4. Song With Orange (Alternate) (6:42)* 5. Diane (Alternate) (7:29) 6. New Now Know How (Alternate) (4:19)   PERSONNEL: Disc 1, 1, 6-10; Disc 3, 1-3: John Handy (as, cl on "Pussy Cat Dues"); Booker Ervin (ts); Shafi Hadi (as on "Bird Calls" and "Jelly Roll," ts); Jimmy Knepper (tb); Horace Parlan (p); Charles Mingus (b); Dannie Richmond (d) • Disc 1, 2-5, 11, 12: John Handy (as, ts on "Goodbye Pork Pie Hat"); Booker Ervin (ts) Shafi Hadi (as on "Open Letter to Duke" and "Girl of My Dreams," ts); Willie Dennis (tb); Horace Parlan (p); Charles Mingus (b); Dannie Richmond (d) • Disc 2, 2-4, 6, 7, 10; Disc 3, 4-6: Richard Williams (t, except on "New Now Know How"); Jimmy Knepper (tb); John Handy (as); Booker Ervin (ts); Benny Golson (ts, except on "New Now Know How"); Jerome Richardson (bs, except on "New Now Know How"); Teddy Charles (vibes, except on "New Now Know How"); Roland Hanna (p, except on "New Now Know How" and "Strollin'"); Nico Bunink (p on "New Now Know How" and "Strollin'"); Charles Mingus (b); Dannie Richmond (d); Honey Gordon (voc on "Strollin'") • Disc 2, 1,5,8,9: Don Ellis (t); Jimmy Knepper (tb); John Handy (as); Booker Ervin (ts); Ronald Hanna (p); Charles Mingus (b); Dannie Richmond (d); Maurice Brown (cello on "Slop" and "Put Me in That Dungeon"); Seymour Barab (cello on "Slop" and "Put Me in That Dungeon")   DATE AND LOCATION: Disc 1, 1, 6-10; Disc 3, 1-3: May 5, 1959, 30th Street Studio, NYC; Disc 1, 2-5, 11, 12: May 12, 1959, 30th Street Studio, NYC; Disc 2, 2-4, 6, 7, 10; Disc 3, 4-6: November 1, 1959, 30th Street Studio, NYC; Disc 2, 1, 5, 8, 9: November 13, 1959, 30th Street Studio, NYC Originally released: Disc 1, 1,4,7: Columbia CS 8171 (1959, LP); Disc 1, 2: Mosaic MQ4-143 (1993, 4LP); Disc 1, 3,5,6,8-12; Disc 2, 1,3-5,10: Columbia (1979); Disc 2, 2,6-9: Columbia CS 8236 (1960, LP); Disc 3, 1-3,6: Mosaic MQ4-143 (1993, 4LP); Disc 3, 4,5: previously unissued Selections marked "*" originally appeared in edited form and are now presented in unedited form for the first time on CD. Selections marked "+" are bonus tracks not included on the original LP.

36. Mingus Revisited (1960, Mercury)   TRACKS: 1. Take the "A" Train (3:34) (Billy Strayhorn)   INTERPOLATION: Exactly Like You (Jimmy McHugh) 2. Prayer for Passive Resistance (3:49) 3. Eclipse (3:45) 4. Mingus Fingus No. 2 (3:22) 5. Weird Nightmare (3:35) 6. Do Nothin' Till You Hear From Me (3:33) (Duke Ellington)   INTERPOLATION: I Let A Song Go Out Of My Heart (Ellington) 7. Bemoanable Lady (4:32) 8. Half-Mast Inhibition (8:12)   PERSONNEL: 1, 2, 3, 5, 6: Ted Curson (t); Jimmy Knepper (tb (solo on 1)); Joe Farrell (ts (first tenor solo on 1)); Booker Ervin (ts (second tenor solo on 1)); Yusef Lateef fl, ts (third tenor solo on 1, solo on 5)); Eric Dolphy (fl); Roland Hanna (p); Paul Bley (p); Charles Mingus (b); Dannie Richmond (percussion); Lorraine Cousins (voc on 3 and 5)   4, 7, 8: Marcus Belgrave (t); Hobart Dotson(t); Clark Terry (t); Ted Curson (t); Richard Williams (t); Slide Hampton (tb); Charles Greenlee (tb); Eddie Bert (tb); Jimmy Knepper (tb); Eric Dolphy (as (solo on 7)); John LaPorta (s); William Barron Jr. (s); Joe Farrell (ts); Yusef Lateef (ts);

Danny Bank (sax); Robert Di Domenica (fl); Harry Shulman (oboe); Don Butterfield (tuba); Roland Hanna (p); Charles Mingus (bass); Charles McCracken (cello); Dannie Richmond (percussion); George Scott (percussion); Sticks Evans (percussion); Gunther Schuller (conductor on 8) Date and Location: 1, 2, 3, 5, 6: May 25, 1960, NYC; 4, 7, 8: May 24, 1960, NYC Original issue: Mercury SR-60627 (1961) as *Pre-Bird* Reissues: Limelight LS-86015 (1965) as *Mingus Revisited*; (198?) as *Pre-Bird*

37. Mingus at Antibes (1960, Atlantic) Tracks: 1. Wednesday Night Prayer Meeting (11:54) 2. Prayer for Passive Resistance (8:06) 3. What Love? (13:34) 4. I'll Remember April (13:39) (Raye/De-Paul/Johnston) 5. Folk Forms I (11:08) 6. Better Git Hit in Your Soul (11:00) Personnel: Ted Curson (t); Eric Dolphy (as, bcl); Booker Ervin (ts); Charles Mingus (b, p); Dannie Richmond (d); Bud Powell (p on 4) Date and Location: July 13, 1960, Antibes Jazz Festival, Juan-les-Pins, France Original issue: Atlantic SD 2-3001 (1976, 2LP) Reissue: Atlantic Jazz 7567-90532-2 (1986, CD)

38. Charles Mingus Presents Charles Mingus (1960, Candid) Tracks: 1. Folk Forms, No. 1 (12:00) 2. Original Faubus Fables (9:15) 3. What Love (15:20) 4. All the Things You Could Be By Now If Sigmund Freud's Wife Was Your Mother (8:32) Personnel: Ted Curson (t); Eric Dolphy (as, bcl); Charles Mingus (b); Dannie Richmond (d) Date and Location: October 20 (Priestley) or November 19 (liner notes), 1960, Nola Penthouse Sound Studios, NYC Original issue: Candid 9005 (1960) Reissues: Barnaby Records BR 5012 (19??)

39. Mingus (1960, Candid) Tracks: 1. MDM (19:52) 2. Stormy Weather (13:25) (Arlen) 3. Lock 'Em Up (6:35) Personnel: Ted Curson (t); Lonnie Hillyer (t); Eric Dolphy (as, bcl); Charles McPherson (as); Booker Ervin (ts); Jimmy Knepper (tb); Britt Woodman (tb); Nico Bunink (p on 1); Paul Bley (p on 3); Charles Mingus (b); Dannie Richmond (d) Date and Location: 1, 2: October 20, 1960, NYC; 3: November 11, 1960, NYC Original issue: Candid 9021 (196?) Reissues: Jazz Man JAZ 5002 (with extra track "Vassarlean" (6:38))

40. Reincarnation of a Lovebird (1960, Candid) Tracks: 1. Reincarnation of a Lovebird (Take 1) (6:58) 2. Wrap Your Troubles in Dreams (Take 4) (3:55) (Moll/Koehler/Barris) 3. R & R (Take 1) (11:51) (Eldridge/Brown) 4. Body and Soul (Take 2) (13:51) (Green) 5. Bugs (Take 3) (8:28) Personnel: 1, 5: Lonnie Hillyer (t); Charles McPherson (as); Booker Ervin (ts); Paul Bley (p); Charles Mingus (b); Dannie Richmond (d) 3, 4: Roy Eldridge (t); Jimmy Knepper (tb); Eric Dolphy (as); Tommy Flanagan (p); Charles Mingus (b); Jo Jones (d) 2: Roy Eldridge (t); Tommy Flanagan (p); Charles Mingus (b); Jo Jones (d) Date and Location: November 11, 1960, Nola Penthouse Studios, NYC Original issue: Candid 9026 (1960) Reissues: Mosaic MD3-111 (*The Complete Candid Recordings Of Charles Mingus*, 3CD)

41. Mysterious Blues (1960, Candid) Tracks: 1. Mysterious Blues (8:35) 2. Wrap Your Troubles in Dreams (3:48) (Moll/Koehler/Barris) 3. Body and Soul (10:41) (Green) 4. Vasserlean (6:38) 5. Reincarnation of a Lovebird (9:13) 6. Me and You Blues (9:54) (Eldridge/Mingus/Flanagan/Jones) 7. Melody from the Drums (9:25) (Richmond) Personnel: 1, 2: Roy Eldridge (t); Jimmy Knepper (tb); Eric Dolphy (as); Tommy Flanagan (p); Charles Mingus (b); Jo Jones (d) 7: Dannie Richmond (d) Date and Location: November 11, 1960, Nola Penthouse Studios, NYC Reissues: Mosaic MD3-111 (*The Complete Candid Recordings of Charles Mingus*, 3CD)

42. Newport Rebels (1960, Candid) Tracks: 1. Mysterious Blues (8:35) 2. Wrap Your Troubles in Dreams (3:49) (Moll/Koehler/Barris) 3. Me and You (9:46) (Eldridge/Mingus/Flanagan/Jones) Personnel: Roy Eldridge (t); Eric Dolphy (as on 1); Jimmy Knepper (tb on 1); Tommy Flanagan (p); Charles Mingus (b); Jo Jones (d) Date and Location: November 11, 1960, Nola Penthouse Studios, NYC Original issue: Candid CANF 6008 Reissues: Candid LP 9022; Candid CCD 79042 (*Mysterious Blues*, CD); Mosaic MD3-111 (*The Complete Candid Recordings of Charles Mingus*, 3CD)

43. The Complete Candid Recordings of Charles Mingus (1960, Mosaic) Tracks: Disc 1: *The Quartet* 1. Folk Forms No. 1 (13:01) 2. Original Faubus Fables (aka Faubus of Fables) (9:03) 3. What Love? (15:19) 4. All the Things You Could Be By Now If Sigmund Freud's Wife Was Your Mother (8:33) 5.

Stormy Weather (13:23) (Arlen) 6. Melody from the Drums (9:21) (Richmond) • Disc 2: The Ensemble 1. Reincarnation of a Lovebird No. 1 (9:17) 2. Vasserlean (aka Weird Nightmare) (6:36) 3. MDM (19:07) 4. Bugs (8:25) 5. Reincarnation of a Lovebird (6:55) 6. Lock 'Em Up (6:41) • Disc 3: The Eldridge Session 1. Mysterious Blues (8:35) 2. Body and Soul (13:45) (Green) 3. Body and Soul (alternate) (10:45) 4. R & R (11:48) (Eldridge/Brown) 5. Wrap Your Troubles in Dreams (3:48) (Moll/Koehler/Barris) 6. Wrap Your Troubles in Dreams (alternate) (3:50) 7. Me and You (9:52) (Eldridge/Mingus/Flanagan/Jones) PERSONNEL: • Disc 1 (1-5): Ted Curson (t); Eric Dolphy (as, bcl, fl); Charles Mingus (b); Dannie Richmond (d) • Disc 1 (6): Dannie Richmond (d) • Disc 2 (1-3): Ted Curson (t); Lonnie Hillyer (t); Eric Dolphy (as, bcl, fl); Charles McPherson (as); Booker Ervin (ts except on 1); Jimmy Knepper (tb); Britt Woodman (tb on 3); Nico Bunink (p); Charles Mingus (b); Dannie Richmond (d) • Disc 2 (4-6): Ted Curson (t except on 4); Lonnie Hillyer (t); Eric Dolphy (as, bcl, fl except on 4); Charles McPherson (as); Booker Ervin (ts); Paul Bley (p); Charles Mingus (b); Dannie Richmond (d) • Disc 3: Roy Eldridge (t); Jimmy Knepper (tb on 1-4); Eric Dolphy (as, bcl, fl on 1-4); Tommy Flanagan (p); Charles Mingus (bass); Jo Jones (d) DATE AND LOCATION: Disc 1 and disc 2 (1-3): October 20, 1960, NYC; Disc 2 (4-6) and disc 3: November 11, 1960, NYC ORIGINAL ISSUE: Disc 1 (1-4) as Charles Mingus Presents Charles Mingus (Candid 9005); Disc 1 (5) and disc 2 (3, 6) as Mingus (Candid 9021); Disc 2 (2) and disc 3 (4) as The Jazz Life (Candid 9019); all others except disc 3 (3, 6) on the 4LP issue MR4-111 in 1985. Disc 3 (3, 6) originally issued as part of this 3-CD set (they were not issued on the 4LP sessions because they were found only later by accident on tape reels marked as by Cal Massey).

44. Oh Yeah (1961, Atlantic) TRACKS: 1. Hog Callin' Blues (7:26) 2. Devil Woman (9:38) 3. Wham Bam Thank You Ma'am (4:41) 4. Ecclusiastics (6:55) 5. Oh Lord Don't Let Them Drop That Atomic Bomb on Me (5:38) 6. Eat That Chicken (4:36) 7. Passions of a Man (4:52) 8. Charles Mingus interviewed by Nesuhi Ertegun (24:30) PERSONNEL: Booker Ervin (ts); Rahsaan Roland Kirk (fl, siren, ts, manzello, strich); Jimmy Knepper (tb); Charles Mingus (p, voc); Doug Watkins (b); Dannie Richmond (d) DATE AND LOCATION: November 6, 1961, NYC ORIGINAL ISSUE: Atlantic #1377 (1962 without the interview, LP)

45. Tonight at Noon (1957/1961, Atlantic) LP TRACKS: 1. Tonight at Noon (5:58) 2. Invisible Lady (4:49) 3. 'Old' Blues for Walt's Torin (8:59) 4. Peggy's Blue Skylight (9:42) 5. Passions of a Woman Loved (9:43) PERSONNEL: 1, 5: Jimmy Knepper (tb); Shafi Hadi (as); Wade Legge (p); Charles Mingus (b); Dannie Richmond (d) 2-4: Booker Ervin (ts); Rahsaan Roland Kirk (fl, ts, manzello, strich); Jimmy Knepper (tb); Charles Mingus (p, voc); Doug Watkins (b); Dannie Richmond (d) DATE AND LOCATION: 1, 5: March 12, 1957, NYC; 2-4: November 6, 1961, NYC REISSUES: 1, 5: Atlantic SD3-600 (Passions of a Man, 1979, 3LP); 1-5: Rhino R2 72871 (Passions Of A Man: The Complete Atlantic Recordings 1956-1961, 1997, 6CD)

46. Passions of a Man: The Complete Atlantic Recordings 1956-1961 (Rhino) TRACKS: Disc 1: 1. Pithecanthropus Erectus (10:33) 2. A Foggy Day (7:47) (George Gershwin) 3. Love Chant (14:56) 4. Profile of Jackie (3:07) 5. Laura (4:52) (David Raksin) 6. When Your Lover Has Gone (2:27) (Einar Aaron Swan) 7. Just One of Those Things (6:06) (Cole Porter) 8. Blue Greens (11:42) (Teddy Charles) • Disc 2: 1. The Clown (12:29) 2. Passions of a Woman Loved (9:43) 3. Blue Cee (7:48) 4. Tonight at Noon (5:58) 5. Reincarnation of a Lovebird (8:31) 6. Haitian Fight Song (11:57) • Disc 3: 1. E's Flat Ah's Flat Too (6:37) 2. My Jelly Roll Soul (6:47) 3. Tensions (6:27) 4. Moanin' (7:57) 5. Cryin' Blues (4:58) 6. Wednesday Night Prayer Meeting (5:42) 7. E's Flat Ah's Flat Too (Alternate Take) (7:16) 8. My Jelly Roll Soul (Alternate Take) (11:51) 9. Tensions (Alternate Take) (5:30) 10. Wednesday Night Prayer Meeting (Alternate Take) (6:56) • Disc 4: 1. Prayer for Passive Resistance (8:06) 2. Wednesday Night Prayer Meeting (11:54) 3. Folk Forms I (11:08) 4. What Love? (13:34) 5. I'll Remember April (13:39) (DePaul, Johnston, Raye) • Disc 5: 1. Devil Woman (9:38) 2. Ecclusiastics (6:55) 3. "Old" Blues for Walt's Torin (8:59) 4. Peggy's Blue Skylight (9:42) 5. Hog Callin' Blues (7:26) 6. Oh Lord Don't Let Them Drop That Atomic Bomb on Me (5:38) 7. Passions of a Man (4:52) 8. Wham Bam Thank You Ma'am (4:41) 9. Invisible Lady (4:49) 10. Eat That Chicken (4:36) • Disc 6: 1. Charles Mingus interviewed by Nesuhi Ertegun (75:00) PERSONNEL: Disc 1, 1-5: Charles Mingus (b); Jackie McLean (as); J.R. Monterose (ts); Mal Waldron (p); Willie Jones (d) • Disc 1, 5-8: Teddy Charles (vibes); Hall Overton (p); Charles Mingus (b); Ed Shaughnessy (d) • Disc 2: Charles Mingus (b); Shafi Hadi (Curtis Porter) (ts); Jimmy Knepper (tb); Wade Legge (p); Dannie Richmond (d); Jean Shepherd (improvised narration on "The Clown") • Disc 3:

Charles Mingus (b); John Handy (as); Jackie McLean (as); Booker Ervin (ts); Pepper Adams (bs); Willie Dennis (tb); Jimmy Knepper (tb); Horace Parlan (p except 1 and 7); Mal Waldron (p on 1 and 7) • Disc 4: Charles Mingus (b, p on 2, 3); Eric Dolphy (as, bcl on 5); Booker Ervin (ts on 1-5); Ted Curson (t); Bud Powell (p on 6); Dannie Richmond (d) • Disc 5: Charles Mingus (p, voc); Roland Kirk (ts, fl, siren, manzello, strich); Booker Ervin (ts); Jimmy Knepper (tb); Doug Watkins (b); Dannie Richmond (d) DATE AND LOCATION: Disc 1, 1-5: January 30, 1956, Audio-Video Studios, NYC; Disc 1, 5-8: November 12, 1956, NYC; Disc 2, 1: February 13, 1957, Audio-Video Studios, NYC; Disc 2: 2-6: March 12, 1957, Atlantic Studios, NYC; Disc 3: February 4, 1959, Atlantic Studios, NYC; Disc 4: July 13, 1960, Antibes Jazz Festival, Juan-les-Pins, France; Disc 5: November 6, 1961, Atlantic Studios, NYC; Disc 6: late 1961/early 1962, Nesuhi Ertegun's office, Atlantic Records, NYC ORIGINAL ISSUES: Disc 1, 1-5: Atlantic 1237 as *Pithecanthropus Erectus* (July 1956); Disc 1, 5-8: Atlantic 1274 as Teddy Charles's *Word from Bird* (June 1958); Disc 2, 1, 3, 5, 6: Atlantic 1260 as *The Clown* (August 1957); Disc 2, 2, 4; Disc 5, 3, 4, 9: Atlantic 1416 as *Tonight at Noon* (June 1964); Disc 3, 1-6: Atlantic 1305 as *Blues & Roots* (March 1960); Disc 3, 7-10: previously unissued; Disc 4: Atlantic 2-3001 as *Mingus at Antibes* (October 1979); Disc 5, 1, 2, 5-8, 10: Atlantic 1377 as *Oh Yeah* (April 1962); Disc 6: previously unissued extended interview; edited version originally appeared on CD reissue of *Oh Yeah*, Atlantic 90667-2 (1988)

47. The Complete Town Hall Concert (1962, United Artists) TRACKS: 1. Freedom—Part One (3:45) 2. Freedom—Part Two (aka Clark in the Dark) (3:11) 3. Osmotin' (2:47) 4. Epitaph—Part One (7:00) 5. Peggy's Blue Skylight (5:17) 6. Epitaph—Part Two (5:08) 7. My Search (8:06) 8. Portrait (4:31) 9. Duke's Choice (aka Don't Come Back) (5:09) 10. Please Don't Come Back from the Moon (7:22) 11. In a Mellotone (aka Finale) (8:18) (Duke Ellington) 12. Epitaph—Part One (alternate take) (7:22) PERSONNEL: Snooky Young (t); Ernie Royal (t); Richard Williams (t); Clark Terry (t); Eddie Armour (t); Lonnie Hillyer (t); Rolf Ericson (t); Quentin Jackson (tb); Britt Woodman (tb); Jimmy Cleveland (tb); Willie Dennis (tb); Eddie Bert (tb); Paul Faulise (tb); Eric Dolphy (as); Charles McPherson (as); Charlie Mariano (as); Buddy Collette (as); Romeo Penque (oboe); Zoot Sims (ts); George Berg (ts); Jerome Richardson (bs); Pepper Adams (bs); Danny Bank (contrabass cl); Jaki Byard (p); Toshiko Akiyoshi (p); Les Spann (g); Charles Mingus (b); Milt Hinton (b); Dannie Richmond (d); Warren Smith (vibes, percussion); Grady Tate (percussion); Melba Liston (arranger); Bob Hammer (arranger); Gene Roland (arranger) DATE AND LOCATION: October 12, 1962, Town Hall, NYC ORIGINAL ISSUE: United Artists UAS 15024 (*Town Hall Concert*, 1963)

48. Live at Birdland 1962 (Jazz View) TRACKS: 1. Take the "A" Train (10:38) (Billy Strayhorn) 2. Fables Of Faubus [Mr. Faubus] (10:47) 3. Eat That Chicken [Theme] (0:13) 4. I Can't Get Started [The Search] (6:27) (Vernon Duke) 5. Monk, Bunk and Vice Versa [King Fish] (6:49) 6. Please Don't Come Back from the Moon [Moonboy] (7:35) 7. Eat That Chicken [Theme] (0:06) PERSONNEL: 1-3: Richard Williams (t); Charles McPherson (as); Booker Ervin (ts); Jaki Byard (p); Charles Mingus (b); Dannie Richmond (d) 4-7: Eddie Armour (t); Don Butterfield (tuba); Charles McPherson (as); Pepper Adams (bs); Jaki Byard (p); Charles Mingus (b); Dannie Richmond (d) DATE AND LOCATION: 1-3: March 24, 1962, Birdland, NYC (broadcast); 4-7: October 19, 1962, Birdland, NYC (broadcast) ORIGINAL ISSUE: Session Disc 118 (*Hooray for Charles Mingus*) REISSUES: 1,2: Musica Jazz 2 MJP 1067 (*Charles Mingus, 2/1988*)

49. Vital Savage Horizons (1951/61/62, Alto) LP TRACKS: 1. What Is This Thing Called Love (Porter) 2. I'm Beginning to See the Light 3. Improvisation 4. Ecclusiastics (Ecclesiastes) 5. Monk, Bunk and Vice Versa PERSONNEL: 1, 2: Billy Taylor (p); Charles Mingus (b); Marquis Foster (d) 3, 4: Jimmy Knepper (tb); Yusef Lateef (ts); Rahsaan Roland Kirk (ts, stritch, manzello); Doug Watkins (b); Charles Mingus (p); Dannie Richmond (d); Pee Wee Marquette (announcer) 5: Richard Williams (t); Charles McPherson (as); Booker Ervin (ts); Toshiko Akiyoshi (p); Charles Mingus (b); Dannie Richmond (d); Symphony Sid (announcer) DATE AND LOCATION: 1, 2: November 6, 1951, Storyville, Boston (Billy Taylor Trio); 3, 4: October 21, 1961, Birdland, NYC; 5: March 31, 1962, Birdland, NYC ORIGINAL ISSUE: 3, 4: Alto 714

50. In Concert (1962, Jazzman) TRACKS: 1. Eat That Chicken (3:13) 2. Reets and I (6:52) 3. Monk, Bunk And Vice Versa (10:25) 4. Devil Woman (9:42) 5. Eat That Chicken 6. Peggy's Blue Skylight (13:52) 7. Ysabel's Table Dance (11:33) 8. Eat That Chicken (1:04) PERSONNEL: 1-4: Richard Williams (t); Charles McPherson (as); Booker Ervin (ts); Toshiko Akiyoshi (p); Herman Wright (b (according to Tempo di jazz issue)); Charles Mingus (b); Dannie Richmond (d) 5: Richard Williams (t); Charles McPherson (as); Booker Ervin (ts); Toshiko Akiyoshi (p); Henry Grimes (b); Herman Wright (b); Dannie Richmond (d) 6-8: Richard Williams (t); Charles McPherson (as); Booker Ervin (ts); Toshiko Akiyoshi (p); Henry Grimes (b (according to Tempo di jazz issue)); Charles Mingus (b) DATE AND LOCATION: 1-5: May 5, 1962, Birdland, NYC; 6-8: May 12, 1962, Birdland, NYC ORIGINAL ISSUE: 6-8: J for Jazz 808 (?) REISSUED: Tempo di jazz CDTJ 704 ("Charles Mingus", CD, Italy)

51. Charles Mingus (1962, Musica Jazz) LP TRACKS: 1. Take the "A" Train (Strayhorn) 2. Fables of Faubus 3. Ysabel's Table Dance 4. Monk, Bunk or Vice Versa PERSONNEL: See various other 1962 releases for personnel information. DATE AND LOCATION: ORIGINAL ISSUE: 1,2: Session Disc 118; 3: J for Jazz 802; 4: Ozone 19

52. The Black Saint and the Sinner Lady (1963, Impulse!) TRACKS: 1. Track A—Solo Dancer (6:20) 2. Track B—Duet Solo Dancers (6:25) 3. Track C—Group Dancers (7:00) 4. Mode D—Trio and Group Dancers (17:52) Mode E—Single Solos and Group Dance Mode F—Group and Solo Dance PERSONNEL: Rolf Ericson (t); Richard Williams (t); Charlie Mariano (as); Jerome Richardson (ss, fl); Dick Hafer (ts, fl); Quentin Jackson (tb); Don Butterfield (tuba); Jaki Byard (p); Jay Berliner (g); Charles Mingus (b, p); Dannie Richmond (d) DATE AND LOCATION: January 20, 1963, NYC ORIGINAL ISSUE: Impulse! AS35 (1963?) REISSUE: MCA Impulse! MCD05649 (1986, CD)

53. Mingus Plays Piano (1963, Impulse!) TRACKS: 1. Myself When I Am Real (7:39) 2. I Can't Get Started (3:40) (Vernon Duke) 3. Body and Soul (4:31) (John Green) 4. Roland Kirk's Message (2:40) 5. Memories of You (4:35) (Eubie Blake) 6. She's Just Miss Popular Hybrid (3:08) 7. Orange Was the Color of Her Dress; Then Silk Blues (4:14) 8. Meditations For Moses (3:39) 9. Old Portrait (3:45) 10. I'm Getting Sentimental Over You (3:44) (George Bassman) 11. Compositional Theme Story: Medleys, Anthems and Folklore (8:35) PERSONNEL: Charles Mingus (p) DATE AND LOCATION: July 30, 1963, NYC ORIGINAL ISSUE: Impulse A-60 REISSUES: Jasmine (1980, LP); MCA Victor Inc. MVCZ-83 (199?, CD, Japan—special cardboard jacket with the original artwork exactly reproduced)

54. Mingus, Mingus, Mingus, Mingus, Mingus (1963, Impulse!) TRACKS: 1. II B.S. (4:46) 2. I X Love (7:38) 3. Celia (6:12) 4. Mood Indigo (4:43) (Duke Ellington, Barney Bigard) 5. Better Get Hit in Yo' Soul (6:28) 6. Theme for Lester Young (5:50) 7. Hora Decubitus (4:41) 8. Freedom (5:10) PERSONNEL: 1, 4-8: Eddie Preston (t); Richard Williams (t); Britt Woodman (tb); Don Butterfield (tuba); Jerome Richardson (ss, bs, fl); Dick Hafer (ts, cl, fl; Booker Ervin (ts); Eric Dolphy (as, fl); Jaki Byard (p); Charles Mingus (b, narration on 8); Walter Perkins (d) 2, 3: Rolf Ericson (t); Richard Williams (t); Quentin Jackson (tb); Don Butterfield (tuba); Jerome Richardson (ss, bs, fl); Dick Hafer (ts, fl, oboe); Charlie Mariano (as); Jaki Byard (p); Jay Berliner (g); Charles Mingus (b, p); Dannie Richmond (d) DATE AND LOCATION: 1, 4-8: September 20, 1963, NYC; 2, 3: January 20, 1963, NYC ORIGINAL ISSUE: 1-7: Impulse! AS54 (1963, LP); 8: Impulse! AS99 (an Impulse! compilation The Definite Jazz Scene, LP) REISSUE: MCA Impulse! MCAD-39119 (19??) COMMENTS: "II B.S." is "Haitian Fight Song," "I X Love" is "Duke's Choice," "Theme for Lester Young" is "Goodbye Pork Pie Hat," and "Hora Decubitus" is "E's Flat, Ah's Flat Too.".

55. Town Hall Concert (1964, OJC) TRACKS: 1. So Long Eric (17:48) 2. Praying With Eric (27:31) PERSONNEL: Johnny Coles (t); Eric Dolphy (as, bcl, fl); Clifford Jordan (ts); Jaki Byard (p); Charles Mingus (b); Dannie Richmond (d) DATE AND LOCATION: April 4, 1964, Town Hall, NYC ORIGINAL ISSUE: Jazz Workshop JWS-005-S (1964) REISSUES: Prestige P-24092 (Portrait, 2LP with My Favorite Quintet, 1980, liner notes by Jaki Byard); Fantasy/Original Jazz Classics OJC-042 (1983, LP)

56. [April 10, 1964, Amsterdam] **a. In Amsterdam 1964** (DIW) TRACKS: 1. Ow (Dedicated to a Genius) (21:23) (Dizzy Gillespie, B. Green) 2. So Long Eric (Don't Stay Over There Too Long Eric) (22:18) 3. A.T.F.W.U.S.A. (A.T.F.W.Y.O.U.) (4:52) (Byard, Mingus) 4. Orange Was the Color of Her Dress Then Blue Silk (13:55) 5. Meditation on a Pair of Wire Cutters (23:06) 6. Sophisticated Lady (5:36) (Duke Ellington) 7. Fables of Faubus (part 1) (23:14) 8. Fables of Faubus (part 2) (7:14) PERSONNEL: Johnny Coles (t); Eric Dolphy (as, bcl, fl); Clifford Jordan (ts); Jaki Byard (p); Charles Mingus (b); Dannie Richmond (d) DATE AND LOCATION: April 10, 1964, Concertgebouw, Amsterdam, The Netherlands *b. Concertgebouw Amsterdam, Vol. 1* (Ulysse AROC) TRACKS: 1. Ow (aka Dedicated to a Genius, aka Parkeriana) (20:42) 2. So Long Eric (21:42) 3. A.T.F.W.Y.O.U.U.S.A. (4:00) 4. Orange Was the Color of Her Dress, Then Blue Silk (13:47) PERSONNEL: Johnny Coles (t); Eric Dolphy (as, fl, bcl); Clifford Jordan (ts); Jaki Byard (p); Charles Mingus (b); Dannie Richmond (d) DATE AND LOCATION: April 10, 1964, Concertgebouw, Amsterdam, The Netherlands REISSUE: DIW 323/324 (2CD) *c. Concertgebouw Amsterdam, Vol. 2* (Ulysse AROC) TRACKS: 1. Meditation on a Pair of Wire Cutters (22:50) 2. Sophisticated Lady (5:25) (Duke Ellington) 3. Fables of Faubus (Part 1) (23:01) 4. Fables of Faubus (Part 2) (7:40) PERSONNEL: Johnny Coles (t); Eric Dolphy (as, fl, bcl); Clifford Jordan (ts); Jaki Byard (p); Charles Mingus (b); Dannie Richmond (d) DATE AND LOCATION: April 10, 1964, Concertgebouw, Amsterdam, The Netherlands ORIGINAL ISSUE: AROC 50608 (LP) REISSUE: DIW 323/324 (2CD)

57. [April 12, 1964, Oslo] *a. Live in Oslo 1964* (JazzUp) TRACKS: 1. So Long Eric (22:20) 2. Orange Was the Color of Her Dress (15:10) 3. Parkeriana (aka Ow, false depart) (2:35) 4. Take the "A" Train (12:45) (Strayhorn) PERSONNEL: Johnny Coles (t); Eric Dolphy (as, fl, bcl); Clifford Jordan (ts); Jaki Byard (p); Charles Mingus (b); Dannie Richmond (d) DATE AND LOCATION: April 12, 1964, Oslo, Norway *b. Orange (Moon)* TRACKS: 1. So Long Eric (22:06) [mistitled "Fables of Faubus"] 2. Orange Was the Color of Her Dress (15:11) 3. Ow! (2:29) (Dizzy Gillespie) 4. Take the "A" Train (9:42) (Billy Strayhorn) PERSONNEL: Johnny Coles (t); Eric Dolphy (as, fl, bcl); Clifford Jordan (ts); Jaki Byard (p); Charles Mingus (b); Dannie Richmond (d) DATE AND LOCATION: April 12, 1964, Oslo, Norway (??) *c. Live In Oslo 1964—Vol. 1* (Landscape) TRACKS: 1. Announcement 2. Orange Was the Color of Her Dress (14:17) [14:20] PERSONNEL: Johnny Coles (t); Eric Dolphy (as, bcl, fl); Clifford Jordan (ts); Jaki Byard (p); Charles Mingus (b); Dannie Richmond (d) DATE AND LOCATION: April 12, 1964, University Aula, Oslo, Norway *d. Live In Oslo 1964—Vol. 2* (Landscape) TRACKS: 1. Meditations (19:25) [23:00] 2. Parkeriana (18:38) [20:50] PERSONNEL: Johnny Coles (t); Eric Dolphy (as, bcl, fl); Clifford Jordan (ts); Jaki Byard (p); Charles Mingus (b); Dannie Richmond (d) DATE AND LOCATION: April 12, 1964, University Aula, Oslo Norway

58. [April 13, 1964, Stockholm] *a. Live In Stockholm 1964* TRACKS: Disc 1: 1. So Long Eric (2:38) 2. Meditations (false depart) (2:06) 3. Meditations (16:40) 4. So Long Eric (6:54) 5. Orange Was the Color of Her Dress, Then Blue Silk (13:10) • Disc 2: 1. Peggy's Blue Skylight (11:03) 2. When Irish Eyes Are Smiling (11:35) 3. Fables of Faubus (17:46) PERSONNEL: Johnny Coles (t); Eric Dolphy (as, bcl, fl); Clifford Jordan (ts); Jaki Byard (p); Charles Mingus (b); Dannie Richmond (d) DATE AND LOCATION: April 13, 1964, Stockholm, Sweden COMMENTS: Disc 1's 1-4 are from rehearsals, the others are from the actual concert. *b. Meditations on Integration* (Bandstand) TRACKS: 1. Peggy's Blue Skylight (11:06) [11:03] 2. Fables of Faubus (17:40) [17:46] 3. Orange Was the Color of Her Dress (12:59) [13:10] 4. Meditations on Integration (22:15) [22:14] PERSONNEL: Johnny Coles (t); Eric Dolphy (as, bcl, fl); Clifford Jordan (ts); Jaki Byard (p); Charles Mingus (b); Dannie Richmond (d) DATE AND LOCATION: 1-3: April 13, 1964, Stockholm, Sweden; 4: April 14, 1964, Copenhagen, Denmark

59. [April 14, 1964, Copenhagen] *a. Astral Weeks* (Moon) TRACKS: 1. Fables of Faubus (33:58) 2. Meditations (22:31) PERSONNEL: Johnny Coles (t); Eric Dolphy (as, fl, bcl); Clifford Jordan (ts); Jaki Byard (p); Charles Mingus (b); Dannie Richmond (d) DATE AND LOCATION: April 14, 1964, Copenhagen, Denmark *b. Live in Copenhagen 1964* (Landscape) TRACKS: 1. Orange Was the Color of Her Dress (14:18) [14:40] 2. Meditations (22:39) 3. ATFW U.S.A. (4:13) [4:01] 4. Fables of Faubus (34:11) [33:57] PERSONNEL: Johnny Coles (t); Eric Dolphy (as, bcl, fl); Clifford Jordan (ts); Jaki Byard (p); Charles Mingus (b); Dannie Richmond (d) DATE AND LOCATION: April 14, 1964, Old Fellow Palaet's Store Sal, Copenhagen, Denmark

60. [April 16, 1964, Bremen] *a. Hope so Eric Vol. 1* (Ingo) LP TRACKS: Side A: 1. So Long Eric, part 1 (18:15) (titled "Hope so Eric") • Side B: 1. So Long Eric, part 2 (8:10) (titled "Hope so Eric") 2. AT FW USA (4:30) 3. Sophisticated Lady (3:45) (Duke Ellington) PERSONNEL: Johnny Coles (t except B2, B3); Eric Dolphy (as, fl, bcl except B2, B3); Clifford Jordan (ts except B2, B3); Jaki Byard (p); Charles Mingus (b except B2); Dannie Richmond (d except B2, B3) DATE AND LOCATION: April 16,

1964, Bremen, Germany ORIGINAL ISSUE: Ingo ten *b. Fables of Faubus Vol. 2* (Ingo) LP *c. Parkeriana Vol. 3* (Ingo) LP

61. [April 17-18, 1964, Salle Wagram, Paris] *a. Revenge!* (Revenge) TRACKS: ▪ Disc 1: 1. Peggy's Blue Skylight (12:50) 2. Orange Was the Color of Her Dress Then Blue Silk (11:35) 3. Meditations on Integration (22:30) 4. Fables of Faubus (24:53) ▪ Disc 2: 1. So Long Eric (28:28) (mistitled "Goodbye Pork Pie Hat" on 1st pressing) 2. Parkeriana (24:53) PERSONNEL: Johnny Coles (trumpet on "So Long Eric"); Eric Dolphy (as, fl, bcl); Clifford Jordan (ts); Jaki Byard (p); Charles Mingus (b); Dannie Richmond (d) DATE AND LOCATION: April 17/18, 1964, Salle Wagram, Paris, France ORIGINAL ISSUE: several unauthorized recordings, including ▪ Disc 1: Le Jazz CD 19 ("*Paris 1964*", 1993, CD); Disc 2: Le Jazz CD 38 (*Paris 1964, Vol. 2*, 1995, CD); Disc 1 (1,3,4): France's Concert FCD 102 (*Meditation*, CD); Disc 2: France's Concert FCD 110 (*Vol. 2: Live In Paris, 1964*, CD); Jazz Collection (*Fables Of Faubus*); Disc 1 (2,4), Disc 2 (1): Jazz Time 64036-2 (1995) and Jazz Hour/Qualiton 75316 (*Goodbye Pork Pie Hat*), both recordings have mistitled "So Long Eric" as "Goodbye Pork Pie Hat." *b. Meditation* (France's Concert) LP

62. [April 19, 1964, Theatre des Champs-Elysees, Paris] *a. The Great Concert*, Paris 1964 (Musidisc) TRACKS: Disc 1: 1. Introduction et Presentation (1:33) 2. So Long Eric (mistitled "Goodbye Pork Pie Hat") (27:10) 3. Meditation For Integration (23:04) 4. Sophisticated Lady (6:12) (Duke Ellington) ▪ Disc 2: 1. Orange Was the Color of Her Dress Then Blue Silk (16:00) 2. Parkeriana (23:35) 3. Fables Of Faubus (27:47) PERSONNEL: Eric Dolphy (as, fl, bcl); Clifford Jordan (ts); Jaki Byard (p); Charles Mingus (b); Dannie Richmond (d) DATE AND LOCATION: April 19, 1964 (from Sunday 12:10 a.m. to 2:45 a.m.), Théâtre des Champs-Elysées, Paris, France, except "So Long Eric," which was recorded April 17/18 at Salle Wagram (?) ORIGINAL ISSUE: Prestige 34001 (1970, 3LP) OTHER ISSUES: SAAR srl CD 56047 (*Parkeriana*, 1993, CD) - liner notes claim this to be from Salle Wagram, but timings and personnel indicate that this is from Champs-Elysees: 1. Parkeriana (23:38) 2. Meditations for Integration (21:53) 3. Orange Was the Color Of Her Dress, Then Blue Silk (14:12)

63. [April 26, 1964, Wuppertal] *a. Mingus in Europe, Vol. 1* (Enja) TRACKS: 1. Fables of Faubus (37:35) 2. Starting (5:27) (Eric Dolphy) 3. Meditations (22:23) PERSONNEL: Eric Dolphy (as, bcl, fl); Clifford Jordan (ts except 2); Jaki Byard (p except 2); Charles Mingus (b); Dannie Richmond (d except 2) DATE AND LOCATION: April 26, 1964, Wuppertal Townhall, West Germany *b. Mingus in Europe, Vol. 2* (Enja) TRACKS: 1. Orange Was the Color of Her Dress Then Blue Silk (17:00) 2. Sophisticated Lady (3:44) 3. AT-FW-YOU (5:09) 4. Peggy's Blue Skylight (11:32) 5. So Long Eric (22:51) PERSONNEL: Eric Dolphy (as, fl, bcl); Clifford Jordan (ts); Jaki Byard (p); Charles Mingus (b); Dannie Richmond (d) DATE AND LOCATION: May 26, 1964, Wuppertal Townhall, Wuppertal, Germany REISSUE: 1, 2: Jazz Masterworks-Intermezzo CJZLP 10 (*Mingus & Duke*, 1985, Italy, LP)

64. [April 28, 1964, Stuttgart] *a. Mingus in Stuttgart* (Unique Jazz) LP TRACKS: 1. A.T.F.Y.O.U.U.S.A. 2. Sophisticated Lady (Ellington) 3. Peggy's Blue Skylight 4. Orange Was the Color of Her Dress, Then Blue Silk 5. Fables of Faubus 6. So Long Eric 7. Meditations 8. These Foolish Things (Strachey/Link) PERSONNEL: Eric Dolphy (as, fl, bcl); Clifford Jordan (ts); Jaki Byard (p); Charles Mingus (b); Dannie Richmond (d) DATE AND LOCATION: April 28, 1964, Mozartsaal, Stuttgart, Germany ORIGINAL ISSUE: 1, 2, 5: Unique Jazz UJ009; 3, 4, 6-8: Unique Jazz UJ007/008

65. *Right Now: Live at the Jazz Workshop* (1964, OJC) TRACKS: 1. New Fables (23:18) 2. Meditation (For a Pair of Wire Cutters) (23:44) PERSONNEL: John Handy (as on 1); Clifford Jordan (ts, fl (?)); Jane Getz (p); Charles Mingus (b); Dannie Richmond (d) DATE AND LOCATION: June 2-3, 1964, Jazz Workshop, San Francisco ORIGINAL ISSUE: Debut DLP-86017

66. *Mingus at Monterey* (1964, JVC/Fantasy) TRACKS:1. Duke Ellington Medley: 1. I Got It Bad and That Ain't Good (4:14) (Duke Ellington) 2. In a Sentimental Mood (1:46) (Ellington) 3. All Too Soon (1:53) (Ellington?) 4. Mood Indigo (0:59) (Ellington, Barney Bigard) 5. Sophisticated Lady (1:46) (Ellington) 6. Take the "A" Train (13:54) (Billy Strayhorn); 2. Orange Was the Color of Her Dress, Then Blue Silk (13:04) 3. Meditations on Integration (22:49) PERSONNEL: Lonnie Hillyer (t); Charles McPherson (as); John Handy (ts on "Take The 'A' Train" and "Meditations on Integra-

415

tion"); Jaki Byard (p); Charles Mingus (b); Dannie Richmond (d); plus on "Meditations On Integration": Bobby Bryant (t); Melvin Moore (t); Lou Blackburn (tb); Red Callender (tuba); Buddy Collette (as, fl, piccolo); Jack Nimitz (bs) DATE AND LOCATION: September 20, 1964, The Monterey Jazz Festival, Monterey, California ORIGINAL ISSUE: Jazz Workshop JWS 001/002 (1965) REISSUES: Prestige P-24100 (1981, 2LP, liner notes by Charles Mingus); 1: Jazz Masterworks-Intermezzo CJZLP 10 (*Mingus & Duke*, 1985, Italy, LP)

67. My Favorite Quintet (1965, Charles Mingus) LP TRACKS: 1. So Long Eric (18:24) 2. Medley (15:58) She's Funny That Way (Moret/Whiting); Embraceable You (Gershwin); I Can't Get Started (Duke); I Don't Stand a Ghost of a Chance With You (Young); Old Portrait 3. Cocktails for Two (8:15) (Johnson/Coslow) PERSONNEL: Lonnie Hillyer (t); Charles McPherson (as); Jaki Byard (p); Charles Mingus (b); Dannie Richmond (d) DATE AND LOCATION: May 13, 1965, Tyrone Guthrie Theater, Minneapolis ORIGINAL ISSUE: Charles Mingus Records JWS 009 (1965) REISSUES: Prestige P-24092 (*Portrait*, 2LP with *Town Hall Concert*, 1980, liner notes by Jaki Byard); America 30 AM 6105 (misleading front cover title *Town Hall Concert—Charles Mingus & His Quintet featuring Eric Dolphy*, LP, 198?)

68. Village Gate (1965, Ozone) TRACKS: 1. The Arts of Tatum and Freddie Webster (Majonet) 2. Don't Let It Happen Here PERSONNEL: Hobart Dotson (t); Lonnie Hillyer (t); Jimmy Owens (t, fluegelhorn); Julius Watkins (Fr horn); Howard Johnson (tuba); Charles McPherson (as); Charles Mingus (b, p, narration on 2); Dannie Richmond (d) DATE AND LOCATION: September 10, 1965, Village Gate, NYC ORIGINALLY ISSUED as Ozone 19

69. Charles Mingus Octet Recorded Live at Monterey (1965, East Coasting) EP TRACKS: 1. They Trespass the Land of the Sacred Sioux (part 1) 2. They Trespass the Land of the Sacred Sioux (part 2) All compositions by Charles Mingus PERSONNEL: Jimmy Owens (t, fluegelhorn); Lonnie Hillyer (t); Hobart Dotson (t); Charles McPherson (as); Julius Watkins (Fr horn); Howard Johnson (tuba); Charles Mingus (b, piano); Dannie Richmond (d) DATE AND LOCATION: September 18, 1965, The Monterey Jazz Festival, Monterey, California

70. Monterey Jazz Festival (1965, Malpaso) TRACKS: Don't Let It Happen Here (8:52) [music 8:45, applause 0:07] PERSONNEL: Charles Mingus (narration, b, p); Jimmy Owens (fluegelhorn); Julius Watkins (Fr horn); Hobart Dotson (t); Lonnie Hillyer (t); Garnett Brown (tb); Howard Johnson (tuba); Charles McPherson (as); Dannie Richmond (d) DATE AND LOCATION: September 18, 1965, Monterey Jazz Festival

71. Music Written for Monterey 1965, Not Heard (1965, Jazz Workshop) 2LP TRACKS: 1. Meditation on Inner Piece 2. Once Upon a Time There Was AaHolding Corporation Called Old America 3. Ode to Bird & Dizzy 4. They Trespass the Land of the Sacred Sioux 5. The Arts of Tatum & Freddie Webster 6. Muscrat Ramble 7. Don't Be Afraid, The Clown's Afraid Too 8. Don't Let It Happen Here PERSONNEL: Jimmy Owens (t); Lonnie Hillyer (t); Hobart Dotson (t); Charles McPherson (as); Julius Watkins (Fr horn); Howard Johnson (tuba); Charles Mingus (b, p); Dannie Richmond (d) DATE AND LOCATION: September 25, 1965, Royce Hall, University of California at Los Angeles ORIGINAL ISSUE: Jazz Workshop JWS 013/014 (196?)

72. Charles Mingus (1961-1966?, Frequenz) TRACKS: 1. unknown title (7:25) (mistitled "Blue Cee") 2. Take the "A" Train (10:41) (Billy Strayhorn) 3. Monk, Bunk or Vice Versa (10:43) 4. O.P. (8:20) 5. Sophisticated Lady (3:56) 6. So Long Eric (7:17) 7. Fables of Faubus (17:32) 8. Don't Let It Happen Here (3:20) PERSONNEL: 1: Jimmy Knepper (tb); Yusef Lateef (ts); Roland Kirk (ts, strich, manzello); Roland Hanna (p); Charles Mingus (b); Dannie Richmond (d) 2, 3: Richard Williams (t); Charles McPherson (as); Booker Ervin (ts); Jaki Byard (p); Charles Mingus (b); Dannie Richmond (d) 4: Ed Armour (t); Don Butterfield (tuba); Charles McPherson (as); Pepper Adams (bs); Jaki Byard (p); Charles Mingus (bass); Dannie Richmond (d) 5: Jaki Byard (p); Charles Mingus (b) 6, 7: Johnny Coles (t); Eric Dolphy (as, bcl); Clifford Jordan (ts); Jaki Byard (p); Charles Mingus (b); Dannie Richmond (d) 8: Lonnie Hillyer (t); Jimmy Owens (t); Julius Watkins (Fr horn); Howard Johnson (tuba); Charles McPherson (as); Charles Mingus (bass, recitation); Dannie Richmond (d) DATE AND LOCATION: 1: October 21, 1961, Birdland, NYC; 2: March 24, 1962, NYC; 3: March 31, 1962, NYC; 4: October 26, 1962, NYC; 5: April 16, 1964, Bremen, Germany;

6,7: April 13, 1964, Stockholm, Sweden; 8: January 18, 1966, NYC COMMENTS: This bootleg originates from Italy.

73. Lennie's-on-the-Turnpike (1966, soundtrack) 1. All the Things You Are (Kern) 2. Peggy's Blue Skylight 3. Take the "A" Train (Strayhorn) 4. Secret Love 5. Portrait 6. unknown title PERSONNEL: Lonnie Hillyer (t except 4); Charles McPherson (as except 4); John Gilmore (ts except 2, 4, 5); Walter Bishop (p except 1, 2); Charles Mingus (b, p, voc); Dannie Richmond (d) DATE AND LOCATION: November 1966, Lennie's-on-the-Turnpike, Peabody, Massachusetts (1-5) and November 21, 1966, Mingus's loft, NYC

74. [March 31, 1970, Slug's, New York] *a. Dizzy Atmosphere—Live at Historic Slug's Vol. 1* TRACKS: 1. Ray's Idea 2. So Long Eric 3. If I Should Lose You 4. I Can't Get Started (Duke) 5. Dizzy Atmosphere 6. Peggy's Blue Skylight 7. Better Git It in Your Soul 8. Orange Was the Color of Her Dress PERSONNEL: Bill Hardman (t); Charles McPherson (as, fl); Jimmy Vass (as); Charles Mingus (b); Dannie Richmond (d) DATE AND LOCATION: March 31, 1970, Slug's, NYC *b. Fables of Faubus—Live at Historic Slug's Vol. 2* TRACKS: 1. Fables of Faubus 2. In a Sentimental Mood (Ellington) 3. Take the "A" Train (Strayhorn) 4. Billie's Bounce/Koko (Parker) 5. O.P. 6. Greensleeves PERSONNEL: Bill Hardman (t); Charles McPherson (as, fl); Jimmy Vass (as); Charles Mingus (b); Dannie Richmond (d) DATE AND LOCATION: March 31, 1970, Slug's, NYC

75. Statements (1970, Lotus) LP TRACKS: 1. Orange Was the Color of Her Dress (18:05) 2. The Man Who Never Sleeps (16:30) 3. O.P. (8:40) PERSONNEL: Eddie Preston (t); Charles McPherson (as); Bobby Jones (ts); Jaki Byard (p); Charles Mingus (b); Dannie Richmond (d) DATE AND LOCATION: October 25, 1970, Teatro Lirico, Milano, Italy (according to discography by Mario Luzzi) · probably correct; October 1970, Rotterdam, The Netherlands (according to ?); 1969, Amsterdam, The Netherlands (according to LP) ORIGINAL ISSUE: Joker UPS2072 (197?)

76. [October 28, 1970, Paris, France] *a. Charles Mingus in Paris 1970* (DIW) TRACKS: 1. O.P.—Tribute to Oscar Pettiford (9:24) 2. The Man Who Never Sleeps (14:37) 3. Orange Was the Color of Her Dress (17:15) 4. Fables of Faubus (10:36) 5. She's Funny That Way (18:49) (Moret/Whiting) 6. Ellington Medley (19:01): 1. In a Sentimental Mood (Ellington) 2. Sophisticated Lady (Ellington) 3. Mood Indigo (Ellington/Bigard) 4. Take The "A" Train (Strayhorn) PERSONNEL: Eddie Preston (t); Charles McPherson (as); Bobby Jones (ts, cl); Jaki Byard (p); Charles Mingus (b); Dannie Richmond (d) DATE AND LOCATION: October 28, 1970, Theatre National Populaire du Palais de Chaillot, Paris, France REISSUES: 1-3, 6: Ulysse Musique AROC CD 1003 (*Paris, TNP, October 28th 1970*, 1988, CD); (*Charlie Mingus Sextet Live*, CD) *b. Charlie Mingus Sextet Live* (Blu Jazz) TRACKS: 1. So Long Eric (13:50) 2. The Man Who Never Sleeps (14:30) 3. Pithecanthropus Erectus (9:30) 4. She's Funny That Way (18:00) (Moret/Whiting) 5. Ending Theme (2:00) PERSONNEL: Eddie Preston (t); Charles McPherson (as); Bobby Jones (ts, cl); Jaki Byard (p); Charles Mingus (b); Dannie Richmond (d) DATE AND LOCATION: October 28, 1970, Theatre National Populaire du Palais de Chaillot, Paris, France

77. [October 31, 1970, Paris, France] *a. Pithycanthropus Erectus* [sic] (1970, Musidisc) TRACKS: 1. Pithecanthropus Erectus (16:35) 2. Peggy's Blue Skylight (12:43) 3. Reincarnation of a Lovebird (13:00) 4. Blue Bird (17:55) (Charlie Parker) PERSONNEL: Eddie Preston (t); Charles McPherson (as); Bobby Jones (ts); Jaki Byard (p); Charles Mingus (b); Dannie Richmond (d) DATE AND LOCATION: October 31, 1970, Paris, France ORIGINAL ISSUE: 1, 2: America 30 AM 6109 (*Pithecanthropus Erectus*, LP); 3, 4: America 30 AM 6110 (*Blue Bird*, LP) REISSUE: Prestige 24028 (*Reincarnation of a Lovebird*, 2LP) *b. Reincarnation of a Lovebird* (1970, Prestige) 2LP TRACKS: 1. Reincarnation of a Lovebird (13:00) 2. I Left My Heart in San Francisco (4:10) (Cross, Cory) 3. Blue Bird (17:00) (Charlie Parker) 4. Pithecanthropus Erectus (16:35) 5. Peggy's Blue Skylight (12:46) 6. Love Is a Dangerous Necessity (4:01) PERSONNEL: Eddie Preston (t); Charles McPherson (as); Bobby Jones (ts); Jaki Byard (p); Charles Mingus (b); Dannie Richmond (d) DATE AND LOCATION: October 31, 1970, Paris, France ORIGINAL ISSUE: 1-3: America 30 AM 6110 (*Blue Bird*, LP); 4-6: America 30 AM 6109 (*Pithecanthropus Erectus*, LP)

78. Charles Mingus Sextet in Berlin (1970, Beppo) LP TRACKS: 1. History (8:15) 2. O.P. (10:48) 3. Reincarnation of a Lovebird (10:52) 4. The Man Who Never Sleeps (13:15) PERSONNEL: Eddie Preston (t); Charles McPherson (as); Bobby Jones (ts, cl); Jaki Byard (p); Charles Mingus (b); Dannie Richmond (d) DATE AND LOCATION: November 1970, Berlin, West Germany ORIGINAL ISSUE: Beppo 508 COMMENTS: This is probably an unauthorized recording.

79. Charles Mingus Group with Orchestra (1971, Denon) TRACKS: 1. The Man Who Never Sleeps (16:19) 2. Portrait (8:13) 3. O.P. (7:25) All compositions by Charles Mingus and arranged by Jaki Byard PERSONNEL: Eddie Preston (t); Bobby Jones (ts, cl); Charles Mingus (b)—with Toshiyuki Miyama and His New Herd—big band including; Shigeo Suzuki (as on 2); Hiroshi Takamu (as); Masahiko Sato (p); Yoshisaburo Toyozumi (d) DATE AND LOCATION: January 14, 1971, Tokyo, Japan ORIGINAL ISSUE: Columbia NCB7008 (Japan, LP) REISSUE: Denon DC-8565 (1990, unauthorized, CD)

80. Shoes of the Fisherman's Wife (1959/1971, CBS) TRACKS: 1. Slop (6:12) 2. Song With Orange (6:37) 3. Gunslinging Bird (5:03) 4. Things Ain't What They Used To Be (7:36) 5. The Shoes of the Fisherman's Wife Are Some Jive Ass Slippers (9:30) 6. Far Wells, Mill Valley (6:11) 7. Mood Indigo (8:13) (Ellington/Bigard) PERSONNEL: 1, 4, 7: Don Ellis (t); Jimmy Knepper (tb); Booker Ervin (ts); John Handy (as); Roland Hanna (p); Charles Mingus (b); Dannie Richmond (d); Maurice Brown (cello); Seymour Barab (cello) 2, 3, 6: Richard Williams (t); Jimmy Knepper (tb); Booker Ervin (ts); Benny Golson (ts); John Handy (as); Jerome Richardson (bs, fl); Roland Hanna (p); Teddy Charles (vibes); Charles Mingus - bass; Dannie Richmond - drums 5: Snookie Young (t); Jimmy Nottingham (t); Eddie Bert (tb); Urbie Green (tb); Julius Watkins (Fr horn); Danny Banks (reeds); Jerry Dodgion (reeds); Charles McPherson (reeds); Bobby Jones (reeds); Roland Hanna (p); John Foster (p); Charles Mingus (bass); Richard Davis (b); Homer Dench (b); Ron Carter (b); Milt Hinton (b); Dannie Richmond (d) DATE AND LOCATION: 1, 4, 7: November 13, 1959, NYC; 2, 3, 6: November 1, 1959, NYC; 5: September 23, 1971, NYC COMMENTS: This CD contains unedited versions from Mingus Dynasty sessions.

81. Let My Children Hear Music (1971, CBS) TRACKS: 1. The Shoes of the Fisherman's Wife Are Some Jive Ass Slippers (9:34) Transcribed, arranged, orchestrated, and conducted by Sy Johnson. 2. Adagio Ma Non Troppo (8:22) Transcribed by Hug Miller, orchestrated and conducted by Alan Raph. 3. Don't Be Afraid, the Clown's Afraid Too (9:26) Conducted by Teo Macero, transcribed, arranged, and orchestrated by Sy Johnson. 4. Taurus in the Arena of Life (4:17) Arranged, orchestrated and conducted by Sy Johnson. 5. Hobo Ho (10:07) Arranged by Charles Mingus and dictated to Bobby Jones; conducted by Sy Johnson. 6. The Chill of Death (7:38) Orchestrated by Charles Mingus, conducted by Alan Raph, recitation by Charles Mingus. 7. The I of Hurricane Sue (10:09) Scored by Charles Mingus, especially for this date, for small jazz orchestra with ten-piece traditional orchestral accompaniment. Large band arrangement by Sy Johnson. PERSONNEL: Lonnie Hillyer (t); Joe Wilder (t); Snooky Young (t); Jimmy Nottingham (t); Julius Watkins (Fr horn); Bobby Jones (ts); James Moody (ts); Charles McCracken (cello); Charles McPherson (as); Jerry Dodgion (as); Sir Roland Hanna (p); Jaki Byard (p); Jimmy Knepper (tb); Charles Mingus (b); Ron Carter (b); Richard Davis (b); Milt Hinton (b); Dannie Richmond (d); etc. DATE AND LOCATION: 1, 7: September 23, 1971, NYC; 5: September 30, 1971, NYC; 3: October 1, 1971, NYC; 4: September 23-November 18, 1971, NYC; 6, 2: November 18, 1971, NYC ORIGINAL ISSUE: Columbia KC31069 and Columbia CK 44050 (USA) in 1972 without "Taurus in the Arena of Life"

82. Charles Mingus and Friends in Concert (1972, CBS) TRACKS: Disc One: 1. Introduction by Bill Cosby (1:06) 2. Jump Monk (7:28)* 3. E.S.P. (9:25)* 4. Ecclusiastics (9:31)* 5. Eclipse (4:03)* 6. Us Is Two (10:12)* 7. Taurus in the Arena Of Life (aka Number One Grandson) (4:53)* 8. Mingus Blues (5:33)*** 9. Introduction to Little Royal Suite by Bill Cosby (0:14) 10. Little Royal Suite (20:20)** • Disc Two: 1. Introduction to Strollin' by Bill Cosby (0:50) 2. Strollin' (10:14) (Charles Mingus, George Gordon)* 3. The I of Hurricane Sue (11:12)* 4. E's Flat, Ah's Flat Too (aka Hora Decubitus) (17:08)*** 5. Ool-Ya-Koo (3:54) (Walter "Gil" Fuller, Dizzy Gillespie) 6. Portrait (3:58)* 7. Don't Be Afraid, the Clown's Afraid Too (10:36) PERSONNEL: Teo Macero (conductor); George Dorsey (as); Richie Perri (as, fl); Lee Konitz (as); Charles McPherson (as); Gene Ammons (ts); Bobby Jones (ts, cl); Gerry Mulligan (bs); Howard Johnson (bs, bcl); Jon Faddis (t); Lloyd Michaels (t); Eddie Preston (t); Lonnie Hillyer (t); Sharon Moe (Fr horn); Dick Berg (Fr horn); Eddie Bert (ttb); Bob Stewart (tuba); John Foster (p); Charles Mingus (b); Milt Hinton (b); Joe Chambers (d) GUESTS: Honey Gordon (voc on "Eclipse," "Strollin'" and "Portrait"); Randy Weston (p on "E's Flat,

Ah's Flat Too") Dizzy Gillespie (voc on "Ool-Ya-Koo"); James Moody (fl on "E's Flat, Ah's Flat Too"); Bill Cosby (MC, voc) DATE AND LOCATION: February 4, 1972, Philharmonic Hall at Lincoln Center, NYC ORIGINALLY RELEASED: Columbia KG 31614 (1973, 2LP, US); CBS S 67288 (1973, 2LP, Europe) REISSUES: Sony Music Entertainment, Inc. CBS Sony SRCS 7089-90 (19??, 2CD, Japan)*Arranged by Sy Johnson, **arranged by Charles Mingus, Teo Macero and Sy Johnson, ***arranged by Charles Mingus.

83. Newport in New York Jam Session (1972, Cobblestone) 1. Jumpin' at the Woodside 2. Lo-slo-bluze PERSONNEL: Cat Anderson (t); Jimmy Owens (t); Charles McPherson (as); Buddy Tate (ts); Roland Hanna (p); Milt Buckner (organ); Charles Mingus (b); Alan Dawson (d) DATE AND LOCATION: July 6, 1972, Radio City Music Hall, NYC ORIGINALLY ISSUED as Cobblestone CST9025-2

84. Ronnie Scott's (1972, CBS unissued) 1. unknown titles PERSONNEL: Jon Faddis (t); Charles McPherson (as); Bobby Jones (ts, cl); John Foster (p); Charles Mingus (b); Roy Brooks (d, musical saw) DATE AND LOCATION: August 14 and 15, 1972, Ronnie Scott's, London UNISSUED, recorded by CBS (Europe)

85. In The Kingdom of Glass—Jazz i Glasrike (1972, Jazz på Rällen) TRACKS: Disc 1: 1. Introduction by Charles Mingus (1:45) 2. Intro—When the Saints (8:17) 3. The Man Who Never Sleeps (18:49) 4. Mindreaders Convention in Milano (29:20) • Disc 2: 1. Fables of Faubus (24:59) PERSONNEL: Charles McPherson (as); Bobby Jones (ts, cl); Jon Faddis (t); John Foster (p); Charles Mingus (b); Roy Brooks (d) DATE AND LOCATION: August 19, 1972, Emmaboda Jazz Festival, Sweden ORIGINAL ISSUE: Disc 1: unissued, recorded by Sveriges Radio (aircheck, mono); Disc 2: unissued, recorded by Sveriges Television, SRT (aircheck from TV, October 26, 1972) COMMENTS: These are noncommercial compact discs made from private broadcast tapes.

86. Live in Chateauvallon, 1972 (France's Concert) TRACKS: 1. Duke Ellington Medley (26:46): 1. Blues in G (bass solo) (3:45) 2. In a Sentimental Mood (Duke Ellington) 3. Sophisticated Lady (Ellington) 4. ?? (Ellington) 5. Mood Indigo (Ellington, Barney Bigard) 6. Take the "A" Train (Billy Strayhorn); 2. Fables of Faubus (19:10) 3. Diane [Body And Soul] (6:56) 4. Blues Medley (15:32): 1. John's Blues aka Blues for Roy's Saw [Blues for Some Bones] 2. Noddin' Ya Head Blues PERSONNEL: Charles McPherson (as); John Foster (p, voc); Charles Mingus (b); Roy Brooks (d, musical saw) DATE AND LOCATION: August 22, 1972, Chateauvallon, France COMMENTS: The track listing on the CD liner notes is almost completely wrong and it is fixed here, except for Eddie "Cleanhead" Vinson tune (?) "Blues for Some Bones," which appears also as "John's Blues" on Stormy & Funky Blues. Liner notes also list "Stormy Weather" (even that is mistitled "Stormy Monday") and "I'll Remembered April" [sic] to have been played as part of Ellington medley, but neither of them are recognizable.

87. Parkeriana (1972, Bandstand) TRACKS: 1. Body and Soul (Green) 2. Stormy Weather (Arlen) 3. In a Sentimental Mood (Ellington) 4. Take the "A" Train (Strayhorn) PERSONNEL: Charles McPherson (as); John Foster (p); Charles Mingus (b); Roy Brooks (d) DATE AND LOCATION: 1972

88. Blue Skylark (1972, Original Revival Collection) TRACKS: 1. Peggy's Blue Skylight (11:38) [mistitled "Blue Skylark"] applause, announcement Mingus (0:20) 2. Celia (fragment) (6:14) applause insert (0:25) 3. Blues for a Saw (18:56) [mistitled "Blues For Roy Saw"] applause (0:52) PERSONNEL: Hamiet Bluiett [CD: Barry Blue] (fl, bs); Joseph Gardener (t); John Foster (p); Charles Mingus (b); Roy Brooks (d, musical saw) DATE AND LOCATION: October 20, 1972, Warsaw, Poland (according to CD: May 3, 1968, Atlanta—Mingus was inactive during that period) ORIGINAL ISSUE: 2: Muza SXL0929 (stereo) and XL0929 (mono) (Jazz Jamboree 1972, LP)

89. Mingus Quintet Meets Cat Anderson (1972, Unique Jazz) TRACKS: 1. Celia (Mingus) 2. Perdido (Tizol) PERSONNEL: Joe Gardner (t); Hamiet Bluiett (bs); John Foster (p); Charles Mingus (b); Roy Brooks (d, musical saw); Cat Anderson (t on 2) DATE AND LOCATION: November 5, 1972, Philharmonie, Berlin ORIGINAL ISSUE: Unique Jazz UJ20

90. Mingus Moves (1973, Atlantic) TRACKS: 1. Canon (5:28) 2. Opus 4 (6:39) 3. Moves (3:43) (Doug Hammond) 4. Wee (8:57) (Sy Johnson) 5. Flowers for a Lady (6:44) (George Adams) 6. Newcomer

DISCOGRAPHY

(7:13) (Don Pullen) 7. Opus 3 (10:26) 8. Big Alice (5:44) (Pullen) 9. The Call (7:15) (composer unknown) PERSONNEL: Ronald Hampton (t, tambourine); George Adams (ts, fl); Don Pullen (p, organ); Charles Mingus (b); Dannie Richmond (d); Honey Gordon (voc on 3); Doug Hammond (voc on 3) DATE AND LOCATION: October 29-31, 1973, Atlantic Recording Studios, NYC ORIGINALLY ISSUED: 1-7: Atlantic #1653 (April 8, 1974); 8-9: previously unissued

91. Mingus at Carnegie Hall (1974, Atlantic) TRACKS: 1. C Jam Blues (24:32) (Duke Ellington) 2. Perdido (21:53) (Juan Tizol) PERSONNEL: Jon Faddis (t); Charles McPherson (as); George Adams (ts); John Handy (as, ts); Hamiet Bluiett (bs); Roland Kirk (ts, strich); Don Pullen (p); Charles Mingus (b); Dannie Richmond (d) DATE AND LOCATION: January 19, 1974, Carnegie Hall, NYC ORIGINAL ISSUE: Atlantic #SD-1667 (January 1975) REISSUE: Mobile Fidelity (19??) COMMENTS: Priestley lists following unissued tracks: "Peggy's Blue Skylight," "Celia," "Fables of Faubus," "Big Alice," and "C Jam Blues Ending."

92. Changes One (1974, Atlantic) TRACKS: 1. Remember Rockefeller at Attica (5:56) 2. Sue's Changes (17:04) 3. Devil Blues (9:24) 4. Duke Ellington's Sound of Love (12:04) PERSONNEL: Jack Walrath (t); George Adams (ts, voc on 3); Don Pullen (p); Charles Mingus (b); Dannie Richmond (d) DATE AND LOCATION: December 27, 28, and 30, 1974, NYC ORIGINAL ISSUE: Atlantic #1677 (1975)

93. Changes Two (1974, Atlantic) TRACKS: 1. Free Cell Block F, 'Tis Nazi U.S.A. (6:52) 2. Orange Was the Color of Her Dress, Then Silk Blue (17:31) 3. Black Bats and Poles (6:20) (Jack Walrath) 4. Duke Ellington's Sound of Love (4:13) 5. For Harry Carney (7:57) (Sy Johnson) PERSONNEL: Jack Walrath (t); George Adams (ts); Don Pullen (p); Charles Mingus (b); Dannie Richmond (d); Jackie Paris (voc on 4); Marcus Belgrave (t on 4); Sy Johnson (arranger on 4) DATE AND LOCATION: December 27, 28, and 30, 1974, NYC ORIGINAL ISSUE: Atlantic #1678 (1975)

94. Mingus in Åhus 1975 (1975, Jazz på Rällen) TRACKS: 1. Intro by producer Inge Dahl (3:21) 2. The Devil Blues (19:12) 3. Sue's Changes (34:35) PERSONNEL: Jack Walrath (t); George Adams (ts, voc (on 2)); Don Pullen (p); Charles Mingus (b); Dannie Richmond (d) DATE AND LOCATION: July 19, 1975, Åhus Jazz Festival, Piratenteatern, Sweden ORIGINAL ISSUE: commercially unissued radio broadcast (Sveriges radio P3, November 9, 1975, mono)

95. Keystone Korner (1976, Jazz Door) TRACKS: 1. Remember Rockefeller at Attica (10:15) 2. Devil Blues (17:02) 3. Duke Ellington's Sound of Love (13:37) 4. For Harry Carney (16:51) (Sy Johnson) PERSONNEL: Jack Walrath (t); George Adams (ts, fl); Dannie Mixon (p); Charles Mingus (b); Dannie Richmond (d) DATE AND LOCATION: May 1976, Keystone Korner, San Francisco (April 1976 according to the CD)

96. Stormy & Funky Blues (1972-77, Moon) TRACKS: 1. Blues Medley (9:38): 1. John's Blues aka Blues for Roy's Saw 2. Noddin' Ya Head Blues; 2. Flowers for a Lady [Angry Reeds] (9:09) (George Adams) 3. Stormy & Funky Blues (7:38) (Mingus, Adams) 4. Opus 3 [Squeezed Strings] (15:44) 5. Cumbia & Jazz Fusion (15:35) PERSONNEL: 1: Jon Faddis (t); Charles McPherson (as); John Foster (p, voc); Charles Mingus (b); Roy Brooks (d, musical saw) 2-4: George Adams (ts, voc); Hamiet Bluiett (bs); Don Pullen (p); Charles Mingus (b); Dannie Richmond (d) 5: Jack Walrath (t); Ricky Ford (ts); Bob Neloms (p); Charles Mingus (b); Dannie Richmond (d) DATE AND LOCATION: 1: August 1972, Stuttgart, Germany (according to CD: 1971); 2-4: July 28, 1974, Todi, Umbria Jazz Festival, Italy (according to CD: 1975, Perugia, Italy); 5: 1977, Milano, Italy (according to CD: 1976) COMMENTS: The track listing on the CD liner notes is almost completely wrong and it is fixed here, except for Eddie "Cleanhead" Vinson tune (?) "John's Blues," which appears also as "Blues for Some Bones" on *Live In Chateauvallon*, 1972, and for "Stormy & Funky Blues." which seems to be a blues jam with an improvised riff theme. Bobby Jones might playing tenor sax on "Blues Medley."

97. Three or Four Shades of Blues (1977, Atlantic) TRACKS: 1. Better Git Hit In Your Soul (4:35) 2. Goodbye, Porkpie Hat (7:00) 3. Noddin' Ya Head Blues (10:29) 4. Three or Four Shades of Blues (12:03) 5. Nodoby Knows (10:06) All compositions by Charles Mingus. "Three or Four Shades of Blues" arranged by Charles Mingus, others arranged by Paul Jeffrey. PERSONNEL: Jack Walrath (t); Ricky Ford (ts); Bob Neloms (p); Charles Mingus (b); Dannie Richmond (d); George Coleman (as, ts except on 5); Sonny Fortune (as on 5); Jimmy Rowles (p on 4); Philip Catherine (g except on 4); Larry Coryell (g except on 5); John Scofield (g on 4, 5); Ron Carter (b on 5); George Mraz (b except 4, 5) DATE AND LOCATION: 1-3: March 9, 1977, NYC; 5: March 11, 1977, NYC; 4: March 29, 1977, NYC ORIGINAL ISSUE: Atlantic SD 1700 (1977)

98. Cumbia & Jazz Fusion (1977, Atlantic) TRACKS: 1. Cumbia & Jazz Fusion (27:58) 2. Music for "Todo Modo" (22:18) 3. Wedding March/Slow Waltz (take 9) (1:55) (trad.) 4. Wedding March/Slow Waltz (take 12) (2:14) (trad.) PERSONNEL: 1; Charles Mingus (b, voc, Latin percussion); Jack Walrath (t, Latin percussion); Jimmy Knepper (tb, btb); Mauricio Smith (fl, piccolo, ss, as); Paul Jeffrey (oboe, ts); Ricky Ford (ts, Latin percussion); Gary Anderson (bcl, contrabass cl); Gene Scholtes (bassoon); Bob Neloms (p); Dannie Richmond (d); Candido Camero (congas); Daniel Gonzales (congas); Ray Mantilla (congas); Alfredo Ramirez (congas); Bradley Cunningham (Latin percussion) 2; Charles Mingus (b); Jack Walrath (t); George Adams (ts, afl); Quarto Maltoni (as); Anastasio Del Bono (oboe, Eng horn); Roberto Laneri (bcl); Pasquale Sabatelli (bassoon); Dino Piana (tb); Danny Mixon (p, organ); Dannie Richmond (d) 3, 4; Charles Mingus (p) DATE AND LOCATION: 1: March 10, 1977, NYC; 2: March 31 and April 1, 1976, Rome, Italy; 3, 4: May 1, 1977, NYC ORIGINAL ISSUE: 1, 2: Atlantic #8801 (May 1978); 3, 4 ("Wedding March/Slow March"): previously unissued

99. Spain '77 (1977, Excelsior) LP TRACKS: 1. For Harry Carney (16:10) (Sy Johnson) 2. Three or Four Shades of Blues (9:40) 3. Cumbia & Jazz Fusion (26:28) PERSONNEL: Jack Walrath (t); Ricky Ford (ts); Bob Neloms (p); Charles Mingus (b); Dannie Richmond (d) DATE AND LOCATION: July 16, 1977, Sitges, Spain COMMENTS: This is possibly an unauthorized recording.

100. Final Work (1977, CMA Jazz) TRACKS: 1. Peggy's Blue Skylight (5:16) 2. Fables of Faubus (6:12) 3. Caroline Keikki Mingus (6:18) 4. Slop (5:05) 5. So Long Eric (4:32) 6. Farewell Farwell (5:59) 7. Just For Laughs (part 1) (4:26) 8. It Might As Well Be Spring (5:32) (Richard Rodgers) 9. Duke Ellington's Sound of Love (5:54) 10. Just for Laughs (part 2) (2:35) PERSONNEL: Jack Walrath (t); Woody Shaw (t); Ricky Ford (ts); Paul Jeffrey (ts, arranger); Gerry Mulligan (bs); Bob Neloms (p); Lionel Hampton (vibes); Charles Mingus (b); Dannie Richmond (d); Peter Matt (Fr horn (according to CMA issue)) DATE AND LOCATION: November 6, 1977, NYC ORIGINAL ISSUE: 1-4, 6, 7, 9, 10: Who's Who 21005 (197?) as *Lionel Hampton Presents the Music of Charles Mingus*; 5: Who's Who 21014 as *Giants of Jazz Vol. 2*; 8: Gateway GSLP 10113 REISSUES: (*Jazz Classics*, CD); CLEO CLCD 65005 (*The Sound of Jazz*, CD); Kingdom Jazz CDGATE 7016 (*His Final Work*, CD); Who's Who In Jazz WWCD 21005 (*His Final Work*, CD); Galaxy Music 3886052 (*The Sound Of Jazz, Vol. 5*, CD)

101. Me, Myself An Eye (1978, Atlantic) LP TRACKS: 1. Three Worlds of Drums (30:20) 2. Devil Woman (8:12) 3. Wednesday Night Prayer Meeting (9:42) 4. Carolyn "Keki" Mingus (7:40) PERSONNEL: on all tracks: Charles Mingus (leader); Randy Brecker (t); Mike Davis (t); Jack Walrath (t, arranger); Akira Ohmori (as); Ken Hitchcock (as, ss); Daniel Block (ts); Michael Brecker (ts); Ricky Ford (ts); Pepper Adams (bs); Ronnie Cuber (bs); Craig Pupura (bs); Jimmy Knepper (tb); Larry Coryell (g); Ted Dunbar (g); Jack Wilkins (g); Bob Neloms (p); Eddie Gomez (b); Joe Chambers (d); Dannie Richmond (d); Paul Jeffrey (conductor) on 1: George Coleman (ts); Slide Hampton (tb); Sammy Figueroa (percussion); Ray Mantilla (percussion); George Mraz (b); Steve Gadd (d) •on 2-3: Lee Konitz (as); Yoshiaki Malta (as); John Tank (ts); Keith O'Quinn (tb) DATE AND LOCATION: 1: January 19, 1978, Atlantic Studios, NYC; 2-3: January 23, 1978, Atlantic Studios, NYC COMMENTS: Jack Walrath's comment on "Me, Myself An Eye" was published in *Down Beat*'s June 21, 1979, issue.

102. Something Like a Bird (1978, Atlantic) LP TRACKS: 1. Something Like a Bird, Part 1 (19:10) 2. Something Like a Bird, Part 2 (12:14) 3. Farewell Farwell (6:57) PERSONNEL: • on all tracks: Charles Mingus (leader); Mike Davis (t); Jack Walrath (t, arranger); Ken Hitchcock (as, ss); Lee Konitz (as); Akira Ohmori (as); Daniel Block (ts); Ricky Ford (ts); Pepper Adams (bs); Ronnie Cuber (bs); Craig Pupura (bs); Jimmy Knepper (tb); Bob Neloms (p); Ted Dunbar (g); Larry Coryell (g); Jack Wilkins (g); Eddie Gomez (b); Joe Chambers (d); Dannie Richmond (d); Paul Jeffrey (conductor) 1, 2: Randy Brecker (t); Charles McPherson (as); Michael Brecker (ts); George Coleman (ts, as); Slide Hampton (tb); Danny Toan (g); Kenny Werner (elec p); George Mraz (b); Ray Mantilla (percussion) 3: Yoshiaki Malta (as); John Tank (ts); Keith O'Quinn (tb)   DATE AND LOCATION: 1, 2: January 18, 1978, NYC; 3: January 23, 1978, NYC   ORIGINAL ISSUE: 1980

COLLECTIONS AND ANTHOLOGIES (WITHOUT DETAILS)

103. In a Soulful Mood (1960, Candid)

104. Great Moments (1963, MCA Impulse!) 2LP (Includes both *The Black Saint and the Sinner Lady* and *Mingus, Mingus, Mingus, Mingus, Mingus* plus four tracks from *Mingus Plays Piano*)

105. The Art of Charles Mingus (197?, Atlantic) 2LP

106. Passions of a Man (1979, Atlantic)   TRACKS: Side One: 1. Pithecanthropus Erectus (10:41) 2. Profile of Jackie (3:07) 3. Reincarnation of a Lovebird (8:31) ▪ Side Two: 1. Haitian Fight Song (11:57) 2. Wednesday Night Prayer Meeting (5:39) 3. Cryin' Blues (4:58) ▪ Side Three: 1. Devil Woman (9:38) 2. Wham Bam Thank You Ma'am (4:41) 3. Passions of a Man (4:52) 4. Tonight at Noon (5:58) ▪ Side Four: 1. Passions of a Women Loved (9:43) 2. Duke Ellington's Sound of Love (12:04) ▪ Side Five: 1. Better Git Hit in Your Soul (4:35) 2. Sue's Changes (17:04) ▪ Side Six: 1. Canon (5:30) 2. Free Cell Block F, 'Tis Nazi U.S.A. (6:52) 3. Goodbye, Porkpie Hat (7:00) 4. Mingus on Mingus (3:30)   PERSONNEL: Various personnel, see original Atlantic recordings for more information   DATE AND LOCATION: from January 30, 1956 to March 9, 1977   ORIGINALLY ISSUED: Side 1-1, 2: Atlantic SD 1237 as *Pithecanthropus Erectus*; Side 1-3 and 2-1: Atlantic SD 1260 as *The Clown*; Side 2-2, 3: Atlantic SD 1305 as *Blues & Roots*; Side 3-1, 2, 3: Atlantic SD 1377 as *Oh Yeah*; Side 3-4 and 4-1: Atlantic SD 1416 *as Tonight at Noon*; Side 4-2 and 5-2: Atlantic SD 1677 as *Changes One*; Side 5-1 and 6-3: Atlantic SD 1700 as *Three or Four Shades of Blues*; Side 6-1: Atlantic SD 1653 as *Mingus Moves*; Side 6-2: Atlantic SD 1678 as *Changes Two*; Side 6-4: previously unissued

107. Thirteen Pictures (199?, Atlantic/Rhino)

108. This Is Jazz #6 (1996, Columbia)

MINGUS AS SIDEMAN: TITLES ONLY

1. *Louis Armstrong and His Orchestra* (1943, AFRS Jubilee)
2. *Russell Jacquet and His All Stars* (1945, Globe)
3. *Billie Holiday: At Jazz at the Philharmonic* (1945, Verve)
4. *Howard McGhee and His Combo* (1945, Modern Music)
5. Illinois Jacquet and His Orchestra: *The Fabulous Apollo Sessions* (1945, Apollo)
6. *Wynonie Harris: Meets the Master Saxes* (1945, Apollo)
7. *Ernie Andrews and the Baranco Trio* (1945, G & G)
8. *Bob Mosley and His All Stars* (1945, Beltone)
9. Dinah Washington: *Mellow Mama* (1945, Delmark/Apollo)
10. *Wilbert Baranco and His Rhythm Bombardiers* (1946, Black & White)
11. *Wilbert Baranco and His Rhythm Bombardiers* (1946, AFRS Jubilee)
12. *Ivie Anderson and Her All Stars* (1946, Black & White)
13. The Stars of Swing (1946, unknown)
14. Howard McGhee and His Orchestra (1946, Melodisc)
15. Darby Hicks Quartet (1946, Indigo)
16. Gene Morris Quintet (1946, Cleartone)
17. Gerry Wiggins (1947, private recording)
18. *Lionel Hampton And His Orchestra* (1947, Decca)
19. *Lionel Hampton And His Sextet* (1947, Decca)
20. Lionel Hampton: *Hamp: The Legendary Decca Recordings of Lionel Hampton* (1947, Decca)

21. Earl Hines and His Orchestra/Curley Hamner And His Orchestra (1947, Sunrise/Pickwick/Bravo)
22. Lionel Hampton and His Orchestra (1948, JDS)
23. Red Norvo Trio: *Move!* (1950, Savoy)
24. Red Norvo Trio: *The Savoy Sessions* (1950/1951, Savoy)
25. Red Norvo Trio: *The Standard Sessions* (1950, Standard)
26. Charlie Parker: jam session (1951)
27. Miles Davis: *The Birdland Sessions* (1951, Charly/Le Jazz)
28. *Billy Taylor Trio* (1951, Roost)
29. Melvin Moore (1951, King)
30. Jazz '52 (1952, airshot)
31. Dizzy Gillespie/Charlie Parker (1952, VOA)
32. *Stan Getz Quintet* (1952, Alto/Session Disc)
33. George Wallington: *George Wallington Trios* (1952, Prestige/OJC)
34. Charlie Parker: jam session (1952)
35. *Oscar Pettiford Quartet* (1952, Roost)
36. John Mehegan (1952, Perspective)
37. Duke Ellington and His Orchestra (1953, airshot)
38. Bud Powell Trio (1953, Session Disc)
39. Bud Powell Trio: *Inner Fires* (1953, Discovery)
40. The Gordons (1953, Debut) see Debut Rarities Vol. 4
41. *Quintet of the Year & Bud Powell Trio: The Greatest Jazz Concert Ever* (1953, Debut/Prestige)
42. Miles Davis: *Blue Haze* (1953, Prestige)
43. Charlie Parker: *Charlie Parker and His Orchestra* (1953, PolyGram)
44. Charlie Parker: jam session (1953)
45. Charlie Parker: jam session (1953)
46. Charlie Parker: jam session (1953)
47. *Four Trombones: The Debut Recordings* (1953, Debut)
48. *Bud Powell Trio with Dizzy Gillespie and Charlie Parker: Summer Session* (1953, Session Disc)
49. Bud Powell: various sessions (1953, Fantasy/airshot)
50. Sonny Stitt: *Stitt for Starters* (1953, Roost)
51. Paul Bley: *Introducing Paul Bley* (1953, Debut)
52. Teo Macero: *The Best Of Teo Macero* (1953, Stash/Debut)
53. Oscar Pettiford: *The New Oscar Pettiford Sextet* (1953, Debut) LP
54. Thad Jones: *Thad Jones* (1954/55, Debut)
55. J.J. Johnson and Kai Winding: *Jay and Kay* (1954, Savoy)
56. Thad Jones/Don Senay (1954, Debut)
57. J.J. Johnson: *The Eminent Jay Jay Johnson Volume 1* (1954, Blue Note) LP
58. Vin Strong (1954, Regent/Savoy)
59. Teddy Charles: *Evolution* (1955, Fantasy/OJC)
60. Hazel Scott: *Relaxed Piano Moods* (1955, Debut)
61. John Mehegan Trio (1955, Savoy)
62. Wally Cirillo Quartet (1955, Savoy) see Jazz Composers Workshop (1955, Savoy)
63. Little Jimmy Scott (1955, Savoy) LP
64. Thad Jones/John Dennis: *Jazz Collaboration* (1955, Debut)
65. John Dennis: Debut Rarities, Vol. 5 - New Piano Expressions (1955, Debut)
66. Ralph Sharon All Star Sextet (1955, London)
67. Miles Davis: *Blue Moods* (1955, Debut/OJC)
68. *Metronome All Stars 1956* (Clef/Verve)
69. Quincy Jones: *This Is How I Feel About Jazz* (1956, ABC)
70. Teddy Charles Quartet: *Word From Bird* (1956, Atlantic) see *Passions Of A Man: The Complete Atlantic Recordings 1956-1961* (Rhino)

71. *The Birth of the Third Stream* (1957, Columbia)
72. Hampton Hawes Trio (1957, Jubilee) see Charles Mingus Trios (1957, Jazz Door) and *Mingus Three* (1957, Roulette)
73. Jimmy Knepper Quintet (1957, Debut) see Debut Rarities, Vol. 1
74. Blossom Dearie Trio (1957, VOA)
75. Langston Hughes: *Weary Blues* (1958, Verve)
76. *All Night Long* (1961)
77. Duke Ellington: *Money Jungle* (1962, Blue Note)
78. Pepper Adams (1963, Workshop Jazz)
79. Lionel Hampton: *Presents the Music of Charles Mingus* (1977, Who's Who) see Final Work
80. Joni Mitchell: *Mingus* (1979, Asylum)

Acknowledgments

Many people have been in my corner over the last few years as I wrestled with this book.

Mingus's two living ex-wives—Celia Mingus Zaentz and Judy McGrath—have been slighted or overlooked by most writing about Mingus. They were active in helping me fill in gaps and correct errors and find Mingus sources, people and documents. They were also generous enough to deal with an endless series of interviews, from sweeping to single-question. In the process, they taught me a great deal about life with Mingus, and afterward.

So did Mingus's children: Charles III, Dorian Mingus Zaentz, Keki, and Eric. These four shared more with me than their memories, however traumatic and joyful; they told me about their father, a person no one else could possibly know.

Mingus's sisters, Grace and Vivian, were helpful and forthright in the manner their brother made famous. They don't mince words. Grace, who good-naturedly dealt with many interviews, also offered me documents and pictures that were invaluable new material. Both women filled out the picture of their family in new and dramatic ways.

Sue Mingus graciously agreed to several formal interviews and any number of quick impromptu ones. Her fierce devotion to keeping his name and music alive has helped create a new generation of fans.

Mingus's two oldest friends, Buddy Collette and Britt Woodman, submitted to epic-sized interviews and multiple phone calls and escorted me to times and places they knew in ways no one else did. Chico Hamilton made Watts and Mingus's early days on the road come alive. Kate Mulholland made vivid connections I only intuited had to exist. Max Roach helped me uncover additional sources, people and print, as well as himself uncovering other sides of Mingus in New York. David Amram, Jaki Byard, Janet Coleman, Paul Jeffrey, Howard Johnson, Sy Johnson, Jimmy Knepper, Charles McPherson, Robert Palmer, and Jack Walrath all taught me at great length about the man and artist they knew over the years.

Nearly everyone I contacted about Mingus was unhesitatingly generous with time and stories, viewpoints and ideas—another proof of the man's charisma. Whatever this book captures of the humanity and genius of Charles Mingus owes a great deal to these witnesses from his lifelong orchestra, as unexpected as their testimony often turned out to be. Some of them, too, spent hours answering questions and sharing their pasts. They are Toshiko Akiyoshi, Jody Alsop, George Barrow, Bruce and Roxanne Bethany, Eddie Bert, Paul Bley, George Coleman, Ornette Coleman, Wendy Cunningham, Ted Curson, Bob Dorough, Morris Eagle, Jim Paul Eilers, Philip Elwood, Nesuhi Ertegun, Jon Faddis, Tal Farlow, Jane Getz, Sally Caen Gilbert, John Garcia Gensel, Lorraine Gordon, John Handy, Nat Hentoff, Shirley Holiday Chatters, Phoebe Jacobs, Rhoda Karpatkin, Lee Konitz, Magda Lewis, Julie Lokin, Frank Mabry, Teo Macero, Ann MacIntosh, Jackie McLean, Reese Markewich, Maureen Meloy, Dan Morgenstern, Red Norvo, Robert Palmer, Miriam Patchen, Gust Peterson, Dr. Edmund Pollock, Valerie Porr, Don Pullen, Sonny Rollins, Grover Sales, Bob Stewart, John Stubblefield, J. C. Suares, Shelley Taylor, Joe Termini, Roberto Ungaro, Mal Waldron, George Wein, Art Weiner, Randy Weston, Bill Whitworth, Gerald Wiggins, Estella Williams, Rudy Williams, Richard Wyands, Al Young, Saul Zaentz.

A number of people directly aided my research, making this book both possible and as accurate as possible. Lloyd Pinchback, the Library of Congress archivist responsible for the Mingus Archives, did an exceptional job of organizing a mass of disparate material; his detailed and thorough categories allowed me to surf avidly, and with maximum bang for time spent. And he became a willing and useful ear as I uncovered new connections, suggested new interpretations of data, told stories. As did Larry Appelbaum, whose duties as video archivist at the Library of Congress led him to some excellent Mingus material. Dan Morgenstern at the Rutgers Institute for Jazz Studies graciously let me prowl his files as well as his acute memory. For Mingus family background, I am grateful and indebted to remarkably helpful staff at the Great Smoky Mountains National Park, park historian David L. Chapman and archaelogical technician Jacqueline Lott.

David Grogan and Billy Bergman read the manuscript at various stages and helped clarify its strengths and weaknesses. I talked this book nonstop as I was writing it; many other sympathetic ears listened, and their owners offered reactions. Among them: Gene Seymour, Peter Guralnick, Gary Giddins, Bob Blumenthal, Peter Keepnews, Phil Valenti, Gregg Geller, Jeff Levenson, Jim Macnie, Mark Helias, Marty Ehrlich, Ray Drummond, Ron Givens, Bill Whitworth, Sam Fromartz, Yvonne Ervin, Tom Everred, J.R. Rich, Terri Hinte, Martin and Paddy McLaughlin, Helene Greece, Ellen Spross, Shelby Fischer, Thea Crist, and Michael Martone.

My editors at the New York *Daily News* over the last few years—Ron Givens, Larry Hackett, Kevin Hayes, Alan Mirabella, Jane Freiman, Jim Melanson, and Phil Roura—let me disappear for ever-increasing stretches of time into the Mingus morass with unstinting support, and tolerantly let me surface when I wanted or needed to.

My agent, Tom Wallace, has been patient and illuminating in guiding me through this process of making a book. My assistant, Chuck Bock, a writer in his own right, was both tape transcriber and willing ears with ideas; his feedback was buoying and gratifying.

My veteran editor, Sheldon Meyer, gently steered me through a project that grew to twice the size he'd commissioned, and different from anything else either of us had done. His belief in me was invaluable.

Also at Oxford, Penelope Anderson kept track of all of this book's necessary pieces and developments with keen professionalism and humor, making a complex maze as straightforward as possible. And veteran production editor Joellyn Ausanka eased the sometimes difficult transition from manuscript to book.

And despite my long disappearances and author's mood swings, my wife, Tesse, and daughters, Donna and Linda, never let me stop believing that what I was doing mattered, and let me know clearly that they believed it too.

Index

429